Mary Shelley

By the same author

A Different Face: The Life of Mary Wollstonecraft

Mary Shelley
ROMANCE AND REALITY

by
EMILY W. SUNSTEIN

The Johns Hopkins University Press
Baltimore

Originally published in 1989 in a hardcover edition by Little, Brown and
Company. Johns Hopkins Paperbacks edition, 1991, published by arrangement with
Little, Brown and Company.

Designed by Robert G. Lowe

The Johns Hopkins University Press
701 West 40th Street
Baltimore, Maryland 21211-2190

The paper used in this book meets the minimum requirements of American National
Standard for Information Sciences—Permanence of Paper for Printed Library
Materials, ANSI Z39.48-1984.

Library of Congress Cataloging-in-Publication Data

Sunstein, Emily W.
    Mary Shelley : romance and reality / by Emily W. Sunstein.
       p.   cm.
    Originally published: Boston : Little, Brown, 1989.
    Includes bibliographical references.
    ISBN 0-8018-4218-2
    1. Shelley, Mary Wollstonecraft, 1797–1851. 2. Authors,
English—19th century—Biography. 3. Romanticism—England.
I. Title.
PR5398.S86   1991
823′.7—dc20
[B]   90-23541

Contents

List of Illustrations

Acknowledgments

IN THE COURSE of preparing this biography, a far more complex and lengthy undertaking than I anticipated at its inception in 1975, I have consulted and corresponded with a great number of specialists and institutions. I am especially indebted to the following: Donald H. Reiman for his counsel and his comments on a portion of my manuscript; Betty T. Bennett for reading a preliminary draft and responding to many questions; my reader, Joan Dulles Wallace; Mrs. Stuart Rose of Illustration Research Service, London; and my editors, Christina H. Coffin and Betsy Pitha.

I am grateful as well for the repeated and generous help of Dr. Bruce Barker-Benfield of the Bodleian Library; Paula R. Feldman; Mihai Handrea and the late Robert Yampolsky of the Carl H. Pforzheimer Shelley and his Circle Collection, the New York Public Library; and William St. Clair.

For giving me access to their manuscript collections, I wish to thank Lord Abinger, Peter Beauclerk Dewar, The Hughendon Manor, the Keats-Shelley Memorial House, Rome, and John Murray.

Joan Patterson Del Pozzo helped me with problems of Italian literature and translation. Lenora D. Wolfgang translated Prosper Mérimée's letters.

For other assistance I am grateful to the late Seymour Adelman; Valerie Alderson; Les Amis du Vieux Chamonix; John Baxter; The Beinecke Rare Book and Manuscript Library, Yale University; Biblioteca Labronica "F.D. Guerrozzi," Livorno; The Bodleian Library, Oxford; The British Library; G. Philip Brown; Alison Byerley; Sir Joseph Cheyne; David R. Cheney; Columbia University Library; Gino Conti; Stuart Curran; Rosemary Cullen; P.M.S. Dawson; David de Laura; Wilfred S. Dowden; Celia Eckhardt; Dr. Paul Ecker; Dr. Frank Elliott; The Folger Shakespeare Library; Ferdinando Gatteschi; Giancarlo Gatteschi; Christina M. Gee; The Grolier Club; Hertford County Record Office; David Holmes; Melissa Holmstead; The Huntington Library, San Marino, California; Steve Jensen; Nicholas Joukovsky; Keats House, Hampstead; Mark Kipperman; Dr.

Thomas Kyle; Lambeth Palace Library; Celeste Langen; The Library of Congress; The Library Company of Philadelphia; Libraries, London Borough of Camden; Lilly Library, Indiana University; University of Iowa Libraries; The Henry W. and Albert A. Berg Collection, New York Public Library; John McCoobrey; George S. MacManus Co.; Leslie A. Marchand; The Mitchell Library, State Library of New South Wales; Alice-Leone Moats; E. B. Murray; Marcella Londini Narbona; The National Library of Scotland; Iona and the late Peter Opie; The Osbourne Collection of Early Children's Books, Toronto Public Libraries; The Pierpont Morgan Library; Burton K. Pollin; Public Record Office of Northern Ireland; Ramsgate Branch Library, Kent; Rice University; Charles E. Robinson; the late Joan St. George Saunders; Justin G. Schiller; Diana Scott-Kilvert; the late David Stocking; Marion Kingston Stocking; The Robert H. Taylor Collection, Princeton; Daniel Traister; The Traveller's Club, London; Dr. Louis Tufts; Humanities Research Center, University of Texas; Alexander Turnbull Library, Wellington, New Zealand; Wendy Wall; Washington University Libraries, St. Louis; Patricia Wells; Dr. Louis A. Wikler.

Permission to quote was given by Lord Abinger; The Bodleian Library, Oxford; The British Library; Katherine Haramundanis, for the Garnett Papers; The Houghton Library, Harvard University; The Huntington Library, San Marino, California, for P. B. Shelley's *Queen Mab;* Johns Hopkins University Press, for *The Letters of Mary Wollstonecraft Shelley,* Betty T. Bennett, ed., and for *Mary Shelley: Collected Tales and Stories,* ed. Charles E. Robinson; Keats-Shelley Memorial House, Rome; Oxford University Press, for *The Letters of Percy Bysshe Shelley.* F. L. Jones, ed., Oxford at the Clarendon Press, 1964; The Historical Society of Pennsylvania; The Carl and Lily Pforzheimer Foundation; Rosenbach Museum and Library; The Master and Fellows of Trinity College, Cambridge, for the Houghton MSS.; University of London Library; Dr. Williams's Trust, London.

Emily Dickinson's "The Life that tied too tight escapes" is reprinted by permission of the publishers and the Trustees of Amherst College from *The Poems of Emily Dickinson,* edited by Thomas H. Johnson, Cambridge, Mass., The Belknap Press of Harvard University Press, Copyright 1951, 1955, 1979, 1983 by The President and Fellows of Harvard College.

Permission to publish the illustrations was given by: The Bettmann Archive; The Bodleian Library, Oxford; The Trustees of the British Museum; Bibliothèque Nationale, Paris; Bibliothèque Publique et Universitaire, Ville de Genève; The Keats-Shelley Memorial Association; London Borough of Camden; Réunion des Musées Nationaux, The Louvre; National Museums and Galleries on Merseyside (Walker Art Gallery); The Mitchell Library, State Library of New South Wales; The National Portrait Gallery, London; Newstead Abbey, Nottingham Museums, England; General Research Division, The New York Public Library, Astor, Lenox and Tilden Foundations; The Carl H. Pforzheimer Shelley and his Circle Collection, The New York Public Library, Astor, Lenox and Tilden Foundations; Sotheby's, London; The Victoria and Albert Museum, London.

In this second printing for the Johns Hopkins University Press, I have corrected errors, and, upon reviewing Mary Shelley's works, revised four attributions. "The Clouds; a Dream," apparently by H. F. Cary, has been deleted. The translation of Guidiccioni's "Sonnet to Italy," review of Thomas Roscoe's *The Italian Novelists,* and "Byron and Shelley on the Character of Hamlet" have been changed to probable works by Mary Shelley.

I am grateful to Charles E. Robinson and to the Johns Hopkins University Press for their assistance in these alterations.

Mary Shelley

Introduction

MARY WOLLSTONECRAFT GODWIN SHELLEY is the only stellar English Romantic author for whom there is no complete or definitive biography; the only one, moreover, whose image has become clouded during the almost century and a half since her death. This book aims to rectify both of these inequities.

Historians of European civilization have named the period from 1780 to 1830 the age of Romanticism for a cultural phenomenon that flourished between rather than began or disappeared at those dates, and that was too complex, diverse, and cross-cut by other trends to be perceived at the time as a "Romantic movement." The same is true for those whom we view as the movement's protagonists or contributors.

If there was never a pure Romantic, however, Mary Shelley was a Romantic by any definition, indeed by birthright. The namesake daughter of the pioneer feminist Mary Wollstonecraft, who died giving her birth in 1797, and the philosopher and novelist William Godwin; the lover and wife of Percy Bysshe Shelley, she literally embodies the English Romantic movement. Her parents were principal shapers of its emergent sensibility and the revolutionary ideas of its left wing; she herself, along with Shelley, Byron, and Keats, was a major protagonist of Romanticism's "second generation" and last efflorescence; and whereas the poets died young in the early 1820s, she participated in the movement's final years and absorption into Victorian culture.

Her concept of romance as supra-normality captures what Romanticism meant at its height to many of her contemporaries and encompassed a cluster of vital meanings that have long since been lost or vulgarized: intensity not merely in love and sex but in all the passions; expressiveness, imagination, innovation, risk, exploration, exoticism, glory; but also ordeal and woe — Lermontov longed to be as unhappy as Byron had been. What distinguishes Mary Shelley is her love of justice, learning, wisdom, and freedom, the essence of which she defined in her novel *Valperga* as regenerative conflict with the real, imperfectible world: "that clash and struggle which awaken the energies of our nature, and that operation of the elements of our mind, which as it were gives us the force and power that hinder us from degenerating . . ."

Whereas romance and reality, like utopianism and realpolitik, are certainly different things, they cannot be polarized since what we conceive could or ought to be affects our perceptions, beliefs, the course of our lives, and the development of society. Mary Shelley was the kind of Romantic who understood this, lived it, and created from it.

"Whoever can imbue mankind with a myth has accomplished more than the most daring inventor," Elias Canetti has said. Mary Shelley has that rare distinction as the author of *Frankenstein*, which she wrote at the age of nineteen. A sensation on publication, again a sensation when its authorship by a young woman was discovered, as her story has expanded into the world public domain it has gained richness and mysterious mastery until today critics recognize it as the first modern myth. "After a century and a half," as George Levine and U. C. Knoepflmacher write, "*Frankenstein* begins to look both inexhaustible and inexplicable."

While she specialized in "the romantic, the ethereal, the terrible," her contemporaries recognized her "protest against society" in the content, for her breed of Romantics were as engaged with social issues as with self-expression. With *Frankenstein* she founded the genre we call science fiction, which at its best fuses this dual engagement, and enlarged its possibilities in *The Last Man*, the first futurist catastrophe novel and one of the most ambitious novels ever undertaken by a woman. Muriel Spark has justly observed that she is a genuine prophetic novelist who anticipated "the ultimate conclusions to which the ideas of her epoch were headed."

She was her mother's successor as the most important woman of letters between Wollstonecraft and George Eliot. At the age of ten she published her first juvenilia. Her oeuvre includes six novels, a novella of father-daughter incest unpublishable during her lifetime, literary biographies, an unfinished memoir of her father, travel books and short biographies, stories, essays, reviews, and poems of which unsigned examples are still being identified. Besides these, her notes on Shelley's life and work innovated a mode of literary criticism since become standard: relating the work to the circumstances in which the artist created it.

Posterity, furthermore, owes Mary Shelley an as yet only partially paid measure of gratitude for her contributions to Shelley's stature. But for her, he might possibly have concentrated on philosophy rather than poetry. Throughout his career he was generally unappreciated, unread, and abhorred, while she provided the companionship and support essential to a man of his idiosyncrasies and hypersensitivity. He might have remained little known if after his death she had not gathered and edited his many unpublished poems and prose pieces, published his complete works, and vindicated his character. And if she did not create the myth of the poet as modern secular saint, she cast Shelley perfectly in that role for which the spirit of her age longed, and for which there has been a continuing demand since.

From Coleridge and Charles and Mary Lamb, to Shelley, Byron, and Keats, to Mérimée and Carlyle, she associated with many of the major talents of her time. Her writing, and her dramatic life as well, have influenced Peacock, Beddoes, the Brontës, George Eliot, Poe, Hawthorne, Melville, Stendhal, Balzac, Sand, Spark, and many others.

Mary Shelley was a distinctive compound of "fire under snow," youthful rebel, overreacher, scholar, moralist, heroine of a great love story and of a life — and an afterlife — of storm and stress. She was famous, or infamous, for experiencing both the pleasures and penalties of the Romantic feminism her mother had originated: claiming sexual fulfillment among women's rights, when those rights were inordinately difficult to act out. Punishment went with the territory for male dissidents, too, nor were the orthodox necessarily *méchants* to defend against attacks on their values and status, but the worst sufferers were women like Mary Shelley who lacked money and power.

She was born in the eighth year of the French Revolution when hopes for a just, free new order were succumbing to reaction. An aspiring youngster, she was reared by Godwin to be "great and good," and embraced her parents' more revolutionary beliefs. At sixteen she ran away to live with twenty-one-year-old Shelley, the unhappily married radical heir to a wealthy baronetcy, who personified the genius and dedication to human betterment she passionately admired all her life. Although she was cast out even by her father, the dynamism of this liaison produced her masterpiece, *Frankenstein,* which she conceived during one of the most famous house parties in literary history with Shelley and Byron on Lake Geneva, and wrote while being battered by a series of calamities. The worst of these was the suicide of Shelley's wife. Albeit reluctantly, the lovers married, but fierce public hostility drove them to Italy. Here their two children died, a trauma from which Mary Shelley never entirely recovered. Nevertheless, Shelley empowered her to live as she wished: to enjoy intellectual and artistic growth, love, freedom, and a "wild, picturesque mode of living . . ." When she was twenty-four he drowned, leaving her penniless with a two-year-old son.

For her remaining twenty-nine years she engaged in a different mode of "clash and struggle" with the internal and external punishments consequent on her union with Shelley. Poverty forced her to live in England whose social system, moralism, and dullness she loathed, and where she was shunned by conventional circles. She made herself into a professional writer, helped to support her father as well as her son, and tried to continue the essence of her former life in retirement with a woman friend, also an outcast. Then, after a traumatic disillusionment, she lived in the world.

Her circle included prominent literary and theatrical figures, artists, scientists, and politicians. She came to more traditional views of women's dependence and difference, like her mother before and George Sand after her. That is no reflection on their courage and integrity but derived from their socialization, their punishment, and a dialectic that still continues between equality and "difference" feminists. She welcomed the revolutions and reforms of the 1830s and was an ardent partisan of Italian national liberation. Gradually, however, a series of disappointed hopes and ambitions impaired her, until she was invalided at the age of forty-eight. She died of a brain tumor in 1851, with poetic timing, just as Prince Albert opened the Great Exhibition, a showcase of technological progress against which she had warned in her most famous book.

It is one of biographical history's more remarkable miscarriages of justice that Mary Shelley, a legend in her own time, came to be misunderstood, or belittled, or maligned in specious comparisons to Shelley. Her life has been collapsed into his. Neither her formative girlhood, nor her part of her union with Shelley, nor, most important, her years from the age of twenty-five to fifty-three, have ever been thoroughly explored. Yet her reputation has been clouded, even smeared, in a train of circumstances that will be amplified in the last chapter of this book but require note here.

Never an easy character to understand, Mary Shelley herself made it harder to do so after Shelley's death, for reasons that constitute much of the drama of those years. Proud, sensitive, and self-denigrating, she made misleading statements about herself that have been taken at face value. While she was instrumental in placing Shelley in the pantheon of English poets and culture heroes, she diminished herself in her few accounts of both their careers and hid from public notice. As a result, her later contemporaries viewed her as inordinately lesser to Shelley and his inconsolable widow by choice — whereas she had hoped to remarry a radical patrician. After her death her adoring son and daughter-in-law, Sir Percy and Lady Shelley, along with most liberal Victorians, sentimentalized her and Shelley and minimized his radicalism — which radicals have always tended to exaggerate. There followed a counterreaction launched by Mary

Shelley's ancient enemy-friend Edward John Trelawny. It is a question as to which misrepresentation did her the most damage.

In 1878, when there was no other contemporary of the Shelleys alive to disprove him, Trelawny brutally assailed Mary Shelley, declaring that she had been Shelley's opposite in everything: indifferently educated, intellectually mediocre, antipathetic to his radical views, shrewish, a "slave of convention" who only wanted respectable domesticity and genteel society and allied herself with his ideological enemies after his death. In response, Lady Shelley withheld Mary Shelley's original letters and journals — a policy more or less continued by her heirs until the mid-twentieth century — and censored the authorized biography published by Florence T. Marshall in 1889. That work was the more inadequate because Marshall and most specialists, then and thereafter, believed much of what Trelawny had said. Thus the next important biography, by Rosalie Glynn Grylls in 1938, more or less confirmed his views.

On the overtly Trelawnyan side, a succession of hostile commentators have seemed to vie for putting the worst construction on everything about Mary Shelley. Shelley being a subject of enormous interest, she has repeatedly figured in studies of him by scholars who perforce relied on previously published material about her. *Frankenstein* is an egregious example of the consequences. Although both Victor Frankenstein and his monster derive from and illuminate Mary Shelley's Promethean ambition, her rebellion, gifts, and cultivation, until the late 1970s the prestigious studies of *Frankenstein* featured Shelley's life, thought, and art rather than hers.

As a result of these accreted misconceptions and biases, some who approached Mary Shelley with the best intentions have lacked conviction, while her detractors have been full of scornful intensity.

Near the centenary of her death, Mary Shelley began to attract interest in her own right. Her original papers were made available, and a good many literary scholars since have studied her seriously. But what has been believed about a person for a century is hard to change. In the absence of a fair biography the Trelawnyan cloud over her has persisted despite an increasing number of informed champions.

When I began to study Mary Shelley in 1975, I held the general view that she was Shelley's satellite, dimly and erratically pulsing around him in the brilliant constellation of Shelley, Keats, and Byron, and I thought to present her as the conservative daughter of a radical mother. But in researching her life, particularly the years after Shelley's death, I gradually realized that I was not finding the person I expected. I began again from the beginning, testing prior assumptions, trying to dig out all the facts and to understand her character and beliefs. What was originally meant to be a complete biography of a figure whose reputation was essentially settled, therefore, has ended as a revisionary work.

Mary Shelley's career traces the full trajectory of a Romantic's life, and her special significance lies in her role both as an actor in the glorious time and a survivor of it. Her life offers as well a close study of "superior womanhood," literary creativity, and problematic Romantic feminism. In the process of studying it, this biography has become a labor of respect and conviction that Mary Shelley constitutes her own vindication.

1 THE ASPIRING CHILD

The careful rearer of the ductile human plant can instil his own religion, and surround the soul by such a moral atmosphere, as shall become to its latest day the air it breathes.

Mary W. Shelley,
Lodore

Give me the Boy at the plough, and the Girl at her spinning wheel, rather than Master learning metaphysics, and Miss learning life and manners, in the pages of <u>Wolstonecraft</u> and <u>Godwin</u>.

Jane West,
Letters to a Young Man

1 "My brilliant star"

"I WAS NURSED and fed with a love of glory," Mary Shelley wrote of her childhood. "To be something great and good was the precept given me by my father."[1] Exceptional aspirations for a female child born in 1797, but she was born exceptional: Mary Wollstonecraft Godwin the younger, only child of the brief union of the famous feminist Mary Wollstonecraft and William Godwin, then a philosopher and novelist whose stature approached Rousseau's. Parentage was destiny for her in the sense that it would have been for a daughter of royalty, or as it was for Germaine Necker de Staël: not that it necessarily determined her gifts or the course of her life but that she and the people around her expected it to, and in fact her particular career would have been virtually impossible without it.

Themselves children of an age when Enlightenment, Romanticism, and revolutions fused to engender a surge of explorative and transforming energy, Mary Wollstonecraft and William Godwin were born in the late 1750s in the ascendency of the English and French *philosophes* and of Rousseau. They were young adults when Watt invented the steam engine and Cook discovered a new continent, Australia; when the boy poet Chatterton committed suicide and, art following life, Goethe's *Werther* took young Europe by storm; when the American Revolution endowed theories of perfectibility with probability. As they turned thirty the French Revolution began.

Wollstonecraft's history was prologue to her daughter's, who would confront essentially the same condition of women and take her mother as guide, or rather as patron saint; indeed, one can discern quotations from Wollstonecraft's career and writings in her own. The child of an erratic, marginal gentleman farmer and an unloving Anglo-Irish mother, Wollstonecraft was an early example of an emerging cultural type, "a gentry child in revolt." She began her protest as a youngster, protecting her mother from her father's drunken abuse and resenting her oldest brother's favored position. She was a passionate, demanding, generous girl with

bright auburn hair, a devout Anglican, who combined the sensibility of "a female Werther" with sureness, daring, and drive, and who seized every opportunity to enlarge her limited formal education.

Even before her father lost his fortune, reputation, and her tiny portion as well in a shady speculation, she determined to be independent, an uncommon aspiration when most gentlewomen, however poor, worked outside the home only when forced to it. At nineteen she found a position as a paid companion, practically the only job opportunity for a young girl of her class. In the next nine years she ascended in accepted lady's work to become mistress of her own school, author of a book on girls' education, and governess to the daughters of Viscount and Lady Kingsborough in Ireland. Her favorite and most deeply influenced pupil, Margaret King, later Lady Mount Cashell, was to be closely associated with the Godwins and the Shelleys.

"I will not marry," Wollstonecraft flatly declared at twenty-one. Marriage not only gave the husband legal ownership of his wife's person, property, and issue, it was indissoluble, except that an influential man could obtain a divorce by act of Parliament. The double standard of sexual conduct for middle-class wives, moreover, was rigorously enforced by women, whose stature it enhanced. In the always more permissive aristocracy, wives had substantial freedom, hypocritical but useful, to take lovers and remain in society, and their variously fathered children — like the Harleys, known to wags as the Harleian Miscellany — were not stigmatized as bastards. If a man divorced his wife, however, she was ostracized; if they separated, he retained rights to their children and to her property. Wollstonecraft's first major social defiance was to rescue her frantic younger sister Eliza from an unhappy marriage and a postpartum breakdown by literally snatching her out of her husband's home, perforce leaving behind her baby.

More elemental, women were hostages to their anatomy. Contraceptive devices were primitive and unreliable until the 1870s, as well as generally abhorrent on religious and moral grounds in England, so that sexual activity meant probable pregnancy for the overwhelming majority of women, regardless of class. The redoubtable Duchess of Leinster (with whose family Mary Godwin would later be intimate) had twenty children by her first husband, and after his death scandalously married her sons' tutor and had two more. But the sensitive, gently bred writer Melusina Trench confessed that her otherwise happy marriage had meant "an annual day of torment and terror" until menopause.[2] There were no anesthetics, death in childbed was common, and the child mortality rate was appalling.

Whereas most women took their situation as a given of Nature and God, Wollstonecraft chose the sole dependable way of life for a "woman who wishes to be free": spinsterhood. To fulfill her need for shared love and commitment, she had an older friend, Fanny Blood — who later married and died in childbirth — and after her mother died and her father remarried, she took charge of her two younger sisters and a brother.

Frustration with a governess's life and friction with the aristocratic Irish mother of her pupils decided Wollstonecraft to veer off her conventional career track at the age of twenty-eight. She wrote a semiautobiographical novel, *Mary,* and went to London to become "the first of a new genus" of woman, a full-time professional writer and editor specializing in women, children, and education. She worked under the aegis of Joseph Johnson, a liberal publisher, through whom she entered London's intellectual society.

Two years later, in 1789, the French Revolution began, a cataclysm that toppled the great brittle superstructure of the ancien régime, taking with it the divine right of king and church. As the French constructed a new order, English enthusiasts were convinced that, despite mob atrocities in Paris, a new epoch had opened in which immemorial misery, injustice, and constrictions were to be eradicated, and in which man had the power to reshape the world: its politics and literature, social and personal relationships, the human condition itself.

Wollstonecraft, hitherto apolitical, was definitively radicalized. In late 1790 she published *A Vindication of the Rights of Men,* an answer to the renowned Edmund Burke's early attack on the French Revolution. Then she was inspired to apply the rights of man to woman's condition, and in 1792 published a feminist social study cum manifesto that first made women's rights into a cause, *A Vindication of the Rights of Woman.* Her demands for "JUSTICE for one-half of the human race" were too profoundly revolutionary for most revolutionaries, but she won a following among radicals and educated women — the feminist Lucy Aikin would recall fighting her boy playmates about the rights of women — and augmented a trend already under way toward regarding women as an important social force.

Both as a rationalist and a feminist, Wollstonecraft denigrated Eros in her second *Vindication* on grounds that sexuality and its consequences blocked the development of female character, autonomy, and achievement. But she herself had become infatuated with Henry Fuseli, a brilliant Romantic painter and intellectual, and a married man. She hoped to realize the famous triangle that Rousseau had romanticized in his novel *La Nou-*

velle Héloïse, and proposed to live with the Fuselis as the celibate member of a ménage à trois. When she was spurned, she determined to enjoy a man's freedom of action, including sexual fulfillment.

At the end of 1792, just before Louis XVI was guillotined, Wollstonecraft went to Paris, where she associated with the Girondists and worked on a plan for public education, until the spring, when the Jacobins seized power and initiated the Terror, to her vehement indignation. As she turned thirty-four, she began a rapturous first affair with a rakish American freebooter-frontiersman, Gilbert Imlay, on whom she projected her image of the artless, uncorrupted New World man. When war with England began, Imlay saved her from prison or death by declaring that she was his wife.

The lovers settled at Le Havre. Wollstonecraft wrote a book affirming the long-term promise of the Revolution, discovered that she adored domesticity, and in May 1794 bore a daughter, named Fanny after her dead friend. Imlay meanwhile concentrated on making money, over her protests. Besides, she was too soaring and serious for him, and she expected a durable bond. Hoping to shake her off without a scene, he left on business for London, where he remained and lived with an actress. Wollstonecraft asserted that no motive whatsoever should compel a man and wife to live together a moment after their mutual love and regard had gone. Yet at first incredulous, then desperate, she followed Imlay, momentarily swayed him, undertook an extensive Scandinavian business trip for him, offered to live with and "improve" his mistress, and twice attempted suicide.

At last, in early 1796, her passion began to wear itself out. She published a poignant, lovable, and masterful travel memoir based on her letters to Imlay from Scandinavia, her first appearance as a Romantic feminist. Now thirty-seven and a tragic celebrity, she resumed her former London life and by summer became intimate with William Godwin, three years her senior and currently at the zenith of "the firmament of reputation."

Godwin has declined into relative obscurity. It was his peculiar fate to write works that seemed to possess revolutionary importance but proved in the perspective of history to have derived from or to have influenced people of greater moment, so that he has been swallowed up in the fame of others, subsumed in the spirit of the age he was once thought to have formed. Moreover, as will appear, his own life demonstrated that some of his key beliefs were untenable and that others could be applied to dishonorable or destructive effect.

Godwin is a strange character, at once impressive, sad, and endearing. Quite unlike Wollstonecraft, he was a product of the English subculture of Calvinist dissent, of Puritan and republican tradition. Reared in a strict, penurious minister's family in Norfolk, the ambitious young provincial was educated for the ministry at an academy led by broadly erudite radical clergymen, where he characteristically prided himself on Toryism and doctrinal extremism. Reading the *philosophes,* however, converted him to atheism and republicanism. He left the pulpit and made a meager living in London as an obscure novelist, historian, and editor, affiliated with left-wing Whigs. High-minded, celibate, remarkably unworldly for his age and intelligence, he formed an intimate circle of poor, earnest, argumentative intellectuals like himself.

When Godwin first met Wollstonecraft briefly in 1791, her writings had led him to expect a stalwart virago, but he found a lovely, engaging woman. In his own case, his appearance both fit and belied the man. Ordinary-looking except for a bold forehead and intellectual expression, slow-moving, dressed like a parson, Godwin was reserved, usually placid, even cold in manner, kept his hands in his pockets or his arms folded. He was constitutionally inhibited and resistant to emotion on principle as a danger to self-control and judgment. His benign smile, however, bespoke a kind-hearted man. Thus far, he manifested his self-ideal of the calm, benevolent, fearless, dispassionate philosopher, "considering the legitimate object of discussion to be the development of truth, and not victory."

Nevertheless, he was an enthusiast intellectually, imaginative, thin-skinned, and aware that ductility was a "leading" feature of his mind. Godwin quested for truth and intellectual and moral greatness, but without gut certainty as to precisely what these consisted of — an example of talent straining for genius. Lacking empathy and insight, dependent upon cerebration, he examined and reexamined his positions "without end," had a passion for reviewing them in ruthlessly frank discussions with his colleagues, pronounced them with such extremism that he invited people to "come kick" him — and yet his record of conversions and adaptations is extraordinary.

Moreover, he resembles Julien Sorel, hero of Stendhal's novel *The Red and the Black:* vain, self-conscious, craving supreme distinction. Owing to his class and to the fact that he was not an Anglican, he was excluded from England's glittering prizes and harbored Jacobin envy of and resentment against the ruling aristocratic oligarchy, on whom he tended to fawn: "who will listen to him?" he wrote of a poor man's situation. "His appearance is mean . . . he is alarmed and overwhelmed with confusion before he opens his mouth. Filled with the conscience of his worth, he anticipates the unmerited contempt that is prepared to oppress him, and his very heart dies within him."[3]

As it did Wollstonecraft, the French Revolution gave Godwin his great opportunity. "That was the period of theory and enthusiasm," Mary Godwin would write in an unfinished memoir of her father. "All free-spirited men enquired what was best, while the more eager endeavoured also to attain that best — Metaphysics became the basis for schemes of government — and armies were despised when put in the balance with the spirit of liberty. Man had been reigned over long by fear and law, he was now to be governed by truth and justice."[4] In 1793 Godwin published a weighty anarcho-utilitarian treatise, *An Enquiry Concerning Political Justice,* which rocketed him to fame. All the literate classes of society debated his ideas. "Perhaps no work of equal bulk ever had such a number of readers," it was said at the time.

Godwin argued that humankind is capable of constant improvement because reason is our governing attribute. Reason must necessarily lead us to understand and to follow truth, in particular to recognize that our greatest happiness is the happiness of all. What preserves injustice, selfishness, and evil are institutions. We should eliminate nations, governments, organized religion, wealth, rank, customs, and marriage, forgo all private affections — friendship, love, family — for Universal Benevolence, and share property, lovers, and children. The truly enlightened, Godwin asserted, will devote their lives and resources to the general good, and, by means of free discussion, convince others to improve society gradually and peacefully. "Truth can never gain by passion, violence, and resentment . . . ," he wrote elsewhere. "It is by calm and recollected boldness that we can shake the pillars of the vault of heaven."[5]

His younger friend William Hazlitt claimed in 1825 that Godwin, like another Prospero, spoke words that were to change the world. Still later, Mary Godwin would observe more accurately in her Memoir that he gave "a promethean spark to the dead letter of mere philosophy." What excited people about Godwin's "Modern Philosophy" was not his keystone of reason, which was disproved as he wrote in the living political laboratory of France; he himself stressed that reason would become dominant, especially in the lower classes, only with education, led by an elite, over a long period of time. Rather, he offered a faith and a high moral code in a period of dissolution of the old order and religious certainties, when new political, social, and industrial systems were still inchoate.[6]

William Wordsworth was one among many of Godwin's then liberal friends who had serious doubts about his arguments, but *Political Justice* created disciples, especially among the young. Robert Southey and Samuel Taylor Coleridge planned a Godwinian colony in western Pennsylvania; Henry Crabb Robinson, the diarist, left the law for scholarship; the wealthy Wedgwood brothers began to support needy intellectuals.

Godwin redoubled his acclaim in 1794 with a gripping novel of crime and pursuit, psychological depth, and social criticism, *Caleb Williams; or,*

Things as They Are, which was said to have opened a new era in literature, and is today considered the original detective novel. It was the first of three that would establish him as perhaps the premier living male novelist until Walter Scott. "The characteristic strength, the depth of thought, the heart-grappling interest, the terrible graces"[7] of his fiction were prized by his daughter, whose *Frankenstein* derives from his work, and by Byron, Shelley, and Stendhal, and influenced Dickens, Dumas, and Hugo among others.

That same year Godwin performed what Mary Godwin always viewed as his most glorious exploit. As the Tory government, capitalizing on fears of English Jacobinism and war with France, initiated a policy of draconian suppression of dissent, Godwin risked his liberty and possibly his life to defend twelve prominent advocates of parliamentary reform who were tried for high treason in a crucial test case and acquitted largely due to his efforts. One freed defendant, the cynical John Horne Tooke, kissed Godwin's hand in public. The reaction had only begun, but, as Mary Godwin wrote in her memoir, "a boundary [was] placed to the encroachments of arbitrary power."[8]

Now lionized by the liberal elite, Godwin reveled in his extensive celebrity. Nevertheless, he continued to practice his principles, which he had elucidated in *Political Justice.* Though tempted, he refused to accept a parliamentary seat from the Whigs lest he forfeit his all-precious independent judgment and become "the last of gentlemen, who am now the first of plebeians."[9] He owned no property and lived by his pen, residing frugally in the cheap new suburban village of Somers Town. He always had and always would share his funds, for he believed that if any person needed money that another could spare, the needier person had an absolute right to it, unless the money could be more beneficially employed, and there was no question of gratitude since justice was served. He himself asked for minor aid when he needed it, and had a way of calling benefactors who expected repayment "opulent men," as if they were unconscionable sybarites.

Mary Wollstonecraft and William Godwin became secret lovers in August 1796 — probably his first love affair. By late November they knew she was pregnant and confronted the dissident's perennial difficulty: how to live a principled life in the world as it is. She was calling herself Mrs. Imlay, in dread of an outcast's fate for herself and her two-year-old Fanny, legally a bastard. Godwin was notoriously against marriage: "property — and the worst of properties." But he was too kind and conscientious to subject her to further suffering. In late March 1797 they married at St. Pancras church with only his close friend James Marshall as witness, and let the sensational news leak out as they settled at No. 29, The Polygon, in Somers Town.

Some people sneered, conservatives feared the union of two influential radicals, and many of Wollstonecraft's female acquaintance ostracized her, as they could no longer pretend to believe that she had been married to Imlay; even the great actress Sarah Siddons and the radical author Anna Letitia Barbauld "were too correct to visit her as Mrs. Godwin."[10] But for admirers like Godwin's friend the playwright Thomas Holcroft, they were "the most extraordinary married pair in existence."

The couple instituted an innovative co-equal marriage. She worked at home on *The Wrongs of Woman: or, Maria,* a novel of purpose, which called for a single standard of sexual morality and liberalization of marriage and divorce laws. He had a study nearby. They kept their separate friends and social engagements. With her fire and "intuitive perception of intellectual beauty," in his famous phrase, she completed a revolution of his belief system. He had been something of an idiot savant until she introduced him to the aesthetic, sensuous, and domestic pleasures he had rejected without ever experiencing; he would never again be content without them.

The politically turbulent summer of 1797, during which the couple awaited the birth of their "William," was also a season of natural phenomena, which people of the period commonly interpreted as Nature's symbol or reflection of happenings on the earth. Prodigious tempests swept England, actually due to volcanic eruptions in the Ecuadorian Andes months before: tidal bores and waterspouts on the coast, killer floods, apocalyptic electrical storms with fireballs and lightning "seeming to threaten the earth with universal conflagration"; horses reared and screamed in their traces. A freak hail storm killed so many birds that country people cleared them from the fields by the basketful. On August 14, an unpredicted comet arose over the London area, a soft globe of light visible for eleven suddenly calm nights before stormy weather resumed.* The expectant parents called it their child's benign star.

Wollstonecraft, attended on principle by a female midwife, gave birth to a daughter on the night of August 30 at twenty past eleven. The placenta would not expel. A hastily summoned physician operated, leaving the patient fatally infected. The infant, named for her mother, was put to her

* This siege of tremendous, terrifying storms (some of which hit France) and their bizarre consequences were reported in detail in the monthly *Gentleman's Magazine and Historical Chronicle* from July through September 1797 (vol. LXVII, Part The Second; see p. 819 for Capel Loft's letter on the comet). There would be nothing like it until 1816, when the volcanic eruption in 1815 of Tambora in Indonesia caused global meteorological phenomena, including the aberrant storms that contributed to the genesis of *Frankenstein*.

fate
crazy storm the summer she was born
+ the summer she wrote Frankenstein

breast, but had to have a wet nurse on the third day, and was brought in to the sickbed from time to time to encourage the sinking, agonized Wollstonecraft to hold on to life. Poor Godwin entreated his wife to recover, then gently elicited her last wishes. Mary Wollstonecraft died on the morning of September 10.

That day the infant was taken to a family friend, Mrs. Maria Reveley, to let Godwin mourn in peace, while his friend Thomas Holcroft rushed to The Polygon urging him to " 'have Mrs. Godwin opened for a remarkable woman.' "[11] Though Godwin refused to let the illustrious dead be dissected, he had a death mask made and tresses of her hair cut for relics. He was still too stricken to attend the burial on September 15 at St. Pancras, where six months before he had married because of his new baby.

Suddenly, this grieving, methodical, forty-one-year-old intellectual, who had lived until his marriage in a couple of rooms on some hundred pounds a year, who knew nothing of young children, least of all female, found himself solely responsible for an infant daughter and a three-year-old girl who was not even his, a large household, and heavy debts. It was not in Godwin's nature, philosophy, or financial situation, however, to languish in inconsolability, much less succumb to despair. The baby Mary had fallen frighteningly ill at Mrs. Reveley's. On her eighteenth day he brought her home, where she gratifyingly recovered "as by a charm." He resolved to give Fanny his name and let her believe she was his daughter until she was old enough to know about Imlay.

Godwin promptly began his *Memoirs of the Author of A Vindication of the Rights of Woman*, followed by an edition of Wollstonecraft's posthumous works, including her private letters to Imlay, which he published in 1798. It was the worst of times. Except for a suspect and silenced minority, the literate English public was united in fear and loathing of what the French Revolution had become, and by war fever. To the east, Napoleon, soon to be dictator, threatened invasion; to the west, the United Irishmen Rebellion broke out; at home, a small Jacobin conspiracy was uncovered, and there were sporadic working-class protests against inflation. Nelson was the national hero. Godwin now thrust himself into the pillory with his memorials of Wollstonecraft. For, with the implacable innocence of a philosopher of truth, he revealed the details of her intimate life, which comparatively few had known about: her love for Fuseli, her liaison with Imlay, her premarital affair with him — "stripping his dead wife naked," said Robert Southey, who had himself been in love with Wollstonecraft but spoke for many who were revolted by Godwin's candor.

In his next novel Godwin announced that while "philanthropy is a

godlike virtue," to live celibate and without natural affection is to be bereft
of the great joys of life. Since most people already thought so, this conversion did not add to his intellectual luster, although admirers rightly
saw it as Godwin at his finest, asserting truth as he discovered it.

The vicious "anti-Jacobin" press, already engaged in a wholesale witch-
hunt, made prime scapegoats of Godwin and the "lascivious whore" Wollstonecraft in three years of atrocious abuse that destroyed their reputations
with the general public, while the massive rising tide of disillusion with
revolutionary ideas would impact on the thinking of progressives and
conservatives alike into the 1830s. Whereas the *Monthly Visitor* magazine
had just printed extracts from Wollstonecraft's works "For the Entertain-
ment and Instruction of the Rising Generation," in 1815 her edifying
Original Stories for youngsters had to be published anonymously; most
mainstream feminists disavowed Wollstonecraft until mid-century. Godwin was forced underground, his book sales and creativity were damaged,
and whenever he put up his head to try to retrieve his solvency and
celebrity, as with his first play, the hostile press howled him down. He
made Fanny one of the notorious bastards of her generation, and he hardly
enriched the infant Mary's dower by proclaiming that she was conceived
well before her parents' wedding. On the other hand, there were those,
like the young Percy Bysshe Shelley, who came to adore Wollstonecraft
through Godwin's *Memoirs*. When the time came for Mary Godwin to
prepare family memorials, she would be hypersensitive to the enormous
potential effects of such works.

After five brief years of glory, Godwin plummeted to a nadir of public
disfavor. Frightened or disgusted London hosts no longer invited him to
the salons he had loved. Some of his admirers had already recanted liberalism in toto because of the French Revolution; of these some, like
Wordsworth and Coleridge, remained personally loyal, others shunned
him, and a few blasted him publicly.

Staunch progressives, nevertheless, considered Godwin an immortal
martyred leader of the great cause that would rise again. Granting his lack
of common sense in *Political Justice,* they compared him to a great, if failed,
explorer on humanity's behalf — a Promethean paradigm that Mary Godwin would immortalize in her scientist, Frankenstein, whose confidant,
Walton, is a polar explorer. From Francis Place, a London tradesman and
activist who would become a leader of the nonviolent 1830s mass movement for reform, through Shelley and two generations of utopian socialists,
and on into the 1860s, *Political Justice* fired political idealists. In its logical
yet utopian extremism, its "fantasy of Reason," and its demonstration that

morality could be built on a free yet dedicated self rather than on religion, it was a seminal Romantic work, a masterwork of the age, declared Benjamin Constant.

Himself serene in that faith, Godwin behaved with exemplary philosophy. He preserved his papers for future biographers and carried on, revising some of his views as truth or circumstance dictated. His need for love and for a mother for his two little girls impelled him into two clumsy, rejected marriage proposals — first to Harriet Lee, an important writer of fiction whom he hardly knew; later to the newly widowed Maria Reveley, whom he genuinely cared for. Undeterred, he paid his greatest tribute to Wollstonecraft by devoting himself to her children.

Romance and reality merged from the start of Mary Godwin's life. She entered the world like the heroine of a Gothic tale: conceived in a secret amour, her birth heralded by storms and portents, attended by tragic drama, and known to thousands through Godwin's *Memoirs*. Shelley would elevate the event to mythic status in his Dedication of *The Revolt of Islam:*

> They say that thou wert lovely from thy birth,
>   Of glorious parents, thou aspiring Child.
> I wonder not — for One then left this earth
>   Whose life was like a setting planet mild,
>   Which clothed thee in the radiance undefiled
> Of its departing glory: still her fame
>   Shines on thee, through the tempests dark and wild
> Which shake these latter days; and thou canst claim
> The shelter, from thy Sire, of an immortal name.

From the cradle, surrounding adults regarded the child as peerless, imbued her with pride in her parentage, quickened her by their expectations, and emboldened her with intimations of her lucky star. Actually, the comet could be said to have portended her mother's death and her father's fall. True Godwinians, however, saw human history sub specie aeternitatis as a progressive flow kept in motion by generations of great individuals, and Mary's star emblematized that promise. "And thou, strange star! ascendant at my birth," she would write in "The Choice" in 1823, "Which rained, they said, kind influence on the earth, / So from great parents sprung, I dared boast / Fortune my friend . . ."

The man "who is a friend to general happiness," Godwin wrote shortly before Mary's birth, "will neglect no chance of producing in his pupil or his child, one of the long-looked-for saviours of the human race."[12] He was convinced that babies are born with their potential waiting to be developed. The day after he brought Mary home from Mrs. Reveley's, her nineteenth day, he persuaded his friend William Nicholson to analyze her physiognomy, and preserved the report among his papers. Since the baby was wailing, "The mouth was too much employed to be well observed," Nicholson wrote, but elsewhere he did see, quite accurately, "considerable memory and intelligence . . . quick sensibility." He concluded that "her manner may be petulant in resistance, but cannot be sullen. . . ."[13]

Godwin's ultimate hopes for Mary were somewhat different from, and lower than, those if she had been a boy. He had never agreed with Woll-stonecraft that "mind has no sex," holding that by nature and education women generally excelled in "the empire of feeling" and men in logical analysis, and furthermore that women were incapable of being Newtons or Shakespeares. All the same, he believed that the range of possibilities within each gender was vast, and that every child's individual character and talents should be developed to the utmost. Moreover, he did not differentiate between male and female children where primary education was concerned or in his demand for high moral standards. Princess Char-lotte, two-year-old daughter of the disreputable future Prince Regent, was heir apparent to the throne, and the question of her education was being widely discussed. It would be like Godwin to vow to show the world that he would educate his and Wollstonecraft's unique child for true superiority.

From now on he studied the progressive educational authorities, among whom he himself and Wollstonecraft were eminent, from Rousseau through the more recent, and new works as they were published. He adopted many of Wollstonecraft's child-care practices, and kept in his service her French maid, Marguerite Fournée, who had taken care of Fanny almost since birth. The surrogate mother-housekeeper he selected, Louisa Jones, a friend of his sister, Hannah Godwin, was a devotee of Wollstonecraft.

Godwin kept a meticulous, cryptic, multivolume record of daily activities in his journals until the day before his death. During Mary's crucial first year, the anxious novice father recorded her progress: "Mary ill" the first winter and dangerously so; "How wonderful was her escape of her life," his aged mother wrote. "Wet nurse dismissed" when Mary was eight months; "Send to Dr. Combe," an eminent physician, about her feeding; consultation with leading specialists about her inoculation for smallpox. (The inoculation would not prevent her from catching a mild case in 1804 and again in 1828.) Thereafter she thrived.

When Mary was nine months old, George Taylor, one of Godwin's fervent admirers, traveled from the north country to meet the great man and was doubly honored to hold the celebrated baby. "So you really have seen Godwin and had little Mary in your arms!" his wife marveled, "the only offspring of a union that will certainly be matchless in the present generation. . . . If you do not remember every word you heard Godwin utter, woe be to you!"[14] On his second visit, Taylor reported, Mary, sitting on Miss Jones's lap, keen and trusting, "knew me instantly and stretched out her arms."[15]

"Talk of parental affection" with another father, Godwin notes. If he began by treating Mary as a great experimental opportunity, he developed the strongest attachment that was in his nature. He was a besieged middle-aged widower. She was his first baby, the first whom he observed growing, and pretty as well, with bright gold curls, very white skin, and large light eyes. Loving, precocious, sensitive, and spirited, she was everyone's favorite, most of all her father's. While he was scrupulously conscientious, observing Fanny's privilege as the elder even in his journal, where "F" always precedes "M," he referred to his own daughter as "pretty little Mary," relished evidence of her superiority, and gently rewarded Fanny for submitting to inferior status.

In Godwin's novel in progress, *St. Leon*, he described Mary at about a year old as the daughter of the hero and his beloved wife, Marguerite de Damville, an idealized Mary Wollstonecraft. Little Marguerite junior is full of "innocent tricks, and smart, unexpected sallies":

> Nothing could possibly be more ingenuous than this admirable infant; nothing more kind, considerate and enthusiastic in her tenderness and grief. . . . But, the moment the sorrowful occasion was over, she would resume all her vivacity . . . she certainly oftenest contributed to [our] amusement and pleasure.[16]

Fanny was the antithesis of the proverbial love child, angular, sallow, and "plain," a nice way of saying ugly. As Mary gilded the liaison that produced her, Fanny smirched the Wollstonecraft–Imlay connection — convenient to Godwin's chagrin that his wife's first lover had been an inferior man. Understandable in view of her past traumas and present admonitions by the adults to "behave like an angel to Mary," Fanny was a sensitive, passive child who expected little and could not afford to express her anger about it. In *St. Leon*, she is six-year-old Julia: "profoundly depressed by every mark of unkindness . . . by no means capable of her mother's active beneficence and heroic fortitude."[17]

Another St. Leon daughter, Louisa, resembles her mother, probably Godwin's recompense for Louisa Jones's Wollstonecraftian practice in the nursery, and maybe her most material, as he was hard put for money. It was her "pride and boast" to foster the children as Wollstonecraft had taught: hugging, holding, stimulating — "rousing infant faculties by strong impressions" — bathing them in cool water and dressing them in light, loose garments consisting of only a dress and a chemise. Fanny never liked her, probably because she was mad about Mary, but Mary loved this adoring, energetic woman who was as close to a mother as she ever had. "Your fair Daughter Mrs. Mary . . . ," Miss Jones once wrote Godwin while holding the insistently grabbing baby, "does not choose that I should write and nurse or pretend to nurse her at the same time."[18]

That bond was fractured when Mary was fifteen months old, an age when fears of abandonment are said to be particularly strong. Miss Jones left The Polygon, possibly because Godwin dashed her hopes of becoming his wife, and one of his more erratic disciples was in love with her. She offered to come by the day several times a week, but the infuriated Godwin threatened that she could never see Mary again if she left. Miss Jones went off in tears, assuring him that the nursemaid, Cooper, was "*extraordinarily attached* to Mary"; "Cooper told me this morning that she would lay down her life for the child if it were required of her."[19] But Godwin limited Cooper to basic physical care, since, like most enlightened parents, he believed that servants spoiled, frightened, or corrupted children. After about a month, he let Louisa Jones return on her terms, and her sister Margaret Jones filled in. Without a resident foster mother, Godwin sent Fanny to a local day school, after twice interviewing the "schooldame," to give her scope and companionship.

As Godwin himself said, he was the last person to compensate for Mary's motherlessness. Wollstonecraft had not changed the essential man. He rejoiced to observe in Mary that even infants had a will of their own. "We may say to them, as Adam to [Eve] . . . ," he wrote in *St. Leon,* "thou standest before me, vested in the prerogatives of sentiment and reason; a living being, to be regarded with attention and deference. . . . I rejoice in the restraint to which your independent character subjects me, and it will be my pride to cultivate that independence . . . "[20] But, though he had bitter memories of his own father's severity and had long since rejected original sin as a rationale for stringent child discipline, he substituted original insubordination, which was precious evidence of "our high destination," but which necessitated early control; the violence unleashed by the French Revolution may have intensified his conviction. Like many high-minded parents of the time, he would not tolerate anger or jealousy in his children. Moreover, he was reserved and to a child, awesome. Mary and Fanny knew he loved them, but as God might love.

Coleridge, a younger father who enjoyed his own little boys' rumbus-tiousness, first dined at The Polygon when Mary was two years and three months old, and was distressed by the "cadaverous silence" of Wollstone-craft's children. Nevertheless, Godwin treated them with uncommon "mildness, kindness and respect," and with deep affection; indeed, he reproved Wollstonecraft's Irish former pupil, now Lady Mount Cashell, who refrained from "frivolous exhibition of tenderness" with her chil-dren.[21] He wished not to crush but to regulate children's urge for freedom, to encourage it in exercise and the "games of romps" Louisa Jones played with Mary and Fanny. Furthermore, he worked on his sensibilities in his pedantic way, influenced by Coleridge, whom he thanked for improving his "poetic and physiopathic feelings." "My dear Godwin . . . ," the touched Coleridge replied, "I more than suspect that dear little Fanny and Mary have had more to do in that business than I."[22]

Somers Town was not particularly attractive, but it had a Gallic tone, being an enclave of French refugees from the Revolution, and it was set in pleasant countryside. The Polygon, located at the edge of town, was a ring of thirty-two attached houses, each with an interior walled garden.* Number 29 overlooked the fields to the north, and comprised two nicely finished lower floors with a streetside balcony, a modest third floor for the nursery, and a garret for servants. Mary ran free out-of-doors, a Woll-stonecraft practice rarely permitted to female children, worked in the family vegetable plot with the gardener, and was taken for walks in the meadows and along country lanes; she was always to need and love outdoor exercise.

The child had a warm, extended family. The bachelor James Marshall was a fixture, *in loco avunculi* to the little girls, whom he adored. Every Sunday Aunt Hannah Godwin and the Jones sisters came to dinner, and Mary and Fanny were often taken to see them in London. Godwin loved company. Among his regulars were Charles Lamb, merry, teasing, and whimsical, who played whist and drank gin with Godwin, and Coleridge, whose little son had a childish crush on Mary. "Hartley sends his love to Mary," Coleridge wrote, adding his own "Kisses for Mary and Fanny. God love them!"[23] Wollstonecraft's sisters, Aunts Everina and Eliza, were schoolmistresses in Dublin, but Uncle James, a tall, impressive naval officer, visited twice.

Mary's day was organized around her father. Everyone kept quiet throughout the morning, which he spent in his study writing the books on which the household depended. At one o'clock he rang a bell for light

* Charles Dickens's family would live at The Polygon in the 1820s.

lunch and for the children to sit with him for half an hour. His cozy, book-lined study was the heart of the house. Over the fireplace hung John Opie's magnetic, soulful portrait of Wollstonecraft, painted when she was pregnant with Mary. Godwin then took the children for a walk. Often they crossed the meadows to nearby ancient, stubby St. Pancras church and its quiet graveyard, and stood at her mother's pedestal-like tombstone between a pair of weeping willows Godwin had planted. He taught Mary to read and spell her name by having her trace her mother's inscription on the stone.

Godwin received in the afternoon: colleagues with whom he chatted about politics, the war, the latest art exhibit or play; callers from as far away as France or America; solicitors for the "Great Master's" advice on education, career, or philosophic questions. Most of his visitors asked to see the children, and his young bachelor disciples made much of affectionate "little sister Mary."

His first concern in schooling was to inculcate an early taste for reading, in order to generate "an active mind and a warm heart." Mary's primer was a tender book of lessons her mother had written for Fanny and "William" before her death. Godwin followed that with the best imaginative works — he abominated "fact-filled little monsters" — such as Perrault's *Mother Goose,* La Fontaine's *Fables, Valentine and Orson,* later Fénelon's *Fortunatus.*[24] To develop Mary's precocious reading skills he sent her to day school with Fanny the summer before her fourth birthday,[25] while continuing to teach the girls himself.

Mary was two and a half when she began to accompany her father and Fanny on regular jaunts to London for dinner with his friends, Astley's circus, musical comedies, and menageries. They would have been an interesting sight to knowing Londoners: the dark-suited, grandfatherly Godwin and the deceased Wollstonecraft's two simply dressed little girls, the pretty fair one his own daughter, the plain one Wollstonecraft's bastard by Imlay. He waited to take a long vacation, in Ireland, until two months before Mary's third birthday, leaving Louisa Jones and James Marshall in charge. Mary, reported Marshall, worried that Godwin had given her to her sitters. "Tell Mary," Godwin tenderly replied, "I will not give her away, and she shall be nobody's little girl but papa's."[26]

Mary's day ended with a prayer. Under the influence of Coleridge, a Christian, Godwin had shifted from atheism to abstract theism: "a reverent and soothing contemplation of all that is beautiful, grand, or mysterious in the system of the universe, and in a certain conscious intercourse and correspondence with the principles of these attributes . . ."[27] He believed, however, that little children need a simple faith in an omniscient, all-loving God, revealed in the wonder of nature. He also adapted Bible stories for Fanny and Mary, which he later published pseudonymously.[28]

But it was Godwin whom Mary worshiped. Love for a father, she wrote at twenty-three, is "the first and the most religious tie."[29] His very name and his followers' admiration intensified the child's reverence, while he, naturally, was gratified by and cultivated her veneration. At the same time, however, being a man, he developed early strengths in her that, she believed in retrospect — and probably proudly felt in childhood — "are folded up, and often destroyed, under mere feminine tuition." "Nothing was dreaded, indeed, by her, except his disapprobation," she would write of one of her numerous father-reared heroines, Ethel Lodore:

> Her earliest feeling was love of her father. She would sit to watch him, guess at his thoughts, and creep close, or recede away, as she read encouragement, or the contrary, in his eyes and gestures . . . she felt proud and elate when she quitted her [nurse] for her father's side.[30]

"My own domestic scene is planned and conducted solely with a view to the gratification and improvement of children," Godwin warmly declared in late August 1801, the day before Mary's fourth birthday — dismayed by a charge that he advocated infanticide. "Are not my children my favourite companions and most chosen friends?"[31]

Still, the forty-five-year-old man was frustrated by celibacy, hounded by unending political attacks, and ripe for an adulatory widow ten years his junior, a Mrs. Mary Jane Clairmont, who had moved next door with two children near the ages of his. They met on May 5, when she is said to have come out on her balcony at No. 27 while Godwin was taking the air on his at No. 29 and hailed him as "the immortal Godwin," whereas most strangers blenched at his name. They began taking their children on joint excursions; the Clairmonts helped celebrate Mary's birthday at No. 29, shortly after which Charles Lamb observed disapprovingly that the love-struck philosopher was courting Mrs. Clairmont.

Godwin's second romance was a repetition of his first, which probably clouded his judgment and clarified the enamored Mrs. Clairmont's, familiar as she was with his *Memoirs* of Wollstonecraft. By October they were secret lovers. She became pregnant. Moreover, she was not really Mrs. Clairmont, as Wollstonecraft had not really been Mrs. Imlay. The lovers married in London on December 21 — twice. The first church ceremony between Godwin and Mrs. Clairmont, widow, was again witnessed only by James

Marshall, but this time for show. The couple then proceeded by themselves, secretly, to a second church where she married Godwin under her legal name and status: Mary Jane Vial, spinster.

The newlyweds spent their wedding night at a country inn, returning next day to dine at No. 29 and to announce the news to their assembled children. Godwin, in love and convinced that he was bestowing a softer Wollstonecraft on her children, had in fact brought a snake to live in young Mary's Eden.

2 "To be something great and good"

NO WOMAN under Heaven, not even Mary Wollstonecraft had she descended from it, would have been readily accepted as her father's consort by four-year-old Mary Godwin. She was a proud, sensitive, deep-feeling child, then entering the most overt and sexualized stage of her childhood attachment to him. She had been a jealous witness to his courtship of her stepmother, who, according to Mary's adult version, hooked and played Godwin by outrageous flattery, and landed him when she became pregnant. Mary is unlikely to have grieved when the baby, who would have been named William, Junior, died at or shortly after birth in June 1802.

Her venerated "elderly" father, moreover, conspicuously returned his voluptuous wife's love. After a year of marriage, Charles Lamb complained, Godwin acted like a honeymooner, after six years the couple were still exchanging mildly erotic letters, and in old age Godwin would tell her that they were a veritable Philemon and Baucis.

That said, Godwin imposed on young Mary an obnoxious stepmother, for he had married a woman as compelling as Wollstonecraft but morally beneath him. As he realized, she was not so much bad as driven. Her Vial antecedents were noble Huguenot immigrants to Geneva, and she had lived in the prosperous class from which, she regularly reminded Godwin, she had descended to marry him.[1] She also had had a superior education. But she had been born illegitimate. Possibly to escape the humiliations of bastardy, she managed at the age of eleven to be sent to the Continent. Until she was twenty-seven, she apparently lived with expatriate mercantile families, in France until the Revolution, then in Spain until war drove her back to England, where her children, also illegitimate, were born: Charles, who was Fanny Godwin's age, and Jane, eight months younger than Mary. "Mr. Clairmont" may have been two men; Charles's father a Swiss entrepreneur with patrician English relatives, Jane's unknown. Mary Jane Vial had a married sister in Rochester and probably had come to Somers Town because of its French inhabitants.

The second Mrs. Godwin struggled ceaselessly to wrest esteem and security from a world in which she saw practically everyone as sneering, grasping, and maddeningly advantaged compared with herself. She was clever, alert for audacious coups, determined, energetic, and talented, but her strategies were those that misogynists and feminists alike attributed to the "frail" sex, namely, prevarication, duplicity, and guile. Behind her company manners, "smooth as velvet," Mary later said contemptuously, lay "storms" of temper and envy. She opened people's mail, acted behind their backs, lied, pried, and slandered. She reminded Lamb and his sister, Mary, who "HATED" her, of the spiteful sister in Perrault's story "Toads and Diamonds." Godwin's old friends walked on eggs with her, and it is a tribute to him that they continued to visit The Polygon, though they also enjoyed getting the latest on his impossible wife.

Godwin expected her to give his little girls maternal care, and she tried to be a good stepmother. But she could not do the only thing that might have won Mary: love her. Understandably, she was aggrieved by odious comparisons with her illustrious predecessor: "to take another wife with the picture of Mary Wollstonecraft in his house! Agh!" exclaimed Robert Southey. But she was also ridden with jealousy of Wollstonecraft, whose glamorous shade haunted her home, and of Wollstonecraft's namesake daughter, whom Godwin and his circle cherished. For the whole of their thirty-five-year marriage she accused Godwin of preferring Mary to herself. Mary, furthermore, outshone her favorite Jane. The illegitimate Fanny represented a Wollstonecraft she could pity yet scorn.

For all her faults Godwin liked having a wife who looked up to him, especially in this obscure second half of his career. Whereas he and Wollstonecraft had had their squabbles, he treated his inflammable second wife with invariable sweet patience, as if she were a "Bad Baby" — another of the Lambs' epithets. He set out to improve her. Ductile as he was, however, he accommodated to her. He deprecated "first mamma" in order to reassure the jealous second, assuring Mrs. Godwin, for example, that her love letters to him were as fine as the misguided Wollstonecraft's impassioned letters to "a fusty old pisant of a painter" (Fuseli) and an "unprincipled debaucher" (Imlay).[2] Mrs. Godwin's ways were more conventional than his; the context in which he reared Mary became more so. "I think, quite contrary to the vulgar maxim . . . that love is never love in its best spirit, but among unequals," Wollstonecraft's widower would declare, the love of parent and child being its highest model, and the love of woman who "by the nature of things" must look up to man, and enlightened, modern man who treats her not merely as a convenience but with courtship, consideration, and fealty.[3]

As Godwin also knew, Mrs. Godwin's anxiety about money brought out the worst in her. His family had doubled, but he had the same resources as before: advances on each volume of his painstakingly written books, which were eaten up long before he began the next volume, and modest help from a rich admirer. She made some money translating books from the French, one on Voltaire, and planned a compendium of foreign articles on the Middle East, then of interest because of Napoleon's Egyptian campaign. She also had a small estate of her own. Still, she was driven to distraction by shortages of cash, having to give promissory notes to the grocer and butcher. In her former station in life she had lived well, had had vacations, she told Godwin, who regretted what he had brought her to. Worried also about her children's future, within months of her marriage she maneuvered her husband into exploiting his influential acquaintances, approaching one, without telling Godwin, to get her son, Charles, into Charterhouse School. Godwin apologized for her "impertinence" but followed up her initiative.

Godwin, who could not work well under pressure, feared that his intellectual powers were failing, while his wife dreaded eventual destitution. In 1805, when Mary was eight, Mrs. Godwin "forcibly" persuaded him that they could make their fortune by publishing children's books for schools and the trade — a genuine market of opportunity due to the growing middle class. He not only knew nothing about business, he had an intellectual's contempt for it, intensified by his particular philosophy. But he borrowed the capital from two publisher friends and set up offices in London with a manager.

Since his name, which stood for subversive views, would doom the business — government spies were watching him — the enterprise was called the Juvenile Library of M.J. Godwin & Co. Godwin, the principal producer, wrote for it under pseudonyms in addition to publishing serious works elsewhere under his own name; Mrs. Godwin did translations and probably wrote stories. Although Godwin has received insufficient credit for the Juvenile Library, in fact it was innovative in format and in its amusing but liberal and richly informative content, and reads delightfully today, which is not surprising considering the qualifications of some of its authors: Godwin himself; Charles and Mary Lamb, who contributed *Beauty and the Beast* and *Tales from Shakespeare;* William Hazlitt; Lady Margaret Mount Cashell; and Richard Sheridan's niece, Alice Lefanu. Godwin asked Wordsworth to write for him, but he declined. That young Mary Godwin profited from books of this caliber is indubitable, and though the author of *Political Justice* and his friends felt that he had come down in the world, he kept M.J. Godwin & Co. going until 1825 — but at a price he could not have anticipated: his honor. Mary herself would be the enterprise's worst victim.

The time when Mary Godwin was the universal favorite in her little world terminated when her father installed the stepmother and her children. Daily life at No. 29 was the worse for fuller rooms, louder voices, vehement Clairmont scenes. The child had less time alone with a father grown more self-conscious. In making her own arrangements, "second mamma" expelled the people Mary loved best after her father. Her nursemaid, Cooper, and Wollstonecraft's former maid, Marguerite Fournée, were given immediate "congé." Then James Marshall, who had practically lived at The Polygon, was eased out, "pained almost to torture" and begging to be allowed still to see the children. In time, all relations with Aunt Hannah Godwin and Mary's former foster mother, Louisa Jones, ceased.

When Mary was five and a half, her stepmother gave birth to a strapping son, William Godwin, Junior. The triumphant Mrs. Godwin arranged for a churching at St. Paul's to which the proud father took the whole family, a rare concession to orthodoxy on his part. Mrs. Godwin, of course, eschewed St. Pancras with its Wollstonecraft associations.

Most of Godwin's old friends felt sorry for Mary and Fanny. As the classic Cinderella fairy tales attest, because so many women died in childbed it was not uncommon for daughters to be subjected to bad stepmothers. Coleridge utilized the theme in *Christabel,* in which the unfortunate heroine's father remarries an ingratiating, secretly deformed witch, and though Coleridge conceived the poem before Mrs. Godwin appeared, people in the know, and later Mary, associated it with Mary's situation. Closer to home, the dying mother in a children's story that Godwin published in 1812, "The Widower Remarried," in *The Parent's Offering* by Mrs. Caroline Barnard, makes her husband promise to give their little Matilda to an aunt if he marries again — though in adolescence Matilda discovers that his second wife is lovely and she joins his family.[4]

Young Mary may have identified with Cinderella's plight, but not with her exemplary submission. She herself responded as if she conjoined the male twins in another children's classic of the time, *Valentine and Orson*. Valentine, reared by nobles, is an aspiring young knight, while Orson, who was abandoned and brought up by bears, is a mute, savage wild boy — forerunner doppelgängers of Mary's Victor Frankenstein and his monster. Indeed, her early circumstances could have nourished an innate fascination with violence, duality, metamorphosis, and the uncanny where nothing is what it seems, which she would later put to literary use.

If certain strengths in a male originate in his mother's preference, Godwin's favoritism contributed to Mary Godwin's characteristic pride, optimism, and courage. Moreover, she may have been ambivalent about her motherlessness, which deprived her of tenderness but also of a rival for Godwin; in fact, if Wollstonecraft had lived, Mary might have developed into a less original woman. "Force of mind is developed only by attacking power," said Madame de Staël, in a favorite aphorism of the Romantics. Young Mary attacked by going into silent resistance to "mamma," unbroken by her stepmother's alternating cajolery and annoyance. When she was seven, her father wrote a novel with many family references, *Fleetwood*, in which he spliced his daughter and wife by giving the forty-five-year-old hero a girl-bride named Mary who possesses attributes of both. But he satisfied neither party.

Mary denied that Godwin truly loved her stepmother and sensed that many of his friends despised her. She refused to believe that a son by this woman could supersede her, Wollstonecraft's heir. All that hurt Mary in her father's conduct she blamed on her stepmother. It remained the rock upon which her life was founded that Godwin loved Mary herself more than anyone else in the world, and intimates of the family agreed with that judgment. The unremarried widower and his daughter in her story "The Elder Son" (1834) may well depict Mary and Godwin's relations:

> He never caressed me; if ever he stroked my head or drew me on his knee, I felt a mingled alarm and delight difficult to describe. Yet, strange to say, my father loved me almost to idolatry; and I knew this and repaid his affection with enthusiastic fondness, notwithstanding his reserve and my awe.[5]

Whether a lovable stepmother might have induced Mary to moderate her devotion to Godwin, Mrs. Godwin helped to concentrate it at an idolatrous level, which remained Mary's way of loving for many years. "Until I met Shelley," Mary said long after, "I may justly say that he was my God."[6] Few fiction writers have explored father-daughter love more persistently. Imagining live good mothers rarely interested her. Many of her heroines are motherless, only children of adoring fathers they adore and with whom they live in retirement; three — Euthanasia in *Valperga,* and Ethel Villiers and Fanny Derham in *Lodore* — have unloving mothers, all of whom are alienated from the fathers. Both internalized morality and benign tenderness are signified by paternal figures for Euthanasia, who imagines Conscience as a king with a diadem of thorns and a whip, "his countenance, though severe, majestical"; more remarkably, she sees the

evening star as masculine, "the good genius of the world watching his
children in their repose . . ."[7]

Certainly Mary strengthened her psychic musculature by exercising it
on the family field, and yet she compensated for a fault line along her self-
confidence and trust. Already motherless, she had been "abandoned" by
Louisa Jones, then by Godwin. One of her self-referential heroines, the
orphaned Perdita in *The Last Man* (1826), is withdrawn and diffident due
to a solitary, loveless childhood, and both needs approval and is too proud
and stubborn to court favor.

To complicate Mary's motherlessness, her mother had died giving her
birth, and if she needed reminding, her own birthday was celebrated by
the family on August 30 and on September 10 Godwin commemorated
Wollstonecraft's death by taking Mary and Fanny to lay flowers on the
grave. With reason to believe that she had caused her mother's death and
possessed her father's exclusive love, she seems to have been enraged at
his rejection and to have attributed it not only to her stepmother but to
those sins in which he himself had complicity.

Living up to her formidable parentage might have daunted as well as
inspired Mary in any event: her half brother William, qualitatively less
gifted and strong than she, was to be practically disabled by being his
famous father's son; Mary had both Godwin and Wollstonecraft to contend
with. But Godwin's "desertion" may have intensified her anxiety about
her intrinsic value. "I am ever afraid of being proud of what I do not
really possess," she would note privately five years after she had written
Frankenstein, "of being fine with borrowed feathers."[8] This fear of success
had less to do with the usual female worry about being "unfeminine" than
with ambivalence about rivaling her parents.

Manifold as its interpretive possibilities are, *Frankenstein* is rooted in
Mary's family drama — and not only *Frankenstein*. In the apparently incestuous nightmare that engendered the book when she was eighteen, a
"natural philosopher" flees from the hideous "child" he has created from
dead bodies and vivified with a powerful "engine" (slang for phallus). In
the novel, the enraged monster kills his creator's little brother William
and his bride, and destroys Frankenstein and himself. In *Matilda*, which
Mary wrote at twenty-two when she was working out of a depression,
Matilda's father abandons her because her birth killed her mother. Later,
he falls in love with his daughter and kills himself, and she, feeling guilty
of patricide, dies. At thirty-one, again under stress, Mary wrote "The
Mourner": once more, a story of excessive father-daughter love, patricide,
and filial suicide.

Thornton Hunt would later suggest that Mary's "force of natural af-

her excessive D of for her father made her suppress her affections?

fection . . . had somehow been stunted and suppressed in her youth."[9] In fact, that force was intensified while she had to keep covert what she later knew to be "excessive and romantic" love for her father, along with jealousy and anger, which were suppressed by her inhibitions as a female, an idealist, and by her training. She had as well an early sense of the sadness of things. Her problematic means of fending all this off were denial, escape, and absolute faith in her star, but her positive course was achievement.

A casual observer at The Polygon, where Mary lived until she was ten, would notice little difference between the Godwins and other enlightened middle-class families. The parents and five children worked at their appointed duties and went out *en famille* to London sights and shows, country outings, the local fair. Mrs. Godwin efficiently managed the household, which she set up as that of a gentleman-scholar of moderate means, and maintained the proper English distance between herself and her servants — a practice Wollstonecraft had deplored — while "the first of plebeians" expected his correspondents to address their letters to William Godwin, Esquire. The children had a governess, Miss Maria Smith, to whom Mary was devoted, and on whom she probably modeled Elizabeth Raby's upright, orderly, unemotional Miss Jervis in her last novel, *Falkner* (1837).

On closer inspection the children were a miscellany; the five, after all, had four fathers. Mary was dainty, very pale, with fair hair turning a lighter auburn than her mother's, usually reserved, tending to keep to herself, and aware that she was considered the prodigy because of her parentage and gifts. She felt closest to gangling, sparrow-colored, dour Fanny and yet divided from her because Fanny accepted their stepmother, though she confessed to Mary that she could not love her. The Wollstonecraft aunts offered to take Fanny in Dublin but Godwin would not consider it. When she was eleven he told her that Imlay had been her father,[10] after which she was more submissively devoted to Godwin, dutiful to her stepmother, and melancholy.

The Clairmont children looked down on Fanny but were mightily impressed with Mary. Mary got on well with Charles, an attractive boy of moderate capacity, with whom she shared an interest in drawing. Jane, however, who was to be a major figure in Mary's life, was troublesome from the beginning. A clever, "capering," sometimes sullen, dark little brunette with speaking black eyes and a musical gift, Jane was her mother's darling and had many of her ways; prating extravagantly in what Mary later called "Clairmont style" to get attention, and sheltering behind babyishness when called to account. She was also as envious as Mrs. Godwin

Mary = reserved but full of pride + ambition

Claire = babyish when in a pickle talking incessantly

of Mary and resented Mary's private contempt for her mother. Yet Jane admired her stepsister and developed an ambivalent fixation on her that Mary never found a way to live with comfortably or to escape. William, Junior, was a rough, unmanageable little boy, though he could do no wrong in his mother's eyes.

Mary was aspiring and teeming with imagination, a fiction writer both by nature and by the example of her famous parents. She began writing early. And yet her writing showed little promise of her future forte, for she channeled her imagination into more pleasurable, and unrevealable, private fantasizing. "As a child I scribbled," she would write too dismissively in an 1831 Preface to *Frankenstein,* her brief, incomplete, and sole autobiographical account of her early years, "and my favourite pastime, during the hours given me for recreation, was to 'write stories' ":

> Still I had a dearer pleasure than this, which was the formation of castles in the air — the indulging in waking dreams — the following up trains of thought, which had for their subject the formation of a succession of imaginary incidents. My dreams were at once more fantastic and agreeable than my writings. In the latter I was a close imitator — rather doing as others had done, than putting down the suggestions of my own mind. What I wrote was intended at least for one other eye — my childhood's friend and companion; but my dreams were all my own; I accounted for them to nobody; they were my refuge when annoyed — my dearest pleasure when free.[11]

Probably her stories were intended for her governess's eye, but that "at least" is typical of her public reticence in middle age — except in her fiction. Her father saw her better work, and she was writing in the hope that it would be seen by many eyes, namely, be published by M.J. Godwin & Co. for other children. Moreover, she remained a daydreamer for most of her life.

Mary tried to confide her enthusiasms and something of her troubles to her father, who loved the idea of bright, eager, trusting youngsters, but discouraged her without meaning to. "Often," she recalled, "did quiescence of manner and tardiness in understanding and entering into the feelings of others cause him to chill and stifle those overflowings of mind from those he loved, which he would have received with ardour had he been previously prepared."[12]

Especially in low moods when she felt unloved or unworthy, she went — as does orphaned Elizabeth Raby in *Falkner* — to be "with mamma" at Wollstonecraft's grave and to fantasize. But her father, who himself had been a daydreamer as a boy, worried about this habit and tried to comfort her. Three weeks after her ninth birthday, ten days after the ninth anniversary of her mother's death, he wrote a theist story for "My dear child" in which a father takes his youngster to a graveyard and explains material death and the "secret meaning of life": that we, animals, and all Nature share the universal spirit that some call God. The child cannot draw well, "but suppose your pencil was in the hand of Mr. Turner, the great landscape painter that we dined with. . . . The world is all like Mr. Turner's landscape: all is order, and regularity, and beauty." The father speaks of the child's tendency to want to be alone to think, daydream, or simply withdraw. But, he says, the child can be certain that "No, I am not alone: I am not in the midst of a wilderness of desolation and death . . . the Great Spirit is with me."[13]

He was not the only adult to write for Mary's encouragement. Witness the first story of Mary Lamb's *Mrs. Leicester's School,* published by M.J. Godwin & Co. when Mary was eleven, about Elizabeth Villiers (names Mary would use in her own fiction), whose father taught her to read from her mother's tombstone and who clings too much to the grave until her Uncle James, a naval officer, inspires her to strive to become the superior girl her mother would have wanted.

Mary found out everything about her mother that Wollstonecraft's former circle would tell, and always heard what she wished to hear, even from brusque Aunt Everina, who visited London on family business: "no one who has ever seen her," Mary wrote in middle age, "speaks of her without enthusiastic veneration."[14] Godwin would not yet allow Mary to read his *Memoirs* of Wollstonecraft because of its revelations about her sex life, but she devoured those of her mother's works that he considered suitable to her age — textbooks, stories, her first novel, *Mary*. The daughter always signed her name in full, an eponym of intellectual aristocracy: Mary Wollstonecraft Godwin. That her parentless monster in *Frankenstein* must ipso facto be "unnameable" would be her powerful personal metaphor for deranging deprivation and alone-ness.

In cultivating her "good" mother Mary had the gratification of adding to the pangs of her "bad" stepmother. Though Polygon habitués knew better than to mention Wollstonecraft in front of Mrs. Godwin, she was chronically affronted by strangers' enthusiasm for her great predecessor. An American among the steady little stream of callers to Godwin's study reported that the second Mrs. Godwin was charming but that he could not take his eyes off Mary Wollstonecraft's portrait.[15] Some visitors asked Mary to stand under the painting and found resemblances. One can imagine Mary watching for her stepmother's chagrin on such occasions. When

Mary was seven, Aaron Burr, the vice-president of the United States, had the portrait copied for his daughter, Theodosia.

Mrs. Godwin made it clear that while she herself was a superior woman, she was no extremist like Wollstonecraft. Godwin entirely supported her. When asked, as happened annoyingly often, if he was rearing Mary and Fanny according to Wollstonecraft's system and ideas, he icily replied, under his wife's fiery eye, that "The present Mrs. Godwin" did not accept all "the notions" of their mother, and that neither she nor he had time enough "for reducing novel theories of education to practice."[16]

Under his own system, nevertheless, Mary developed habits of the mind and heart that set her apart from youngsters of either gender and put her at odds with most girls in crucial respects. Though each of the Godwins retained primary jurisdiction over his and her own children, Godwin as a young minister had tried to start a seminary, and he brought up the five youngsters in what amounted to a little Godwinian sect.

All the children were deeply influenced by him, but Mary was his star disciple, the most powerfully engaged and permanently affected, the one from whom he demanded and gave most. Her most felicitous, intimate, even thrilling intercourse with her father was that of pupil and teacher, and inordinate as her later tributes to him might seem, it was homage to mentorship that few fathers gave their daughters. And she had, further-more, a model of all she did not wish to be in her stepmother.

"I learned from [my father] . . . ," says *Valperga*'s Euthanasia, "to believe that content of mind, love, and benevolent feeling ought to be the elements of our existence; while those accidents of fortune or fame, which to the majority make up the sum of their existence, were as dust of the balance."[17] As Jane Clairmont was to say more prosaically, Godwin reared the children "to think it was the greatest misfortune to be fond of the world, or worldly pleasures or of luxury or money."[18] Both sons and daughters performed domestic duties such as waiting on table. Food was plain and strictly for nourishment, not gastronomic delectation. "We might eat —" Mary would recall, "but were never allowed to talk of eating."[19] She was so accustomed to a Spartan bed in childhood that she could never sleep on "any but a *hard* bed — I care not how hard, so that it be matresses."[20] Mrs. Godwin and Maria Smith taught the girls handwork; Mary especially liked to net and embroider.

As Godwin talked of the beauty of content, however, he more persua-sively fed Mary's love of glory and excellence. Though it is still generally assumed that she had little systematic education and developed the cultural sophistication manifest in *Frankenstein* during her two years with Shelley prior to writing it, she could not have done so in such a short time. Living with Godwin was an education; she loved learning; he encouraged her, and gave her the background Wollstonecraft had not had and regretted having missed. One of his favorite women was the Renaissance intellectual Countess of Pembroke, "the glory of the North."

Godwin, who was often consulted on education, prepared the youngsters for what he wished them to continue autodidactically throughout their lives: cultivation of knowledge and feelings through the liberal arts he had studied in Dissenting schools — more the liberal arts as they are defined today than they were in the nineteenth century. His two major fields were history and literature: the history of the Roman Republic, Greece, and England "as a means of becoming acquainted with whatever of noble, useful, generous, and admirable, human nature is capable of designing and performing"; Latin and Greek classics, Shakespeare and Milton and their contemporaries, and "the first rate poets of every language."[21]

To these eventual ends Godwin instructed the older children as a little class in mythology, Roman and English history, followed by the Greek, and wrote his splendid books on the subjects for M.J. Godwin & Co. He tried out these works on Mary, Fanny, Charles, and Jane, "placing themselves in a circle before me, and each one repeating his paragraph in turn. . . . How *easy* this is! Why we learn it by heart, almost as fast as we read it!" he quotes them as improbably exclaiming.[22] Every week they composed an essay that they memorized and recited to Godwin. Maria Smith handled more prosaic lessons.

In her memoir of Godwin Mary would criticize his faults as a teacher. He expected too much from education, and his views about it were rigid. "His strictness was undeviating. . . . He was too minute in his censures, too grave and severe . . . at once too far divided from his pupil through want of sympathy, and too much on a level from the temper he put into his lectures."[23] His strengths were enthusiasm and erudition, a gift for synthesizing, and emphasis less on accumulation of knowledge than on truly understanding it with a constantly active mind and through imagination. More than the ability to make things up, imagination to his circle meant intellectual, emotional, and aesthetic involvement. One can hear in his textbooks the drive and feeling that Mary absorbed. "I should have a poor opinion of the student that did not say, 'Well, but I will learn who Praxiteles and Protagenes were,'" he writes, and recommends going on to Lemprière's *Classical Dictionary*, which will "fill the soul with instruction and awe."[24]

Mary's eleventh birthday treat was a visit to Westminster Abbey, where Godwin gave the youngsters the first of several history lessons from the tombs, always decrying selfish ambition and tyranny and glorifying men and women who had benefitted humankind — among whom Mary counted her parents. Her enduring mythological hero was the Prometheus whom Godwin depicted in *The Pantheon,* her first mythology text, who created man and vivified him with divine fire. In her adult metaphors great men and women give off light and fire; they "leave a radiant track," "gild humanity," energize with "a promethean spark."

If Mary had been a boy, Godwin would probably have done what he did with Charles and William, entered her at eight as a day pupil in Charterhouse School, a small London public school, while instructing them at home in subjects not covered there, since public schools, the most prestigious of which were Eton and Harrow, concentrated on the classics. There were no comparable schools for girls. Not that all female schooling was as frivolous as critics ranging from Wollstonecraft to Jane Austen complained. For instance, in the *Juvenile Library* magazine (1800–1802; the Godwins had appropriated that title for their publishing house after the magazine went out of existence), which gave prizes for essays, translations, poetry, and scientific experiments, over a third of the winners — who included Mary's future friends Thomas Love Peacock and Leigh Hunt — were girls educated at school and at home, and they won for Latin and science as well as "softer" subjects. There would be many women of letters and learning in Mary's age group. Nevertheless, most girls were discouraged from serious "mental accomplishments." The future mathematician Mary Somerville was ridiculed at school for wanting a Euclid, and home-taught Melusina Trench felt that her adult work was not what it could have been because she had been overflattered for second-rate early writing: "Trop d'encouragement lasse le génie," Mrs. Trench ruefully quoted de Staël.

Mary probably had at least as fine an education at home as any girl in England, especially considering the enrichment of her father's circle. For if Godwin was almost totally out of the public eye he still enjoyed superlative company. One evening when Coleridge was to recite, Mary hid under the parlor sofa with Jane; they crawled out when discovered by Mrs. Godwin, who ordered them to bed, but Coleridge interceded and they were permitted to hear the poet declaim "The Ancient Mariner."[25]

One would never know from Mary's later compulsion to believe that Shelley "drew her from obscurity," that Godwin's callers included the poets Wordsworth and Samuel Rogers, the painters Thomas Lawrence and James Northcote, the musician Muzio Clementi, the actor-manager Charles Kemble, the hydrographer Admiral Francis Beaufort, the scientist Humphry

Davy, the French economist Jean-Baptiste Say, the Irish authors Sydney Owenson (later Lady Morgan) and Maria Edgeworth — and this is only a minuscule sample. Novice and established writers brought him presentation volumes. Inventors came with designs, as he was enthusiastic about new technology. At the age of five, Mary had watched the first parachute jump in England with her father, when the aeronaut André-Jacques Garnerin descended from a balloon into the fields behind St. Pancras. As Godwin wished the children to emulate achievers, they dined with his guests.

When Godwin took the family to the theater, a treat so "exquisite" for Mary that she could not eat beforehand, they sat in the manager's free seats, and the play might be by James Kenney, who had married the widow of Godwin's friend Thomas Holcroft, twice by Godwin himself, or by Shakespeare starring Godwin's cousin Thomas Cooper, or might be a comedy with the Listons, who played whist at The Polygon. At art exhibitions, Godwin introduced his family to painters like John Flaxman and J. M. W. Turner, to whom he referred in his story for "My dear child."

Inevitably, Mary absorbed the general view, and Godwin's, that Nature reserved the ultimate in genius to men. Moreover, though her early experience made her feel sufficiently akin to males that she would choose men to narrate two of her novels, that was also because they had scope denied to her gender. One of Godwin's early books for youngsters, also written to inspire Mary and Fanny, was a *Life of Lady Jane Grey,* a girl-prodigy of scholarship and wisdom as well as feminine accomplishments and virtues, who, however, had no option but to submit to parents whose ambition led to her beheading. Godwin does not seem to have started Mary on Latin until she was an adolescent, and never taught her Greek, which was viewed as a male preserve and unnecessary for females, so that she looked up to those "more cultivated" males who had read and written Greek and Latin since boyhood.

Despite this, Mary took female unorthodoxy and achievement for granted, not just her mother's but women in her family circle. The ardent republican Madame Harriet de Boinville hosted a salon for radical intellectuals. Helen Maria Williams, an author and former friend of Wollstonecraft, lived in Paris in a common-law marriage, and Lady Mount Cashell, who besides writing for Godwin had been active in the Irish Rebellion of 1798, had left her husband and eight children to live with her lover, with whom she subsequently went to Italy. Charlotte Smith, whose country home Mrs. Godwin visited, was an eminent novelist and adapter of Petrarch. Mary

Lamb — guarded by her brother, Charles, since she fatally stabbed her mother in one of her chronic spells of madness — wrote delightful works when she was well. Even Aunt Everina Wollstonecraft did literary hack work, not to mention Mrs. Godwin.

Mary's own writing was first published when she was ten and a half — a feat that she omitted, typically, from her *Frankenstein* Preface. In late 1807 she wrote an expanded version of the popular comic song "Mounseer Nong Tong Paw," from Charles Dibdin's 1796 musical comedy *The General Election*, about a dense John Bull who goes to France and ludicrously misunderstands the language. Godwin sent it and another manuscript to an acquaintance on January 2, 1808. "That in small writing is the production of my daughter in her eleventh year," he wrote, "and is strictly modelled, as far as her infant talent would allow, on Dibdin's song."[26] "Mounseer Nongtongpaw," illustrated by young William Mulready, was published that month, became an M.J. Godwin & Co. staple, and was pirated in the United States.

 Godwin took care to condition Mary not to think too well of herself, however, and to scorn what he most deplored in himself: seeking applause. While he had such an aversion to personal publicity that he never allowed his portrait to be printed as a frontispiece in his books, he particularly disliked girls and women who put themselves forward. Knowing that his circle regarded his and Wollstonecraft's daughter as something of a personage, he instructed them not to treat Mary with special attention: "I am anxious that she should be brought up [in that respect] like a philosopher, even like a Cynic," he said. "It will add greatly to the strength and worth of her character."[27]

He worried also about her Wollstonecraft sensibility, the more so because Wollstonecraft's sister Eliza had had a breakdown. In *Fleetwood*, he described the three girls of his family, older by some ten years, in the McNeil sisters. Poor Fanny is plain, sensible Amelia. Jane is Barbara, whose "dark eyes flashed with meaning." Mary is the youngest, Fleetwood's bride, Mary, whose very skin is sensitive: "the soft white of her hands and neck looked as if they would have melted away beneath your touch; her eyes were so animated; and her whole physiognomy so sensitive, that it was scarcely possible to believe a thought could pass in her heart, which might not be read in her face."[28]

Godwin made a special effort to impose stoicism on Mary: "the sincerest warmth is not wild, but calm," he wrote, "and operates in greater activity in the breast of the stoic, than in that of the vulgar enthusiast."[29] In particular, he taught her that superior persons conquer sorrow with activity. "Idleness generated by grief would become a bad habit if indulged,"[30] she wrote at nineteen, when she was in mourning.

In other respects Godwin's moral training applied to all the children, though he expected most of Mary and least of flighty Jane, and had its perils. Whereas religious conservatives told youngsters they were tainted with original sin — especially girls, whose mother Eve had perpetrated a double "primaeval rebellion" against God and Adam — and must submit to authority, Godwin believed that youngsters were pure-hearted and should think for themselves. A parent, he wrote, should never say " 'this is rash; that is singular; this is contrary to the judgment of the world; you must learn to think like others, or you must expect to be disliked;' . . . he who is afraid to think unlike others, will soon learn . . . not to think at all."[31]

True, like other progressives who held that parental despotism prepared a child for "slavish" submission to tyranny in the polity, Godwin contradicted himself in his family. When her children were naughty, Mrs. Godwin whipped Charles and slapped Jane, which cleared the air. Godwin never laid a hand on Mary, but punished her nonetheless with cold silent disapprobation, one of the few things that could make her cry. He spoke only to give orders until she made heartfelt contrition, perhaps approximating the recital of Gilbert's "My Mother," which Godwin enforced on Charles when the boy was bad to his mother: "Who fed me from her gentle breast, / And hushed me in her arms to rest, / . . . My Mother," and ending fearsomely: "For God, who lives above the skies, / Would look with vengeance in his eyes, / If I should ever dare despise, My Mother!"

That was Godwin angry, however, for he himself insisted that belief in a vengeful, tyrannical God was a perversion of religion. He taught Mary to revere the teachings of a human Jesus, and, less successfully, to respect the religion of her country; that Mrs. Godwin, herself a Voltairean, occasionally took her own children, and sometimes perhaps Mary, to St. Paul's on Sundays, doubtless diminished Mary's respect. Nor was Godwin capable of feeling even the equable theism he offered the children, humanism being his genuine religion. Mary, who needed transcendence, probably laid at Wollstonecraft's grave the foundation of her idiosyncratic faith, initially that her mother's spirit lived on, watching and inspiring her, later that the spirits of all aspiring and great individuals were imperishable.

On Godwin's tablets of moral law, the first commandment was to trust in the truth and adhere to it, for the property of truth was fearlessness and eventual victory over every adversary. When he caught Charles in a

lie he was so upset that he recorded it in his journal: "Mendacio." Telling
the truth was Mary's hallmark from childhood, and she observed it strictly
since lying was considered a minor, even endearing fault in ordinary females, and her stepmother lied. She was not bound to tell anything she
wished to conceal, but she must never falsify. When Mary was twenty-
four, Godwin said that he had never known her to utter a falsehood, and
to the end of her life she believed that adherence to truth was "the noblest
attribute of human nature."[32]

"Never shrink from the candid examination of another" was a corollary
and more hazardous Godwin maxim, in order to improve one's fellows
as one hoped to be improved by their frankness. One was supposed to
speak "with affection and benignity," though Godwin himself sometimes
failed in that regard. Whatever the tone, examinees were unlikely to appreciate the practice.

Godwin also instilled in Mary the discipline of self-examination that he
recommended to all his disciples, to search herself for faults and failures
and for virtues and achievements. Although she sometimes dwelt on the
negatives, the purpose was to gain understanding and self-approbation
and to act rightly. In *Valperga* and *Lodore,* her heroines' fathers teach them
"to fathom" their sensations, and "discipline" their minds, "to penetrate,
anatomize, to purify" their motives, but once assured of their integrity,
"to be afraid of nothing."[33]

The most radical precept Mary Godwin incorporated from her father
was to act as she believed right, defying the world if necessary — and most
of her major heroines, sometimes for better, sometimes for worse, were
to do so.[34] With the fundamental exception of Godwin's views on females,
Wollstonecraft would have instilled many of his other concepts in Mary.
Wollstonecraft, however, would have feared and warned Mary of the
consequences. Given "the dependent and oppressed state of her sex," she
had said when Fanny was a baby, "I dread to unfold her mind, lest it
should render her unfit for the world she is to inhabit."[35] But Godwin
had the kind of temperament that could conceive *Political Justice*'s inflam-
matory condemnation of society's evils and enkindling vision of what it
could be, and yet require his followers to refrain from any action except
proselytizing. It does not seem to have occurred to him that Mary might
come into conflict with the world, much less with himself, and he underestimated the penalties for women, as he did the power of passion, illusion,
and despair.

Jane Clairmont would declare in old age that his rearing had unfitted
her for living in the real world that contained immutable evil and vicious

characters. "Nothing could be more refined and amiable than the doctrines instilled into us," she said, "only they were utterly erroneous."[36] Although it was easier for Jane to blame Godwin than herself for her misfortunes, there was some truth in her criticism. Mary Godwin's, even more than Jane's, was a high-risk preparation for life, things being as they were in her society.

3 "The time of my girlish troubles"

IT HAPPENED that Mary Godwin's adolescence coincided with one of the worst periods in her father's life. In 1807 the Godwins made a total commitment to their book business and that November moved into central London to live on the new, larger premises of M.J. Godwin & Co. To finance the move and to restore his literary celebrity, Godwin had written a second play. It closed after one night. M.J. Godwin & Co. encountered a series of problems, so, discarding her class pride, Mrs. Godwin became manager and saleswoman, while Godwin, who had recurrences of the fainting fits to which he was liable, gave almost all of his time to the firm.

"But such a husband and such a wife do not make one man of business," Godwin told the Scottish publisher Archibald Constable. Despite heroic labors, growing sales, and the fact that owing to a legal tangle they paid no rent, the inexperienced Godwins struggled to avoid bankruptcy. They had capitalized the firm with borrowed money and had to keep on borrowing to pay debt installments, high interest, and running costs, and to cover somewhat extravagant living expenses. Mrs. Godwin clung to the enterprise as to life itself, pinching pennies and splurging pounds, assuring Godwin that one creditor would forgive a loan, that a friend would bequeath him money. Meanwhile, she played on his vanity and philosophy of sharing to convince him that since he had sacrificed himself for humanity his admirers had an obligation to provide him a secure old age. This is one of the few if not the only opinion of her stepmother's with which Mary passionately agreed.

In 1810, when Mary turned thirteen, Godwin raised a fifteen-hundred-pound subscription from eminent Whigs, but at year's end he was faced with demands for another thousand. The master-tailor Francis Place, who told Godwin that he owed him everything he most valued in himself, tried to straighten out Godwin's affairs and enlisted a few other men to lend him money, which was eventually meant to total three thousand pounds and clear him from debt. Godwin and his wife — "a prime mover," Place later said — led Place on by doctoring their books.

"Riches corrupt the morals and harden the heart, and poverty breaks the spirit and courage of a man," Godwin said grimly, "plants his pillow with perpetual thorns, and makes it all but impossible for him to be honest, virtuous, and honourable."[1] He began to extract loans, large and small, from everyone he could inveigle, which vanished into M.J. Godwin & Co.'s insatiable "maw," while he trudged forward just ahead of cracking ice, dogged, adept, persuasive, and increasingly notorious for sponging. Some people avoided him. "I dare say they would rather shun my society, than do what I shrewdly suspect is their duty," he said.[2] To sustain his self-respect, the more dubious his conduct the more he appeared to be without qualms, even snubbing "this tradesman" Place to the Earl of Lauderdale. In fairness, M.J. Godwin's books sold well, and Godwin continually expected something to turn up; Dickens is said to have drawn on him for Mr. Micawber. And he never stopped sharing what he had, with the needy widow of a scholar he barely knew, with his brothers and their children, with a young disciple whom he helped to attend Cambridge.

The Godwin family lived a curiously schizoid existence. M.J. Godwin & Co. was located at 41 Skinner Street in the commercial district of Holborn, surrounded by warehouses, tanners, cheese wholesalers, and second-rate shops. Nearby, epitomes of political injustice, were Newgate Prison for debtors, where the Godwins dreaded they might end, and Old Bailey, which drew avid mobs through Skinner Street to watch public hangings. The first summer, Mrs. Godwin took Jane to a friend who ran a boarding school at Ramsgate. The following June 23, Mary was escorted by her stepmother to Notting Hill, then a health spa with several good schools, where she may have stayed until November with a couple named Corrie, coming home for weekends — while the other youngsters summered with The Polygon's owner, Leonora Knapp, a family friend.

Number 41 was a cheap new five-story corner building with a curved display window and a carved head of Aesop over the door. Occupying the ground floor were the bookshop and offices, where Mrs. Godwin endured creditors, drudgery, exhaustion, and the humiliation of selling behind the counter, sometimes to social acquaintances. The upper four stories comprised Mary's home. Over the curved shop window was her father's quadrant-shaped study, adorned with Mary Wollstonecraft's portrait, lined with a lifetime collection of great books, where he now wrote mostly children's books and did the accounts on Sundays. Up the "stump-a-stump" staircase, on which the maid was constantly carrying trays and breaking Mrs. Godwin's "elegantissimo" china, were the private quarters. And through the shop door, the front entrance to her father's house, continued to pass his distinguished callers, fewer, but still choice; "indeed," said Henry Crabb Robinson, one of Godwin's new young regulars at Skinner Street, "I saw none but remarkable persons there."[3] One of the first visitors was Aaron Burr, who, though acquitted after his trial for treason, had been driven from the United States and who became close to the Godwins before going on to the Continent.

"Les goddesses," as Godwin called the three girls, had a floor to themselves with bedrooms and an ample schoolroom where they worked with their governess, Maria Smith. Masters came to the house for French and Italian lessons, art for Mary and Charles, music and singing for Jane. The girls took turns helping Mrs. Godwin with housekeeping, cook's accounts, laundry lists. Domestic matters annoyed Mary, and she complained that Jane was expected to do less than she and Fanny. But she learned to cook rudimentarily and make her modest dresses; Mrs. Godwin believed that girls should stay young and simple. Otherwise the three had uncommon independence. They were expected at four o'clock dinner but took other meals when they pleased and used their schoolroom as a parlor to entertain their friends and make evening tea at nine.

Since Fanny was expected eventually to teach at the Wollstonecraft aunts' Dublin school, Godwin gave her some training at the London school of Joseph Lancaster, founder of the progressive Lancastrian system, who taught poor children by using unpaid older students. Mrs. Godwin, however, increasingly relied on her for housekeeping. Fanny had good independent judgment and shared a passion for poetry with Mary, but she irritated the younger girls by being the good, admonishing elder sister. Her perfect husband, Jane once said wickedly, would be Harley in Henry Mackenzie's *The Man of Feeling,* who continually burst into tears from excessive admiration of goodness. But nobody thought Fanny would marry.

Jane's mother, who cherished her favorite's "blithe looks and affectionate, obliging ways," said she was "always delighted with everything, always admiring, always content, and finding people heavenly and delightful."[4] To Mary's eye Jane also resembled the girls Wollstonecraft had deplored: a show-off who got away with naughtiness, a screamer frightened of ghosts and robbers, and a sulker with an abject streak. Jane admired Mary vastly and echoed her — when she was with her — but her envy discomfited the older girl. They sometimes larked together but were not friends.

In Mary's intense definition of Friend, she had few if any near her age, and she preferred to be lonely rather than to compromise. She would distribute elements of her youthful self among the heroines of her fifth novel, *Lodore:* self-sufficiency and aspiration in the fearless, radical scholar, Fanny Derham; pride and spirit in spoiled Cornelia Lodore; dependency and need for love in gentle Ethel Villiers. She was usually self-contained, and looked fragile even to Jane, who knew she was strong and active; "whether it be from your excessive fairness of skin and your auburn hair, I have always thought you of a very delicate constitution," Jane said at thirty-seven.[5] But she had strong feelings and opinions, passionate enthu-siasms, exceptional loyalty and perseverance, and she loved danger. She balked at coercion, though she was easily led by affection and by her quick sympathy.

Mary was forming the habit of a Godwinian schedule that, like a ballet dancer, she would follow most of her life: study and writing until early afternoon, then exercise and recreation. In addition to reading history and literature, she started Latin, may have tried Chapman's *Homer,* studied French by means of an original text and a translation, such as Helen Maria Williams's bilingual edition of Louis XVI's poignant letters from prison,[6] and learned some etymology, geometry, geography, and natural history. She loved the chivalric romances. Apparently Miss Smith paid less atten-tion to Mary's large scrawling handwriting and imperfect spelling — "Teueday," for example — than to her work habits. Godwin was also training her to take notes, make extracts and chronologies, and use cross-references; "to read one book without others beside you to which you may refer is mere childs work," he always insisted.[7]

She missed living in the country and disliked London. Her father was entrapped there in "sordid" business, for which she blamed her step-mother's mercenary nature. Moreover, she was peculiarly sensitive to and interactive with her physical surroundings, despite Godwin's stoic teaching that superior persons remain impervious to externals. She was becoming a devotee of Wordsworth's nature poetry and like him loathed London's coal-smoke–polluted air, clangorous streets, "getting and spending," opu-lence and squalor.

M.J. Godwin & Co. had its compensations, however. All over the house were manuscripts, proofs, freshly printed volumes. Books informed the girl's existence, and there was no boundary between them and daily life: M.J. Godwin books for income; serious books like her father's *Essay on Sepulchres,* which was inspired by the family visit to Westminster Abbey; books by or mentioning people she knew; books in her father's library from which he selected works for her studies and pleasure, books to live by. "Like all young and ardent minds," she would describe herself as Elizabeth Raby in *Falkner,* she found models in biography, especially Plutarch's heroes, "whereby she measured her own thoughts and conduct, rectifying her defects, and aiming at that honour and generosity which made her heart beat."[8]

Mary's and Charles's first art instructors were young illustrators for M.J. Godwin & Co., William Mulready and George Dawe and his sister, who themselves studied with John Varley. They were succeeded when she was thirteen by Varley's most gifted student, John Linnell.[9] Linnell, following Varley — "Go to Nature for everything" — pioneered in painting landscapes out-of-doors, and took Mary and Charles to Hampstead Heath to sketch. Judging from the few surviving examples of Mary's later drawings — a portrait, scenery, a human figure — she would not have made an artist. But art was considered good training for writers, and Linnell's close observation of naturalistic detail and especially his poetic pantheistic feeling may have strengthened these faculties in Mary. She also worked with Hannah Hopwood, painter-daughter of the artist James Hopwood — the Hopwoods, friends of her family, had lived in Wollstonecraft's hometown of Beverley — and went to the Royal Academy annual opening and other art exhibits with Godwin, an indefatigable, rapt gallerygoer.

Whenever the weather permitted, Mary walked in the afternoons to the gardens of the Temple, or those of Charterhouse School, or farther out to St. Pancras graveyard. She did not see herself as religious; religion was coming to mean superstition, empty ritual, Hebrews slaughtering their enemies in the name of an imaginary, exultant God, Christian conquests, hierarchies, and hypocrisy. But the quiet country graveyard was in effect church for her intertwined faith in the immortal human spirit, her communion with nature, romantic inspiration, and her fantasizing. The boy poet Chatterton had strolled among these tombs a few hours before he committed suicide; when Mary was ten the great Corsican patriot Pasquale Paoli was buried there; when she was thirteen, so was the transvestite Chevalier d'Eon, who passed as a woman until found otherwise upon his deathbed. And here Mary was free to "obey Fantasia," daydream, and imagine the shining future promised by her star: "my dreams my darling sun bright dreams!" she wrote in her journal years after. "They peopled the Churchyard I was doomed so young to wander in — hope drank at her [Fantasia's] fountain — and she fed on the Ambrosia of hope."[10]

Godwin's circle now constituted Mary's intellectual marketplace, where she became aware of contemporary ideas; she loved its energy and diversity. The talk might be about Itard's education of Victor, the Wild Boy of Aveyron; or Crabb Robinson might report on his stay in Germany, where he discussed Godwin with Goethe and interviewed Adam Weishaupt, former leader of the underground revolutionary Illuminati sect, now a misanthrope and a conservative, like so many who had been disillusioned by the French Revolution. Godwin's good friend the Irish politician John Philpot Curran had defended the romantic young leader of the 1798 Irish Rebellion, Lord Edward Fitzgerald, and was, according to Byron, at once the ugliest man and most scintillating and boldest conversationalist he ever knew. Later, when Mary read Plato's *Symposium* she imagined that its participants had been free spirits like Curran.

Of all Godwin's friends Coleridge probably had the greatest influence on Mary. He was her first living model of erratic genius, "miraculous" monologues, and brilliant, subtle, wide-ranging intellect. His periodical *The Friend*, which both she and Jane read, was among the formative works of her girlhood, particularly his insistence on the primacy of individual genius, his critical ability to connect great minds, works, and events, and his sense of past and present as an unbroken chain. It was in the audience of his lecture series on Shakespeare and Milton, which the Godwins attended *en famille* when she was fourteen, that she first glimpsed Lord Byron, muffled up against the curious but recognizable by his limp from a clubfoot. Shortly after, she became Byron's admirer for the first cantos of *Childe Harold*, which made him world-famous, and for his opposition in the House of Lords to the death penalty for Luddites.

The familiar differences between her father and Coleridge would be at the heart of *Frankenstein*. Godwin believed that government in its largest sense formed the virtues and vices of its citizens, whereas Coleridge had deeper psychological insights. No one articulated better than Godwin the optimistic spirit of the age, which was to prevail until World War I: "What the heart of man is able to conceive, the hand of man is strong enough to perform. . . . I firmly believe that days of greater virtue and more ample justice will descend upon the earth."[11] While Coleridge profoundly admired Godwin for the nobility of his views, he believed in essence that those two sentences were a sanguine non sequitur, since the hand may produce evil unless the heart is governed not only by morality but reverence and a sense of sin.

Mary was incorporating her father's political concepts — with an ardor for justice and liberty and indignation at their opposites that Godwin considered natural for young people but tried to temper. He was a republican in theory, a champion of freedom of expression, press, and religion who despised party spirit and fanaticism, and an egalitarian who nevertheless repudiated the idea that all men were alike, least of all an uneducated, susceptible populace and an intellectual and moral elite. He believed in social and economic equality and universal education on grounds of justice and as means for gradual, orderly, uplifting renovation of society; grand comprehensive plans to benefit humankind, he said, must inevitably fail. She would adhere to these ideals for all of her life. The Roman Republic, the English Commonwealth, and the achievements of the French Revolution (up to the overthrow of the Gironde) were his historical apexes, but he taught Mary to put them in perspective as systems vulnerable to demagogues, dictators, and currently to reaction, until the next cycle began.

Britain was ruled by an aristocratic oligarchy, Whig as well as Tory. In practical politics the Godwins supported the Whig left wing, the faction advocating civil liberties and reform of Parliament, then elected by a small, grossly anachronistic suffrage that excluded the middle classes — the very sector of society on which Godwin and Wollstonecraft relied for progress. Mary's family talked politics and took the Whig *Morning Chronicle,* of which Godwin kept a complete set. He knew its editor, James Perry; once when he visited Perry's country house, he took his own youngsters along. Godwin had a sneaking admiration for Napoleon, but Mary hated "Bonaparte" for his dictatorship and bloody imperial wars that dominated the news; the Tyrolean Andreas Hofer and the Haitian Toussaint l'Ouverture, who died fighting French imperialism, were among her lifelong heroes.

Although repression had not abated and the Tories had been in power for nearly two decades, activists like Francis Burdett, with whom Godwin was in touch, were keeping the still weak reform movement alive. When Mary was fifteen, Leigh Hunt, editor of *The Examiner,* was sentenced to two years in jail for libeling the Prince Regent, but turned it into a triumph by decorating his cell like a bower and receiving eminent sympathizers, including Godwin and Byron.

The times seemed promising for women. Princess Charlotte, presumptive future queen, was the liberals' darling, a strong-minded teenager who defied her father, the Prince Regent, by supporting the Whigs. Though conservatives deplored women authors, they dominated English fiction, and if friendly male critics claimed that they excelled in poeticizing common life, that was disproved by Jane Austen, Fanny Burney, Maria Edgeworth, Harriet and Sophia Lee, Lady Morgan, Jane Porter, Ann Radcliffe, Charlotte Smith — and Madame de Staël, the premier female author and personality in what Coleridge called the age of personality. De Staël would note that writing fiction was a source of power for women, that they had entered the field to dominate men or avoid being dominated by them. When Mary was fifteen, her father met Madame de Staël at a dinner party.

Within a consensus of woman's importance, intellectuals debated her proper role. The Wollstonecraftian spinster Lucy Aikin argued for independence and achievement: "Improve, excell, surmount, subdue your fate!"[12] Wollstonecraft's example provided a favorite argument on the other side, however, on grounds that she had succumbed to a suicidal passion for Imlay and died of the ordained female infirmity, childbirth. Both conservative Jane West and liberated de Staël believed that women had a high special mission. West claimed that women's task in a world rightfully led by men was to refine manners and conserve morals; thus "we become *legislators*," though excluded from Parliaments."[13]* De Staël, one of history's great egotists, declared that woman's glory and destiny was her selflessness. Robert Owen, Saint-Simon, and Fourier — and young Percy Bysshe Shelley — were arriving at grander ideas about woman's redemptive capacity. While they were free thinkers, they had a religious counterpart in the millenarian Joanna Southcott, who claimed to be the New Savior sent to raise women and redeem humanity; she attracted thousands of followers during Mary Godwin's girlhood until her death in 1814, following a hysterical pregnancy that was supposed to deliver Shiloh, the second Christ.†

Mary was also becoming a partisan of women's rights. Though Godwin doubtless worried about the effect, he could no longer prevent her from reading his *Memoirs* of her mother, Wollstonecraft's *Vindication of the Rights of Woman*, her letters to Imlay, and her last novel, *The Wrongs of Woman: or, Maria*. In fact, Mary learned her mother's history in more intimate detail than if Wollstonecraft had lived, and worshiped her both as rational intellectual and romantic heroine who had defied injustice, custom, and prudence. As for marriage, Wollstonecraft acknowledged in *Maria* women's need for "protectorship as mothers": "With proper restrictions . . . I revere the institution which fraternizes the world."[14] But the proper restrictions did not exist, and when Mary read her father's *Political Justice* she found his arguments incontrovertible, that marriage was an outworn superstition, legalized slavery for the wife, and an unreasonable enchainment for both spouses. She believed she was reading her mother's testament to herself in the narrative of *Maria*'s heroine, which is addressed to her daughter in case she dies before she can instruct her: condemnation of the social, economic, and sexual wrongs done to women and a call to her daughter to pursue happiness while she is young.

This in an age when both the enlightened and the conservative mainstream agreed that it was imperative to restrain girls, that conventional mores for them were a matter of survival. Godwin had long since averred that his advocacy of free love and condemnation of marriage in *Political*

---

* West's ideological enemy, Shelley, would alter her rationalization of executive powerlessness in his famous claim that poets were the world's legislators.
† Southcott, along with de Staël's *Corinne*, would be Mary's model for the prophetess Beatrice, a heroine of *Valperga*.

Justice were purely speculative, and discouraged people from writing about Wollstonecraft's love life. Love, he wrote in one of Mary's textbooks, is "one of the best of our feelings, but when it leads human beings to trample on all that is honourable and well-regulated in society, as by licentious poets and other writers it is too frequently described, it is one of the deepest blots to which our nature is exposed."[15] Mary's future social utility and her happiness, he told her, depended upon her capacity to live by judgment rather than by passion.

But Mary's allegiance to her mother was intensified by the fact that Wollstonecraft was still being libeled in the press and warned against in fiction — which suggests that Wollstonecraft stirred other young females. Mary would always scorn the otherwise liberal Maria Edgeworth, whose Angelina in *Moral Tales* for girls "foolishly" aspires to combat "the system of social slavery," as does a young woman in Edgeworth's novel *Belinda*. Such works, of which *Sense and Sensibility* is the supreme artistic example, typically contrast a self-restrained, high-minded, realistic young woman with one who comes to grief because of her romanticism or Wollstone-craftian beliefs.

Thus Mary had parental sanction for protest against familial as well as social authority when, in early 1811 at thirteen and a half, she entered puberty (menarche then generally occurred nearer to fifteen) with a re-belliousness that Godwin was in no mood to countenance. Desperately juggling debts, he had taken Charles Clairmont — admittedly no scholar — out of school to learn accounting to reassure his creditors about his firm's future, and that November apprenticed him to Constable in Edinburgh. Furthermore, he had to let Maria Smith go, and though she remained close to the family there was no buffer at Skinner Street between the Godwins and Mary.

What Mary could read may have been one source of conflict. "Observe," Godwin told his wife when Charles obtained a copy of Thomas Paine's *Age of Reason,* which Godwin considered superficial and impudent, "I totally object to Mary's reading in Charles' book."[16] Mary apparently set-tled for Godwin's substitution, the sober, learned deist Anthony Collins. The flashpoint, however, was Mary's now overt hostility to her stepmother. The girl showed her contempt for "mamma" and her incessant talk about money, protested "stupid" instructions, and drove her into tantrums. God-win invariably took his wife's part and demanded that Mary admit her fault and submit. When Mary refused, Godwin overawed her or punished her with inexorable silence. Mary became depressed, withdrew, and had to be "*excited* to industry."

That spring Mary developed a severe skin eruption on one hand. On

May 13 Godwin took her to the renowned surgeon Henry Cline, who ordered the pustules opened and poulticed several times a day and put her hand in a sling. Cline warned that heroic treatment might be required, perhaps surgery, and prescribed six months of salt-water therapy. On the seventeenth Mrs. Godwin, now all sympathy, rushed Mary to Ramsgate. "Tell Mary," the unforgiving Godwin wrote his wife, "that, in spite of unfavourable appearances, I have still faith that she will become a wise and, what is more, a good and a happy woman."[17]

Mrs. Godwin installed Mary at one of Ramsgate's several boarding schools where Jane had stayed in 1808, Miss Caroline Petman's at 92 High Street,[18] and vacationed nearby with William, Junior, for a month. It was June 10 before she could report to Godwin that Cline's extremely painful prescriptions were doing Mary good. "Mary is decisively better today, has had her dip. . . . So far she has had but one *fresh* water poultice which I put on last night, seeing her a little spent with pain. The pustules when pricked, die away, and others succeed. In the bathing machine today, she made . . . efforts to assist herself with the sick hand. . . . I indulge the hope of all yet being well and that our poor girl will escape the dreadful evil we apprehend."[19]

Whatever the emotional component of Mary's skin condition, Ramsgate initiated her collaboration with the Godwins in self-exile and banishment respectively.* Uneasiness about Mary may have contributed to a rare fight Godwin had with his wife in late August, but he did not visit his daughter even for her fourteenth birthday, when he went on vacation to the west of England. However, Miss Petman was solicitous of her distinguished pupil, and if Mary did not derive much advantage from the work or from the thirty-some pupils, she was accustomed to independent study and pleasantly placed. For her hand, she bathed daily in the sea or in the bathhouse's warmed salt water. She could inspect Ramsgate's harbor installations, walk the beach and cliffs, select books at the library, or go to the assembly rooms where the chaperoned girls met pupils from the local boys' schools. She did not flourish, however, and was not called home for eight months, coming just in time for the Godwins' tenth anniversary celebration on December 21. "Mary . . . looks very lovely, but has not the air of strong health," noted Aaron Burr, who was in London through March.[20]

Burr's journal entries while he was in the bosom of the Godwin family are vignettes of delightful, enlightened parents and children — though the old libertine made advances toward Mrs. Godwin and seems to have been

* Similarly, in *Lodore*, Fanny Derham spends her girlhood away from home owing to friction between herself and her mother.

aroused by the ingenuously affectionate, nubile girls. They took him along to see their friends and dragged him up to the schoolroom for tea, which Fanny or Jane (never Mary) made, sometimes so strong that he had "vigils" all night. He bought "the lassies" stockings to wear to a great ball at the home of the editor J. P. Collier — one of the few parties they seem to have attended — and they presented themselves for his inspection in gowns they had made for the occasion, "extremely neat, and with taste," and told him all about it next day. When he came to dinner the girls entertained afterward with an hour of singing or dancing. Once, eight-year-old William, who lectured weekly on a little pulpit, delivered a speech called "The Influence of Government on the Character of the People." Mary had written it, though her authorship was not announced, owing to her father's and her own resistance to "putting herself forward."[21]

All the while, however, Mary's conflict with her stepmother and father had resumed. In February Godwin began taking her back to Cline. Her whole arm was now affected; if it was the right arm she could not write. After Cline prescribed another six months at the seaside, Godwin arranged for her to live near Dundee with the family of William Thomas Baxter, a prosperous sailcloth manufacturer. Though he and Baxter had met only once, the Scot had contributed to his subscription for the Treason Trials defendants of 1794, and was the father-in-law of his friend David Booth. Godwin asked Baxter to "consider the first two or three weeks as a trial, how far you can endure her, or, more fairly & impartially speaking, how far her habits & conceptions may be such as to put your family very unreasonably out of their way." Granting that he had been remote from Mary and kept her in a degree of awe and restraint, "I am not therefore a perfect judge of Mary's character. I believe she has nothing of what is commonly called vices, & that she has considerable talent. . . . In all other respects except her arm, she has admirable health, has an excellent appetite, & is capable of enduring fatigue."[22]

On June 7, 1812, Godwin, Fanny, and Jane saw Mary aboard the packet *Osnaburgh,* her arm in a sling, dreading the motion sickness she suffered at sea and in carriages, knowing no one. Her suddenly anxious father found a lady passenger with daughters to take charge of her. After about a week's sail north the ship turned into the protected Firth of Tay, and Mary revived. On the high northern bank at Broughty Ferry, just before Dundee Harbor, the captain pointed out Baxter's extensive grounds and landmark residence, The Cottage, formerly the Countess of Strathmere's dower house, which overlooked a promontory crowned by a romantic fifteenth-century castle. Mary had a hearty welcome and got on so beautifully with the Baxters that they became her second family, with whom she would spend sixteen of the next twenty-two months.

The relaxed, light-hearted, permissive Baxter home was pure delight to Mary, who for the first time was free to live in the way that was always to make her happiest: with privacy, intellectual and loving companionship, exotic new experiences, and closeness to Nature. Baxter was a dear man, ten years younger than Godwin, easygoing and weak. His children were older than Mary, which she preferred, and treated him with relative irreverence; he was dominated by his son-in-law David Booth, who was his age although married to his eldest child, Margaret. Honored to have Mary Wollstonecraft Godwin as his guest, Baxter put himself out to please her and otherwise left her at liberty. She was extremely fond of him, as of an indulgent uncle.

His youngest daughter, Isabel, a serious, studious, "violently" affectionate girl four years older than Mary, became her first intimate friend, a rare relation for both. Isabel idolized Mary Wollstonecraft and Madame Roland, the Girondist leader guillotined by the Jacobins, shared Mary's love of poetry and history, and introduced her to botany. The two girls studied together, and ranged the beach below The Cottage, selecting shells for Isabel's collection. The whole Baxter family were enthusiastic painters.

Of equal importance with the company were the natural attractions of the place and the opportunity for solitude. From her bedroom window Mary could see the distant, snow-topped Grampians, a sight that exhilarated her. Besides bathing in the Firth, she took advantage of Cline's prescription of fresh air for her arm to spend a great deal of her time out-of-doors alone to read, write stories, and to fantasize while she climbed down the dunes to walk the extensive beach along the Firth, wide as an inland sea, or up into the barren windy hills behind the house. This was her "eyry of freedom," where she could lose herself in daydreams for as long as she wished. Years later the locals claimed that she began *Franken-stein* in her favorite retreat, the Baxter pine grove, but she was still writing in what she later termed "a most commonplace style."

Isabel's older sister Christina, a gruff, downright Scotswoman, was not as close to Mary as Isabel was, and may have resented it. But Christy having precedence as Isabel's elder, Mary brought her home in early November for a return six-month stay. The girls arrived at Skinner Street in time for breakfast on the tenth.

Next afternoon, Mary briefly met a glamorous new disciple of her father's, about whom she and her whole family had been excited since January, and who was leaving for Wales after six weeks in London. Twenty-year-old Percy Bysshe Shelley, radical heir to a rich baronetcy and a poet, came to dinner with his girl-bride, her older sister, and the Godwins' physician, William Lawrence.

If Mary loved Scotland's novelties, provincial Christy Baxter marveled at Mary's London privileges, for they went with the artist David Wilkie to an exhibit of Reynolds's paintings, attended the theater, including the opening night of Coleridge's *Remorse,* saw a good deal of Coleridge himself, Charles and Mary Lamb, and the James Kenneys, met the Henry Fuselis, Robert Owen, and Thomas Moore. Mrs. Godwin put herself out to be lovely to Christy, who thereafter would not let Mary speak against her stepmother. In old age Christy recalled the girls' debate on woman's role; she and Fanny for domesticity, Mary and Jane against.[23] The Wollstonecraft faction had an ally in John Philpot Curran's daughter Amelia, then on one of her visits from abroad. As salaciously witty as her father, Amelia Curran was an amateur painter, musician, and writer, who had turned down Lord Cloncurry's proposal of marriage and lived independently in Rome.[24]

Godwin himself was so impressed with his fifteen-year-old daughter that he reread her mother's early novel *Mary* that January, as if to savor the likenesses. Mary's resemblance to her mother was less physical than impressionistic, especially in her presumably dichotomous feminine looks and manner and "masculine" qualities. "My own daughter," Godwin informed an inquirer, "is considerably superior in capacity to [Fanny], the reverse of her in many particulars," and went on to describe Mary quite as her future Frankenstein's father might have described his adolescent son: "She is singularly bold, somewhat imperious, and active of mind. Her desire of knowledge is great, and her perseverance in everything she undertakes almost invincible."[25]

She was also, he added, very pretty. Under middle height, small-boned, slender but rounded, Mary enjoyed Titian coloring, with "clear bright white skin" and gold-bronze hair, thick, silky, and luxuriant, "of a sunny and burnished brightness like the autumnal foliage when played upon by the rays of the setting sun," Jane would describe it.[26] She had an oval face distinguished by her high forehead and especially by her large, deep-set, very light, clear hazel eyes, the left eye with a touch of green, which could change to or appear gray. Her look was calm, penetrating, and earnest, or pensively sidelong. She had a short upper lip and delicately curved, rather thin mouth, which firmed when she listened and became mobile and redder when she spoke. Her voice was high and clear, her smile sweet. She had plump, tapering fingers and double-jointed thumbs that she could bend back to the wrist. Jane, who sometimes dressed as a boy, thought her a model of girlish beauty and talent, herself comparative clay. One suspects that Mary did not altogether disagree.

By this age Mary had developed a tranquil, poised persona, and a peculiar calmative power, when she chose to exert it, on excitable Jane or mournful Fanny. "Aegis to my sensibility," her fantasizing accounted for some of that serenity, and for the rest, pride, Godwinian philosophy, a sure sense of direction and beliefs, and faith that "Fortune was her friend." Mrs. Godwin complained that she thought of nothing but herself, and Fanny, that Mary left others to cope with disagreeables; "I know you hate thinking of unpleasant things," said poor Fanny. Even so, Mrs. Godwin admired Mary's "great talents, her sagacity, her steady industry,"[27] while Fanny and Jane envied her independence and the gratification she had in her work.

She turned passionate, however, when she was deeply stirred, and cross in her rare low moods. Whereas she was too devout a learner to intrude into the talk of her superiors, when she spoke it was with decidedly more candor and boldness than expected in young girls. She enjoyed disputations with her peers, "démêler le vrai avec le faux," as her father said of his own debates. Her humor was ironic and teasing. Before introducing Christy to Charles Lamb, who was shy with strange females, Mary warned her not to be shocked, as he "always kissed ladies when he met them for the first time." Nervous Christy found that Lamb simply shook her hand.[28]

It would be surprising if Godwin did not publish some of the stories Mary was writing at this age,[29] nor was publication uncommon for talented youngsters, among them Anna Maria Porter, Leigh Hunt, and Caroline Norton. She may also have contributed to her upkeep now with a bit of copying and proofreading for M.J. Godwin & Co. She hoped someday to write biography, history, and most of all novels in what came to be called the Godwinian school and included Wollstonecraft, defined by William Hazlitt as fiction in which "the work and the author are one" in philosophy and fervid feeling. Godwin, however, continually impressed her with the need for long apprenticeship, and her standards were very high. Spenser, Sidney, Shakespeare, and Milton were her favorite older English poets; Wordsworth, Coleridge, Southey, and Byron among the modern. She herself wrote poetry only when moved by strong emotion.

On June 3, 1813, Mary and Christy sailed for Dundee, taking along Mary's artist friend Hannah Hopwood for the summer. Mary remained for ten happy months, during which she was cured of her skin problem for good. She and Isabel visited the David Booths' Gothic-revival mansion across the Tay at Newburgh, where they wrote their joined names on a lancet window with a diamond ring. Booth was one of her father's more formidable colleagues; a wealthy retired brewer, brilliant lexicographer and scholar, autocratic and tough — and a practical joker. He promised to show the girls the most beautiful place on earth, and had them put on tarpaulins and oilskin hats and descend a deep shaft on a succession of long, steep leaders until at the bottom they found themselves in a coal mine, "very irate."[30]

An older Baxter son, Robert, who worked in Edinburgh and brought Charles Clairmont home to see Mary, may have been in love with her. With Baxter's stables at her disposal she became a good horsewoman, and she learned to sail and row. Whatever respect for Christianity she had, however, was lost when her hosts took her to church. They were Glassites, members of Godwin's original harsh Calvinist sect. The Glassite God predestined men, women, and children to hellfire at will, whatever their piety, visited retribution upon them, and his worshipers spoke in tongues.

With Isabel as guide, Mary delved into the occult with which Scottish culture abounded: legends, the Evil Eye, dealings with the devil, raising witches, sympathy and antipathy, humanoid monsters, and so on.[31] The girls experimented with "Sortes Evangelicae" — opening a Bible at random and interpreting a passage as Providence's intent — and with second sight. Isabel had had one spectacular experience when she was strolling the beach with her father and "saw" a friend who had died that day, unbeknownst to her. Mary began to cultivate her own premonitory capacities, to look for signs in nature, and to free-associate about her future, "to picture my future life," she later explained, "not drawing the colours from probability or desire — but letting them take their own course."[32] Sometimes she had extraordinary success.

And Mary went off alone to commune with the figures of her imagination. Years later when she was famous, an admirer visited the beach where she had walked "in sweet and sinless reverie." "Was she ever, like Mirza, overheard in her soliloquies . . . ?" he asked. "Did the rude fisherman of the place deem her wondrous wise, or . . . mad, with her wandering eye, her rapt and gleaming countenance, her light step moving to the music of her maiden meditation?"[33] Among her imaginings may have been those of her future sixteen-year-old heroine of *Matilda,* who lives by the sea in Scotland, reads Shakespeare and Milton (Pope, Cowper, and translations of Livy, and Rollin's *Ancient History* as well), and brings "Rosalind and Miranda and the lady of Comus to life . . . imagining myself to be in their situations." Rosalind, disguised as Ganymede, boy-beloved of Jove, spirited, courageous, adventurous; and Miranda, beloved daughter of the powerful magician Prospero, both find worthy lovers. Milton's chaste Lady resists Comus's lust, temptations, and magic powers: "thou canst not touch the freedom of my mind." Matilda also fantasizes meeting the widowed father she has never seen: "I was to be his consoler, his companion . . . his first words constantly were, 'My daughter, I love thee'!"[34]

Being good hosts and proud Scots, the Baxters took Mary touring, and it was on these excursions that she first discovered and satisfied a craving for grand scenery, strange customs, places whose very names had evocative power for her; she loved reading a pertinent work in situ. She saw Edinburgh and St. Andrews, toured up the Tay through the Grampians to Inverness and perhaps to John o' Groat's facing the Orkneys — locales she was to use in *Frankenstein* and *Perkin Warbeck* (1830). She once had a rapturous response to a mountain scene that a traveling companion remembered into old age; "her passionate enthusiasm when taken into a room arranged with looking-glasses round it to reflect the magic view without of cascades and cloud-capped mountains; how she fell on her knees, entranced at the sight, and thanked Providence for letting her witness such beauty."[35] For the rest of her life she had a yearning for mountains and felt profoundly content in their vicinity. Dundee itself was a major port for northern voyages, so she heard of whalers' and explorers' expeditions into the Arctic — like Walton's in *Frankenstein;* explorations of unknown regions were always to fascinate her.

Between the ages of thirteen and sixteen, she would write, "the human heart is nearest moral perfection, most alive, and yet most innocent, aspiring to good, without a knowledge of evil."[36] If that innocence is arguable generally, hers was preserved by insulation in Scotland that was prolonged by Isabel Baxter's engagement. Isabel's sister Margaret Booth had died. David Booth, then forty-eight, fell deeply in love with twenty-one-year-old Isabel, who agreed to marry him. For Mary this December-May love probably seemed more romantic because the engaged couple knew they would be excommunicated by the Glassites for making an incestuous match.

Mary got permission from her father to stay with Isabel until March 1814. On the twentieth, the Baxters gave her a gala send-off, inviting relatives and friends "to see Mary Godwin shipped for London," as the *Osnaburgh,* which had taken on ordinary passengers at Dundee, hove to below The Cottage and Mary was rowed grandly out to board her. She and Isabel had exchanged locks of hair and vowed eternal friendship. "They were all very sorry-like to part," observed one guest.[37] In ten days she arrived at Skinner Street.

4 "My Choice!"

MARY GODWIN was sixteen and a half in the spring of 1814, when she returned to a home she had not lived in for the greater part of her adolescence, a total of two of almost three years, spent mostly in extraordinary freedom in Scotland. She was restively discontent with Skinner Street's monotony. "So much do the young love change," she was to write, "that we have often thought it the dispensation of the Creator, to show that we are formed, at a certain age, to quit the parental roof."[1] She sported tartan dresses and chafed in a role outgrown like the few clothes she had left behind eleven months before: working in the stuffy schoolroom, doing chores, feinting with her stepmother. Her father was rushing about the city on business with Charles Clairmont — who had completed his apprenticeship with Constable and had preceded Mary home — straining to survive the current M.J. Godwin & Co. emergency, and again subject to fainting spells. Francis Place was angrily breaking with him, having lost a large sum trying to help the firm.

As soon as Mary arrived, her old governess, Maria Smith, came to see her, and the interesting Amelia Curran was visiting again from the Continent, but no one could replace Isabel Baxter, soon to be Booth. Fanny, now nearly twenty, was preoccupied with housekeeping, and her prospects were so bleak that Mary could hardly complain to her. Jane, who turned sixteen in late April, had had a semester at a boarding school run by a Frenchwoman, where her fluency in French had improved beyond Mary's, who probably spoke better brogue. Jane was taking music and singing, for which she showed promise, and talked of getting trained in Paris, which Mary doubtless encouraged. But Mrs. Godwin said she was as childlike as if she were only twelve. In any case, Mary had never been close to her.

Additionally, the political situation was dispiriting. Mary had come home to the news that the allied armies had just defeated Napoleon, and she welcomed his fall and the end of two decades of war. But from that week well into summer, as the city celebrated victory, cheering crowds greeted England's autocratic allies, the Czar, the King of Prussia, and glittering processions of generals and diplomats, while the corpulent caricature of Bourbon legitimacy, Louis XVIII, mounted the French throne as if the Revolution had never occurred. The divine right of kings, largely unleavened by rudimentary civil liberties, was restored on the Continent. In England, the Tories seemed invincible, and the Prince Regent was a contemptible, fuddled voluptuary. "It is necessary calmly to await the progress of truth," Godwin always said, but reaction had triumphed for the near future. Equally unsatisfactorily, his frequent visitor that spring, the emerging utopian socialist Robert Owen, insisted that his own system would take effect in a few years; "but how he can expect to make the rich give up their possessions, and live in a state of equality," Fanny once remarked to Mary, "is too romantic to be believed."[2]

An especially infuriating novel, moreover, was published this season, Fanny Burney's *The Wanderer,* whose Wollstonecraftian anti-heroine, a supporter of the French Revolution, asserts the right of woman, "if endowed with senses, to make use of them," and takes the ultimate unfeminine initiative of telling a man she loves him. "I have conquered the tyrant false pride; I have mocked the puerilites of education, I have set at nought and defeated even the monster custom."[3] She attempts suicide when the man prefers a "nice" girl.

On the other hand, Mary relished the sensational current struggle between the heir apparent, eighteen-year-old Princess Charlotte, and the Prince Regent over Charlotte's determination to break her engagement to the Prince of Orange, which she took it into her hands to announce to her fiancé that June.

Returning to St. Pancras, Mary fantasized and tried to foresee the future. While the epitaph inscribed on her mother's tombstone, "Author of A Vindication of the Rights of Woman," bespoke Mary's ambition for the life of an emancipated woman of letters, it also challenged her beyond her current capacity to act. As Wollstonecraft had foreseen, she was alien to standard feminine existence but lacked the resources and social context for the career she was resolved upon — as well as experience, since she had been sheltered more than most girls in her books, dreams, and Scottish retreat.

In her writing she had two mutually exclusive present aims; to attempt more ambitious work than her "commonplace" stories, and to help her father by writing children's books for the firm. Either way, living at home seemed intolerable, yet she was too young to be independent; even her mother had not left home until she was nineteen, and then to work as a

companion before becoming a teacher; she was twenty-eight before she
became a full-time writer. But if teaching was good enough for Fanny,
Mary meant to start her career as an author where Wollstonecraft had left
off, not in lowlier positions where she had begun. Novice authors, however, required a subsistence, and it would be more than four years before
Mary came of age and inherited fifty pounds a year from her mother's
share of Wollstonecraft family properties in London. And Godwin could
not afford tutors or take the time himself to work with Mary on her
studies.

Her own life seemed utterly ordinary compared with her fantasies of
fascinating companions, travel, and high romance. Among the young people she knew she had no intellectual peers, much less the superiors she
preferred, and outside of her father's circle her distinction was a barrier,
as her very name frightened conventional people. Nor could she expect
any immediate gratification of the passion for "the mysterious, the unknown, the wild, the renowned" that she had discovered in Scotland and
would never lose.[4] As for love, one of her mother's great regrets had been
that she was thirty-four before she experienced sexual fulfillment, and Mary
meant to love young and ecstatically, but not a Robert Baxter. She could
not foresee that a deus ex machina for all these ambitions was about to
materialize at Skinner Street, but she was ready to grasp opportunity, as
she had been charged by her mother in the familiar words of the heroine
of *Maria* to her daughter:

> I would . . . with fond anxiety, lead you very early in life to
> form your grand principle of action, to save you from the vain
> regret of having, through irresolution, let the spring-tide of ex-
> istence pass away, unimproved, unenjoyed. — Gain experience —
> ah! gain it — while experience is worth having, and acquire suf-
> ficient fortitude to pursue your own happiness; it includes your
> utility, by a direct path. What is wisdom too often, but the owl
> of the goddess, who sits moping in a desolated heart . . .[5]

There was one promising development at Skinner Street, however.
Godwin's desperate exertions were aimed at stalling his creditors with the
prospect of partial payment in a few months and eventual total reim-
bursement through the generosity of his young admirer Percy Bysshe
Shelley. Mary had met Shelley only briefly eighteen months before, and
her father had always had one or two ardent disciples even in his decline,
but Shelley was qualitatively the most memorable. When she drafted her
novella *Matilda* in 1819, she probably described herself in Matilda's initial
meeting with a young married poet: "he was in the height of his glory

and happiness . . . I had then gazed with wonder on his beauty and listened to him with delight . . . he often made the subject of conversation with us — and we read his poems together."[6]

Eminently the patrician in appearance and accent, Shelley was a tall, frail-looking youth, five years older than Mary, with narrow stooped shoulders and a small head, a shock of brown hair, blue eyes, delicate complexion, elegantly dressed if slightly disheveled. His movements were normally gentle, abrupt when he was excited. His boyish features were not regularly handsome, "yet was the effect of the whole extremely powerful," wrote one of his closest friends, Thomas Jefferson Hogg, who had met him at Oxford:

> They breathed an animation, a fire, an enthusiasm, a vivid and preternatural intelligence, that I never met with in any other countenance. Nor was the moral expression less beautiful than the intellectual; for there was a softness, a delicacy, a gentleness, and especially . . . [an] air of profound religious veneration. . . .[7]

Veneration of Godwin, Wollstonecraft,* and other great dissidents, that is. Mary remembered from the meeting in November 1812 that Shelley was eloquent with Godwin, affectionately playful with Fanny, and had fixed on her with his staring blue gaze. She and Fanny had surmised that Shelley's beautiful, elegantly gowned girl-wife, Harriet Westbrook, had learned her radicalism by rote, with a flat accent, so to speak, and with limited comprehension. Shelley, however, was not only a genuine heir of Godwin but a budding genius, the girls agreed when they read his draft of *Queen Mab,* a long, neo-Godwinian poem of magnificent promise.

When Mary Godwin met Shelley again in the spring of 1814, he was only twenty-one but already had had an amazing career. (His family is a classic case of generational succession: hard-nosed founder, liberal parents, Shelley the radical child, and Shelley's limp son who ended the line.) If Shelley looked like the product of a long line of bluebloods, his grandfather, Bysshe Shelley, had made the family fortune by twice eloping with short-lived heiresses, and was a baronet of fairly recent creation. A blue-jowled old cynic out of Fielding, Sir Bysshe had as his life ambition to found a great family banked by his accumulated properties, which, by the law of primogeniture, he intended to pass on as one large estate to successive eldest sons who could become peers and political powers. While siring a large illegitimate family, he made the most he could out of his ovine heir, Timothy, Shelley's father, on whom he bestowed an Oxford

* Shelley may have delayed his imminent departure for Wales in order to meet Wollstonecraft's namesake daughter.

education, the Grand Tour, a Sussex estate, a Whig seat in Parliament, and a gentry wife. Timothy resembled one of Jane Austen's more limited country squires, being proper, literal, conscientious, and philistine. Instead of the anticipated serviceable heir, Timothy and his wife, Elizabeth Pilfold, produced in their first child a rogue genius who would fight everything they stood for.

Shelley was born the young master on August 4, 1792, at Field Place, his father's Sussex estate. Until he was fourteen, when his brother, John, was born, he was the only son with four adoring younger sisters whom he ruled and tenderly loved — the prototype of his later sexual taste for ménages with several female partners. He was sent young to boarding school, then to Eton, and would always be grateful for the scholarship in classics he had gained there. But these schools also prepared him for alienation from his class and society, for he violently rebelled against unjust masters, caning, schoolboy brutalities, and the fagging system. "Mad Shelley" was a favorite target for bullies who drove him into famous paroxysms of rage. While most Etonians cropped their hair and drilled to fight Napoleon, Shelley wore his hair long, dreamed of a lovelier world, and read social and religious critiques. He was fired in particular by Godwin's *Political Justice* and by Mary Wollstonecraft, both as feminist and martyred heroine, whose betrayal by Imlay he lamented in several poems "To Mary"; he considered writing Henry Fuseli for information about her. Shelley had expected to succeed his father in Parliament someday, but as he entered Oxford at eighteen his fierce adolescent rebellion fused with his radical beliefs and atheism, and he became a born-again, lifelong evangelist in their cause.

To "see Shelley plain" — almost a contradiction in terms — he was at once a quintessential missionary utopian, a remarkable poet and intellectual, hypersensitive, idealizing, loving, self-pitying, aggressive, a patrician of his times, and a saint manqué with an unearthly quality that friend and foe alike stretched to describe. The lines between his imaginings, dramatizing, mischievousness, and pathology are sometimes hard to draw. He had paranoid suspicions and occasional hallucinations, colored situations, played a double game to get his way, usually on grounds that it was a means to a higher end. He was a master at exposing his enemies' sins and rationalizing his own deviations from his high self-ideal.

With young Shelley, to believe or feel was to act without the slightest hesitation, and to go on until he was stopped; all his life he liked to say that he never was stopped. Jeff Hogg observed that "he sprang to meet . . . advances with an ingenuous eagerness which was peculiar to him; but he was suddenly and violently repelled . . ."[8] He was possessed by hatred of evils, oppression, and injustice and by dedication to expunging them from the world: "it was the cardinal article of his faith," Mary Godwin would write,

> that if men were but taught and induced to treat their fellows with love, charity, and equal rights, this earth would realize Paradise. . . . He desired to induce every rich man to despoil himself of superfluity, and to create a brotherhood of property and service, and was ready to be the first to lay down the advantages of his birth.[9]

Shelley believed that his gifts and rank endowed him with genuine power and saw himself as a mythological hero persuading humankind to conform to his vision of what it could and should be. "Shiloh," Byron was teasingly to call him, after Joanna Southcott's hoped-for savior. Love, more than Godwin's reason, was the power he evoked to conquer evil in the world and the hostility in himself that he projected onto other people and external forces. Females personified love, beauty, truth, and harmony in his universe; they were his muses, as well as victims he burned to liberate from oppression and sexual restrictions.

Mary Godwin would observe years later of Shelley's career that in their society "no false step is so irretrievable as one made in early youth."[10] The supremely self-confident boy went to war on the world he expected to convert. During his first term at Oxford he bewitched his fellow-freshman Jeff Hogg into forming a two-man Godwinian cell, tried to manipulate his favorite sister into taking Jeff as her lover, and attempted to convert his own sweetheart to atheism. When his sweetheart "betrayed" him and became engaged to a conventional young man, Shelley exploded in fury, swore revenge on Christianity, and with Hogg published a pamphlet on the necessity of atheism, for which they were expelled from Oxford. Shelley's father was so shaken and bewildered that he negotiated with his son through the family lawyer, William Whitton, while he himself tried to reason Shelley into Christianity and a Whig parliamentary career. But the insolent boy played with him like a picador with a slow bull and talked of breaking up the family estates. He would have no money of his own until after the deaths of his grandfather and father; in fact, Sir Bysshe controlled all of the Shelley property, and Timothy Shelley lived at Field Place only because his own father chose for him to do so.

Sir Bysshe demanded that "the pupil of Godwin" recant and submit unconditionally or be left to ruin himself — while Timothy gave Shelley a two-hundred-pound allowance — and between grandfather and grandson, iron and steel, the conflict escalated. Shelley converted to Godwinism his sister's pretty schoolmate Harriet Westbrook, daughter of a prosperous London innkeeper, whose thirty-year-old sister Eliza he also admired; sisterly love was one of the highest forms of affection in his creed. Even the green boy knew the Westbrooks were encouraging him in the hope that Harriet would make a great match, but when she was "horribly persecuted" for proselytizing his views at school, he took his first major false step: he eloped with her, just as they turned nineteen and sixteen respectively. The young newlyweds agreed to separate if the time ever came when they no longer wished to live together.

Shelley, of course, expected his family to be appalled, but when Timothy stopped his allowance and refused him the funds to live in modest gentlemanly style, the boy accused his mother of adultery and became so wild that the Shelleys feared for their safety. Timothy consulted Whitton about making his younger son, John, heir, which was legally impossible. Thereafter Shelley believed his father was conspiring to have him outlawed or declared insane, even killed, so John could inherit, whereas in fact Timothy soon restored Shelley's allowance. Harriet's father contributed another two hundred pounds.

In need of fathers he could revere, Shelley became friendly with the poet and former radical Robert Southey, who had been in love with Mary Wollstonecraft, but he proved conservative and a Christian, whereupon Shelley first wrote Godwin and asked the author of *Political Justice* to be his mentor. As earnest of Shelley's seriousness, Godwin persuaded him to give up his current political agitating in Ireland and to study history and philosophy in order to change society fundamentally. He also asked Shelley to reconcile with his family, partly for the youth's own good and partly because he and Mrs. Godwin hoped that thereby Shelley could help them financially, something Shelley meant to do in any case.

Meanwhile, Jeff Hogg invoked his own favorite *Political Justice* principle — when two men loved the same woman they should share her sexually if she were willing — and tried to make love to Harriet. Initially, Shelley was shocked, but he soon agreed that this was a high form of disinterested benevolence and tried to talk Harriet out of her "prejudices" against it. Harriet summoned her sister Eliza, and after Shelley had a hallucination in which he saw a demon, the worried Eliza remained with the couple.

At a time when most men preferred women of inferior capacity to their own, Shelley's ideal mate was a colleague as well as a lover; to train Harriet to share his mission and his studies was his cherished vision of their union. But Harriet, though well educated, was an ingenuous teenager with a hearty laugh, ever perfectly groomed, and one-dimensional; "to be once in her company was to know her thoroughly," said Shelley's friend and her admirer, Thomas Love Peacock.[11] At first she followed Shelley enthusiastically, but his development hopelessly outstripped hers, while his erudite friends, some of them cranks or elderly men like Godwin, and his unremitting high seriousness of purpose bored the girl. After their daughter, Ianthe, was born, Eliza Westbrook convinced Harriet that it was time Shelley reconciled with his family and lived as befit his station.

When Shelley came of age in 1813, he asked his father and grandfather for a financial settlement, with which he also hoped to pay large debts he had contracted for amenities like a carriage and for his lavish good works; among the latter, he had saved Peacock from suicide by giving him a subsistence and planned to help Godwin more substantially. Sir Bysshe's price remained that Shelley recant his Godwinian beliefs. Shelley refused. His differences with Harriet grew bitter.

Now Shelley knew he had made a terrible mistake in uprooting Harriet from ordinary life and expecting to transplant her to the rarefied existence that was essential to him. He beseeched her to dismiss Eliza, whom he had come to loathe as her evil genius and could no longer bear to live with. Harriet indignantly refused. Beginning in February 1814, the couple lived apart for weeks at a time; by May he was despairingly begging her in verse to forgo her "remorseless" scorn, and to pity if she could not love him. Harriet's touching expressions after she had lost him — "Oh, no, with all the affections warm, a heart devoted to him" — were understandably self-delusory.[12]

In fact, Shelley suspected she had a lover, a Captain Ryan, and that Ryan was the father of the child she conceived that spring and bore in November. Godwin was later to hear from an independent source that she had had an affair. Possibly they were correct, and it is no derogation of Harriet to suggest it. A beautiful, aggrieved teenaged wife whose husband urged sexual sharing with his friend might take a lover of her own choice; hoist on his Godwinian petard, Shelley could only feel that she had confused a serious ménage à trois with a frivolous affair. Strangely, that winter, after she and Shelley separated for good and she was living at the Westbrooks' with her infant son, Charles, and little girl, her family, instead of petting and indulging Harriet, restricted her so closely that she complained that life was scarcely worth having. They may have feared that Shelley would divorce her for adultery with Ryan, who was then in London. Shelley would always behave as if Charles was his son, but given his Godwinian contempt for blood paternity, that is not conclusive. Moreover, as will be seen, he had urgent financial motives for wanting people to believe that Charles *was* legitimate. On the other hand, he could have deluded himself about Ryan, and he was in such a state that he seems also to have suspected Peacock of having an affair with Harriet.

However interesting, the question is not crucial. It was not over Harriet's "error" that Shelley despaired in spring of 1814, but at being chained for life to a woman whom he believed to be hopelessly unloving and incompatible, and Shelley's despair, like everything about him, went to the extreme. His ideals of chivalry and selflessness barred him from overmastering her or from leaving her, so he curbed his feelings and went into a paralyzing depression. "I felt as if a dead & living body had been linked together in loathsome & horrible communion," he later wrote Jeff Hogg, quoting one of Wollstonecraft's similes in *Maria;* ". . . one revolting duty yet remained, to continue to deceive my wife."[13] This he did with such success that Harriet did not understand her danger. At the same time he himself believed, now and for many years to come, that he had some illness that would kill him young.

Meanwhile, Shelley had made the financial commitment to Godwin that Mary Godwin regarded at first as an unmitigated blessing, but that was to wind a poisonous way through her next eight years. After Godwin informed Shelley about his desperate need for a large lump sum to pay his business debts, Shelley pledged to pay, over time, the totality of Godwin's indebtedness, which Godwin represented as three thousand pounds, though it was closer to five thousand. Shelley needed money for himself, too, so he decided, possibly at Godwin's suggestion, to get a twenty-six-hundred-pound "post-obit" loan on his eventual inheritance and split it with Godwin as a first installment. Godwin undertook the complex, protracted negotiations with a Mr. Nash. Post-obit loans were ruinously expensive, since the lender was not repaid until the borrower inherited, and the more so in this case because if Shelley predeceased his father and had no legitimate son, the Shelley estate would go to his brother, John, leaving Nash high and dry. At this time, not only did Shelley not have a son, the legitimacy of a future one was dubious because Shelley had been underage when he married. Therefore, he went through a second marriage ceremony with Harriet, despite their troubled relations, a week before Mary Godwin arrived home at the end of March.

Mary had been at Skinner Street for five weeks when Shelley arrived on May 5 from his house near Windsor to work with Godwin on the Nash loan. They were immediately attracted to each other. After seeing Godwin, Shelley would come up to the schoolroom to talk about her studies and read with her; they were in essential agreement on politics and women's rights, though they disagreed as between her theism and his atheism. On the sixteenth, before he returned home for a few days, he brought her a notebook for a translation of the *Aeneid* she was about to start, and she thought of commemorating the event in verse. "Shall I write a poem on receiving a cordial shake of the hand at parting from an esteemed and excellent person," she jotted in it; "ah I cannot write poetry."[14]

A week later, Fanny went to her Wollstonecraft relatives in Wales for a vacation, and possibly also because Mrs. Godwin was afraid Fanny was in love with Shelley. Actually, her absence let Mary and Shelley meet more freely, with Jane as innocent co-conspirator, though she knew enough not to betray them at Skinner Street. Every afternoon Mary went with Jane to the garden of Charterhouse School. As Mrs. Godwin subsequently found out from the gardener's wife, "they were always joined by a young gentleman . . . she says the fair young lady and the young gentleman always retired to sit in the arbor and the little young lady used to walk up and down by herself."[15] They were discussing metaphysics, they told Jane, and Jane granted that she knew and cared little for that. Or the three walked to St. Pancras, where Mary put flowers on her mother's tomb. "In early life," she would write in *Lodore*, "there is a moment — perhaps of all the enchantments of love it is the only one which is never renewed — when passion, unacknowledged to ourselves, imparts greater delight than any after-stage . . . we neither wish nor expect. A new joy has risen upon our lives; and we rejoice in the radiance of the morning."[16]

But they were falling in love, though neither said anything, believing it hopeless. Shelley's *Queen Mab* was their theme poem, and if its loving dedication to Harriet made for awkwardness, the work stimulated discussions that were a revelation of companionship to both. As yet unknown, Shelley was undecided whether to make his mark as a philosopher or a poet. He had attempted to be both in *Queen Mab,* appending extensive notes on atheism, republicanism, free love, vegetarianism, and so on. To avoid prosecution for blasphemy and sedition he had printed it privately and distributed some seventy copies. Almost no one had noticed it; none of his circle appreciated it. Shelley had been too demoralized by this "failure" and by his marital troubles to write poetry for publication since. But Mary was enthusiastic over the poetry and most of the content.

Though Mary was too proud and diffident to show Shelley her own writings, she began to confide her aspirations and something of her troubles to him. On June 8 young Robert Baxter arrived from Scotland — according to Baxter family tradition to ask Mary to marry him, but she preferred Shelley. Certainly she was otherwise engaged. That same day Shelley stopped in with Jeff Hogg on the excuse of seeing Godwin, who had gone out. As they waited in Godwin's study, "the door was partially and softly opened," Jeff recalled, by Mary, whose voice, looks, and effect struck him.

> A thrilling voice called 'Shelley!' A thrilling voice answered, 'Mary!' And he darted out of the room, like an arrow from the bow of the far-shooting king. A very young female, fair and fair-haired, pale indeed, and with a piercing look, wearing a frock of tartan, an unusual dress in London at that time, had called him out of the room.[17]

" 'Who was that, pray?,' " Jeff asked, " 'a daughter?' " " 'The daughter of Godwin and Mary,' " Shelley meaningfully replied. As Jeff knew, names had magical power over Shelley, and of all names Mary Wollstonecraft Godwin. But Shelley by all accounts fell desperately in love with Mary for the reason given by Jane Clairmont, that she had "great understanding and both knowledge and liking for the abstract subjects and high thoughts he delighted in."[18] She fulfilled his ideal of the daughter of Wollstonecraft, his goddess of freedom and love, sired by Godwin, his lawgiver: "Thou child of love and light," he would call her. Without pedantry, she was the finest scholar of any young girl he had ever met, and her strengths were in general history and literature, where, Godwin had pointed out, Shelley had weak spots. She was as eager for further learning as he, and her insights and judgments were equally impressive. She was a feminine type he admired, said by others to resemble Eliza O'Neill, who later became his favorite actress and who was known for her classically shaped head, tender simplicity, and force of passion. But Mary was also an original, giving the impression of pure "bright spring" with her singular pallor and light Titian hair, and of character in her steady, probing gaze. When Shelley described her to Jeff that October, he was still in raptures:

> The originality & loveliness of Mary's character was apparent to me from her very motions & tones of voice. The irresi[s]tible wildness & sublimity of her feelings shewed itself in her gestures and her looks – Her smile, how persuasive it was & how pathetic! She is gentle, to be convinced & tender; yet not incapable of ardent indignation & hatred. . . . *Then,* how deeply did I not feel my inferiority, how willingly confess myself far surpassed in originality, in genuine elevation & magnificence of the intellectual nature . . .[19]

Mary sensed and secretly returned his admiration. She scorned aristocrats as a class, but she was thrilled by his dedication to human betterment, renunciation of patrician advantage, and magnificent generosity. No one had ever had such perfectly tuned sympathy for her, such profound admiration for the qualities she prized most in herself. Besides his poetic gift, he was an ideal mentor, a fine classics scholar, with a subtle, penetrating intellect. She felt enlarged and irradiated by his love and companionship, which burst "upon my young life's cloud like sunshine . . . ," she was to write in her poem "The Choice." Between him and Robert Baxter or any other young man she was likely to meet, there was no comparison. And he was quiveringly sensitive, ailing, and obviously badly married. With her predilection for a suffering, public-spirited hero with an unworthy wife, she rapidly lost interest in fantasies of consoling her father in favor of an ardent desire to do so in reality for Shelley. She was ready to defy the world for love of him; prudence, her mother had written, is the resort of weak people.

Ironically, money was the catalyst of the romantic denouement, as it was to dominate the ensuing struggle between Mary, her father, and her lover that endured until Shelley's death. Shelley was ambivalent about money and therefore prone to make gifts he came to resent; he regarded concentrated wealth as an unmitigated evil, yet his future estate gave him present power. On June 18 he came to London to stay until the Nash loan was finalized, meaning then to join Harriet, who was waiting for him at Bath. Bailiffs were pursuing him for debts, so he took rooms at an obscure inn and had his meals at the Godwins'. Now, with the first installment of his pledge to Godwin imminent, instead of loving Godwin's daughter without hope he craved to possess "this inestimable treasure." Honor silenced him for another week. To divorce Harriet would be unthinkably base, even if he had grounds. All he could offer Mary was a liaison that would mean her ruin, particularly since he believed he had only a year or two to live. Still, he could not bear to take the only step that could prevent a disclosure, to stay away from her, and he had the perfect rationale, helping her father.

Seeing him every day, Mary felt more certain of their mutual passion. Young William Godwin, then thirteen, was to describe her as Madeline in his *Transfusion* "wrapt in a novel and irresistible habit of excitement" and sense of power over the glamorous married aristocrat who tries to seduce her while pretending to aid her family. So the Godwins would see it.

The inevitable occurred on the evening of Sunday, June 26. The Godwins went to Amelia Curran's for tea. Mary and Shelley walked to St. Pancras with Jane, who withdrew and left them at Wollstonecraft's grave. "A calm twilight pervades the clear sky — the lamp like moon is hung out in heaven & the bright west retains the dye of sunset."[20] Such was the evening, Mary recalled near its ninth anniversary, when she revisited St. Pancras, that decided her destiny.

For the first time Shelley confided a history of his private life that at once aroused Mary and left the outcome to her; how his quest for love and understanding had been met with "falsity" and hard, cold hearts from his family, from schoolmates who had persecuted him, from his sweetheart, and most lately from his wife, who did not love him and had been unfaithful to him. Now, he intimated, that he had found his deliverance in Mary he had no right to it. He tearfully choked back a declaration and stopped speaking. Mary was trembling. In the first great moment of their life together — which he would memorialize in three poems — she spoke "words of peace and pity" and kissed him. Then, with quiet candor and resolve she told him that she loved him and was entirely his, for the world's conventions were vulgar superstitions to such as they. In Shelley's famous Dedication to her of *The Revolt of Islam:*

> How beautiful and calm and free thou wert
> In thy young wisdom, when the mortal chain
> Of Custom thou didst burst and rend in twain,
> And walked as free as light the clouds among . . .

Shelley poured out his feelings, and they may have made love then and there behind her mother's gravestone, like Dido and Aeneas in their cave. Shivering and laughing, "We will have rites our faith to bind, /" Mary's alter ego Helen tells Lionel in Shelley's *Rosalind and Helen.* "But our church shall be the starry night, / Our altar the grassy earth outspread, / And our priest the muttering wind." His real birthday, Shelley told Mary, was June 27.

Over the next week the young lovers planned what they meant to be a model new way of life. They counted on getting Godwin's and Harriet Shelley's consent to their union. Indeed, regardless of her scorn for custom, Mary wanted her father to give her to Shelley without standing at an altar, a daughterly longing that her reason did not touch; Shelley was to ask Godwin for her hand in a liaison. They factored Shelley's money into their strategy; he was to speak to Godwin immediately after the Nash loan was signed. Shelley hoped that Harriet would agree to a legal separation with an independent income. Mary proposed that they also invite her to join them in a ménage à trois as their "sister." Shelley had the liberal attorney Basil Montagu draw up separation papers, and when Montagu refused to compose an agreement for the ménage Shelley wrote one himself. The lovers pledged themselves to one another before parting; "you are now

Mary going to mix with many and for a moment I shall depart," Shelley said, "but in the solitude of your chamber I shall be with you."[21]

On July 6 Shelley and Nash signed the papers for a loan of twenty-six hundred pounds, of which eleven hundred was for Godwin, with the actual money to be ready in two weeks. That afternoon, after dinner Shelley took Godwin out for what seemed to Mary an excruciatingly long walk. Her father returned alone, grim, told her her plan was insane, and ordered her to her room. She remained there for two days, collecting her arguments, while Godwin expostulated vehemently with Shelley. On the eighth, her father summoned her to his study, where, under Mary Wollstonecraft's portrait, father and daughter engaged in a grand confrontation for which Mary may be said to have been educated.

She was primed to defy Godwin, but he disarmed her by proposing to speak to her as a moral and intellectual equal. He had forbidden Shelley the house, Godwin told Mary, but knew he could not prevent her from joining her lover unless she herself was convinced that she should give him up. He condemned Shelley for seducing her and claimed that if his love were not selfish and purely carnal he would never ask her to become a social outcast. Mary hotly spurned these accusations, declared that she had given herself freely, and cared nothing for the world.

But when Godwin worked on her sense of honor and filial love, Mary wavered. She was taking an excitable youth away from his hapless young wife and little daughter, Godwin argued, abetting Shelley to do to Harriet precisely what Imlay had done to Mary's mother, whereas if Mary firmly discouraged Shelley his passion would subside. Shelley had summoned Harriet from Bath; when the couple met face-to-face they might reconcile. Second, as she could see in his twitching face, Mary was torturing and endangering her father. After all his struggles, Mary's selfish passion threatened to bring infamy upon her mother's memory and the entire family. On top of that, there would be financial disaster if things did not return to normal, since Godwin's creditors were at that moment expecting eleven hundred pounds from Shelley's post-obit — not to mention Shelley's pledge of thousands more, which would secure her father's few remaining years.

Overwhelmed, Mary summoned up her ideals of duty, fortitude, and selflessness, and determined to sacrifice her happiness. She could never love anyone else, she told her father, but she would not see or encourage Shelley. Godwin had her compose an appropriate letter to Shelley and rewarded her with high approbation and assurances of entire confidence in her truthfulness and resolution. Tense, hopeless, and exalted, she confined herself to the house. The shop porter, whom Shelley bribed, slipped her a copy of *Queen Mab* in which she read two notes from her lover: an

Aesopian message in ink under the Dedication to Harriet, conveying that
Harriet was unloving and mercenary and that Mary's fidelity would surely
be worthy of her great mother, and a sentence hastily jotted in pencil
when he gave the little book to the porter: "You see, Mary, I have not
forgotten you." What she forbade herself to reply to him, she wrote on
the endpapers of *Queen Mab* with remembered lines from Byron poems:

> This book is sacred to me and as no other creature
> shall ever look into it I may write in it what I please —
> yet what shall I write that I love the author beyond all
> powers of expression and that I am parted from him
>   Dearest & only love by that love we have promised to
> each other although I may not be yours I can never be
> another's —
>   But I am thine exclusively thine — by the kiss of love
> by

> The glance none saw beside
> The smile none else might understand
> The whispered thought of hearts allied
> The pressure of the thrilling hand

> I have pledged myself to thee & sacred is the gift . . .
>   But ah I feel in this was given
>   A blessing never meant for me
>   Thou art too like a dream from heaven
>   For earthly love to merit thee.[22]

When she later told Byron she had quoted his "To Thyrza" on this
occasion, he must have been secretly amused; "Thyrza" was a deceased
choirboy whom he had loved.

If Godwin now had had the integrity to refuse Shelley's impending gift,
he might have extracted the equivalent sacrifice of Mary from Shelley. But
he was too close to financial salvation, too afraid of his wife, and too
furious with the young patrician who had "seduced" his daughter and
"betrayed" himself. To accept was impeccably correct *Political Justice* doctrine: because of his need and deserts he had an absolute right to Shelley's
money, and Shelley's crimes had no bearing whatsoever. In trying to have
both Mary and the money, Godwin proved that the second was more
important, and he was to demonstrate it consistently in future. He operated
very carefully, waiting until he thought the time was right before he gave
Mary's letter to Shelley. To his relief, though Shelley was extremely agitated

he continued the final formalities with Nash and seemed to accept the situation.

But Shelley was hoodwinking Godwin. He called in his friend Peacock, who found him frantic, beside himself, determined to convince Harriet to release him, to live with Mary or to die with her. "Every one who knows me must know that the partner of my life should be one who can feel poetry and understand philosophy," he exclaimed feverishly, waving a bottle of laudanum. "Harriet is a noble animal, but she can do neither."[23] Harriet, meantime, had become apprehensive about Shelley even before his summons and was forewarned by a mutual friend, Shelley's bookseller Thomas Hookham, Jr.

On July 13 the couple met in an emotional marathon encounter. Harriet pretended to agree to a separation and accompanied him to Skinner Street to so inform the Godwins. In his blind infatuation Shelley wanted her to comfort Mary in her sufferings and the "tyranny" exercised on her, but that Harriet spurned. "I murmur not," he conceded, "if you feel incapable of compassion & love for the object & the sharer of my passion."[24]

Harriet kept up with Shelley her pretense about separation, though she declined a ménage à trois. But she was determined to fight for him. And no wonder, since, beyond her feelings for him, separation doomed her, at nineteen, pregnant with her second child, to loneliness, the social stigma that attached to a separated wife, and to chastity or to affairs that would make her a pariah. She secretly begged the Godwins to keep the lovers apart until Shelley came to his senses. "She was very much agitated, and wept, poor dear young lady, a great deal," said Mrs. Godwin.[25] Harriet also wrote to Mary and probably informed her of her second pregnancy. Mary promised her not to yield to Shelley.

On July 19 Godwin sent the trusty James Marshall to pick up his eleven hundred pounds from Nash's office; he took the high road when it came to receiving the money from Shelley's hand. Now he planned to send Mary out of Shelley's reach, to Helen Maria Williams in Paris, or to another friend he had not seen in years, Maria Reveley, now Mrs. Gisborne, in Italy. Mary would undoubtedly have gone. Then, one afternoon when she was in the schoolroom with Jane, she heard a commotion rushing up the stairs, Mrs. Godwin and Shelley shouting. The door burst open and Shelley ran in, rumpled, red-eyed, distraught, shrill. Shoving Mrs. Godwin out of his way, he "walked straight to Mary," Mrs. Godwin later wrote Lady Mount Cashell:

'They wish to separate us, my beloved; but Death shall unite us,' and offered her a bottle of laudanum. 'By this you can escape from tyranny; and this,' taking a small pistol from his pocket, 'shall reunite me to you.' Poor Mary turned as pale as a ghost, and my poor silly [Jane] . . . filled the room with her shrieks. . . . With the tears streaming down her cheeks, [Mary] entreated him to calm himself and to go home. She told us afterwards she believed she said to him, 'I won't take this laudanum; but if you will only be reasonable and calm, I will promise to be ever faithful to you.' This seemed to calm him, and he left the house . . .[26]

"Poor Mary," Mrs. Godwin told Lady Mount Cashell, "one must feel sorry for her. She showed so much serious intention of not encouraging him."[27] Shortly after, the household was awakened at midnight by the doorbell; someone from Shelley's inn announced that he had taken an overdose of laudanum. While Mary agonized, the Godwins rushed out to him, walked him up and down, and called in their mutual friend Madame de Boinville to nurse him.

Mary was on the rack, and Shelley turned the screws in frantic smuggled letters. "He declared unless she joined him as Partner of his Life — he would destroy himself," Jane recalled. "Poor Mary was agitated by these letters and by the recollection of [his recent] attempt at suicide . . . she knew not what to do — if she shewed these letters to her Father and he took measures to prevent the correspondence she believed firmly Shelley would destroy himself — thus much she told me and wept bitterly . . ."[28] Moreover, if Shelley had not already told Mary that Ryan was Harriet's lover and the father of her coming child, he did so now. As for Mary's promise to Godwin, doubtless Shelley reminded her of Princess Charlotte, who, on July 12, had tried to run away from her father and had been confined incommunicado; would Mary Wollstonecraft's daughter submit to such tyranny?

Mary passed word to her lover that she would run away with him. "Love, youth, fear and fearlessness," she said, brought her to her decision. She did not lie to her father but simply hid her intention, remembering that in *Political Justice* he had condoned deception if it saved a life. The lovers were to meet at the corner of Hatton Garden and Holborn on July 28 at four in the morning and flee to the Continent. When Jane saw Mary preparing to leave, she begged to go along, for the Godwins suspected her of collusion and she would be insufferably restricted at home and lose any chance of Paris; besides, she could help the lovers by speaking French. The distracted and sympathetic Mary agreed if Shelley would agree, one of the unwiser decisions of her life; one suspects she also sensed that nothing could distress her stepmother more than losing Jane. The two girls quietly packed and put on proper black silk traveling dresses and bonnets. Just before four, Mary crept downstairs, left a letter on her father's dressing table, then ran a short way in the muggy dawn to Shelley, who was waiting fearfully with a chaise, got his consent about Jane, and ran back to fetch her stepsister and the baggage.

The three piled into the chaise, Mary fell into Shelley's arms, and Jane drew awkwardly to the window as the driver whipped up for Dover. During the eleven-hour drive on a record hot day, Mary was so faint and queasy from motion sickness that despite their fear of being followed they halted at each stage to let her rest. They reached the port at four. Mary restored herself with a swim while Shelley hired a small boat. By six they pushed off from the beach in a falling breeze. For most of a windless night the craft weltered on the channel swells, while Mary lay seasick on Shelley's knees. Abruptly, a squall hit, the skiff heeled, shipping water. In thunder and lightning, the sailors reefed, and a northwester drove them straight to Calais. When the boat ground onto the sand, Mary woke from a doze to see the sun come up. "Mary look," Shelley said, as if it were for them alone, "the sun rises over France."[29]

II ROMANCE

France — Poverty — a few days of solitude & some uneas-iness — A tranquil residence in a beautiful spot — Switzer-land — Bath — Marlow — Milan — The Baths of Lucca — Este — Venice — Rome — Naples — Rome & misery — Leg-horn — Florence   Pisa — Solitude   The Williams — The Baths — Pisa — These are the heads of chapters — each con-taining a tale, romantic beyond romance.

Mary Shelley, Journal,
December 19, 1822

The Life that tied too tight escapes
Will ever after run
With a prudential look behind
And spectres of the Rein –
The Horse that scents the living Grass
And sees the Pastures smile
Will be retaken with a shot
If he is caught at all –

Emily Dickinson

5 "France — Poverty — a few days of solitude & some uneasiness"

ONLY A TEENAGER of Mary Godwin's singular qualities could have contrived or survived her first year with Shelley, a year of exaltation and ordeal, reckless adventure and focused experiment, living on the stretch and in straits.

Liberated from all restrictions for the first time in her sixteen years, madly in love, she launched with Shelley on a gypsying honeymoon that landed them back home in six weeks, to confront realities that both were too naive and obsessed to have anticipated. As they put their ideals into practice with the righteous defiance peculiar to privileged young radicals, they had no mature counselor — not that they would have heeded one. They believed that they were incapable of perpetrating evil, and that whatever mistakes they made could be forgiven or undone. In regard to Harriet Shelley, they were blinded by a folie à deux of the most compelling kind: passion justified by principle.

Mary in particular had begun a "warfare with society" on the enemy's ground. For though youth constituted some excuse for a girl who lived "in sin," that Mary Wollstonecraft Godwin did so openly, something even her parents had not dared, and with a married man, started her off in life with an ineradicable brand. She would never regret the liaison for herself, however. One can only speculate on what she or Shelley would have become without their union, but together they created an existence that, for all its punishments and tragedies, came closer than could any other to fulfilling her ultimate desires.

"It was acting a novel, being an incarnate romance," she would recall of her arrival in France.[1] She and Shelley played the juvenile ingenues, amorous, self-conscious, endearing, impudent, short on money and baggage, obviously runaway lovers, while Jane Clairmont played soubrette. Had she too "run away for the sake of Love[?]" a bemused Swiss gentleman asked Jane. "Oh! dear No," she twinkled. "I came to speak french."[2]

In Mary's schema she had declared independence from the world's anachronistic, oppressive system for a dangerous but charmed, supremely gratifying new existence. "She feels as if our love would alone suffice to resist the invasions of calamity," Shelley noted in their new joint journal. "She rested on my bosom & seemed even indifferent to take sufficient food . . ." [3] Intensifying her bliss, he was as superexultant with her as he had been suicidal without her. "How great is my rapture," he cried at one point. "I a fiery man with my heart full of Youth, and with my Beloved at my side . . ." [4] Like unloosed prize colts they ran for the love of velocity and exploration, veered from obstacles, dropped down to repose and nest, galloped off again, an anapest rhythm they were to maintain for some five years.

Their activity sprayed out from intense, youthful purpose. At the first opportunity, in their hotel room in Paris, Mary showed him the emblematic trousseau she had packed in her trunk; her girlhood writings, "productions of her mind" he was avid to study, letters from her father, friends, Shelley himself, Harriet Shelley, and the works of Wollstonecraft, Shakespeare, and Byron, whose love poems she forthwith read to her beguiled lover. Throughout their tour they read enhancing works aloud: Wollstonecraft's *Mary* at twilight on a castled hilltop, her *Letters from Sweden* while boating down the Rhine, Tacitus's account of the ferocious siege of Jerusalem during a violent storm.

They intended to live by the Godwin-Wollstonecraft teachings that Mary had declared at her mother's grave, but to avoid Wollstonecraft's error with Imlay, so possessed by love for a sensual deceiver that she had clutched him desperately, contrary to her belief in free unions. Theirs was to be the voluntary companionship of two autonomous individuals, and while they could not imagine ever wishing to part, they forbade themselves to speak of loving forever. They abhorred de jure unions, but in their code Harriet remained Shelley's de facto responsibility, and they were utterly serious about her living with, or, if she preferred, near them; Shelley wrote her to bring their little girl, Ianthe, and join him on the Continent. The only qualm that occasionally penetrated Mary's joy, and pricked Shelley's guilt as well, was the thought of Godwin; "and she loves him so much," Jane wrote when she recorded one such incident in her journal:

> Mary laughed and said Men always were the sources of a thousand difficulties — then Shelley asked her why she of a sudden looked so sad — and she answered I was thinking of my father — and wondering what he was now feeling. He then said, "Do you mean that as a reproach to me —" and she answered "Oh! No! Don't let us think more about it."[5]

After landing at Calais on July 29, the lovers and Jane went to Dessein's famous hotel, where Sterne had begun his *A Sentimental Journal through France and Italy*. Shelley and Mary took the premium room, the bed-sitting chamber that had been Sterne's.[6] Here, as had Sterne, they made their first entries in a journal, which Mary was to rework in 1817 for a travel book of her own, *History of a Six Weeks' Tour*. "Mary was there," Shelley wrote. Mary took the pen: "Shelley was also with me."

That evening her stepmother arrived, frantic to retrieve Jane. Mrs. Godwin shunned Mary, but pleaded through the night with Jane to come home, only to see Shelley next morning win her back with a word. Though Mary exulted at her stepmother's defeat, her own was a Pyrrhic victory beyond her present capacity to comprehend, for Mrs. Godwin turned on her heels for home, well on the way to becoming a dangerous enemy, while Jane would burden Mary's entire union with Shelley. Heedless and triumphant, Mary and her companions sped off for Paris.

The Continent had just been opened to English travelers after two decades of war, so that Mary Godwin was among the first tourists of her generation in the area. "With extasy" the trio delighted in the exotics of their first foreign land, where even annoyances were amusing, went into sophomoric giggles at the food, the *couture*, the children talking French. But they detested the restored Bourbon monarchy. Their destination was the republic of Switzerland: Lake Uri, where William Tell had fought for liberty and an enlightened character in Godwin's *Fleetwood* had resided, then Rousseau's Geneva, later perhaps Italy.

But Shelley had brought insufficient funds and Mary of course had nothing, so that everything depended on money forwarded by his friends Hookham and Peacock, which they neither could nor would do. "Imprisoned" in Paris, they sold Shelley's watch, celebrated his twenty-second birthday on August 4, and saw a few sights, Mary's favorite being St. Denis Gate, modeled on Roman triumphal arches she longed to see. They were unable to find Helen Maria Williams, Mary's parents' friend, for a loan; Shelley finally borrowed sixty pounds from a M. Tavernier. This they decided to stretch by hiking to Neuchâtel, a mad tomboy escapade even for a daughter of Wollstonecraft accustomed to range the moors, especially since she was uncommonly fatigued from love, strain, and (unbeknownst to her) the first days of pregnancy — but irresistible on account of its "romance." Shrugging off their landlady's warnings that the girls could be raped by roving demobilized soldiers, they bought an ass, left their trunks to be forwarded — the one containing Mary's writings and letters was retained in Paris and lost — packed a portmanteau and picnic basket, and set merrily off, Mary in black silk perched sidesaddle on the beast, "thinking of Don Quixote and Sancho Panza."

As they approached eastern France, recently ravaged by Cossacks pursuing Napoleon's troops, they encountered verminous inns, wretched food, and brutish peasants, who glared from hovels worse than Mary had seen in dirt-poor Scotland, and muttered against these well-dressed vagabonding young national enemies. While Mary's hatred of war flamed at her first sight of its depredations — "this plague," she wrote in *Six Weeks' Tour*, "which in his pride, man inflicts upon his fellow man" — the enlightened trio was so naive and arrogant as to expect smiles from the victims: "we could hardly pity the people when we saw how unamiable they were." After 154 kilometers, Shelley sprained his ankle. They bought an open cart, hired a mule and a surly driver, and proceeded to Neuchâtel, increasingly excited as they climbed into the picturesque Jura. Every so often the lovers would go off "walking" to make love.

In this strenuous adventuring they quickly defined their individuality. Mary enjoyed facing danger but greeted minor disagreeables "in a very complaining tone," she noted in self-mockery in the journal, or "Mary groans," while Shelley waxed alternately angelic or savage. She asserted her own ideas and comparative sagacity against his sometimes alarming wildness and his visionary enthusiasm, Jane taking her side. At a mountain stream, he tested the limits of Mary's liberation, begging her to strip and bathe with him, but she stoutly refused, mindful of their driver's glares, her buttoned black silk and multiple undergarments, and most of all her self-respect: "first, she said it would be most indecent," the wide-eyed Jane noted, "and then also she had no towel . . . He said he would gather leaves from the trees . . ."[7] Another time, when they were picnicking in a glen rather than dining in a squalid inn, "Shelley said there would come a time when no where on the Earth, would there be a dirty cottage . . . Mary asked what time would elapse before that time would come — he said perhaps in a thousand years — We said perhaps it would never come, as it was so difficult to persuade the poor to be clean."[8]

When they crossed the border into Switzerland, the Godwinian Mary was gratified to observe here and now the virtues of a Protestant, mountain republic where everything seemed spruce, cheerful, and prosperous. Just as they went into raptures at their first sight of the Alps gleaming on the horizon, their local driver began an unsublime dissertation on dairy farming and politics. "Shelley got into a fever and got out . . . to be to his own thoughts," Jane noted, but Mary listened, remarking that the mountain air had imbued this Swiss citizen with "freedom and warmth."[9]

On August 23 they arrived at Brunnen, Tell's headquarters on Lake

Uri, "and indeed," Mary would write in *Six Weeks' Tour,* "this lovely lake, these sublime mountains, and wild forests, seemed a fit cradle for a mind aspiring to high adventure and heroic deeds."[10] They sent out the laundry and took a house. Shelley began a prose fantasy, "The Assassins," about a Lebanese terrorists' Shangri-La, probably expecting Mary to collaborate, but it was not her style and she mostly took his dictation. Far from their ideal of Switzerland, Brunnen proved to be petit bourgeois and dirty, and Shelley had only twenty-eight pounds left. Giggling at their illusions and vagaries, the moment the laundry dried they headed back home by the cheapest mode, boating down the Rhine.

As travelers of their class coached along the banks rather than ride the public boats, Mary Godwin always prided herself on being the first English girl to take the then venturesome water route. But the lovers were offended by their "disgusting" plebeian fellow passengers; "'Twere easier for god to make entirely new men than attempt to purify such monsters as these,"[11] noted the future author of *Frankenstein.* They hired smaller craft, and were swept downriver by the dangerous current, circling in whirlpools, skirting rocks. On Mary's seventeenth birthday, August 30, they reached Basle; on September 2 they tied up for the night at Gernsheim, below the ruined castle of the Frankenstein counts.

Following this thrilling descent the diligence (comparable to a bus) trip from Cologne to Rotterdam was "most detestable," Mary noted, "being five times slower than a snails walk." They were detained for two stormy days at the port of Marsluys, during which she left Shelley to "The Assassins" to begin a story titled "Hate," "& gives S. the greater pleasure," he noted ardently on September 10. The uncompleted "Hate" has been lost, but it would be like Mary to presage what awaited her at home.

After a violently rough passage, she and her companions arrived in London on September 13, penniless. What seemed a last hilarious holiday lark deflated that afternoon into the first lesson of an intensive eight-month education. They took a cab to Shelley's bank, to find that Harriet had withdrawn all his funds; drove on to a friend of his and Harriet's who "treats us very ill," Mary noted; finally went to Harriet at the Westbrooks', where "poor Mary & Jane are left two long hours in the coach," while Shelley induced his pregnant wife to give him money to share with his lover.

wow --

Somewhat sobered, next day Mary tried to consult Maria Smith on Skinner Street's mood, but her old governess had been condoling with Godwin and refused to see her. Shelley wrote her father, whereupon Fanny and "Mamma" (crossed out in the journal by Mary and permanently substituted by "Mrs. Godwin") rushed to their lodgings but fled when Shelley

tried to bring them inside. They were reconnoitering for Jane only. There
followed a week of ominous silence. Then a harsh note from Godwin
arrived, in which, in an extreme application of his habitual punishment,
he excommunicated Mary so absolutely that he addressed his note to
Shelley, and had forbidden the family to speak to her; it was to be two
years and four months before she had any direct word from him. Within
days she discovered that all of her old circle shunned her, intimates who
had cherished her, friends who professed the most liberal principles: Maria
Smith, James Marshall, the Baxter family, the Hopwoods, the Lambs,
Madame de Boinville and all, some out of regard for Godwin and for
Harriet Shelley, some because Mary had leaped outside the pale of their
acquaintance.

In short order, Harriet Shelley discarded all pretense of Godwinism,
refused Shelley's request that she join him, and demanded that he give up
his mistress and return to her. He disabused her bluntly. "My attachment
to Mary neither could nor ought to have been overcome: our spirits and
[bodies] are united. We met with passion, she has resigned all for me."[12]
Turning vindictive, Harriet hired an attorney and spread a slander against
her rival's beloved father, which she knew to be false and which was cruelly
harmful to Jane as well: that Godwin had sold Mary to Shelley for eight
hundred pounds and Jane for seven hundred. At this, Shelley informed
Harriet that she was no longer his wife, though he would support her,
after which she ran up bills and eventually sent her suspected lover, Ryan,
to dun him.

The young lovers seized on Harriet's iniquities as the incontrovertible
justification of their union and decided that from the beginning she had
cared only for Shelley's money and position. They could not conceive that
they, acting on the highest, most beneficent principles, had driven her to
misbehave, or had ever wronged her in any way. As had already happened
in France, if either seemed uneasy about their liaison it was a reproach to
the other. Passion, absolute conviction of their unique rightness for each
other, the realization that Mary was pregnant, further blinded them to
Harriet's case; mutually reinforcing denial would keep them so. Since
Harriet chose to live with the Westbrooks rather than with them, and
Shelley intended to support her, in effect they wrote her off, without any
conception that in her anomalous situation she might come to harm.

Besides, they were engrossed in their own victimization. Pointed by
Harriet, creditors for thousands of pounds immediately set on Shelley's
trail, forcing them to move to Pancras; by May they had moved four more
times, leapfrogging about the metropolis to escape bailiffs. Soon they were
actually poor for the first time in their lives, scrimping in cramped, shabby

lodgings. A sense of right sustained them, yet they were unnerved by cavalier treatment from their peers, plebeian insolence, even "foul self-contempt," which the patrician Shelley felt in his unprecedented impotence. Loathing the city, they were unable to move to the country, and spent hours at business offices while Shelley tried to raise cash and a large post-obit. Exasperated, Mary jotted a "motto" in the journal: "Here are we three persons always going about, & never getting anything. Good God, how wretched!!!!!"[13]

Of all these troubles, Godwin's repudiation most staggered Mary, and Shelley as well. But as Godwin's one hand cast them out, the lovers, like followers of some flawed guru, more Godwinian than Godwin, zealously helped him grasp Shelley's money with the other. Mrs. Godwin allowed Charles Clairmont to see them, in order to keep them informed of M.J. Godwin's financial emergencies. As she calculated, Shelley stood by his pledge to clear Godwin of debt, raised what small sums he could, and offered to share his next post-obit. And Godwin accepted, though he refused to see or write Shelley. "Oh! philosophy," noted Mary tersely.

The configuration of this knot of emotion, principle, and money derived from the consensus of the major parties that Godwin represented sacred authority. If they had transmigrated directly from Jacob's tents instead of leading the avant-garde of an enlightened age, father, daughter, and lover could not have played out a more elemental patriarchal drama, one that was to end only with Shelley's death.

Godwin was in a cold, implacable rage, steeled by Mrs. Godwin's fear and rage over Jane. "Mary has committed a crime," he declared, against hallowed social arrangements, morality, her family, and Harriet Shelley. In his heart he knew that if Mary was not doing exactly what he had done, she was doing what he had said in *Political Justice*, and Godwin defensive was at his worst. He loved Mary as much as he could love anyone and he remained fascinated by Shelley, who possessed what he lacked — genius of the first order, rank, and charisma. But by enacting theories that he had moderated with experience, they threatened his hope for a secure old age and for immortal fame, the grand solace of his inglorious recent years. William, Junior, had run away for two days; Jane was ruined unless they could rescue her; Fanny was loyal in action, but defended Mary. Creditors who had been promised Shelley's next installments were turning ugly, and the world was sneering gleefully, as nothing more delights the unreformed than the spectacle of a reformer whose child goes bad.

Godwin's mortification and jealousy were unbearable, and he meant to make Shelley pay, literally, for bride rape. Mary posed a lethal threat to Godwin's authority; she was dead to him unless she confessed that she had misinterpreted his teachings and quit Shelley. He knew precisely how dangerous his repudiation might be, from the experience of his close friends: Holcroft's runaway son had killed himself in terror of his infuriated father, and Curran's daughter Sarah died following her father's excommunication over her love affair with the Irish rebel Robert Emmett. But at the very moment when he was reproaching his irate disciple-creditor Francis Place for failing him "in tenderness, in love, in anxiety," he cut off his child to demonstrate his righteousness to the world and to punish her. He had refused to pursue her to Calais and now complained that with her "as it were at our door," he could not forget her as he wished.

No girl in England was better suited intellectually than Mary Godwin to surmount her father's rejection. She expected to be ostracized by the world and prided herself that she was perfectly careless thereof. And she expected her father to be hurt and angry at her forfeited word, justifiably so. But she counted on him to see that she was putting into practice his revolution against the old order, and to forgive and uphold her, not to take her actions as a revolt against himself and succumb to "prejudice" and fear of what people would say. Incredulous, she once stood in the street under his study window, only to find herself utterly disregarded, while Fanny emerged to speak to Jane with eyes dutifully averted from herself. "Slavish submission," charged Mary, who took some time to understand that Fanny felt bound to repay Godwin's years of kindness with strict obedience.

Determined to win her father, she spent the next month rereading *Political Justice* and *Maria* in order to marshal from her parents' mouths a vindication of her right to live with Shelley. She could demonstrate further to Godwin that her liaison was not simply indulgence in "licentious love," as he alleged, but a continuation of her growth. Beginning in their first London lodgings, she and Shelley initiated the studious regime they were always to follow, reading Wordsworth's new "The Excursion," Coleridge, Southey, Godwin's works. On her fifth day in London, Shelley began teaching her Greek, though she objected that she ought first to perfect her Latin. In the journal entries, which now became primarily her office, reviewed by him, she recorded their daily work; "read two odes of Anacreon before breakfast," she notes of a typical day. "M. draws PBS read Diogenes Laertius I read Political Justice — walk out with Shelley."[14]

But in her soul Godwin was Creator to her Eve, and she loved him so strongly that she could only break away violently, and had not broken at all in the sense that Shelley was his disciple. Apparently, she also felt that her liaison balanced Godwin's remarriage to her stepmother, even revenged it, and when Godwin rejected her "bargain" she was not only bereft of a

father but left guilty of mutiny and of rage she could not admit. Clinging
to hope of having both father and lover, she was positive Godwin would
eventually soften and blamed much of his behavior on her stepmother.
Thus she usually maintained remarkable equilibrium, but peace of mind
became entangled with financial compensation to her father.

Since Shelley had robbed Godwin of his "treasure," he gave money in
recompense as well as to redeem his boyish pledge; indeed, he tended to
overpromise. But opposition to fathers was his mythic role. Moreover, he
tended to blame others for troubles of his making: in a year he would
blame Godwin for the isolation he himself caused by persuading Mary to
live with him, and later would blame Godwin for having accepted the
pledge he had rushed into in boyhood.

As Godwin's *Memoirs* had described her mother's fortitude in ostracism
over Imlay, so Mary "disdained to sink" under the injustice of universal
rejection. (Actually, Wollstonecraft, twenty-one years older than Mary at
the time, had taken her situation harder than Godwin allowed.) She refused
to be intimidated or shamed and went with Shelley to museums, art
exhibits, the parks, the aeronaut Garnerin's popular scientific lectures. Once
they saw her father, who cut them dead.

Shelley introduced Hookham and Peacock, supposedly unprejudiced
about females in Mary's position. Hookham acted like a "prig" in her view,
and though Peacock, a man of twenty-nine, was witty and a gifted writer,
Shelley warned her of his "cold calculation." Typically, Shelley had suspicions of people to whom he gave money unless they were weaker than
he. Mary's sole female companion was Jane, herself dependent and wavering between the lovers and the Godwins, who were trying every means
short of abduction, and even considered that, to get her away.

But despite her "careless, fearless spirit" and her wry journal entries,
Mary was too sensitive not to be hurt and anxious. Fortifying herself on
the Wollstonecraft side, she spent hours at her mother's grave, reading,
drawing strength from conviction that her mother's spirit approved her
liaison. She was utterly dependent upon Shelley, whom she had known
for only six months, and if they were separated she sometimes felt a child's
needfulness and self-pity. From October 23 to November 9 he went into
hiding to avoid arrest for debt. After furtive, humiliating meetings with
him in obscure inns or unlikely public places, "return gloomy," she noted.
Once, she and Jane had to pawn Shelley's microscope to buy dinner. The
lovers exchanged letters between meetings:

> *Mary:* For what a minute did I see you yesterday — is this the
> way my beloved we are to live . . . in the morning I look for

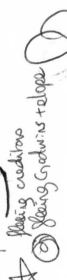

fleeing creditors + debts

leaving Godwins + debts

you and when I awake I turn to look on you — dearest Shelley . . . I was so dreadfully tired yesterday that I was obliged to
take a coach home forgive this extravagance . . . I had been so
agitated . . . a morning rest however will set me quite right
again . . . I send you Diogenes as you have no books —[15]
Shelley: Oh! those redeeming eyes of Mary that they might beam
upon me before I sleep! Praise my forbearance oh beloved one
that I do not rashly fly to you . . .
  . . . a thousand of the sweetest kisses live in memory . . . If
you are inclined to work over any latin, read Cicero's Para-
doxa . . .[16]

Now Mary composed a grand vindication of her liaison (unfortunately
lost) and sent it to Fanny to give Godwin. Shelley was in raptures: "The
simple & impressive language in which you clothed your argument —
the full weight you gave to every part, the complete picture you exhibited . . . was more than I expected. How hard & stubborn must be the
spirit that does not confess you to be the subtlest & most exquisitely
fashioned intelligence . . ."[17] But she had scorned to make an emotional
appeal, and Godwin spurned her "cold, indelicate" brief by means of
a stinging note from her stepmother. "I detest Mrs G.," the girl wrote
Shelley:

  . . . why will not Godwin follow the obvious bent of his affections
  & be reconciled to us — no his prejudices the world & she — do
  you not hate her my love . . . hug your own Mary to your heart
  perhaps she will one day have a father till then be every thing to
  me love — & indeed I will be a good girl and never vex you any
  more. I will learn Greek . . . a poor widowed deserted thing no
  one cares for her . . . I shall dream of you ten to one when naughty
  one — you have quite forgotten me —[18]

The approach of a planned November 4 meeting restored her spirit,
despite a shocking disappointment. She had been counting on Isabel Booth's
support, but on the third she received a letter from Isabel's husband, David,
in Isabel's name, repudiating her for her liaison and for afflicting her father.
"I did think Isabel perfectly unprejudiced — she adores the shade of my
mother —" Mary wrote Shelley,

  but then a married man it is impossible to knock into some peoples
  heads that Harriet is selfish & unfeeling and that my father might
  be happy if he chose . . . Higho love such is the world . . . I shall
  meet you tomorrow love & if you do but get money love which

indeed you must we will defy our enemies & our friends (for aught I see they are all as bad as one another) and we will not part again —[19]

The girl resolved to wait for her father to come around. Having begun her adolescent lesson of disillusion, she classed him with other aging erstwhile liberals: such as Wordsworth, whom she called "a slave," and Shelley's favorite author, Christoph Wieland, "one of those men," she noted challengingly for her lover to read in the journal, "who alter all their opinions when they are about 40 and then thinking that it will be the same with every one think themselves the only proper monitors of youth."[20]

She and Shelley were reunited on November 9, in new lodgings at 2 Nelson Square. Three days later, she started a short biography of J. B. Louvet de Louvray, author of the racy novel *Faublas* and an audacious Girondist who had voted against Louis XVI's execution and later led an anti-Jacobin guerrilla movement with his mistress, Madame Loidoiska.* Soon, however, Mary stopped, as she began to suffer the bleeding and pain of a threatened miscarriage. Following her mother's preference for female practitioners for female problems, she sent Shelley for Mrs. Knapp, landlady of The Polygon and a midwife — who promptly informed the unmoved Godwin. On her advice Mary stayed in bed, feeling childishly aggrieved and caged in. "Very ill all day," she noted. "S and J. out all day hopping about the town."[21] Whenever the bleeding stopped, she confidently returned to normal activity until the next episode, and did not consult her family physician, Dr. William Lawrence, until late December, when she was entering her sixth month.

On December 6, Shelley had a letter from Harriet — calling herself "a *deserted wife*," Mary noted indignantly, when the lovers believed that Harriet had deserted Shelley and was no wife — announcing the birth of his supposedly eight-month son, Charles, a week before (a delay that suggests possible anxiety about his paternity). Gleeful, Shelley sent out birth notices and went to see the baby. But his excitement was strictly monetary, as poor Harriet realized, giving him up for good; a legitimate son meant better terms for loans.

At the turn of 1815, Shelley gave up seeking loans when his implacable grandfather died, and his father, now Sir Timothy, dealt more generously with his still insolent son. The Shelley lawyer, William Whitton, also

---

* Mary Godwin intended to vindicate Louvet from an attack by Abbé Augustin Barruel that she had recently read. She also identified with Louvet because she saw herself and Shelley as comrades in arms against tyranny. Louvet and Loidoiska would be an inspiration for Shelley's Laon and Cythna in *The Revolt of Islam*.

changed, advising Sir Timothy to leave the way open for Shelley to return
to his family. In effect, Sir Bysshe's will protected the bulk of the family
fortune by giving Shelley the choice of inheriting, after his sixty-one-year-
old father's death, an enlarged but entailed estate valued at two hundred
thousand pounds, or an eighty-thousand-pound estate outright.[22] Shelley
promptly chose the latter, partly because in return his father granted him
a thousand-pound annuity and seventy-four hundred pounds for his debts,
in which Shelley duplicitously included one thousand pounds for Godwin
and two hundred for himself, and after which he still owed many creditors.

The lovers could not leave for the country until after mid-May, when
the settlement was to be signed. Meantime, money was short, bailiffs
lurked, and Shelley's health declined from the strain of negotiations with
lawyers, with court officials, and with Harriet. As their poverty promised
to end, the lovers discovered that their isolation eased. Godwin ended his
ban on writing to caution Shelley about his choice of estates: "all this is
very odd & inconsistent —," Mary noted sagely on February 5, mistaking
it as an augury of reconciliation, "but I never quarrel with inconsistency —
folks must change their minds." Her father also let Fanny, Maria Smith,
and James Marshall see Mary. Peacock asked for money. But their standing
alone and helplessly poor *contra mundum,* which Mary would memorialize
in *Lodore* through the newlywed Ethel and Edward Villiers, had made "a
marriage of the heart." As Shelley would write in his Dedication of *The
Revolt of Islam* to Mary:

> There is the wisdom of a stern content
> When Poverty can blight the just and good,
> When Infamy dares mock the innocent,
> And cherished friends turn with the multitude
> To trample: this was ours, and we unshaken stood!

Both Mary Godwin and Shelley envisaged their liaison as the core of
a pastoral Godwinian commune, in which affection, money, and intellectual pursuits would be shared, and they had begun that experiment as
soon as they arrived in London. Mary saw the solution to multiple claims
of affection in the kind of ménage that she and Shelley had offered their
"sister" Harriet, and she agreed with Shelley in principle on sexual sharing,
based upon Godwin's theories in *Political Justice.* What she discovered was
that she lacked the patience, submissiveness, and capacity to compromise
required for contented communal living, and that Shelley was the only
man who fulfilled her demands for a lover.

Shelley's sexual tastes and ideology, by contrast, were a continuum. He
had stage-managed his friend Jeff Hogg's abortive efforts to become his

own sister's lover and had encouraged Harriet to sleep with Jeff. He cherished the idea of loving and being loved by a bevy of girls, and it was a prime part of his mission to enable them to enjoy sexual freedom and equal rights. In France he had tried to adopt a little peasant girl, and just recently had so dazzled Mary and Peacock with a vision of kidnapping his sisters and settling all together in darkest Ireland, à la "The Assassins," that he half-persuaded them to try. Jane was irresistible disciple material at hand, and, thanks to her "vulgar" mother, badly in need of reeducation, which Shelley undertook with Mary's assistance. "Content yourself with one great affection, with a single mighty hope . . . ,"[23] he told himself when annoyed by Jane's childish sullenness and untrustworthiness, but returned to his task. Mary and Jane were no more friends than before; it was Shelley who told Jane that Mary was pregnant. But when the Godwins convinced Jane to return home, Shelley was so crushed that Mary persuaded Jane to stay.

Exerting his seductiveness, when Mary went to bed early because of her pregnancy, Shelley instructed Jane late into the night to the point of mutual arousal, explaining why he had wanted Harriet and Jeff Hogg to be lovers. Then he would change to safer "ghostly" talk, send Jane into her ready hysterics, bring her to Mary's bed, and watch adoringly while Mary performed a role that enraptured him, calming Jane with her "all powerful" feminine benevolence. Jane, a volatile compound of idealism and folly, swallowed Shelley's concepts whole and flew off into his orbit, rhapsodizing for years to come about "a new world where truth and perfect freedom abound." Struggling to match Mary, she studied one step behind her and began a novel, *The Ideot*, about a girl who acts on her natural impulses.

Shelley came to love Jane as an engaging youngster whose clever sallies and naughtiness alike made him smile. She, however, fell in love with him. When she saw the lovers amorous, she got sulky, and even returned to Skinner Street, until she learned of Mary's endangered pregnancy and came back for good. In token of her resolve, she changed her name to Clara — as she will be known until her next change, of which there would be two in five years. But Clara took advantage of Mary's incapacitation to make up to Shelley, and then played the innocent as to why Mary was so often "cross" with her.

Shelley's friend Hogg entered the equation in mid-November and provided a new factor. Thomas Jefferson Hogg was a stocky, hawk-nosed, learned young man whom Shelley once compared to an oyster; truculent, sardonic, and rough, yet a pearl of a friend. The oldest son of a northern family with his living to make, he had bid farewell to romantic youth in a pseudonymous novel, *Memoirs of Prince Alexy Haimatoff,* which Mary had just read attentively, and was now reading for the bar. The lovers were unsure of his fitness to be their friend, since lawyers were panderers to the evils of society in the Godwinian canon, and Shelley meant to discard Jeff if he did not approve of the liaison and of Mary.

Shelley need not have worried, for he himself was the love of Jeff's life; at least, all Jeff's loves were to be first Shelley's, starting with Shelley's sister and Harriet. Both young men, furthermore, dreamed of consummating with Mary their unfinished business of sharing Harriet. Jeff charged Shelley with abetting Harriet's refusal and assumed that Godwin and Wollstonecraft's daughter was sexually available — as would other men — while Shelley chafed at the charge and hinted that Mary was indeed "enlightened."

To Shelley's proud delight Mary began by challenging Jeff's philosophic positions, noting her triumphs in the journal: "get into an argument about virtue in which Hogg makes a sad bungle . . ."; "an argument upon the love of Wisdom and free Will & necessity — he quite wrong but quite puzzled . . ."[24] But Mary knew Shelley missed his old closeness to Jeff; she had need of new friends and Jeff was amusing, erudite, and fascinated by her. She engaged him to help her read Ovid, a sure sign of her favor.

By Christmas, Mary was lapped in adulation by Jeff as well as by her adored Shelley, in whom "my whole soul is wrapped up" as she rhapsodized in total sincerity, bringing tears to Jeff's eyes. "Dormouse," they called her, as she often had to stay in bed like a pet in its cage; or "Pecksie," for the exemplary good and wise fledgling in Mrs. Trimmer's tale of a robin family; or "Maïe," for the Pleiade of the beautiful hair and for the mad month of youth and joy. Shelley wrote a jocular verse to her triple nature: "On her hind paws the Dormouse stood / In a wild & mingled mood / Of Maïeishness & Pecksietude."[25]

Jeff declared his love on New Year's Day, and asked to become her lover. Startled but flattered, eager to prove that she had none of Harriet's "prejudices" and to please the overjoyed Shelley, Mary promised to try to progress from affection to love, which she hoped to feel after her expected delivery in May. To her annoyance, instead of letting things develop naturally, Shelley and Clara, who saw her chance for Shelley, made transparent excuses to leave her alone with Jeff. But in late January she was anticipating their "joy & delight":

> — in the summer when the trees are green . . . when . . . I have
> my little baby with what exquisite pleasure shall we pass the
> time — you are to teach me Italian you know & how many books

we will read together but our still greater happiness will be in
Shelley — I who love him so tenderly & entirely whose life hangs
on the beam of his eye . . . you who have so sincere a friendship
for him to make him happy . . . to see his love his tenderness . . .[26]

This peculiar idyll was interrupted by emergencies that penetrated through
Mary's theories to her instincts. On February 22 she suddenly went into
labor and delivered a seven-months' girl before the arrival of Dr. John
Clarke, who had attended her mother after her own birth. He advised
that the tiny premature could not survive. But Mary refused to accept
Clarke's verdict and kept her baby at her breast, trying to make it suckle.
In two days it was taking milk, and Clarke allowed there might be hope.
Triumphant, Mary read *Corinne*, Madame de Staël's epic of woman-artist,
while nursing, and sent Shelley to buy a cradle. Already languid and
coughing, he developed chest pains on the baby's third day (he would
sicken after the births of all their children), suspected he had consumption,
and consulted a Dr. Pemberton, who diagnosed an advanced case. Shelley
was convinced that it was fatal, but Mary, though fearful about his health,
refused to believe it, sustained by Jeff, who would always claim that Shelley
never had the disease.

Again following her mother's teaching, Mary did not spend the usual
postpartum weeks lying about. When they had to move to new lodgings
down the street on the baby's eighth day, she walked there with her infant;
Shelley and Clara followed later. She apparently thought of the baby as
essentially hers, possibly meant to name her Mary Wollstonecraft Godwin
III. On the eleventh night, she assumed the baby was sleeping and did
not wake it to suckle; next morning, March 6, she saw that it was twisted
and dead. "From its appearance, it evedently died of convulsions,"[27] she
wrote Jeff, summoning him to help her quiet the distraught Shelley. Four
days later Jeff moved in with them.

Mary's stoic indoctrination forbade her to "indulge" in mourning, yet
she found herself grieving: ". . . think of my little dead baby," she noted
in the journal on March 13, "this is foolish I suppose yet whenever I am
left alone to my own thoughts & do not read to divert them they always
come back to the same point — that I was a mother & am so no longer."
Six days later: "Dream that my little baby came to life again — that it had
only been cold & that we rubbed it by the fire & it lived — I awake &
find no baby — I think about the little thing all day . . ."

But if she restrained her sadness over the infant's death and worry about
Shelley's illness, they activated her distaste with what her liaison was becoming, and she took steps to reorder it, beginning with Clara. Amusing

and appealing as Clara could be, she got on Mary's nerves and always would, interspersing abject respect with anger, schadenfreude, and sly disloyalty. Moreover, Clara expected a ménage à quatre, claiming to love Shelley as Jeff loved Mary, when Mary believed it was only a crush and sensed that Clara wanted whatever Mary had. Clara was in love with Shelley, but her desire for sex was more philosophic than genuine at this age, and she seems never to have developed an urgent erotic drive.

In puerile bravado, the lovers and Clara had given credence to Harriet's slander that Shelley slept with both girls, for Shelley flaunted the eager Clara everywhere, with and without Mary, who shrugged thoughtlessly. But in a ménage all parties had to be devoted, and by now the two girls were so at odds that Clara sometimes kept to her own room. Moreover, the lovers abominated carnality for its own sake, and Shelley *"explained"* to Clara that he was not in love with her, though privately he probably offered to try, as Mary was trying with Jeff. Clara would later tell Byron that Shelley was her lover this spring. Mary, who trusted Shelley absolutely, never believed it, and whereas he apparently was to hoodwink her about Clara a few years later, it is highly unlikely that he did so now.

Two days after her baby's death, Mary announced that Clara must return home, as she could no longer bear to live under the same roof with her, and she was too clever not to remind Shelley that he had felt the same about Harriet's sister Eliza. Besides, she meant to separate, not to break, from her stepsister. Shelley had to agree, though sorely disappointed. But the lovers had converted Clara too successfully and made her, at just seventeen, an outcast dependent upon them; she refused to return home, and to poor Mrs. Godwin's anguish Godwin refused to have her because the Wollstonecraft aunts said her delinquency would endanger Fanny's chances in life. In a typical division of labor, Shelley comforted Clara, while Mary enlisted Fanny and James Marshall to persuade Mrs. Knapp to board Clara at The Polygon. Clara advertised to be a companion, but chose the romantic and untenable course of living alone in Lynmouth, where she meant to finish her novel. Mary took her shopping for her kit; Shelley paid for everything and intended to leave her an independence, though he had no will and nothing to give until his father died.

Simultaneously, Mary determined that if Jeff Hogg was worthy to be her lover he would give up the study of law and devote himself to love and literature. Pride and awareness that Imlay had exploited her mother made her demand a lover's total dedication. Her prescribed six-week post-partum abstinence ended about April 10, and toward the end of the month she may have gone so far as to allow Jeff lovemaking without consummation. At that point, she put him to the test, perhaps in agreement with

Shelley. She may have suspected Jeff would fail. Though aroused, she did not really love him, nor would she sacrifice herself to Shelley's desire for a triangle. Her own jealousy warned her that Shelley might feel it, despite his declaimers, and that she should not risk the relationship that meant everything to her.

On April 25 the lovers ran off for a short holiday near Eton — during which Mary apparently conceived another child — and summoned Jeff to enjoy the "shared treasure" of Mary. Being once again in her natural country habitat and reading Wordsworth "among green shades" thrilled her with delight, she wrote Jeff, assuring him that she loved him wherever she was: "For Maië girls are Maië girls / Wherever they're found / In Air or in Water / or In the ground."[28] Jeff would not leave his work. She sent "Prince Prudent" an ultimatum, echoing her mother's words to Imlay: "if you do not come I am off . . . I shall believe that your love is all a farce . . . Yours — as we shall see when we know how you behave."[29] "We" responded to Jeff's refusal by terminating the sexual triangle, though he lived with them until they left London.

On May 13, after private farewells between Shelley and "his friend," Clara, as Mary noted emphatically in the journal for his edification, he put Clara on the early coach to the west, and spent a long, disturbing day with his father, uncle, Harriet's representatives, and assorted attorneys for the signing of his financial settlement. He arrived home late, exhausted and ill. That night after writing her journal entry, Mary scored a line across the page and wrote, "I begin a new journal with our regeneration." (This second journal notebook, which covered the next fourteen months, was later lost.) They decided to tour the Devon coast and Wales for Shelley's health, alone for the first time in ten months.

As Shelley was to describe in *Rosalind and Helen*, the lovers left London in his repossessed carriage and spent "the azure time of June" on a second honeymoon — "one soul of interwoven flame" — staying at Torquay, a resort for consumptives,* then visiting Clara and the spa of Clifton. Here Shelley had a severe "pulmonary" attack. He envisioned dying in Mary's arms, but she persuaded him to rush to London to consult Dr. Lawrence. He left her all he had if he should die, a check for three hundred pounds to cash immediately before creditors seized his funds: "I intreat my own sweetest Pecksie . . . that she will go without a day's delay to London with it herself; or it may be of no use."[30]

After several "days of uneasiness," which in fact should have been dread

---

* Torquay would inspire the opening episodes of *Falkner,* the motto of which, celebrating Fidelity, is taken from *Rosalind and Helen.* The first scene is set at the grave of a young man who died of tuberculosis.

if only because of her position if he died, Mary received his letter announcing a miraculous recovery, or a faulty prior diagnosis: Lawrence
found no tubercular symptoms whatsoever. As a pledge of his safety,
Shelley sent her a diamond brooch in the form, oddly enough, of a cross.
He was looking for a house at Windsor and then intended to fetch her in
the carriage. After a few more days, about ten in all, Mary became frightened and angry. The first anniversary of her flight impended, and Shelley's
 birthday. She suspected, correctly, that while she waited compliantly for
him, Clara had rushed to join him, an infuriating "freak" typical of Clara.
Most seriously, Mary realized she was pregnant and had flashes of fright
about Shelley's intentions. On July 27 she wrote him a poignant child-
woman's letter, saying nothing of her pregnancy, struggling between fear
and confidence, submission and assertiveness, praying him to come back,
give her leave to join him, or "expect me without it. . . . do not be angry
dear love — Your Pecksie is a good girl . . ."[31]

Shelley may already have been on his way. Within the week they were
settled at Windsor for the first relatively serene period of their union.

6 "A tranquil residence in a beautiful spot"

FOR THEIR FIRST HOME, Shelley brought Mary Godwin to the area near Eton where he had roamed in his schooldays, lived with Harriet, and always loved best in England. To Mary, the place he had chosen at Bishopsgate, just outside the eastern entrance to Windsor Great Park, was idyllic: an isolated brick cottage with a flower garden, and for their pleasure grounds the park's Chapel Wood and Virginia Water, the charming countryside and the Thames.* For company, Peacock walked downriver from the nearby village of Marlow, where he lived with his widowed mother; Jeff Hogg came up from London on weekends. Here the lovers spent nine quiet months, during which Mary's second pregnancy proceeded normally, and the pattern of their union took shape.

Money was always short, since Shelley's thousand-pound annuity was inadequate for his extraordinary benevolences and the patrician style of living that, to his friends' amusement, he took for granted despite his radicalism, and to which Mary became accustomed. It was his fortune; she disliked thinking about money and believed as he did in sharing, but it promised them freedom of action, to her new and precious, and sustained her family, so she knew something about his finances.

The annuity was deposited in quarterly payments of two hundred and fifty pounds, so that he had to borrow if he needed a sizable sum. Such loans added to his heavy indebtedness, including five hundred pounds for his carriage, which the carriage maker periodically repossessed. But he always expected momentarily to inherit six thousand pounds a year on the death of what seemed a totteringly aged father — a vast underestimation of Sir Timothy, who would survive for almost thirty years. Actually, Shelley now had less than six hundred pounds a year, since two hundred went to

* The cottage, near Rhododendron Walk, is still standing. In *The Last Man*, Mary Shelley transmuted Windsor into a metaphorical Garden of Eden, where the narrator, Lionel Verney, lives with his loved ones until they are expelled by a plague that destroys the human race except for him alone. The cottage is his sister Perdita's solitary maiden residence. In "The Mourner" it becomes Clarice Evesham's post-exilic hermitage.

Harriet Shelley and their children, Ianthe and Charles, at the Westbrooks';
he gave about a hundred to Clara Clairmont, who had scrambled back to
Lynmouth; another hundred to Peacock, who acted as his sometime agent;
and a stipend to Charles Clairmont, who "broke loose from horrors" of
his impossible mother's making at Skinner Street, and came to Bishopsgate
counting on Shelley.

That fall Shelley scraped up funds for Charles to take Clara to Ireland
and investigate a distillery business, and offered to raise three hundred
pounds for Godwin. Godwin had begun his first novel in a decade, *Mandeville,* so the lovers were eager to give him peace to write. In addition,
Shelley gave away uncounted sums or impetuously undertook projects,
seldom sure where his outlays had gone and often repenting them.

Mary adored Shelley for his generosity and regarded his improvidence
as rather fun. She disliked seeing him exploited, however. When Harriet
(ever mercenary, in the lovers' view) demanded more child support, Shelley
offered instead to rear Ianthe, something Mary was eager to do, but Harriet
refused. And when Charles asked for capital for the distillery, Mary agreed
with Shelley that this was beyond the call, though after Charles got into
some kind of a scrape, Shelley paid his way to emigrate to the Continent
and thereafter sent him occasional checks.

To keep their options open, Shelley had rented the cottage furnished,
for a year. Touring in his carriage had so delighted Mary that she suggested
continuing to Wales to read "Tintern Abbey" in situ before settling, and
though at Bishopsgate both discovered a love of home life they would
always oscillate between it and wanderlust. Rather than Mary's being
victimized by Shelley's restlessness, as has been part of their legend, travel
was not only one of her ways to escape unpleasant situations, she craved
new impressions and equated change with growth. He was drawn to the
squire's life in which he had been reared, and he would propose putting
down roots between their continual moves; until she was fifty she had no
permanent home and few possessions.

Like other uncommon aspects of Mary Godwin's career, however, this
motility was aggravated by her social stigma. Bishopsgate was only the
first example. Shelley had disregarded the fact that friends of the Godwins
and of Harriet Shelley lived in the vicinity, and Mary, who scorned "stupid"
circumspection, left important letters lying about for her local servants to
peruse. As people learned who she was, she met with glazed or prurient
stares when she went out into the neighborhood. Peacock's mother was
too starchy for Mary's taste, but she was the only woman in the area who
would know her.

Thus, for temperamental and pragmatic reasons, the ideal of home she

developed at Bishopsgate was portable, consisting of space to live pleasantly, work, and receive a few friends, set in an attractive landscape preferably near water and mountains, with furnishings that were disposable
except for her and Shelley's box-desks and expanding book collection.
Their style was a moderate primitivism with the luxuries of fresh flowers,
moonlight rambles, saddle horses, and a sailboat, Shelley's passion. She
dressed for comfort and for exercise and rarely bothered with a parasol;
he wore his shirts open at the neck. During pregnancy she refused to lace
herself, though respectable women of all classes did so, and wore loose
clothing that most people considered eccentric and unattractive. She preferred colors that set off her Titian skin and hair: pink, buff, lilac, and her
favorite white.

Mary hired her first cook and a maid or two to whom she delegated
domestic affairs as much as possible, and returned to her customary day
divided between work and relaxation — a schedule that Shelley, hitherto
disorganized, found beneficial and paralleled. "We had our separate occupations and our common amusements,"[1] says her narrating alter ego of
The Last Man, the scholar-writer Lionel Verney, through whom she would
describe her life at Windsor. She selected a little room for her study, where
she retired after breakfast to work until early afternoon dinner; in fine
weather she and Shelley sometimes spent the day reading under the trees
in Windsor Great Park. "I felt convinced," says Lionel:

> that . . . no man's faculties could be developed, no man's moral
> principle be enlarged and liberal, without an extensive acquain-
> tance with books. To me they stood in the place of an active
> career, of ambition, and those palpable excitements necessary to
> the multitude. The collation of philosophical opinions, the study
> of historical facts, the acquirement of languages, were at once my
> recreation, and the serious aim of my life.[2]

Shelley supported her with exalted enthusiasm and pride: "among women
there is no equal mind to yours," he said, "and I possess this treasure.
how beyond all measure is my felicity."[3]* He was "always most earnest
and energetic in his exhorations that I should cultivate any talent I possessed, to the utmost," she writes.[4] They studied together as well as alone,
read many of the same books; sometimes he tutored her, a relationship
both cherished. Except when they were separated and Mary wanted to
preserve special thoughts for him, she used her journal as Godwin had
his, to record their daily reading and writing, with cryptic references to

---

* His Cythna in *The Revolt of Islam,* Asia in *Prometheus Unbound,* and Beatrice in *The Cenci*
possess the intellect and skill in disputation as well as the character that he admired in Mary.

other matters. At year's end she made lists — usually not complete — of the books they had read singly and jointly and proudly added them up to assess their accomplishment.

Around Mary's eighteenth birthday, the lovers hired a shallow draft boat and rowed with Peacock and Charles Clairmont to the source of the Thames and back, stopping at Oxford to see Shelley's former haunts and to let Mary, who was studying Commonwealth history, locate the spots where Charles I had collected his army and "the patriot" John Hampden had died fighting the royalists.

Mary had a sense of order about things that were important to her, but took for granted that Shelley would live as he pleased. He drifted in and out of the house, wandered and composed al fresco, and ate when he felt like it, perhaps standing with a book in one hand. "Mary, have I dined?" he would sometimes ask. Like protesters against impure societies through the ages, he abstained from meat and alcohol; she laid in a store of vegetarian foods, occasionally made him a passable pudding, without sugar, which they boycotted because it came from slave plantations. She liked her tea sandwiches cut neatly, but dinner with proper courses was a rarity unless they had company, and throughout their union friends complained about the quality of her table.

The second half of the day was for recreation. Mary, a skeptic in medicine, was convinced that regular amusement and exercise were better than physicians for Shelley's fragile health and sensitive nerves, and took him on long daily walks in all seasons, one of their favorite times for conversation. "Don't over walk Shelley," Clara admonished her the following autumn, "and pray *make* him get a new great coat."[5] In the evenings they read aloud, most often he, while she embroidered. At either side of their bed were tables with books, inkstands, and paper.

Mary was perennially indignant that Isabel Baxter Booth had sacrificed their friendship to opinions about marriage that Mary supposed had been condemned by "every enlightened reasoner upon moral science."[6] Otherwise, except for rare outbursts, she seemed calmly indifferent to her ostracism. She believed that she was Wollstonecraft's last regret solaced, her last wish fulfilled: a daughter who chose young to pursue joy and greatness with a worthy companion regardless of a benighted, hypocritical world. Beyond that, she placed herself in the grand tradition of lawbreaking passion with Francesca and Paolo, Juliet and Romeo, and identified in particular with Desdemona, who fell in love with her father's friend, eloped, and was disowned; she was always to see *Othello* played whenever she could. The Godwins' enmity was part of the romance. "Because a young Poet fell in love with a beautiful and quite young girl and persuaded her to run away and marry [*sic*] him . . . ," Clara Clairmont would recall, "Papa took to being chilling haughty and stern, and Mama to being lively and furibonde . . ."[7]

Shelley shielded Mary, had her called "Mrs. Shelley" when they traveled, and made her the center of a little court whose charter members were Hogg and Peacock, where she was treated as befit her "hereditary aristocracy" encapsulated in "thy beloved name" and her personal merits. He set the tone with exquisite courtesy. "She is accustomed to be surrounded by her own coterie," Clara would warn Byron, "who treat her with the greatest politeness."[8]

After Shelley, Jeff Hogg was Mary's first, if troublesome courtier. The lovers had relegated Jeff to the status of friend with an unfortunate misconception of what was important in life — which they did not let him forget. "Mary . . . unites with me in saying," Shelley once wrote, "that she shall be happy to see you as soon as you can get free from the numberless briefs which are no doubt pouring into your vestibule."[9] She felt so little shame about her abortive affair with Jeff that she never retrieved her indiscreet letters — which he probably told her he had burned (his to her have disappeared).* But Jeff remained in love with her for several years and showed that her rejection had hurt him by exalting her, in a sardonically critical tone, to what she called "a slippery and turbulent eminence." She was annoyed that he could not settle for simple, sincere friendship, which was never again possible, and distrusted his goodwill, so that she alternated between coolness and the facetious-to-serious sparring with which they had begun their acquaintance.

Her relations with Peacock were not confidential but usually were calmer and in the long run steadier. Though fond of Harriet Shelley, Peacock chose the lovers' side not simply out of self-interest as they suspected, but because he admired them. Behind his mask of aloof, evenhanded wit he was a devotee of Wollstonecraft, whose eulogy by Southey he recited with emotion even as an elderly man. Mary enjoyed his rapier wit, scholarship, literary gifts, and extraordinary ear for disputations. Apparently through associating with the argumentative lovers and Jeff, Peacock found his true métier of fictionalized intellectual satire in his first novel, *Headlong Hall*, published that December, in which he brilliantly parodied opinions across the spectrum of ideas.

In his next novel, *Melincourt*, which he conceived during the Bishops-

her letters to Jeff still exist then

---

* Mary Shelley's essay "Madame D'Houtetôt," *The Liberal* (1823), concerns a similar real situation, with which she obviously identified, and concludes that d'Houtetot's incongruous reasoning led her threesome "to the brink of a precipice." In an 1839 short biography of Rousseau, however, Mary Shelley is more severe and perceptive, stating that d'Houtetot did not immediately reject Rousseau because she enjoyed his attentions.

gate spring, Peacock used Mary Godwin as model for Anthelia Melincourt, a fearless, proud, independent heiress whose mother died giving her birth and whose father cultivated her mind. (Anthelia is Greek for a reflected image of the sun — Mary Wollstonecraft). Surrounded by a circle of admirers, composed, self-possessed, looking with Godwinian calm "on the course of necessity," Anthelia works in her study from breakfast to dinner, practices a system of rigorous sincerity, and is "perfectly indifferent to private malice or public misrepresentation." She seeks a husband who is "champion of the feeble, the firm opponent of the powerful oppressors," and finds him in the Shelleyan Sylvan Forester, who is looking for a Loidoiska to his Louvet, and immediately decides to teach her Greek. "O Freedom," she sings, "Be thou guide of all my thought," and she envisions their sailing the world in a magic bark until Freedom overcomes Fraud, Slavery, Fear, and Ignorance. Stella in Peacock's *Nightmare Abbey* — "I submit not to be an accomplice in my sex's slavery" — and the titular heroine of *Maid Marian* are of similar character.

This superlative mini-society, with her lover for fellow student and tutor, constituted Mary Godwin's university. Between January 1815 and the summer of 1816, the eighteen months before she conceived *Frankenstein,* she read some ninety works that are representative of her permanent interests. One important course was her study with Shelley of the major English poets: Spenser, Shakespeare, Milton, Coleridge, Wordsworth, Byron, and Southey, as well as Scripture for its poetry. Her other reading included *The Canterbury Tales* and Godwin's *Life of Chaucer,* William Beckford, Samuel Richardson, Joanna Baillie, Matthew "Monk" Lewis, Walter Scott, Ann Radcliffe; she also read Goethe and Schiller in translation, Shelley having interested her in German literature. In history and related fields she read Gibbon's *Decline and Fall* and his *Life and Letters,* Edward Clarendon's *History of the Civil Wars,* Edmund Burke's *Vindication of Civil Society,*[10] William Robertson's *History of America;* memoirs of modern philosophers, historically important figures, and travelers, such as Admiral George Anson's narrative of his voyage around the world and Carl Phillipp Moritz's *Tour of England.*

She read Voltaire, d'Holbach, and the major works of Rousseau and de Staël in the original, and, with Shelley tutoring, Ovid, Sallust, Virgil, Quintus Curtius, and Petronius ("detestable," she noted). She would become an accomplished scholar in Latin and Romance-language literature.[11] She studied Italian and Greek through the *Iliad* and the satirist Lucian, aided by Shelley, translations, and lexicons. In addition, the lovers followed current political-literary debates in the major arbiters of taste and opinion, the Tory *Quarterly* and Whig *Edinburgh Review*s.

One can trace to Bishopsgate concepts that would contribute to *Fran-kenstein*. Probably through Shelley, she was attracted to Bishop Berkeley's philosophy, which placed the human mind at the center of existence as the perceiver, interpreter, and maker of reality. Among other contemporary applications of the power of the mind over Nature, her circlet discussed the benefits and costs of technological progress, in conversations Peacock may have used in *Headlong Hall:* "Profound researches, scientific inves-tigations: to what end . . . ?" asks one speaker, when new factories are operated by "death-doomed" child workers, to which the Godwinian char-acter replies that nevertheless science is producing unprecedented im-provement in the lives of ordinary people. To the first speaker Prometheus symbolizes a disaster to man, to the second a drive essential to human progress.

Paradise Lost, which Mary reread with Shelley that autumn, put defiance of the status quo in mythic context. She followed it with de Staël's *De l'Allemagne*, the importance of which to *Frankenstein* has not so far been recognized. Here de Staël reviewed Schlegel on Classicism and Roman-ticism (of which Mary had intimations from Coleridge's lectures), and Goethe's *Faust* with its overreaching philosopher.[12] In her account of current German scientific research, de Staël declared that revolutionary discoveries impended about the principle of existence, specifically noting that a brilliant young physician, Koreff, had made new observations on the principle of life and the action of death. (Koreff turned out to be a charlatan.)

It was characteristic of Mary, however, perhaps in part because she was a female sensitive to the limits of power and had borne a child, that while the possibility that men could seize the prerogatives of Nature thrilled her as the ultimate ambition for knowledge, power, and glory, she also sensed on a deeper level the potential consequences of that ambition.

As for her own writing, Mary was blocked, for the first time since childhood. This was a severe disappointment since, after producing only fragments during their agitated first year, the lovers hoped for better results at Bishopsgate, and Shelley composed *Alastor,* his first mature long poem. To some degree the still fresh excitations of her liaison prepossessed her: "reality stood in the place of fiction," she would explain in her Preface to *Frankenstein*. Shelley, she added, was "for ever inciting" her to write — and in terms that articulated her real ambition: "to prove myself worthy of my parentage, and enrol myself on the page of fame." Whereas he meant to overcome her diffidence, however, he sharpened her conflict between ambition and "impious" rivalry with her parents. In her view, he wished her to write "not so much with the idea that I could produce any thing worthy of notice, but that he might himself judge how far I possessed the promise of better things hereafter."[13] More likely, Shelley already believed that she promised to equal her parents. At the same time, though he stood eager to act as coach and critic as she climbed Parnassus, she was frightened of losing his love and esteem if she failed.

Nevertheless, she was reading great literature not just for mastery but to advance beyond her "commonplace" girlhood stories to original fiction, for both she and Shelley always held that original genius in any field could evolve only from continual study of the greatest predecessors. And she was studying psychic phenomena relating to genius, which fascinated Shelley, too: the sources and functioning of imagination, fantasizing, dreams, and waking dreams in which the artist is possessed by and attempts to shape unconscious material, such as Coleridge's purported dreaming of "Kubla Khan" entire. Still, more than intellectualizing was required to break the inhibition that kept her from releasing her imagination into her writing. Actually, the compression of these months at Bishopsgate would serve that purpose.

Even in normal circumstances, Mary Godwin's connection with another young original like Shelley would have produced rare dynamics, and their particular situation complicated and intensified her relations with the poet and affected her development. Her purpose was to live in a union resembling Godwin and Wollstonecraft's marriage, and ostensibly she achieved it: equal partners enjoying both autonomy and the reciprocal benefits and enhanced voluptuousness of intimacy, intellectual and otherwise.[14] But going so early from Godwin to Shelley, Mary lacked the confidence and the power to act in genuine freedom; she would not be able to grow into them as had Wollstonecraft during two decades of being on her own.

It followed from Mary's first sixteen years that she sought the father-lover-tutor-colleague she found in Shelley, who would be everything to her. He also enabled her to bypass the world and to live in what she later called "a dream." Thus sheltered, she preserved an adolescent naïveté, idealism, and trust, despite her precocious sagacity, particularly in regard to him. She had her share of jealousy, but she seems to have felt none in his case once she was sure of his fundamental commitment — and she was never possessive with anyone. Though people in general fascinated her, her insight suffered from wishful thinking and from refusal to perceive — and carelessness about — the true measure of resentment or envy harbored by Jeff Hogg or Clara Clairmont.

Moreover, she chose Shelley because she looked up to greatness, and while he abhorred "the tyranny of command" in personal as well as political life, his moral vision, intellect, and personality were so compelling "as to constitute him a sort of tyrant" over his intimates, including those older and wiser than she. The intellectual and inspirational returns for Mary were unique, but inwardly she always felt that he was superior to her, even though Shelley, another excellence-worshiper, felt that she might be the mentor to him that he had been for Harriet, that Mary ruled over. him.

Mary's youth, her sacrifice, her dependence, their passion, led Shelley to inflate his normally extravagant chivalry with her, and Mary to accept it with gratitude and a sense that her ostracism, if not her self, legitimized it. In his seductive vision she was a juvenile Spenserian lady to his "Elfin Knight." Neither saw any conflict between their advocacy of women's rights and his "submission to the great general laws of antique courtesy," which, he declared, "is my religion,"[15] and which increased his power over women, who loved him for it. His lavish praise could not cure Mary's diffidence, however, since she attributed it more to his love than to his discernment.* He spoiled her, took care of tiresome business, even wrote her doctor. He consulted her about most matters out of respect for her superior judgment — Mary is always "wise" to Shelley — and because she often had decided opinions. While she declared herself freely, both expected him to make final decisions and carry them out. "If I have interfered in the legislative," she was to say, "I have had nothing to do with [the] executive part of our little government."[16]

Though some Shelleyans claim she was sexually cool, she seems to have been a passionate partner until her great tragedy of 1818–1819,[17] when Shelley was desolated at the change in her. And Shelley himself may have had qualms about sex: the male's death following intercourse occurs in two of his poems, and consumptives, as he continually suspected that he was, were warned not to "spend" their failing powers in sex. Her first two pregnancies were probably due to ignorance and romantic heedlessness. After her second baby was safely born, she wanted more children, but a moderate number and well spaced, and after the third they used some form of mechanical birth control.

Between them the pair created androgynous ideals of a feminine woman with power, wisdom, and intellect, and a morally strong man who was tender, selfless, and sensitive. There were interesting ambivalences. If Shelley was indecisive Mary became impatient, but at the same time she had a perennial weakness for strong men in trouble and "delicately healthed Poets" in particular. Being chronically ailing and transcendentally idealistic

* Elizabeth Raby in *Falkner* feels similarly about her foster father's admiration.

gave Shelley a sizable advantage, but Mary loved sustaining him, and if he was attacked, defended him fiercely. He loved the idea of a forceful, militant young woman upholding her failing lover, and yet cherished "angelic mildness" in females, which was not one of Mary's consistent attributes.* Likewise, he told Clara Clairmont there were two Claras: bad Clara being irritable, melancholy, and sarcastic; good Clara, gentle, cheerful, and the most engaging person he knew.

Living as a social outcast, confined to Shelley's not wholly *sympathique* friends, reinforced Mary's tendency to suppress her emotions generally, and to concentrate on Shelley. With him alone, she was to note in her journal, her voice could "assume its natural modulation. . . . How often . . . I thought how superiorly gifted I had been in being united to one to whom I could unveil myself, & who could understand me."[18] This shedding of inhibition as if he were part of herself, however, was neither entirely wise nor reciprocal.

For Shelley oscillated between "seeking all sympathies in one" ideal mate and being enchanted with diverse excellencies in members of the sex he loved. Furthermore, it was an integral part of his self-ideal to subdue his "internal irritability" and practice systematic forbearance with his friends. According to his theory, taking people as they are leaves them what they are, but treating them as if they were what they should be improves them. When Mary was cross he submitted, and when she apologized he tenderly pardoned her. Any annoyance he felt he concealed from her. While he was confrontational to an extreme with opponents and in some of his poetry, his vibrating receptivity and need for admiration and harmony often made him diplomatic or even double-dealing; he told people what they wanted to hear, while confiding more critical opinions to others. Though Mary's ideal of candor ran counter to his of harmony, she excused what she saw of his deception on grounds of his tender heart.

Mary Godwin was later said to resemble the pensive, feminine, Roman bust familiar to Victorians as "Clytie," except for a "tall and intellectual forehead" and the "bright, animated, and sweet expression that so often lighted up her face"[19] with people she knew and liked. However, Godwinian frankness and sincerity were her pride, and she refused to temper them to her precarious status, expecting her little circle to value this "want of tact" — her favorite phrase about herself, complained Jeff Hogg. Paradoxically, at her most independent she was the most dependent upon

---

* In *The Last Man*'s Perdita and Idris, Mary Godwin would reflect the duality of her relation to Shelley. In married happiness the reserved, mistrustful Perdita becomes more open and contented, but her disposition is never "saintly." Princess Idris, Lionel's "golden treasure" who elopes to marry him and is excommunicated by her mother, is a sweet-tempered, yielding wife.

[handwritten top margin: Mary - ruled by emotions but keeps them hidden from everyone]

Shelley's protection and understanding. Though their associates deeply respected her character and gifts, most of them had an ideal of malleable, unassertive, sweet-tempered femininity, and privately criticized her as a young woman who for all her devotion to Shelley had been trained in "antagonistic ideas of independence" and did not always fulfill her obligation to serve him.[20] "Strength in a woman should be merely symbolic; we are frightened at finding it real," as Balzac would write.

Her inculcated ideal of Ciceronian stoicism, moreover, had the result that even she herself and Shelley were to understand her emotionality only after tragedy broke her down. Independently, Shelley and Leigh Hunt were later to compare her to an apparently cool volcano. Her reserve and ironic badinage prevented her associates from perceiving her diffidence or her passionate essence, and none probed beyond the apparent persona. In her journal and many of her letters, except to Shelley, one has to tease out not what she thinks but what she feels or prefers not to say; one begins to know her in her silences and in her works.

[handwritten right margin: she kept everything inside until it burst]

Their friends understood what bonded the couple, however. While Shelley was in large part, as she said, her guide, teacher, and interpreter, after his death she exaggerated her inferiority to "his far more cultivated mind" and muted her part in their life virtually to the point of silence, so that it is not sufficiently understood that she was a major actor and his principal interlocutor, crucial to his artistic career. For all his forcefulness, Shelley compared himself to "an harp responsive to every wind," a "passive Earth" under the influence of sun and moon. He needed her steadiness. Troubles made him ill, and he was subject to extreme self-pity, manic elation, and deep despondency, shuddering fears and occasional delusions, all of which she soothed with her "all powerful" calm — as once at Bishopsgate, when he was overcome by horror while recording a dream and ran to the refuge of her voice and presence.

[handwritten right margin: She was the steady rock to his wild currents]

At the beginning of their liaison she, as it were, pulled his gifts, passions, beliefs, and aspirations into alignment. "You alone reconcile me to myself & to my beloved hopes," he wrote her, and of her to Jeff Hogg, "I never before felt the integrity of my nature."[21] Apparently, it was after they had lived together for several months that he decided to dedicate himself to poetry rather than philosophy.[22] Although typically she never mentioned herself in that connection, her belief in his poetic genius and in a mission of poets that accorded with his contributed to his decision.

Having chosen poetry, he "educated himself for it" by studying the major Greek and Italian poets with Hogg and Peacock, and the English poets with Mary. In the case of Coleridge, an old family friend, she wrote out some of his poems from memory, perhaps not having his printed work at Bishopsgate,[23] and her account of him is reflected in Shelley's "Oh! there are spirits in the air" of this period. In discussing *Christabel,* she informed Shelley that Coleridge's original idea for the villainess's deformity was "two eyes in her bosom,"[24] a detail that gripped Shelley's imagination. Sometimes, but never to the detriment of her own work, she made fair copies of his often chaotic drafts. That he entrusted the fruits of his genius to her eyes first to decipher and study she regarded as a privilege — and it would uniquely enable her to edit his manuscripts.

They shared a common cultural language rich in allusions and quotations. Her dynamic interpretation of sympathy says much for what both she and he cherished in their association. "No people need so much sympathy as poets," she would write. "The interchange of thought and feeling, the fresh spirit of inquiry and invention, that springs from the collision or harmony of different minds, are for them a necessity and a passion."[25] Both would sustain the other's creative struggles. "The act of writing may compose the mind," she writes, "but the boiling of the soul, and quake of heart, that precede, transcend all the sufferings which tame spirits feel."[26]

Shelley was a Manichaean who divided existence into evils of tyranny, injustice, hatred, guilt, and pain, which he hated violently, and "holy" virtues of love, freedom, justice, genius, compassion, and harmony, which he adored; his poetic subtlety and power lay in delineating these as entities, not in their shadings and interconnections. That humankind could perfect the world was the faith he lived on for many years, and he hoped to convert the cultivated leaders of society to his moral and political vision, an illusory goal that could only be frustrated, so that he was dashed to despair or enraged.

He professed martyrdom but worked at cross purposes, publishing poetry that deliberately shocked. Thus he insulted his readers' intelligence and sense of the sacred by blasting Christianity, on which he in fact blamed much of the evil in the world, and loved horrifying them by proclaiming his atheism. If Mary seems to have induced him seriously to consider the immortality of the spirit, he acidulated her scorn for Christianity. His extremism, and his arcane, surreal, and novel art as well, deprived him of the audience he sought. At this time poets were not yet glorying in the role of dissident. Without Mary's supreme faith in his work, he might possibly not have maintained enough himself to keep writing.

Fox to his hedgehog in the classic typology, Mary Godwin had opposite affinities, which she prized and indeed strengthened to balance his utopianism. For one fundamental difference, she was in concordance with her parents' beliefs, whereas Shelley was in rebellion against his; to her Prometheus was a catalyzer, to him Jove's martyred challenger. Shelley

would represent her steadier faith in long-term progress in Cythna's reassurance to discouraged Laon that while "This is the winter of the world,"
buried seeds of truth, justice, and freedom await inevitable spring. But
her optimism was tempered by modulated expectations and acceptance of
an irreducible human condition. A natural novelist, she liked detail, complexities, perversities, and paradox for themselves, and studying people
who differ from herself; he loved to consider "the moral or the physical
universe as a whole" and the resolution of human differences. She believed
that humor contributed to a saving sense of proportion; he imaged laughter as a "heartless fiend."

She helped him to become less driven, self-righteous, and angry, to
recognize the potentially destructive and self-destructive abyss he created
between the real and the ideal — a theme of *Alastor*. "Maie says that if we
had met the Emperor Julian in private life he would have appeared a very
ordinary man," he noted as a new insight.[27] He encouraged her aspirations,
enriched her mind and spirit, and energized her. So absolutely did he fulfill
her dreams that a favorite subject of her fantasizing was their marvelous
joint future. Above all, their union magnified her confidence in her star,
an irrepressible faith that persisted into her forties. Against all reason and
experience, bad fortune was repeatedly to take her by surprise; but given
any reason to hope, she would revive.

On January 24, 1816, eleven months after her first ill-fated delivery,
Mary Godwin gave birth to a healthy full-term boy, "the offspring of
freedom and love, of Beauty and strength,"[28] as Clara Clairmont, who
returned for the lying-in, would rhapsodize, exalting the martyrlike defiance and singular bliss of voluntary unmarried motherhood. In feminine
triumph Mary named her son William Godwin and loved him with a
special sense of fulfillment and joy.

This illegitimate boy would be the most cherished of Mary and Shelley's
children, and as his birth seems to have marked the passing of their bond
into the equivalent of marriage, so they believed it should be the turning
point for his grandfather. Mary dreamed that her father would come to
embrace her and his namesake; Shelley tried to see him, consulted Maria
Smith, urged the intimidated Clara, who was now received at Skinner
Street, to speak for them. "It has perpetually appeared to me to have been
your especial duty," he wrote Godwin, "to see that, so far as mankind
value your good opinion, we were dealt justly by, and that a young family,
innocent and benevolent and united, should not be confounded with
prostitutes and seducers."[29]

Godwin remained adamant, even interlined his demanding business letters about the three hundred pounds Shelley offered to raise for him with cold insults that made Shelley tremble and sicken in fury. In the rabidly jealous, vengeful hate that his titular hero of *Mandeville* feels for the Shelleyan character Lionel, who marries Mandeville's sister, Godwin expressed what he felt, and would feel to the death of Shelley. Regardless, Shelley undertook complicated efforts to raise the money and Mary actively assisted him. "Her sentiments in all respects coincide with mine," Shelley wrote Godwin agitatedly, "her interest is perhaps greater, her judgement from what she kn[ow]s of our situation of what ough[t or] can be done is probably more ca[lm] & firm."[30]

But Mary became depressed when she realized that her father's excommunication stood. The anniversary of her first baby's loss, thoughts of the certainty of death, a chill, rainy, spring that made winter seem endless, all added to her sadness, and she was anxious about Shelley, whose health worsened because of the cold and their ill treatment — and perhaps because of William's birth. They planned to summer in Italy with Clara and Jeff; meantime, she kept her mood private and struggled against it.

Shelley had to make business trips to London. Mary sometimes took the baby, whom she was nursing, to be with him at their London pied-à-terre in Marchmont Street, and to see Fanny. Her half sister's melancholy brought her out of her own. Fanny was wretched at Skinner Street, her sole alternative the uncongenial Dublin aunts, though her heart was with the lovers: "perhaps . . . because I found the world deserted you, I loved you the more," she told Mary, and she adored William: "kiss him again and again for me."[31] Mrs. Godwin was at her worst. Clara refused to live at Skinner Street and instead took lodgings and investigated a stage career, for which Mrs. Godwin blamed the lovers, and blamed them too for depriving her of Charles. She tried to turn Fanny against them, telling her that they made scornful fun of Fanny. She also claimed that Fanny's upkeep strained Godwin's health, while he asked Fanny to press the lovers for his three hundred pounds, so that Fanny was forced to urge his demands on Mary and Shelley. They did not comprehend her plight and disliked her incessant admonitions.

Suddenly, Clara provided a sensational escape from these troubles when she confided to the dumbfounded Mary that she had become acquainted with the great Lord Byron himself, and that Byron had asked her to introduce him to Mary before he left England. As all the world knew, after the recent birth of their daughter, Ada, Lady Byron had left the poet, and debts and horrendous scandal about his perversions and incest with his half sister were driving him to the Continent. That Byron took the time to see Mary Godwin is a measure of her hereditary prestige. Mary was thrilled by this request on the part of the stormy poet whose works she and thousands knew by heart, and whose sexual allure was legend. In intriguing secrecy, she went with Clara to his grand Piccadilly mansion, probably on April 19, for a brief meeting, and found him amazingly soft. "How mild he is! How gentle! How different from what I expected,"[32] Clara quoted her to Byron.

In fact, Clara was using Mary as cat's-paw to consummate a bizarre seduction of Byron. As she approached eighteen, Clara made an audacious leap for glory that, she later said, gave her ten minutes of happiness and discomposed the rest of her life; it would also disturb much of Mary's. Byron's separation had struck Clara as the chance of a lifetime; she concluded that he would replace Lady Byron and Ada with an unmarried girl who would bear his child and whom he would treat as his wife,[33] a delusion born of Mary's liaison with Shelley and sad ignorance of Byron. Byron, whose desk bulged with letters from love-struck females, ignored Clara's attempts to see him until she wrote that she was Godwin's stepdaughter. (Byron had recently considered assisting Godwin financially.) Clara offered herself to Byron, adding that she longed to give him a child. To prove her aptitude she confided "the most important secrets," a mélange of truth and lies, claiming not only that she, Mary, and Shelley practiced Godwin's free-love theories, but that Shelley had been her lover, helped her abort their child, and then discarded her, as Byron would have the right to do.

Byron was the kind of Regency swordsman that Wollstonecraft-Godwin followers abhorred. He carried a condom, tumbled chambermaids, took stunning, sensual women for his serious mistresses, and talked freely about his exploits. There were few amatory experiences, including schoolboy homosexual love and incest — compulsively confessed to a few intimates — that Byron at twenty-eight had not had. Moreover, though Clara had become a handsome young woman with Iberian looks and sparkle, this girl-radical, "Atheist and Murderer,"[34] was not to his taste, and he had no intention of taking an official mistress. He warned her on both points, discouraged her, but she persisted and he would have felt like a poltroon to reject her. Two days after meeting Mary he slept with Clara. Apparently, she proved to be virgin.[35] That only convinced him that she was immoral for the worst reason: principle.

Clara's initiative with Byron, though courageously forthright, had much to do with impressing Mary and Shelley, and she had loved Byron as adolescents love matinée idols. Now she was overwhelmed by him. To mark her transformation she again changed her name, to the more elegant Clare, which she would keep as long as she loved him. But she was incapable of the autonomy she professed, and even abased herself. Knowing he did not care for her, she masochistically dangled the unwitting Mary before him. "You will, I daresay, fall in love with her," she wrote. "She is very handsome and very amiable, and you will no doubt be blest in your attachment; nothing could afford me more pleasure. . . . I will redouble my attentions to please her . . . do everything she tells me, whether it be good or bad."[36]

After Byron sailed on April 23, Clare told Mary and Shelley that she was his mistress, doubtless one of the great moments of her life. Having set Mary up by her interview with Byron, Clare easily persuaded the lovers to meet him in Geneva, where he planned to summer before proceeding to Italy and would supposedly be delighted to have their company. They made up excuses for a hasty departure, as their real purpose had to be secret. Mary had a tiff with Fanny, who accused them of going on an unconscionable holiday instead of raising three hundred pounds for Godwin, to which Mary retorted that Fanny cared only about Shelley's money. On May 2, the trio, with baby William, rushed off from London in Shelley's carriage, leaving Jeff in the lurch and Peacock to close down the Bishopsgate cottage.

Elated to be traveling again and on this adventure, Mary sped in style and comfort, except for her bedeviling motion sickness, along her elopement route through France and into magnificent new terrain ascending the Jura. Late in the day of the fourteenth, her party rashly crossed the deeply snowbound summit, with four horses to pull and ten men to support the carriage, and descended to Lake Geneva in pelting snow near dark. It was "sublime," this "awfully desolate" soundless icy expanse invaded by a handful of humans who dared Nature's power. Her *annus mirabilis* had begun.

7 "Switzerland — Bath"

AFTER MONTHS of studious incubation and depressing weather, Mary Godwin was exhilarated as rarely before in her eighteen years by Geneva's "divine" summery air and light and picturesque scenery, and by a sense of liberation and efflorescence. "I feel as happy as a new-fledged bird," she wrote Fanny, "and hardly care what twig I fly to, so that I may try my new-found wings."[1] As the interaction between her circumstances and her writing are teased out, that the girl produced her masterpiece in her first adult book this year seems less improbable if no less remarkable.[2] For *Frankenstein* was the product of her extraordinary parabolic passage into adulthood, launched in Switzerland "when first I stepped out from childhood into life,"[3] accelerated with unnatural velocity by prodigious events during the next eleven months, and descending, as she completed the book, "an old woman."

The gamble on summering with Byron paid off, founding one of the richest relationships of her career. For two felicitous weeks of study, sailing, and sight-seeing she and her companions waited for him at Dejean's fashionable lakeside hotel facing the Alps at Secheron outside Geneva. Their initial meeting on May 27 was awkward, since Byron was displeased to find Clare and had with him his young traveling physician, John Polidori, who was agog at this confusing, irregular trio: "M Wollstonecraft Godwin . . . called here Mrs. Shelley," Polidori recorded in his journal, and her married lover, who also "kept" her "sister," who was Byron's mistress.[4]

But the acquaintance rapidly warmed. Byron and Shelley rented neighboring houses on the opposite shore at Cologny. On June 1 Mary Godwin's party moved into Maison Chapuis, a cottage on the water with a little bedroom for the lovers overlooking a cove where the poets' jointly bought sailboat was moored. On the tenth Byron moved a ten-minute climb away, through a hillside vineyard, into the grander Villa Diodati, where Milton had stayed, with a prominent iron balcony and a splendid view of the lake and Jura. On Clare's initiative he had resumed their sexual

Show that they had ended before? ([illegible handwritten note])

How to show that Clair is already pregnant?

relations, and she, who soon realized that she had conceived his child in April, hoped to become his official mistress — an illusion shared by Mary and Shelley.

Byron being the preeminent member, the little colony accommodated to his routine of late nights and after-noon rising, which enabled the lovers to continue their morning work. In her initial euphoria at Dejean's, Mary had begun writing, possibly a children's book to meet part of her father's needs, which Fanny had accused her of neglecting.[5] Doubtless for the same reason, she and Shelley worked briefly on a French translation of *Political Justice*. She concentrated on reading French literature to solidify the language while she was speaking it to Genevans; she also read Tasso with the bilingual Polidori, and the *Aeneid*, sketched the scenery and drew a portrait of Byron, which she sent to Fanny.

Mary's activities

Sailing was the daily adventure, and the uncommonly exuberant Mary, free of her usual seasickness, enjoyed that summer's rough lake waters to the point of "hilarity." Often she took William: "Rocked by the waves, o'er which our vessel swept, / Beside his father, nurst upon my breast, / While Leman's waters shook with fierce unrest" ("The Choice"). Byron came down for a sail at dusk to foil avid Byron-watchers who spied on his every move. When bad weather forced them indoors, the Chapuis household went up to Diodati's elegant Louis Quinze salon and talked "grave or gay" into the small hours, the most brilliant conversations Mary had known since the best at her father's house. One evening Byron had fascinating guests, the recently exiled Italian patriot Pellegrino Rossi, who had fought with Murat, and elderly Charles Bonstetten, who had known Voltaire and Rousseau.

Everything combined to charge Mary's excitation and deepen her soundings: the elements, the place, the company. As she moved into Chapuis, the weather suddenly changed from radiant to melodramatically tempestuous. Great electrical storms and torrential rains bombarded the area for the rest of the season, similar to the summer she was born (and likewise due to a volcanic eruption, Tambora in Indonesia, the year before). Mary scorned the idea of God more than ever with this show of Nature's power, exulted in the towering Alps — "higher one would think than the safety of god would permit," she quipped, and crowned by Mont Blanc, "highest and queen of all,"[6] — Earth's symbols of human challenge. Likewise she *"enjoyed"* the storms, "grander and more terrific" than she had ever seen, with awesome lightning, the cosmic power harnessed by Franklin and Nature's simile for illumination in the human mind.

Through Milton, Voltaire, Rousseau, and Gibbon, who had resided on its shores, and currently Madame de Staël at nearby Coppet, the lake was sacred to enlightenment; Mary thought of her group as a modern Promethean cadre, she carrying forward her mother's torch of female liberation. That their cause would prevail had been confirmed for her in France by signs of mounting popular hatred for the Bourbons. Geneva, Rousseau's birthplace, had recently been restored to a Calvinist republic following its own bloody revolution a few years after the French. Even the world's hostility exhilarated Mary, as she, Shelley, and Clare were spotlighted in Byron's notoriety and became the scandal of the visiting international set. These included Robert Southey, once Shelley's friend, who had turned adamantly against him since Shelley left Harriet for Mary. Rumor had it — "Monstrous, deformed, titanic Rumor" in the *Aeneid* — that Byron, the incestuous lover of his sister, Shelley, Mary Godwin, and her "sister" had formed a League of Incest in which Godwin's daughters slept with both men. Canny Dejean rented telescopes to his guests, who took Diodati's tablecloths drying on the balcony for the girls' petticoats. The lovers deliberately went further *épater les bourgeois* when they visited Chamonix in July; in four public registers, which became a tourist attraction, Shelley inscribed Mary as "Mad. M. W. Godwin," Clare as "Mad. Clairmont," himself in Greek as "Atheist" and the three as "Atheists one and all."

Detesting the English distance between "haughty" mistress and ignorant servant, Mary took advantage of Geneva's freer, literate, and more refined lower orders to engage a permanent nursemaid equivalent to her mother's Marguerite Fournée, a ruddy-faced twenty-one-year-old seamstress, Louise Duvillard, called Elise, who had taken care of her own younger siblings, including a baby William's age.[7] The republic disappointed Mary to some degree. Genevans were mercenary and puritanical, local children were put out to work and suffered almost as much as child laborers in the kingdom of Britain,[8] and in the Alps, presumably purer and engendering love of freedom, the peasants, especially women, were ground down by immemorial toil and yet were "very indifferent" about government. But she made pilgrimage to Geneva's Plainpalais park, where local revolutionaries had executed the city fathers and erected an obelisk "to the glory of Rousseau," as she wrote Fanny in a letter that coupled ironic insight and ringing affirmation:

and here (such is the mutability of human life) the magistrates, the successors of those who exiled him from his native country, were shot by the populace during that revolution, which his writings mainly contributed to mature, and which, notwithstanding the temporary bloodshed and injustice with which it was polluted,

has produced enduring benefits to mankind, which all the chi-
canery of statesmen, nor even the great conspiracy of kings, can
entirely render vain.[9]

Shelley and Byron meanwhile were articulating the pertinent philosophic issue in what would become their running debate. A determinist
and misanthrope, Byron argued that we can only endure or protest what
our nature, society, and destiny make of us, while Shelley insisted that if
inspired truly we can overcome everything and perfect ourselves and human
existence. Out of "incapacity and timidity," Mary contributed little, but
in defining her own position she granted the forces limiting humankind
and nevertheless remained convinced that we are capable of ruling or
"tacking" through them. On a deeper level, however, she was ambivalent.

Mary shed a certain jeune fille provincialism this summer, thanks to
Byron. Adding to her excitement, she was his favorite; indeed, she would
apparently list him among "the beautiful & glorious & noble" men who
had looked at her "with the divine expression of love" but became her
friends rather than lovers.[10] He denied the general belief that they were
lovers with an indignation unique in his career, primarily to defend a
traduced young woman he esteemed, but also as if he were annoyed at
not getting credit for having resisted trying. He saw that she was of another
order than Clare and respected her courage and devotion to Shelley and
her baby; her reserve appealed to him who was perpetually pursued by
overeager women, and he drew her out by talking of mutual acquaintances
like Curran and Coleridge.

Although she would never quite admit it, Byron attracted Mary sexually,
but even so, his moral incompatibility confirmed her preference for Shelley.
The two men were fascinating foils — even in the timbre of their voices,
Byron's mellow, Shelley's high, in the discussions she heard as both duet
and dialogue.* For her fascination with intriguing characters, Byron displayed the infinite variety of the premier charmer-genius of the time,
spoiled, capricious, docile, cynical, and above all radiating "intellectual
energy." "Beauty sat on his countenance and power beamed from his
eye —," she would write.[11] The lovers saw him as a great, potential, progressive leader — Shelley would have given his right arm for Byron's command of world attention — though he was surprisingly conservative socially,
"Lord Byron" even to Clare. Among themselves they called him "Albè."
He seems to have advised the startled lovers to marry if possible.[12]

Byron at this time was writing superb poetry, including the third canto

---

* In *The Last Man* she would portray them as brilliant, spoiled Lord Raymond and dedicated
utopian Adrian, and her Perdita-self as Lord Raymond's wife.

of *Childe Harold,* which Mary always cherished because it incorporated their summer experience,[13] and versified a comment she made one moon-lit night when they glided in to shore from sailing: that their boat was being "saluted" by the scent of flowers and mown hay and the sounds of grasshoppers and evening songbirds. Byron hated copying his poems for the press, so Clare was his major copyist. But Mary made him extra copies of the canto and of "The Prisoner of Chillon"; being especially interested in the circumstances in which he wrote the canto (a critical approach she would take later as Shelley's editor), she noted on her copy where and when he had composed each group of stanzas.[14] She may have been unwise to show her enthusiasm so freely, since Shelley was writing comparatively little; despite Byron's respect for Shelley's aristocracy and talent, he daunted the younger poet.

Mary was also the favorite of Polidori, whom she treated with teasingly affectionate firmness: "Mrs. S. called me her brother (younger)," he noted dismally.[15] He was clever, handsome, and interesting in regard to science and psychological phenomena, but so unstable and offensive that Byron was to fire him that fall. As for many contemporary young men, Byron was his role model, but he could not come up to the mark. One afternoon as Mary was climbing up to Diodati he was incited by Byron to leap from the famous balcony to offer her his arm, and ingloriously sprained his ankle. When the poets decided to sail around the lake without him, he became suicidally distraught.

While Mary was expanding with such provocations, they also undoubt-edly turned her inward, to her birth, which had killed her mother in just such a stormy season; to her prototypical genius-father; to Harriet Shelley. The excitement intensified during the week of June 16. On the sixteenth Chapuis was caught at Diodati by a wild downpour and spent the night. They all gathered at the fireplace and read aloud a German book of ghost stories translated into French, *Fantasmagoriana, ou Recueil d'histoires d'ap-paritions de spectres, revenants, fantômes, etc.* From the introduction's ref-erence to the occult in Scotland that had fascinated Mary in adolescence, the contents probed to her quick. In "La Morte fiancée," a man who abandoned his beloved for another girl is killed by her pursuing ghost. In "Le Revenant," a girl who married against her father's will loses her baby and is abandoned by her husband.[16]

A group of travelers in "Les Portraits de famille" relate ghostly en-counters they have had, and this inspired Byron to propose that they each write a ghost story. "You and I," he told Mary, "will publish ours to-gether."[17] At this thrilling prospect Mary set herself to think of a story that would "speak to the mysterious fears of our nature" and prove her worthy of her parents. Next day Shelley started a tale; Byron read the beginning of his own. "The ghost-stories are begun by all but me," Polidori goaded himself,[18] apparently meaning all the men. Keeping up the "ghostly" tone near the following midnight, Byron recited *Christabel,* to Mary a poeticization of her own childhood situation, but Shelley suddenly "saw" Mary as the villainess with eyes for nipples (possibly blaming Mary for seducing him from Harriet) and ran screaming out of the room. Mary quietly left Polidori, the professional, to calm Shelley, but this attribution of monstrosity and guilt made its mark.

The poets dropped their stories, but Mary persisted and became the houseparty joke. "Have you thought of a story?" they asked each day, to which she had to reply "with a mortifying negative."[19] Her ambitions and her value were at stake, however, and she focused that pressure on her failure, determined to break it. On June 22 Byron and Shelley were to leave to sail around the lake, perhaps adding to Mary's anxiety; Shelley, who could not swim, would come close to drowning in a storm. The night before their departure the company speculated on a subject Mary may have brought up from de Staël's *De l'Allemagne:* whether the principle of life could be discovered and whether scientists could galvanize a corpse or manufactured humanoid.[20] When Mary went to bed, still worrying about her ghost story, she had a "waking" hypnagogic nightmare:

> I saw the pale student of unhallowed arts kneeling beside the thing he had put together. I saw the hideous phantasm of a man stretched out, then, on the working of some powerful engine, show signs of life . . . His success would terrify the artist; he would rush away . . . hope that . . . this thing . . . would subside into dead matter . . . he opens his eyes; behold the horrid thing stands at his bedside, opening his curtains . . .[21]

Opening her eyes in terror, Mary tried to shake off the dream, thought again about her failed ghost story, and realized that she had found it. Next morning after the poets sailed off, she sat down at her work table and with the words that open Chapter IV of *Frankenstein* — "It was on a dreary night of November" — began a tale of a few pages narrating her dream. When Shelley returned on June 30, he was impressed and urged her to go on.

The nightmare imploded on the barrier that had always dammed her imagination from her writing. During the next three weeks she evolved her mature creative mode, deploying her imagination among actualities that in turn catalyzed it,[22] and developed the core plot of *Frankenstein* in the form of a story. Her use of place was masterful.

The Modern Prometheus, as she would subtitle her novel, Victor Frankenstein, is the son of an elderly oligarch of Geneva, who has a nearly ideal childhood, except that his father disapproves of the boy's quest for knowledge of Nature's secrets. After his mother's death he goes to Ingolstadt University (cradle of the radical Illuminati sect and mentioned by de Staël as a scientific center). Here he discovers the principle of life and, obsessed by ambition for glory and mastery, manufactures a creature from corpses. In his secret attic "work-shop of filthy creation" he vivifies his creature and suddenly sees that it is hideous. He flees in horror and breaks down. The monster has disappeared. Victor recovers with the help of his closest friend, Clerval. He learns from his foster sister Elizabeth that his little brother William has been murdered in Plainpalais park — locale of revolutionary executions — and when he arrives in Geneva, he sees the monster and knows he is the killer.

With astounding ruthlessness, Mary named the murdered boy for her father, half brother, and baby son, using "William" as a bellows to flame her imagination. "Victor" has compound connotations: an eponym, a juvenile nom de plume of Shelley's, and the name of the Wild Boy of Aveyron — which relates the maker to his monster. As for "Frankenstein," Shelley had reported that the ruined Château des Allignes near Evian, which he and Byron had seen on their sail around the lake, resembled castles he and Mary had seen on the Rhine, reminding Mary of Castle Frankenstein, one of whose counts was said to have died pursuing a dragon.

On July 21, apparently at about this point in her story — and despite press reports of "ravages affreux" in the Alps, dangerous avalanches and flooding due to the rain — the lovers and Clare went to Chamonix for a week, the very week during which, two years before, Mary had decided to flout her father and live with Shelley. Possibly that coincidence inspired the idea that the monster would demand a mate from his creator, and with it the decision to make the monster a second protagonist. Confined to the hotel by rain on the twenty-fourth, she noted "write my story" in her journal.[23] Next day she visited the Mer de Glâce. Thus she brought Victor, who has become engaged to Elizabeth, to Chamonix along her own route, and had Victor encounter the monster in the colossal setting of the Mer de Glâce. Here the monster softens Victor by telling the story of his solitary, groping "childhood," his brutal rejection by people terrified of his appearance whom he tried to aid, and his enraged murder of William. He vows to live peacefully at the ends of the earth if Victor will manufacture him a mate.

Returning to Chapuis on July 27 — "kiss our babe & go to bed" —

next day Mary observed the second anniversary of her elopement and continued her story. Victor begins work on the female, then realizes that she will breed an evil race, and destroys her. The maddened monster kills Victor's friend Clerval, his bride, Elizabeth, on their wedding night, and brings on his aged father's death. To set the scene where Victor swears revenge on the graves of his loved ones, on August 22 Mary went to see Geneva's disappointingly ugly cemetery: "nothing more than part of a field enclosed in with palisades," she noted in her journal. Victor sets out in long, arduous pursuit to kill the taunting monster and dies of exhaustion. The remorseful monster rushes off to commit suicide.

"Shelley & I talk about my story," Mary noted on August 21. Thanks to his "incitement" she decided to make it into a full-length novel. By now she saw its connection to *Paradise Lost*[24] and began to think in terms of mythic scope, itself a Promethean ambition given her inexperience and reverence for Milton. The Ur-*Frankenstein* manuscript has not survived, but Polidori dined out for the rest of the summer on Byron's story-telling contest, an outline of the tale Mary Godwin "hatched" in a dream, and his own seminal story, "The Vampyre,"[25] which was inspired by Byron's unfinished tale.

Meanwhile, Byron had given Mary her most shocking lesson of the summer. In a meeting with Clare and Shelley (which to Mary's bewilderment Byron asked her not to attend) he announced that his affair with Clare was terminated. He had always warned Clare that it was temporary, felt bored and mortified by her Godwinian prating, and did not believe she loved him, because she was not sexually passionate. The wretched Clare got him to promise to rear their child after its birth in January, which was to remain secret so that she could resume a normal life; besides, the thought of Mrs. Godwin's knowing terrified Clare and worried the lovers, who knew they would be blamed.

On every count Mary was appalled; by Byron's Regency code, by Shelley's unworldliness and her own blindness and naïveté, by Clare's folly, deceit, and present piteous misery. Henceforth she entertained no illusions whatsoever about Byron, fewer about Clare, and slightly fewer about Shelley. Clare, furthermore, was totally on their hands, since she could not be alone, and Shelley refused to let Byron support her. The lovers gave up their dream-plan of a marvelous boating voyage down the Danube and around the Mediterranean. Shelley, for whom Switzerland had been a revelation of how deeply he loved England, wanted to live near Windsor in a "fixed, settled, eternal home." Mary preferred a "mousehole" near "noble trees and divine mountains." But as Shelley's father had ordered

him home for a financial consultation, they decided to stay in
from the Godwins until Clare's delivery.

Mary saw little of Byron during the last half of August bec
friends Scrope Davies, John Cam Hobhouse, and the Gothic
"Monk" Lewis were staying with him, and though Shelley socialized at
Diodati she would not expose herself to these men of the world. On
August 29, the day before her nineteenth birthday, her party, augmented
by the nursemaid, Elise Duvillard, started home via Versailles and Le Havre
to Portsmouth.

While Shelley went to London on business, Mary took her charges to
Bath and found lodgings in the center of the fashionable spa in Abbey
Churchyard. Except for a week when she joined Shelley and Peacock in
Marlow and enjoyed the ripening autumn, she serenely resumed her work
routine, planned *Frankenstein*'s novelization, and found a local painter for
art lessons. "I cannot help envying your calm contented disposition,"
Fanny wrote, "and the calm philosophic habits of life which pursue you,
or rather, which you pursue, everywhere."[26] Mary's companions leaned on
her steadiness. Shelley was despondent for several reasons. First of all, he
blamed himself for Clare's predicament. In London he had made a will
with "Mary Wollstonecraft Godwin" his major legatee and handsome
bequests for Clare and her coming child. Harassed by creditors, he could
send the angry Godwin only two hundred of the three hundred pounds
he had promised. And the reviewers disliked *Alastor;* one even censured
it for indecency. Mary quietly said, " 'Why the world must be going
mad.' "[27] "I am an outcast from human society," Shelley lamented; "my
name is execrated . . . by those very beings whose happiness I ardently
desire."[28]

Clare was sad and fractious, flared up when "Your *favourite* Mary," she
wrote Byron in one of several loving letters to which he never replied,
was "*impertinent* and *nauseous* enough" to be surprised that Byron sent
Clare a promised book.[29] Yet, "She says," Clare reported, "that if she were
ever so much determined not to like you she could not help doing so . . ."[30]
Mary rented a piano for Clare to cheer her, hoping also that she could
become independent by performing or teaching music instead of living in
the lovers' new establishment. "Give me a garden & *absentia Clariae,*" she
told Shelley, "and I will thank my love for many favours."[31] They could
not return to Bishopsgate because of ugly local gossip, for which Mary,
losing her calm when she thought of her child's future, unjustly blamed
Mrs. Godwin, whom she accused of pursuing her and little William "like
a hound after foxes."

"On this day, Mary put her head thro the door & said — Come & look, here's a cat eating roses — she'll turn into a woman . . . ," Shelley noted in the journal on October 6. Mary's imagination was now primed for her novel. She had reread the last three volumes of Richardson's *Clarissa Harlowe,* the modern epistolary equivalent of *Paradise Lost* with a doomed, rebellious Eve, and had decided to frame her novel in the letters of a young explorer, Walton, to his sister. Walton's ambition for knowledge and glory parallel Victor's; he is searching for the North Pole when his ship is caught in ice. Victor stumbles upon it, fatally exhausted by his pursuit of the monster, and relates his own and the monster's story to Walton. At the end Walton describes Victor's death and the monster's brief appearance and exit to immolate himself.

For her protagonists' formative experience, which she had not fleshed out in her tale, Mary consulted the Abbé's letters in Rousseau's *Emile,* which discuss how children develop consciousness of themselves and the world. She set the novel in the eighteenth century, prior to the French Revolution, but gave it currency by quotations from Coleridge, Lamb, Shelley, and other modern authors.

Bath and Abbey Churchyard might seem a curious backdrop for her blasphemous story, but the locale's complacent English norms symbolized everything to which she was contrasting her story, and gave it at once sharper and broader focus. She also realized that the League of Incest story, then filtering back to England, endangered her, Shelley, and Clare — in fact, it would hound them for the rest of their lives. She felt their aloneness as never before, and the menacing power of society arrayed against defective and defecting individuals. During *Frankenstein*'s novelization her education in that regard would be completed. Likewise she came home to a postwar depression and a campaign for parliamentary reform, which was spreading from longtime advocates like Burdett and Place to mass meetings, along with outbreaks of working-class violence, including a riot in Skinner Street — all met by harsh governmental repression. In particular these uprisings by an inflamed, long-suffering populace throughout the coming year would resonate in her monster's rage.

Above and beyond all this, she was shocked as she wrote by three successive traumas; she would put on mourning five days after she began her novel. That she was young and raw to such experiences, that by character she contained her feelings and by circumstance had *Frankenstein*'s plot in which to express them, account for the novel's focused power that would prove unique in her work.

She began to write on October 7. Next day she had a letter from Fanny announcing that she was coming through Bath on her way to their Wollstonecraft relatives in Wales. The lovers met her briefly at the coach stop.[32] Actually, it was Fanny's farewell. On the ninth Mary had a note from her half sister indicating that Fanny intended to kill herself. Shelley rushed after her, Godwin had followed her. Both turned back after seeing a Swansea newspaper report that a young woman had committed suicide by taking laudanum. She was identified only by a gold watch (which the lovers had brought Fanny from Geneva), by corset stays marked M W (which had been her mother's), and by an unsigned suicide note referring obliquely to her bastardy; she knew Godwin dreaded publicity. Godwin returned to London through Bath, where he wrote Shelley but did not address Mary either in that letter or in his terse reply to her condolence letter. At his request the lovers left the body to be buried by the parish; less respectable unclaimed corpses often were given to students (like Victor Frankenstein) for dissection. Later the Godwins told people she had died of natural causes.

"Fanny died this night," Mary added in small writing to the journal entry she had written for the ninth, but the embittered grief and consternation she felt at her victimized sister's death appears in her novel. "Before," says Victor's sweetheart, Elizabeth, when the Frankensteins' innocent servant Justine is executed for the murder of little William, "I had looked upon the accounts of vice and injustice, that I read in books or heard from others . . . as remote, . . . but now misery has come home."[33]

On October 18 Mary launched full into Victor's early life, and in ten days noted completing "Chap. 2½" with his mother's death and his departure for Ingolstadt University. For his researches, she consulted Sir Humphry Davy's *Chemistry,* and for Walton's expedition, books of voyages, probably from the Bath library.[34] In the evenings Shelley read aloud other contributory works: *Paradise Lost,* Locke, Shakespeare, Gibbon, *Political Justice.* She finished Volume I on November 20,[35] and prepared for the second in which the monster tells Victor his story.

She changed to longer sheets of paper to accommodate her large, looping handwriting, and worked fast and with few strike-outs, as she was always to do when engrossed by her subject. Shelley corrected ("enigmatic o you pretty Pecksie," for her "igmmatic") and edited, mostly to embellish her style, which, as she was making a transition from story to novel, he thought too "bald" and "abrupt," so that he added as much as several sentences at certain points. Irked at the perennial few (still extant) who were later to exaggerate his part, particularly those who claimed he created the plot, she would declare that she "certainly did not owe the suggestion of one incident, nor scarcely of one train of feeling" to him, and the manuscript bears her out.[36] Despite her grimness, she made private jokes, naming William's childhood sweetheart Louisa Biron, another character "the rich M. Duvillard" for Elise, whose father had been a modest clockmaker.

On December 5 Shelley left to look for a house at Marlow, and to meet Leigh Hunt, editor of *The Examiner*, who was championing his poetry. Mary was finishing Chapter IV of Volume II,[37] in which the monster hopes to be accepted by a poor family, the De Lacys, whom he is secretly aiding, "& I think you would like it," she wrote Shelley, adding that he must buy her a Livy as she had shamefully neglected Latin.[38] So as not to give credence to the League of Incest story and lead people to believe that Shelley was the father of Clare's child, they had moved Clare into separate lodgings. Mary gave her Elise for company and to Shelley's annoyance took William into their own bedroom. "Tell me shall you be happy to have another little squaller?" she teased him about living with Clare and her baby. "You will look grave on this . . ."[39] Actually she herself had just conceived.

The morning after Shelley's return, December 15, when Mary was about halfway through *Frankenstein,* a second tragedy came to light. Harriet Shelley's whereabouts had been unknown since the autumn. That day Shelley received a letter from his friend Hookham informing him that Harriet, heavily pregnant, had drowned herself in the Serpentine.

The lovers were shocked, but only and inappropriately shocked, for they denied the enormity of Harriet's suicide. Shelley's first thought was to get his children, whom he had not seen for months, from the Westbrooks. He got Mary's consent to marry him, to ensure custody, and rushed off to London, while she decided to send for a fashionable Bath upholsterer to choose furniture and drapes for the house he had just leased in Marlow. "Yes, my only hope my darling love, this will be one among the innumerable benefits which you will have bestowed upon me . . . ," he wrote.[40] "Ah! my best love to you do I owe every joy . . . ," she replied with a shaking hand and a wry twist: "Love me, sweet, for ever — But I [do] not mean —— I hardly know what I I mean I am so much agitated . . . there will be a sweet brother and sister for my William who will lose his pre-eminence as eldest . . . as his Aunt Clare is continually reminding him —"[41]

The story told by Harriet's sister, Eliza Westbrook, which was essentially correct, was that Harriet had become pregnant by an officer who was ordered abroad, and that Eliza hid Harriet in lodgings, where she succumbed to despair. But Shelley believed Hookham's version, that Harriet had gone from man to man, ending with a "low" groom. In her pitiful suicide letter Harriet begged Shelley to leave their daughter, Ianthe, with Eliza, but he refused on grounds that Eliza would prejudice the child against Mary, "the wife of her father's heart."[42] Now Shelley felt certain of custody, so he and Mary decided not to marry. Despite appeals from Mrs. Godwin, who wrote Mary to expect a third suicide, her father's, and from Godwin to Shelley, the lovers held out until Christmas Day, when Mary received an entreaty from her father, his first direct word in two and a half years, which she could not resist.[43]

She went to London to marry so Godwin could attend. All the same, she would not fall into his arms; she and Shelley stayed with the Leigh Hunts in Hampstead, and a cautious, ingratiating Godwin came to her for a constrained reunion. Witnessed only by the Godwins, they were married on December 30 at St. Mildred's Bread Street — probably Mary's choice because of its connection to Milton, who had advocated divorce — and immediately returned to Bath. "A marriage takes place on the 29th," noted the new Mrs. Shelley simply and erroneously in her journal.

On January 3, 1817, Mary Shelley recommenced *Frankenstein* at about the point where the monster is driven off by the horrified De Lacys, shot by the father of a drowning (*sic*) girl he has rescued, and goes on to murder little William Frankenstein. On the sixth Shelley went back to London on business. On the twelfth Mary again had to stop writing, to take care of Clare, who gave birth to a daughter. "4 days of idleness," she confided impatiently to the journal. But she intensely pitied Clare, who dried up her milk and tentatively named the baby Alba, expecting "Albè" to come take his child from her. By now, however, Byron's revulsion had become so strong that she had ceased annoying him by writing. Shelley therefore had to be intermediary, and Mary was convinced that Byron would not take Alba if Clare persuaded Shelley to make demands on him. "Be kind but make no promises . . . ," Mary begged Shelley, "for you are warm-hearted & indeed sweetest very indiscreet —"[44] Mary notified Byron of the birth in cheerful terms and announced her marriage in cryptic mis-chievousness as "Another incident" which "allows me to sign my-self . . . Mary W. Shelley."[45] She made no mention of Harriet's suicide. (When Byron heard that Shelley's wife had killed herself, "do you mean his *wife* — or his Mistress? — Mary Godwin?" he asked. "I hope not the last —"[46])

Clearly, Mary wished to put Harriet out of her mind. But now the Westbrooks filed in Chancery Court for custody of Ianthe and Charles, citing Shelley's radical beliefs and unlawful cohabitation with "Mary God-win." Mary felt sick with anxiety. On her William's first birthday she prayed that his star might be fortunate and influence the case, and on the twenty-fifth left him with Elise and Clare and went to join Shelley. Herself almost two months pregnant, she had all she could do to steady him. He was in a dreadful state of mind, anticipating prison and total ruin,[47] and suffering agonizing side pains as well. He accused his family of instigating the Westbrooks, Eliza of murdering Harriet for her inheritance. And yet he had written Eliza that she might "excusably" regard Mary "as the cause of your sister's ruin," a letter Mary now read in the Westbrook brief. She excused him, of course, but her first confrontation with responsibility for Harriet's death had come from him. That, however, was wiped out by a threat that would haunt her for years, that Chancery Court might take William and her unborn child away on grounds that she and Shelley were unfit parents.

For the next month she lived between Hampstead, with the Hunts, and Skinner Street, working with Shelley and his lawyer Basil Montagu and adviser Henry Brougham, a prominent Whig. While Lord Chancellor Eldon agreed with Shelley's argument that the Westbrooks were too "illiterate and vulgar" to have the children, the question of Shelley's custody turned on how he would educate them about sexual morality and marriage. Counsel advised him to plead that he had changed his doctrines: witness his recent marriage to Mary, who would have continued to live with him as before. Mary Shelley bristled: "Shelley would by no means deny his principles," she declared.[48] Despite Godwin's vehement objection, she copied Shelley's own brief denouncing the institution of marriage and arguing that if his children were taken from him no citizen's private life was safe from the state. Lord Eldon refused Shelley custody, a precedent-setting decision, but allowed him to select guardians.

During this month, the Hunts, ten years older than the Shelleys, cheered the couple, introduced them to a few friends, notably young John Keats, whom they saw several times, had the William Hazlitts and the eminent musician Vincent Novello for a musical evening, took them to the theater and the opera. By February 5 the four were so intimate that Mary told Marianne Hunt about Clare, and arranged for Marianne, who had four children, to keep Alba while Clare lived nearby, and later to bring the baby to Marlow, where Clare would join them.

Mary summoned the Bath contingent, and on the twenty-seventh took William to Marlow, where she stayed with Peacock's mother since her own residence, Albion House, was not ready. Her ordeal now made itself felt in a sense of fleeting time, futility, and death, and in a nightmare "of the dead being alive" so clinging that she got out of bed at one in the morning to write Leigh Hunt.

Sore, taut, and morbid, she immersed herself in *Frankenstein,* apparently near the end of Volume II, which concludes with Victor in torment over the ghastly consequences of his experiment. "Can you wonder," he says, "that sometimes a kind of insanity possessed me, or that I saw continually about me a multitude of filthy animals inflicting on me incessant torture . . . ?"[49] Working long hours every day, she built up momentum as she wrote straight through until the end of the last volume on April 9, through the move into Albion House, visits from Godwin and Jeff Hogg, the arrival of Clare, and then of the Hunts, who brought Alba and stayed. On the tenth she began correcting the manuscript; from the eighteenth until May 13 she made a recorrected fair copy for the press. Shelley copied the last thirteen pages. On the fourteenth he did a final correcting and wrote a preface. "Finis," she wrote — eleven months after her *Frankenstein* nightmare.

Frankenstein drew out of Mary Shelley the ultimate she was capable of at her age: a young woman "saturated with literature and ideas" who had freed her imagination and prophetic gift to dramatize emerging trends and follow them to ultimate conclusions. The discrepancy between her social self and the depth and force of this novel has always startled people to the point of incredulity. But as Balzac was one of the first to observe — specifically in regard to Mary Shelley — certain women of her time had a gift for highly imaginative horror fiction, the function of which as an outlet of repression is today a truism; not that this was confined to women authors, but that their social situation gave it subjectively and objectively greater import.

Obviously, the monster created from corpses reflects the primitive Mary Shelley: her guilt at being her mother's killer-reincarnation, her rage that her father abandoned her, and her resentment of her half brother, William.* The monster and Victor are also universally recognized as a double. That this identifies Victor with Mary Shelley, however, has been ignored until quite recently. But given what her break with her father, society, and the feminine ideal meant for a girl of her time, she is the modern Promethean defier of "natural" limits. Both she and the monster, furthermore, are of Victor's party: exceptional, fearless, imbued with the oppositional energy she prized in herself and others.

Moreover, Victor is only the first of the characters on whom she projects a lifelong preoccupation with ambition, which she sees as the problematic motivation for human endeavor in a universe in which man has become God. In her first four novels, individuals who possess "good" ambition

---

* Ellen Moers interprets *Frankenstein* as a myth of female revulsion against child-bearing. In my view, however, she overlooks Mary Godwin's sense of guilt for having caused her mother's death and rage at her father's remarriage, and supports her theory with traumatic events that Mary Godwin did not experience until *after* she conceived *Frankenstein*'s plot in the summer of 1816: the suicides of Fanny Godwin and Harriet Shelley, and the deaths of her two children in 1818–1819.

for knowledge, glory, power, self-perfection, for service to a domestic circle or to humanity, are vulnerable to their own delusions and instability, to corruption, fate, and Nature; or they are overwhelmed by the destructive ambition of others for power and dominance. In *Frankenstein* her answer is commitment to human happiness and a reverence for Nature: the first sign of Victor's fatal flaw of egotism is that he forgets his "natural" bonds to the people he loves and to Nature in the frenzy of his work. It follows that he fails his duty to his monstrous child and brings on doom.

Frankenstein was also Mary Shelley's outlet for a lurking black pessimism astounding in a girl so young, so enthusiastic for all her apparent stoicism, and so emboldened to overreach by faith in her star. Perhaps because of her early lessons in death, mutability, and deprivation, it is as if a monster pursued her whom she normally believed she had outstripped and who, if felt approaching, she could force back or escape. When she was thirty-two, the two currents in effect changed places, and whereas heretofore her fiction had concluded with death, her endings became relatively happier.

In *Frankenstein,* mutable Nature evokes and reflects the instability of the human mind and of fate. After his "abortion" disappears, "happy inanimate nature" frees Victor from sorrow and care. Then in quick succession, night makes him prophesy evil, during a storm he is excited by "this noble war in the skies," and lightning reveals the "filthy daemon" he created. Subsequently, the Alps console and elevate him, he swells "with something like joy," only to see the monster bounding toward him.

Nevertheless, as the "noble and godlike" Victor dies, knowing the destructive potential of ambition and warning Walton to "Seek tranquillity and avoid ambition," his last words are, "Yet why do I say this? I have myself been blasted in these hopes, yet another may succeed."[50] Walton, however, accedes to his mutinous crew and gives up his expedition. With extraordinary clairvoyance and integrity Mary Shelley recognized that what her father trusted as the promise of humankind — "What the heart of man is able to conceive, the hand of man is strong enough to perform" — was also its gravest threat. It is perhaps her greatest and most characteristic accomplishment in *Frankenstein* that the issue remains unresolved and unresolvable.

8 "Marlow"

MARY SHELLEY welcomed Marlow as a place to recoup and regularize her life after six months of shocks. In some ways this would be a normal year for a young woman-artist turning twenty: her new marriage, a second child, a "permanent" house, an enlarged circle, progress in work. What Marlow defined, however, was the impossibility of satisfactory life in England.

When she first saw Shelley's choice of a home in late February 1817 she was delighted. It was an exurban gentleman's property on which they had spent two thousand pounds for a twenty-one-year lease, furnishings, and remodeling and landscaping that Peacock had taken charge of to their specifications. The house itself sat on the street, but there was an extensive garden, four acres of grounds, a large, elegant, purple-draped library fit for "luxurious literati," five "best" bedrooms, separate nurseries for William and Elise, and Alba and her nurse, Amelia Shields; (one water closet) and attics for the cook, four maids, and gardener-butler. To minimize the servants' mixing and gossiping with the locals, they were recruited in London. Alba was supposedly "Miss Auburn," Clare her dead mother's friend.

In residence from April through July was the Leigh and Marianne Hunt household, seven strong, with four young children and Marianne's sister, Elizabeth Kent, moving from Hampstead to Lisson Grove. Hunt was the Shelleys' most significant new associate, both as political ally and friend. Although he was taunted by enemies as a "cockney," his weekly political and cultural journal, *The Examiner,* voiced the progressive cause in the then highly politicized English press. Furthermore, he was a cultivated, versatile man of letters, mad about music and Italian literature.

Hunt supported himself by his pen and continual help from his many friends, which he took with notoriously ineluctable and shameless charm; Dickens would draw on him for *Bleak House*'s Horace Skimpole. The Shelleys had yet to learn that when the Hunts had money they ran through it extravagantly. Hunt was sensitive about his class, vain, and limited in taste — preferred Zerlina's pretty arias to the "too loud and crashing" chords of Don Giovanni's descent to Hell, and wrote honeyed poetry. But he had a gift for making the ordinary festive and the festive enchanting, and for dispelling gloom.

About as far as it could go, moreover, Hunt had widened the Shelleys' circlet, most importantly with the stockbroker-poet Horace Smith and Keats, then twenty-two and still a novice poet — though Keats declined their invitation to join the Hunts at Marlow, feeling that the Shelleys treated him de haut en bas, and that Shelley might influence him artistically. Thanks also to Hunt, Mary discovered a love of music, for he played the piano and sang delightfully, and took her to her first Mozart opera, for which she developed an abiding preference, and fjurthermore accompanied her to the theater — which Shelley had disliked — so that her girlhood excitement for theater revived.

Though far less Mary's intellectual equal than Leigh Hunt, and burdened with household cares, "poor dear" Marianne Hunt was her first woman friend since the elopement. She cut fine silhouettes and "scraped" sculptures, including busts for the Shelleys' library and a head of Shelley; Mary, who was hard to portraitize, sat to her, with results that evidently did not please and have not survived. Their strongest bond was a common sister problem: Marianne's incompatible sister, Elizabeth Kent, a clever professional writer, a strong, irascible woman, and patently in love with Hunt, lived with them. More demanding than his charm indicated, Hunt exhorted the two women to live in harmony: "Will is the devil," he said, of others, while Marianne tippled and Bessy took opium. This trio's Marlow visit was taken as reinforcement of the League of Incest by such as Robert Southey, who claimed that Hunt was becoming as infamous as Shelley in his domestic life.[1]

In May, entering her sixth month of pregnancy, Mary emerged from completing *Frankenstein* to a writer's letdown and to tense, sad contemplation of everything that had occurred since Fanny's suicide. Shelley sailed her down the Thames to London on his new boat for a holiday and to give her manuscript to Byron's publisher, John Murray, whom he had met the previous autumn when he delivered the third canto of *Childe Harold* — though Mary doubted that the conservative Murray, proprietor of the leading Tory *Quarterly Review,* would accept *Frankenstein.* Since Shelley felt that her name and youth would spoil the chances of a work bound to be attacked in any case, and Godwin feared more opprobrium, it was represented as by a very young friend of Shelley's who wished to remain anonymous, a common form of publication. And Mary herself wished it so, as she worried about trading off her parents and bidding for attention at her age with a major novel. Assuming a "natural" career progression, her circle regarded *Frankenstein* as a remarkable beginning, but no more.

Shelley had already fallen back under Godwin's sway: "nothing gives me serener & more pure pleasure than your society," he told him.[2] Mrs. Godwin being in France on business, Shelley had arranged to leave Mary at Skinner Street for a week to rehabilitate her relations with her father. Here she too succumbed as they talked books and ideas, and went as in the old days to her mother's grave and to the theater, where Mary was dazzled by the magnificent actor Edmund Kean. She saw the Lambs and others of her old circle to whom she was now, as a married woman, persona grata and impressively matured. "Mrs. Shelley . . . is grown quite a beautiful woman," the playwright James Kenney told Crabb Robinson.[3] Robinson himself avoided her, exemplifying the censoriousness she would face henceforth because of her liaison with Shelley and presumed participation in the League of Incest.

Godwin rejoiced to have his daughter again, safely married; "Be happy, be respectable (worthy of respect)," he told her. But the resources of her husband, a "future ornament of the English baronetcy" as he now maddeningly called Shelley (in part to irk) figured large. Shelley had authorized him to arrange another post-obit loan, of two thousand pounds, to be divided as before, and Godwin, readying Mary to take Fanny's place as his pleader, dwelt upon his financial needs, loneliness, comedown in the world, aging, and worry about boorish, unstable William, Junior. "I wish I could see him happy," she wrote Shelley. She had just reread Byron's third canto of *Childe Harold* on the Geneva summer, and it intensified her depression and nervousness:

> It made me dreadfully melancholy . . . the moment of enjoyment lives only in memory and when we die where are we? . . . I am very well here but so intolerably restless that it [is] painful to sit still for five minutes . . . I will not close this letter just yet that if I feel in better spirits after dinner I may say so.
>
> Good bye pretty one — I smile now and shall again when I see you saturday[4]

Back at Marlow, she settled into a routine of work, companionship, and pastoral pleasures: "beautiful walks, uplands, valleys, wood, water, steeples issuing out of clumps of trees . . . brooks, nooks, and pretty looks. (Here a giggle, and a shake of the head from the ladies)," Hunt wrote Vincent Novello one sunny afternoon when they were all sitting in the garden. "The other day a party of us dined in a boat under the hanging woods of Clevedon."[5] They often gathered in the library, browsing and chatting; Clare remembered that once Shelley came in from his study to read them a beautiful line from Plato.[6]

After her work hours, Mary played and walked with William — "blue eyes," "Will man," or "Wilmouse" — whom she dressed in fine red smocks and in the fall a fur hat with gold braid that had to be just right. In rearing him she followed Wollstonecraft and the Hunts' free ways ("Yahoos," Byron would call the Hunt children). Elise, who was on close terms with Mary and intimate with Clare, took care of William's cold baths and morning outings and was permitted only "frequent and poignant re-monstrances" in French to curb him, while Godwin predicted that Mary's system would make the child peevish and imperious. Mary took William's naughtinesses as passing, though they discouraged Shelley, who expected the child's innate goodness to be perfected by ideal handling. She believed children's minds were often as intelligent as adults' "and differ only by containing fewer ideas,"[7] which she meant gradually to enlarge. For a time the Shelleys took in a neighborhood child to educate, Polly Rose, who remembered that Mary, "fair and very young," talked to her at bedtime about what she and Shelley had been reading or discussing, "always wind-ing up with, 'And now, Polly, what do you think of this?' "[8]

Frankenstein was turned down by Murray, as Mary expected, then by a new publisher and friend of Hunt's, Charles Ollier, who returned it by the next post. But in late August, just before Mary delivered her baby, Shelley's booksellers, Lackington, accepted the novel, despite her refusal to make some alteration they requested. The firm meant to retain all the profits from the first edition; Shelley, however, contracted on the mys-terious young author's part for one third of its profits, "because it is possible there may be no demand for another."[9] Meanwhile, on his assurance that it was not too trivial Mary occupied the last three weeks of her pregnancy writing a spirited, idiosyncratic little travel book based on the journal of her elopement trip, *History of a Six Weeks' Tour*.

Shelley was engrossed in a major poem, *The Revolt of Islam*, which he was to head with a long and beautiful Dedication to Mary.* The work was intended as a risk-all test of public receptivity to his artistry, and to political, religious, and sexual opinions he knew would result in perse-cution by "depraved" or mistaken enemies: careless of the consequences to himself, he wrote Byron, "I can but die; I can but be torn to pieces, or devoted to infamy most undeserved."[10] Clare studied and tried as well

---

* Shelley's militant Cythna is drawn from Mary Shelley: her mother died giving her birth, she is a "child of glory" "with a still and earnest face," "without fear of evil or disguise," and she is an inspiration to and passionate lover of Laon, with whom she is martyred.

to write, including a review of *Frankenstein;* Peacock composed much of his long poem *Rhododaphne* at Albion House.

"Our house is very political as well as poetical," Mary had told Hunt that March. In what seemed to be a prerevolutionary climate, with populist journalists like William Cobbett stirring the working classes and outbreaks of civic disorders, the Tory administration declared a national emergency, suspended habeas corpus, and passed a seditious meetings act. Mary and her circle were talking political philosophy and strategy, discussing monarchies and republics one evening until three in the morning with Hazlitt; all but Hunt were for republics — he said that crass America had ruined republics for him.

To tease Hunt about republics, and about his fluency in Italian, Mary sent him the *Marseillaise* ("Macellois" in her phonetics) to improve his French: "for convenience sake you must either learn that or I italian that we may not always shock one another with our vernacular tongue."[11] Mary took "extreme pleasure" when Hunt's political articles were bold, assuring poor Marianne that he was unlikely to be jailed again. Her political reading this year included Tacitus, Spinoza, whose *Tractatus Theologico-Politicus* she translated with Shelley over the next four years, Montesquieu, Montaigne, Hume, Junius, Godwin, and Lady Morgan's new *France;* as Morgan was a liberal, the *Quarterly* viciously attacked her in a review Mary read with indignation.

Both Mary and Shelley believed that bloodshed was justified to overthrow intransigent autocrats and oligarchies; indeed, Shelley was glorifying just such an uprising led by Laon and his sister-lover Cythna in *The Revolt of Islam*. In the poem, however, the revolt is brutally crushed. The burning issue in England was how to make gains out of current upheaval. If progressive intellectuals, actually more or less radical on the nineteenth-century political spectrum, were comparable to what Mary called the "intrepid reformists" of the French Revolution's Gironde party, the Revolution had proved that liberty, equality, and fraternity were vulnerable to susceptible mobs, dictators, and restored oppressive monarchies. Shelley, moreover, tended to think from the point of view of a landed aristocrat,[12] and despised the "purse-proud" commercial class — while Byron feared that "low designing dirty levellers" might bring on "democratical tyranny."[13] What Mary hoped for was bloodless revolution in which leadership by the middle classes would allay violence on the part of the lower orders and their oppressors, and what Shelley more realistically now proposed in an anonymous pamphlet was moderate expansion of the suffrage to the middle classes — among whom, however, support of the Tories was being solidified by current disorders.

Thus Mary, Shelley, and Hunt feared anarchy and vehemently deplored men like Cobbett who incited the populace: "a revolution in this country would [not] be *bloodless* if that man has any power in it," Mary wrote Shelley. "He is I fear somewhat of a Marius perhaps of a Marat . . . He encourages in the multitude the worst possible human passion *revenge* or as he would probably give it that abominable *Christian* name retribution."[14] Hunt published her letter in *The Examiner* as by a lady of "masculine understanding," and though pleased to find it in print Mary protested that if she had known she would have worded her too "femininely expressed" opinions with more dignity.

This she hoped to do in a major historical romance, a genre popularized by Jane Porter and more recently by Walter Scott. In her twofold zeal for liberty and social betterment, and for high culture and morality, she believed that superior individuals were essential models and leaders, and if history taught that even the greatest were fallible, their ambitions, struggles, and failures were the stuff of romance and the compost of progress. Looking through the library, she thought of writing her novel on the conflict between a tyrant and republicans, although it would be a year before she found the "body" for this work, which would eventually be published as *Valperga*. *Frankenstein* had convinced Shelley that she had a gift for drama, and he urged her to try a play, which strongly attracted her. She felt, however, that she needed a thorough grounding, and began what would be a two-year course of reading essays on drama and the great English, French, Latin, and Italian plays.

Nevertheless, until October she continued to feel edgy. She discovered that she did not care for country gentry life. Shelley liked keeping open house, but the responsibility devolved upon her, and everyone had maddeningly proprietary presumptions. Besides the Hunt seven, Peacock expected to dine every day and Jeff Hogg to come on weekends. Marianne teased Mary about Jeff's being in love with her, but he was particularly churlish, since he and Hunt, and Peacock and Hunt, each vying for first place in the Shelleys' favor, did not always get on. Shelley being unwilling to offend, she insisted that Jeff sleep at Peacock's.

Her recent trials, her marriage, the new command she felt from *Frankenstein,* Shelley's fallibilities, made her more assertive. "My sweet Love," she wrote him in a new tone shortly after their wedding, about one of his lovable but extreme benevolences:

> You were born to be a don Quixote and if that celebrated personage had ever existed except in the brain of Cervantes I should certainly form a theory of transmigration to prove that

you lived in Spain some hundred years before & fought with
Windmills.[15]

While she upheld Shelley and Clare, themselves troubled, she had outbursts of nervous irritability when she felt especially worried or depressed,
and grew more critical and ironic. As with everyone she liked, she spoke
her mind to the Hunts, declared that if Hunt took exercise he would not
get ill, "preached" to Marianne, pregnant with her fifth child, against
wearing stays in her condition and for birth control; "a woman is not a
field to be continually employed either in bringing forth or enlarging
grain,"[16] she would later admonish. And she had discovered that they were,
if endearingly, childishly feckless. "Adieu little babes —" she quipped when
they left for Lisson Grove, "take care not to loose one another in the
streets . . . but take hold of one another's hands & walk pretty."[17]

Moreover, when she disagreed with Hunt, sensitive and stubborn as
she, she argued tenaciously. "Marina," he fondly called her, for the peerless
heroine of Shakespeare's *Pericles* ("Born in a tempest, when my mother
died," and suffering a wicked stepmother), and "nymph of the sidelong
looks." Though he admired her he much preferred Shelley, for she antag-
onized him by her will, irony, directness, and "peevishness." Others agreed.
Dr. Furnivall of Egham, who attended her lying-in, said years later that
she ordered Shelley around and he submitted like a child. Keats, who had
resented both Shelleys for advising him not to publish his early poems,
found Mary's teatime precision threatening. "Does Mrs S cut bread and
butter as neatly as ever?" he asked Hunt. "Tell her to procure some fatal
scissors and cut the thread of life of all to-be-disappointed poets."[18]

Hunt's tack was to swallow his disapproval and charmingly diminish
her when she was "a good girl." "Did I not detect her lurking faculty of
giggle at the theatre," said he, "when she sat shaking her white shoulders"
at a comedy.[19] Although he championed his friends' work in *The Examiner,*
he was never to review *Frankenstein,* which in fact he did not like. He
told Mary she was too serious, too prone to dwell on the dark side of
human affairs.

But what really harassed Mary were far graver problems. Both she and
Shelley were harrowed by charges that they had caused Harriet Shelley's
suicide. Apparently out of pride, principle, and determination to protect
Harriet's children, they made a tacit compact to remain silent about the
fact that Harriet had been pregnant by a lover and about any previous
lovers. Peacock either never knew why Harriet drowned herself, refused
to believe it, or, later, lied about it. The Shelleys also knew that the greater
Harriet's "sins," the more Shelley would be blamed; as Southey said, "She

was thoroughly corrupted by him, followed the example which he had set her, and then in shame at the consequences, threw herself in the Thames."[20] The word around London was that she had turned to prostitution because Shelley refused to support her. John Murray called Shelley "the vilest wretch now living"; the best believed of Mary Shelley was that he had suborned her, the worst that she was the vicious heir of Wollstonecraft and Godwin, Byron's mistress, atheist, and so on.

Moreover, from now on there were things unsaid and unsayable between the Shelleys. If they were not the immediate cause of Harriet's suicide, they had still to contend with their part in her ruin. Mary had convinced herself that Harriet was incapable of serious feelings, but the suicide linked her to Wollstonecraft, who had twice attempted suicide over Imlay; in a sense, Mary had caused two women's deaths, her mother's and Harriet's. The Chancery case made her feel as if she had been stripped and exposed to a hostile world — or "as if I were walking on the edge of a precipice, towards which thousands are crowding, and endeavouring to plunge me into the abyss," as Elizabeth says in *Frankenstein* — and had been literally brought to judgment. But after examining herself and her actions according to her habitual practice, she denied that she or Shelley should have done anything differently in regard to Harriet or had any responsibility for her death. As Shelley's was the greater blame, Mary could not accept blame herself without accusing him, whom she was determined to exonerate. "Reproach not thine own soul, but know thyself," Cythna tells Laon in *The Revolt of Islam,* as Mary in prose told Shelley. "O vacant expiation! Be at rest. — / The past is death's, the future is thine own."

Likewise Shelley's feelings were complicated and impossible for him to confide to Mary. Though he was tormented about Harriet, the only self-reproach he could admit was that before marrying her he should have realized that she was incapable of properly enacting his principles. His hostility and aggrievance intensified; witness the unprecedented ferocity and self-pity of *The Revolt of Islam*. But there were private hours when he was despondent or aghast. Clare observed that Harriet's death changed him, that he became much less self-confident and "wild." From this time on he sublimated to almost superhuman effect, while projecting his guilt onto others, society, and even Mary. When the witty, worldly Horace Smith visited Marlow, even though he deplored Shelley's atheism he was moved to reverence as the frail poet, heaving with emotion and irradiated by spirituality, expanded on his faith that reason, natural religion, and love would gradually uplift the human race to a higher state.

That Mary and Shelley had married over Harriet's dead body, so to speak, evoked a vague dread that sometimes became acute and made it harder for them to find peace in their new marriage, about which they remained ambivalent in any case. They asserted their unaltered disdain for this unenlightened "sanction" and resented having compromised principle without even getting Shelley's children or surcease from public hostility. Betwixt and between the name she and Shelley prized and the new one, Mary asked the Hunts not to call her Mrs. Shelley, not only to be on a first-name basis but also because "I do not half like the name" — which she always signed "Mary W.," for Wollstonecraft — "Shelley." Since they had refused to publicize their marriage, one newspaper reported Shelley's continued "cohabitation" with the "woman" for whom he had left his wife, upon which they allowed Hunt to reply in *The Examiner* that "the Lady with whom he lives, and who inherits an intellect equally striking and premature, from celebrated parents . . . *is* his wife,"[21] something that was still not universally believed.

When, after three years of rejection, Mary tried to restore her intimacy with Isabel Baxter Booth, she reiterated her opposition to marriage so vehemently that Isabel declined to correspond. To avenge and solace Mary, Shelley began what he called "my pretty eclogue," a long, quasi-biographical poem, *Rosalind and Helen,* in which Rosalind is remorseful about her rejection of Helen because of Helen's liaison with Lionel. And in his Dedication of *The Revolt of Islam* he panegyrized Mary's courage and wisdom in flouting tyrannical custom to live with him, a challenge that was to outrage their enemies.

On the other hand, marriage had certain "conveniences": it reconciled them with Godwin, legitimized future children (though not William), and increased their circle; Marianne Hunt might not have associated publicly with Mary otherwise. In fact, one of Mary's first thoughts about her marriage was that if it had taken place sooner Fanny Godwin could have found asylum with her and Shelley instead of killing herself. Furthermore, Isabel's father, William Baxter, Mary's fondly loved Scottish foster father, now came to visit her and to meet Shelley. And Shelley himself acknowledged that one could not always practice one's principles in private life.

Another problem, Clare, dominated Albion House and created difficulties between the Shelleys. Lest people think that Alba was Clare's child by Shelley, they barricaded the place against the neighborhood, and each time Godwin visited they held their breath, while Mrs. Godwin was never invited and smoldered at her exclusion. Morose and irritable, Clare sequestered herself with the baby she could not acknowledge, and could hardly be persuaded to play a fine, unpaid-for piano Shelley got her through Novello. She also suffered occasionally from what was later diagnosed as scrofula. When she had hopes of Byron, she was at her best, an irresistible entertainer ("rubs her hands and twinkles her head," said Hunt, who called her Prima Donna), cracked wicked jokes about her situation, and sang at the piano in a beautiful contralto.

At moments she could not bear the thought of giving Alba to Byron, but she had had the child in the first place for him, and Fanny's suicide hardened her determination, since without Byron's protection Alba might end like Fanny, and with it could have a secure, even splendid life. Mary, who could not look at Alba without thinking of Wollstonecraft's descriptions of Fanny as a baby, agreed absolutely. And Clare anticipated reopening relations with Byron through Alba; the name Albion House had probably appealed to all of them because they expected Albè-Byron to visit and take his Alba.

After the suicides of two desperate young women, Mary had no present thought of *"absentia Clariae."* Beyond family loyalty, she felt bonded to Clare by sisterhood in rebellion, like lone amazons at war with society who shared rewards and punishments that only they two could understand. She always respected that avatar of her stepsister, whatever her personal discomfort with Clare. In addition, she knew Shelley blamed himself for converting Clare to his sexual theories and sensed that he was giving Clare the protection and love he had failed to give Harriet.

Shelley set the model for relating to Clare based solely on her status as the weakest party; even when Clare was wrong in some quarrel, he expected Mary to ask her pardon and Mary felt guilty for being harsh. She intended to name her baby for Clare if it was a girl, and vowed that until Clare's fortunes improved she would live contentedly with her as Shelley so intensely desired, and even admonished Marianne Hunt at least to *"appear* so" with Bessy Kent if only to please Hunt. Mary would persist more or less successfully in this resolve for three years, despite uncommon provocations.

Clare's respect for and resentment of Mary intensified with Mary's comparatively better fortune, her marriage, her general development, and her genius as manifested in *Frankenstein*. "No one could believe it was written by so young a woman," Clare would write Byron. "Whatever my private feelings of envy . . . how I delight in a lovely woman of strong and cultivated intellect . . . to hear all the intricasies of life and arguments, hanging on her lips. If she were my mortal enemy . . . I would serve her with fidelity and fervently."[22] Though Clare would remain in love with Byron for three more years — she declined Peacock's marriage proposal at Marlow — she and Shelley had their own intimate friendship, with Mary's knowledge. Marriage had not altered either of the Shelleys' belief in free, nonexclusive unions. But Clare exploited the advantage of victimhood, crept as close to Shelley as she dared, looked over her shoulder to see how Mary was taking it, criticized her to Shelley, and gave him the opportunity to do likewise.

Moreover, this intimacy encouraged the belief that they were lovers. "Mary is not a woman if, notwithstanding all her apparent stoicism, these things do not give her pain," said Isabel Booth's husband, David, who suspected them.[23] Though Mary scorned such evil-minded presumptions, her trust invited deception and her permissiveness worked against her preoccupying fear: that Alba would be identified as Shelley's "incestuous" child, that he would be prosecuted, and that William and her coming child would be taken from her. Although she loved Alba, she saw no alternative to Byron's taking the child. Partly out of jealousy of Byron, Shelley wanted Clare to say the baby was hers by a Swiss marriage and stay with them. "But the wise heads [Mary, the Hunts, possibly Peacock] suppose that such a tale would make people consider it as mine . . . ,"[24] he wrote Byron, in which event he himself admitted that they would have to flee England. While Mary felt that every day increased their danger, as well as their hateful precautions and lies, instead of coming for Alba Byron settled in Venice, where, Mary told Shelley, he was probably "over head & ears in love with some Venetian." Clare was crushed.

Godwin constituted another divisive problem. While Mary assumed that Shelley was as devoted as she to relieving his financial problems, Shelley increasingly felt that Godwin had gotten him to pledge to redeem his debts when he was too young to know what he was doing, or to foresee his present needs and desires. Indeed, to Godwin's apprehension he was trying to raise money for Hunt, feeling that M.J. Godwin & Co. swallowed whatever he gave whereas the Hunts would be made secure. Actually, Shelley felt that his account with Godwin was close to even, on which balance sheet his marriage to Mary may have counted, and that it was his money to give, not hers.

Heavy with child, "ennuied" and anxious, for a time Mary considered having her baby in London near Marianne Hunt, who neglected, with other commissions, to send the nurse Mary asked her to hire, when Mary was frightened of having a local woman who would gossip about Alba; "did not your naughty heart smite you with reproach," she wrote Marianne. The baby was born September 2, a girl who resembled Shelley. Mary named her Clara Everina, the latter for her mother's sister.

She had an exceptionally disturbing postpartum month. Byron asked them to send Alba to Venice, when they had neither money nor escort; meanwhile there was so much Marlow talk about Alba that they decided they must leave the village. Shelley's creditors were dunning him; on one occasion he was arrested for debt. Worst of all, he had been ailing and now, as before when she gave birth, his health precipitously declined and he believed his "constitutional" consumption would prove fatal. While she helped him to hope and resist, he also envisioned her as his posthumous vestal, a role he continually imagined for her from now on, as if preparing her. "Death and Love are yet contending for their prey," he wrote in the Dedication of *The Revolt:*

> Yet in the paleness of thy thoughtful cheek,
>   And in the light thine ample forehead wears,
>   And in thy sweetest smiles, and in thy tears,
> And in thy gentle speech, a prophecy
>   Is whispered, to subdue my fondest fears:
> And through thine eyes, even in thy soul I see
> A lamp of vestal fire burning internally.

The first proofs of *Frankenstein* arrived, which diverted Mary somewhat. On September 23, Shelley went to London for two months to oversee their various publications, consult Dr. Lawrence, and try to raise money. "Ah! my love you cannot guess how wretched it was to see your languour and encreasing illness," she wrote him. "I now say to myself perhaps he is better — but then I watched you every moment & every moment was full of pain . . ."[25] "I am just now surrounded by babes," she wrote four days later. "Alba is scratching and crowing — William amusing him-self with wrapping a shawl round him and Miss Clara staring at the fire . . . Adieu — dear love — I cannot express to you how anxious I am to hear from [you] —"[26] "Dearest & best of living beings," he replied, "how much do your letters console me . . . So soothing so pow-erful and quiet are your expressions that it is almost like folding you to my heart."[27]

But she was tight-strung, annoyed with the Hunts, who came to keep her company but went about on their own; so irritated by Peacock, who came as usual to dinner and drank his bottle of wine, that they had a fight and Peacock told Shelley he had a good mind not to come to the house again.[28] Her milk supply dwindled and supplementary cow's milk disagreed with the baby. William hung on Elise because of the infant, and sometimes Mary felt too exhausted to do justice to *Frankenstein*. "I send you my dearest another proof . . . ," she wrote of one batch she had corrected, "but I am tired and not very clear headed so I give you carte blanche to make what alterations you please."[29]

Dr. Lawrence recommended Italy or the English coast for Shelley's health, and Shelley asked Mary to decide. The thought of Italy made her

glow; "a clear sky — pure air & burning sun" she believed would improve
Shelley's health. And they could take Alba to Byron. But now Mary feared
that Clare did not really wish to part with Alba and was putting obstacles
in the way by asking Shelley to make conditions that Byron send regular
reports; "but promises with Albe! . . . ," Mary said; "why it is the labour
of several months to get any kind of answer from him . . ."[30]

Whereas it was Shelley's "manly part" to decide, after two days with
no satisfactory answers about anything, she bombarded him. "You have
advertized the house but have you given Maddocks [the agent] any orders . . . And have you yet settled for Italy or the Sea — and do you know
how to get money to convey us there and to buy the things that will be
absolutely necessary . . . ? And can you do anything for my father before
we go?"[31] In a "wild" crescendo, she threatened to wean Clara and come
to London if he did not return for the weekend, and when he agreed she
panicked because someone had just been killed in a local coach accident.
Shelley came, and since Clare agreed with Mary about Italy, he decided
to go, for his health and because they could take Alba to her father, "a
thing of incredible importance to the happiness perhaps of many human
beings." Now Mary was afraid of what Godwin would say in view of his
need for Shelley's money:

> if my Father said — Yes you must go — do what you can for
> me . . . I should far from writing so melancholy a letter prepare
> every thing with a light heart — arrange our affairs here and come
> up to town to wait patiently . . . I know not whether it is early
> habit or affection but the idea of his silent quiet disapprobation
> makes me weep as it did in the days of my childhood. I am called
> away by the cries of Clara . . . God knows when I shall see you —
> Clare is forever wearying with her idle & childish complaints . . .[32]

Once they settled upon leaving for Italy in the spring, Mary became
her old self. Her own temper, Clare wrote Byron, was "inconstant and
volage; . . . I do not like our Mary, sail my steady course like a ship under
a gentle and favourable wind."[33] Mary apologized and made up with
Peacock, and copied his *Rhododaphne* for penance; Jeff stayed at Albion
House on weekends. While she was correcting *Frankenstein* proofs she
did not want to get out of the habit of writing, and considered a major
project her father suggested, but there was insufficient time to start on it.
However, she edited her and Shelley's travel letters (written with eventual
publication in mind) for *Six Weeks' Tour;* Shelley wrote a preface. Hookham was publishing it anonymously, though the authors were quite recognizable.[34]

In mid-October Mary was sent the first, unbound volume of *Franken-stein* and translated some of it, probably into French. At Shelley's suggestion she also translated Apuleius's "Cupid and Psyche," the myth of a girl's ordeal for love with which she identified. She weaned Clara at about two months, and in November joined Shelley in London for ten days, saw friends, and went to a dressmaker. In rebellion against the sumptuary puritanism of her girlhood, or perhaps to suit her repute as a scarlet woman, she ordered a crimson evening gown with deep decolleté that showed off her white bust and sloping shoulders, of which she was becoming vain.

When she returned to Marlow, she began preparing for Italy by reading Dante and Italian opera libretti and practicing her drawing. She was more than ever eager to leave England; in fact, she had become Anglophobic. On top of vicious gossip about Albion House, the campaign for parliamentary reform had failed; Princess Charlotte died giving birth to the first child of a recent marriage, dashing hopes for a future liberal monarch; and prosecutions for publications considered seditious, blasphemous, or immoral were multiplying. Ollier stopped publication of *The Revolt of Islam* until Albion House constituted itself a committee of bowdlerizers so that among other alterations the lovers Laon and Cythna were not brother and sister.

The radiant Clare planned to give Alba to Byron, with Milly Shields for nurse, and to live near them to supervise. Though she knew Byron accused her of being immoral, she simply could not take him — of all people — seriously, and wrote with intimate jollity that she was studying the Shelleys and Plutarch's heroes as models of worthiness and abstinence respectively. She assured Byron that she had not had "one *hot* moment" since she last saw him — which set his teeth on edge and hardened his determination to have nothing to do with her. Shelley, now more jealous, drew closer to her — although, unknown to Clare, he had "capitulated" to Byron, promising to tell her nothing Byron did not authorize. Like children about a teacher, they commiserated over Mary's flaws and "wise head." As Clare was jealous of Shelley's poems to Mary — "He wrote you verses that immortalized you and made you the envy and glory of your sex," she would tell Mary[35] — he wrote Clare two poems to "Constantia," constant to him despite Byron, and published one secretly,[36] though he later let Mary see the drafts.

Albion House was so cold and damp that winter that William, though swathed in flannel, had chapped skin, and the books mildewed in the library. But it was a time of great literary excitement in the family. Godwin's *Mandeville* was published, which Mary read straight through, and then immediately sent Lackington a dedication to Godwin to be inserted in *Frankenstein*'s front matter. The *Six Weeks' Tour* came out and was praised, most gratifyingly, by Thomas Moore, who recognized the authors and congratulated them. "Mrs. Shelley, tho' sorry that her secret is discovered, is exceedingly delighted to hear that you have derived any amusement from our book," Shelley replied.[37] "She has another literary secret," he added, for he was stirring interest in *Frankenstein,* sending advance copies to several illustrious authors, and supervising its advertisement as "a Work of Imagination." Ollier published *The Revolt of Islam,* and Shelley wrote his sonnet "Ozymandias," which he signed "Glirastes," Latin for lover of the dormouse, and which may have been inspired by a travel book to which Mary called his attention.[38]

On the last day of 1817 Mary Shelley had her first bound copy of the three volumes of *Frankenstein.* Booksellers took 459 of a run of 500, and after Lackington deducted the Shelleys' sizable book bill, the anonymous author received twenty-eight pounds. Official publication date was to be March 11, but from the dedication to Godwin and the book's daring, the few outsiders who read advance copies assumed it was by Shelley, something Shelley had feared and Mary did not appreciate. Jeff Hogg set a friend straight: "In plain terms Frankenstein is written by Mrs Shelley & is th[ere]fore estimable not for its own sake alone but as a present pledge of future excellence."[39]

Godwin took the news about Italy calmly, since he had finalized Shelley's post-obit loan of two thousand pounds and received a thousand for *Mandeville.* The Albion House lease and furnishings were sold, but for three months Mary was so concerned about money that she kept account of their expenses. Moreover, she had outgrown her nonchalance about their possessions. "Remember," she told Shelley, "we lost all the little property we had at Bishopsgate . . . here we have much more to loose & I must not leave this house untill such things as we do not dispose of are put in a place of safety."[40] She selected some hundred volumes for shipment to Italy and a smaller number to take along, and packed the rest of their library and papers for Peacock to store. The others preceded her to London. On February 10 she closed down the house and joined them.

For a month they enjoyed the Hunts, Jeff, Peacock, who came to be with them, and Horace Smith, visited the newly installed Elgin marbles at the British Museum, the Oriental Library at East India House, stocked up on stationery and notions. Mary, who had packed a dozen lightweight white dresses, had a new riding habit made. They took their fill of theater and opera in the best box seats, Mary in her red dress, Shelley in a formal coat: "a thin patrician-looking young cosmopolite yearning out upon us," recalled Hunt, who sat in the pit, "& a sedate-faced young lady bending in a similar direction with her great tablet of a forehead, & her white shoulders unconscious of a crimson gown."[41] The children were christened, for purposes of legal identification only; Alba became Allegra at Byron's request.

Because of the Godwins, however, it was a disagreeable, in fact a fateful, month. They were so enraged on two counts that Mary's father refused to see her until a week before she sailed. After leading Godwin to count on half the post-obit, Shelley presented him with five hundred pounds less, implying that he needed it himself, and gave fourteen hundred pounds to Hunt. (The Hunts were to squander it in a year.) "In the calmness of philosophy," actually icy rage, Godwin justly accused Shelley of inconstancy and cruelty, letting him work for a year on the loan, then breaking his promise and leaving him embarrassed for five hundred pounds he had pledged to his creditors. Mary may not have known about Shelley's decision until the last moment, and although she defended him, it dismayed her.

On the second count, the Godwins knew Allegra was Clare's child. Clare had been so afraid that her mother would drag the secret out of her that she had not spent a single night at Skinner Street since Allegra's birth, or even visited without one of the Shelleys as shield. That fall she had sometimes stayed with Shelley in London to see her mother and to take care of him, and Mary told her not to hurry back, as she had the Hunts or Baxter for company. Whereas they probably meant to show their indifference to the League of Incest story, this "cohabitation" gave David Booth, then in London, a needed weapon.

William Baxter had told Mary that Booth had influenced Isabel against the Shelleys and that she was wretched in her marriage. "So she is to [be] another victim of that ceremony," said Mary grimly,[42] and launched a plot with Baxter's help to get Isabel away from her husband (as Wollstonecraft had rescued her sister Eliza) by inviting her to come along to visit Italy. When Booth, fighting for his wife, saw that Clare was staying with Shelley, he drew the logical conclusion and convinced Isabel they were lovers and Allegra their child. Isabel, now a sad, intimidated young woman, remained with Booth. She and Mary managed, however, to see one another secretly before Mary's departure.

Booth informed the Godwins of his conclusion, so Clare had to confess that Allegra was hers, by Byron, but the Godwins always believed Shelley was the father. Mrs. Godwin, anguished at her beloved daughter's ruin and at losing her to Italy, loaded the entire blame on Mary, the greatest enemy she had in the world, she declared, the author of all her misfortunes.

The score remained unendurably out of balance at Skinner Street; both Godwins were determined on revenge and redress. For the next four years Mrs. Godwin would see no one who spoke fondly of Mary; Godwin would be obsessed by his lost five hundred pounds and pressure the Shelleys for the sum, though he knew he was straining Mary's relations with Shelley — and perhaps the money was one rationale for just that.

More eager than ever to depart, Mary Shelley crossed the Channel from Dover in rough seas on March 12, 1818.

9 "Milan — The Baths of Lucca — Este — Venice — Rome — Naples — Rome & misery"

MARY SHELLEY began what was to be the most extreme chiaroscuro period of her life in a spirit of release, hope, and adventure. On Friday, March 13, she set out from Calais for the third time in four years, in a little cavalcade consisting of Shelley's carriage and a temporary calêche loaded with baggage, five adults, and three children: herself, Shelley, two-year-old William, seven-month-old Clara and their nurse, Elise Duvillard, Clare Clairmont, fourteen-month-old Allegra and her nurse, Amelia Shields.

For novelty they went via Burgundy, passing dour backwater towns; "Who ever heard of Douai?" she tossed off in the first of her regular letters to the Hunts. Shelley read Schlegel aloud as they traveled hard, stopping to let the children stretch, "and after the sun has set," she noted in her journal, "the horned moon — Orion & his brothers lend us their light." They rested at Lyons, where she could see the ever-inspiriting Mont Blanc massif, "queen" of Europe, around which she would pivot to Milan.

In the oppressive Continental political climate, Lyons pleased her because of its traditional, now suppressed republicanism. Having gained the confidence of their local driver, a covert Bonapartist, she reported to Hunt on the White Terror of 1815, little known in England, when followers of the fanatic Duchesse d'Angoulême, Marie Antoinette's daughter, had slaughtered Protestants and anti-Bourbons, "which could never have been committed if there was liberty of the press," though Mary allowed that "ce Monsieur q'on appelle Louis XVIII is a better man and restrained them."[1] Possibly also for Hunt's *Examiner,* she began an unfinished satiric letter in the Lucianic mode from Bloody Queen Mary in Tartarus congratulating the Duchesse.[2] On the next leg of the journey through Savoy, the censor at Chambery tried to confiscate the Shelleys' books. Here Elise had a prearranged reunion with her family, who came from Geneva to see her.

Crossing the Alps was an adventure in itself, especially in off-summer months. On March 30 they crossed deeply snowbound Mont Cenis, along precipices and one fragile bridge that gave Mary the "nervous bores," and descended the steep but gentle windings of the superb Napoleonic road to the timber line, down through greening foliage and fragrant blossoming fruit trees, and in the balmy radiance of an Italian late afternoon arrived at verdant Susa. She and Shelley deposited the others at an inn and drove straight to the Augustan triumphal arch in a meadow thick with violets, through which she visioned the storied enchantment of her beloved ancient Italia, and felt the voluptuous charm of living Italy in their graceful blonde guide, who reminded her of Fuseli's *Eve*.

They proceeded through Turin[3] to Milan for a three-week stay, expecting Byron to summer with them as at Geneva, on Lake Como. Byron declined, however, and it began to dawn on the Shelleys that while he was willing to have Allegra he meant never to see Clare again. Of the various modes of expatriate-hood, he had gone native in Venice with a vengeance against British proprieties and Lady Byron, who personified them, gorging on sexual exploits that astounded dissolute Venice and were the talk of Milan: "Albe, Albe every where!" noted Mary. As his excess was in part defiance of mores he respected, it inflamed his aversion to Clare, whom he rightly suspected of pursuing him with Allegra as bait and irrationally accused of making him a focus of scandal. He refused to allow Clare to live near Allegra, on grounds that she would corrupt the child with her views, and only Shelley's diplomatic letters persuaded him to agree that Clare could even come to see or have Allegra for a visit, and then only if the Shelleys were also present.

Though Clare was wretched, and the Shelleys would have supported her if she had kept Allegra, she accepted Byron's fiat. "I send you my child because I love her too well to keep her," she wrote. "With you who are powerful and noble and the admiration of the world she will be happy, but I am a miserable and neglected dependant."[4] Mary realized that Milly Shields was too provincial for Byron's lordly *garçonnière,* so she persuaded the more sophisticated Elise to accompany Allegra, and, knowing that Byron was fond of herself, she had Shelley write him that she felt almost as much affection and anxiety about Allegra as she would for one of her own children. On April 28, the day after Clare's twentieth birthday, Allegra and Elise left for Venice, taking choice new English books, including *Frankenstein,* which Mary had thought to give Byron in person.

From her felicitous entrance at Susa into "the land of blue skies," Mary Shelley would crisscross the peninsula and gravitate toward the Italophilia for which she, like Byron and Stendhal, was later noted. More than most cultivated tourists, she was making a long-desired pilgrimage to a land not only beautiful and exotic but sacred to what she considered the greatest civilization human beings had ever created, heir to the Greek. To drive along Roman roads, to see landscapes, sites, and monuments where political and literary history had been made, while reading Livy or Virgil in "that language which once awoke the pauses of this Roman air with words of fire,"[5] to pass vineyards and large-eyed oxen out of Homer, to see works of art she had known only through engravings if at all, and places described by Dante, Petrarch, Tasso and Ariosto, to people Venice with Desdemona or Rome with Corinne — these were almost religious experiences to her even more than to Shelley with his predeliction for Greece.

In Milan the modern city impressed her: at La Scala a "infinitely magnificent" ballet, or, rather, tragic pantomime, of, "strange to say," her talismatic tale of Othello; and the bel canto tenor Giovanni Davide, for whom the gossiping, card-playing box patrons fell silent as his arias "stole upon the ear like a murmur of waters" while the piercing soprano "ran up the octaves beside him in a far different manner." She and Shelley visited "divine" Lake Como, where they tried to rent the famous Villa Pliniana with its exquisite loggia and ravishing view. During the morning work period, which she and Shelley kept to on their longer stops, she read some French literature but plunged into Italian studies with a Milanese teacher, reading Richardson's novels in Italian, Tasso and Ariosto with Shelley, later Gozzi, Monti, Metastasio, Boccaccio, and Ricciardetti, until most of her reading related to Italy. Italian literature would become one of her fortes.

From Calais on, Shelley was acutely homesick, often depressed, and repeatedly complained that "we do not know a single human being." Though Italy abounded with English tourists and the Shelleys followed the standard routes, staying at first-class hotels catering to the English, they avoided their compatriots out of general antipathy and specific fear of being insulted. Nor had they come with the usual entrée into local society, where literati and artists mingled with an international gentry; even a cadet like Polidori had a marvelous time in Milan, where he met the poets Pellico, Monti, and Breme. For several months Mary would not miss home for traveling, "when," as she would always feel, "the excitement of something new prevents regret for the old."[6] But the Shelleys were so unnaturally isolated after Byron disappointed them that finding English company became an almost equal priority with seeing Italy.

Besides, to them, followers of Gibbon, Italians were the Grand Illustration of Mary's girlhood lecture, "The Influence of Government on the Character of the People": virtuous and wise during the Roman Republic, morally degenerating though artistically great ever since as they submitted to the empire, Catholicism, authoritarian princes, and foreign domination.

("A tribe of stupid and shriveled slaves," Shelley called them.) This was an article of faith for most English liberals, whereas conservatives blamed Italian vices on Napoleonic rule, only recently replaced by restored ancien régimes. The few English Mary met this year had such stereotypical animus against Italians — one, explaining that Italians had great interest in art and none in morality, recounted that when he praised a young lady as "virtuosissima," his Italian friend assumed he meant musical virtuosity — that it was the land Mary loved at first, not its people.

The Shelleys now planned to summer in Florence, see Rome, and winter in Naples. But first, to divert Clare and find some of their own kind, they decided to cross to the west coast and present Godwin's letters of intro-duction to two of his old friends, Lady Mount Cashell in Pisa and Mrs. John Gisborne in Leghorn. Missing Allegra and Elise from their original party of eight, they sped along the Via Emilia through countryside "bloom-ing and fertile like a perpetual garden," and crossed the Apennines with an overnight stop in a windstorm: "Listen, listen, Mary mine, / To the whisper of the Apennine, / It bursts on the roof like the thunder's roar / Or like the sea on a northern shore . . . ," Shelley wrote.

They arrived at Pisa on May 7 and left the same day without contacting Lady Mount Cashell because Mary could not bear the sight of a chain gang at labor in the city streets. At Leghorn, they went directly to the waterfront to see the veritable Mediterranean that had borne the ships of Ulysses and Aeneas. The bustling modern port they disliked, but Mrs. Gisborne proved so delightful that they stayed for a month, during which Mary and Maria Gisborne founded an intimacy that would last until the older woman's death.

Mary had been eager to know Mrs. Gisborne, who could have been her stepmother, and she now repined at the difference that would have made in both their lives. The antithesis to Mrs. Godwin, Maria James Reveley Gisborne was a charming, self-effacing, softly affectionate woman of forty-eight. Her early career had been uncommonly glamorous and promising. Her father had kidnapped her from her mother,* and she had spent her girlhood with him in Constantinople and Rome, where she studied with Angelica Kauffmann and knew Jeremy Bentham. Her father had disowned her when she married the distinguished architect-historian Willey Reveley, with whom she went to London. She had been Godwin's favorite and Mary Wollstonecraft's friend, and her son, Henry Reveley, who still lived with her, had played with Fanny Godwin. The week fol-lowing Wollstonecraft's death, she had taken care of the newborn Mary

---

* Mary would adapt this kidnapping in *Lodore,* in which Lord Lodore kidnaps his daughter, Ethel, from his wife.

in her home. When she was widowed, Godwin proposed to her, but she refused him for John Gisborne, a retired businessman with sisters married to the painter John Varley and the musician Muzio Clementi, but himself quite ordinary.

Economy-expatriates, the Gisbornes had lived in Italy for eighteen years because their two-hundred-pound income went twice as far as in England — which, to Mary's chagrin, they missed and refused to condemn. Mary considered Mrs. Gisborne a potentially notable, defeated, overly modest woman who had narrowed herself in petty domesticity and deference to an extraordinarily dull husband. Moreover, having lost a child, both Gisbornes were smotheringly devoted to her son, Henry, an engineer trained by the famous John Rennie and currently building a steam engine, which he hoped would revolutionize Mediterranean shipping, but a remarkably submissive son: "he is only thirty years old," Mary wrote Marianne Hunt, "and always does as he is bid."[7]

Still, Maria Gisborne took to Mary with maternal affection and was intellectually companionable, a scholar of Iberian languages and literature, with a delicious way of dropping Italian phrases that Mary began to emulate. She explained with Britannic amusement about Italian customs, such as *conversazione,* or open-house evenings, found them a courier named Paolo Foggi, a seamstress for sheets, a physician for Clare's scrofula, and agreed to be their factotum at the entrepôt of Leghorn, where many English goods were available; Peacock would ship notions and books from home. She was also ignorant of her new young friends' notoriety, and her unshadowed friendliness was such "a treat," in fact enormous relief, that Mary refrained from enlightening her — new acquaintanceship required " 'not telling all the truth,' " she would soon write in a tale, " 'if you have any thing you wish to conceal (and who has not), but promising not to falsify any thing.' "[8] — until that winter when Mrs. Gisborne, especially inquisitive in her confined existence, heard "reports" about them.

Mrs. Gisborne informed them that low-lying inland cities like Florence were unsafe in summer because of dangerous fevers, and recommended the Apennine resort of Bagni di Lucca. Having failed to persuade the homebound Gisbornes to join them, on June 11 the Shelleys drove to the Bagni, where they leased Casa Bertini near a house once occupied by Montaigne, on the topmost of the spa's three levels, in a fold of the wooded hills. From here they could hear the rushing Serchio river, where Mary took her children to bathe, and enjoyed long hikes and horseback rides. "We have but one wish," wrote Mary, who longed for Mrs. Gisborne. "Now we see no one —"[9]

Being ignorant of the Shelleys' relations with their compatriots, Mrs.

Gisborne had sent them to the resort of the English Florentine colony who, to Mary's disgust, acted as if they owned the place: "We see none but English, we hear nothing but English spoken — The walks are filled with English Nurserymaids, a kind of animal I by no means like, & dashing, staring Englishwomen . . ."[10] And Napoleon's sister Princess Pauline Borghese socialized with these "high ministerial English" although they had dethroned her brother, whose modernizing influence in Italy Mary now valued. As the English eschewed the dances at the Casino because they were held on Sundays, the Shelleys made a point of attending, but they did not dance and could speak only haltingly to the Italians present.

"We live in our studious way," Mary wrote Mrs. Gisborne, with their crate of books which had arrived from England. Shelley translated Plato's *Symposium,* and Mary studied the original while she copied his version. As both were planning plays, she translated Alfieri's *Mirra* for practice, a retelling of Ovid's familiar daughter-father incest myth, and considered dramatizing the famous sixteenth-century Cenci murder, a period account of which she had copied in the Gisbornes' library — and was to copy another version in Rome.* In this lurid historical episode, Beatrice Cenci was raped by her horrible father, had him murdered, and was executed with her mother and brothers. Alternatively, Mary planned a play on Charles I, for which Shelley read Hume's *History of England* aloud in the evenings; this project was inspired by Godwin's suggestion that she undertake a history of the Commonwealth, which he had contemplated for a decade but did not expect to write himself.

Godwin's political news excited Mary: the Whigs had made gains in recent local elections, and her father had begun a rebuttal to Malthus's *On Population,* his first such work since *Political Justice.* "Malthus," she advised Mrs. Gisborne, "is the work from which all the rich have . . . borrowed excuses and palliations for their luxury and hard-heartedness —"[11] In separate letters to Shelley, however, Godwin was demanding his five hundred pounds, by which the last post-obit was short. Shelley replied that he needed money himself (they were traveling expensively) and was determined not to reduce his children's fortune by ever again raising post-obits. The two men stopped corresponding, but Godwin went on jabbing at Shelley in his letters to Mary. A few months later she would offer Godwin the profits of a possible second edition of *Frankenstein,* for which she did some correcting, and which he "peremptorily" declined.[12]

By now Mary had learned from letters and reviews that her novel was a sensation. Along with the expected denunciations for impiety and ex-

---

* Stendhal used similar sources for his Cenci story.

travagant wildness, critics lauded the book's "highly terrific" power, even the *Quarterly* and the women's magazine *La Belle Assemblée*. Above all, *Blackwood's* glowing lead review by Sir Walter Scott, to whom Shelley had cannily sent the book, established *Frankenstein*'s stature and novelty in "supernatural" fiction, and the author's "original genius."[13] (Scott subsequently said he much preferred *Frankenstein* to any of his own novels.) The next issue of *Blackwood's* praised the "sweet-blooded" wife-author of *History of a Six Weeks' Tour*, added "sincere wishes for her future happiness," tantamount to calling quits to Mary's past — and reprinted part of Shelley's "Mont Blanc," "a little poem by the husband . . . rather too ambitious" but "often very beautiful."[14]

For all her delight, Mary did not immediately, if ever, incorporate an appropriate measure of confidence from this early achievement of her ambition. Even now, after the study she had invested in playwriting, which was to attract her for years, she worried about her competence for drama, and Shelley had regularly to "incite" her, paraphrasing her father's words, " 'There is nothing which the human mind can conceive, which it may not execute.' " "Shakespeare was only a human being,"[15] he added, which may further have daunted her.

Nevertheless, there was a limit to her diffidence. Scott, like most people, assumed that Shelley had written *Frankenstein*. Whereas Mary had just asked Byron to keep her secret, this so piqued her that she immediately revealed herself to Scott, though her brief note (an "intrusion") of thanks and explanation was self-denigrating: "I am anxious to prevent your continuing in the mistake of supposing Mr Shelley guilty of a juvenile attempt of mine; to which — from its being written at an early age, I abstained from putting my name — and from respect to those persons from whom I bear it."[16]

Word spread that the author of *Frankenstein* was a young novice and the daughter of Wollstonecraft and Godwin, and by spring the fact of her authorship was published, whereupon the éclat was magnified. There would always be those who said Shelley must have conceived the idea or even written the novel, and this always galled her. "There is nothing to which contemporaries are more prone, than to discover that an author does not write his own works," she would remark in 1837.[17]

As for *The Revolt of Islam*, there were a few laudatory reviews, but most condemned Shelley's ideas, even the small number impressed by his artistry. He was too demoralized to start the poetic drama he had contemplated. To restore his confidence, Mary persuaded him to finish her "pretty eclogue" *Rosalind and Helen*. Now he reset the poem in Italy, where Helen lives in exile mourning her dead Lionel, with their little son "all the solace of my woe." Not one of his greatest, this work proved one of his most uncanny, a prophecy followed by confirmatory events, so that Mary came to believe it had magical power and could never reveal its private significance.[18]

In mid-August while Mary was making a fair copy of this poem, Clare heard from Elise that Byron had transferred her and Allegra to the home of the Venetian British consul, Richard Belgrave Hoppner and his Swiss wife; in fact, Byron's disorderly palazzo was no place for a child. Clare, horrified that she had given him her daughter for this, packed for Venice, swearing histrionically to confront him and drown with Allegra. Unable to stop her, Shelley set out with Clare on the seventeenth, accompanied by the indispensable courier Paolo Foggi. The carriage was in storage and express vehicles were too expensive, so they traveled by *vetturino*, a slow covered wagon hired by several travelers with the same destination. Mary, though uneasy to the point of feeling sickish at being left alone with the children, cheerily again invited the Gisbornes, who were so dismayed by her situation that they arrived on the twenty-fifth.

On the twenty-eighth she heard from Shelley. The Hoppners had warned him to conceal Clare's presence from Byron, who spoke of her with "horror"; Shelley therefore let Byron assume that Mary was at hand waiting permission for Allegra to visit them for a month. Not only did Byron readily agree, but Shelley was so thrilled by his cordiality that he sent Paolo back to Mary and asked her to rush by *vetturino* with the children to the east coast before Byron discovered the deception: "my own beloved Mary you must soon come & scold me if I have done wrong & kiss me if I have done right — for I am sure I do not know which — & it is only the event that can shew." The Hoppners, furthermore, were "unprejudiced" about their history, agreeably detested Italians, and Mrs. Hoppner was "so good so beautiful so angelically mild that were she wise too, she would be quite a Mary . . . Her manne[rs] are like yours when you know & like a person."[19]

The Gisbornes helped Mary hurriedly to pack the Shelley-Clairmont gear and give over the house to the landlord, and agreed to take the crate of books to Leghorn. With an anxious Mrs. Gisborne accompanying her on the first stage, Mary set out with the children and Paolo on the thirty-first, the day after her twenty-first birthday. On September 5 she arrived exhausted at Este, where Shelley, Clare, Allegra, and Elise were waiting at Byron's villa, I Capuccini, which he had lent them. But by now the whole point of her forced march was moot; as Byron had insisted on paying his respects to her, Shelley had had to confess that she was en route from Lucca.

The villa sat above Este castle, where three-year-old William promptly devised a new game, shouting to make echoes against the walls, and the open view of the green Lombardy plains was a relief to Mary after Lucca's narrow ravines. Shelley greeted her with a poem: ". . . As sunset to the sphered moon / As twilight to the western star, / Thou, Belovèd, art to me." Brimming with news, he had begun a poetic drama, *Prometheus Unbound,* was planning a long narrative poem, *Julian and Maddalo,* and expected they might soon be Sir Percy and Lady Shelley with a large income, for he had heard his father was ill (he recovered). Given Byron's good mood, he might even agree to give Clare another month with Allegra.

But on the long, torrid trip, with overnight stops in cheap accommodations, Clara, who passed her first birthday en route, had contracted dysentery, until quite recently the major killer of weaned babies. After a week at Este the child became dehydrated, thin, and weak. The Shelleys were dissatisfied with the local physician and sent for another from Padua, but Clara did not improve. Shelley made a flying pleasure visit to Byron, who recommended the famous Venetian doctor, Francesco Aglietti. At Shelley's summons Mary started from Este with the baby at three in the morning on September 24, in order to meet Shelley in Padua and make the twenty-mile trip to Venice before dark. As they barged the lonely Brenta canal to Fusina, where one then embarked for Venice, Clara grew worse, twitching convulsively, but they could only press on, while Mary focused so desperately on the passing surroundings that when she returned a quarter-century later she would recognize every detail.

Around five that afternoon they reached an inn at Venice. Shelley rushed on for Aglietti, Mary called another physician, who said there was no hope. Frantic, she ran out into the hall to meet Shelley, and when she saw Clara die, collapsed in such unprecedented utter despair that Shelley allowed the Hoppners to take them to their house. She could not bear to see the child buried next day at the Lido's Protestant cemetery. But she had Shelley ask Byron in her name to grant Clare another month with Allegra; next day when she visited the grave and saw Byron riding on the beach, he assured her of his assent. During the next two days she visited the Doge's Palace, the Accademia and Library, trying to subdue and divert her grief, until longing for William and refuge made her return with Shelley to Este.

"This is the Journal book of misfortunes," she noted tersely in the notebook that included the deaths of Fanny Godwin and Harriet Shelley. With her stoic-trained conscience, she did not need her father's acknowledgment of Clara's death, which was delayed in the mails until winter, to agree with his message that only very ordinary, "pusillanimous" persons sink under such calamities. For fear of giving way, it was a month before she informed Mrs. Gisborne, and then baldly. She continued reading Livy and Alfieri. As a mutual service, to divert her and provide him with a copyist he did not have in Venice, Byron sent her his drafts of *Mazeppa*, "Venice: An Ode," and the first canto of *Don Juan*, for which she made press copies.

But Godwin's version of stoicism, based on reason and his cooler heart, proved artificial and unsupportable to Mary. She had taken repeated blows in the four years since her elopement, including the death of her first premature baby, with remarkable fortitude, mastering or else escaping them; then she was at an age of maximum resilience and hope, and these had seemed eccentric misfortunes in a brilliant existence promised by her star. Now, probably for the first time in her twenty-one years, that faith was shaken; the only way she could contain her grief and bitterness was to withdraw, cornered, depressed, and sometimes captious, and she remained largely so until winter; like bereaved Ugolino in Dante's *Inferno*, "I did not weep, so I turned to stone inside."

Contrarily, though despondent, "it must be borne," said Shelley, in a more Christian response of resignation, sense of sin, and search for grace. Unlike more fortunate parents who find bittersweet comfort and deeper bonds in mourning, Clara's death left the Shelleys in unprecedented self-engrossment and distance. Mary blamed the calamity on her "deceptive" star, but she must also have blamed herself, Shelley, and Clare. And she knew that Shelley did not feel this loss as painfully as she; William was his favorite. William was infinitely more to her now, her solace and the foundation of her hope, a child so beautiful that her Italian servants looked in his bedroom to admire him sleeping, and who was attached to her with all the happy passion and charm of a beloved three-year-old boy.

Shelley always needed her comfort and sexuality when he was sad; this time she could not provide them. Moreover, Harriet Shelley had in effect risen from her grave and interposed between them. Shelley was convinced that they were atoning for what Harriet had suffered, while for both their sakes Mary tried to push away that unbearable thought, which fractured the justification for their union on which they had staked everything. He thought of Harriet with excruciating remorse and "relenting love," as he now wrote in "Lines Written among the Euganean Hills." "Forget the dead, the past? Oh, yet / There are ghosts that may take revenge for it . . . ," he wrote in another poem.

He did not show Mary these or subsequent morose poems so as not to hurt or burden her further. At other times he believed Clara's death was sufficient punishment and transcended it, in the exalted development of "Euganean Hills" and above all in his visionary *Prometheus Unbound*, in which the martyred Titan and his wife, Asia, both act to free themselves from enforced separation into sublime, Creation-transforming rapture. This ecstatic reunion could not take place in reality, and Shelley blamed Mary in part for the deprivation.

On October 10, Mary was panicked by minor symptoms of William's. They rushed him to Venice. After the doctor reassured them, they remained until the end of the month at a hotel on the Grand Canal, between the Hoppners' house and Byron's Palazzo Mocenigo, with a view of the Rialto bridge. But Mary was more often disgusted with Venice's stench than enraptured at wonders along the Canal, or with the "wretched" Rossini *Otello* rather than at the gilded rococo theater where it played. Mrs. Hoppner went with her to Clara's grave, and introduced her to the chevalier Mengaldo, a dashing Bonapartist who regaled the author of *Frankenstein* with "true" ghost stories, which she recorded at length in the journal, and accounts of his campaigns with Napoleon's Italian army.

Since *Frankenstein*, which he vastly admired, Byron and Mary were on more equal terms, spiced with the disingenuous camaraderie of a pair whom people link sexually, so that she teased him about his operatically jealous Venetian mistress, whom she met at his palazzo, and he showed her his memoirs for her advice as to whether they were publishable, which she endorsed. And sometimes when Shelley stayed late at Byron's, she gazed from the window at Venice in moonlight, savored the gondoliers' soft cries, and felt her old rapture.

Don Juan's rollicking, mocking brilliance initially struck Mary as emblematic of Byron's moral decline in corrupt Venice, but neither she nor Shelley could ever resist him in person. Moreover, mutual enemies at home and in Italy bound the three. Byron reported that "the filthy English" in Rome and Florence had been full of the League of Incest story a year ago, for which — unfairly in this instance — they all blamed Robert Southey. "The Son of a Bitch," Byron wrote Hobhouse, not only lied but had been in love with Mary Wollstonecraft, "which might have taught him to respect the fame of her daughter."[20] The Shelleys declined ever to answer such charges. "In modern times," Mary would contemptuously observe, "domestic circumstances appear to be that part of a man's history most worth enquiring into."[21]

Now Byron offered to give Allegra to Clare and support them. Shelley strenuously urged Clare to accept. Elise, moreover, insisted on remaining with the Shelleys, because she had fallen in love with the courier, Paolo. But in late October Clare sent Allegra back to the Hoppners, where Mary spent two days with the child. "If argument or entreaty can turn any one

from a desperate purpose, whose motive and end depends upon the strength
of affections only," Mary would write of an equivalent situation, "then it
is right so to turn them . . . If they are proof against expostulation . . . it
becomes the duty of those who love them, to assist."[22] That was the gist
of her rejoinder to Mrs. Hoppner, who disliked Clare and told Mary that
her stepsister was sacrificing Allegra's childhood happiness for what Byron
would eventually do for the child.

On November 5, the Shelley party, reduced to five adults and William,
left Este and traveled for three and a half weeks toward Naples, sight-
seeing at Ferrara and Bologna, crossing the Rubicon to Terni, where the
waterfall reminded Mary of Sappho's suicide leap "and her form vanished
as in the shape of a swan." They spent a dazzling week in Rome, during
which Mary visited the Colosseum three times and fell in love with the
city. Shelley went ahead to Naples to reserve rooms. Mary followed in the
carriage with the others, through the malaria-breeding Pontine marshes
and ancient Latium, notorious for murderous banditti, to Gaeta with its
magnificent wild bay "sanctified by the fictions of Homer," and, in the
garden below her inn, by the ruins of Cicero's villa. "The waves of the
sea broke close under the windows of his villa which was perhaps then
shaded as it is now by an olive grove & sented by orange and lemon
trees —,"[23] she wrote in a long journal entry; because of the same fierce
onshore wind she felt, Cicero could not take ship to escape Octavian's
soldiers, who assassinated him in the woods about a mile inland. The
Roman Republic perished with him.

Naples, the farthest south she had ever been, with its semitropical light
and color, brightened her spirits. During their three-month stay her acute
mourning for Clara passed, and toward the end she conceived a child.
Shelley had taken splendid rooms overlooking the Royal Gardens and the
gorgeous bay. Besides the museum and Davide's performance at San Carlo,
they visited Herculaneum, Pompeii, the Bay of Baiae with the Elysian
Fields, Lake Avernus, and the Cumean Sybil's cave, ascended Vesuvius,
and made an excursion to Paestum, then too rugged and remote for most
tourists. When Shelley was too ailing to sight-see, she read Virgil's *Georgics*
at the hotel window: "looking at almost the same scene that he did —
reading about manners little changed since his days, has made me enjoy
his poem, more, I think, than I ever did any other."[24]

As she grew better, Shelley lapsed into secret morbidity. He was being
subjected to painful, heroic treatments for supposed liver disease by a local
physician, but usually appeared cheerful, so she attributed his occasional
visible melancholy to constant pain, and was besides absorbed in efforts
to sustain her own still volatile spirits. Later, she would be gnawed by

remorse for not having been more sensitive and solacing, but in fact she heartened him at the time, and he seemed tenderly grateful. When she came on his draft of "Lines Written among the Euganean Hills" she may have transcribed for his encouragement those parts she thought worthy of salvaging.[25] In any case she persuaded him to complete it and send it with *Rosalind and Helen* to Ollier for publication. Shelley ended it with a hopeful coda, and explained in an introduction that he retained the morose opening at her request, "a dear friend . . . who would have had more right than anyone to complain, that she has not been able to extinguish in me the very power of delineating sadness."

Meanwhile they read Winckelman, Livy, Dante, *Corinne,* and Sismondi's *Histoire des republiques italiennes du moyen âge.* Thanks to the affirmations of Sismondi, a republican, that Italians still loved "liberty, virtue and glory," Mary began to believe in Italy's resurgence, which seemed confirmed by the current Liberales revolt in Spain, and to connect the personages of republican Rome, and Rome's successor the medieval Republic of Florence, with what Shelley still termed Italy's "filthy modern inhabitants."

In Sismondi she also found her tyrant-protagonist for the historical romance she had first thought of in Marlow, which was to occupy her for the next two and a half years; the early fourteenth-century Ghibelline *condottiere* Castruccio Castracani, superb, gifted, ambitious, and ruthless, who made himself Duke of Lucca and warred against Florence. His republican adversary would be the fictional young Countess of Valperga, who gives up their love on political grounds — and for whom Godwin, Mary's future editor, would change the title from *Castruccio* to *Valperga.* Mary was also struck by Sismondi's account of the Manichaean Paterin heretics (the Italian name for Cathars or Albigensians) who believed in a universe in which forces of Evil clash with those of Good, a belief that inspired *Valperga's* second fictional heroine, the Paterin Beatrice, and was so congruent with Mary's own oscillating moods since Clara's death that she incorporated it into her thinking. It was a perfect novel to write in Italy; Mary planned to research exhaustively in the oldest sources available, and to see those settings which she had not yet visited.

In mid-January Mary was presented with a new problem: "when I set my foot on the shore at Calais," she wrote Mrs. Gisborne, "I seemed to break the thread of my annoyances. but I find care to be the thing that Horace describes it to be ["behind the horseman sits black Care"] . . . We shall see you, the good spirit willing, next June —" she ended in her Paterin mode, "but the devil is getting more and more power in the world every day —"[26] The devil she knew was that Paolo Foggi had been cheating them outrageously and that Elise was pregnant by him. They dismissed him, and when Mary could not talk Elise out of leaving with him, she made Paolo marry Elise at the British Legation Chapel. Thereafter, Elise turned Catholic and settled in Florence, and Mary predicted that she appeared "in the high road" to becoming a complete Italian.

The devil Mary knew not of for eighteen months was the pernicious uses the Foggis would make of their knowledge of the Shelleys' and Clare's intimate affairs. Clare had probed Elise about Byron's doings in Venice, and Elise had told her, among other luridities, that he talked of making Allegra his mistress someday. Given that information and Byron's blatant scorn for herself, Clare began including "insolent" remarks in her letters, which infuriated him. Soon she would in effect divorce on her side, and again change her name, permanently, to Claire.

The Foggis were also cognizant of Shelley's "Neapolitan child," a mysterious business he hid from Mary, probably so as not to hinder her recovery from Clara's death. Apparently for the sake of an unknown English lady, he secretly undertook the charge of an illegitimate baby girl born December 27, 1818, to the lady or a connection of hers. He found and paid local foster parents, probably through Paolo, before discovering his dishonesty, and later had the infant baptized Elena Adelaide Shelley and illegally registered as his by his wife, "Maria Padurin," after the unwitting Mary's Paterin philosophy.[27] He seems to have hoped that Mary would agree to adopt Elena after she got over Clara's death.

On February 28 the Shelleys, now a party of four adults and William, left Naples, and on March 5 made a circuit of Mary's favorite Colosseum as they drove into Rome, which seemed to her even more moving and grand after "sparkling, dancing Naples"; "Penseroso after Allegro," she said. They took rooms in the Corso, and for three months she explored the city with supreme pleasure. "Rome repays for every thing," she wrote Marianne Hunt, a city "thrice holy" in paintings, architecture, and statuary, of which Marcus Aurelius at the Capitol, the Vatican Cupid and Psyche, and Castor and Pollux at Monte Cavallo were among her favorites. William exclaimed, "O Dio che bella" at the sights, and became a connoisseur of marble female feet from seeing so many statues at his eye level.[28]

If she objected to St. Paul's Corinthian columns, "taken by that wretch Constantine from the tomb of Hadrian," it was Rome the Eternal City that most impressed her with its magnificent Roman, medieval, Renaissance, and baroque aggregation, and its current Easter ceremonies. As she

was to describe in *Valperga,* Rome was a restorative epiphany on the night
she watched moonlight streaming through the Pantheon's ceiling aperture
and lighting the interior columns:

> It seemed as if the spirit of beauty descended on my soul, as I
> sat there in mute extasy; never had I before so felt the universal
> graspings of my own mind, or the sure tokens of other spiritual
> existences. . . . I became calm; amidst a dead race, and an extin-
> guished empire, what individual sorrow would dare raise its voice?[29]*

In this mood she worked on "Valerius: The Reanimated Roman," the
story of an encounter between a resurrected first-century republican who
despises what Rome became thereafter, and the contemporary young Lady
Isabel Harley, who asserts the inspirational value of imperial Rome and
its literature to moderns, points to the uselessness of bewailing the past,
and tries to make him feel the "existence of that Pantheic Love with which
Nature is penetrated."[30] This inter-century conceit always intrigued Mary,
since it illuminated the divergent preconceptions of two periods. She also
began the unfinished "An Eighteenth Century Tale" in a mode inspired
by Boccaccio.

Shelley urged her to write the play on the Cencis, but she protested
her incompetence and preferred her projected novel. At her insistence that
he was wrong to think he himself lacked dramatic talent, Shelley began
The Cenci, for which he used her notes and departed from his usual practice
to discuss the scenes with her. Later he was to take over her idea for a
play on Charles I. It was always her pride that she helped him discover a
new aspect of his genius and contributed to *The Cenci,* her favorite of his
works.

As always at Easter, Rome was thronged by pilgrims of rank and fashion
including multitudes of "rich, noble — important and foolish" English,
declared Mary. Despite her father's maxim "a man is better than a stock
or stone," one had only to see a supercilious dandy eying the Apollo
Belvedere to disagree, she said. In Naples, she had mocked the "ghastly
and laughable" ceremonies of reactionary King Ferdinand and Queen
Maria Caroline, aunt to the Duchesse d'Angoulême. In Rome, the exemplary autocrat Emperor of Austria stalked past worshipers held at bay
by his guards; "a curious thing," wrote Mary à la Montaigne to Mrs.
Gisborne, "that a fellow, whose power only subsists through the supposed

* Eight years later, in *The Last Man,* Rome becomes a monument to and metaphor of all
that was great in the history of human creativity. "hardly more illustrious for heroes and
sages, than for the power it exercised over the imagination of men . . . the wonder of the
world, majestic and eternal survivor of generations." (III: 331, 332.)

conveniences of the state of the complaisance of his subjects, should be thus insolent."[31]

Shelley's aristocratic Roman banker could have introduced them into the grand palazzi, where such international luminaries as Lady Morgan, Davy, Canova, Thorwaldsen, Turner, and Lawrence were appearing. The Shelleys, however, remained alone amidst the crowds for fear of being insulted. The League of Incest story had been revived by the April *New Monthly Magazine,* which published Polidori's *Vampyre* as, mistakenly, by Byron, along with a letter denying that the author of *Frankenstein,* "Miss M. W. Godwin," and her sister had been Byron's mistresses at Geneva. Simultaneously, *The Vampyre,* with the offensive letter in the preface, was published as a separate volume. Godwin persuaded the publisher of the volume to omit the letter from the second printing.[32] The *New Monthly Magazine* reached Rome, however, and excited one Englishman to knock Shelley down for "a damned Atheist."

An English acquaintance in Naples had given them a letter of introduction to a distinguished elderly intellectual, Signora Marianna Dionigi, whose musty *conversazione* they attended, but who was not what they had in mind for society: "very old — very miserly, and very mean," Mary said. However, Signora Dionigi got them seats for the magnificent Easter observances, and an art teacher for Mary named Delicati, who also did a portrait of her that was too bad to keep. Mary invested in art supplies, sketched in the Borghese Gardens and the Baths of Caracalla, where Shelley was continuing *Prometheus Unbound,* and began a painting. The Signora also found a singing instructor for Claire; since Allegra was settled, Mary hoped Claire would train to become a professional singer or teacher, and for the next year saw to it that she had the best instruction.

On April 19 Mary's suspicion of pregnancy was confirmed by Dr. John Bell, an expatriate employed by Princess Pauline Borghese, and a liberal who had visited The Polygon when she was small. Although the child was probably planned, she confessed to Hunt that she had moments of worse depression than over Clara's death, along with "evil" thoughts she could not shake off. In fact, a terrible vision similar to Shelley's *Rosalind and Helen* had come to her during her usually pleasurable daydreaming about the future: "in this kind of second sight, I saw myself desolate and alone — My William . . . gone . . . beloved Shelley vanished —"[33]

Frightened and mistrusting Italian *"Medicos"* since Clara's death, she was unsure whether to have the baby in England or stay in Italy under Dr. Bell's care. "Although continually seeing novelties," she admitted to occasional homesickness and yet feared a return to England's hostile "simoonic wind." Besides, Dr. Bell was taking charge of Shelley's case and prescribed a hot climate. Confidence in Bell fixed the Shelleys on Italy. Since he was to accompany Princess Borghese to Naples in June, before the Roman malaria season began, they decided to do likewise and asked the Gisbornes to join them so they would not be so alone. "I wish you would; but how many things do I wish as uselessly as this," Mary wrote, and broke out: "I am sick of it — I am sick of seeing the world in dumb show . . . ," and, moreover, "so devoured by ill spirits, that I hardly know what or where I am."[34]

Ominous news had just arrived from Godwin. He was being sued for fifteen hundred pounds' back rent at Skinner Street, a suit that had brought on a slight stroke and that, if he lost, meant "horror and death." He asked Mary to sound out her "inconstant" husband about the five hundred pounds owed him.

Shelley, however, assured Mary that he would help her father if necessary. Mary became more cheerful and more confident about her pregnancy, and a seashore home near Naples seemed so alluring that they pushed up their departure from Rome to early May. But then they decided to wait until early June, for they had some interesting English callers, including Godwin's acquaintance the philosopher Sir William Drummond. Best of all they discovered that Mary's family friend Amelia Curran had just returned from a visit to London. Enjoying Rome and talking with this keen, amusing woman was such a pleasure for Mary that they moved next door to her, to 65 Via Sistina above the Spanish Steps. Miss Curran promptly painted portraits of Mary, Shelley, Claire, and William holding a rose — all of which sitters and amateur artist agreed were unflattering and bad likenesses, except for William's.

Without warning, on May 25 William, a strong, rosy child who had rarely been ill, came down with a serious case of worms. Dr. Bell purged the worms, but advised that the child was weak and delicate, in fact dangerously anemic, and needed great care in a cool climate. As Princess Borghese had changed her destination and Bell's from Naples to Tuscany, they decided to proceed to Lucca, Castruccio country, where they would be within reach of Bell for William and for Mary's expected delivery in late October.

On June 2 William suddenly fell desperately sick with an enteric disease, probably cholera or typhoid. As the Shelleys agonized over the child in all too recognizable death throes, Bell managed to revive him, but had little hope. Mary and Shelley took turns at his bed helplessly watching the little boy, who was raging with fever. "We do not quite despair yet we have the least possible reason to hope," Mary hastily wrote Maria Gisborne.

"The misery of these hours is beyond calculation — The hopes of my life are bound up in him."[35] At noon on the seventh William died.

The Shelleys buried him in the Protestant cemetery near Cestius's pyramid-tomb, and fled northward in terror for their coming child, to Maria Gisborne in Leghorn. Their carriage now held four silent adults and Miss Curran's portrait of William. At Leghorn, Mary Shelley broke down.

10 "Leghorn — Florence   Pisa"

"WHEN I LOOK BACK on all I suffered at Leghorn, I shudder with horror . . . ," Mary Shelley told Marianne Hunt in late November 1819, after the worst was over.[1] Shell-shocked, she cried out against her children's deaths, and foresaw more calamity: "in excessive agony I called for death to free me from all I felt that I should suffer."[2] Then she sank into severe depression.

Shelley rented the manor house of a farm on the city's outskirts, convenient to the Gisbornes. In this four-story, airy mansion cooled by sea breezes, with peasants singing Rossini under her window, Mary sat in her room with William's portrait, marble-pale in black, withdrawn, weak, trembling, "so melancholy and sickly," Claire wrote Byron, giving up a plan for Shelley to take her to see Allegra, "that I cannot imagine how she could be left alone."[3]* Shelley was afraid she would go insane or kill herself, but when he tried to reach her she broke out in bitter fretfulness, protest, and despair — "irritate for very taste of grief," he noted — ended in tearful apologies, and withdrew the worse for shame. "How blind we mortals are . . . ," she wrote Marianne Hunt on June 29:

> We came to Italy thinking to do Shelley's health good — but the Climate . . . has destroyed my two children . . . I never know one moments ease from . . . wretchedness & despair . . . to loose two only & lovely children in one year — to watch their dying moments . . . I feel that I am no[t] fit for any thing & therefore not fit to live . . . But all this is all nothing to any one but myself . . .[4]

And on September 24, the anniversary of Clara's death:

> . . . I am much changed — the world will never be to me again as it was — there was a life & freshness in it that is lost to me —

---

* See the mourning mother in "The Ritter von Reichenstein," a previously unidentified short story by Mary Shelley published in *The Bijou* for 1828.

on my last birthday . . . I repined that time should fly so
quickly . . . now I am 22 . . . & only repined that I was not older —
in fact I ought to have died [with William] on the 7th of June . . .[5]

Though her depression eased in November, when she delivered the
child she was carrying, it persisted for another nine months, and thereafter
her inner landscape had shifted: the eruption and ash-covering of a loving
heart, Shelley was later to image it. Watching children die was a fact of
life acknowledged to be more agonizing and indelible for the mother. It
was not the worst loss a man can have, Hunt told Hogg, and advised the
Shelleys to weep "quietly, but not for long." The mother's expected responses were submission to God's will, dedication to others, gentle broken-
heartedness. Though the diaries of Lady Holland and Melusina Trench
testify to private "savage despair" and refusal to resign themselves, Mary's
circle considered her more overt reaction as inordinate — except for Mrs.
Gisborne, who came to admire and love her "beyond all other women."

Mary would later recognize William's death as a watershed of her life:
on the far side had been zestful anticipation, certainty, a sense of trust and
belonging, fruitfulness, and above all fearlessness; after, "this world seemed
only a quicksand, sinking beneath me."[6] William's death eclipsed the faith
in her benign star and her power to master life on which her stoicism was
based; indeed, for months her hope was transmogrified into belief that an
evil Providence ruled the whole of existence. Beatrice, the maddened Paterin of *Valperga,* would pronounce the anathema Mary had felt:

> Then reflect upon domestic life, on the strife, hatred, and un-
> charitableness . . . think of jealousy, midnight murders, envy, want
> of faith, calumny, ingratitude, cruelty, and all which man in his
> daily sport inflicts upon man. Think upon disease, plague, fam-
> ine . . . oh! Know you not what a wretch man is? . . . Look into
> your own heart . . . gaze on mine; I will tear it open for your
> inspection. There is remorse, hatred, grief . . . misery. . . .
> I see the cruel heart, which lurks beneath the beautiful skin of
> the pard . . . the blight of autumn in the green leaves of spring,
> the wrinkles of age in the face of youth . . . storm in the very
> breast of calm, sorrow in the heart of joy, all beauty wraps de-
> formity.[7]

She did not torment herself that any negligence of hers contributed to
William's death: "without experience," Claire would say years later, "with
no one to warn you of the effects of the climate, but bestowing every care
a mother's heart could devise, and most guiltless . . . you loved your child

and would give your life to preserve his."[8] Rather, she was overwhelmed by worse than pure grief: a partial return of what she had repressed. Whereas she believed that she and Shelley had been disinterested, justified, and principled in forming their union, she felt that she was being punished for having defied her father and ruined Harriet Shelley.* Her children had been proof that she had "won," and now the fruits of her hubris were destroyed, as the gods slew Niobe's children for her boasting and punished Prometheus for overreaching.

Her conscience substituted a retributive Fate for the biblical God whose code of retribution she execrated. If her four years with Shelley could be "blotted out," she said, she might now be happy starting over again with him, or alternately she wished they had a dozen children. But these were graspings. She dreaded more calamity because she loved Shelley as entirely as before and knew she would choose him again, even knowing what would happen. Because of her career and love of movement she never wanted a large family, and certainly not now when she dreaded for the child she was carrying.

In Rome she had previsioned William's absence; from now on she was certain that her fears were warnings. Shelley may have considered changing *Rosalind and Helen*'s tragic ending, to reassure her. "Is there not a principle in the human mind," she would write in *Valperga*, "a feeling which would warn the soul of peril, were it not at the same time a sure prophecy that peril is not to be avoided?"[9] The uncanny fact is that she wrote that very passage, and the ending of *Matilda*, which she composed that summer, with unknowing second sight.

While she closed in on herself, Shelley took for his study a small glazed pergola on the roof of the high house, with an infinite view of the sea and countryside, a perfect metaphor for his compulsion to transcend reality. Here he completed three of his greatest works; her *annus terribilis* following Clara's death was his *annus mirabilis*, culminating in the ultimate of utopian sublime, the fourth act of *Prometheus Unbound*. But he expressed his sense of abandonment in the private notebook he had used for such purposes since Clara's death:[10] "My dearest Mary, wherefore hast thou gone, / And left me in this dreary world alone? / Thy form is here indeed — a lovely one — / But thou art fled, gone down the dreary road, / That leads to Sorrow's most obscure abode; / Thou sittest on the hearth of pale despair, / Where / For thine own sake I cannot follow thee."

Most unions change imperceptibly; the terrible second shock of William's death, coming so soon after Clara's, decisively divided the Shelleys.

---

* Mary reread *Clarissa Harlowe* that summer.

For Mary, making love seemed a cruelly ironic, impossible affirmation, whereas death increased his desire. In another secret poem, "Invocation to Misery," he summons her, "mourning in thy robe of pride, / Desolation — deified!" to make the best of their evil lot in sensual delight. "Ha! thy frozen pulses flutter / With a love thou darest not utter, / . . . Kiss me; — oh! thy lips are cold; / Round my neck thine arms enfold — / They are soft, but chill and dead; / And thy tears upon my head / Burn like points of frozen lead."

Yet Shelley himself, haunted by the conviction that he was doomed and a carrier of doom to everyone he loved, sometimes felt that his life was in ruins, that he and Mary were paying for what they had done to Harriet Shelley. "That time is dead for ever, child! / Drowned, frozen, dead for ever! / We look on the past / And stare aghast / At the spectres wailing, pale and ghast, / Of hopes, which thou and I beguiled / To death on life's dark river."[11] In *Julian and Maddalo,* the maniac's oscillating responses to his mistress's abandonment, a section he withheld from Mary for months, are his own: self-pity and resentment, love for a compassionate and wise "spirit's mate," and pity for an unfortunate "Child" (also meaning Mary) who with himself must endure what they had inflicted on another.

Shelley was the only person who could deal with Mary on her level, and he believed that it was his duty to protect and uplift her. His concealments, however, also betray hostility. The final version of *Prometheus Unbound* marks an important shift from his prior image of their union as one of "twin stars" to an attribution of greater power and responsibility to her. Prometheus's wife, Asia, irradiated all Creation with love, hope, and joy; when grief "cast eclipse" on her, Earth suffered "the contagion of a mother's hate / Breathed on her child's destroyer" until her reunion with Prometheus. Given his poems about men who die after sex, possibly her inhibition was doubly frustrating, for if she were passionate he might escape to death.[12]

Although she too was tempted by doom, Mary Shelley turned to study and writing. Around the fifth anniversary of her elopement she began a novella in which she attempted to work through her tragedy. An important Romantic fiction, it is also a crucial biographical document, and one of the first case histories of an acute depression, the more rare for being written by the patient. She titled it "Fields of Fancy" and completed a draft in September, then revised it for publication as *Matilda.* "I sought the end of my being & I found it to be knowledge of itself," says Diotima, Matilda's spiritual mother-adviser.[13]

The novella is an alternative scenario to Mary's own mother's early "Cave of Fancy," one of whose characters, unlike Mary, resisted her passion for an unhappily married man. Here Mary approached the psychic level and some of the themes of *Frankenstein,* but focused, with extraordinary audacity for the period, on a girl's incestuous involvement with her father. It was as if she were fantasizing what sin might have occurred if she had not committed her real "crime." Again the "child" is motherless; Matilda's mother died giving her birth. Again the father abandons the baby, to a cold aunt in Scotland. Matilda grows up with "somewhat unnatural" day-dreams of being her father's consolation. When she is sixteen he returns, to their mutual joy. Soon he dismisses a potential suitor, the Shelleyan poet Woodville, and eventually reveals that he himself is in love with her; Matilda, the cause of his wife's death, should be as his wife was to him. Aroused but horrified,[14] Matilda sends him away, then fearfully rushes to him, and finds his corpse by the sea in which he drowned himself, leaving her guilty, like Frankenstein's monster, of patricide.

Though fictionally heightened and ruthlessly self-accusatory, the balance of the novella essentially describes Mary's situation at that time. Feeling unfit to live — "I with my dove's look and fox's heart" — Matilda with-draws into a hermit's existence and cannot be retrieved by the efforts of the angelic Woodville, who is mourning his dead fiancée. Once affectionate and openhearted, Matilda is encased in "impenetrable and unkind silence"; she has become peevish, suspicious, "captious and unreasonable":

> . . . even with Woodville, the most gentle and sympathizing crea-ture that existed. . . . When for a moment I imagined that his manner was cold I would fretfully say . . . "I was at peace before you came . . . but you forced yourself upon me and gave me these wants which you see with triump[h] give you power over me . . . go: the sun will rise and set as before. . . . You are cruel . . ."
>
> And then, when . . . I saw his countenance bent with living pity on me . . . I wept and said, "Oh pardon me! . . ."[15]

As Woodville with Matilda, Shelley tried to make Mary see evil not as destiny's work but as our own "willful ill," which we may alter if we so determine, to hope, to believe in *Prometheus Unbound*'s message of the ultimate omnipotence of Good and Love. Love was "the law of life" for him, she later wrote, "and all woe and pain arose from the war made against it by selfishness, or insensibility, or mistake."[16] The more she de-viated from this ideal, the more he exemplified love, kindness, and for-bearance.

Shelley made her hate herself more by denying that her violent reaction was natural and legitimate. Nevertheless, her instinct was to wrestle with authentic demons. She repudiated his *Prometheus* vision, in which "he sheltered himself," she wrote two decades later, still with a tinge of irony, "from . . . disgusting and painful thoughts in the calm retreats of poetry, and built up a world of his own, with the more pleasure, since he hoped to induce some one or two to believe that the earth might become such . . ."[17] She had never accepted his utopianism, and now scornfully denied that one could rely upon Good and redeem the world, or that Love protected and saved. "I had no idea that misery could arise from love," Matilda says, "and this lesson that all must learn was taught me in a manner few are obliged to receive it."[18]

Grim and violent, *The Cenci* corresponded more with Mary's vision, as well as with Shelley's darker views. Probably he consulted her on it this summer to divert her, and both benefitted from its purgation. While she was using him as model for the celestial Woodville, she knew that she was a model for *The Cenci*'s mad scene where Beatrice, formerly of "subtle mind," falls into frantic delirium, then lucid, tortured desperation, then "proud, impenetrable grief."* In *Matilda* the heroine resents this: "I am, I thought, a tragedy; a character that he comes to see me act: now and then he gives me my cue that I may make a speech more to his purpose: perhaps he is already planning a poem in which I am to figure . . . he takes all the profit and I bear all the burthen."[19] She dies, reconciled to return to maternal Nature and believing that her spirit will live on with those of her father, Woodville — and, in her draft, his fiancée.

Depressives turn everything into fuel for wretchedness; but Mary's was exacerbated and prolonged until the following summer by unremitting troubles. Godwin's very condolence letter, reiterating his fears of his impending lawsuit and need for the fatal five hundred pounds, so agitated her that she wrote to Ollier about an advance on her projected *Valperga*. "On account of the terrible state of her mind," Shelley asked Godwin to write more soothingly, but both Godwins were enraged beyond pity over the money, Claire, and in Godwin's case his daughter's unshakable devotion to and trust in her "disgraceful and flagrant husband," who, Godwin insisted, had fathered Allegra on Claire. "My misfortune has not altered the tone of my father's letters . . . ," Mary wrote Amelia Curran, whom she asked to design a pyramid tomb for William's grave; "can you wonder that my spirits suffer terribly —"[20]

"He cannot . . . place a shade of enmity between her and me —" Shelley wrote Hunt, "but he heaps on her misery, still misery."[21] Shelley never said a harsh word to her about her father, whom he never ceased to revere

---

* She was also one of the models for the maniac in *Julian and Maddalo*, with his twining pale fingers and his laments shifting from passionate to "unmodulated, cold, expressionless."

for his work and even his character, but he was bitter, and she knew he resented Godwin's financial demands. No situation is as terrible and agonizing, she declared in her forties, as that of a young woman torn between father and lover. Certainly it was agonizing for her.*

Like Shelley, but deliberately, Godwin intensified Mary's sense of shame and failure. He claimed that she was overreacting selfishly to her losses instead of to his own, and gave her good advice that he was making it impossible to enact, that if she continued her "selfishness and ill humour" her intimates "will finally cease to love" her, even fail to endure her:

> I cannot but consider it as . . . putting you quite among the commonality and mob of your sex, when I had thought I saw in you symptoms entitling you to be ranked among those noble spirits that do honour to our nature. Oh, what a falling off is here! . . . You have the husband of your choice, to whom you seem to be unalterably attached, a man of high intellectual endowments, whatever I and some other persons may think of his morality. . . . You have all the goods of fortune, all the means of being useful to others. . . . But . . . all is nothing, because a child of three years old is dead.[22]

On Shelley's twenty-seventh birthday Mary started to keep her journal again, albeit irregularly for many months. Since she could not bear to continue where she had left off, at William's fatal illness, she started a new journal book. She had been reading Livy; now she read Dante with Shelley. They began an eleven-month course in deist-political critique, for which she read the Scriptures, Paine, Voltaire, Rousseau, More, and d'Argens, while continuing their translation of Spinoza; she also copied Shelley's latest poems for the press. For spiritual strength she turned to Cicero's stoic courage, Horace's ripe acceptance of life, Virgil's *Georgics,* celebrating nature and human labors. Charles Clairmont arrived from Spain for a three-month visit en route to teach in Vienna. The Shelleys learned Spanish with him and Mrs. Gisborne, their fifth tongue, which Mary studied with a Cervantes play and a Beaumont and Fletcher adaptation. By October she was reading Alemán, later Calderón, and in time most of the important Spanish as well as Portuguese literature.

Shelley was investing in Henry Reveley's steam engine and money was

* As plangent evidence, her relevant fictional heroines either are orphaned of their fathers before they fall in love, or oppose their fathers and lose their lovers or even their own lives. Note "The Sisters of Albano," "Transformation," "The Dream," "The Brother and Sister," "The Invisible Girl," and perhaps "The Pilgrims." Only in her last novel, *Falkner,* completed after Godwin's death, are father and husband reconciled.

short, so Mary determined on "oeconomies," hoping also to save for Godwin. Henry proposed to Claire; though Claire declined, the dismayed Gisbornes' strategems to save him from a tarnished, penniless wife made the still-tremulous Mary tease them in her old style about Henry's marrying an heiress; "you could not refrain from . . . innocent little quizzes, notwithstanding your hand trembling," Mrs. Gisborne replied affectionately.[23]

As Mary entered her eighth month, the Shelleys left for Florence to await her delivery by Dr. Bell.* They stopped in Pisa, where they found an instant friend in Lady Margaret Mount Cashell. This towering nononsense *grande dame*, whom Mary had not seen since childhood, lived with her longtime lover, George Tighe, under the name of "Mrs. Mason," a fictional character created by Mary Wollstonecraft, who had been her governess. She knew the second Mrs. Godwin too well not to have discounted her vicious letters about the Shelleys, and being an amateur medico she was full of authoritative concern for Mary. Mary had Maria Gisborne send her a half pound of the best tea "at whatever price" and *Frankenstein*, which Mrs. Mason read promptly, as she did everything, and approved, which she did rarely, with her highest accolade: "I think it the production of a strong mind."[24]

In Florence they stayed economically at Madame Merveilleux du Plantis's *pensione* for respectable English, near Santa Maria Novella. Mary visited the opera and the Uffizi before confining herself to walks in the neighborhood. But just when security and promptitude would have been a blessing, it developed that Dr. Bell was fatally ill and could not attend her, and she had five more weeks to go. Meanwhile on November 9 she plunged into despair when she heard from her father that he had lost the lawsuit and was ordered to pay back rent of fifteen hundred pounds, which he hoped to compromise for, of course, five hundred. That day she began to rewrite "Fields of Fancy" as *Matilda* for publication for his benefit.

On November 12, after a mercifully short two-hour labor, Mary delivered a boy, quite small but active and ravenous at the breast. She notified Maria Gisborne before she even saw him unswaddled, curbing her welling joy with irony. "The little boy takes after me, and has a nose that promises to be as large as his grandfather's — I have not yet seen his form, but I enput it to be the quintessence of beauty . . . he becomes quiet the moment I take him."[25] The ladies of the *pensione* came to congratulate her: "sweetly pretty . . . beautifully fair . . . very delicate and interesting" in the conjugal bed.[26] They baptized the baby Percy Florence. The second name was

---

* On leaving, she pressed into Mrs. Gisborne's hand a slip of paper with lines from Byron: "Reflect on me as on the dead / And think my heart is buried here." (Houghton Library, MS Eng. 822.1 [13]. Quoted by permission of the Houghton Library.)

suggested by Miss Sophia Stacey, a distant young relation of Shelley's, also staying at Madame du Plantis's, and *"entousiasmée,"* Mary said, about Shelley despite her conservative views. To Mary, the name signified Florence's former glory.

Now everyone expected Mary to return to normal, but her losses had been too traumatic. Until the end of the dangerous summer, she concentrated on suckling this child, "in whose life, after the frightful events of the last two years, her own seems wholly to be bound up," Shelley told her father that August.[27] She put aside her habitual schedule for his feedings, airings, and "provoking trifles," complicated by Milly Shields's quitting, and walked so vigorously to encourage her milk that she blistered her feet. When she watched him "taking a right down earnest sleep with all his heart in his shut eyes" after nursing, "for the life of me I cannot fear . . . ," she wrote Marianne Hunt, "yet even now a sickening feeling steps in the way of every enjoyment when I think — of what I will not write about."[28]

Still unconsoled and beset by troubles, she gave vent to bitterness and irritability that made her hard to live with. She prepared for *Valperga* in her spare time, compiling from Sismondi a chronology and a list of sources that she asked the Gisbornes' and Mrs. Mason's help in locating. "I admire Mary's courage & industry," the latter declared.[29] But Mary's letters are replete with Paterin jibes at "Jehovah's" cruelty. "Are you not in a passion, my Dear Mrs Gisborne?" she wrote. "I am sure I am, and have every reason;" the severe cold, Shelley's deteriorating health and spirits, her incompetent Italian nurse; "All goes on de pire en pire . . ."[30]

Shelley had impulsively offered Godwin all the help in his power, but even after he sold his carriage he had nothing to send. His own English creditors were threatening legal action; the Gisbornes were actually suffering from the cold and in dire need of his investment in the steam engine. Mary implored her friend to insulate the windows: "It almost seems like a treason to my affection for you to have been living so miserably while we at least have . . . plenty of firing — You must not do this — Indeed you must not —"[31]

The Shelleys were tired of roving and wanted to settle for a time. Mary preferred Rome, where "my heart is," or Florence because she had not yet explored it, and Claire was taking her music studies seriously, even consulted Madame du Plantis, who taught music, about teaching. But Mrs. Mason decided them on Pisa for its cheap prices, the famous university where Mary could find research material for *Valperga*, a mild healthy climate, the great physician Andreà Vaccà, and the indomitable Mrs. Mason herself, who observed that she might be as good a physician for Shelley as anyone. On January 26, just after a visit from Elise Foggi, who was now in service with an Englishwoman, they left for Pisa.

Though Mary had so little intention of settling there that she left their crate of books with Mrs. Gisborne for another eighteen months, Pisa would be her home for three and a half years. Nine miles from Leghorn, a major city in Castruccio's period, it had declined into "a quiet half-peopled" town. Mrs. Mason recommended the north bank of the Arno, which bisects Pisa in a long gentle arc lined on both sides with fine old residences and wide streets where everyone then promenaded. Mary, who was economizing even on Percy's baby clothes, chose a furnished apartment so small that they soon moved to a larger one. On this side of the river, winter sun flooded in the windows, where Mary set potted plants, and the front rooms were laced with wavering light reflected up from the water.

Mrs. Gisborne produced a nurse, Caterina. When Mary told Mrs. Mason that Mrs. Gisborne said Italian servants were rascally, she returned that she thought the less of Maria Gisborne, found a housekeeper, Maria, who like Caterina became a fixture, and gave Mary instructions about time off for mass, the customary cut for tradesmen, and so on. Cooks came and went, dinner was sometimes unaccountably late, but Mary found that a crown went as far as a pound in England and for the first time ever did not worry about weekly bills.

Dr. Vaccà revolutionized their view of Shelley's life expectancy, moreover, by convincing them that he had no mortal disease, that his pains were nephritic and his chronic bad health due to extreme excitability acting on a hypersensitive physique. Vaccà prescribed a sensible, strengthening regime and tranquil living.

Despite "idleness — & nursing," Mary now wrote the greater part of *Matilda;* "miserable as I was," she recalled, "the *inspiration* was sufficient to quell my wretchedness temporarily."[32] And she began her research for *Valperga* in numerous old Italian histories, which she loved working with, and considered learning shorthand for her copious notes. Apparently in this period, she also wrote a short history of the ancient Jews, mocking biblical "falsehoods and inconceivable absurdities" and modern Christian hypocrisy. Noah's curse on Ham, she wrote, "must quiet the conscience of those traders in negroes who believe in the Jewish mythology," and if the "unequaled barbarity" of Joshua's conquest of the Promised Land is accounted holy, why reprobate patriots of national liberation who "shed the blood of man for the benefit of man [and] their country . . . ?"[33]

In Florence the Shelleys had come to consider themselves no longer travelers but exiles. The *Quarterly Review* had set a new level of execration in a review of *The Revolt of Islam,* which Mary sent Mrs. Gisborne along with favorable reviews in *The Examiner* and *Blackwood's,* "the bane & the antidote." The *Quarterly* attacked Shelley for atheism, subversion, fornication, incest, cruelty to Harriet Shelley, and for his "disgusting" praise in the Dedication of Mary's decision to live with a married man. Mary Shelley, the review pointed out menacingly, was the original of Cythna: heinous, flagrant, and fair game in future: "we have more consideration for her than she has had for herself, and will either mortify her vanity, or spare her feelings, by not producing her before the public . . . [but] when the season arrives, she will be forthcoming."[34]

Along the same lines, an anonymous versified "biography" of Byron castigated the Geneva "Vampyre family," "that knot of scribblers, male and female, with weak nerves, and disordered brains, from whom have sprung those disgusting compounds of unnatural conception, bad taste, and absurdity, entitled 'Frankenstein' . . . the 'Vampyre,' etc. . . . "[35] The *Literary Gazette* followed with a series of vicious attacks on Shelley and his "associate strumpets."

Attacks like these stiffened Mary's spine, while the political scene, which the Shelleys followed in *Galignani's Messenger* (the exiles' Paris *Herald Tribune*), stirred both fear and hope. Since the Peterloo Massacre the fall before, when a cavalry charge killed eleven demonstrators for parliamentary reform, she believed that while England's "poor and middling classes" were united against a despotism supported by the rich alone, Foreign Secretary Castlereagh plotted dictatorship. "There are great spirits in England," she had written Maria Gisborne in January. "So there were in the time of Cesar and Rome. Athens flourished but just before the despotism of Alexander — Will not England fall? I am full of these thoughts."[36]

She was thrilled by the current Liberales uprising in Spain — "I should love to be in Madrid now" — which forced the king to grant a constitution. In a long hot letter to the Hunts she vowed that she would not return to England's degradation and maddening cant. "No — since I have seen Rome, that City is my Country, & I do not wish to own any other untill England is *free* & *true* . . ." England should adopt the name "Castlereagh land," she proposed, import subjects from oppressed countries, and swear in any man self-styled "a slave — a fool — a bigot — & a tyrant . . . ," which would save "a world of trouble in grinding & pounding, & hanging & taxing."[37]

Godwin now claimed that Shelley had "promised" him five hundred pounds and expected it forthwith. On April 6 Mary began *Valperga,* though still researching, and got Shelley to ask Horace Smith, their only well-to-do English friend, to advance her father five hundreds pounds on it.

She wanted Godwin to sell the business, "that load of evils," and come to Italy, but Godwin retorted that that would throw him on Shelley's never-forthcoming bounty. Shelley was miserable over this wretched business: ". . . it is one of the blessings of a moderate fortune," Mary wrote in *Matilda*, "that by preventing the possessor from confering pecuniary favours it prevents him also from diving into the arcana of human weakness or malice."[38] To bestow is a "Godlike atribute," she added, but like Adam and Prometheus the giver pays the penalty of being "martyr to his own excellence."

She herself was sharp and negative with everyone. Shelley bought her coarse combs that tore her fine hair, forgot to subscribe to *Galignani's*. Mrs. Gisborne sent her requested dress goods and a Bible; "The pink is not at all the thing I mean, being both cold and ugly," she said of one; and of the other, "you were sadly cheated." Then she would cry and beg Shelley's pardon. In early March she grasped at a means of curbing herself and asked Maria Gisborne, in a deceptively casual tone, to stay with them instead of accompanying Gisborne to England on business, but in vain.

"Don't you hear Mr Gisborne?" she wrote them: " 'Maria! Where are these stockings to go?' Now Henry — 'Mamma! Don't forget my razors—' Mamma! Maria! run for god's sake or the house will be out of the windows."[39] She went to Leghorn shortly before their departure and gave them gifts for the Hunts and Horace Smith, and *Matilda* for Godwin. "I am well persuaded that the author will one day be the admiration of the world," Mrs. Gisborne noted.[40] But that was the end of *Matilda*. Godwin said the subject was "detestable" and unpublishable without a preface stating that Matilda was not guilty of incest, although, he added, "one cannot exactly trust to what an author of the modern school may deem guilt."[41] Mary could not get him to return the manuscript.

Shelley too had asked Mrs. Gisborne to stay in Pisa, and with express urgency, for the Shelleys' relations were in worse crisis than he allowed Mary to sense. Since the deaths of Clara and especially William, he wrote, Mary had undergone an "inward change" and expressed her sufferings in temper and irritation in spite of "her strong understanding, and of her better feelings, for Mary is certainly capable of the most exalted goodness. . . . Mary considers me as a portion of herself, and feels no more remorse in torturing me than in torturing her own mind."[42] He subdued his own irritation, when some good screaming fights might have cleared the air, and tried gently to restrain her, which only exasperated her. As he could not stop or punish Mary, she went on punishing them both.

For Shelley, 1820 marked the start of a two-year mid-life crisis. He had counted on Mary's complete recovery after Percy's birth, which made the cause of her suffering "obsolete." By January he felt like a deserted child, powerless, frail, and dependent upon a female nurturer-muse. In his "The Sensitive Plant" of that spring, a young Spirit-Lady dies, leaving the plant and the garden she had tended with exquisite love to grow rank and die; the ideal relationship exists, he ends the poem, only "we" have changed.

Mary's bitter depression was only one cause of his own "extreme nervous irritability" and his wretched health. He may have resented her focus on Percy. Learning that he had no life-threatening disease may have come as a mixed blessing. And he had cooled off about helping Godwin, unfairly suspected him of lying about his crisis, enlarged on his villainy to lessen his own contributions to Mary's situation, and even felt that "people" would think she was using him to help her father. Furthermore, he had written *The Cenci* expecting, despite the unplayability of the subject of incest, that a Covent Garden production would bring him wide popularity. It was rejected, and Ollier would not publish it; Shelley had to do so himself. Nor did Ollier publish *Julian and Maddalo*, and Shelley knew that few would appreciate *Prometheus Unbound*, which he judged his greatest work. Meanwhile, Byron and Moore, "much better and more successful poets than I," were acclaimed, and Shelley's repute was so vile that Walter Savage Landor, who was then in Pisa, ignored his overture for acquaintance.

On top of all this, Byron had become so angry at Claire's hostile letters and "Bedlam behaviour" that he told the Hoppners she was "a damned bitch," turned hostile to the Shelleys as well, and refused to let Allegra visit them. To allay friction and obtain the gratifications he needed, Shelley juggled multiple concealments, told Byron he did not disagree with the decision but "pray *don't quote* me" to Claire, and sought sympathy from friends for various troubles with selective confidences.

Shelley and Claire may have become lovers in 1820. Claire had turned back to Shelley from Byron, who had a serious new mistress, Countess Teresa Guiccioli, whom he followed to Ravenna. While lavishing "sweet consolation" upon Shelley, Claire encouraged him to complain about her stepsister, at long last cast down from her superiority. "We speak," he noted, "As to a second conscience when we speak / To friends what otherwise the heart would break / Concealing and containing."[43] But his second conscience's journal was barbed with hostility: two is "the symbol of division," hence marriage's "unhappy querulous state"; "A bad wife is like Winter in a house," Claire quoted from the Greek, possibly cited by Shelley.[44]

Actually, Shelley and Claire were only intensifying their long-standing intimacy, a function of which was to discharge resentment of Mary: on his side because Mary did not give him all that he yearned for, on Claire's because of her envy. Their solution is revealed in Shelley's suggestion to the doubtless startled Gisbornes that if Mary could meet and love a superior man, she would control herself and find happiness in making that man happy. He had also told the Gisbornes that "some fatal end" might result if Mary did not change, and in fact Claire encouraged him to think of leaving Mary.

Mary knew that Shelley and Claire were commiserating, but she was blind to their disaffection with herself. It would be years before she grew up enough to realize how easily she could be duped by those on whom she projected her own loyalty. Perhaps because she tended to distrust in general, she denied that Shelley in particular was not perfectly trustworthy, at the same time that she proudly invited abuse. She despised secret intrigue; it was unthinkable that Claire, much less Shelley, could betray her. Mary was not entirely wrong. It is a curious fact that while excessive nobility in the deceived drives deceivers to find fault in order to justify their own shortcomings and to act without serious qualms, even with sadistic pleasure, they may at the same time cherish the deceived out of love, respect, and gratitude for gullibility.

Although she loved Shelley's genuinely chivalrous (at least in part) protection of Claire, she knew that Claire's conflict with Byron agitated Shelley and worsened his health. She also knew that for Byron to allow Claire to see Allegra, Claire had to convince him that she was not irresponsible; furthermore, to quell the spreading League of Incest story, she had to leave the Shelleys. The last straw was Claire's carelessness and her juvenile Godwinism, which had alienated Madame du Plantis and which Mary tried to rectify, while Claire secretly mimicked, "*Mary says*" do this, "*Mary says*" do that. The stepsisters began to bicker. Claire, unfortunately for her own sake, had given up any intention of teaching or professional singing — having Shelley. Mrs. Mason, who was fond of Claire and knew everything, relieved the pressure by often having Claire stay at her own Casa Silva, and began looking for an alternative home. When that lady took charge, not even Shelley gainsaid her.

The anniversary of William's death, June 7, might have marked the start of Mary's recovery, but a harrowing coda delayed it. On the twelfth, Shelley got a blackmailing letter from Leghorn from Elise's husband, Paolo Foggi, whom they had fired in 1819, threatening to publicize the League of Incest story and the "fact" that Allegra was Claire's child, by Byron or by Shelley. Terrified, the Shelleys and Claire rushed to Leghorn, where they stayed for two months in the Gisbornes' vacant house while Shelley worked with his lawyer, Frederico del Rosso. Shelley had been consulting del Rosso for months on business, which secretly included paying the foster parents of Elena Shelley, his little charge in Naples. Shelley had also told the Gisbornes about Elena.

Mary never had a full account of this nasty imbroglio. Paolo threatened to have Shelley tried in Naples for illegalities relating to Elena, so Shelley eventually told Mary about the little girl, who to his horror now died: the third dead child in less than two years.[45] But he hid "the actual state of my delicate & emergent situation which the most sacred considerations imperiously require me to conceal from Mary," as he mysteriously told Godwin.[46]

Mary may have been right in refusing to believe that Elise was involved in Paolo's blackmail. But his extortion attempts were in part based on Elise's information, which she repeated to the Hoppners when she was in Venice that summer. First, she claimed that Claire had been pregnant by Shelley in 1818, and that after failing in attempts to abort, Claire had given birth to Elena in Naples. Whereas this has been disproved,[47] Elise's second accusation has the ring of truth. When Elise had come to see them in Florence, Claire took her for a walk to confide that Mary had alienated her and Shelley by behaving badly. Thus Elise told the Hoppners that Claire hated Mary and was urging Shelley, now "indifferent" to Mary, to leave her, and that the lovers had been abusing Mary brutally, Claire telling Shelley to Mary's face that she did not see how he could stand to live with her. Such frontal abuse was impossible, but it is no wonder that when Shelley was forced to reveal Elise's story to Mary the following summer, he omitted most of that second charge.

Shock and fear at what she knew of Paolo's doings affected Mary's milk and gave Percy diarrhea, which threw her into hysterical panic. The baby recovered promptly, but she was still weak and fearful when Godwin reported that Horace Smith had advanced only one hundred pounds on *Valperga*, and demanded the remaining four hundred. This so agonized her that she wrote the Gisbornes to ask if they could supply the sum, which Shelley agreed to repay, for the sake of peace, while he influenced the Gisbornes to decline by warning separately of Godwin's "implacable exactions" and "boundless and plausible sophistry."

Claire's silent gloating infuriated Mary. " 'Better than a sop to Cerberus or the music of Orpheus to the furies is a £100 to a philosopher!!,' " Claire noted in her journal, and, " 'Heigh — ho the Clare & the Ma[i] / Find something to fight about every day —' "[48] If only Mary were sufficiently "wise," Shelley wrote the Gisbornes, "poor" Claire could remain with them, which Claire was pressing him to insist upon. But he knew perfectly well what Mary and Mrs. Mason took as inarguable, that it was now impossible; del Rosso had gotten Paolo expelled from Leghorn, but his charges were spreading.

Shelley convinced Mary to let him withhold any of her father's letters about money, on grounds that they tormented her and threatened Percy and their peace. When he intercepted Godwin's next he disgorged his real feelings for the first time, condemned Godwin for having accepted his boyish pledge, and declared that after forty-seven hundred pounds he neither could nor would give more. He accused him of torturing Mary to "apalling effect," announced that she authorized himself to be censor, and forbade Godwin to seek funds through her, which "leads to imputations against both herself & you. . . . She has not, nor ought she to have the disposal of money, if she had poor thing, she would give it all to you. . . . Such a father (I mean a man of such high genius) can be at no loss to find subjects on which to address such a daughter. . . . I cannot consent to disturb her quiet & my own by placing an apple of discord in her hand."[49]

At last Mary saw an end to troubles. She intended herself eventually to provide her father's four hundred pounds by means of *Valperga*. Percy was "blither than ever"; Mrs. Mason was working to remove Claire. In July she began to recover from her terrible year and became, Shelley said, "very good." They heard that Keats had tuberculosis, and invited him to live with them in Italy. Instead of an impressive pyramid tomb for William, Mary decided on a simple slab (which was never installed). She also began seriously to study Greek.

"I give you joy of London smoke," she wrote Mrs. Gisborne. Her friend had seen the Godwins and reported that Mrs. Godwin was choked to glowering silence at meeting this woman whom her husband had loved and who loved Mary. "Poor Mrs. Godwin! I knew it w^d be thus," chortled Mary.[50] Two weeks later, she mocked the current uproar over the farcical divorce trial of adulterous Queen Caroline by her adulterous husband, who was to be crowned George IV, and hailed another constitutional revolution, in Naples:

> The Queen! The Queen! The Queen! Does it not rain Queens in England, or at least orations sent post from Heaven . . . in favour of our heroic — magnanimous — innocent — injured — virtuous — illustrious and lion-hearted British one . . . to be sure, she is injured, but it is too great a stretch of imagination to make a God of a *Beef-eater*, or a heroine of Queen Caroline. — but I wish with all my heart downfall to her enemies . . . Besides her,

you have the coronation . . . Oh! they are a pretty set! [Tory]
Castlereagh's impudence and [Whig] Brougham speechifying . . .
. . . Thirty years ago was the era for Republics, and they all
fell — This is the era for *constitutions*, I only hope that these latter
may in the end remove the motas [muds] of the former . . . I do
not hear from you, and I am vexed — that is my last word, except
indeed I add that I am ever your's [51]

By late July Leghorn became dangerously hot for Percy. They had found
one friendly Englishman, the bibliophile George Jackson;[52] otherwise the
English were gossiping "prodigiously" about them. They wanted a quiet
place where Mary could concentrate on *Valperga*. At Mrs. Mason's recommendation of a local summer resort they left Leghorn on August 5,
the day after Shelley's twenty-eighth birthday, for the Baths of Pisa.

11   "Solitude   The Williams — The Baths"

"RAIN TILL ONE OCLOCK — at sunset the arch of clouds over the west clears away . . ." Fall of 1820 at the Baths of Pisa was so wildly beautiful that Mary Shelley was moved to describe it in her journal, and seven years later would recall in Italian this paradigmatic, mutable autumn: "Allora le nuvole . . . clouds driven across the moon by the raging wind, magnificent clouds . . . seeming as solid as the mountain and under the tyranny of the wind revealing themselves more fragile than a veil of finest silk — then the rain fell — the trees despoiled themselves . . . beautiful — terrible — melancholy."[1]

A quiet little provincial spa, the Baths of Pisa sits at the foot of Monte Pisano, four miles from Pisa. Mrs. Mason came with her daughter to see them settled, and Mary took a day to write a story for the girl. Shortly after, she, Shelley, and Claire went to Lucca, so Mary could see Castruccio's ducal city and the terrain. Then she plunged into writing *Valperga*. As for Claire, Mrs. Mason followed through to disengage her from the Shelleys and from the "Miss Clairmont" who was even more notorious as Allegra's mother and Shelley's lover after Paolo Foggi's dirty work. On August 21 Claire went to Mrs. Mason in Pisa, then to Leghorn to bathe in the sea for her scrofula while Mrs. Mason arranged for her to live in Florence as paying guest with the family of a prominent physician, Dr. Botji. At the end of October Mary went to Pisa to see Claire off. Shelley escorted Claire on all of these comings and goings.

For the first time in five years the Shelleys were in solitude — without Claire. They spent a quiet two and a half months working, walking, and horseback riding in the foothills and along the canals that intersected the fertile plain. The chance to be alone with Shelley, the marking of her twenty-third birthday, the revolving season, her natural resilience, the inspiration of *Valperga* all combined to restore what Mary prized most in herself, "hope & genius — self approbation & enthusiasm."[2]

The only cause for disturbance was the Gisbornes, who returned to

Leghorn but declined Mary's invitation to visit and report on London. When the Shelleys innocently went to see them, Mary found that her father and "that filthy woman," her stepmother, had made them doubt Shelley's character and his investment in the steam engine. "I see that the ban of the Empire is gone out against us . . . ," she wrote Mrs. Gisborne hotly, "what terms need be made with Pariahs — And such, thank God a thousand and a million times, we are, long — very long, may we so continue . . . join them, or us —"[3] It was "an affair of pelf," she said contemptuously, and remained aloof from them for months. Mary's father, correct but fuming after Shelley's "scurrilous" letter, wrote her only when he had specific news, though Shelley gave him minor financial aid.

Mary was reluctant to leave the baths until in rainy late October the Serchio river flooded the village and drove them to Pisa. They rented furnished apartments at Palazzo Galetti, an unpretentious residence on the sunny side of the Arno, next to a proper marble palace noted for a pro- vocative inscription, "Alla Giornata." In spring they moved to nearby Casa Aulla. Though Mary had some difficulty settling in town, and Pisans gave her an eerie feeling, "crawling and crablike through their sapping streets" (a quote on Venetians from Byron, which she was using in *Valperga*), she began to enjoy Pisa.

They were all on familial terms with Mrs. Mason, her lover, George Tighe, and their daughters, Lauretta and Nerina, then eleven and five. As a young woman Mrs. Mason had written pamphlets, which Mary was reading, in support of the 1798 Irish Rebellion, and had known young Lord Edward Fitzgerald, a martyr for liberals, who died in it. When she left Lord Mount Cashell he exercised his legal right to keep their children, though he gave her a thousand-pound annuity. She was the first expatriate Mary knew who loved Italians; indeed, she refused to meet any English. Ostracized by respectable compatriots at home and abroad, she had retired with Tighe to Pisa, Tuscany being the most enlightened of the Italian states. The present Grand Duke Ferdinand, son of a reforming Enlight- enment Austrian prince, had retained much of the progressive legislation of the Napoleonic interregnum, and though an absolute ruler he had declared, to Mary's gratification, that if Tuscans wanted a constitution, *ebbene,* he would grant one *subito*.

The reclusive Tighe, an agronomist nicknamed "Tatty" because he grew potatoes, was Mary's model for Guinigi in *Valperga*, the soldier turned farmer who tried to teach young Castruccio to "think only of the duty of man to man." Dr. Vaccà too, Mary observed, was "a great republican and no Xtian." As a medical student in Paris he had taken part in the storming of the Bastille, and now treated the Pisan poor at a dispensary where Mrs. Mason assisted.

At Shelley's invitation, his cousin Thomas Medwin had come from Geneva to spend the winter as their houseguest, and since Shelley was suffering deep dejection and agonizing nephritic pains, Mary was initially happy to have Medwin, who fervently admired Shelley and his poetry. "In calumny," she wrote in *Valperga,* "it is to the friends of our youth that we must turn; for they alone can know how pure the heart is . . ."[4] The cousins had been moderately close during their school days and Medwin's short career as a man about London, but had not met for seven years. Medwin had served in the Indian army, from which he was now retired at half pay and footloose. After some weeks, however, Mary especially found him tiresome, an intellectually pretentious "seccatura," who of a quiet evening insisted on interrupting their reading to recite what he had just written of his clumsy translation of Dante.

Medwin was not impressed with Mary's looks, and she startled him by speaking unashamedly about her premarital liaison, but he thought her an eminently fit wife for his unworldly, hypersensitive, dejected genius of a cousin. That winter, he recalled, Shelley sought repose from his troubles "in the tenderness of affection and sympathy of her who partook of his genius, and could appreciate his transcendent talents."[5]

Like a healed veteran, Mary had become more detached, smiling in her serene way — "the lucent eyes, and the eternal smile," Shelley wrote, of a blue Italian day — and apparently cooler. If she had stabilized, however, it was on "shifting sands": "joy returned," she later noted, "& life was dressed in other charms for me. Yet never for a moment did I cease to wish to die — It was not discontent — it was fear that stamped this unvaried feeling on me —"[6] What would today be diagnosed as severe anxiety seems to have stemmed from guilt about Harriet Shelley, which she was more or less to repress for another decade; yet it was also battlewise anticipation and a genuine prophetic gift, which, however, absolutely excluded fear for Shelley, her "bark of refuge." He was "so tempest worn and frail" that she believed his very weakness proved he was meant to live.[7] Her defense against fate was to try to foresee the future in free association or, as Charles I had done by "Sortes Virgiliae," by opening the *Aeneid* and interpreting the first passages she saw.

She was both newly eager for lively, diverse company and concerned, following Spinoza, "not to ridicule human actions, nor bemoan, nor detest, but to understand." She had always been fascinated by discoveries of any kind and by mythic descents into the underworld such as those of Psyche and Orpheus, and she now applied these to the human mind. Lord Shaftesbury became one of her favorite authors for his adoration of nature and prescriptions of humor against melancholy and moralism, and particularly for his recommendation "to explore the interior *Regions* and *Recesses* of the MIND" — the latter echoed in Hume, whom she apparently reread. She would describe the change in herself through Lionel Verney in *The Last Man:*

> In early youth, the living drama acted around me, drew me heart and soul into its vortex. I was now conscious of a change. I loved, I hoped, I enjoyed; but . . . I was inquisitive as to the internal principles of action of those around me: anxious to read their thoughts justly. . . . All events, at the same time that they deeply interested me, arranged themselves in pictures before me. . . . This undercurrent of thought, often soothed me amidst distress, and even agony. . . . Attentively perusing this animated volume [of life], I was the less surprised at the tale I read on the new-turned page.[8]

Matilda had been the first fiction in which she focused on self-analysis; from now on that would be intrinsic to her serious work. *Valperga,* an undeservedly little-known work of rich Romanticism, serious philosophy, and fine scholarship, is her epic of this period when she found meaning in what she had been through since Clara and William died. She felt that she had grown; her literary ambition was stronger: "With books in their hands against glory, / whereto they set their names —" she quoted Sir Philip Sidney in her journal.[9] Her major heroine in *Valperga,* Euthanasia — Greek for good death — affirms Mary Shelley's own love of wisdom and of "its parent, its sister," liberty, and a Romantic view of the value of upheaval in personal and political life:

> . . . the essence of freedom is that clash and struggle which awaken the energies of our nature, and that operation of the elements of our mind, which as it were gives us the force and power that hinders us from degenerating, as they say all things earthly do when not regenerated by change.[10]

The male protagonist Castruccio is a politicized version of Victor Frankenstein, whose gifts and aspiration are perverted by lust for power. But he becomes relatively less important except as the common unhappy love interest and symbol of male dominance for the two far more original young heroines, Euthanasia and Beatrice, polar "sisters," each of whom represents aspects of Mary Shelley.

The ruling Countess of Valperga — inspired by the eleventh-century Tuscan countesses Beatrice and Mathilda — Euthanasia had been trained by her father in the highest principles, rigorous self-examination, historical perspective, and love of wisdom and liberty — Mary Shelley's tribute to Godwin at his greatest, which she never allowed his behavior to obscure. She and Castruccio are in love. Euthanasia intends to abolish class distinctions in Valperga; princes and priests are among the novel's villains. When Castruccio becomes a tyrant, she painfully gives him up and joins republican Florence in war against him. Beatrice represents unbridled passion, energy, and imagination. Orphaned daughter of a mother who claimed to be the Holy Ghost — drawn from Joanna Southcott and de Staël's Corinne — she is a young religious prophetess who begins by believing that she is infallibly inspired. Passionately in love, certain that her mother's spirit approves "days of error, vanity and paradise," she gives herself to Castruccio. When he leaves her, she turns Paterin and goes mad.[11]

More explicitly than in *Frankenstein*, Mary Shelley states her fundamental position: given the ungovernable forces of Nature, flawed human nature, and "things as they are," the source of individual and social progress and happiness is the self-aware human mind. Euthanasia prescribes exploring the psyche, which she describes as a vast cave. At the entrance are Consciousness and emotions; in the vestibule, Memory, Reason, aspirations, and drives. Conscience, imaged as a majestic, severe male, sits outside the innermost cavern but cannot penetrate it. Anyone who does must carry an inborn light, intuitive moral sense, in order to avoid evil, excuse for crime, even madness, and to find creative imagination, the highest virtues, and contentment.*

Idolizing anything is error; Beatrice idolizes her lover, Euthanasia her principles, Castruccio his power. No matter how highly evolved women may be, however, they are subject to a world ruled by power-hungry men and to their own emotions; this is true both of Euthanasia, Mary Shelley's first stoic heroine, and for Beatrice, like Matilda the antithesis of a stoic. Euthanasia has cold comfort with "the owlet Wisdom" and feels that Castruccio can be hers only if he is defeated, "an extinguished volcano." Castruccio banishes her from conquered Valperga; ironically, she feels mystic oneness with the beauty of Nature and "the eternal spirit of the universe" just before she is drowned in a storm at sea, "which, as an evil stepmother, deceives and betrays all committed to her care." Cas-

---

* In *A General Introduction to Psycho-Analysis*, Sigmund Freud compares the unconscious to a large anteroom crowded by mental excitations adjoining a second, smaller reception room guarded by a censor, in which consciousness resides.

truccio, however, flourishes and at his death "pays his debt to Nature with a calm mind."

Mary Shelley never discarded the Godwinian assumption that to be conquered by emotion is to have failed, but she had come to a riper stoicism, more like Seneca's. She also applied to herself the Humean concept that though everyone sees the same actualities, each sees and feels them differently, and differently at different times: she had reacted Beatrice-like to her children's deaths with irrational self-hate and hatred of life; she now saw this reaction as a part of her nature she had constantly to struggle against, the mind, as Seneca said, being itself the cause of its own happenings. "They say that Providence is shewn by the extraction that may ever be made of good from evil — that we draw our virtues from our faults — so I am to thank God for making me weak . . . ," she would write in her journal, "but I can never applaud the permitter of self degradation though dignity & superior wisdom arise from its bitter & burning ashes."[12]

Her apparent coolness extended to Shelley, partly involuntary defense against feeling too much and becoming depressed and fretful. Moreover, instead of comforting him she tried to make him resolve to remedy a major cause of his own suffering: his isolation and conviction that he was hated, unread, and doomed to be so. Because it dealt with human emotions and actions, *The Cenci* had been more praised and widely reviewed than any of his previous works, and she argued that he should follow it with a drama on Charles I, gain wider public recognition of his genius and appreciation of his true character, and thereby relieve his morbidity. But Shelley gravitated irresistibly to more abstract, difficult poetry like *Prometheus Unbound*. Thus one of his recent and loveliest "visionary rhymes," "The Witch of Atlas," became a minor bone of contention between them, while he wrote Peacock that she had "raked" *Valperga* out of "fifty old books."

More was involved here than literature. It was a question of their divergent reactions to life. Although he had lost some hope for a redeemed world, he retained his longing for the ideal. "Shelley shrunk instinctively from portraying human passion, with its mixture of good and evil, of disappointment and disquiet," she was to write, that very mixture that was attracting her as never before. "Such opened again the wounds of his own heart; and he loved to shelter himself rather in the airiest flights of fancy, forgetting love and hate, and regret and lost hope."[13] He himself now said that their isolation and his abstract way of thinking had been bad for them and for Claire, but like many lovers of humanity in theory he avoided it in the flesh except for a chosen few. She was convinced that his poetic and antisocial sheltering was a shackle to unhappiness that only he could break. "Be strong, live happy, and love," she wrote in one of their joint notebooks,[14] quoting the Archangel's exhortation to Adam and Eve after their expulsion from Eden in *Paradise Lost*.

Medwin's testimony to the Shelleys' compatibility highlights Shelley's compartmentalization of his feelings for Mary into admiration and devotion, and dissatisfaction and resentment. He considered escaping everything. Mary, Percy, his "failed" career, and traveling to the Levant with Medwin or Claire. He had everything he could do, he told Claire, who reproached him for their separation, in "taming his will" to have her with him.

He knew that Mary's coolness was the result of their children's deaths, and that she loved him, perhaps more than he liked at this stage; he referred to her "idolatry" in "The Witch of Atlas." It is likely that she remained cool because he detached himself from her. Apparently he now chose to have separate sleeping arrangements. His study was two floors above her; "congratulate me on my seclusion," he wrote Claire.[15] When Claire came from Florence on holiday, their reunion was such that he afterward told her he lived on the memory of "certain intoxicating moments." She returned to Florence because Mrs. Mason chided her for being weak and unreasonable and Mary expected it, but sent her letters to Shelley to Mrs. Mason at Casa Silva until the latter put a stop to it. Mary meanwhile regularly wrote Claire long, newsy letters.

The Shelleys had been together for more than six years; both knew they were no longer lovers but companions in marriage, which ideally was "warm and kind," he wrote in "The Witch of Atlas." He was miserable both at his duplicities and at the loss of her tenderness: "When passion's trance is overpast, / If tenderness and truth could last, / Or live, whilst all wild feelings keep / Some mortal slumber, dark and deep, / I should not weep!" "Couldst thou but be as thou hast been" in tenderness, he felt that he could dream the rest and be content, but in fact he longed to commingle rapturously with an uplifting sister-soul, "not mine but me," and was about to fall in love again.

Though he was more reclusive, Mary had decided to mix in Pisa society, and by early December was enjoying stimulating company. Her introducer was Francesco Pacchiani, formerly a lecturer at the University of Pisa, an unbelieving, polymath priest out of a Hoffman tale. At first he struck her as the only Italian she had met who had a heart and soul, then as a combination Machiavelli and Boccaccio, for he talked like a Lucifer, shocked Shelley with a dirty joke, and made a pass at Claire. In *Valperga* he is

Benedetto Pepi, who corrupts Castruccio. Later, the Shelleys were to avoid him.

One of Pacchiani's most important introductions was to Tomasso Sgricci, a famous *improvvisatore,* practicer of the art, peculiar to Italy, of impromptu poetic declamation on elevated subjects suggested by the audience, which Mary knew from de Staël's *Corinne* and which now dazzled her. The first evening in her drawing room Sgricci declaimed on the destiny of Italy in his exquisite Italian, and thereafter the Shelleys attended, even once subsidized, his performances. Mary wrote Hunt an extensive description: "The ideas and verses & scenes flowing in rich succession like the perpetual gush of a fast falling cataract. The ideas poetic and just; the words most beautiful, *scelte* and grand."[16] Shelley having a bad case of boils, Pacchiani took her to hear Sgricci at Lucca, where she sat at the theater with the learned Marchesa Eleanora Bernardini; when the Duchess of Lucca gave Sgricci an unfamiliar subject, Inêz de Castro, they concocted her story for him.

Now fluent in the language and literature of "this divine country," Mary thought in Italian and loved its vivid expressive sinuosities, particularly as revealed by Sgricci. What especially interested her, and what she discussed at length with him, was the interplay between the improvisor's inspiration and the warming audience, and the art as an integration of the genius of Italy, "fervent fertile and mixing in wondrous proportions the picturesque the cultivated & the wild until . . . they mingle and form a spectacle new and beautiful."[17] She saw the connection to religious inspiration, and introduced this art into *Valperga* with Beatrice. In *The Last Man*'s segments of prose poetry she would produce an equivalent of improvisation, the influence of which and of the Italian language shows in her richer, more expansive novelistic style.

Sgricci was, as Byron said, a "celebrated Sodomite," though she, who had possibly never met a man she knew to be homosexual, could hardly believe it of one so admirable. She ventured to ask him about it, and wrote Claire that he denied it with "frankness." Shelley shared her present prejudice, having eliminated the homosexual from his translation of Plato's *Symposium* just, as Mary once said, when the subject was about to be discussed.

Pisa was the Italian headquarters for a Greek movement of national liberation from the Turkish empire, and Pacchiani introduced the Shelleys to its chief, twenty-nine-year-old Prince Alexander Mavrocordato. He also introduced them to several British locals whom Mrs. Mason avoided, including Count John Taaffe, an Irish Knight of Malta who was writing a commentary on Dante. An unconscious comic relief, Taaffe paid fussy court to Mary, once sending her two guinea pigs for Percy with a note that convulsed her and Shelley, wishing he were one of the guinea pigs so that he could see her that morning.

Mary was too busy during the winter to do much on *Valperga*, and for "amusement" wrote two short verse dramas adapted from Ovid, "Proserpine" and "Midas," which, Medwin observed, Shelley read with delight, now and then altering a word. She also wrote, with Shelley, a poem on Orpheus.

Mary would call Pacchiani a "Black Genius" for introducing them to Emilia Viviani, nineteen-year-old daughter of the governor of Pisa. Initially, she was the object of their indignant sympathy and of the visiting Claire's, as she had been confined for years in the convent of Santa Anna first as pupil, now until her family arranged the customary marriage in which the bride had no say. Mary was amused that instead of the dim Gothic vaults of fiction, the convent was an ordinary, rather unclean building smelling of garlic; against this background Emilia, pale and elegant, with a Roman nose and magnificent black hair and languorous eyes, seemed romantic and pathetic. She was "always lamenting her pitiful condition," Mary wrote Hunt. "Her only hope is to marry but . . . how they marry in this country,"[18] and she quoted a "masterpiece" of a standard marriage contract in which the groom's attributes but not his name were included. Mary visited Emilia regularly, bringing books and blotting paper, as Emilia wrote poetry.

Shelley was enraptured by this beautiful victim and fell patently in love, just as Mary came to know her well enough to see that she was rather common, quite worldly-wise beneath her effusive rhetoric, and acting a romantic part with him. As Mrs. Mason said, Emilia's chief talent was intrigue, and the fire was in her head more than her heart. "You seem to me a little cold sometimes . . . ," Emilia wrote her "very dear and beautiful sister," making her confidences with Shelley clear, "but I know that your husband said well when he said that your apparent coldness is only *the ash which covers an affectionate heart*."[19] After that, Mary certainly remained cool.

Despite Pacchiani's hints that Emilia was not as guileless as she seemed, her supposedly pure, radiant soul enchanted Shelley, and while he denied to the jealous Claire feeling "what you call love," he was in love. "Oh my beloved," he noted, kissing flowers she sent him. "Oh love! I am all love," she wrote. They became the talk of *tutto Pisa*, where Mary later said, gossip was incredibly "eager and pertinacious" because politics was forbidden and people had nothing else to talk about.

In early February Shelley composed *Epipsychidion*, a long, autobiographical love poem of gorgeous form and questionable content, which he published anonymously in England. (Simultaneously, he deceived Claire about his intent to publish *Julian and Maddalo,* which Claire feared because of its references to Allegra.) In *Epipsychidion* he views his life as a quest for a divine Pilot-Love. He obliterates Mary's former passionate love and her tenderness; she was like a Moon that "warms not but illumines" and he had lain asleep beside her, bright or dim as she smiled or frowned on him. And there he lay "within a chaste cold bed." "For at her silver voice came Death and Life" — Harriet Shelley's suicide, the births and deaths of Clara and William, who in his dream seem to be "masked" as his still living Ianthe and Charles: "the wandering hopes of one abandoned mother," Harriet. Surely these are the most terrible lines Shelley ever wrote: Mary's voice, not his, brought on all tragedy; only his own emotional state can excuse it.

After the deaths of her children, Mary-Moon "Then shrank as in the sickness of eclipse," leaving his soul "as a lampless sea." "And who was then its Tempest" as well as his "Planet of that hour" — Claire — he did not identify. But when she was "quenched" — forced to leave him — his being fell into "a death of ice," split by "earthquakes" of secret anger and protest, "The white Moon smiling all the while on it."

Emilia appears: the Sun. He envisions Moon and Sun ruling "this passive Earth" with "beautiful and fierce" Comet-Claire sharing their lives, and all love one another in despite of a reproving world. Whereas in monogamy, "poor slaves" tread the beaten road with one "chained friend," "True love in this differs from gold and clay, / That to divide is not to take away" — something any child knows is not true. His apostrophes to Emilia — "Seraph of Heaven!"; "Thou Wonder, and thou Beauty, and thou Terror"; "Emily, I love thee" — exceed any he ever addressed to Mary, and he ends with an ecstatic vision of flight with Emilia.

It has been said that Shelley would have left Mary at some point had he not feared she would kill herself. But he knew she did not believe in suicide and would never abandon Percy. Though he was repeating his situation vis-à-vis Harriet (and would do so again with Jane Williams) — the misunderstood, scorned husband who has found his ideal in another woman — he was no longer a boy. Moreover, after having persuaded Mary to elope, watched her suffering over their children, and still blaming his *Thanatos* touch for Claire's misfortunes and the deaths of Fanny Godwin, Clara, William, and Elena, Shelley could not have lived with himself if he had left Mary. More positively, he admired and respected her, needed her companionship and strength, and loved her.[20] Significantly, he wrote a draft of *Epipsychidion* in a *Matilda* workbook she was no longer using. In his foreword he stated that the poet had been confused and was dead.

Nevertheless, he was alternately excited and dejected about Emilia for months.

He probably did not show Mary the unmistakably Shelleyan *Epipsychidion* until summer, around the time of its publication. Its exposure of his passion for another woman and account of her own role wounded her deeply. But she had known as of late winter that Shelley was in love and that Emilia was encouraging him.* Typically, it was only after the affair had ended that she commented on it to anyone, and then satirically, though six years later in *The Last Man* she conveyed her anxiety, anger, pain, and hurt pride in Perdita's reaction to her husband Lord Raymond's adultery. But whereas Perdita — like Lady Byron — confronts her husband and leaves him, Mary hoped that Shelley would sacrifice Emilia for her, and that his "Italian Platonics," his longing for Emilia as an embodied ideal, would end when he saw her as she was. She understood that he was the sort of man who might continually love in this way, and yet she trusted that their union was essentially impregnable.

She continued to visit Emilia, the victim of a system she abhorred, and conducted herself toward Shelley with calm, unmartyred normality, except for an ironic undertone. She was too proud to consider seducing him, and apparently took for granted that they would not be sexually intimate as long as he loved Emilia. But what she later called her "shell" hardened, and it was easier for her to express her affections for anyone but Percy in writing than in speech.†

That spring of 1821 came early and was exquisite. "One is not gay — at least I am not —" Mary wrote Claire on April 2, "but peaceful & at peace with all the world —"[21] By mid-month, Emilia was still toying with Shelley but also enjoying the rivalry of two parentally approved suitors. He assured Claire that he was greatly relieved and Mary said "things got calmer," but in fact, as he wrote the next year, he felt like "a widowed dove" whose mate had sighed but flown their nest.

Meanwhile, Mary was enlarging her circle of friends. Medwin agreed with her that Shelley needed to be brought out of his morbid isolation, and had invited to Pisa a young couple whom he had met in India and lived with in Geneva. Edward and Jane Williams arrived in January. Mary was always unsure how she would be received by even enlightened English people, especially women, so that she was delighted with Edward, "the

* Mary would permit herself the pleasure of giving her version of this affair in "The Bride of Modern Italy" (1824).
† Perdita, in *The Last Man,* "could love and dwell with tenderness on the look and voice of her friend, while her demeanour expressed the coldest reserve."(I:19.)

opposite of a prude," she told Claire. A former Etonian who had been a midshipman before joining the army in India, where he met Jane, Edward Ellerker Williams was retired on a comfortable income. Handsome, endearing, genial, lively, and ingenuous, he obliged Mary by loathing Maria Edgeworth's works and admiring the Shelleys'. He was also an amateur artist and promptly began Mary's portrait.

A lovely brunette, Jane Cleveland Williams was seven months pregnant with their second child, the first a year-old son named for Medwin. Mary began warily with her. Though "tolerant" and always sweetly tactful, Jane, Mary sensed, did not like her, and Mary had reservations. All the uneasiness and defensiveness immemorially felt by women limited in education and scope in their relations with "superior" women, and vice versa, lay between them. But when Edward confided that Jane was a victim of a particularly dreadful marriage, Mary identified her with the heroine of her mother's *Maria* and became attached to her. Jane was the legal wife of an officer named Johnson who had turned out to be so despicable, indeed criminal, that even her brother, a high-ranking army officer, approved of her leaving him. She and Edward had been together for some two years and were very much in love.

It is startling to realize that the Shelleys had never known a couple their own ages; by spring when Medwin left to tour Italy, the four had become intimate. Mary attended Jane when the Williamses' daughter was born, and stood as godmother to the child, named Rosalind after Shelley's poem (known later as Dina). Though Shelley was preoccupied by Emilia, he liked Edward from the start, and Jane increasingly. Both men were more mad than skilled about boating. Shelley bought a narrow skiff to which Henry Reveley fitted a "huge" sail; once Edward tipped it over in the Arno; twice Shelley fell off but was pulled out with refired nautical ardor. In April Mary sailed with them downriver to the Mediterranean.

Prince Mavrocordato had become another of Mary's special friends, and through him she entered the circle of Prince and Princess Argiropoulo and the Pisan band of Greek aristocrats in exile. Already an astute statesman (the future first president of the Greek republic), eager to stake wealth and life for Greek freedom, Mavrocordato personified the best of young Europe to her, and was besides spirited, cultivated, and handsome in a Levantine way. They talked French, which he spoke like a Parisian, and as he was learning English she became his English teacher, and he her Greek instructor with whom she read Sophocles' two Œdipus plays and *Antigone*. "Do you not envy my luck, that . . . an amiable, young, agreeable and learned Greek prince comes every morning to give me a lesson of an hour and a half," she wrote Mrs. Gisborne.[22] Though Greek was difficult for her, she loved it.

As a Greek revolution seemed improbable, "je n'oublierais jamais les consolations que vous m'avez donnée,"[23] the prince wrote Mary in one of many little notes. He gave her inside information on Castlereagh's covert support of the Turks, which Mary passed on to Hunt, hoping to send documentary evidence to important Whigs and "give another knock to this wretched system of things." "Prophet I am of noble combats": Mary having just read this in Sophocles, Shelley, who of course encouraged this friendship, ordered a seal for Mavrocordato with that motto, which he later used for his *Hellas*.

Mary saw the only chance for European freedom and peace in the constitutional revolutions in Spain, Naples, and this spring in Piedmont, Genoa, Massa, and Carrara, which were instigated by the proscribed Carbonari movement that Byron joined in Ravenna. These she hoped would spread north and eventuate in republics. In fact, out of touch with English realities, she asked her father, to his amazement, if England were not on the verge of revolt. Sgricci was said to be a Carbonaro; impossible, Mary declared, or he would be at Naples, where she and Shelley intended to go in summer. To their dismay, the revolutions were quashed and the old regimes brutally restored.

But on April 1, "like a caged eagle just free," Mary exulted, Mavrocordato rushed to Casa Aulla to announce that General Alexandros Ypsilanti had invaded Wallachia. Thus opened six years of war that fired the imagination of a swelling international Philhellene movement among the classically educated, who believed that Greece, inhabited by descendants of Plato, Pericles, Themistocles, and Leonidas — now actually an anarchic, semibarbaric land — would be restored to her former glory. Though ignorant of modern Greek, Mary quickly translated Ypsilanti's proclamation of Greek freedom for *The Examiner,* probably helped by one of the Greek circle; Shelley corrected it; and on the fifth she sent it to Hunt under the title "A Cry of War to the Greeks." Hunt had already published the proclamation but printed her accompanying letter with the latest news from Greece and the Continent where Greek students and exiles were leaving to fight. "Let us hope that no narrow policy and mean fear will tarnish . . . the conduct of those who . . . sway the councils of the British Empire," she concluded.[24] But England and the Holy Alliance quietly supported the crescent over the cross. "Why I am a better Xtian than they," Mary wrote Hunt.[25] Mavrocordato and his aides were wild to reach Greece but were refused transit passports until mid-June.

"But for our fears, on account of our child," Mary Shelley would write in 1839, "I believe we should have wandered over the world, both being passionately fond of travelling."[26] They planned to winter with the Williamses in Florence, someday to live on a free Greek island, perhaps see India. But to protect Percy during the hot months, they returned to the Baths of Pisa in early May with the Williamses, residing on the outskirts of town a half hour walk from the Williamses' villa at Pugnano.

It was one of the charms of this season to float in their skiff on the canals "under verdant banks, sheltered by trees that dipped their boughs into the murmuring waters. By day, multitudes of ephemera darted to and fro . . . at night, the fireflies came out among the shrubs on the banks; the cicale at noon-day kept up their hum; the aziola [owl] cooed in the quiet evening."[27] Amelia Curran invited herself to stay, but Shelley was in a misanthropic mood so Mary put her off. Once when they were sitting outside to enjoy the twilight, she harkened him to the aziola. "And I," Shelley wrote, "who thought / This Aziola was some tedious woman / Asked, 'Who is Aziola?' How elate / I felt to know that it was nothing human, / No mockery of myself to fear or hate: / And Mary saw my soul, / And laughed, and said, 'Disquiet yourself not; / 'Tis nothing but a little downy owl."

Taaffe visited; Mavrocordato came in military dress, and sent the latest news from Greece; "they conquer and cut to pieces the forces sent against them . . . ,"[28] said Mary ferociously. When he embarked at Leghorn she sent him a farewell letter, and he promised to have future proclamations translated and sent her. Thereafter she followed his part in the war with urgent concern and considerable pride.

Mary treasured the memory of Pugnano as the perfection of Italy: the Williamses' villa with its cool marble halls, cypresses in the gardens, "the perfume" of surrounding wooded mountains, and the two couples playing "like children." "Very soft society," Shelley told Claire of Edward and Jane, "after authors & pretenders to philosophy."[29] Willowy as a dark-haired Botticelli maiden, Jane did everything gracefully: her hair, her clothing, the decoration of her home, her "pretty" singing, what both Shelleys had taken to be lack of animation and intellectual interest they now saw as "beautiful simplicity." Though Jane much preferred Shelley, she admired Mary's beauty and gifts, and Mary counted her a true friend.

Edward was genuinely devoted to Mary, so much so that he teased about her, to him, novel concept of candor. "According Mary's doctrine," he wrote Shelley when he submitted a play for his corrections, "the more faults you find the greater [I] shall consider the proofs of sincerity";[30] Mary preserved this little note. They exchanged locks of hair, had confidential conversations. "Dearest girl," he wrote on a memento, "I shall not forget!" After Shelley she loved him better than anyone. Both Edward and Jane followed Shelley in treating her as the center of an admiring little court.

Shelley's bad health and febrility were their joint concerns. Mary and Jane relieved his side pains by mesmerism, which Medwin had taught them. Apparently quoting Mary, Edward wrote his friend Edward John Trelawny that Byron and other authorities considered Shelley to be the premier living imaginative poet, that Byron sought his advice and had been influenced by him in recent works, adding that if Shelley wrote more intelligibly he would be popular. On hearing of Keats's recent death in Rome, Shelley wrote his great elegy, *Adonais,* but was disturbed that *Queen Mab,* which he now called "villanous trash" injurious to liberalism, had been published in a pirated edition — though to his relief without the "foolish" Dedication to Harriet.

Basking in this gaiety and closeness, "I was no longer the silent and the serious —"[31] Mary later recalled. Nevertheless, her sense of pursuing fate persisted. When Percy, a sturdy child, had a high fever from teething, she sent for Vaccà in panic. One perfect evening with Shelley and the Williamses, "when the evening star panted in the west . . . ," she suddenly said, "oh that I might now die — & escape the evils in store for me."[32] On Shelley's twenty-ninth birthday "7 years are now gone —" she noted. "I will not prognosticate evil — We have had enough of it. . . . May it be a polar day — Yet that too has an end. —"

Since late winter, Mary had been working full-tilt on *Valperga,* a far longer work than *Frankenstein;* "I will wait until the flood ebbs and then channel my thoughts,"[33] she jotted in Italian in a workbook. In late July she finished the third and last volume, and began copying the whole for the press. "Be severe in your corrections & expect severity from me, your sincere admirer," said Shelley, who had not yet read the work. "I flatter myself you have composed something unequalled in its kind, & that not content with the honours of your birth & your hereditary aristocracy, you will add still higher renown to your name."[34] He was equally proud of a recent French translation by Jules Saladin of *Frankenstein,* which was reviewed by some critics with disgust at its unfeminine subject and treatment,[35] by others with recognition of its originality and power.

Mary had sent Hunt a narrative in Italian of a colorful episode in Florentine history for *The Indicator,* his new magazine, which failed before he could publish it. Now, when the Gisbornes visited before leaving permanently for England, she gave them a children's story, "Maurice," for her father. "Very pretty," he wrote sulkily, but did not publish it on grounds that it was too short to print alone and would not bring much money.

Claire spent a day at the baths en route to summer in Leghorn with new Florentine friends; the Botjis had introduced her into society where she was a great success, since no one knew she was Byron and Shelley's Miss Clairmont and she was extremely attractive. She had accepted her independent life, and was learning German in order to become a German aristocrat's paid companion. Byron, however, had put Allegra in a convent school, to which Claire furiously objected and urged the Shelleys to do likewise. But unbeknownst to her, Shelley had invited Byron to Pisa, since she was living in Florence. Both Shelleys were unwilling to antagonize Byron, and were convinced that diplomacy was essential given his hatred of Claire and possession of Allegra. Shelley wrote Byron that if he ever changed his mind about the convent school, Mary "intreated" him to believe that she was most anxious to help place the child in another situation.

Meanwhile, Emilia Viviani's parents had forbidden Shelley to see her, and Mary observed his mournfulness with silent irony. Probably around June 26, the seventh anniversary of their declaration of love in St. Pancras graveyard, he drafted a poem recalling that evening when he stood silent, and Mary had broken the impasse and united them. He asks her to speak again:

> We are not happy, sweet! our state
>   Is strange and full of doubt and fear:
> More need of words that ills abate; —
>   Reserve or censure come not near
> Our sacred friendship, lest there be
> No solace left for thee and me.
>
> Gentle and good and mild thou art,
>   Nor can I live if thou appear
> Aught but thyself, or turn thine heart
>   Away from me, or stoop to wear
> The mask of scorn, although it be
> To hide the love thou feel'st for me.

Apparently he did not show her this draft,[36] because he knew their distance stemmed not only from her inhibitions since their children's deaths, but also, as he wrote John Gisborne the following summer, from his own conviction that it was his duty to deceive Mary — as he had deceived

Harriet. "Sacred friendship," however, meant telling her everything, about Emilia, Claire, and thoughts and feelings that can hardly be shared without destroying a loving spouse unless the purpose is full rapprochement. Shelley wanted it both ways.

Though Mary was to accuse herself of "cold neglect," when Shelley did confide in her, partial and manipulative as it was, she responded wholeheartedly. On August 3 he left to visit Byron, who was still in Ravenna with his mistress, Countess Teresa Guiccioli, but first he went secretly in the opposite direction to Leghorn, where he spent his birthday with Claire. When he got to Ravenna, he wrote "Dearest mine" to have Claire visit during his absence but not to tell her he was with Byron.

That same letter contained news that horrified Mary. From Hoppner, Byron had heard Elise Foggi's story about Shelley and Claire, which Byron now confided to Shelley and which he and the Hoppners believed. It was, Shelley wrote Mary, "the old story" that he and Claire were lovers, which if true would have been "a great error & imprudence," plus new charges (which he had concealed from Mary for a year) that Elena was their child whom they tried to abort and put in a foundling home — "unutterable crimes" — and that Claire and Shelley had abused Mary shamefully; he said nothing about Elise's accusation that Claire had encouraged him to leave Mary: "imagine my despair of good," he wrote, "how . . . so weak & sensitive a nature as mine can run further the gauntlet through this hellish society of men . . . *You* should write to the Hoppners a letter refuting the charge in case you believe & know & can prove that it is false."[37]

Mary responded on cue. Fighting tears, she sent him a vehement letter ' to show Byron before forwarding it to Mrs. Hoppner, which bears the physical signs of her shock and which she had sufficient acuity to send as it was, to be more convincing.

> You knew Shelley, you saw his face, & could you believe . . . the testimony of a girl [Elise] whom you despised? . . .
>
> It is all a lie — Claire is timid; she always shewed respect even for me — poor dear girl! . . . if ever we quarrelled, which was seldom, it was I, and not she, that was harsh, and our instantaneous reconciliations were sincere & affectionate.
>
> Need I say that the union between my husband and myself has ever been undisturbed — Love caused our first imprudences, love which improved by esteem, a perfect trust one in the other. . . .
>
> . . . Claire has been seperated from us for about a year . . . her connexion with us made her manifest as the . . . Mother of Al-

legra. . . . she wished to appear . . . [worthy] of fulfilling the maternal duties — you ought to have paused before you tried to
convince the father of her child of such unheard of atrocities. . . .

Those who know me well believe my simple word . . . I swear
by the life of my child, by my blessed & beloved child, that I
know these accusations to be false —[38]

Shelley then minimized the matter, and it is doubtful that Byron showed
this letter to Mrs. Hoppner, who in any case in 1834 was still telling
people that Claire had had a child by Shelley. While Mary did not write
the complete truth, generously overdid her defense of Claire at her own
expense, and denied the disturbances in her marriage, she did not falsify
what she believed to be its essence: love, esteem, and perfect trust. Indeed,
her response may have made him know he would never leave her: "beloved
friend —" she wrote him, "our bark is indeed tempest tost but love me
as you have ever done & God preserve my child to me and our enemies
shall not be too much for us.

"Consider well if Florence be a fit residence for us —" she added, since
Claire would be there. "I love I own to face danger — but I would not
be imprudent —"[39] However, Byron, who seemed eager to see Mary, had
agreed to move to Pisa. It was time, Shelley proposed, to put down roots,
urge the Williamses to stay, and "to form for ourselves a society of our
own class, as much as possible, in intellect or in feelings."[40] Mary agreed,
and the couple resolved to settle in Pisa.

12 "Pisa" — The Last Chapter with Shelley

DURING THE AUTUMN of 1821 at the baths, unlike the previous stormy year, the weather was so radiant and the events so happy that Mary Shelley took them as a hopeful sign for settling in Pisa. She and Shelley were probably making love again, at least on occasions. Countess Guiccioli had preceded Byron by two months, and on September 1 drove out to meet Mary, who found her pretty, amiable, and "unpretentious," and made her welcome. On the eighth, Emilia Viviani's wedding day, Shelley took Mary and the Williamses to the remote, ruggedly beautiful Gulf of Spezia to explore sites for the next summer. Shortly after, on a hot, pellucid day, the four rode horseback up Monte Pisano to an old fortified town, picnicked on flowered grass and rested in the shade, rapt at the felicity of their friendship and the view.*

Mary was so busy copying *Valperga* and furnishing her new house in town during October that she did not touch her journal. On the twenty-fifth, a week before Byron's arrival, they moved into Pisa. Though they had one tenth his income (and Shelley knew that his own debts in England totaled over twenty-two hundred pounds), they meant to live partway up to him in their first permanent home since Marlow: the entire top floor of Tre Palazzi di Chiesa, with a panoramic view, and directly across the Arno from his historic Palazzo Lanfranchi. They splurged on the furnishings, which, with their portable belongings, included seven beds, Percy's small one, a sofa bed for Shelley's study, implements for four fireplaces, bookshelves and work tables, thirty-two chairs, Mary's looking glass and bidet, and a *batterie de cuisine*.[1] From Mrs. Gisborne in England Mary ordered large damask tablecloths, counters and letters for Percy, who turned two in November, and their box desks. Peacock sent the rest of their library. Besides Maria and Caterina, the staff consisted of a cook and manservant. The Williamses rented a house near theirs.

* Mary Shelley described this day in "Recollections of Italy" (1824).

Byron was ensconced *en prince* with numerous servants, his famous hulking gondolier Tita, superb horses, and his menagerie of geese and other curious animals, while Countess Guiccioli lived nearby with her father, Count Ruggero Gamba, and young brother Pietro, whom Mary liked exceedingly. At Shelley's instigation, Byron had agreed that Leigh Hunt should emigrate to Pisa with his family that winter to edit a new magazine for which they would all write, later titled *The Liberal,* and assigned them the ground floor of Lanfranchi the modest decor of which, rather to her annoyance, he delegated Mary to oversee. Medwin, drawn by Byron's presence, arrived in late November.

Claire had spent October at the baths, staying mostly with the Williamses before returning to Florence just as Byron arrived in Pisa; the former lovers were close to irrational about one another. To mollify her resentment of the Shelleys' association with Byron, Shelley told her they hoped gradually to get him to remove Allegra from the convent school, which they too considered an utterly noxious education. This Claire accepted from Shelley, even his strategy of defaming her to Byron in order to disarm him: "He told himself . . . ," she later informed Mary, "that it was absolutely neccessary he should traduce me and that he expected I should submit . . ."[2] But she fumed over Mary, telling her that she should not be seen in public with Byron's paramour, to which Mary retorted that Claire was invoking the identical hypocritical moralism that Byron applied to Claire. Mary, who hoped to get Teresa on their side, began soon after she met the countess; she "never mentions Allegrina's mother," Teresa wrote Byron, "but she often speaks of Allegrina with the utmost concern."[3]

In fact, even if there was ambivalence on both sides, both Shelleys were eager to be with Byron, as he with them. Mary rightly said that she was "part of the Elect" for the next six months, which many of the participants were to remember as a summit of their lives. Byron's glamour, his flow of new poetry, his conversation, his captivating and maddening personality, were uniquely electrifying. That winter Mary resumed her role of his copyist for *Sardanapalus, The Two Foscari,* and *Werner,* and was so struck by the last that she broke off to read it to Shelley and Edward.

She saw less of Byron than she liked, however. Teresa Guiccioli had separated from her husband for love of Byron, who had become her *cavalier servente.* This Italian relationship demanded the lover's total abnegation, which, Mary observed, "no matrimonial exigence can equal" (Byron had stopped work on *Don Juan,* which Teresa considered pernicious), and studious uninterest in other females. While the woman's life revolved about her lover, with jealousy and quarrels, the more dramatic the more admirable, both were bound to fidelity, a system Mary preferred to secret adultery. To maintain a degree of independence, Byron hosted a masculine circle of which Shelley was a reluctant part and professed affectionate scorn for "womankind."

In the afternoons, "Our good cavaliers flock together," Mary wrote Marianne Hunt, "and as they do not like *fetching a walk with the absurd womankind*, Jane . . . and I are off together, and talk morality and pluck violets by the way."[4] Then she rode horseback with Teresa or drove out in Teresa's carriage to watch the men shoot at targets, returning with them in cavalcade and all Pisa staring. When the men went to Byron's drinking suppers, she attended Teresa's *conversazione*. Considering their different cultures and educations, the two got on well, speaking French or Italian. Teresa tended to judge Mary as a wife, an excellent "esprit practique" to an unworldly, eccentric husband, but she was impressed by the Shelleys' intellectual companionship and Byron's respect for Mary, and thought of becoming studious if it would tie Byron closer, until he, doubtless horrified, assured her otherwise. Possibly it was due to Mary's persuasion that Teresa now permitted Byron to continue *Don Juan*.

After Mary completed her fair copy of *Valperga* on December 1, she put off planning another novel and went back to her studies. These studies included Greek and advanced Italian, with masters — Homer, Plato's *Ion*, Tacitus, Virgil, Dante, Machiavelli's *History of Florence;* memoirs and letters of the period of Charles I, probably in aid of Shelley's drama on the subject; Bacon's *Apophthagmes* and *Naturall Historie* and Kant's *Physische Geographicie,* natural science being a new interest. She reread Milton's *Samson Agonistes,* Fénelon's *Télémaque* and Rousseau's *Emile;* among newer publications, the novels of Thomas Hope, Sir Walter Scott, and Lady Morgan, and Ugo Foscolo's *Last Letters of Jacopo Ortis*. She was particularly enthusiastic over Alessandro Manzoni's "Cinque Maggio," an ode to Napoleon upon his death that was circulating in manuscript before publication.[5]

In a surge of hope for Greek restoration to her former glory, Shelley had composed *Hellas,* which Mary considered one of his greatest works. But his Charles I drama did not go well, and he was so overcome by envy, wonder, and despair at Byron's current poems and popularity — the only living poet worth contesting, he told Mary — that he wrote only occasional verses, one an abject sonnet to the older poet: "the worm beneath the sod / May lift itself in homage of the God." Antisocial except for Byron's command performances, he dressed so oddly that Claire would not be seen with him on the street when she visited, and he slipped off for hours into the pine woods outside town.

The Shelleys had arrived at considerable autonomy, by mutual consent.

On December 10, "A divine, cold, tramontano day," Mary went shopping, walked with the Williamses and Teresa to the public garden; Medwin came to tea. "Afterwards we are alone," she noted as a special happy event; she and Shelley read Herodotus together, he read Chaucer to her, and they finished off with Tacitus. But she rarely recorded his daily work in her journal, and he completed their Spinoza translation with Edward, who became his copyist.

At the turn of 1822 Mary was so busy that for the first time she did not make a list of her and Shelley's reading in her journal. Prince and Princess Argiropoulo and a group of their compatriots arrived for the winter. In addition, there were two newcomers who would be prominent in Mary's future. Edward John Trelawny, a friend of the Williamses and of Medwin, was infinitely the more original, a Herculean twenty-nine-year-old who looked more like a Moorish marauder than the younger son of a titled Cornish family, and talked to match: "he is clever —," Mary wrote Maria Gisborne, "for his moral qualities I am yet in the dark he is a strange web which I am endeavouring to unravel —"[6] using a metaphor more intuitively keen than she understood for many years.

Trelawny, who resented the inferior status and income awarded a younger son, had accomplished little, had no specific aims except for dreams of being a unique machismo character, and was seeking attachment to solid eminences: Byron, Mary because of her "pedigree of genius" and *Frankenstein*, and Shelley, many of whose opinions he was to adopt. A wild, rebellious boy, he had joined the Royal Navy, served in the Indian Ocean, and retired at twenty. After a few years of marriage, he divorced his wife for adultery, left two daughters in England, and wandered about on five hundred pounds a year while melding his fantasies into a lurid *alter vita*, in which he deserted the navy to join a pirate chief in the Indian Ocean for butcheries, buried treasure, beautiful female victims. To hear him, he had reluctantly cleaned his nails of grime, blood, and gunpowder, asked only to foul them again, and being devastating to women though never bound by them, had bastards in every port. As Byron amusedly recognized, Trelawny was a signal example of life following art, specifically Byron's Giaour, Corsair, and Lara.[7] But for all his incurable mendacity and braggadocio, his gruff-sailor manner and streak of bloodthirsty crudeness, his spotty education, he was generous, brave, and a remarkable storyteller.

Mary was the one of the Pisan circle who took Trelawny seriously: as a sort of genie whose "horrific" and comic if dubiously true adventures stimulated her imagination, unlike the "everyday sleepiness" of ordinary talk; as a character she did not immediately understand and therefore enjoyed studying; and as a man whose good heart she and Shelley trusted.

Emboldened by her sexual reputation, he tried his luck, but accepted her rebuff. Indeed, he was one of the few men she ever knew who scorned the female ideal, and became attached to her as a fellow "cross grained" character, who was "not of the sect who profess or practise meekness, humility, and patience."[8] When he confided that he was lonely, indolent, and discontent, she gave him Godwin's works to read, told him in her father's words that he was devoid of two vices, insincerity and an abject, servile nature, and bore on "untired," he said gratefully, "with my spleen, humours, and violence."

The second, quite different personage, Mary's first great lady, wintered in Pisa with what Edward Williams called a "litter" of seven daughters. Mrs. Charles Beauclerk, daughter of the Duchess of Leinster, was a Regency brunette beauty of forty known for her gallantries, and the half sister of one of Mary's heroes, the dead Lord Edward Fitzgerald. Medwin, whose family and Shelley's were the Beauclerks' neighbors in Sussex, took Shelley to call on her, and despite Mary's notoriety Mrs. Beauclerk was pleased to make her acquaintance. Her adolescent daughter Georgiana was especially taken with Mary.

This elect grouping flared brilliantly for its very instability. While Byron was the undisputed sun around whom all revolved, he and Shelley, two antagonistic personalities, each dominated constellations of talents ranging from Mary Shelley to more or less cultivated amateurs, flanked by the circles of Mrs. Beauclerk and the Greeks; weaving in and out were Trelawny's eccentric comet, Medwin, and visiting luminaries like Sgricci and the elderly poet Samuel Rogers, who had known Mary's mother.

Proudly they played to the great, duller audience of Pisa and all Europe; dazzled, envious, many hostile. The Grand Duke's court being in residence, the duke himself walked to and fro outside Lanfranchi hoping to catch a glimpse of Byron. The conservative English press had a field day excoriating the Shelleys and Byron in their conveniently assembled League of Incest and Atheism (to promote which, according to *Blackwood's,* was Shelley's purpose in *Epipsychidion*), with "vain and vulgar" Hunt in the offing — whose own reputation for incest led Shelley to warn him not to bring Bessy Kent to Italy. Byron challenged Southey to a duel (via a friend in England who did not deliver it), partly because of Southey's old charge that Mary was Byron's lover.

At twenty-four, holding an eminent place in this company, Mary Shelley was in her young prime, and "so full of spirits & life," she later recalled to Trelawny, "that methinks . . . you must have thought me even a little wild"; "I had nothing to desire."[9] Percy was blooming, Shelley in fair health; she felt she was the loved center of a beloved inner circle of Shelley and the Williamses, sought affection from other people, had Medwin and Trelawny regularly to dinner, attended the opera in Teresa's box. Since Shelley shrank from social festivities, Trelawny squired her to the riotous three-day Carnival for which she got up a Turkish costume, like Cythna in *The Revolt of Islam* or her Wollstonecraftian character Safie in *Franken-stein*. Jane was stunning in genuine Hindustani dress.

Byron decided they should play *Othello* to all Pisa in his great hall at Lanfranchi and organized the perfect cast: Mary the faithful Desdemona, Trelawny the violent Moor, Byron a sinister Iago, Jane Emilia, Edward Cassio, Medwin Roderigo. They rehearsed late into the night, and once Trelawny went to strangle Mary with such a roar that he woke Jane, who had fallen asleep on a sofa. As Teresa could not participate and besides was jealous of Mary, she stopped this production.

"The most striking feature in her face," Trelawny later wrote of Mary Shelley in this period, "was her calm, grey eyes":

> She was rather under the English standard of woman's height, very fair and light-haired, witty, social, and animated in the society of friends . . . she had the power of expressing her thoughts in varied and appropriate words, derived from familiarity with the works of our vigorous old writers.[10]

"She was delicately fair . . . ," Jane Williams was to write in a later memorial, "and her warm and vivid imagination decked all things with its own bright hues. while on her expansive brow sat reason triumphant over youth."[11] The Greek Count George de Metaxa did her "miniature" in French: "These are the prettiest little ways, the prettiest little looks, the prettiest little figure . . . the prettiest little movements in the world . . . how prettily she expresses herself and if in conversation after some little story or joke in good taste or some kindness of hers, there is an opportunity to talk, feel or test her sensibility, her pretty eyes and all her person express it so well that one sees that her soul is in accord . . ." Unable, as was common, to integrate her femininity and powers, "You will excuse if when finished will not say all what deserves . . . ," he concluded in English, "the heart conceived that the pen can not describe what he feels . . . you are the goddess of Athenes . . ."[12]

If Mary put aside writing, she was engrossed in an "animated volume of life," thronged with new people and situations, which she craved and yet protected herself against, for she had always been sensitive to them and was peculiarly raw. She could never forget her dead William and Clara, or her hostage to Fortune, Percy — "se Dio vuole," she added whenever she spoke of his robust health and liveliness. Autumn was her favorable season, she had decided, spring the ominous, and though she joked about it to Claire, she was in deadly earnest. At times she wondered if that winter's were gallows pleasures and wished to die before they ended.

Furthermore, she had led a high-minded existence in an isolated, minuscule circle, needed to be solitary, and to integrate new experience with her aspirations: "When I would tear the veil from this strange world & pierce with eagle eyes beyond the sun —" she wrote in her journal, "when every idea strange & changeful is another step in the ladder by which I would climb . . ."[13] She took to sitting up late in the "hermitage" of her room to sort things out.

Among the elect there was more friction, vying for position, and power playing than Mary had ever encountered. Trelawny was fond of Edward but disliked Jane, hated Medwin, whom he accused Mary of raving about, while she rather disliked Tom, who was Jane's particular friend. Medwin, who had tried to marry a fifteen-year-old heiress, pursued Mrs. Beauclerk and hinted that he was successful, borrowed from Shelley and never repaid, courted Byron and elsewhere disparaged Teresa. Byron got drunk with him and to Mary's disgust talked even about his relations with his half sister, though he knew Medwin was taking notes for a book. At times Mary wished she and Shelley could go off and live by themselves on an island.

Nevertheless, she began short-lived, tentative forays into the English world represented by the colony in Pisa. Medwin and others were presented to the Grand Duke, which Mary thought might be amusing. Shelley would not make the arrangements, "and so we go on in our obscure way —" she wrote Mrs. Gisborne, "the Williams's live the same life as us, and without a sigh, we see Medwin depart for his evening assemblies — Yet though I go not to the house of feasting, I have gone to the house of prayer —"[14]

Vaccà had reported that their first-floor neighbor, Dr. George Frederick Nott, an English clergyman, had called Shelley a scoundrel. Taaffe repeated this all over town, whereupon Nott denied it via Medwin and supposed this was why Mary never attended his Sunday services. She accompanied the Williamses there once a month for three months to prove she believed him, knowing that he was soon leaving Pisa, until she heard he had preached against Shelley's atheism. She challenged him, he denied it, and the English gossiped the more.

Hogg, to whom Mrs. Gisborne showed Mary's letter about Nott, affected to be scandalized, as Mary had scorned his own rare churchgoing. Actually, she had gotten herself into a false position trying to be polite, for simultaneously she was attacking Christianity for Byron's benefit. Often a target for believers, Byron had been sent Charles Leslie's *Short and Easy Method with the Deists,* a famous demonstration of the truth of Christianity by "true" biblical miracles as distinct from "the Fabulous Histories of the Heathen Deities." Leslie's proofs were "staggering," Byron declared, and challenged Shelley to answer them.

Both the Shelleys wrote answers, his a serious argument that he did not finish, telling Mary that Byron needed the moral check of religion. She appealed rather to Byron's sense of the ridiculous in her sketch "The Necessity of a Belief in the Heathen Mythology to a Christian," in which she juxtaposed Jewish scripture and Greek myths and claimed they were equally plausible: Jupiter revealed himself to the Greeks; Jehovah to the Jews; Mercury to Priam, Calypso, and Ulysses; archangels to Abraham, Lot, and Tobit. "If the revelations of God to the Jews on Mt. Sinai had been more peculiar & impressive than some of those to the Greeks, they w^d not immediately after have worshipped a calf. A latitude in revelation . . ."[15] Byron was later to remark that he had doubts of Leslie's demonstration.

In January Mary ventured on "feasting" in her own house and decided to give a party with the English tenor Sinclair to entertain, until the horrified Shelley deputed Edward to dissuade her. During February, however, she realized that the world was not for her. On the seventh Trelawny escorted her to her first great ball, one of several given by Mrs. Beauclerk for her older, marriageable daughters, with a crowd in full dress, irresistible music, dancing, compliments, laughter, masses of candles and flowers. Shifting sensations rushed over Mary: intense excitement, delight and hope, tearfulness, sudden renewed exhilaration. On such an evening, "life seems to weigh itself —," she wrote in her journal after she got home late that night, "and hosts of memories & imaginations thrus[t] into one scale makes the other kick the beam:

> You remember what you have felt — what you have dreamt — yet you dwell on the shadowy side and lost hopes, and death such as you have seen it . . . The Time that was, is, & will be presses upon you & standing [in] the centre of a moving circle you "— slide giddily as the world reels" . . . The Enthusiast supresses her tears — crushes her opening thoughts and —
>
> But all is changed — some word some look exite . . . laughter dances in the eyes & the spirits rise proportionably high . . .

"Sometimes I awaken from my ordinary monotony — & my thoughts flow," she noted the following night, "until as it is exquisite pain to stop the flowing of the blood, so is it painful to check expression & make the

A French engraving of Mary Wollstonecraft by Roy;
it is not known whether this was done
from life or was imaginary.

William Godwin at the height of his fame
by an admirer, James Northcote.

"Shelley and Mary in St. Pancras Churchyard."
A Victorian conception by W. P. Frith, who sketched the site
in the 1870s and modeled the heads on works owned
by Sir Percy and Lady Shelley.

An unsigned miniature,
possibly Mary Wollstonecraft Shelley,
inscribed "Mary Shelley 1815" on the back.

LORD BYRON AT THE VILLA DIODATI NEAR GENEVA 1816.

Clear, placid Leman! thy contrasted lake   Which warns me, with its stillness, to forsake
With the wide world I dwelt in, is a thing   Earth's troubled waters, for a purer spring

Childe Harold. LXXXV. Canto III.

Two of several artists' conceptions of the famous Geneva summer of 1816. Mary Shelley,
then Mary Godwin, was often on the balcony depicted in "Lord Byron at the Villa Diodati
near Geneva, 1816." In the 1833 "Promenade sur Le Lac de Genève" by I. A. Deveria,
she is probably supposed to be the seated young woman clasping a child.

This miniature of Mary Shelley was painted by Reginald Easton after her death
but probably bears some resemblance to her at about twenty-two. Easton's
sources were a pencil sketch made by Edward Ellerker Williams in 1821–1822,
Mary Shelley's death mask, and the advice of Sir Percy and Lady Shelley.
An engraving after the miniature was printed in France.

Percy Bysshe Shelley, a revision by Alfred Clint of the 1819 portrait by Amelia Curran, and probably a better likeness since Mary Shelley and Jane Williams supervised Clint.

Lord Byron, painted by Richard Westall.

Amelia Curran's portraits of William Shelley, aged three,
painted in Rome in 1819 just before the child's death,
and of twenty-one-year-old Claire Clairmont.
Miss Curran's portrait of Mary Shelley was later
in Trelawny's possession, but it has disappeared.

Mary Shelley's draft of a Lucianic satire in the form of a letter
from Bloody Queen Mary congratulating the Duchesse d'Angoulême on the
slaughter of French pro-revolutionaries (1818). Note her sketches of trees.
Her drawing of a man lying on a pallet is possibly meant to be
the murdered father of Beatrice Cenci (1819).

Casa Magni in a moderate surf. By Henry Roderick Newman.

Though Mary Shelley was not actually present, she kneels at the left while Byron, Hunt, and Trelawny mourn in "The Cremation of Shelley's Body," by Fournier and Gérôme.

William Hazlitt and Thomas Allsop saw Mary Shelley's "beautiful and very peculiar expression" in Titian's *Young Woman at the Toilet*, while Thornton Hunt said that her best portrait, except for her "tall and intellectual forehead" and sweet smile, was this bust of a Roman lady — "Clytie" to Victorians, with whom it was a widely reproduced favorite.

Le Romantisme ou le Monstre littéraire by J. Vigné.
Here an androgynous *Frankenstein*'s monster, costumed in a toga
like T. P. Cooke, who first played the role in 1823, but with
long flowing hair, symbolizes the monstrosity of Romanticism
and Romantic authors such as Mary Shelley.

The Last Man, an oil painting by John Martin.

Some of Mary Shelley's close friends.
Edward John Trelawny by Joseph Severn; Jane Williams by Alexander Blaikley;
Mrs. Leicester Stanhope in a celebrated portrait by C. Macpherson, engraved
for the Annual *Forget-Me-Not* for 1833; and Leigh Hunt by Margaret Gillies.

William Godwin in old age by Daniel Maclise.

Possible sketches of Mary Shelley, William Godwin,
and Edward John Trelawny by Richard Rothwell,
in a Rothwell sketchbook.

Mary Shelley at forty-two, painted by her friend Richard Rothwell
shortly after she finished her editions of Shelley's complete works,
and exhibited at the Royal Academy in May 1840.

Photograph of Sir Percy Florence Shelley
in middle age. He was said to have had his
mother's nose and his father's eyes.

Sir Percy and Lady Shelley in costume for one
of the plays they presented at their theater.

Monument to Percy Bysshe Shelley and Mary Shelley at Christchurch Priory, Dorset, by Henry Weekes, and an engraving of the monument.

overflowing mind return to its usual channel — I feel a kind of tenderness to those . . . who awaken this train & touch a chord so full of harmony & thrilling music . . ."

But by the twenty-fifth, after calling on Mrs. Beauclerk, she knew where she stood:

> . . . The most contemptible of all lives is where you live in the world & none of your passions or affections are called into action — I am convinced I could not live thus . . . Let me love the trees — the skies & the ocean & that all encompassing spirit of which I may soon become a part . . . where goodness, kindness & talent are, let me love & admire them at their just rate . . . & above all let me fearlessly descend into the remotest caverns of my own mind — carry the torch of selfknowledge . . . but too happy if I dislodge any evil spirit or ensh[r]ine a new deity . . .

"Dearest *Children* . . ." she wrote the Hunts, who were delayed by lack of money, winter storms, and Marianne's illness, "under the bright sky of dear Italy — My poor Marianne will get well and you all be light hearted & happy —"[16] More than any of her intimates she loved and felt at home in Italy. When Edward first met Teresa, Mary wrote Mrs. Gisborne, her formal politesse drove him crazy, and he stayed away from *conversazione* rather than learn the necessary expressions, which Mary tried to "drub into him"; " 'ora la levo l'incommodo.' 'Incommodo! no, anzi è un piacare.' — the answer alone makes him mad . . ."[17] Her servants addressed her in the familiar second person; Maria embraced her, drew up a chair, and joined the conversation; Caterina was marvelous with Percy, who spoke only Italian.

As for England, "even at this distance it sometimes strikes me with sudden fright to think that any chain binds me to it."[18] Shelley's *Adonais* had been abused in the *Literary Gazette*. Everyone they knew, the Gisbornes reported, was insipid, intellectually dull, or "a century behind hand," save for Hogg and Peacock, and Peacock had taken a job at the East India Company and married an innocent, conventional former sweetheart.

Mrs. Godwin was so violent against Mary that Godwin asked Mary to address her letters to him elsewhere and broke with the Gisbornes. To pay the four hundred pounds Godwin still demanded, Mary had tried for months to get the sum for *Valperga* from Ollier, who backed and filled; Shelley's poems had sold so pitifully little that Ollier had lost money, and Shelley, misguidedly, did not want the novel published with "Author of Frankenstein" on the title page lest its chance for popularity be jeopardized. Finally, when Godwin was about to be evicted from Skinner Street, Mary sent him the manuscript to sell and keep the profits, a truly generous gift, he acknowledged, though against nature unless Shelley actually did possess a fortune — which Godwin had talked himself into believing. "I long to hear some news of it —" she wrote Mrs. Gisborne, "as with an authors vanity I want to see it in print & hear the praises of my friends —"[19] But Godwin put off publication, hoping to get a better price after his current emergency ended.

For the Shelley-Williams boating summer on the Gulf of Spezia, which Byron intended to join, Trelawny was having two yachts built in Genoa by his friend Daniel Roberts, a retired navy captain. Shelley's, named *Don Juan* by Byron somewhat to Shelley's chagrin, was to be twenty-four feet long and swift as a seabird for racing Byron's *Bolivar,* a heavy ocean-going vessel with cannon, which Trelawny would captain; Edward bet Byron five crowns that *Bolivar* would not sail eleven knots an hour.[20] Mary said to Jane, "laughing each to the other, 'Our husbands decide without asking our consent, or having our concurrence; for, to tell you the truth, I hate this boat, though I say nothing.' Said Jane, 'So do I; but speaking would be useless, and only spoil their pleasure.' "[21]

Summering with Byron was problematic, however, for their relations had become tense. Shelley had sent Hunt money for his voyage, which Hunt had used up. When Shelley, in debt to Byron and jealous, resisted asking Byron for more, Hunt asked Byron directly, for which sum Byron accepted a post-obit pledge from Shelley — having become parsimonious since his recent inheritance of a large estate. Hunt's only income was a share in *The Examiner,* now edited by his brother, and the prospective *Liberal,* while Byron half-regretted that project, which depended entirely on his participation, and read Shelley letters from Tom Moore and other English friends warning that he would be tarred by his association with Shelley and degraded by Hunt.

Moreover, Claire was seeing Elise Foggi in Florence, and Elise told her that Byron had said Shelley was Allegra's father, which so enraged Shelley that he might have challenged Byron, except that if Byron killed him Mary and Claire would be penniless. But since Hunt needed *The Liberal,* Shelley could not even break with Byron and settled on writing a new will substituting Hogg for Byron as executor. Elise also denied having said that Elena was Claire's child by Shelley, and agreed to deny it in writing to Mrs. Hoppner; Claire asked Mary's advice about phrasing this disclaimer, which Mrs. Hoppner never credited.

In addition, Claire, who was thinking of leaving Italy, had a premonition that she would never see Allegra again, that her child would die in the convent — which the Shelleys discounted — and begged Byron to let her see Allegra before she left. Shrugging this off as histrionics, Byron refused. At Mary's instance Claire came to discuss her plans. After she returned to Florence, Shelley's appeal for her sent Byron into a tantrum, whereupon Claire asked the Shelleys to help her to kidnap Allegra by force if necessary. By now Mary was hot "to extricate all belonging to me from the hands of LB, whose hypoccrisy & cruelty rouse one's soul from its depths," but advised waiting for some change, as they had no money, Byron would hunt Claire down, and might kill Shelley in a duel, while Shelley added in the same letter that he was shocked at Claire's "thoughtless violence. . . . give up this idle pursuit after shadows . . . Live from day to day . . . cultivate literature & liberal ideas to a certain extent . . . let the *past* be past."[22]

Shelley was speaking of his own pursuit as well, for he had finally lost his illusions about Emilia, starting before her marriage when she asked for money, which he had borrowed from Byron, and accelerating afterward to shamed revulsion when she hinted they could be lovers. That winter he told Mary about the money, withdrew *Epipsychidion* from publication, and could not bear to look at it. Hunt teased him about having fallen in love with someone who did not deserve it, and Shelley, seeing this as a paradigm of his sometimes more destructive idealism, was left "prey to the reproaches of memory, & the delusions of an imagination not to be restrained."[23] He despaired too at his vile repute, believed he had even less audience than was true and no reason to write, and lost faith in his poetic gift — though he admitted that enmity fascinated him.

He turned to the Williamses for pity and comforting, lamented Emilia's play-acting, his failed career, his "cold home," Mary's "scornful" urging of him to be resolute and believe in his genius — and trained his imagination on the quite ordinary if charming, safe Jane, who adored Edward, and to whom he wrote exquisite verses. Jane was not only ignorant of the Shelleys' entire history, and too shallow to understand them, she was vain, envious of Mary, and devoted to Shelley. She readily believed that Mary was unfeeling and had never made Shelley happy. As Claire before her, she commiserated with him over Mary's faults and encouraged his hidden discontent.

Mary, who trusted Jane's affection for her, waxed sarcastic to Mrs. Gisborne on Shelley's disillusion with Emilia. And yet both the Shelleys felt that they had turned a corner. Mary conceived a child in early March. A month or two later he began a major poem, *The Triumph of Life*.[24] Her *Matilda,* and her current reading of Rousseau, may have contributed to this unfinished work; more significant, it is the first in which the female principle dims and a male, Rousseau, becomes his familiar Spirit. In June he wrote John Gisborne that he was unusually at peace, except for missing his old friends:

> I only feel the want of those who can feel, and understand me. Whether from proximity and the continuity of domestic inter- course, Mary does not. The necessity of concealing from her thoughts that would pain her, necessitates this, perhaps. It is the curse of Tantalus, that a person possessing such excellent powers and so pure a mind as hers, should not excite the sympathy in- dispensable to their application to domestic life.[25]

It is hard to be the wife of a saintly character who lacks a saint's fortitude and straightforwardness. Their old impasse persisted: her shell, his con- viction that he had to deceive her about his needs and feelings, his demand that she perceive them even while his love and praise deluded her into believing all was well. Moreover, it was not that she did not feel, for he knew better, nor that she did not understand (with the exception of his double-dealing), but that she did not always agree with him. When Shelley confided to Hunt in early July that a "cloud" hung over their union, Hunt was probably correct to believe that "it only wanted a certain kind of address to explain to both of them and do away,"[26] and he intended to talk to them.

With spring, Mary began to wait for the season's misfortune. At first she feared for her pregnancy. Since Percy's birth she had had a presentiment that he would be her last child. Now, she tried to "see" her future with a second child, but could not. "I wished it — I tried to figure it to myself but in vain —"[27]

On March 24, there occurred what she hoped would serve as the spring adversity. As she and Teresa followed their cavaliers in Teresa's carriage, an anti-English Pisan dragoon galloped through the men. In the ensuing melée the dragoon knocked Shelley off his horse and slashed another man; Byron's servants wounded the dragoon. Shelley was dazed but unhurt, Teresa fainting, but Mary, to Edward's bafflement, looked "philosophically upon this interesting scene,"[28] actually, in huge relief that it was no worse. Despite outcries against the English among university students and the local soldiery, she went to the hospital and found that the dragoon was improving: "bustle & nothings," she noted. The authorities launched an investigation for which she and Teresa underwent a five-hour examination that struck her as farcical: a "talkative buffoon" officiating, a servile little clerk behind a mountain of papers. But Byron took the in fact serious affair seriously, so she coordinated the writing of several white papers for the police, the press, and friends.

On March 31 her pregnancy seemed irregular and she began to fear again: "Not well," she noted, "read Homer & Telemaque — a hateful day," and was unwell again in early April. But on the twenty-third she thought the real spring misfortune had struck: Allegra. That day Claire, who had come for a visit, left for a two-day excursion with the Williamses to look for summer houses on the Gulf of Spezia, where she was to vacation with the Shelleys; Byron had decided, to their relief, to summer near Leghorn since no port on the sparsely inhabited gulf could accommodate the *Bolivar*. A few hours after Claire left, Teresa came to tell Mary that Allegra had died of typhus in her convent school.

Shelley, who was afraid Claire would go insane or try to kill Byron, determined to move to Spezia the instant she returned and tell her of the tragedy there. Though only one house had been found, Casa Magni at San Terenzo near Lerici, on the twenty-sixth he rushed Mary off with Claire and Percy, while he and the Williamses packed their goods. For five days Mary put up a front with Claire while searching the Spezia area for rentals, until it was clear that only Casa Magni was to be had, and they met the others and all moved in together.

A dreadful week followed. When they told Claire about Allegra, she accused Byron in furious despair of hating her so viciously that he put her child in a fatal situation where no one could blame him for murder, and whatever the others' protestations that Byron was grieving and remorseful that he had ignored their advice to move the child, Claire believed for the rest of her life that he had murdered Allegra. Byron sent her Allegra's portrait and let her decide funeral arrangements, which she agreed should be at Harrow, Byron's former school. Soon she returned to Florence, staying until early June, surprisingly reconciled to her loss, "more tranquil than, when prophesying her disaster," Mary wrote Mrs. Gisborne. Byron gave Mary a letter of Allegra's as her memento of the child.

Once the crisis was over, Mary was horrified by this latest of a series of beloved children's deaths and possessed by the conviction that another disaster was imminent — miscarriage, the loss of Percy, or some unknowable calamity. She fell into the acute anxiety she had suffered just after William's death: fear, exhaustion, hours of dreadful irritability ending in tears.

Like a pegged animal sensing an impending earthquake, she was in terror without knowing why or being able to make herself understood and to flee, for Shelley adored the place and talked of their staying permanently. The magnificent wild site, everything she had always loved, made her weep and shudder. Directly on the water like a ship broached on a Salvator Rosa coastscape, backed by steep wooded hills, Casa Magni looked out at the semienclosed bay of Lerici and beyond to the Mediterranean. To the east, almost inaccessible by land, two miles by boat, was Lerici, whose promontory forms one arm of the bay; to the distant west, Porto Venere; at hand an extensive rocky beach vacant except for the wretched huts of San Terenzo, a fishing hamlet with filthy, raucous inhabitants whose dialect was unintelligible to her Tuscan servants.

"Mary still continues to suffer terribly from languor and hysterical affections . . . ,"[29] Shelley wrote Claire at the end of May. "I regret the loss of Mary's good health and spirits . . . ," Mrs. Mason wrote Shelley. "I dread Claire's being in the same house for a month or two, and wish the W———s were half a mile from you."[30] Too small for two households, Casa Magni was a converted boathouse with a ground floor for storage and second-story living quarters. A large center salon gave onto an open terrace that ran the length of the house over the water. Mary took the left front bedroom, Shelley the right; the Williamses' room was behind his; the children, and Claire when she returned, camped in secondary quarters. The servants were in outhouses. With a young hand for Shelley's boat and Byron's Tita hiding out after the dragoon incident, there were some thirteen adults plus Percy, Dina, and Meddy (the Williamses' children). The Williams and Shelley servants "fought like cats and dogs"; Jane complained they ruined her kitchenware. Food and supplies had to be fetched from Sarzana, a three-mile walk away. Townsfolk, Mary's servants fussed about the primitive conditions; after three weeks the cook and manservant quit.

In heavy weather the exposed house was battered by the elements, swells pounded the beach like artillery, foam hissed among the rocks. But Mary was ridden by fear on normally calm, clear days, when the bathing and walks were perfect, the men hunted, fished, and boated, and in the evenings they sat under the stars on the terrace, singing to Jane's guitar. "There is a terror," she was to write in her fourth novel, *Perkin Warbeck*:

> whose cause is unrevealed even to its victim, which makes the heart beat wildly; and we ask the voiceless thing — wherefore, when the beauty of the visible universe sickens the aching sense; when we beseech the winds to comfort us, and we implore the Invisible for relief . . . ? We endeavour, in our impotent struggle with the sense of coming evil, to soar beyond the imprisoning atmosphere of our own identity. . . . To one thus aware of the misfortune that awaits her, the voice of consolation is a mockery. Yet, even while she knows that the die is cast, she . . . sits smiling on any hope brought to her, as a mother on the physician who talks of recovery while her child dies.[31]

Shelley believed that her fear and nervous irritability were an irrational but excusable revival of her sufferings over their dead children. As she was too proud to explain this to the Williamses, they attributed her state to Allegra's death, her pregnancy, and bad sportsmanship: " . . . I am proud," Edward told Jane, "that *wherever* we may be together you would be cheerful and contented."[32] Jane drew closer to Shelley, who was happier and stronger than in years, and writing her love poems that he warned her not to show Mary; Jane believed that he would have married her if they had been free.

Meanwhile, the Godwins were evicted from Skinner Street and appealed to Mary for money in letters that Shelley intercepted, replying that as her condition was "always distressing, & sometimes alarming" he could not allow them to torture her over her father's situation, "which she would sacrifize all she possesses to remedy."[33] But at Mrs. Mason's urging that things which cannot be concealed are better told promptly, he showed Mary the Godwin mail — which actually relieved her. This, she wrote Mrs. Gisborne, "was the summit and crown of our spring misfortunes"; she joked about Casa Magni's "disorderly order": "you may imagine how ill a large family agrees with my laziness, when accounts and domestic concerns come to be talked of. — 'Ma pazienza.' " They were trying to erase the name "Don Juan," which Byron had had painted on the sail of Shelley's boat:

> — for days and nights full twenty one did Shelley and Edward ponder upon her anabaptism, and the washing out the primeval stain. turpentine, spirits of wine, buccata, all were tried, and it became dappled . . . the piece has been taken out, and reefs put . . . I do not know what L^d B— will say, but Lord and poet as he is, he could not be allowed to make a coal-barge of our boat.[34]

Mary was most at peace on the *Don Juan*, cutting smoothly across the protected bay, when she lay with her head on Shelley's knee, closed her eyes, and forgot everything but the wind and swift motion. "A perfect plaything," the boat had been built to Trelawny's model of an unseaworthy miniature schooner. To a hull so light that it required extra ballast to sit properly in the water, Shelley and Edward had Captain Roberts add bow and mizzen sprits and two top masts for more canvas to make her "sail like a witch." Moreover, she had no decking so that heavy seas would fill her quickly.

On June 13 Trelawny sailed Byron's impressive *Bolivar* into the bay, booming a cannon salute. Mary, who had been feeling unwell, watched from the terrace as Shelley and Edward sailed out to bring him ashore. Two days later she was well enough to sail over to Lerici to inspect the

Bolivar. Trelawny learned of Mary's nervous condition, but Shelley explained that "she had excuses of suffering little known to anyone but himself,"[35] and Trelawny sailed off "loath to part from what I verily believed to have been at that time the most united, and happiest, set of human beings in the whole world."[36]

On the morning of June 16, some three and a half months into her pregnancy, Mary miscarried, hemorrhaging uncontrollably. They kept her conscious by brandy and vinegar massages. In their isolation it was mid-afternoon before they could get ice, and the doctor had not come. Shelley finally saved her from bleeding to death by lifting her from bed and sitting her in a tub of ice. She believed she was dying and felt tranquilly sure of going into a world as beautiful as that she was leaving, "a passive satisfaction" though she did not actively wish to die; "my own Shelley could never have lived without me, the sense of eternal misfortune would have pressed to heavily upon him, & what would have become of my poor babe?"[37]

Extremely weak from massive loss of blood, Mary stayed in bed for over two weeks, during which her recovery was retarded by weird excitations. One night Shelley ran screaming, half awake, across the salon into her bedroom for comfort; he had had a nightmare in which a bloodstained Edward and Jane told him the sea was rushing into the house and he had strangled Mary. Later he confessed that he had been having visions and once saw Allegra rise naked from the sea, while the usually prosaic Jane claimed to have seen Shelley on the terrace when actually he was miles away.

Unnerved, convinced that Percy would die at Casa Magni, Mary implored Shelley to take them to the Baths of Pisa. When he and Edward decided to sail to Genoa to surprise the Hunts, who were en route to Leghorn, her bleeding resumed, possibly induced by fear, but stopped when Shelley gave up his excursion. On July 1 the two men, with Captain Roberts, sailed to meet the Hunts at Leghorn. Mary was just strong enough to crawl from bed to the terrace, frantically called him back two or three times, clung to him, wrote a desperate note to Hunt — "I wish c^d write more — I wish I were with you to assist you — I wish I c^d break my chains & leave this dungeon —"[38] and cried bitterly as she watched the *Don Juan* disappear behind the promontory.

Mary later told Mrs. Gisborne that when Jane and Claire took their evening walk she got out of bed to pace the terrace, "oppressed with wretchedness, yet gazing on the most beautiful scene in the world . . . it added only to my wretchedness —

I . . . told myself the tale of love peace & competence which I
enjoyed — but I answered myself by tears — did not my William
die? & did I hold my Percy by a firmer tenure? — Yet I
thought . . . when my Shelley returns I shall be happy — he will
comfort me, if my boy be ill he will restore him & encourage
me.[39]

She wrote to Shelley at Leghorn, begged him to take them away, once
signing herself, "Yours Entirely." She expected the men back Monday,
July 8, but it stormed and rained all day Tuesday. Wednesday was fair,
and several feluccas arrived from Leghorn; "one brought word that they
had sailed monday, but we did not believe them — thursday was another
day of fair wind & when twelve at night came . . . we began to fear": but
only some illness or disagreeable delay. Friday's post brought news from
Hunt, then at Byron's in Pisa, that the men had sailed on Monday, and
asking if all was well: "the paper fell from me — I trembled all over —
Jane read it — 'Then it is all over!' she said. 'No, my dear Jane,' I cried,
'it is not all over . . . we will go to Leghorn, we will post to be swift &
learn our fate.' "[40]

They were rowed to Lerici in heavy swells, where they hired a carriage
and drove thirty-five kilometers to Pisa at top speed, "two poor, wild,
aghast creatures," arriving at Byron's palace at midnight. "I staggered up
stairs . . . 'Where is he — Sapete alcuna cosa di Shelley,' " she demanded
of Teresa. White as marble after her miscarriage, "terror impressed on her
brow . . . ," Byron said, "a desperate sort of courage seemed to give her
energy . . . I have seen nothing in tragedy on the stage so powerful, or so
affecting."[41] The two women coached on to Leghorn, lay down dressed
at an inn until six in the morning, then found Captain Roberts and Trelawny, who confirmed that the *Don Juan* had sailed on July 8.

Still they did not despair; the boat might have been driven to Corsica,
and was said to have been seen in the gulf. Couriers were sent to the
coastal watch towers. Inquiring at each port along the way, they rushed
back to Lerici with Trelawny. At Via Reggio they found some of *Don
Juan*'s gear washed ashore (Trelawny insisted it could have been thrown
over deliberately), and finally arrived at Casa Magni; "Mrs. Wil-
lams . . . more dead than alive —" Trelawny wrote Byron at four that
morning, "and Mrs Shelley is little better — I cannot describe the scenes
here!"[42]

From that night, July 13, they waited so "thrown about by hope &
fear" that Mary remembered the next five days as twelve. Fixed to the

terrace, focusing Shelley's telescope on every boat passing along the coast, some heading into the bay, she took opium for a few hours' sleep, even reproached herself amidst "convulsive gaspings of despair" for influencing the fates by her morbid anticipation.[43] Yet she would not believe the worst. Indefatigably combing the coast, Trelawny went to Leghorn on the eighteenth seeking news. On the nineteenth Mary was near collapse, but when Trelawny had not returned by evening she told Jane she had hope. At seven he came back, with a face that made Caterina shriek. As Jane fainted and Mary listened, gaunt, upright, rigid, Trelawny told them he had seen Shelley's and Edward's bodies, which had been washed ashore. Rather than try to console Mary, he launched into an eloquent eulogy of Shelley, "until I almost was happy that I was thus unhappy to be fed by the praise of him."[44]

Next morning she started for Pisa with Jane and their children. At Via Reggio she walked to the beach where Shelley's body had been buried in quicklime; three white sticks marked the temporary grave. It was a week short of eight years since her flight with him from Skinner Street.

III HEROISM

That Lionel great wealth had left
By will to me, and that of all
The ready lies of law bereft
My child and me, might well befall.
But let me not think of the scorn,
Which from the meanest I have borne,
When, for my child's belovèd sake,
I mixed with slaves . . .

> Percy Bysshe Shelley,
> *Rosalind and Helen*

A solitary woman is the world's victim, and there is
heroism in her consecration.

> Mary W. Shelley,
> review of *The Loves of the Poets*

13 "Magnificent, deep, pathetic, wild and exalted"

"I NEVER SAW such a scene — nor wish to see such another," Byron wrote John Murray[1] two weeks after Mary Shelley had returned from Casa Magni to Pisa: bereft of Shelley before her twenty-fifth birthday, near destitution, with a two-year-old child. He was speaking as well of Jane Williams's similar plight, of course.

But in fact, more than anyone could know, Mary Shelley was in extremis. If Shelley had died of illness over time, she would have expressed all she felt for him, and he would have given her a final benediction. When a union is suddenly terminated by gruesome death, however, the survivor can be left as she was, incredulous, fearful, remorseful for what has been left unsaid and undone, and the entire grieving process is intensified. Moreover, hers was a special case. Shelley's death tore open the shell in which she had pent up her feelings since the death of their son, William; she reproached herself for coldness; and her guilt was compounded by the return of what she had repressed: a degree of acceptance of the "proper" female role, and the gasp of the ghost of Harriet Shelley, also drowned.

Even without these factors, losing Shelley was a cruelly revolutionary disaster. Mary deluded herself, some say, about the gratifications of her union with him, but these skeptics misunderstand what she wanted out of life. She had endured more in their eight years together than do most people in a long life span — "Great God! What we have gone through," she exclaimed to Claire Clairmont. Nevertheless, he had enabled her to overleap ordinary existence, to satisfy her intellectual, romantic, and moral demands, and, despite her inhibitions, her passions. She had been the companion of a genius whose money, charisma, and chivalry had empowered and protected her as she overrode her diffidence, maintained an "unfeminine" heterodoxy displeasing to many of their liberal circle, and defied the hostile world.

By the same token, however, she had moved into waters beyond her individual depth. For all her maturity she had remained a child prodigy to Shelley's impresario, at once spoiled by him and undercut by adversity, while preserving a childlike trust. Trelawny was to tell her that she was "the person in the world most ignorant of it and of character," and she conceded: "I seldom see, I only feel evil."[2]

And while she had steadied Shelley, she herself had much of his excitability and idealism. She vowed herself to him forever, at first felt his spirit hovering near. She had always believed the spirit lived on "if we so will it," and now especially his. "All say that he was an elemental spirit . . . ,"[3] she wrote Tom Medwin — thus Trelawny, Jane Williams, Charles Clairmont, the Hunts. Indeed, Hunt wrote Horace Smith that Shelley had been a "seraphical thing of the elements," and in first flush Byron declared that compared with Shelley every other man was a beast. But with her transcendental urge and her need to deny her loss, Mary initially transfigured him into a god. "People used to call me lucky in my star," she wrote Maria Gisborne. "You see now how true such a prophecy is — I was fortunate in having fearlessly placed my destiny in the hands of one, who a superior being among men, a bright planetary spirit . . . raised me to the height of happiness . . . I would not change my situation as His widow with that of the most prosperous woman in the world —"[4]

After the staggering succession of deaths, she felt destined to misery and longed to die. As the daughter of Godwin, she never considered suicide, though Wollstonecraft had attempted it when her lover Imlay deserted her, but instead she hoped to die like her mother at thirty-six. (Actually, Wollstonecraft had been thirty-eight.) She intended to devote her remaining "eleven long years" to study and to Percy, and saw herself embarking on the terminal chapter of an epic tragedy, sustained only by hope to become worthy to join Shelley's spirit.

Some say, too, that Mary deluded herself about Shelley's virtues. Certainly, she idolized him. He evoked, and still evokes, cultists, and she simply idealized him with more urgency than did most of his intimates, partly through overcompensation, partly through the same mythic compulsion that led Shelley to write *Epipsychidion* for Emilia Viviani. As she later indicated, Madame de Staël's reaction to the death of her father resembled her own to Shelley's,* a parallel suggesting that these women who transcended female norms recognized that they had depended on a beloved male's approval and active help.

But Mary Shelley had neither de Staël's ego nor exhibitionism nor,

---

* See Mary's "Madame de Staël" in *Lives,* 1838–1839, II:331, in which she quotes from de Staël's narrative: "terror and despair" at being left unsupported by her father's unfailing compassion and watchful help, need to continue her loving admiration of him, conviction that he was the most perfect human being, and that in moments of exaltation he was with her still.

perhaps most important, her worldly power. Everyone, above all she herself, counted on her strong mind and will. These are the very qualities
that work against resignation, however, and they could not overcome her
needfulness and self-doubt. Yet she had a man's pride that barred her from
showing need, which the people around her in fact preferred not to see.
Shelley had been her unique Friend, the encourager and supporter she
required for both emotional and pragmatic reasons. Without him, she was
vulnerable to what psychologists today term "social anxiety" stemming
from guilt and/or anger — a sense of being isolated and helpless in an
unfriendly world, a fear of being scrutinized and humiliated, or worse.
Some people become aggressive, some compliant; others, like Mary Shelley, withdraw.

"A wretched thing of aspiration and despair," she called herself in her
journal three months after Shelley's death, chagrined at her weakness. She
marshaled her strengths, but on shaky ground. And at the end of her
formative first year alone the inordinate self-reproach, which by then she
had put into better proportion, was reawakened and extended by the man
who might have relieved or even exonerated her: Leigh Hunt, Shelley's
friend.

Thereafter she was to encounter misfortunes, many the making of aspirations that were practically impossible for a woman in her circumstances
to fulfill, and to protest her fate, even to despair. But Godwin was right
when he characterized her in adolescence as "bold, rather imperious, active
of mind and almost invincibly persevering." One must attend to her resurgence and to what she does, or else one misperceives the essential Mary
Shelley. For though she would eventually wear out, she remained remarkably productive, enduring, resilient, and true to herself.

If her union with Shelley had been "romantic beyond romance," her
life without him would be a Romantic quest to live nobly and happily,
bereft of the very elements that had made her former existence possible.

Mary Shelley began by venting her emotions through activity. Jane
Williams, her two children, and Claire Clairmont moved in with her,
sharing what little they had; "we have one purse," she said. As Godwin
had published her mother's posthumous works and a memoir, so she asked
Peacock to send her those of Shelley's unpublished manuscripts that were
in England and planned to write his biography. She wrote Amelia Curran
for his only portrait, bad as she had thought it (and unavailable, since
Miss Curran was in Paris and the painting was stored at Rome), and
designed little mementos with mottoes. She mourned too for Edward and
worried about Jane, "who withers like a lily."

A common hysteria binds the deceased's intimates prior to the funeral, which in this case was delayed for three weeks. Byron, and particularly Hunt and Trelawny, devotedly attended Mary. Tenacious as an Antigone, she determined to have Shelley buried in William's grave in Rome — where she would have gone to live except that she was still gripped by terror for Percy and believed Rome would kill him — though everyone opposed her plan as expensive and necessitating complex negotiations with various local authorities. She ordered a coffin, which was returned to the maker at a monetary loss when it turned out that quarantine regulations required that Shelley's and Edward's corpses be burned on the beaches where each had been temporarily buried. Mary delegated Trelawny to stage a hero's cremation for Shelley near Via Reggio, like that of drowned Misenus in the *Aeneid*. On August 15 and 16 Byron and Hunt watched Trelawny perform the grisly business. Trelawny burned his hands gathering Shelley's ashes for Mary and fragments of bones for Claire and himself; Hunt took the remnant of the heart.*

Mary remained in Pisa, writing Mrs. Gisborne the first complete account of her ordeal at Casa Magni: horror recollected in despair. When the men returned, she rushed to their carriage and wrangled with Hunt for Shelley's heart, both feeling that it was his unconsumable essence. Hunt declared that not even her right superseded his, as Shelley's closest friend. Mary appealed to Byron, who took her side. Eventually Jane persuaded Hunt to give the relic to Mary, who placed it in her copy of *Adonais,* Shelley's self-fulfilled elegy on Keats. Then she took his ashes to Leghorn to be shipped to Rome without thinking to ask Hunt to escort them.

This macabre spat was emblematic of ongoing appropriations of Shelley by friends vying for importance of place as his intimate, at the expense of his widow, whose superiority they had always envied, and whose powerlessness freed them to act in ways they would not have dared if Shelley had been alive. Jane showed Mary nothing but tender affection, but she confided to Hunt that Mary's "coldness" and "temper" had made Shelley unhappy, and Hunt, who showed Mary his animosity, told Jane about "our Shelley's" report to him, a few days before his death, of the cloud over his marriage. Hunt even felt that Shelley would not have sailed into the fatal storm but for Mary's "petulant" pressure for him to return to Casa Magni; actually, it had been Edward who was impatient to sail.

Claire criticized Mary's temperament to Jane, as well as to Trelawny, who stoutly defended her, and she bitterly resented Mary for welcoming Byron's attentions, while she herself took money from him for a Goethe

* This was common fetishism in a period whose iron man, Napoleon, left his heart to his wife, and whose physician took his penis, which is owned at present by an Englishwoman.

translation. (Mary saw to it that Byron paid.) Claire had a brief affair with Trelawny, who had a mistress in Genoa but probably was attracted to Claire because of her connection to Byron and Shelley; he was to make a career out of being the poets' friend. But Claire refused to stay with Trelawny. She had had enough of Don Juans, was determined to be independent, and had no recourse but to find a position as companion or governess. For two decades she would try to escape being identified as the mother of Byron's child and Shelley's "incestuous" lover, which threatened her livelihood. Mary paid her way to Vienna, where her brother, Charles, lived.

In any event, people were less attentive to Mary after the funeral, as is generally true, and she herself withdrew, expressing herself only in letters to Mrs. Gisborne: "At times I feel an energy within me to combat with my destiny — but again I sink . . . Solitude is my only help & resource; accustomed even when he was with me to spend much of my time alone, I can . . . forget myself — until some idea, which I think I would communicate to him, occurs . . ."[5]

Her anxiety as a new widow was compounded by imminent penury. Shelley's annuity stopped with his death; she would not come into the estate he had willed her until after his father's death. Sir Timothy being near seventy, presumably her inheritance would not be long delayed. Ever to want or need a fortune, however, seemed outlandish; she hoped to live by her pen. But for her, as for Shelley and Byron, writing was a calling that required a financial base, however minimal. Without this she doubted her ability to support herself and Percy: "the idea that my circumstances may at all injure him is [the] fiercest pang my mind endures."[6] She decided to go home and "claim" a small maintenance from Shelley's father in return for signing away her legacy.

Though Shelley had made Byron and Peacock co-executors in his 1817 will, he had written two wills in Italy, substituting Hogg for Byron and leaving Hunt two thousand pounds. Mary therefore declined Byron's help until her search of Shelley's papers failed to discover the later wills, whereupon Byron assumed his office. Godwin urged Mary to come home; "We have now no battle to fight" was his sole reference to Shelley. Mrs. Godwin offered to share her small estate; "I rather suspect that 'tis your own which she means," said Byron,[7] who dissuaded Mary from going to England and sacrificing Percy's prospects for a maintenance that he believed Sir Timothy would provide. On what the journey would cost she could live for months in Genoa, where his entourage and the Hunts were to settle, and she could make money writing for *The Liberal*. Moreover, he bought her furniture but let her keep essentials, and when the *Don Juan* was raised from the sea bottom and auctioned, he gave Mary and Jane the proceeds, though Shelley had owed him money. By fall Mary probably had some one hundred pounds.

Two months after Shelley's death, on September 11, Mary set out from Pisa for Genoa with Percy, her servant, Maria, and Jane Williams and her children, who were going to Jane's mother in London. They took rooms at the Croce di Malta inn. On the seventeenth Jane left, with Mary's letter recommending her to Jeff Hogg — from whom Mary never heard, although Jane sent a message that he was too overwhelmed to write. Mary would have lived alone had Trelawny not warned that she was asking for unbearable solitude and insult, as the local English were "most bitter" toward her and would believe she was continuing her purported sexual relations with Byron. Indeed, that she and Shelley had been married was neither generally known nor believed in England until her friends publicized the fact. So Mary took a large house for herself and the Hunts, despite her uneasy relations with Hunt, near a residence Byron had rented at Albaro, a suburb in the hills above the port. She moved in late September. A week later Byron, the Hunts, and their six children arrived.

Before leaving Pisa, Mary had wandered through her empty house feeling that Shelley was about to materialize: "I would have knelt until the stones had been worn by the impress . . ."[8] But once at Genoa, she felt the full enormity of her loss, grief, yearning, even anger, like Psyche deserted by Eros: "as poets have described those loved by superhuman creatures & then deserted by them —" she wrote Jane, "Impatient, despairing —"[9] She appeared quite normal, nonetheless, and returned to her daily routine. But she waited like a proud child for someone to offer the affectionate attentions she demanded, while confiding to Jane and Maria Gisborne in letters she delayed writing until she was relatively calm. "I can*not speak* . . ." she told Jane, "but I *can write,* & so I scrible —"[10] And to Mrs. Gisborne: "Those about me have no idea of what I suffer; for I talk, aye & smile as usual — & none are sufficiently interested in me to observe that . . . my eyes are blank . . ."[11] Only an Englishwoman she met in Genoa, a Mrs. Thomas, saw through her manner during their "many delightful hours together," and felt for her, "helpless, Pennyless, and broken hearted."[12]

She sensed with reason that Hunt did not like her. Though sometimes kind, he later admitted that he often treated her coldly, almost cruelly. He fussed over the "forty room" house; "any thing but snug . . . costs us 80 crowns," of which Mary paid thirty and besides tutored his older children; he complained about Percy, sneered if Mary spoke lovingly about the child or Shelley, said bitter things to her himself. She usually worked in her own quarters and took her daily walk alone, but Hunt retired early from their common salon, "albeit Mrs. S. . . . looketh not satisfied therewith,"[13] he wrote Bessy Kent with snide vanity. In fairness, Hunt had grave problems of his own. Marianne was ill from apparent tuberculosis and despised Italy and Byron. Byron respected Hunt but disliked being connected with a second-rate "plebeian" poet, while Hunt strove to uphold his self-respect, knowing that *The Liberal* depended totally on Byron's participation.

Byron was very kind to Mary and treated her like an old comrade. (He gave her a lock of his hair.) He saw her rarely, however, which she attributed in part to Teresa Guiccioli's jealousy, and which, she felt, was just as well since his casual tone about Shelley offended her. Still, she trusted that Byron took a personal interest in her. At Godwin's suggestion he had his London solicitor, John Hanson, approach the Shelleys' lawyer, William Whitton, for her maintenance. Byron would have been her banker, but she hated borrowing, and Trelawny was giving her graphic accounts of Byron's tightness. She did, however, borrow books, pens, and sugar from his household, his servant delivered her mail, and she let him pay her for copying his current *The Deformed Transformed, The Age of Brass,* and Cantos X–XVI of *Don Juan.* He had promised Teresa that these cantos would be "immaculate," so Mary edited flagrant indelicacies and also let him know when she thought his work short of his "*highest*" style.

After Trelawny's almost "distressingly" generous help since Lerici, she felt that he was her only friend in Italy. (Having initially felt guilty for designing the *Don Juan,* he was to claim that he had warned about her unseaworthiness.) He, however, was preoccupied with his married mistress, Gabriella Wright, whom he expected Mary to befriend. Mary kept it at acquaintanceship because she could not abide secret adultery. "I hate & despise the *intrigues* of married women, nor in my opinion can the chains which custom throws upon them justify . . . deceit & falsehood . . . ," however pardonable, she wrote Jane. "Truth is the only thing of any worth in ones intercourse . . . where there is not that, vice must follow. Forgive this moral discourse . . ."[14]

In this essential solitude, Mary Shelley nurtured an intense inner life for eight months, like the only nun of some extreme order. As both discharge and affirmation, and an expression of herself to the best of her talents, she began a new "Journal of Sorrow," a remarkable Romantic document, her raw *liber amoris,* diametrically opposite to her former terse recording of daily work and activities, and the best evidence of what losing Shelley meant to her. Here she sounded, purged, and inspired herself on nights when she felt a particular need, as she had done by talking with Shelley, on pages she expected no one ever to see.[15] From now on, that would be the major function of her journals.

"First; I have now no friend," she began on October 2. "For eight years I communicated with unlimited freedom with one whose genius, far transcending mine, awakened & guided my thoughts . . . my mind was satisfied. . . . What a change!" And on November 10: "To see him in beauty . . . To be interpenetrated by the sense of his excellence — & thus to love singly, eternally, ardently . . ."

But " 'death has murdered hope!' — those are the sounds that all Nature echoes to me," for the Genoa winter was closing in, cold and savage, with floods raging down Albaro's high hills. For months she was nervous "to a degree that borders on insanity some times" (possibly in part the aftereffects of her miscarriage), especially about Percy. She could not love him joyously as she had William, and he did not resemble Shelley as Clara had. "Oh my child — what is your fate to be? . . . you are the only chain that links me to time — but for you I should be free."[16] Indeed, she imagined him dead; then feeling that she "shuddered" out of habit since he appeared firmly of this world, she feared he would be unhappy.

Like other survivors of holocausts, she believed henceforth that destiny governed human existence. "Chains" as fetters and lifelines were her frequent metaphor. She was "chained to time," she was bound like overreaching Prometheus on his rock. Every past event seemed a link to her present fate. "Father, Mother, friend, husband children — all made as it were — the team that dragged me conducted me here . . ."[17] Her *Matilda* and *Valperga*, Shelley's *Rosalind and Helen* and "The Sunset," the visions and premonitions at Casa Magni, all seemed to have foretold his drowning; she even hoped for Isabel Baxter Booth to appear in Italy, as her surrogate had in *Rosalind and Helen*. "I see no one who did not know him," she wrote Maria Gisborne, "& thus I try to patch up the links of a broken chain."[18] "I was, as another, the Mother of beautiful children," she noted on October 10, a link to Harriet Shelley quickly suppressed but emerging in an assumption that whereas she would love again, that love would be blighted.

If fate seemed to have confined her to the life of the mind, however, she embraced it. "Activity of spirit is my sphere —," she noted on November 10; her worst moments were when she sank into lethargy "worse than despair." With the vestal fire Shelley foresaw in the Dedication of *The Revolt of Islam,* she vowed to "endeavour to consider my self a faint continuation of his being, & as far as possible the revelation to the earth of what he was. Yet to become this I must change much." She set herself a course of study, not simply for knowledge but for definition. "You will be with me in all my studies, dearest love!"[19]

She granted herself genius. To the degree that diffidence weighed her down, however, Shelley rose in the balance. From the Geneva summer she recalled "my incapacity & timidity" rather than her due degree of collegiality with Shelley and Byron. On November 17: ". . . I am nothing, but I was something and still I cling to what I was," like a ruined house, of interest only because haunted by a "wild & beautiful spirit"; "moon-shine," as Hunt and Byron called her, detached and pale in her black dress as his Moon in *Epipsychidion*. But she was maddened that they "dared" speak of her like any ordinary widow.

> . . . I feel myself degraded before them; knowing that in their hearts they degrade me from the rank which I deserve. . . . I feel dejected & cowed . . . before my judges — for so I consider all who behold me . . . I must get more satisfied with my-self . . . Dearest Shelley! . . . give me some force.
>
> When before did a spirit of the elements, taking an earthly dress, select one of this world for its mate? . . . I shall never be as one of them & they must feel that. . . .[20]

"The weakness of human nature is to seek for sympathy," she wrote Mrs. Gisborne.[21] She began a five-month self-analysis and evaluation. "I have pride & that is useful in the world, but the sincerity of my character destroys its utility. I am ever afraid of being proud of what I do not really possess . . . I am not mean or base — yet I feel at times as if I were . . . I am not imperious — insincere or selfish . . . [but] somewhat generous true & kind."[22] Urgently she denied that she was unfeeling. "Oh my beloved Shelley —" she wrote in her first entry, "It is not true that this heart was cold to thee . . . now you know all things — did I not in the deepest solitude of thought repeat to myself my goodfortune in possessing you?" "A cold heart! have I [a] cold heart?" she asked, citing her anguish to disprove it.

When her emotions were roused, especially by sound — music, or By-ron's voice, to which she had been accustomed to hear Shelley's respond — she fought to preserve her restraint. She felt near hysterics when she heard or saw the sea, "his murderer." If she had anything practical "*to do*" she felt frightened and abused, since Shelley had always acted for her. Oth-erwise, her opinions were as positive as ever, but when she had to state them against opposition she longed to hide like a "dormouse." Neverthe-less, placed between Byron and Hunt, she stuck by the weaker Hunt. When Hunt heard that Byron had disparaged him to Murray (for which he never forgave Byron), she girded herself and asked Byron to soothe Hunt.

To "supply a part of that *real* poetry, brilliancy & sunshine I have lost," she turned to her imagination: daydreaming and fiction. She planned a novel about thirteenth-century King Manfred of Naples, glamorous, intrepid, and as dissolute as Castruccio but warring against Austrian imperialism and the pope.[23] After Godwin advised that this would not interest the public, she used her research for "A Tale of the Passions," which she began in late October for the second issue of the quarterly *Liberal,* the workshop for her professional novitiate. On November 10 she finished the tale, in which she established her mature short-story style: "it has done me great good, & I get more calm." Strikingly, her heroine, Despina, does what she herself had not done — conceals her passion for the married Manfred. Despina disguises herself, like Fidelio, to support Manfred's son, is exposed by a vengeful rejected lover, and is executed.

Conservative critics were already castigating the "unholy Alliance" producing *The Liberal,* and since Mary Shelley explicitly connected her tale to recent failed Italian uprisings against Austria, even the previously friendly *Blackwood's Magazine* attacked "the *soprano* of a female voice . . . pouring forth the rough notes of Jacobinism. One should think, that a female breast, just chastised by a sad calamity, might find other modes of consolation than in feeble railing against kings and gods."[24] In the third *Liberal,* Mary compounded her reputation for immorality with "Madame D'Houtetôt," an essay on her subject's relations with her lover and would-be lover, Rousseau. This triangle resembled that of Mary, Shelley, and Hogg in 1815; Mary may have been sending Jeff an Aesopian explanation of her former rejection, to which she attributed his silence. She also published a few of Shelley's poems in the magazine and assisted Hunt with the editing.[25]

In late November she made an overture to Trelawny and, until he left Genoa at Christmas, talked with him for hours about Shelley and Edward. He offered her money. "Indeed I do believe, my dear Trelawny, that you are the best friend I have —" she replied, "& most truly would I rather apply to you . . . than to any one else . . . at present I am very well off . . ."[26] He wrote Claire that Mary had become more "amiable," but her undiminished mourning astonished and provoked him. Too crude ever to understand her, he liked her because he believed she was like him, "overbearing, self-willed" and "choosing to love in our own fashion"; perhaps he had amorous hopes of her.[27]

Mary planned a complete, *"perfect"* edition of Shelley's works for a public largely ignorant of them, and asked for *"All"* in print and holograph to be sent her. She meant first to issue his unpublished work, and borrowed Byron's copy of Gibbon's posthumous works as a possible model. She began the long process of editing the papers at hand. This editing, sometimes salvaging the many poems for which Shelley left no fair copies, was her proudest feat and one that only she, familiar with his working habits and in the fervor of dedication, could have accomplished. Only those who have seen his papers can appreciate her achievement. In twenty-six workbooks and on copious separate sheets are passages that may or may not belong together, fragments, trials, words smeared or crossed out, written over. Sometimes she had to supply punctuation and connections. In some cases she changed or omitted words she felt to be unsuitable for immediate publication, being determined to present Shelley's "highest" genius. This was common practice (Shelley himself had bowdlerized Plato in his translation of the *Symposium,* and some verses he had not intended to publish as they were, if ever). Moreover, she preserved most of the holographs, with which later editors have worked.

She loved working with Shelley's manuscripts, but she was distressed to find verses about his secret despondency, her "coldness," poems to Emilia Viviani and Jane (Jane, Trelawny, and Medwin had his most revealing verses to Jane). Her remorse and adoration intensified; she was convinced that he had hidden his unhappiness and sacrificed for her because he loved her above all else, and she now beatified him for gentleness, tolerance, "heavenly benignity," love and sympathy, the "flower of love." Meditating on him, and on "our nature, our source & our destination," she found new faith that existence had purpose. On December 19 she wrote: "Would that memory had not pains that sting as well as grieve. I might have been other — & far better . . . But despondance must not intrude . . . Why am I here? — but that I am destined to be wiser, better & happier than I am . . . I go to him, & so, not tearless, not alas! uncomplain[in]g — yet resigned, I nerve myself for the future."

"Rapture, exultation — content, all the varied change of enjoyment have been mine . . . distance shall not dim them." She began Shelley's biography, or rather hagiography, "to make him beloved to all posterity," especially as his death had inspired both eulogies and obloquy. In December she outlined chapters of their union, in February wrote an account of his Eton school days, and in March a votary's foreword adapted from her journal: "I was the chosen mate of a celestial spirit . . . I am a priestess, dedicated to his glorification by my sufferings . . ."[28]

Meanwhile, in her quotidian life her sense of humor returned. She confided to Jane that Teresa saw to it that Byron was "kept in excellent order, quarelled with & hen-pecked to his hearts content,"[29] and passed on his sally about Jane and his half sister: "I love Janey very much . . . as a sister — rather an unlucky phrase for me . . ."[30] When Jane settled her affairs, Mary and she meant to live in Florence, as Mary hated Genoa.

Now Mary missed Shelley also as "lover — husband." She understood her longing for reciprocal love with others not as weakness but human need, an imperative need of her nature, and called him to witness that when her friends treated her well, "in how warm a gush my blood flows to my heart & tears to my eyes — how truly I then love them . . ."[31] She wrote Jane that her affectionate letters came "like the sounds of remembered music"; "I will deserve your love . . . ," she vowed.[32]

Marianne Hunt was pregnant; the doctors said her delivery might kill her. By now Mary was miserable living with the Hunts, but determined to stay with Marianne until she had her baby in June, and consulted Mrs. Mason, with whom she regularly corresponded, on treating Marianne's night sweats and spitting of blood.

In January 1823 she learned that Sir Timothy's solicitor, Whitton, had rejected the overtures of Byron's Hanson. Shelley's father was said to be infirm, but Byron wrote him soliciting her maintenance. She began to economize and list her expenses: Maria's wages, a boy for heavy cleaning, dyeing her clothing black (she did not wear full widow's regalia), new black silk stockings, an outfit for Percy, flowers, cologne, Madeira, laudanum for toothache and tranquilizing.[33] Claire was ill and penniless in Vienna, and the police threatened to expel her and Charles as Godwin's relations. When Mary told Byron that either he or she must provide for Claire, "the choice was too inviting," she told Jane in confidence; he let her send money, and she refused his offer to reimburse her. The hounded, unhappy Claire went to Russia to be a governess.

"I go on from day to day & know that I am unhappy . . . ," Mary noted on February 17; "suddenly . . . it is as a change from narrative to a drama . . . & I on narrow pinacle of isolated rock, stand shuddering." Once she heard Shelley say "Mary"; once saw a distant sail, thought it was his, and almost rushed to the beach. But as spring began, despite moments of "unworthy" despondency, she felt something of her old hope, spirit, and self-approval. She got up at dawn, drank in the view from her balcony, and spent hours outside with a new box of paints and on walks, buoyed by reveries, "nourishing a romantic & exalted tone of mind in thought about that above me —"[34] "I lead an innocent life," she noted on the twenty-fourth, "& it may become a useful one":

> I have talent; I will improve that talent . . . render myself worthy
> of my divine Shelley . . . What is it that moves up & down in my

soul & makes me feel as if my intellect could master all except my fate? . . . I have felt myself exalted with the idea of occupation, improvement, knowledge & peace.

"I am beginning seriously to educate myself," she wrote on March 19. In metaphysics she arrived at a Kantian idealism, studying his *Critique of Judgment* and *Critique of Practical Reason,* apparently in German, which Claire may have taught her. She read Schiller, translating a segment of his *Turandot* as "The Stars"; and Sidney's *Arcadia,* Shaftesbury's *Character-istics,* and Plato's *Menexenus* on orations honoring the illustrious dead, which she continued translating where Shelley had left off. She felt sur-rounded by a host of noble spirits "communing with me, teaching & encouraging me . . ." In particular she identified with Petrarch, inspired by his dead love Laura, and chose two passages from his sonnets as epi-graphs for her edition of Shelley's poems — the second of which she altered for his sex: *"Ma ricogliendo le sue sparte fronde / Dietro lo* [for *le*] *vo così passo passo,"* which may be translated as "gathering his scattered fronds / I follow in his footsteps close behind."*

She marked the scope of her intellectual development in an essay for the fourth *Liberal,* "Giovanni Villani." In the Classic-Romantic contro-versy, she finds excellence in both modes but prefers the latter: the innate impulses of superior minds are "the fiats of intellectual creation." If "well managed," the most interesting and moving works result when authors express their deepest feelings, even display and analyze themselves. Milton, Burton, Sterne, Montaigne, Rousseau, Boswell, Lady Mary Wortley Mon-tagu, Lamb, and Mary Wollstonecraft in *Letters from Sweden:* these are favorites of those who "turn to the human heart as the undiscovered country . . . visit and revisit their own; endeavour to understand its work-ings, to fathom its depths, and to leave no lurking thought or disguised feeling [hidden] for fear of shocking the tender conscience . . . The science of self-knowledge is key."[35]

Godwin had *Valperga* published as "By the Author of Frankenstein," capitalizing on Mary's recent widowhood, while Mrs. Godwin located friendly reviewers for Mary's moral support and income "which can still less wait." Godwin had cut passages of historical detail that impeded the action, but assured Mary that her second novel had more genius than *Frankenstein.* For a new edition of *Frankenstein* she made some re-

---

* For Mary, "fronds" of Laura-laurel equal Shelley's works, deeds, and virtues. (She also quoted from these lines on her packet of Edward Williams's hair.) She later decided not to use the second epigraph, probably because it was too poignant. But in the Introduction to *The Last Man* she would utilize the leaf metaphor in the leaves found in the Cumaean Sibyl's cave, which the author deciphers.

visions revelatory of her present worship of Shelley and her sense of fate.

Mary felt depressed on February 24, and took it as a premonition when Byron received Sir Timothy's refusal to give her a maintenance on grounds that she had lived with Shelley while his first wife was alive and estranged him from his duties. On condition that she give Percy to guardians in England, Sir Timothy would support him. Mary burst into tears. "I should not live ten days seperated from him . . . ," she wrote Byron, "nor shall he be deprived of my anxious love . . . besides, *I* loose . . . all honourable station & name when I admit that I am not a fitting person to take care of my infant . . . I am said to have a cold heart — there are feelings however so strongly implanted in my nature that to root them out life will go with it —"³⁶

To her horror Byron counseled her to accept. When she refused, he advised her to go to England and arrange her affairs. She had declared that Percy's future respect for his father and his moral wellbeing depended upon his not being under the influence of Shelley's relations; Byron countered that Percy would need wealthy, influential relations. Mrs. Mason concurred.

Mary wavered agitatedly for five weeks. She loathed England, had no money for the trip, and hated accepting Byron's offer to lend her the funds. Though "a young beginner," she might support herself in Italy. "My father says that I *can* be independant," she noted on March 17. "I am not, but I will be . . . Shelley! . . . I have need of you!" She longed to remain in the peace, solitude, and beauty of Italy, veiling "hateful" life with studies and reveries; leaving would snap the link binding the present to the past. Personally soliciting Sir Timothy seemed obnoxious and futile. Tom Medwin, who had just missed Shelley's cremation and had been moved by Mary's plight, had reported from Paris to Jane that he knew Shelley's father too well to think he would do anything for Mary, and that on a recent visit to England, he had been disgusted by the whole family's indifference to Shelley.

But Mary needed an English literary agent, a service from which Godwin "slinked." At Jeff Hogg's suggestion Byron agreed to ask his powerful friend Lord Holland to sponsor her with Sir Timothy. In her essays at foreseeing she could not envision inheriting Shelley's legacy: "I shall never fill, what to my indolent disposition, in all that regards the care of money, appears an annoying situation — that of having the management of a fortune," she told Jane.³⁷ All the more did she want Percy to be protected by Shelley's family, who, she said derisively, would be even more prejudiced against her "if I, unprotected, young & tireless, reside abroad — out of their English . . . sanctuary of . . . propriety . . . & foggy virtue —"³⁸

Further, if she contravened Byron she suspected he would quit as executor; "that, to me, confiding & somewhat sanguine, has been a bitter blow."[39] "I can act independantly of the opinion of others," she wrote Jane, "but the expression of that opinion if it be in opposition to mine shakes my nature to its foundations."[40] She wrote Jeff for advice, with implicit apologies for the past: "I do not think that you will find me what I was. but tamed to submission to my harsh fate, grateful for kindness . . . full of affection . . . tolerant — fearful — easily agitated but still reserved & diffident —"[41]

Calmer on March 19, she evaluated herself in her journal as befit the author of "Giovanni Villani": "I have found strength in the conception of [my heart's] faculties, much native force in the understanding of them . . . penetration in the subtle divisions of good & evil. But I have found less strength of self support, of resistance to what is vulgarly called, temptation, far less constancy that [than] I expected; yet . . . true humility . . . an ardent love for the immutable laws of right — much native goodness of emotion & purity of thought."

In early April, Byron decided to go to Greece to aid the revolution, a decision that ended *The Liberal*. Mary thereupon determined to go to England. Optimism gained the upper hand. She trusted that she could get her maintenance. She accepted Byron's offer of travel money, and their relations improved. "I am growing terribly religious," she wrote Jane. "LB. says — what are you a Christian?"; no, she had retorted, if she were she would not be truly religious.[42] "Is Aurora a portrait?" she knowingly queried Byron about Aurora Raby in *Don Juan*, whom he seems to have modeled on Mary: a pale, bookish, self-possessed, sincere girl of proud heritage, whose "best ties" are "in the tomb" but her spirit "strong / In its own strength."*

Mary now walked up to the tops of Albaro's flood-bared hills, and down to a rock overhanging the Mediterranean, at once keen to Nature's savagery and feeling Shelley's spirit in its beauty. "Yet . . . ," she wrote Jane, "this whirl of ideas which is never still is the part of my being I prize & cherish most —"[43] She longed for Rome. Shelley's ashes had been buried in William's supposed grave, which, however, did not contain the child's remains, so Trelawny reburied the urn in a lovely part of the English cemetery, under a plain stone as Mary had requested — and bought the adjacent plot for himself. He and young Pietro Gamba were going to Greece with Byron.

On June 3 Mary Shelley initiated a traumatic conversation with Hunt,

---

* Mary would use the surname Raby for the heroine of *Falkner*.

one of the determinative points of her life. If it drained off some of her empoisoning remorse about Shelley, it also left a corrosive residue and the antidote had its own toxicity. Out of pride and affection she asked Hunt why he disliked her, and out of resentment he explained in full (enhanced by Jane's contribution, though he did not betray her). First, just before his death Shelley had complained to him about her behavior and her "inability" to feel and understand him. And second, Hunt told her, she was willful, impatient, bad-tempered, imperious, critical, and so cold-hearted that she felt no remorse for her treatment of Shelley.

Mary was devastated to learn that at the end Shelley had been so dissatisfied with her as to speak to Hunt, and that this man who loved Shelley found such fault with her. To Hunt's astonishment, she burst out in a passion of words and tears, described her months of secret agony and remorse, and admitted the "evil" she had done. "She is a torrent of fire under a Heckla snow . . . ," he wrote Bessy Kent, only now comprehending that Mary had "worshipped" Shelley; "but I believe, as Mr. Trelawny . . . tells me *he* [Shelley] believed, even when most uneasy with her, that she had excuses of suffering little known to any body but himself, & these ought now to be the more readily granted her on account of the touching remorse she confesses for ever having treated him with unkindness and also her great loss. I believe the impulses of her fire may be turned to good & great purpose & am sure she wishes it to be so."[44]

Remorseful and ashamed, he hastened to console her affectionately, reassured her that she could expiate, and took the occasion to give her the kind of instruction in patience, mildness, and consideration that girls of the period read in courtesy books; "my Pardoner and teacher," she called him.

She appealed to Shelley in her journal that night: "your pupil — friend — lover — wife — Mother of your children . . . I was unworthy of you — I ever felt that — most bitterly & deeply now . . ." Worried about what Jane might have said, she told Hunt that others had seen her "tempers" with Shelley at Casa Magni but not her loving private amends and requests for pardon. Now Hunt blamed Jane for having misled him and wrote Bessy Kent that Jane "has not quite intellect enough to see very far into a case where great thoughts, passions, etc. are concerned."[45] If he had been capable of deflating Mary's excessive self-reproach and of pointing out that Shelley had had flaws, he might have been the teacher Mary needed.

For four years Mary would try to redeem the past by dedication to others. Hunt and Jane were key in her quest because of their intimacy with Shelley, and however they failed her she would cleave to them. She also made the healthy resolve never again to fail to express her affections:

"thus am I changed — too late alas! for what ought to have been," she wrote her "own dear Jane," vowing to be her stay and consolation.[46] Soaring in relief, she composed a long autobiographical poem for Hunt, "The Choice." "All anger was atoned by many a kind / Caress or tear, that spoke the softened mind. — /," she addressed Shelley in her opening "tale of [his] unrequited love."

> It speaks of cold neglect, averted eyes,
> That blindly crushed thy soul's fond sacrifice: —
> My heart was all thine own, — but yet a shell
> Closed in its core . . .
> By this remorse and love — and by the years
> Through which we shared our common hopes and fears,
> By all our best companionship, I dare
> Call on thy sacred name without a fear . . .*

Jane, meantime, discouraged Mary from coming to England, where she was telling Jeff Hogg, as she would tell others, that Mary had made Shelley unhappy throughout their union and that she herself had been his true, if platonic, love. Moreover, Jeff and Jane were about to become secret lovers — even as Mary scoffed at Mrs. Gisborne's belief that he had fallen in love with Jane.

After Mary attended Marianne's safe delivery of a son on June 9, Byron suggested she travel home by fast post coach and made her arrangements through Hunt. Byron was expending large sums for his Greek expedition and worrying about Teresa, who believed he would die in Greece. Byron and Hunt (who was also asking Byron for money for himself) fell into dissension about the Shelleys. Hunt reported Byron's asperities to Mary and Mary's reactions to Byron, with the result that she borrowed from Trelawny just enough to take the cheap, slow *vetturino,* and Byron resigned as Shelley's executor and did not write Lord Holland. Teresa offered to mediate. "Chere Contessina . . . ," Mary replied, "celui qui me n'estime pas ne peut pas etre mon Bienfaiteur."[47] Yet Byron asked Mary to be at Teresa's villa at five on July 13, when he was scheduled to leave to board ship, so that Mary, who considerately arrived just as he drove off, could comfort his sorrowing, fearful mistress.

Mary shipped home two crates of books with a new stock of Italian works and sent a drawing to Mrs. Mason, who told her that misfortune had shown her "in a more amiable point of view" than ever before. The

---

* The poem was inspired by a poem of the same title Hunt had written for *The Liberal* about his ideal of the good life as a response to the Reverend John Pomfret's "The Choice."

Hunts were moving to Florence. Maria returned to Pisa, vowing to return to Mary's service when she came back to Italy. Wrought up, Mary could almost "force my excited feelings to laugh at themselves." On July 25, however, she started home aglow: "let nought earthly approach the sanctum in which thou art enshrined," she apostrophized Shelley, "no wayward weakness bend me from the high destiny marked out for me . . . fill me with faith in thy being — hope of our re-union — patience in the present struggle"[48]

14 "The regions of the has been, is, & to be"

FEELING that she had "dreamt away" her first year without Shelley, Mary Shelley reentered reality via a disorienting "labyrinth" on her month-long journey to England. She was retracing the same roads she had taken to Italy more than five years before, eager and hopeful, in her own carriage with Shelley, Claire, and their children. Now she was traveling by *vetturino*, a lumbering vehicle barely respectable for a lady, with Percy only, thirty pounds to her name, back to her girlhood home. At the same time she was charged by her love of danger, movement, and change, her high resolves, and determination to "take the harvest" of her affairs into her own hands and return to Italy with Jane Williams in the spring. Perhaps it is just as well that, despite her prophetic gift, she did not foresee that she would be trapped in England for the rest of her life.

Early on the ninth anniversary of her elopement — the *vetturino* day began at three — she prepared to cross the Alps, exhilarated by an exquisite, breezy dawn. After crossing, "Consider I am at a dismal inn all alone —" she wrote the Hunts in one of six huge letters en route, "my heart is often on the point of sinking . . . but I strive with the foul fiend & take refuge in the idea of those I love . . . once in the carriage I can defy the *Devil*, for motion keeps up my spirits . . ."[1]

Besides, there were attractions along the way. "Now this pleases me," she wrote of an Alpine religious festa: "one can conceive of animals . . . going to pleasant places to enjoy themselves — but it belongs to that queer animal man alone, to toil up steep & perilous crags, to arrive at a bare peak; to sleep ill & fare worse, & then the next day to descend & call this a feast — the feast of the soul it must be —"[2] The change from Italian imprecations to French suavity also pleased her, particularly the French custom of addressing rich and poor alike "Madame" and "Monsieur" — "a symbol that they claim kindred with & afford sympathy to all."

At Lyons, however, she had to freeze an impudent man, and wept over the loss of her accustomed protection. From there she took the fast post coach to Dijon, arriving dirty and worn after twenty-four hours with Percy on her lap, and on August 12 reached Paris in a state of exhaustion. After buying gifts for the Hunts and her family, she had just enough money to get to London.

She encountered a new aspect of her problematic status on a three-day stay in Versailles with old acquaintances: the Horace Smiths, the playwright James Kenney, Mrs. Kenney (daughter of the author Sebastien Mercier and widow of Godwin's friend Thomas Holcroft), plus their "immense" family of eleven and their lady boarders: "a horde of uninteresting beings." Uneasily proud, after "exhausting my nothings" with the ladies she went into a corner with Kenney, her fellow *"Author,"* and his attractive young stepdaughter, Louisa Holcroft. But they all got into a delectable gossip cum briefing session about London, and everyone was so impressed with her (the Kenneys' six-year-old took her for the Madonna) that she assured her "teacher" Hunt she pleased herself by pleasing them. Her reward was Mrs. Kenney's compliment, the most flattering thing anyone could say, that Mary had become very like Mary Wollstonecraft especially in her manner and way with people. The Kenneys took her back to Paris.

Her father and William, Junior, were on the wharf when her steam packet arrived in London on August 25, 1823, five days before her twenty-sixth birthday. At the Godwins' new bookstore-residence at 125 The Strand, "rather dismal" but better than Skinner Street, Mrs. Godwin raved over her looks and put her and Percy in the attic; both women were determined on the shortest possible cohabitation. Torn between anger at Godwin's former turpitude and daughterly love, Mary had dreaded seeing her father. She waxed ironic to Hunt, telling him that when he wrote her care of Godwin he must address the author of *Political Justice* as "Esq," as Shelley had discovered with "unspeakable astonishment." But she was moved by Godwin's joy at seeing her and his grandson, and she made up her mind to treat the past as moot.

She had to fend off her "fiend" of melancholy. "But lo & behold! I found myself famous!" she wrote Hunt.[3] She knew that a pirated dramatization of *Frankenstein,* called *Presumption,* was playing in London, but she was astounded by its prodigious success, which Godwin had seized on to republish *Frankenstein* — with the proceeds reserved, moreover, *"for my benefit."*[4] On August 29, she made her first public appearance with Godwin and Jane Williams at *Presumption.* While the play (like all its successors) took gross liberties with her novel, the audience was on the edge of their seats, shrieking when Frankenstein cried, "It lives!" and the monster, played by T. P. Cooke with blue body, greenish face, and black lips, costumed in a toga, smashed down the door of a second-story laboratory and leaped onto center stage.* The playbill listed Cooke as " ———"; "this nameless mode of naming the unnameable is rather good," said Mary demurely, more excited than she let on.

She had reunions with the Gisbornes, Charles Lamb, dear and witty as ever, and Isabel Booth, melancholic after a breakdown from which she never entirely recovered. Jane was wretched and ailing: living penuriously with her mother, her tiny income not yet settled, ostracized for her liaison with Edward, whose mother tried to take their children, Meddy and Dina, from her. "I must be rescued or I shall perish," Jane had written Mary. "England is no place for Jane," declared Mary, who was about to be enmeshed in similar circumstances.

Without waiting to consult Peacock or Jeff Hogg, who was on circuit, she immediately tackled one major reason for her "visit": to secure a maintenance. As Shelley's creditors were besieging both Sir Timothy and Godwin, her father despaired of her success. But she wrote Sir Timothy and Lady Shelley at their home, Field Place in Horsham, and with good hopes; the *John Bull* had already reported that she was "compassionated" by Shelley's father. On September 3 she had a reply, from Whitton, and went straight to his office with Godwin and Percy, to begin an unwinnable contest with an old man she was never to see.

When one thinks of what Mary Shelley's future could have been if Sir Timothy had not circumscribed her, he is the villain of the piece, but he acted as he did because he considered *her* a villain. Herself magnanimous and sanguine, she believed he would be moved by his son's widow and little boy if he saw them. It would take her twelve years to surrender that hope; he would live another nine, until she was forty-six.

She began under the misapprehension that he was "laid on the shelf" by illness and age and managed by his wife and Whitton. But he ran his own affairs. He forbade the family to mention Shelley's name, which he hoped would sink into oblivion, and it was he who insisted that Whitton deal with the daughter of Wollstonecraft and Godwin, who had been instrumental in corrupting Shelley and blighting the family honor and estates. He was overseeing the education of Shelley's son Charles, heir to the title and entailed estates, and as Percy was next in line he meant to use Mary's destitution to get Percy from her lest she give him a "Godwin"

---

* The actual vivification of the monster was considered too blasphemous to show on the stage at this period. This play did for Cooke what the 1931 film did for Boris Karloff.

education. If Charles and Percy should predecease him, however, his own son, John, would inherit everything, including what Shelley had willed Mary (and Claire Clairmont).

To Whitton, as to many others, Mary Shelley surely came as a surprise. Instead of the lurid, voluble troublemaker he expected the author of *Frankenstein* and "licentious" woman to be, she was small, young, frail, refined, and spiritual-looking, dressed simply but fashionably, moved gracefully, and spoke in a low, even, melodious voice. Indeed, Sir Timothy was to feel that Whitton took her side.

To Mary, the balding, thin-lipped, long-winded, cautious Whitton seemed the model lawyer she had always scorned. Having expected hostility, she was gratified by his courtesy and heard what she wished to hear. He explained that one of Shelley's wills had to be validated before she had an expectant right to his legacy. She had Mrs. Mason search again for the Italian wills, something that would take until spring and prove vain. Whitton warned her never to contact Sir Timothy and asked her to give up Percy, as he was to do routinely. On her refusal he gave her one hundred pounds for Percy's present needs, indicating that his client would allow Percy that sum annually. Mary believed that her custody was established, that the allowance was for "my" expenses, and would be tripled if she were patient. "This," she blithely said, "relieved me of a load of anxieties" and she moved to neat, cheap lodgings at 14 Speldhurst Street near Coram's Fields and her and Shelley's former pied-à-terre in Marchmont Street, and hired a maid.

Within days, she launched a second project for which she had come to England. Hunt's brother John, now editor of *The Examiner,* agreed to publish Shelley's works. As the Ollier firm, currently closing down, had lost money on the miserably low sales of Shelley's poems, the poet Bryan Waller Procter ("Barry Cornwall") produced guarantors of John Hunt's costs, including twenty-year-old Thomas Lovell Beddoes, one of the coming poetic talents, and the attorney Thomas Kelsall. Mary was excited to find that Shelley had devotees, and that press notices of his death had given him wide if still mostly infamous celebrity. She began preparing his manuscripts for print and seeking pieces she did not yet have. Some people withheld material for its value or private content; many papers stored at Marlow had been appropriated by her former landlord, Thomas Maddocks, or thrown out.*

Her own odium was of course a principal cause of Mary's aversion to England. Hunt had given her a letter to his friend the eminent musician

---

* Apparently among the latter was her second journal.

Vincent Novello, asking him to welcome "Mary Wollstonecraft's daughter" — in which Hunt mentioned Mary's "faults" and assured Vincent that
she would be quiet as a Quaker unless he "put her into a state of pain"
to make her eloquent.[5] She was warmly received, as Jane had been, by
Vincent, his wife, and large family in Shaklewell Green, and their circle:
two bachelors, young Edward Holmes and Keats's former teacher and
friend Charles Cowden Clarke, the tobacco importer Arthur Gliddon and
his wife, Anastasia, who was just as Hunt had described: talkative and
bedizened with an emerald pin. Mary reported to Hunt in Dickensian
style on Mrs. "E.P." and an endless practical joke involving a boiled goose,
for as at Versailles, this group was bourgeois and intellectually second-
rate, if notable for what Mary termed "negative qualities" of amiability
and kindness.

"Vincenzo," however, with whom Mary spoke Italian, was a superior
man, and she was ravished by the music at Shaklewell Green. At Versailles
she had been so near "mortifying" tears when Louisa Holcroft began a
harp melody that she begged her to stop. But now, listening to music,
"the master key" to her emotions, "new ideas rise & develope themselves,
with greater energy & truth than at any other time," she wrote Hunt.[6]
She was inspired to plan an ambitious semiautobiographical novel about
a sole survivor of the human race destroyed by plague in the twenty-first
century: *The Last Man*. This subject was, she rightly said, "more wild &
imaginative & I think more in my way" than historical romances on
Manfred or King Albert, which she had contemplated. Thomas Campbell
and Beddoes had "Last Man" works in progress, but being a survivor
herself she knew she could make the most of the theme. Possibly at Versailles she learned of the satiric *L'An 2440* by Mercier, Mrs. Kenney's
father. Mary Shelley's, however, was to be the first futurist catastrophe
novel.

In October she had reunions with Jeff Hogg and Peacock. She wept
when she first saw Jeff and heard his voice, just the same as always, after
all that had happened to her. Later she wondered about his feelings for
her, since he blushed when they were together, but soon realized that he
was no longer in love with her. Except for a hurt ego she was relieved to
have him simply as a friend. Actually, he blushed because of what Jane
had told him about the Shelleys and herself ("our loss is real . . . ," he had
told Jane, "but hers, however painful, is in fact imaginary").[7] He was also
ashamed of hiding his affair with Jane from Mary, against whose unsus-
pecting head Jane plotted "strategems, and concealments," while Mary
meantime was saying that Jane was incapable of falsity.

Peacock, who had become more conservative in middle age, worked at

East India House, saw a circle of male intellectuals, published occasionally, and was otherwise absorbed in his children — the more attractive, Mary felt, for this "instinctive selfish-unselfishness." Having expected little, and being unsure and impatient with "unholy" business, she was pleasantly surprised to find him a ready, reliable executor. He seems also to have thought she had improved, but saw her only about her business affairs.

Meanwhile, when Mary talked of "cloudless Italy" her father turned "cloudy"; he had his heart set on her staying. Although England seemed more odious than ever after Italy, she reluctantly agreed to make a trial of remaining near him for, perhaps, a year longer than she had planned. While she would be unable to leave when she decided the time had come, her present reasons for delaying were to shape her future.

She was "tied by the leg" to Godwin, as she said, as she was tied to Jane and Hunt, by aspiration to make up for past "derelictions" with moral heroism and emulation of Shelley's selflessness, self-sacrifice, patience, and gentleness. "Love transforms the true lover into a resemblance of the object of his passions," she was to write, of Petrarch.[8] Soon after she left Hunt, she began to protest the "wounds" he had inflicted in condemning her satiric "knife," and her susceptibility to low spirits, impatience, and protest. He had thought too hardly of her heretofore, she wrote him. "I am after all the same as then — the same weak fluctuating creature — but not all you say — yet I dont like myself I promise you —"[9] she added, and admitted to her own "deep and incurable wound" of guilt for having "failed" Shelley. That wound she salved by trust in their bond: "he was mine and loved me," she said.[10]

All the same, "I struggle like an animal in a net," she told Hunt.[11] It was as if she were fallen royalty of a vanished insurgent regime, having lived her young womanhood on a dissident Parnassus: "the spoiled child of my beloved" and the associate of Byron, both of them geniuses and maverick patricians, and in a little international set of elite free spirits; now she was cast down, and onto hostile terrain, alone, and as unresigned as Napoleon on St. Helena.

On the other hand she was inspired by the uncertainty of her situation, the change of scene, and the seeing of old friends. She was young and energetic, with an ironic sense of humor, a disposition so optimistic that Claire Clairmont did not trust her judgments, and irrepressible faith in her star. Once emerged from her solitary Italian exaltation, she reduced Shelley from a god to an incomparable, wondrously spiritual mortal, and was soon to fictionalize him simply as a youthful idealist. She gave a number of his holographs to his admirers if she had a duplicate or a copy. She believed, moreover, that bereaved women had every right to new love, knew she herself needed deep intense love, and hoped eventually to find "another companion" as her mother had found Godwin after Imlay. Meanwhile, she had her mission for Shelley, family, friends, and work.

Her momentum, however, was impeded. It was blocked by poverty and disrepute. In her relations with people, she feared that her superiority would offend, feared overestimating it or being hurt by lack of response, and the more she needed attention and approval the more she shrank from asserting herself. Writing was her natural, in fact necessary, means of revealing who and what she was. But in subject matter she was riveted to the past, and publishing had become a way "to bind the thoughts of my fellow creatures to me in love & sympathy."[12] As for a successor to Shelley, she was afraid of men, of being seduced by an Imlay or having to repulse unworthy men, since she could love only one as "superior" to her as Shelley. Otherwise, she felt that consecration to the dead was right and heroic.

These were the givens of her situation. Her basic aim was to "climb a staircase" of self-improvement, and she did so for the next four years, to a remarkable height. But it was a spiral ascent, when it might have been a forward trajectory, and at the end the whole structure was to collapse.

During her first months in England, Mary Shelley made herself into a professional woman of letters. She had heard that *Valperga* was in great demand, but it had sold only five hundred copies; the public and most critics expected a repeat of *Frankenstein*,[13] nor had its old-fashioned publisher marketed it aggressively; she never felt that it had fair play. The *Literary Chronicle,* however, gave her second novel an enthusiastic lead review, and some critics declared that she had greater dimension than *Frankenstein* indicated. She meant to take her time to make *The Last Man* her best work yet.

Because of her "temporarily" small allowance, she had also to write for money. Probably she used the profits of *Frankenstein*'s second edition to repay Horace Smith for his advance on *Valperga* and to mollify Shelley's creditors. The quickest source of cash was magazines, though she felt that such work cramped her style and capacity; Godwin always refused to write for periodicals. John Hunt offered her a "half-page" in the *Literary Examiner,* which she considered beneath her. Though she hesitated to "put herself forward," which Shelley had always done for her, when Lamb introduced her to the editors of the most serious literary monthly, the *London Magazine,* she found them eager for her work. Identified with liberalism, the *London* published Lamb's "Essays of Elia," Coleridge, Hazlitt, De Quincey, and Stendhal. The pay was a guinea a sheet. On October 14 she submitted a tale which she hoped would appear immediately, in the November number, perhaps "Recollections of Italy" which was published in January.[14]

Her campaign to make the world appreciate Shelley's genius and personal virtues was astutely planned. She decided to publish first his posthumous poems, then his prose. Some private verses she did not consider including, and she omitted his polemic poems — though she circulated them privately — in order to show "how he could write without shocking people," after which the public would be receptive to his complete works. In this decision she also deferred to John Hunt, recently imprisoned for an *Examiner* attack on Parliament and soon to be fined for publishing Byron's "Vision of Judgment."

She declined Procter's suggestion that she write a biographical preface, which, she told Leigh Hunt, "just at this moment would I think better come from you"; "more gracefully" than from Shelley's new widow. Hunt had begun an article on Shelley and would "write what we (you & I) would wish to be written," thus preparing the public for her biography.[15] In that work, remembering the seemingly irreparable damage Godwin had done her mother in his *Memoirs,* and disgusted, as Shelley had been, by public taste for details of private life, she meant to tell the truth and only the truth — but not all the truth, certainly not about Harriet Shelley's "adultery" or Claire Clairmont, who hoped never to see her name in print again.

After waiting for Hunt's preface until just before publication the following June, she wrote one herself. Hunt in fact intended to publish on his own. Moreover, unwisely, she had offered to press his claim on his brother John, who had not sent him the remittances he supposedly owed Hunt. John, an honorable if abrasive man, produced evidence that Hunt owed him eighteen hundred pounds for years of support; Mary then made protracted efforts to resolve the brothers' conflict. For her pains, Hunt suspected her of disloyalty.

As the excitement of London wore off, meantime, Mary dealt with the worsened quality of her life: aesthetic, financial, private, and social. She worked in her "centinal's box" of a study, and when she took her afternoon walk it was under a "whitewashed" sky between rains, through the din and dirt of London, to her friends' drab homes: "it is all so ugly," she said, as well as monotonous and oppressive. Resolved to remain "full of lofty thought, independant & firm," she tried to create an impervious little atmosphere around herself and Percy, kept up her studies and her Italian, sent Mrs. Mason original and translated poems for correction, went to the nearby British Museum for its prints of Italy and classic statues. That summer she meant to live in the suburbs where she could at least enjoy Nature.

Whitton had informed Peacock that she would get only what she needed for Percy: one hundred pounds a year, to be paid in quarterly installments; in purchasing power in Italy, Shelley had had two thousand. "I can earn a sufficiency I doubt not —" she wrote Marianne Hunt. "Mrs. Godwin makes *large eyes* at the quiet way in which I take it all."[16] Her basic needs were modest; Wollstonecraft had supported herself and Fanny by her pen. And Mary blamed her "miserable pittance" on Whitton, trusting that Sir Timothy would soon be more generous.

Of her nearest and dearest, four-year-old Percy could not fill her life, but he was a handsome, loving, clever little boy with his father's staring blue gaze, and she thought she saw other exciting signs of Shelley in him. Like her father before her, she gave him the best imaginative books, and taught him, " 'with his every accent . . . in every circumstance — to tell the truth.' "[17] A tender but firm mother, she had a playful way of relieving children's anger — telling the Kenneys' daughter, who was unjustly punished, that she had already paid for the next time she was naughty.

She saw her father every two or three days (Jeff complained that she forced her "odious" relations on her friends), and they were a familiar sight at the theater: her striking fairness against her habitual low-cut black gown, his bald head and folded arms. Godwin was often too harassed by debts and cares to be good company, and Mary could not talk about Shelley with him, but they had a double bond of devotion and professional work, though she deferred too much to his literary judgment. At his best her father was a ripely impressive old man, one of the great survivors, like an ancient deep-rooted tree in poor soil; Mary had much of his tenacity.

Mary and her stepmother kept on manageable terms, though Godwin's jealous wife made him pay for his joy in his daughter. Young William was a boorish, restless, twenty-year-old, bedeviled by incapacity to live up to his illustrious name. Godwin had had him trained for engineering, then architecture, but he was still dissatisfied. Mary was probably responsible for his finding himself. That fall he wrote two articles that John Hunt published in *The Examiner,* and thereafter he made writing his career, in which Mary was often to assist him.

Mary's relations with Jane Williams were curiously symbiotic. Though Jane was always fondly attentive, Mary sadly and resentfully saw that she was not as loving as her letters had been, while she loved Jane "better than any other human being": her partner in calamity, a victim of society, her link to the past, her means of both identifying with Shelley and expiating her "coldness" toward him. In everything small and large, she tried to give Jane pleasure and satisfaction, reduced her own worldly opportunities by making it clear that to accept her was to accept her friend, who had lived out of wedlock (Edward's mother told people that Mary's disrepute increased Jane's).

Jane spread her tales of the Shelleys beyond Jeff to a few of her and Mary's mutual intimates. But her motive was vanity, and in fact she could not do without Mary, for the duration of Mary's life. Faithful to Edward in her fashion, her secret affair with Jeff notwithstanding, she clung to the past as hard as Mary did; they talked by the hour of their Italian happiness and their return to Italy together. Without Mary to support, introduce, and escort her, Jane would have been even more isolated than she was.

When Hunt reproached Jane for saying "too much (not untruly God knows)" about Mary to others while saying nothing to Mary, Jane replied that if she told Mary her faults it would create an unpleasant discussion and do no good. No one, she added sincerely, better appreciated Mary's noble qualities than she herself. And having Mary enabled Jane, who did not love Jeff, to refuse his pressure to live openly with him. To Mary's annoyance, he reverted to supercilious abuse of both young women.

Of her old friends, Mary regularly saw the Gisbornes, who led a dreary life in the city, and the more stimulating Charles and Mary Lamb in Islington. Delighting in Charles's humor, she passed on to the Hunts his report of a cockney wife who was asked if she knew a particular lady: " 'I can't say I does, Ma'am, but the same Docter as lays me, lays her.' "[18] In her only new circle, that of Shaklewell Green, Edward Holmes swooned over her and over Shelley's "Jesus-Christ like philanthropy,"[19] — she dubbed him "Werther II," believing that Goethe had set youth an unfortunate model in that character — while Charles Cowden Clarke wrote songs to her, bad enough, as he said, to entitle him to be called "an A.S.S."[20] The Novellos' adolescent daughter Mary, who later married Clarke, had a crush on her:

> . . . her well-shaped, golden-haired head, almost always a little
> bent and drooping; her marble-white shoulders and arms statu-
> esquely visible in the perfectly plain black velvet dress . . . cut
> low . . . her thoughtful, earnest eyes; her short upper lip and in-
> tellectually curved mouth, with a certain close-compressed and
> decisive expression while she listened, and a relaxation into fuller
> redness and mobility when speaking . . .[21]

For more equal and attractive company she had Novello and Procter —
both of whom were safe: the first married, the second engaged to the
stepdaughter of Basil Montagu, Shelley's former counsel. By making his
devotion to his wife clear, Vincent put Mary at ease; each playfully acknowledged the other a "prediletto." In lieu of the intellectual exchanges
and exaltation in Nature that had previously triggered her imagination,
she got her literary inspiration from Vincent, who played the piano to fit
her mood: Gluck, Handel, Beethoven, and especially Mozart, whose chief
English champion Vincent was. For deeper sonorities, she heard Vincent
at the Portuguese Embassy Chapel, where he was organist.

Procter had been at Harrow with Byron, and was as frail as Shelley:
she joked about revering delicate minds whose strong thoughts "dilapidate
the walls of sense & dikes of flesh that the unimaginative contrive to keep
in such good repair."[22] She hastened to read his mediocre poetry. "Though
one need not praise an Author to his face — one must have read him,"
she said.[23] Nonetheless, vibrations passed between them during his too
rare calls, as he "bent his dark blue eyes" upon her. She and young Beddoes,
whose oeuvre was to be influenced by *Frankenstein,* were also mutually
impressed.

For the rest, she was annoyed and depressed at being confined to middle-
class inferiors; "a new world" to one accustomed to Shelley and Byron,
and to one whose distinction warranted the best England had to offer.
Godwin's best were a few professionals — the older playwrights Knowles
and Reynolds, the youthful Landseer, and the Prentis brothers, Stephen
a poet, Edward a painter — whom he invited for tea, supper, and whist
at The Strand, where Mary looked so out of place that Henry Crabb
Robinson did not know her at first; "elegant and sickly and young," and
an implausible author of *Frankenstein.* Harriet de Boinville, who had broken with Shelley when he left Harriet but now pitied and admired Mary,
would compare her to "an exotic transplanted unhappily into an unsuitable
soil and shrinking before rude and chilling blasts . . . Your early and intimate intercourse with the most refined of human Beings has left you a
standard for comparison which few in the most polished circles could bear
and from which springs (of necessity) your disatisfaction . . ."[24]

Polished circles, however, were closed to Mary Shelley. "I am under a
cloud," she would write Trelawny, "& cannot form new acquaintances
among that class whose manners & modes of life are agreable to me —
& I think myself fortunate in having one or two pleasing acquaintances
among literary people — whose society I enjoy without dreaming of
friendship."[25] Her position was indeed sharply dichotomous.

In 1823 *Frankenstein* soared beyond literary success into the domain of a classic; a total of four dramatizations were staged, after which some version was often on the boards. And Mary Shelley herself had become a romantic legend; a beautiful young genius who had risked all for love and suffered extreme tragedy. The first of many referential works appeared in 1824. In Medwin's *Ahasuerus* (which Mary said one had to be very patient to get through), the heroine watches for her lover-brother whose body washes ashore. " 'Oh! Why have I nothing to dedicate except this poor heart,' " she cries in Italian, and dies. Laetitia Landon's hugely popular *The Improvatrice* was inspired by Mary and *Valperga*'s Beatrice. One suspects Elizabeth Barrett Browning knew Landon's poem: "I loved him as young Genius loves / When its own wild and radiant heaven / Of starry thought burns with the light, / The love, the life, by passion given. / I loved him too as woman loves — / Reckless of sorrow, sin or scorn."

Mary Shelley had intriguing personal charms, of which she was quite aware. Godwin's "Beauty-daughter," James Northcote called her; "she rather thinks herself one, and yet there is something about her that would pass for such."[26] When Thomas Allsop saw Mary at the Lambs', he knew her because Hazlitt had told him that a Titian in the Louvre — surely his favorite *Titian's Mistress,* now called *Portrait of a Young Woman at the Toilet,* which Hazlitt had copied as a young art student in Paris — resembled Mary's serenely smiling "beautiful and peculiar expression" far more than a contemporary portrait could do; "Hers seemed a face that should be kept to acquire likeness."[27] Allsop observed that at first meeting she appeared unfeeling, even when she talked about Shelley, and seemed to contemplate everything "through the same passionless medium." But, as he added, "this cannot be real." The youthful Richard Henry Horne was moved by her soft melancholy and joy at his enthusiasm for Shelley. When at ease, she was ingenuous, open, direct, and gay, devoid of Britannic stiffness, her language "elegant" but unaffected. Occasionally she talked and laughed like an overflowing "goblet," though afterward she felt mortified.

Yet her obverse image was that of a radical, atheist Jezebel who had lived in sin with Shelley and participated in a League of Incest so promiscuous that when Allegra was born to Claire, Byron and Shelley threw dice to decide her paternity. "It is a notorious fact . . . ," said the editor Alaric Watts (a.k.a. "Attila" for his murderous tongue), "loudly talked of in London."[28] Many people believed that Mary had been Byron's mistress in Italy,[29] and were revolted by *Frankenstein*'s violence and blasphemy. Morals societies posted placards warning "fathers of families" against *Presumption*. A conservative French magazine seized on *Frankenstein* as a

paradigm of Romantic and revolutionary excess in a cartoon, "Le Romantisme ou le Monstre littéraire," picturing the hideously deformed,
enthroned monster in a toga, with a woman's disheveled hair, surrounded
by symbols of destruction.

As Mary Shelley later discovered, nevertheless (or rather consequently)
liberals would have courted her in Paris. If she had been a man she would
now have been welcomed in certain circles in England — even when morals societies were being led by high-minded citizens like the abolitionist
William Wilberforce, when a religious revival preached by the evangelical
Henry Irving induced some of the fashionable to observe Sundays,* and
when prudery, cant, and hypocrisy were pervasive. The serious review of
Valperga in *Blackwood's* regretted that any English lady could have conceived the anathema scene. It gave Mary understandable pleasure that a
clergyman who had attacked Shelley for seducing her and living inces-
tuously with Claire had just been exposed as a homosexual.

Years later, she would feel that she might have "become something" by
writing for a liberal faction if Godwin had not been out of the political
scene or if someone she looked up to had recruited, pushed, and supported
her. In fact, no professional liberal approached her at this time (John Hunt
only for literary work), as some feared that her name would hurt the cause,
nor did she consider a partisan career. Her forte was imagination, and she
lacked her parents' and Shelley's crusading urge, much less their capacity
(long lost in Godwin) to sustain attacks by the vicious opposition press.

Although they were clever and liberal, Procter's fiancée and her mother
refused to know Mary, as did all but exceptionally sympathetic women,
to whom in any case Mary felt more or less alien. As she wrote in 1826,
while she deplored much about Italian mores, the young Italian matron,
"ardent, simple-hearted, undisguising," had the freedom to say and do as
she pleased, whereas Englishwomen were confined "to the toils and dulness
of an English home . . . to the labour of giving dinners and entertaining . . . to the *sotto voce* tone . . . which characterizes our social intercourse,
to the necessity of for ever wearing that thick and ample veil of propriety
which we throw over every act and word . . ."[30] Regardless of gossip,
Mary saw her male acquaintances unchaperoned and told her friends when
she particularly liked a man. "It surely cannot be to her interest, being, as
she is, so utterly destitute of circumspection, to live amongst the lynx-
eyed prudes of England," Jeff had predicted.[31]

Furthermore, Mary found the "middling classes" to whom she had
looked as a progressive force, to be "ignorant, narrow-minded, and big-

* In *The Last Man* Mary was to create an Irving-type preacher who is one of the novel's
villains.

oted."[32] Marianne Hunt's mother, for instance, turned the classic nude statuettes on her piano backside. When Mary visited the Gisbornes, their new daughter-in-law left the room to weep on the housekeeper's shoulder at being required to know a shady woman, who moreover looked at her as if to say " 'that ignoramus does not understand us.' "[33] At this time there were organized groups of prominent women writers,[34] though none was on Mary Shelley's level, but her reputation barred her from belonging to them even had she wished to. Though she scorned aristocrats as a class, she missed their sophistication. If she had had Lord Holland for a sponsor — she lost that chance by refusing to remind Byron to write him — or if she had been rich, she might have enjoyed England.

"Those I would seek, fly me — I have no power," she protested in her journal.[35] Shelley's state in the grave, she said, was not more changed than hers. Indeed, one wonders if he could have survived in her position; his whole persona and his poetry had depended on his patricianhood and unearned income.

No wonder she longed to escape to Italy, her felt home, though she enjoyed debunking it as a romantic vision. One could live there pleasantly on little money, its class structure and female mores were freer, and its English expatriates infinitely nicer to her than most of her compatriots in her "so-called homeland." She had felt her best in Italy not only because of its beauty and culture, but also because of its climate, whereas in England's latitude she had seasonal mood swings; with shortening, gloomy days, troubles she had surmounted or trusted to improve seemed increasingly oppressive, hopeless; she grew diffident and anxious. In spring she recovered confidence, energy, and optimism, and reached a peak in summer, the hotter the better.

Her symptoms were severe that first winter. She could not concentrate on her studies; nothing she wrote pleased her; she felt she had lost her literary powers. She gained weight, and instinctively sought to be outside on rare bright days.

Being short of money, she had to put aside The Last Man to write magazine articles. One imaginative essay, "On Ghosts," appeared in the March London Magazine; another, "Recollections of Italy," in the January issue, and a story, "The Bride of Modern Italy," in April show Mary Shelley in her as it were Don Juan mode — which, unfortunately, she was rarely to employ thereafter. In "Recollections," a sort of sonata in prose, an ironically realistic first segment and coda frame a rhapsodic movement. "The Bride of Modern Italy," crisp, ironic, and realistic throughout, is Mary's version of Shelley's romance with Emilia Viviani; it presents him as a credulous, high-spirited seventeen-year-old, and serves as her comment on Shelley's verse to "E.V.," as she titled it, which she was publishing in *Posthumous Poems*. Godwin introduced her to Henry Colburn,[36] editor of the *New Monthly Magazine,* whose authors included Lady Morgan and Foscolo. He published her "Rome in the First and Nineteenth Centuries" (and a translation of Guidiccioni's "Sonnet to Italy" possibly by her) in March. She also helped Hunt place his work in the *New Monthly.*

The "mud of the magazines," however, made her more miserable. On December 15, for the first time in seven months, she seized her journal: "Was I once the beloved, the happy, the free? . . . the expression 'woman's weakness' truly belongs to my nerveless vacillating mind . . . bare & uncovered now, the evil men will throng round me —" On January 18 she regretted even her melancholy solitude in Albaro: "the resplendent sky was above me . . . Then my studies — my drawing . . . my Greek . . . my metaphysics that strengthened & elevated my mind — Then my solitary walks and my reveries — They *were* magnificent, deep, pathetic, wild and exalted — I sounded the depths of my own nature . . . my grief was active, striving expectant — I was worth something . . .

"I *know* that no good can come to me . . . ," she added. The day before she had visited Coleridge at Highgate: "his beautiful descriptions, metaphysical talk & subtle distinctions reminded me of Shelley's conversations — such was the intercourse I once dayly enjoyed — added to supreme & active goodness — sympathy of affection, and a wild picturesque mode of living that suited my active spirit & satisfied its craving for novelty of impression."

But, as she would later note, "Did I ever despair . . . ? Never! Some latent hope still remained — an untamed spirit still whispered consolation . . ."[37] Excited by the great actor Edmund Kean, she began a blank-verse tragedy for the stage. She threw page after page into her fireplace, but continued attending Kean's inspiring performances on John Hunt's free ticket until she was half-ashamed, and submitted an act to Godwin. Himself a failed playwright, he said that she too lacked dramatic gifts. "As to the idea that you have no literary talent, for God's sake, do not give way to such diseased imaginations," he implored.[38] She dropped her play, though Procter offered to help get it produced. Later she regretted having let Godwin talk her out of drama and was tempted to try again.

By March she was recovering. In spring, she once said, "one fancies change must necessarily ensue — & one looks forward to it with a feeling of hope."[39] Despite Sir Timothy's "professions" she believed he would increase her allowance in June. She and Jane were to summer in suburban Kentish Town. Even she was "sufficiently" pleased when George Canning — the Tory minister whom she admired for changing English policy to support national liberation movements — cited *Frankenstein* in a speech and called the author a "child of genius." She wrote Trelawny that she envied him sunlit Greece, his strenuous activity, and "seeing human Nature . . . among these Greeks and Trojans." But, she added, "One is always ready to throw the blame on the mere accidents of life — I might perhaps be as unhappy any where as here; and the delights of Italy might [be] torture . . . last week we had two really fine days."[40]

When Godwin's first volume of *History of the Commonwealth* (which he had formerly suggested to Mary) was criticized in the *New Monthly,* she went to Colburn for an explanation.[41] In mid-April she had Beddoes and Procter to tea, and she was correcting the first proofs of *Posthumous Poems.* And she reduced her weight with "prodigious" walks: "Ye Gods — how I walk! and starve." As the London season was at its height, she enjoyed a Mozart gala (a partisan event, since the aristocracy was currently lionizing his living rival Rossini) and exhibits of old masters. The Kenneys came from Paris for their annual working visit. Their friend John Howard Payne, the American playwright, to whom they may have introduced her in Paris — Payne was also a familiar of Godwin's and Lamb's — had moved to London and urged her to use his free tickets, so that she saw plays to her heart's content.

Suddenly depressed on May 14, she felt suited to describe her *Last Man*'s feelings, being herself "the last relic of a beloved race." Next day she believed she had had one of her premonitions, for news reached London that Byron had died in Greece: "the dear capricious fascinating Albe," she wrote in her journal, faulty but so often kind, "that resplendent spirit whom I loved" — and more truthfully crossed out the last three words. "Destiny gave to both of us the first spirits of the age," she wrote Teresa Guiccioli, "losing them, there is no second love . . . How much you feared this voyage! . . . But we are all Cassandras . . ."[42] Hesitant to capitalize on her association with Byron, she sent the *London* an anonymous tribute too late for inclusion.

On the "divine" night of June 8, shortly after finishing her preface for *Posthumous Poems,* everything came together for her. She spent that evening at St. Pancras churchyard, remembering her first love passage with Shelley. Byron's death had inspired her to a major alteration of *The Last Man.* To her protagonists representing Shelley and herself, she would add a Byron figure, make him England's future ruler, and give her work sociopolitical dimension. "I feel my powers again — & this is of itself happiness," she noted; "— the eclipse of winter is passing from my mind . . . I have been gay in company before but the inspiriting sentiment of the heart's peace

I have not felt before tonight — and yet, my own, never was I so entirely yours . . . May I die young!"

In mid-month *Posthumous Poems of Percy Bysshe Shelley* was published: it included sixty-five unpublished poems, thirteen out of print, and five translations.[43] Her preface went straight to the point of Shelley's ill repute: "his fearless enthusiasm in the cause which he considered the most sacred upon earth, the improvement of the moral and physical state of mankind, was the chief cause why he, like other illustrious reformers, was pursued by hatred and calumny." Ignoring his controversial private life, she extolled his virtues and gifts, and described her terrible vigil at Lerici.

Some reviewers criticized her "panegyric"; one blamed it on her association with the "cockney" Hunts whom "Mrs. Shelley has strength enough to do without." To her indignation, Hazlitt accused Shelley of having damaged the liberal cause by his extremism.* But most critics were moved by her brief testimony about Shelley and by her "bleeding heart"; in serving him she also served herself.

Posthumous Poems accomplished what Mary Shelley intended: before it, Shelley's immorality, destructiveness, and incomprehensibility were legend, and he was largely unread; upon its publication there was a surge of interest as he seemed at once more accessible and admirable. Moreover, though she has been charged with initiating the legend of the ethereal Shelley, that legend evolved out of his projection of himself and a cultural shift from the Byronic ideal to one of pre-Victorian evangelism, dedication, and earnestness. Besides, he grew to be a hero to radicals as well. The age would seize upon Shelley. In any event she had begun publicly to perform "the historic function of the great disciple,"[44] to dispel the isolation of the master and to compel the public to venerate the man as well as to respect his ideas and artistry. As will appear, she paid for it.

---

* When Mary saw Hazlitt she could not reproach him; he looked dreadful after his disastrous love affair with "Infelice," the subject of his *Liber Amoris* (at which she had earlier scoffed).

15 "The Union of Kentish Town"

ON JUNE 21, 1824, Mary Shelley moved to 5 Bartholomew Place, Kentish Town, one of a group of eighteen houses on the main road at the London end of the village, adjoining an extensive nursery garden and orchard, and near a nonconformist chapel whose Sunday faithful, wearing their "dreary church-going faces," she watched from her window with ironic mirth. Jane was a mile farther out, at 12 Mortimer Terrace. Mary expected to spend only that summer, but as it turned out she would stay for three years.

In point of fact she expected to leave for Italy with Jane the following spring. Though her funds had been so low that she could not move until she got her June quarter, which to her dismay, remained twenty-five pounds, Sir Timothy had accepted Shelley's 1817 will as valid; now, Whitton advised, she could borrow against her future legacy and buy an annuity for the period until Sir Timothy's death. Eagerly she authorized Peacock to investigate the cost of an annuity of three hundred or four hundred pounds a year.

Once the weather became, and even stayed, warm and dry, Mary's summer approached her Italian mode of life. She and Jane saw each other almost every day, Percy grew brown romping outside with Meddy and Dina, and Mary took walks over "Lawny uplands; — wooded paths, green lanes & gentle hills." She worked steadily on *The Last Man*. Her reading included Italian, Spanish, Latin, and Greek literature, and she borrowed classics she did not own from Hogg and Peacock.

About twice a month she and Jane went to the Novellos' at Shaklewell Green. The Lambs had her to Islington with their choice literary friends; sometimes she dropped in unannounced for a chat; and possibly she visited Coleridge again in nearby Highgate. Deriding the country gentry who quit their estates for the London season when the weather was at its finest, she could walk to the center city in forty minutes. Before the season's end that August, she heard the great dramatic soprano Giuditta Pasta, whose performance as Romeo transported her, and Carl Maria von Weber's sensational new *Der Freischütz,* with its Gothic stage effects and "stream of wild harmony."

Louisa Holcroft visited, and, from Genoa, Trelawny's *"brother-in-law"* (the brother of his former mistress), and Mrs. Thomas, who, however, dropped Mary because her inseparable friend Jane was a former "adulteress." The young poet "Arthur Brooke" (John Chalk Claris), author of an elegy of Shelley and himself mourning his wife, came at Mary's invitation, but when he showed signs of falling in love with her she definitively discouraged him.

In late June Byron's body arrived from Greece. She asked his solicitor, John Hanson, to let her view the body privately at the London undertaker's; finding the casket closed, she laid her hand on it in farewell. Byron's rascally black-clad servants tickled her, especially Fletcher, Byron's "Leporello" in carnal adventures, who was attesting to the purity of his master's life. Church authorities refused to entomb Byron's body in Westminster Abbey, so it was taken through Kentish Town to his family vault in a procession Mary was not asked to join. "He could be hardly called a friend —," she wrote Trelawny, "but connected with him in a thousand ways, admiring his talents & with all his faults feeling affection for him, it went to my heart when . . . the herse that contained his lifeless form, a form of beauty which in life I often delighted to behold, passed my window . . ."[1]

The months following taught her more about "that queer animal man" and gave her fresh reason to dislike his world. Byronomania was sweeping the western world and with it an imminent flood of often self-serving or hostile publications. Kenney asked her to meet Byron's friend Thomas Moore, who hoped to write a definitive biography and wanted her help. Mary knew that Moore had warned Byron against associating with Shelley in Pisa, but that had not diminished Shelley's admiration of Moore, man and poet, and Mary intended to give him constructive information only and to make certain he did not expose Claire Clairmont. On July 17 Moore and Kenney came for breakfast.

Mary explained the reasons for Hunt's and Byron's friction and corrected the rumor that Teresa Guiccioli had taken money from Byron. (Mary had told Jane that one advantage to Byron in having the wealthy Teresa as his mistress was that she cost him nothing.) She agreed to give Moore her recollection of Byron's memoirs, which she had read in Italy. Byron had given them to Moore to publish, but Byron's relatives and his executor, John Cam Hobhouse, had recently forced Moore to let them burn the manuscript, which, she privately said, Moore should have had the sense to read carefully before surrendering. Moore was nervous about an impending book on Byron by an "intimate" who he suspected might be Medwin. Naive Mary, who had seen Tom in London the previous winter, thought not.

Moore found Mary Shelley, unexpectedly, "very gentle and feminine," and after he sang one of his celebrated songs for her they went to the studio of Gilbert Stuart Newton (nephew of the American artist), to whom Washington Irving was sitting.[2] A gravely pleasant man of forty, the famous American author was visiting from Paris and enjoying both fashionable London and the particular society that Mary sorely missed; such as General Guglielmo Pépé, who had led the failed Naples Revolution. Irving, she told Charles Cowden Clarke with her usual openness, she found to be a delightful person.[3] Later she attended the premiere of Kenney's play with him, and he promised to call when next in England.

The day after meeting Moore, Mary heard from Tom Medwin at Geneva that he was indeed completing *Conversations of Lord Byron,* based on Byron's talks with him at Pisa and including a brief memoir of Shelley. If Mary did not approve what he had written, he offered to drop the book. Mary had decided not to write her Shelley biography until the Byron fever subsided, and feared that Tom, who had deplored Shelley's "errors of opinion" in *Ahasuerus,* would damage what she had already achieved with *Posthumous Poems* and expected to further with her forthcoming volume of Shelley's prose.

Kindly but firmly, she declined to see Tom's manuscript and asked him to omit Shelley from his book entirely, as well as any mention of herself because she disliked publicity, of Claire for obvious reasons, and of Jane because of her liaison with Edward. Indeed, she urged Tom to drop the whole project, since he had known Byron only four months and printing his capricious half-tipsy remarks was wrong and possibly harmful. Although she had known Byron far better — and could have made more than the five hundred pounds Tom received — she had sworn never to publish anything about him for profit. Moreover (like Peacock, who refused even to have his own works advertised), she had utter contempt for the self-aggrandizement that was one of Medwin's principal aims. "Years ago," she wrote Marianne Hunt, " 'When a man died the worms ate him.' — Now a new set of worms feed on . . . the world's love of tittle tattle — I will not be numbered among them."[4]

On July 23, she was shocked to learn that Sir Timothy was infuriated by *Posthumous Poems* and would terminate her allowance unless she withdrew it from circulation, stopped publication of the prose, and moreover promised not to publish anything by or about Shelley during his own lifetime. Three hundred copies of the poems had been sold, about tenfold more than any of the poems published in Shelley's lifetime, and the projected prose volume was slim. After urgent consultations with Peacock, who negotiated with Whitton, she capitulated to Sir Timothy. "There is no great harm in this, since he is above 70," she wrote Hunt, "& from choice I should not think of writing memoirs *now* . . . Such is the folly of the world . . . Sir T. writhes under the fame of his incomparable son as if it were a most grievous injury . . ."[5]

Equally compelling, Whitton doubled her allowance to two hundred pounds a year by himself supplementing, as a loan, Sir Timothy's hundred, and offered to ask Sir Timothy to fund her annuity; with that she could take Jane to Italy, help Claire, who was miserable in Russia, and live free until Sir Timothy's death made her rich. She made the best bargain possible for John Hunt and the guarantors, and before the unsold *Poems* were surrendered bought forty-one copies. She had also to turn over the prose manuscripts to Peacock, whom Whitton trusted, but she continued to gather Shelley's holographs and keep errata for eventual publication of his work. Peacock was also to recommend Percy's future school, agreeing that he must not have a "Godwin" education.

The emergency had thrown Mary off writing *The Last Man,* but she now told friends that her powers were restored, and Beddoes noted "great alteration for the better and the happier in her appearance and manner."[6] Mrs. Mason sent congratulations, along with the manuscript of her own new novel, *The Sisters of Nansfield* — which curiously combined facets of Harriet Shelley and Mary Shelley.*

Having received a touching letter from Teresa Guiccioli about Byron's death, Mary had the pleasure of seeing Teresa's brother Pietro Gamba, who had accompanied Byron's body from Greece. England would not be a bad country, she reported his saying, "se vedesse mai il Sole."[7] Trelawny had warned her against Pietro and she now understood why. Trelawny had sent Mary and several influential people an account of Byron's death that Pietro revealed to be mendaciously self-aggrandizing. Likewise Pietro refuted Trelawny's claim that Prince Alexander Mavrocordato, now president of the Greek provisional government, was a cowardly "shuffling . . . miserable Jew," whereas he himself had joined a great chief named Ulysses, in reality one of many venal warlords, whose adolescent sister he later married. "Poor Mavrocordato," said Mary, "beset by covetous

---

* The proud, conceited young heroine, named Harriet, elopes, to the fury of her husband's father; chastened by poverty, marital problems, and her husband's death, she and her little boy are eventually supported by her father-in-law, Lord Derham, a surname Mary was to use in *Lodore.*

Suliotes . . . caballed against by the strangers — poor, while every other chief is getting rich . . ."[8]

In late August she was distressed to learn that Medwin was going ahead with his book and with the Shelley memoir, which he sent her for correction. While hardly "one mass of mistakes," as she angrily said, hating inaccuracy, there were many errors, and Tom called Shelley's opinions "wild, visionary and dangerous." Moreover, he assailed Sir Timothy; the timing could not have been worse, just when she hoped to convince her father-in-law to fund her annuity. She returned the memoir, again vainly asking Tom not to publish it. Before *Conversations* appeared in October it was rumored that she was the author and Medwin her stalking horse.[9] If Sir Timothy had credited this, he would have terminated her allowance.

Tom had been more unscrupulous than she expected. His few references to her were respectful, and he omitted mention of Jane and Claire. But he named Teresa Guiccioli as Byron's mistress, claimed that Byron had never loved her, and included cruel, derisive quotations about many of Byron's friends. "By God it is scandalous to ruin people in this way —" Mary wrote Teresa.[10] The infuriated Hobhouse prepared a rebuttal, which, at Pietro's request, Mary checked against her journal and to which she added — though she let pass Tom's false claim to have witnessed Shelley's cremation. But Tom had indelibly impressed her with the uses to which private communications could be put. As Hobhouse had given Pietro his sister's letters to Byron, she asked Hobhouse for "certain letters," probably Claire's (Byron had given her some of Shelley's). Hobhouse wrote thanking her for her help, but kept the letters.*

By the time Hobhouse's article appeared in the *Westminster Review,* however, she had forgiven Tom and wrote to congratulate him on his marriage to a wealthy Swedish baroness. His stationery displayed a coronet and a motto: *Nous ne changerons jamais.* "Happy Medwin," said she dryly. When Tom belatedly challenged Hobhouse, she told the latter it was ludicrous to duel on a literary subject.

"The secret of life appears to me, to be the power of conquering pain & evil . . . ," Mary had written Arthur Brooke in June. "If years do not conquer me, and I trust that I shall die young, I entertain the hope, that I shall overcome misfortune, & continue true to myself & to him with whom my happy years were spent."[11] That, however, was her way of forestalling impossible suitors. On August 30 she turned twenty-seven, and her demand for the real gratifications of life, which neither books nor Percy nor Jane Williams could satisfy, asserted itself.

* In the spring of 1826 Mary tried to help her father retrieve her mother's love letters to Fuseli from the deceased painter's executors.

Procter had married, and dropped her owing to his wife's refusal to know Mary. She recalled the superlative men who had cared for her — Shelley, Byron, Mavrocordato, Williams: "hope & youth are still in their prime, & the pains I feel therefore are ever alive & vivid within me . . . ," she noted on September 3; "they talk of my personal attractions — of my talents — my manners . . . But now I am not loved — I never shall be loved . . . be happy . . . feel life sit triumphant in my frame . . ."

"It is strange also that religious feeling that exalted my emotions in happiness directs me in my misery," she added, however. Jane could not bear to return to London's insults and wretchedness, and deserting her was unthinkable, so Mary decided to stay in Kentish Town for their "last" English winter. "Even in winter the country is most delightful . . . ," she said, "naked woods open sky & green meadows transcend the dirt & gloom of streets."[12] She put Percy in a local day school. Whitton delayed broaching the subject of her annuity to Sir Timothy until October: "he may waste time, but not eternity," she wrote Jeff, "since before the end of that Sir Tim or I will be in kingdom Come, where the acres of the S. estate will probably be of little value . . . while I have bread & potatoes, what is the rest?"[13] Whitton, according to Sir Timothy, had "ever been a powerful advocate in her favour,"[14] but he had to desist when his client fell seriously ill from chronic gout. Mary refused to hope that the old man might die.

Meanwhile, however, the oncoming rainy winter triggered her seasonal depression, worsened by discovering that out of sight in Kentish Town in bad weather was out of mind in London. Once a week she slogged into town to see her father, but no one came out to the village. Vincent Novello was tending his wife, who was disconsolate over an unwanted, ninth pregnancy and, said Mary, "in the horrors of the Month expectant." Neither Moore nor Hobhouse paid their promised calls. Irving remained in Paris. Playfully she reproached her Shaklewell "cavaliers" and Moore. Moore replied that he was terribly busy, but in fact Hobhouse had withdrawn his consent to Moore's biography of Byron, and neither man had further need of her. After all she had done for Hobhouse, a radical M.P. but in her case unconcerned for the weak, Mary later allowed herself to ask him to get her into the ladies' gallery of Parliament to hear the debates on Catholic emancipation and to get background for her parliamentary scenes in *The Last Man*.

Life was drearily monotonous; except for Percy and Jane she was quite alone. "What can I do? how change my destiny? . . . Why is the companion of Shelley companionless . . . ?" she noted on October 26, angry at being reduced to the "pityful" expedient of her journal. "Truly if I am vain, I am sufficiently mortified . . ." Adding to her mortification, instead of being notified personally about a piece she wrote for the *London Magazine* she learned of its rejection by seeing a note to "M. S." in the periodical. She was seized by bitterness at men, "strong only to oppress." Having helped her with Greek, Jeff remarked that intellectual women forfeited men's chivalry. If ". . . I cannot obtain the courtesy of your species I will cut their acquaintance for ever," she retorted.[15] "I endeavour to rouse my fortitude and calm my mind by high and philosophic thoughts," she wrote on December 3, after immersion in Cicero's *De finibus bonorum et malorum:*

> deserted . . . disdained — insulted . . . Ever ready — too ready — to undervalue myself, I might attribute this to the defects of my character . . . [but] it is because I am a woman — poor & unprotected . . . Most women I believe wish that they had been men — so do not I — change my sex & I do not think that my talents would be greater — & I should be like one of these — selfish unkind — either pursueing for their own ends or deserting — because those ends cannot be satisfied . . . Years hence . . . old — ugly — but rich . . . my drawing room may be crouded . . . but now . . . young & affectionate of heart I inexpressibly long for some circumstance that may assure me that I am not utterly disjoined from my species . . . O help me spirits of the wise & ye beloved, to conquer this yearning after unattainable good — & tame my soul, not to ignoble suffrance — but to an haughty bending to the hand that oppresses me — teach me in my little humble room to nourish lofty thoughts & worthy desires . . . patience wisdom & content — I will not stoop to the world . . . I will endeavour to remain unconquered by hard & bitter fortune — yet the tears that start in my eyes shew the pangs she inflicts . . . shall I ever be a philosopher?*

In this impasse, Jane Williams gradually became Mary's second great love, through whom she would be what she wished she had been to Shelley: unstinting, idolatrous, self-sacrificing. That summer Jeff had told Mary that he loved Jane, and Mary, feeling that she would "give worlds to see dear Janey happy," only regretted that Jeff, with his caustic egotism, had not done so, and advised him that if Jane accepted him he should take her to the Continent and give up the law: "I should think myself

---

* For the next two years Mary carried in her reticule a card with a Cicero quotation on it: "Reason possesses an intrinsic element of dignity and grandeur, suited rather to require obedience than to render it, esteeming all the accidents of human fortunes not merely as endurable but also as unimportant, a quality of loftiness and elevation, fearing nothing submitting to no one, ever unsubdued." (Abinger MSS.)

very silly, if I could not find occupation more profitable to mind & body . . ."[16]
"O my Dear," she wrote Teresa on December 30, "if you knew the men
that dare to aspire to be the successors of Shelley and Williams — My
God — we are reduced to this —"[17]

But on January 30, 1825, Jane asked her to leave Mortimer Terrace
because Jeff was there, and it dawned on Mary that the two were lovers.
Jealous, infuriated that she had sacrificed her possibilities in London
for this, shocked at the duplicity of Jane, whom Shelley too had idealized, "So be it! —" Mary noted fiercely. "I w^d not for worlds do other
than I do, & yet — I make not her happiness . . . poverty stricken — deformed squinting lame — bald . . . it is quite just that I should be ejected
from the sight of man . . . I should like to see Shelley just for one half
hour —" And she slashed a great streak across the page.

When she confronted Jane, however, Jane explained that she did not
love Jeff but had been unbearably wretched, frightened, and purposeless
without a man, given her ostracism. Disarmed and hot for sacrifice, Mary
proposed an alternate union of herself and Jane: loving friendship, "confidence and entire sympathy, independent of worldly circumstances."[18]
Jane agreed, if with less ardor, and broke provisionally with Jeff[19] — who
later left for a long tour of Italy to develop his sensibilities. Thus Mary
determined "if she must give up her friend or the world, to make her
election against the world."[20] The world is "a tiger-haunted jungle,"
she wrote in *The Last Man;* its system of social intercourse based on
birth and power false, paltry and futile; "love and life" are our true em-
perors. "I was so ready to give myself away," she later told Trelawny
insouciantly, "— & being afraid of men, I was apt to get *tousy-mousy* for
women . . ."[21] But at the time Jane became "necessary to my existence
almost."[22]

In February Sir Timothy recovered and refused to fund Mary's annuity.
Shortly after, Godwin declared bankruptcy and dissolved M.J. Godwin &
Co. There remained, Mary said, "his pen and me." Charles Clairmont had
married a Viennese woman and expected a child; Claire was saving to
escape Russia; William could just support himself. Mary tried in vain to
raise a large sum for her father from an insurance company with whom
Peacock had begun negotiations for her annuity, and then drained her
funds for the Godwins' move to a pleasant house at Gower Place near the
British Museum. Thereafter, when necessary, she supplied Godwin with
money to bring his income to three hundred pounds a year, a hundred
pounds more than her own allowance and another reason to stay in Kentish
Town rather than expensive London.

As Pietro Gamba was returning to Greece, he put Teresa's letters to

Byron in Mary's safekeeping. Teresa, Mary wrote the countess, should someday use these and Byron's love letters to write the story of their romance, "more romantic than any fictional romance,"[23] which also would disprove Medwin's cruel disparagement. Presumably with Pietro's permission, Mary copied portions of seven of Teresa's letters referring to herself and Shelley, for her future Shelley biography.[24] Mary and Pietro spent their last evening at Kean's *Othello,* which the Pisan Circle had rehearsed, and she gave him a letter for Mavrocordato, congratulating him and trusting that England would be a true friend to the "meilleure et plus noble cause qu'existe."[25]

Spring brought Mary Shelley out to bask in the sun on the grass, reading Virgil's *Georgics* and Lord Shaftesbury, and watching Percy fly kites and garden. "I begin to live again," she wrote Hunt. She wrote, however, in tears, for Hunt (still angry about his brother John) had sent his article on Shelley to the recently founded Benthamite *Westminster Review* without a word to her. She knew about the piece because, of course, the editor of that philosophic radical monthly, John Bowring, submitted it to her for her approval. She approved it, with the proviso that Hunt omit all reference to Claire and not identify Jane. But Peacock, to whom Bowring also sent the piece, fixed on what she had passed over, probably because of her distress over Hunt's unkindness: on the issue most damning to Shelley, his treatment of Harriet, Hunt claimed that the couple had separated "by mutual consent" after Charles's birth — when Shelley had formed his liaison with Mary against Harriet's will and months before the birth. Mary wrote Hunt that this "vital" point must be corrected; "Shelley's justification, to me obvious, rests on other grounds . . ."[26] Then Peacock persuaded Bowring not to publish Hunt's article even if corrected, as it would jeopardize Mary's arrangements with Sir Timothy.

That April, Mary Shelley and John Howard Payne met again and quickly became friends. Much has been made of this episode, which is interesting mainly for highlighting the causes for Mary's attachment to Jane. Then thirty-four, Payne was a veteran, debt-laden man of the theater whose creative level may be judged from his most famous operatic aria, "Home, Sweet Home." Unbeknownst to Mary, he had been struck by her years before they met, when he glimpsed her at the theater in the Marlow period, and more recently feared falling in love with her, since he knew her to be far above him. As he urged her to ask him for seats, she frequently wrote for tickets and treated friends if she could not go — "no sendings back," he insisted. He squired her and Jane to the theater or the opera (Mary paid for her opera seats); a boon, as the English ban on unescorted lady theatergoers was such that when young Harrison Ainsworth met Mary, looking "very handsome," at the Lambs' that spring, she promptly arranged for him to accompany her.[27] Once when Mary and Jane went alone, they pretended to be foreigners.

Mary had Payne to tea and engaged in long fireside chats, shoptalk, and gossip, for which she had a decided taste. He lent her books by his compatriots James Fenimore Cooper, Charles Brockden Brown, and her "favourite," Irving, Payne's friend and professional collaborator, who, she frankly said, interested her. Payne asked why she, young, lovely, and renowned, buried herself in Kentish Town. She explained that she was dedicated to Shelley, Jane, and her bankrupt father, whereupon Payne replied almost worshipfully that she was a "heroine in love and friendship and duty," uniting "superior intellectual endowments with simplicity, fervour, and elevation and purity of character."[28]

Mary demurred that the instinct of self-preservation bound her to Jane, who alone "could alleviate almost unendurable sorrow . . . you must not make me vain — or perhaps worse egotistical — That is the worst part of a peculiar situation, which by making you the subject of over attention . . . creates an undue estimation of self in one's own mind." We "must step lightly on the mosaic of circumstances," she added, to damp his ardor. "The world is a hard taskmaster & talk as we will of independance we are slaves."[29] Payne returned that her real character was inaccessible to any externals "excepting, perhaps, such as can make earthquakes."[30] But he was emboldened by her liveliness during an opera performance over a Spaniard in the audience who ogled her and followed her out. She teased Payne that she was faithful to Irving, took offense at his overfamiliar response, then apologized: "A bad conscience . . . my Dear Payne, is proverbially susceptible — And the feeling that what passed . . . was not quite *en règle* made me captious. I accused myself & so did not like to be accused (as I thought:) by another."[31]

Walking her home from Godwin's on June 25, Payne gave signs of declaring his love. She forestalled him by saying, gently but frankly, that in the hypothetical event that devotion to Shelley permitted her a "second connection" he must be a man whose character and genius approached Shelley's, who "had drawn her from obscurity." Inevitably Payne was hurt; indeed, he felt she had used him to reach Irving. He confessed his long-standing attachment and said he would tell Irving of her interest. He was too upset to see Mary but asked her to write as usual when she wanted seats. It was her hard fate, she wrote in regretful compliance, "either to be deserted & neglected — or, which turns out the same thing, to be liked too well, & so avoided —" Moreover, "How can Irvine surrounded by fashion rank & splendid friendships pilot his pleasure bark . . . into this sober, sad, enshadowed nook?"³²

"Be not a tell tale so God bless you —" she wrote Payne when he left on business for Paris, adding a coquettish come-on: "Give my love, of course Platonic, to I."³³ He showed Irving their correspondence, exposing her to humiliation as she had humiliated him, and probably chilling whatever interest Irving may have had in her. Mary corresponded with Payne with genuine affection, asking him to burn her long letters (some he kept, others he copied in his letterbook): ". . . though I can rein my spoken words — I find all the woman directs my written ones & the pen in my hand I gallop over fence & ditch without pity for my reader — ecce signum!"³⁴ She offered him *The Last Man* to publish in Paris. The following summer he returned to England and thereafter was her true friend.

"The hope & consolation of my life is the society of [Jane]," Mary had written Hunt on June 27. "To her, for better or worse I am wedded — while she will have me & I continue in the love-lorn state that I have since I returned to this native country of yours —"³⁵ Indeed, Jane plus "divine" summer weather made her happier than she had been in years. More than emotions, however, bound her to Jane. For more than three years her private life would be based on an ideal of a little community of outcast women (which Claire Clairmont talked of but never practiced) and on a "difference feminism" that extolled "feminine" attributes and defended women's weakness and flaws,* whether stemming from nature or nurture; given the experience of her own weakness Mary suspected the former to be true, but believed that becoming like men would debase her gender.

For Jane their "union" was an unsatisfactory necessity. Though she bent to Mary's affection, on the rare occasions when she let Mary make serious confidences she withheld the sympathy that Mary equated with love: "the intense essence of sympathy, is love," Mary was to write, and, in the same book, "Love['s] essence is the excess of sympathy."³⁶ All the same, when Jane had the money to go to Italy she would not leave Mary. Mary encouraged her to develop her capabilities. Jane completed a play of Edward's, which Mary offered Payne for production, wrote children's stories, and began a tale about herself, her "idol" Edward, Shelley, and Mary,

* Around this time, when a wealthy friend of Trelawny's and Medwin's, the Reverend John St. Aubyn, seven years Mary's senior, brought her the beginning of a memoir of his long affair with a cruel mistress that he intended to publish for revenge, she performed "the most essential service" anyone had ever done him by insisting that nothing could justify injuring a woman, and that honorable conduct from man to woman "is the first of manly virtues." (John St. Aubyn to MWS, Sept. 10, 1826, Abinger MSS.)

"delicately fair and 'beautiful in her young wisdom' . . ."[37] "Mental occupations," Jane wrote Claire, were her major solace.

Jane's great reciprocal gift was her ability to make Mary laugh. Defying
"every peril," the two young women walked to the Novellos' or the Lambs'
and back to unlit Kentish Town even in rain, "wet thro' & thoroughly
uncomfortable in company," Mary recalled, "laughing the while as if we
were kittens in clover — Happy days those, my Janey."[38] When the Hunts
returned to England that fall, Marianne pregnant with her eighth child,
Mary and Jane trudged about to get them settled in Highgate, and went
there of an evening to talk and dance quadrilles to Hunt's piano. Shelley's
portrait by Amelia Curran finally arrived in September, moving Mary to
an emotional entry in a new (and last) journal notebook, before she turned
again to Jane.

In September Mary spent ten days at Windsor with Jane in order to
vivify her writing about the place, which was prominent in *The Last Man*.
She had hoped to complete the novel months before; the difficulty was
to sustain both the "universal" scene and the particular interest required
for a novel. But she was near enough to the end to ask Colburn to publish
it, he being a cagy, high-powered marketer of books who, said Lady
Morgan, "could not take his tea without a strategem."[39] Horace Smith
(now living in England) acted as Colburn's reader, and after Colburn
accepted the novel, Ollier, who worked for Colburn, filled Mary's need
for books describing "minutely" the environs of Constantinople for her
scenes of Greek-Turkish battle. Colburn rushed the work into publication
on January 23, 1826, preventing Mary from making the revisions she
knew it needed.

Although in this period Mary lived so reclusively that few people knew
her whereabouts, she was currently in the public mind through Lord
Normanby's best-selling novel *Mathilda* — whose heroine, a Carbonara,
elopes with a lover to Naples, where she is ostracized by the English colony;
at the end, she waits on shore for her drowned lover, whose boat has sunk
in a squall. Novels with characters modeled on real people were the rage.
Nevertheless, as England was entering a long financial depression, Colburn
paid only three hundred pounds for *The Last Man*, one hundred less than
Valperga had brought.

Second to *Frankenstein, The Last Man* is Mary Shelley's most original
and impressive fiction. Huge, part prose poem, part novel, and pushing
the limit of the tragic-sublime, it is an extended metaphor of her life
experience, as well as a mine of her vocabulary of images, history, myth,
literature and the arts, and of her prophetic gift. Above all, it constitutes

both intrinsically and purposefully her current manifesto of the power of the human mind — "So true it is, that man's mind alone was the creator of all that was good or great to man, and that Nature herself was only his first minister," she begins[40] — despite the ensuing dramatization of human flaws, blindness, and subjection to Nature.

Characteristically, she tried to forecast what the twenty-first century might be, not what she wished it to be, and depicted varieties of good and bad ambition in her characters. Particularly in England, a world leader, science has brought abundant food, labor-saving machines, and swift transportation including balloon flight. Social conflict and injustices have been ameliorated, not eliminated, likewise, the female condition. In the Shelley-utopian Adrian and the Byronic-egotist Lord Raymond, she makes the first analysis of two polar Romantic mentalities: their philosophic positions, their psychological makeup, and the private and political actions that might follow from them.

She delineates aspects of herself in a double alter ego, the narrator, Lionel Verney, and his sister, Perdita. As children, both were unloved orphans. Thanks to Adrian's instruction, Lionel becomes a humanist author-intellectual and a loving family man. Unschooled, withdrawn, proud young Perdita is misgiving of herself and others; after marrying Raymond, she is happy living at Windsor with him, Lionel, and his wife, Idris (who partakes of Mary Shelley and Jane Williams), their children, and the unmarried Adrian.

The English monarchy had ended when Adrian's father had abdicated the throne. After debate among "willing slaves" of monarchy, republican-libertarians led by a demagogue, and Raymond, who argues that the "commercial spirit" of republicanism leads to rule by the wealthiest, Parliament elects Raymond as Lord Protector. He initiates public programs to end poverty and make England fertile, magnificent, and orderly.

Raymond, "wrapt in visions of power and fame," takes a mistress, an emancipated, ambitious former Greek princess. Perdita leaves him, the more bitterly because a woman cannot launch out "with pleasure or ambition at the helm." As with Victor Frankenstein, their egotism creates fatal familial disorder, here paralleled by cosmic calamity. Raymond leads a Greek revolution against the Turks and is killed in a huge explosion that generates a plague-contaminated cloud spreading fatal disease throughout the earth:

> Nature, our mother, and our friend . . . shewed us plainly, that,
> though she permitted us to assign her laws and subdue her ap-

parent powers, yet . . . She could take our globe, fringed with mountains, girded by the atmosphere, containing the condition of our being, and all that man's mind could invent or his force achieve . . . and cast it into space, where life would be drunk up, and man and all his efforts for ever annihilated.[41]

In remorse over Raymond, Perdita drowns herself. Dying nations are reduced to struggling groups, some sustained by selfless leaders, others betrayed by self-servers, one by a fanatic religious cultist. All Lionel's loved ones die. He alone survives on earth: ". . . I will sit amidst the ruins and smile."[42] But he goes to Rome, repository and symbol of human greatness and creative imagination, which he himself affirms by writing *The Last Man*. At thirty-seven, rather than degenerate he sails out on the world's oceans, driven by "fierce desire" for change, danger, experience, and action, watched by spirits of the dead and "the ever-open eye of the Supreme." Thus, through her fiction, Mary Shelley ends as one unresigned to fate, refusing to live in the past, and launching out.

Mary presented a copy of *The Last Man* to Jane, with a poem to the "dear solace of my life." Jane reciprocated with five stanzas, "An emblem fit of thy dear love." One admirer sent Mary a poem, "Awe-striking Dame!"; another predicted that her novel would endure "while Love remains in the world . . . while Liberty is sought after by men . . ."[43] Jeff was moved to tears at the achievement of his "Sybil." Due to its subject, author, and advertised "portraits" of Byron and Shelley, the book was initially in demand. There were some appreciative reviews. John Martin showed *An Ideal Design of The Last Man* at the British Artists' exhibition that year, and subsequently did two watercolors and an important oil on the subject. Procter told Beddoes she had outclassed Campbell's "Last Man"; "in almost every respect she will do much better than either of us," replied Beddoes, who gave up his own "Last Man," "indeed she has no business to be a woman by her books."[44]

However, the public and most critics disliked the novel's grimness, mix of genres, and high Romanticism, then going out of fashion. It became more an "in" topic than a book actually read. (In 1828 the publisher Rudolf Ackerman put out a card game: "The Sybil's Leaves; or a Peep into Futurity.") One reviewer called the book an "elaborate piece of gloomy folly." Some criticized Mary Shelley for unfeminine coarseness, brutality, and pretension, calling her "Lady Metaphysics." The concept of the human race ending, which today seems plausible, affronted progressives, while conservatives castigated her godlessness and political views. *The Last Man* was banned in Austria, though it was published in France.

The reception of the book into which she had poured herself so demoralized Mary Shelley that she did not begin another novel for a year and a half. To make matters worse, Sir Timothy was furious to see her name and Shelley's in advertisements and reviews. He demanded that she give up writing and stopped her allowance, which Whitton thereupon lent her. Peacock protested that the publicity was Colburn's doing, that the title page read simply "Author of Frankenstein," and that it was unreasonable to expect her to give up her career and needed income. Whitton agreed, but each time his client saw "the name" he got angrier. John Bowring, an admirer of *The Last Man* and a fine linguist who lent her Spanish and Portuguese works, found her a Greek teacher, whom she could not afford. Bowring, secretary of the Greek Committee, had also gotten her news of Trelawny, who had been seriously wounded.

That spring was perversely late and rainy. "The English are a wonderful people — but it is melancholy to see them expend their energies on the cultivation of a swamp —" Mary wrote the playwright John Poole, who sent her complimentary tickets to his new play.[45] Being "amphibious," she got in to London, attended the intellectual *conversazione* of Dr. William Kitchner, and was asked by Newton to sit for her portrait; this she declined because poverty prevented her from buying it and "aristocrasy" from letting him put it up for sale. And she was bored: "being early inocculated with a love of wandering and adventure," she wrote Payne, "my monotonous present existence grows insupportably tedious."[46]

Unable to launch out, by summer Mary was genuinely in love with Jane; "passionate and engrossing love." While she had Jane, "my soul's sunshine," she wrote Payne, she looked on her troubles as a tribute paid to fortune. "She is in truth my all — my sole delight —" she told Hunt. "This excessive feeling . . . has grown slowly, but is now a part of myself —"[47] Sometimes when she got home from Jane's, she shed tears of happiness, or of pain that Jane did not fully reciprocate her love. While refraining from extravagant endearments face to face, she wrote Jane without inhibition, speaking of her "Sweet loveliness," her "perfections of grace & beauty," or, more raunchily: "in fact, dear, except the feminine what is amiable except our pretty N———" ("Notches," slang for female genitals).[48]

Concurrently, Mary turned misanthropic, referring scornfully to God as "Person." "This is [the] prerogative of Manhood!" she wrote Jane of a debased aristocrat who was received everywhere while his wife, a professional singer, was ostracized. In a critically astute letter to *The Examiner*, signed "Anglo:Italicus" (and a second letter that was not published), Mary defended the artistry of the castrato Giovanni-Battista Velluti, whose effeminacy offended many English, and said privately that she preferred Velluti's delicacy to "the boasted energy of that vain creature *man*."[49]

During the past year, furthermore, Mary had befriended a brilliant, bizarre social outcast, Mary Diana Dods, whom Lamb may have recommended to her. By this time "Doddy" was a visiting member of the Kentish Town union and had entrusted to Mary and Jane her life secrets, which have only recently been uncovered.[50] Mary Diana Dods was one of two illegitimate daughters of the Scottish Earl of Morton. Unlike the Ladies of Llangollen, who were visited by Godwin among many others,* she was a "living lie,"[51] a secret lesbian and sometime transvestite. She had achieved literary success as "David Lyndsay." Ambitious and audacious, she had written *Dramas of the Ancient World* as a challenge to Byron's genius, and sent it to him at Pisa, where Mary had judged it powerful but as unlike Byron as "Short life" was to "Immortality." Recently she had published *Tales of the Wild and Wonderful.*

Even "Lyndsay's" publishers never saw her, a "grotesque-looking," cropped-haired, slightly humpbacked figure in a shapeless dress, who looked like a man in women's clothes. Mary, however, firmly took her friend to Dr. Kitchner's. A Tory and a contributor to *Blackwood's,* "Doddy" proved to Mary that the magazine was not hostile to Shelley, as Mary had thought, and wrote the editors that Mary was "a million times too good for the party to which she is so unlucky as to belong . . . she has a very powerful mind, and with the most gentle, feminine manner and appearance that you can possibly imagine."[52] She had warmer feelings, which Mary gently discouraged, judging from a poem in Italian she left Mary when she went abroad in October of 1826; since Mary could not love her as a lover, Mary would be to her like a "young bride whose mother misses her," "the beloved sister of a brother."[53] Mary acted as her literary agent during her absence.

Prior to Doddy's departure Mary took another victim of society under her wing, Isabel Robinson, who was in Claire Clairmont's former plight. A clever, seductive, dark-haired *mignonne* of about twenty, Isabel had become pregnant by a lover who could not or would not marry her.[54] Somehow she concealed her pregnancy even from her family and put her baby out to nurse at Highgate. She suffered from migraines and asthma and had "great talents," according to Mary, who encouraged her to write and began plotting with Jane to help their new young friend.

In early July Mary had news from Whitton that both shocked and filled her with hope: Shelley's son Charles was dying of tuberculosis; Percy

* Melusina Trench and her highly respectable minister son were proud of knowing the Ladies.

would be heir to the Shelley title and entailed estates. Of course, if Percy should die before Sir Timothy, Mary would have nothing, but while she was oppressed by the fatality that destroyed Shelley's children, she was convinced, accurately, that Percy was impervious. And she had flashes of ineffable relief at the prospect that Sir Timothy would deal more generously with his heir's mother.

She, Jane, and their children spent the August of 1826 together in Brighton, with an excursion to one of Percy's prospective properties, Castle Goring. Mary disliked the resort's glare, barren landscape, and the fashionable bustle from which the "hermitresses" were willingly shut out, as she wrote Payne, who had returned to England. But it was a delight being with Jane all day long, and she was full of ideas for articles.

On September 14 Charles Shelley died. Sir Timothy restored Mary's allowance and took under five months' advisement what he would give her in the future. She wrote Hunt a letter of intent to leave him the two thousand pounds Shelley had willed him and tried to help him — dilatory in his work, improvident, and harassed by poor Marianne's alcoholism — to raise money on it. Serene as in her happy years, though her life was as yet unchanged, she prophesied that change was coming. Even that winter was not to discontent her.

Between Mary's discouragement over *The Last Man*'s reception and her sense that it was a dead end in style and content, she had lowered her sights and begun research for a history of Perkin Warbeck, medieval pretender to the throne. That summer she used the material for "Lacy de Vere," a story of revenge: "HATRED alone can survive all change."[55] This was her first of many works for a well-paying and expensive, popular new genre, called Annuals, which had an August deadline for publication in November as Christmas gifts. The Annuals commissioned engravings by the best artists, then prominent authors wrote stories and poems for which the engravings could serve as illustrations.

In October, Bowring's *Westminster Review* published Mary Shelley's first book review, of Lord Normanby's *The English in Italy* and related books by Anna Jameson and Charlotte Eaton. *Westminster* articles were unsigned, but her authorship was evident. She opened with reference to her elopement tour, and posited the existence of an Anglo-Italian cult, fathered by Byron, to which she adhered; she praised the Italians for their attempted revolt against Austria, and chided Normanby for "offensive display" of his rank and, mischievously, for the ending of his *Matilda*. (Her probable second *Westminster* review, of Thomas Roscoe's *The Italian Novelists*, appeared in January.)

She also wrote "A Visit to Brighton" for the December *London Mag-*

azine, and two pieces that the *New Monthly Magazine* rejected, one an amusing essay on the purported "reanimation" of a seventeenth-century Englishman; the magazine had already accepted an article on the subject. Alaric Watts (apparently low on her list) solicited pieces for his Annual from her and "David Lyndsay" but declined her 1820 dramas "Proserpine" and "Midas." By now she decided to write *Perkin Warbeck* as a historical romance, but Colburn did not seem enthusiastic, so she offered to translate Augustin Thierry's *Histoire de la Conquête de l'Angleterre par les Normands* or *L'Osservatore Fiorentino.*

"Happy when with Jane — happy while studying Greek," in her dreams of change that winter she envisioned Trelawny's arrival; he was divorcing his child-bride in an ugly lawsuit, and intended to visit Mary before settling in Florence. "Commonplace as I am become," she told Payne, she longed to see this comrade of her days "of Paradise before the fall." When Sir Timothy again fell ill, she dreamed that she would be rich, free to publish Shelley's works, to go to Florence. Change was coming, indeed revolutionary change, but not in any form that she had anticipated.

16 "Ingratitude, caprice, and change"

"SINCE LAST AUTUMN I expected change — I said it would come — & strangely enough it has come," Mary Shelley wrote in her journal on February 14, 1827. Again strangely, "Thus speak the Sortes Virgilianae": she had opened her *Aeneid* three times, twice to lines describing Dido's emotions after she knows that Aeneas is leaving her; Jane Williams had told Mary that she was accepting Jeff Hogg's long-standing proposal for a common-law union. And stranger: in the third line to which Mary opened, Aeneas's son and his men reenter a battle and again expose their lives to danger; the very next day Mary would learn from Whitton that she would have to renew her struggle with Sir Timothy over Percy and her finances. Even after that, she felt that more change was coming in 1827, but she could not foresee any specific event, much less the earthquake that was to redirect her life.

Jane was either already pregnant by Jeff or soon conceived their child, who was born in late November. Mary was happy for her, but doubted Jeff's suitability, grieved for herself, and fought back jealousy, "the most terrible and selfish of human emotions," she later wrote, "and the most interesting, from its being the most universal."[1] She did not intend to follow Jane's example, she wrote Teresa Guiccioli. "Dear Friend, how could the wife of Shelley condescend to love the men of today. Maybe there are some who are worthy, but they don't show themselves — and therefore here I am always Signora Shelley — and I hope that this beloved name will be written on my tomb."[2] (Teresa had taken a lover some two years after Byron's death.)

Far worse in the event was Sir Timothy's decision about Mary's allowance, which among other constraints obviated any thought she might have had of leaving her beloved Jane for Italy. Finally, he conceded her custody of Percy, but only if she lived in England, where he could keep the boy, she said contemptuously, on "the virtuous road" of British manhood. He denied harboring "unchristian-like feelings" for Mary, but it was antipathy and intent to keep her on a strait path that determined him to set her just above actual want with an allowance of two hundred fifty pounds a year, to become three hundred when Percy, now seven, entered school.

Lastly, and justly in her view, on inheriting Shelley's legacy she must repay the entailed Shelley estate her accumulated allowances. For what she had received since 1823, seven hundred fifty pounds from Sir Timothy and two hundred fifty from Whitton, Whitton drew up a bond. Her lawyer, Shelley's former solicitor, Samuel Amory, objected to a provision, so Sir Timothy once again withheld her allowance, until September. His back was up. One J. J. Stockdale had published accounts of the youthful Shelley's extremism, along with condemnation of Sir Timothy's miserliness with Mary: "What degredation and self-abasement might have been spared to the widowed wife . . ." "Infamous trash!" said Mary. Further, whereas Sir Timothy's son, John, married respectably, his married daughter eloped that spring with a lover.

Since Sir Timothy tied them to England, Mary hoped he would accept her and his grandson as part of the family, give Percy the advantages he needed as he grew older, and make her own life easier. He did ask to see Percy, but excluded Mary. She believed he was "enchanted" by Percy. Actually, he was surprised that her son was "very clean in his Person," and so disturbingly reminded him of Shelley that thereafter he and Lady Shelley saw the child only once a year.

Her "magnificent" allowance meant also that Mary was still "*obliged*" to write for money, instead of what she pleased, and that she could not help Hunt, Payne, and Trelawny, all poor, as all her friends seemed to be, "all great of soul, generous, and incapable of valuing money except for the good it may do." Trelawny, whose fortune was reduced by his participation in the Greek war, lamented that he could not leave for England. "You will come," she urged, "Ah, indeed you must . . . to be consoled by my sympathy, exhilarated by my encouragements, and made happy by my friendship . . . From the ends of the world we were brought together to be friends till death."[3] She assured him he could do no more for the Greek cause, recently tainted by the English Committee's mishandling of Greek bonds and by Greek atrocities against the Turks. Pietro Gamba had died of typhoid in Greece, and Mary wished she had discouraged another recent volunteer, a Captain Bannister, from embarking. Even so, she was thrilled for Greece and for England that Canning became prime minister, expecting him to "regenerate our liberty." His sudden death that summer distressed her.

Mary planned to live near the Hoggs' new home at Maida Place in London, for while she knew better than to believe Jane that their intimacy would remain as before, she treasured Jane's society above all other. Besides, being another man's legal wife, Jane would otherwise be almost totally ostracized. Jeff's family disowned him, and he lost part of his law practice.

But Mary had begun to branch out to new acquaintances who, as it turned out, would constitute a saving bridge. In her singular way and circumstances she was attracted to them, and they to her, variously. Two she had met at Dr. Kitchner's; the young poet Eliza Rennie, of the famous engineering family, and the literary Lord Dillon, who was said to be Miss Rennie's lover. Eliza Rennie was one of those people with whom Mary perennially got involved out of responsiveness, more than their qualities warranted. Though too shallow to plumb Mary Shelley, Eliza Rennie nevertheless was to be her friend for many years and from the first was struck by her compound of romantic persona and strong character.

"If not a beauty, she was a most interesting, *lovable*-looking woman," Rennie would write in 1860, "with a skin exquisitely fair, and expressive gray eyes; features delicate, yet . . . 'aristocratic'; hair of a light but bright brown, most silky in texture and luxuriant in profusion, which hung in long drooping ringlets over her colourless cheek, and gathered in a cluster behind, fell wavingly over her shoulders; a large, open forehead . . ." Her "low, soft, murmuring" voice was melodious. Naturally graceful in her movements, "she did nothing for effect" and seemed invariably gentle. "But with this softness there was neither irresolution nor feebleness . . . but the most steadfast purpose." Nor was she, as some fancied, cold, but had "warm, strong affections" and was "a faithful, unswerving friend."[4]

That same apparent discordance mystified Lord Dillon, a married man, who, notoriously, loved women of strong, "blunt" passions, and who later told Mary that she looked more "sly" than he thought she really was. She always rather enjoyed people's continual puzzlement and no doubt was particularly reserved with a man like Dillon. If he had only read her writings, he said, "I should have thought you . . . outpouringly enthusiastic, rather indiscreet, and even extravagant; but you are cool, quiet, and feminine to the last degree — I mean in delicacy of manner and expression."[5] She probably thought the reverse of him: imposing as a picturebook royal, owner of a great country house, Ditchley, he was voluble, enthusiastic about Shelley, and proudest of his own writing, particularly his immense forthcoming verse epic, *Eccolino*. He had lived for a decade in Florence, so Mary had him to dinner with the modest Maria Gisborne, who was leaving for five years in Italy, and with Godwin.

In February, Mary had spent several days in Paddington with the family of her young friend, Isabel Robinson (carefully keeping, of course, the secret of Isabel's baby), with whom she had founded a friendship that would last until 1841. Fifty-year-old Joshua Robinson was a successful London builder and a cultured man who had received a B.L.C. from Oxford in middle age. A widower, he had ten children: in order, George, an amateur of antiques; Alfred, a solicitor; Isabella, Julia, Louisa, Rosa, Julian and Charles — Percy's playmates — Ellen, and Eliza. That he, with young daughters, welcomed Mary Shelley to his home evidences his liberalism and the courage of the "Paddington nymphs," as Thomas Moore, an old friend, called them.

Set amid fields, with a large garden, Robinson's Park Cottage would become Mary's second home. She also enjoyed his noted intimate dinners for friends such as Thomas Campbell, Lord Dillon, Cyrus Redding, and the artists Richard Rothwell (now Sir Thomas Lawrence's assistant), Thomas Stoddart, and Gilbert Stuart Newton; "the most agreeable I ever remember," recalled Redding, "strictly a 'conversable table' " of some nine guests "and all kinds of subjects freely discussed — poetry, philosophy, economy, politics, and sometimes religion . . ."[6]

"*El tempo bruelve y bullen esperanzas* . . . ," Mary copied Boscán's apposite poem in June. That month she made her most gratifying new friend: Thomas Moore, whom she had known before only professionally. Having contracted with John Murray to write Byron's biography, he had come to breakfast to ask her help, and this time instantly charmed her. "Tommy dearly loves a Lord," Byron used to say of his friend, who divided his time between London aristocratic society, which he adored and whose patronage was important to his living, and his family in the country. But Mary believed he was falsely charged with worldliness, for he seemed warm and genuine, and his songs moved stalwart men to tears: "something new & strange & beautiful," she said when he performed for her, and gave him Boscán's poem, which inspired his "Hope comes again . . ." She talked to him with rare freedom, feeling at home again with a man of Shelley's and Byron's class. "He seems to understand & to like me . . . a new and unexpected pleasure — I have been so long exiled from the style of society in which I spent the better part of my life —" she noted on July 2.

To some extent, Moore was ingratiating himself, since he now realized that she had known Byron far better than he had previously supposed — so well had she proudly hidden that light under a bushel — and that he could get unique material. In fact, she became his minor collaborator, seeing a way to get around Sir Timothy's prohibition of her Shelley biography. After Moore promised not to publicize her contribution or to expose Claire Clairmont, she volunteered to write an account of Byron and Shelley in Geneva and Italy, and showed him some of their letters. Besides that, she agreed with him that since Medwin had slandered Teresa Guiccioli, a sympathetic presentation of her romance with Byron was in Teresa's interest. After he promised to let Mary approve what he wrote, she asked Teresa to help him. She offered to make "a *rough outline*" of the romance from Teresa's letters to Byron, which Pietro Gamba had left with her, but Teresa preferred to do as Mary had previously suggested: write it herself. She did not wish her letters to be printed, and Mary reassured her on that point.[7]

By now Mary had also involved herself in quite another project, a wild and wonderful scheme to rescue Isabel Robinson from her cruel position as a secret unmarried mother with a baby, Adeline, with whom she dared not live. Mary's transvestite friend Mary Diana Dods had returned and was much taken with Isabel. Mary, Doddy, and Isabel concocted, and were to bring off, an incredible coup. That August, Doddy was to become "Mr. Sholto Douglas" and elope with Isabel to Paris, where they would live as man and wife with "their" child. In two years "he" would disappear and "Mrs. Douglas" would come home with Adeline, supposedly born abroad.*

Naturally, Jane was privy to this scheme; so was Eliza Rennie. Jane, however, had made Isabel and Doddy privy to secrets of her own, which, she also informed them, she had confided to several other people. Shelley's love was Jane's only means to satisfy an irresistible need for glamorous distinction. As soon as she got on close terms with anyone of her and Mary's inner circle, she told them that Mary's "coldness" and "temper" had made Shelley unhappy throughout their union, that she herself had been the poet's last, great love, and furthermore that gossip about Mary's "affairs" with other men might well be true; indeed (and in fact), Vincent Novello's wife and friends suspected him of being Mary's lover. Moreover, Jane told Isabel and Doddy, she only pretended to care for Mary — initially because she and Edward wanted to console Shelley, later because she felt sorry for Mary.

At last, after years of defaming Mary, Jane had confided in someone as deceitful as she was. Whether for Mary's sake or pure mischief-making, in "fatal" July, shortly after the fifth anniversary of Shelley's death and six weeks before Mary's thirtieth birthday, Isabel told Mary every word Jane had said.

The blow was more traumatic for Mary's having both invited it and

---

* Probably for Isabel and Doddy's delectation, in *Perkin Warbeck* Mary would note that Mary Boyd, mistress of James IV of Scotland, had a daughter who eventually married an Earl of Morton.

denied its possibility. In effect, it was as if a spouse or lover found out about a beloved's long-standing deception; she was devastated and, at the time, bludgeoned into clearing vision. Ever since Pisa, the woman she had idolized and sacrificed for during the past four years had simulated fondness while poisoning her to their friends, above all to Shelley. It was bad enough to find out that Shelley had complained to Jane, but Mary rightly believed that if Jane had come to her or gotten him to do so, instead of encouraging him in order to gratify her vanity, the problems of their union might have been largely resolved. Nor had Mary had any inkling of the Novello circle's suspicions about herself and Vincent.

Eleven years later Mary still writhed at Jane's falsity. "I had faults —" she would write in her journal in 1838, "instead of exposing these to a candid mind & tender conscience — I was villified behind my back . . . I discovered the sad influence exercised there when the grave permitted no appeal [to Shelley] — & the sense of my own faults redoubled (erroneously perhaps) the bitter sense of unjust treatment."[8]

Most unbearable, by her sweeping sentence on Mary's entire union with Shelley, Jane left a "serpent's tooth" in memories that had radiated comfort, pride, and strength. "The whole wide world of misery contains no pang so great, as the discovery of treachery where we pictured truth," Mary was to write in *Perkin Warbeck*, "death is less in the comparison, for both destroy the future, and one, with Gorgon countenance, transforms the past."[9]

"Am I not a fool!" Mary wrote in her journal on July 13. She could make sense of this latest of her calamities only by believing that the Furies were pursuing her for some unfathomed past crime. "What hast thou done? Nothing! I cannot charge my memory with much — save sorrow; but I have been so beyond the common lot Chastened & visited that I must needs think that I was wicked."

She would be wretched for months, but she showed nothing to Isabel or to Jane. Never one to stop loving because she had been betrayed, she refused to disturb Jane's already melancholy pregnancy; as she had feared, Jane and Jeff were not getting on. A setback in Isabel's "elopement" provided escape. About July 18 Doddy heard that her father had died, and she rushed to Scotland to see to her affairs. Mary sent Isabel and her baby to the village of Sompting on the Sussex coast, quickly prepared to follow (she was trying to find a Latin teacher for the Lambs' ward), and took Percy to join Isabel on the twenty-fourth.[10] Out of pity for the Hunts' difficult adolescent daughter Mary, who Marianne claimed was incorrigibly bad but who Mary Shelley believed was simply neglected, she took the girl along but sent her back after a time.

Through a beautiful, clear August Mary's little group waited for Doddy near Sompting, in an isolated location where no vacationers would see Isabel and her baby. They went to the beach, roamed along the ripe grain fields and elm-lined lanes, and at sunset climbed the upland behind their cottage to view the coast. "We seem to have got to the very uttermost verge of the world — a few steps more, & one could get out of it —" Mary wrote Payne.[11] She resolved to yield stoically to a destiny that "forbade" her happiness in love, to live permanently in the country, and to serve the few good souls "who are like stars in the night of Life." She nursed the apparently devoted Isabel's fevers, mesmerized her for pain, relished her sallies (Doddy was "this person"), and condoned her duplicitous letters to her father: "poor baby how she hates her task." Melting over Claire's currently acute misery in Russia, she invited her stepsister to live with her, while dreading the prospect.

Isabel took Mary's normal demeanor as proof of insensibility, but Payne worried about the tone of her letters, and Godwin contrasted himself, "all cheerfulness" despite his seventy-two years and no clue as to how he could pay an impending debt. "Would to God you were my daughter in all but my poverty!" he wrote. "But I am afraid you are a Wollstonecraft."[12] Godwinian nevertheless, after a month in Nature, diverted from "selfish" sorrow, "I am again at peace . . . ," Mary wrote Payne, grateful for his concern. "I have a friend with me . . . we form altogether a loving family . . . my sympathies expand . . . tell me how you are getting on —"[13]

Along with Wollstonecraft's sensibility Mary had her temper. She began to let out years of resentment of Jane, Jeff, and Hunt, to whom she had clung despite their indifference, even enmity — and to disengage. In her usual amusing cum idolatrous letters to Jane, she also looked back "with disgust" to the three years at Kentish Town as a disturbed and unreal dream. She announced that she would not live near Jane and Jeff, he having "no very enthusiastic affection" for her, and that she was quitting the Hunt coterie. "I . . . cannot continue . . . always seeking — never sought . . . there must be some shew of equality — & no longer for the sake of the past, can I fight so hard to link it with the present. — I have been a good, yielding, obedient, much enduring young person — but I am now ahime! *thirty* —"[14]

She taught Percy Latin and wrote her material for Moore's biography, mailing him six heavy packets, including papers Teresa had sent to her in London, which Payne discreetly picked up. Moore praised the "interest and brilliancy" of Mary's work, and kept her up to date on his transcription of Byron's *"presentable"* letters. She wrote "The Ritter von Reichenstein"

for a new Annual, *The Bijou*.[15] For another, *The Keepsake,* edited by her
friend Frederic Mansel Reynolds, she contributed the first of several pieces
by Shelley, chancing that Sir Timothy would not attribute their publication
to her. Again too late, she sent Watts a story, recent poems,* and a work
by Isabel.

On September 3 Mary and Isabel moved to Arundel, where Mary put
Percy in school. About the twenty-third Isabel's "sposo" arrived: Doddy
in men's clothes. Early in October, when storms lashed the coast, Mary
began *Perkin Warbeck,* recalling in Italian in her journal that she had begun
Valperga seven years before in a similar autumn, but when she had been
exalted and happy. She was in a miserable limbo, casting off her old circle,
about to lose Isabel, and suspecting that living alone in the country would
be unbearable. As it happened, she now met one of the more extraordinary
acquaintances of her career, and ten months later would meet a second,
each of whom posed polar alternatives for her future; even though she
accepted neither, each clarified her own course.

Mary had received a letter from Frances Wright, wealthy Dundee-born
radical, colleague and rumored lover of the aged Lafayette, and an abolitionist whose *Views of America* Mary knew. She and her "little family"
considered spending October in Dieppe, but they remained at Arundel so
that Mary could meet Wright, the most daring utopian socialist of the
period, and initiate an exchange between two remarkable women possessed
by dedication: the one, private; the other, public. Miss Wright had founded
a model colony, Nashoba, on the Tennessee frontier, to demonstrate the
validity of her plan to end slavery: she bought slaves who were to work
out their purchase price, while being educated to be prepared for freedom.
Miss Wright informed Mary that she had returned to recruit a free-love,
anarchic commune of whites for Nashoba, inspired by Robert Owen and
by Godwin's *Political Justice.* "What we want," she told her young lieutenant, Owen's son Dale, "is a few of elevated sentiment who will say, I
take my stand for the cause & not for myself."[16]

She addressed Mary Shelley as the daughter of great parents and companion of Shelley. Honored, admiring, self-deprecatory, Mary answered
"on the instant" that she touched the right chord to excite her interest.
"The memory of my Mother has always been the pride & delight of my
life; & the admiration of others for her, has been the cause of most of the
happiness I have enjoyed":

---

* Mary's passionate poem to "Isabel," "A Night Scene," may date to this period though it
was published in *The Keepsake* for 1831.

Her greatness of soul & my father['s] high talents have perpetually reminded me that I ought to degenerate as little as I could from those from whom I derived my being . . . Mr. Shelley . . . fostered this ambition & inspired that of being worthy of him . . . single among men for Philanthropy — devoted generosity — talent & goodness. — yet you must not fancy that I am what I wish I were, and my chief merit must always be derived, first from the glory these wonderful beings have shed [around] me, & then for the enthusiasm I have for excellence & the ardent admiration I feel for those who sacrifice themselves for the public good. . . . You do honour to our species & what is perhaps dearer to me, to the feminine part of it. — and that . . . makes me tremble for you — women are so per[pet]ually the victims of their generosity — & their purer, & more sensitive feelings render them so much less than men capable of battling the selfishness, hardness & ingratitude w^h is so often the return made, for the noblest efforts to benefit others.[17]

While she admired Owen and his followers,* however, she doubted the practicability of communes, particularly after her recent trauma. Could idealism, she asked, "tame that strange human nature, w^h is perpetually the source of wonder to me? . . . can enthusiasm for public good rein in passion[,] motive [motivate] benevolence, & unite families? . . . My life has been not like yours publicly active, but . . . one of tempestuous suffering," though she was always willing to sacrifice her being for her beloved narrow circle, "& derive my only pleasure from contributing to the happiness & welfare of others."[18]

Being "so much of a woman," Mary admitted to more interest in Fanny Wright than in Nashoba. But Miss Wright was so eager to recruit her that she came to Arundel, staying from October 9 to the thirteenth. An imposing, charismatic woman, she was disappointed in Mary's refusal of Nashoba, until Mary recounted her history and explained that even had she the faith and stamina she could not risk Percy in the wilderness. Now on a first-name basis, Fanny appreciated Mary as she was, and her devotion to Percy and the "fondly dependent" Isabel.

Moreover, Fanny herself admitted to longing for male love and support. In response, Mary wrote a potential Nashobite to whom Fanny was attracted, and later urged young Dale Owen to remember that even Fanny had woman's "inherent" desire for support, and, until such time as Fanny

---

* In *The Last Man*, Lionel Verney carves the date 2100 on St. Peter's dome, as Owenites carved "C.M.," Commencement of the Millennium, on their buildings.

found a lover, to be a brotherly inspiration to "the best being that exists —
a lofty minded, sensitive and talented woman —"[19] At her suggestion,
Fanny sent pamphlets on Nashoba to Moore, and later discussed her
Godwinian commune with Godwin himself, who was "perplexed" by her
plan but admiring of her courage and intentions.

After Mary secured Fanny's introduction to Paris friends for "Mr. and
Mrs. Douglas," that couple left for France. In late October, Mary went
to Harrow, where Fanny was staying with Thomas Anthony and Frances
Trollope (parents of the novelist), remaining until the Wright party, including Mrs. Trollope and three of her children, embarked on November
4. She went out by lighter to see them aboard ship. "Dear love how your
figure lives in my mind's eye," Fanny wrote. "I saw you borne away from
me until I lost sight of your little back among the shipping."[20]

As Dale Owen sailed by a later ship, he spent five memorable days in
Mary Shelley's company. Apparently he took her to a phrenologist who
assayed her as being of "frail clay," confirming Dale's opinion that with
all her impressive intellect she needed loving encouragement, guidance,
and support. Like many children of enlightened materialists, he was drawn
to the spiritual, which he was later to embrace. He then regretted having
come under Frances Wright's influence rather than Mary Shelley's. "Few
women have ever attracted me so much in so short a time":

> Genial, gentle, sympathetic, thoughtful and matured in opinion
> beyond her years . . . essentially liberal in politics, ethics, and the-
> ology, indeed, yet devoid alike of stiff prejudice against the old
> or ill-considered prepossession in favor of the new; and, above
> all, womanly, in the best sense, in every sentiment and in-
> stinct. . . .[21]

Mrs. Trollope was appalled at Nashoba's primitive conditions and
promptly left. Within months, the colony broke up owing to internal
dissension, to mismanagement of its slaves, and to public horror at its
advocacy of miscegenation. Fanny Wright worked for the cause in America
until 1830. "You I must love as a bright specimen of our sex,"[22] Mary
wrote her that year, and kept a lock of her hair among her relics.

Mary took lodgings in London for the winter at 51 George Street,
because Godwin sorely missed her and she had to choose a school for
Percy, which Peacock was investigating. "How anxiously I think of you,"
Fanny Wright wrote. "That dark dismal wet London — cold within &
cold without — so little in unison with your dear self!"[23] There, at the
end of Mary's worst year since 1822, she wrestled with a mid-life crisis
intensified by a crisis of faith that would not be resolved for a year. She

could not forgo seeing Jane, who had had a daughter she named for Mary (the child was to die in eighteen months), but was so constrained that Jane, uncomprehending, accused her of being loath to associate with a woman living out of wedlock.

Mary saw that with Jane she had "fabricated" her own misery and sacrificed for an illusion. Illusion or not, however, the world, in which the best and ostensibly loving were capable of treachery, would never again be the same to her. Add to this her habitual withdrawal, the diffidence Jane had intensified, and the fact that she had been punished by public odium since her elopement with Shelley, then by Sir Timothy, and now by Shelley's intimates, and the result was an invasion of anxiety from which she would never again be entirely free.

That January of 1828, the *Ladies Museum* asked to do her portrait and memoir for their series on prominent women. Of course, she could not because of Sir Timothy, and indeed she was, as she brusquely replied, "a great enemy to the prevailing custom of dragging private life before the world." But she said as well that she was too "insignificant," that as her sex precluded public employment, the public should not be interested in her, and that nothing could annoy her more "than in any way to be brought out of my proper sphere of private obscurity."[24]

Nevertheless, she rebounded in a healthier direction. A month later she confided some of Jane's treachery to Moore. On his good advice she told Jane that she knew of her falsity. Horror-struck, Jane protested her innocence and love in such floods of tears that Mary left rather than succumb, and wrote Jane a long, passionate letter, in which one passage resonates: "I have committed many faults — the remorse of love [in regard to Shelley] haunts me often . . . but for four years I committed not one fault towards you —"[25]

Sick at heart, Mary then kept her tone light, with occasional bitter interjections, until Jane was ready to tell the truth. She closed a friendship Jane had poisoned, sending "mio caro Vincenzo" Novello a farewell note in Italian and a lock of Mary Wollstonecraft's hair — and turned elsewhere. She saw Lord Dillon, the Robinsons, cheered melancholy Isabel Booth, and renewed acquaintance with a young woman who had been a girl when they had met in Pisa, Mrs. Beauclerk's daughter Georgiana, now Mrs. John Paul and a future close friend.

She was at her wit's end for a hundred pounds for Godwin. Moore offered to ask his publisher, John Murray, to give her the sum for her help with the Byron biography, which presently included encouraging Teresa Guiccioli to send her as yet unreceived narrative (it arrived that spring), and persuading Bowring to show Moore his Byron letters. But

Mary had sworn never to make money out of Byron, whose ghost, she said, would "taunt" her if she broke her vow. Instead, she let Moore take her to Murray to offer him *Perkin Warbeck*. Like Shelley, who had offered their work to Murray, she valued Murray's prestige and high payments. His *Quarterly Review,* moreover, had become more liberal.[26]

Murray temporized, still unwilling on ideological grounds to publish her, though she assured him that historical novels had no scope for "opinions." Finally, at Moore's insistence (he was getting two thousand guineas from Murray), Murray sent her a check for a hundred pounds.[27] Adamant about her vow, she insisted she owed him a book.

Though she hated to part with Percy, now eight, on Peacock's recommendation she put him in Edward Slater's boarding school in Kensington, which she inspected before entering him.[28] Percy was a good, truthful, promising child, unsocial as Shelley but docile and phlegmatic; she felt he needed awakening and a male environment. When he liked Slater's, she decided to take young Julia Robinson to see Isabel in Paris. After giving a supper party for Moore, Newton, and the Robinsons that did not break up until three, she left for Paris on April 11, with Fanny Wright's latest Nashoba bulletins, and "milles choses tendres" from Moore to Isabel.

En route, she felt increasingly ill, and went to bed when she arrived at the Douglas apartment near the Champs Elysées. She was told it was chicken pox — "I am so easily duped," she reminded Jane — until she was well enough to know she had smallpox. Having had the disease as well as inoculation in childhood, she was not to have permanent marks. Her swollen, blotched face, however, was such a "fright" that she remained in seclusion until May 12, when zest to see the people who were expecting her overcame vanity. Besides, she had foreseen a "teasing annoyance" in the spring.

Isabel and Doddy, playing "Mr. and Mrs. Douglas" with total and lasting success,[29] were already launched by Frances Wright's intimate friends Mrs. Maria Garnett and her daughters, themselves friends of the great historian Sismondi. But the pair were Mary's only discomfort on an otherwise exhilarating vacation, for their masquerade in action seemed ugly and corrupting. To set the scene for "Douglas" to leave "his wife," Doddy acted the disconsolate husband to Isabel's heartless coquette. Isabel told Mary that she suffered dreadfully in her false part; Doddy, however, was perversely engaged. (The Garnetts wrote Fanny Wright that the Douglases complained of Mary's "insensibility"; given Isabel's effusive show of affection for Mary, Fanny replied, Mary's deficiency was a minor negative compared to Isabel's hypocrisy.)[30]

Mary Shelley was renowned in Paris for her romantic career, her novels, and an 1826 stage version of *Frankenstein* (which Stendhal reviewed in the *Courier Anglaise*), and she discovered that here, where there was traditional scope for intellectual women, she was courted by a brilliant, sophisticated elite. She stretched her vacation three more weeks to partake of the first equal society she had had since Pisa, finding it "droll" to be ugly and know that her face was not her fortune. Mary Clarke, a clever, amusing Irish expatriate and one of Paris's best-known characters, presided over a salon "doctrinaire, libéral et classique," current French Romanticism being Christian and royalist; her lover, Claude Fauriel, was Manzoni's friend and an authority on folk literature. Here Mary also met de Staël's former lover Benjamin Constant, the young explorer Victor Jacquemont, liberal Spanish and Italian exiles, and perhaps the Dr. Koreff to whose "discoveries" of the principles of life and death de Staël had referred in *De l'Allemagne,* the book that had helped inspire *Frankenstein.*[31] It was Mary's boast that she had an interview with the "most illustrious" of all: the legendary Lafayette. In addition, she attended a play on Byron's death, and probably Louis Marie Fontan's drama *Perkins Warbec.*

Twenty-four-year-old Prosper Mérimée, with whose innovative writing she was familiar, was Mary Shelley's second important new friend of this period, and the antithesis of Fanny Wright. Only a Stendhal, Mérimée's close friend, could do justice to this brief encounter between a thirty-year-old English enthusiast-moralist and a precocious French cynic-dandy. Indeed, Stendhal, an ardent Shelleyan, had drawn on Mary Shelley and Shelley for his recent novel *Armance.** Seeing the ripe Aspasia in Mary Shelley, Mérimée confided his malaise to her. "Already wrinkled inside," comfortably supported by his family, he had to struggle with himself to do anything, wrote when he felt like it, and had had many mistresses. He introduced her to Stendhal's concept of "crystallization," that transformation by which the lover sees everything about the beloved, no matter how ordinary or distasteful, as radiantly beautiful, and himself promptly fell in love with her.

If fascinated and flattered, Mary was neither in love nor convinced of the solidity of his instant crystallization. In despair, he wrote asking at least for her friendship. She returned his letter, suspecting he would repent

---

* Armance is a young orphan fallen from high estate. Proud, reserved but passionate, noble-minded, her brow too prominent, her principles too elevated, she never lies but is forced into caution to preserve her integrity in an alien society that prizes money, rank, and appearances. The man she loves is worthy but sexually impotent, and commits suicide at sea en route to fight for Greece. Though Mary frequented Stendhal's circle, it is not certain they met. As he had falsely claimed in one of his works to have met Shelley, perhaps he avoided Shelley's widow.

it, and replied that she would always be his sympathetic, true, and tender friend — but only "if always you desire it — if always (pardon this woman's way of speaking, not coy [coquette] but proud) you should prove yourself worthy . . ."[32] Having momentarily elicited his Shelleyan qualities, she judged him a rare, true poet of sensibility, active mind, "the softest sweetness" and "chivalrous daring."[33]

Mary Shelley began to consider living in London. If society was "nothing as an end" it was a means of discovering distinguished people and making new friends. "My world is enlarged," she said. The Douglases gave her a farewell tea, a flirting party, said the Garnetts, who thought Mary was overfond of admiration: Mary tête-à-tête with Mérimée; Isabel engaging Fauriel "and all others."[34]

On June 4, Mary Shelley and Julia Robinson ("who is perfectly attached to me," Mary pointedly wrote Jane) landed at Dover and presently went to Hastings for sea bathing to heal Mary's disfigured face, since she would not show herself to people who had known her before. When Godwin visited, he was shocked by her "squalid" face and thin, bobbed hair. Joshua Robinson brought Percy down from Slater's for his summer vacation. The great news was that after four years of separation Trelawny, "the good and true one," was in London. He wanted to see her there; she asked him to come to her. "How the contest will end I know not," said Godwin. Trelawny, however, while assuring her of his unchanged devotion, went to the west of England. That puzzled her but did not affect her anticipation of their reunion. Being caught in the country, she wrote Jane, made her hate it "devotedly."

She also missed "poor" Medwin, who had dissipated his wife's fortune and tried to recoup by selling Italian paintings. With "his passion to *far figura*," Mary said, "Tom, had he a million a year, would get incumbered."[35] It would be many months before she saw Hunt. That winter he had published *Lord Byron and Some of His Contemporaries,* a vengeful account of Byron, in which Mary was also dismayed to read the "fiction" she had asked him to correct, that Shelley had separated from Harriet by mutual agreement and "courted another lady" only after Charles Shelley's birth. The critics slaughtered Hunt for his attack on Byron, which drove him into exile, with his family, at Epsom and almost destroyed him: "& if we say it is partly his own fault," Mary wrote Jane, "must one not accuse the Gods who formed him to his own ruin — it is the only comfort one has (& that a sorry one) . . . that it is impossible to render them service —"[36]

Catching up on her work, she wrote "The Sisters of Albano" and "Ferdinando Eboli" for *The Keepsake,* and for *The Bijou* translations of Schiller's "Division of the Earth" and "Song of the Sword" by C. T. Korner, a

German poet-patriot who died fighting Napoleon. She offered Bowring a review of Mérimée's oeuvre, which would appear in the January 1829 *Westminster*. Recognizing the importance of Manzoni's new *I Promessi Sposi*, she proposed to Murray to translate it, but he declined.

Upon publication of *The Keepsake* that November, the influential new *Athenaeum* placed Mary Shelley at the top of its second rank of the leading modern English authors who were represented in that issue of the Annual, while stating that she at times approached the first rank of Coleridge, Scott, Southey, Shelley, and Wordsworth.[37]

By mail, Jane at last made full confession of her treachery and implored Mary to restore their intimacy, adding that Mary had become lovable and less critical since Italy. "I cannot tell why, but we seem to stand more equally now," Mary returned, "tho' now more just to myself I was then as just to others as now." Jane asked what good Isabel's revelations had done; "I must feel the truth a good —"[38] She decided they should begin again, as friends, Jane lamenting the loss of Mary's love, Mary never able entirely to "cicatrize" the wound of Jane's treachery.

After six years, Mary Shelley's post-Shelley interregnum was drawing to a close. Old specters obtruded as she searched herself for the crime for which the Eumenides pursued her; she perceived it in her liaison with Shelley, which her father had interdicted, and which had eventuated in Harriet Shelley's death. That judgment made its first appearance in "The Sisters of Albano," the story of a girl's love for an outlaw that was forbidden by her father and resulted in the deaths of her sister and her lover and crushed her father: "the mingling of love with crime . . . [brings] on the criminal, and all allied to him, ineffable misery."

She recognized that she had idealized Jane and clung to Shelley's intimates out of her need for them and for a life independent of the world, and she now knew that they, who prided themselves on their moral superiority and liberalism, were as flawed as men and women of the world. She continued, with Godwinian integrity, to admire their virtues and to be their friend, but she would never again depend upon them.

Moreover, she had almost expended her capital of countercultural defiance. If she had been free she would have gone to Italy and lived among its congenial natives and expatriates. As it was, she accepted the "cold reality" of human beings and the world as they were. She regretted, she fluctuated, at times she longed for pastoral seclusion; nevertheless, she resolved to make the best possible life for herself in London and to secure her son in the world he would inhabit.

Meanwhile, in June she and Mérimée began a nine-month correspondence of considerable literary interest, but farcically at odds. She had been so hurt by slander that she insisted he keep the correspondence secret; ignorant of her circumstances, he said she was "anti-philosophical." Though she claimed to be disgusted with life, when he asked what he should live for, "amour et gloire," she replied. "Alas, Madame . . . ," he returned, "I was asking you for advice . . . ," not high metaphysics.[39] He had his friend Sutton Sharpe meet her; she said he was a matter-of-fact man; Mérimée responded that he seemed so because he was unhappily in love, "for you must have observed how false it is that love inspires poetic ideas."[40]

In early August Julia fell ill. Mary rushed her to Paddington and remained until Christmas. On the threshold of London, she was beset by troubles she would not explain in letters, while Mérimée chided that she lacked the pride to despise petty problems. Petty they were not. Sir Timothy was so angry about her trip to Paris that he reneged on increasing her allowance for Percy's school. Claire and the Charles Clairmont family arrived for a year's visit, and needed her financial help. Not knowing about *Perkin Warbeck*, moreover, Mérimée scoffed at historical novels ("After that, morality and mores!")[41] and urged her to work like a serious "femme *auteur*" when she had little pleasure, enthusiasm, or conviction in her painstaking work on *Perkin*.

Perhaps worst, Trelawny, the last of her golden links to the past, proved barbed brass. Before they met in November, she so raved about him that Mérimée assumed she was "crystallized"; indeed, he heard they were married. She expected hours of mutual confidences, deeper friendship. But Trelawny was aggressively surly with all his Pisa friends, who had known him "when." The Greek war had been the apex of his life; unsure now what to do with himself, he was trying to prolong his glory and to amplify it with his bogus claims of youthful piracy and intimacy with Byron. Since some people called him a lying charlatan, he both feared exposure and persuaded himself of his veracity.

Expecting Mary Shelley still to be beating against her cage, he found her accepting it. He shrugged off her dependence on Sir Timothy and resented that she could not write Shelley's biography, in which he himself hoped to figure magnificently. When she told him she was helping Moore — Byron's real friend — he gleefully gave her an unusable contribution about Byron's sodomy with a Greek boy. To establish himself in the class to which, as a younger son long absent, he tenuously belonged, he went into society and fascinated that year's debutantes with his great athletic figure, swarthy face worn by hardships, and exotic aura. He had been a minor lady-killer; henceforth he operated in elite circles. Jane indignantly called him a "worldling"; he shunned her for her "degrading connection with a hog." When Claire refused his amorous overtures, he called her "fish-like."

Mary did not yet understand the new Trelawny and could not get his confidence. However, she told him she had resolved to struggle no more to hold on to the past, and to live in the world as it was. Trelawny, enjoying the society to which she was drawn, a nouveau Shelleyan radical, a Byronic Giaour with two grown daughters he had farmed out for ten years and a two-year-old in Corfu, Zella, by his Greek wife, scornfully disapproved and told her that her motives were worldly. His opposition shook and depressed her, so much so that it was months before she tried to explain: "I neither like life — nor the mechanism of society — nor the modes in which human beings present themselves — but I cannot mould them to my will, & in making up my mind merely to take them as they are, enthusiasm fades . . ."[42] When he left suddenly for Florence without saying good-bye, she knew that her former life was indeed over.

"Is it possible," Mérimée wrote, "that having *girato il mondo,* as you have done, you are still up to making castles in Spain? . . . You do not want to represent the world as it is, that is, stupid and wicked . . . it follows . . . that you are continually disappointed . . . *Only the worst is a certainty* — voilà le fin de la philosophie."[43] That degree of cynicism and pessimism she could not accept, but she privately answered his question in the negative. The age of English Romanticism is said to have ended in 1830; at the turn of 1829 it ended for Mary Shelley.

IV THE WORLD

. . . as Sterne says that in solitude he would worship a tree —
so in the world I should attach myself to those who bore the
semblance of those qualities which I ~~had~~ admire —

— Mary Shelley, Journal
February 25, 1822

Full of rebellion, I would die,
Or fight, or travell, or denie
That thou hast ought to do with me.
        O tame my heart;
      It is thy highest art
To captivate strong holds to thee.

— George Herbert, "Nature"

17 "A new kind of life"

MARY SHELLEY did not go readily into her post-Romantic age. When she left the Robinsons' Park Cottage at the end of 1828 for London, the world's venue, she took lodgings just through Percy's Easter holidays and made stabs at retreating to live in the country with ill-contrived companions: first, Claire Clairmont, who refused to prolong her year in England, where she was beset by gossip and snubs; then Isabel "Douglas" (despite Mérimée's quip that she was better fit to be "mounted" by a succession of dandies than to be Mary's friend), who replied to Mary's invitation that she dared not leave Paris yet.

In May 1829 Mary signed a year's lease for a furnished apartment at 33 Somerset Street off Portman Square: "this one year I give to try my fate in the world —" she noted on the thirteenth. "When over I will bury myself in Nature's deepest recess & live to my single sensations . . . let me not deceive myself — I could not do so & be happy." She would remain at Somerset Street for four years, managing largely to achieve her three aims: in order of priority, securing Percy's future, giving her father a "green old age," and rebuilding her own life.

That she had to set priorities was a matter of money. Sir Timothy would not increase her allowance to three hundred pounds until June, after she submitted Percy's school and "taylor's" bills to prove he cost her a hundred pounds a year, what with expenses when he was with her during his vacations. Then she ordered school extras — a dancing master, a drill teacher to cure his stoop; later, riding lessons — so that she reduced the two hundred pounds she reserved for herself. It was the dream of her life that Percy, now nine, would be worthy of Shelley, but happier.

She continued to help her seventy-three-year-old father financially and dreaded the day he could no longer publish. For his current novel, *Cloudesley*, Charles and Claire Clairmont helped with the Austrian and Russian background and Mary with the Italian. She sent *Blackwood's* an unsolicited review of *Cloudesley* in 1830, which was published though the editor said it was "rather a little partial." Even more so was her Memoir of Godwin for an 1831 edition of *Caleb Williams*. In declaring that since ancient Greece no man had so embodied the great philosophers, and making similar claims, she gratified her father's passion for immortal fame at the risk of her credibility.

During her first year in London Mary completed *Perkin Warbeck*, wrote three stories for *The Keepsake*, translated two Italian poems and a German one for the last issue of *The Bijou*, and did two reviews for the *Westminster*: "Modern Italy," her review of works by Best and Sismondi, attests to her passion for Italian liberty and the land where she longed to be. A pirated edition of her *History of a Six Weeks' Tour* appeared with only Shelley's name as author and of course no fee.[1]

Claire Clairmont stayed with Mary for several months. She tutored Mary in German while Mary improved Claire's rusty English, as Claire hoped to publish. After six years apart, the stepsisters were as ambivalent about each other as ever. While Mary pitied Claire and admired her courage and refusal to "vegetate," Claire uniquely discomfited her with disarmingly amusing, fulsome compliments barely concealing a sting, for example, about "the vastness of your intellect" in comparison with "us poor mortals of the secondary and third order," or about Percy's being so interesting that she pardoned him for not being interested in anyone but himself. She was always afraid something would happen to Mary or to Percy, on whose survival her own legacy from Shelley depended: "he little thinks how much I am attached to him!"

At its worst, Claire's hostility verged on the sinister, owing to her undiminished idolatry of Shelley and hatred of Allegra's "murderer," Byron. Although much of the public still condemned Shelley, she saw evidence that year of the transformation Mary had initiated. "His name is now growing up to a stately immortality in a country where he has been accused of unmingled folly and error," *The Athenaeum* observed,[2] while the formerly hostile Walter Savage Landor now presented Shelley as a great and good genius in *Imaginary Conversations*. In his biography of Byron, Thomas Moore condemned his own "presumption" in having warned Byron against Shelley, and gave the fullest, fairest portrayal yet of Shelley. But because of Mary's association with Byron after Allegra's death, "the instant she appears I feel . . . the sickening crawling motion of the Death Worm," Claire would write privately; it was as if Mary had "looked coolly on" Allegra's execution, "rejoiced in the comfortable place she had got in the shew," and shaken hands with the executioner.[3]

In September, Claire borrowed her fare from Mary and returned to her aristocratic Russian employer, who took her to Nice. In November, Mary parted bitterly with Charles Clairmont. Despite her and Godwin's aid, Charles had failed to make his way in London. Under his pressure, she resentfully raised money so that he and his family could return to Vienna. He repaid her bit by bit as he became a successful teacher in the highest Viennese circles. She also helped her father's ancient friend James Marshall.

But Mary Shelley's vital struggle continued to be with Jane Hogg's treachery, which left her morbid and anxious to the point of phobia — though even paranoids can have enemies, and she had real reasons for fear. Three decades later, Eliza Rennie described her "settled sadness, a grave, gentle melancholy, in her face, and voice, and gait"; fits of despondency, when she would see no one; her shrinking from "note or observation" in everything, dress, manner, deportment, even authorship. "To call on her and find her table covered with . . . copy, proofs for correction, etc. . . . made her . . . nervous and unself-possessed . . . Sometimes, to tease her, I would say — 'Well, Mary, how much have you written today?' . . . A pout of the lip and shrug of the shoulder was the only answer elicited."[4]

Trelawny, now living in Florence, unwittingly smoked out this syndrome in the spring of 1829. He had the great idea of validating his claims of youthful brigandage and intimacy with Byron and Shelley by writing them as facts in an autobiography. He meant to include the biography of Shelley that Sir Timothy forbade Mary to write, and asked her to supply the material "without which it cannot be done" (he having known Shelley for six months). Mary refused.

"Shelley's life must be written," she replied — she believed it would exonerate his treatment of Harriet Shelley and prove that he had acted on principle — "I hope one day to do it myself," but it was not to be published in her lifetime or Percy's. "Many men have his opinions — none fearlessly and conscientiously act on them, as he did — it is his act [leaving Harriet for her] that marks him —" She was frightened that a biography would drag her, a lone woman who wished only to be obscure and "insignificant," before the public. "This is weakness — but I cannot help it — to be in print — the subject of *men's* observations . . . attacked or defended!"[5] She feared equally that a biography would damage Percy's chances in life. And there was probably no one of Shelley's admirers she trusted less to present his life with sensitivity and intellectual depth than Trelawny.

Trelawny glowered, especially because he and Claire agreed that Mary had "betrayed" Shelley by helping Moore with Byron's biography — regardless of the fact that Shelley himself had always admired Moore. That winter, at her seasonal nadir, "while fog and ennui possesses London," Mary appealed to Trelawny: "Ah have pity on my miserable clouded faculties . . . the peculiar situation of my relations is heavy on me — my spirits are depressed by care . . . Dearest friend — seal up . . . warm tokens of kindliness . . . Shelley's life as far as the public had to do with it consisted of very few events and these are publickly known — The private events were sad and tragical — How would you relate them? as Hunt has, slurring over the real truth — wherefore write fiction?"6 Though he knew Sir Timothy would cut her off, Trelawny threatened to publish that she had assisted Moore. She did not wish that fact to be secret from friends (only from Sir Timothy), she replied; but if published, "it would destroy me."

She agreed to help Trelawny if she (the cause of Shelley's "act") could somehow be left out of his biography, in which case the most painful portion would be eliminated — and duly killed herself off that summer in a story for *The Keepsake,* "The Mourner." In this variation of *Matilda,* a girl whose willfulness led to the drowning of her adored father hid in a Perdita-like but decrepit cottage in Windsor Park and killed herself; eventually a young man who had been darkly influenced by her marries an innocent girl.

At the very time that Mary turned down Trelawny, however, she was helping Cyrus Redding with a biographical sketch of Shelley that was to preface Redding's edition of the poems of Coleridge, Shelley, and Keats for Galignani. She wanted Shelley's poems published; if a short notice was to accompany them, she meant it to be factually correct. That spring, Horace Smith (perennially distressed at assumptions that he shared Shelley's moral opinions and atheism) declined to help Redding and referred him to Mary Shelley. She was Redding's principal source for his sketch; indeed, to make certain of its accuracy she was tempted to write it herself though fear of Sir Timothy stopped her. After her death Redding revealed that she had helped him and declared that she was "incapable of double dealing in her words," and his sketch proves it: here, Shelley eloped with Mary before his separation from Harriet, lived with her for more than two years until Harriet's suicide, and married her only because Godwin insisted.

To ensure the accuracy of Shelley's poems in Redding's edition, Mary gave him *Posthumous Poems,* errata she had collected, and lines Ollier had suppressed for fear of prosecution. There being no published likeness of Shelley, Galignani thought of commissioning an imaginary portrait, "the drollest, stupidest idea — ever man intent on selling an edition hit upon," she said. She made a sketch of Amelia Curran's portrait, trying to correct its flaws, then let an artist make a drawing, with her advice and that of Miss Curran, who was visiting in London.

After failing to enlist Claire's help, who was herself terrified of publicity,

Trelawny wrote an account of his youth, ending at 1812. In Trelawnyese, Moore was one of those "base, sycophantic, and mercenary wretches who crouch and crawl and fawn on kings, and priests, and lords," and Mary as unlike her real self as "hell from Helicon." While he still admired and cared for her, he was incapable of empathy with anyone. Meanwhile, he was anchoring to Shelley and Byron, as he would to other notables, to ride on their crests, preening himself on rugged individualism. He would have hitched to Mary, to whom he proposed at intervals in the future, and he was to blight her reputation in order to exalt his own.

While he saw degeneration in Mary, Eliza Rennie was so impressed by her extraordinary consistency that she could not perceive her underlying conflicts: "I never knew, in my life, either man or woman whose whole character was so entirely in harmony: no jarring discords — no incongruous, anomalous, antagonistic opposites . . ."[7] Actually, at the age of thirty-two Mary was making a passage in character with remarkable integrity, as well as with the equally remarkable endurance, grit, and resilience that her numerous sad journal entries and letters to intimate friends, her safety valve, have too often obscured. In fact, most of these ventings (analogous to Shelley's despondent private poems) had been grouped and continued to be grouped in periods when she was under extreme pressure; each time, often at the same time, she recovered her serenity and sense of humor.

The seven years since Shelley's death had taught Mary Shelley that she could not master all except her fate by her mind; furthermore, because of what she had been forced to see about Jane, and thereby about herself, she now had a deeper and subtler understanding of the complexities of the human mind, in particular its compulsion to rationalize needs and desires. Into that understanding rushed recognition that if she and Shelley had been justified and disinterested in forming their liaison, there had been "alloy in what they deemed pure gold,"[8] for they had also been passionately in love, and had inadvertently brought about Harriet's death.

It was in the second half of *Perkin Warbeck*, heretofore written in prosaic impersonal style, and completed more richly and intensely during 1829, that she began to work through the emotional and philosophic ramifications. Young Perkin claimed to be Richard Plantagenet, and his war for Henry VII's throne was supported by James IV of Scotland, who married him to his cousin Katherine Gordon. Though he confessed to being an impostor before his execution, Mary Shelley believed that he was Richard. While she condemns feudalism, her Richard and his beloved and adoring Katherine personify its "fidelity, self-devotion, and chivalric attachment," contrasted to "cold, avaricious" Henry and a dawning materialistic age.

Richard's flaw, like that of Victor Frankenstein and Lord Raymond — and of Shelley and Mary — is intrinsic in human nature: we "make ourselves the central point of the universe." Richard lacks the love of human betterment that creates truly improved social structures.[9] He sacrifices thousands of lives for his monarchic ambition in the belief that it is glorious, just, and favored by God. "It is thus . . . ," Mary Shelley glosses, in a decisive shift from *The Last Man,* that the human mind, "that mystery," manifests its transformative power, which, if put to right uses, might "turn evil to good, foul to fair; then vice and pain would desert the new-born world!" But "It is not thus: the wise have taught, the good suffered for us; we are still the same . . ."[10]

The widowed Katherine was kept at Henry's court, and married three more times. In the Conclusion, Mary Shelley turns that unromantic fact into an answer to Trelawny and an affirmation. Reproached by a Plantagenet loyalist who has become a hermit, Katherine declares that she is devoting herself to educating the crown prince, who may repair Henry's crimes and bestow happiness on the realm; "Meanwhile I am human . . ." Still bound by reason and duties, still loving dead Richard,

> And must my living heart be stone . . . ? . . . I venerate also the freer impulses of our souls. My passions, my susceptible imagination, my faltering dependence on others, my clinging to the sense of joy — this makes an integral part of Katherine, nor the worst part of her . . . I am content to be an imperfect creature, so that I never lose the enobling attribute of my species, the constant endeavour to be more perfect.[11]

Perkin Warbeck is Mary Shelley's last novel on a grand scale, and the first in which the heroines, Katherine and Monina (who disguises herself as a man to support Richard's cause), survive to live as nobly as may be within their individual capacities and circumstances. Her subsequent two novels would feature modern women and their heroism or service in more ordinary life.

"I am doomed to a divided existence, and I submit," says Katherine.[12] Mary Shelley, however, was not the passive, one-dimensional Katherine who had never had ambitions. She submitted, based on a sense of reality belatedly acquired, her drive for the preservation of herself and her son, and the mature branching of her rooted philosophy. "I never was more worthy of your love and esteem," she told Trelawny.[13] Although one of its healthier elements was that she no longer built her life on Shelley's memory, she was following the course he had recommended to Claire

Clairmont: "cultivate . . . liberal ideas to a certain extent . . . let the *past* be past."

The past could not be past for her, however, or for Claire. Mary tried to accept but never resigned herself to lesser life; she was, after all, a Romantic survivor. Her acceptance tore at live roots of ambition and love of glory that, along with her succession of misfortunes, left her more vulnerable than before to what she called her "domestic enemy": discouragement, protest, and brooding. English society, moreover, never forgot her past.

And finally, she herself was in conflict about her youthful liaison with Shelley because of Harriet Shelley's death, and indeed that conflict was to intensify. She never repented on her own account what she called her "first step in life . . . what ever may have been its effects,"[14] which had and continued to dominate her life, yet she believed that it had been wrong and that fate had punished her. In *Perkin Warbeck*, her deist Supreme Power is no longer simply watching but is ordering, in inscrutable ways "we strive to believe are good." And her belief that the past, present, and future are linked has evolved to acceptance of "the cruel law of religion" which she had repudiated since girlhood: retribution, sometimes long delayed, inexplicably withheld or repeated, follows wrongdoing even to the next generation. That belief, henceforth manifest in her writing, intensified her drive to make Percy happy and secure, as he was already suffering from his parents' error.

Moreover, she came to place major responsibility for Shelley's "act" — including persuading her to elope — on him, where it in fact belonged. In *Perkin Warbeck* she explained that Perkin rationalized involving Katherine in his dangerous quest by believing he would better her lot — not that Katherine regretted it. In her 1830 "Transformation," however, a mutinous boy who loved his Maryish foster sister, "child of love and light," "harrowed her child's heart, and profaned her child's lips with an oath, that she would be" his against her father's wishes. That, however, was one of her few implied reproaches, for her admiration of Shelley's genius and virtues remained intact — though she no longer questioned her worthiness to join his spirit after death.

"I do not wish at present to renew the recollection of the past," she told Trelawny, a cri de coeur, and yet it would seep into her writing, like the "ghastly tale" the Ancient Mariner was impelled sporadically to retell — though in disguises that only a handful of her contemporaries could penetrate — because Shelley's "act" stuck in her moral throat. But she could not write his biography without specifying her own qualms, which she refused even to attempt until four years after Sir Timothy's death freed her to publish a life. She was, however, to do him the ultimate service one can do an artist.

"You want more than a man and true demi-gods are very rare," Mérimée wrote in their last exchange, at the same time questioning if she had ever had any passions[15] — a bitter irony to a woman of her temperament. Yet she recognized that she had loved her father and Shelley like gods and "almost deified" Jane, a folly for which Jane was suffering as well as herself. She would love again but never again with idolatrous passion. She felt the "tears of things" in friendship as well: "blind miserable beings," she wrote Trelawny, "thus we grope in the dark — we depend on each other yet we are each a mystery to the other — and the heart which should be in the hand of a friend, either shuns the contact, or is disdainfully rejected."[16] From now on her insights were quite remarkable, though her emotions often overrode them.

In other areas she had modified rather than changed. She had learned from experience with Hunt, Jane and Jeff Hogg, and Trelawny that even the best liberals were capable of prejudice, injustice, and cruelty. Her response was Shelleyan and Godwinian: she laid new stress on love, self-restraint, peace, and tolerance. In her 1830 story "The Swiss Peasant" she deplored the violence and bigotry of both revolutionaries and aristocrats. "Brothers should not fight . . . ," she would declare in 1833, shocked at threats of civil war in America. "What is the use of republican principles & liberty, if Peace is not the offspring? War not Kings is the *fleau* [scourge] of the world —"[17]

Though she would never be a Christian, she now believed that most people need religious faith of some sort, respected latitudinarian Protestants as well as principled atheists, and was even tolerant of Catholics while deploring their particular tenets. In her 1830 review of Mérimée's historical novel *Chronique du règne de Charles IX* for the *Westminster,* she excerpted a long portion on the good death of a frank atheist who, though indifferent to "the mysteries of eternity," is far superior to a weaker man who grasps at deathbed absolution out of fear. Mérimée had boldly sketched "the reality of things," she stated: "the best lesson a novelist can give is that of toleration; nor can that lesson be injurious, while the truth is impartial and the book mirrors the world, where the irreligious feel sorely the want of future hope . . . ," and the wicked among them, however wealthy, are the unhappiest of all.[18]

She had come also to realistic acceptance of women's powerlessness, their need for male protection, the unhappy consequences for children, girls in particular, who were reared uncontrolled — something that made Trelawny afraid for his half-Greek daughter Zella and place her with conventional ladies. She continued to believe that women's characteristics differed from men's, but no longer idealized the feminine (relatively speaking) or derogated the masculine. Her view of women's sphere and capacity was to vary with her own self-confidence; she never deviated, however, from admiration of female achievement, from personally supporting oppressed women, or from a single standard of right conduct, in sex as in all aspects of life. "It is probably one among the many superstitions which rather injure than exalt the characters of women, which makes us, in spite of ourselves, set so high a price on their constancy even to the dead," she wrote in her 1829 review of Anna Jameson's *Loves of the Poets*.[19]

By the time Mary Shelley finished *Perkin Warbeck* in late 1829, her transition into the world was under way. In November she was cutting her overlong novel hard. For primary sources she had consulted Moore's friend Thomas Crofton Crocker, an authority on Ireland; Sir Walter Scott for Scotland; Mérimée for France; and many English works. She knew it was a fine book and anticipated its success. "Indebted" to Murray for the hundred pounds he had given her for helping Moore with his Byron biography, she offered him her novel. When he declined, she confidently went back to Colburn, splurged on Christmas gifts, and refused to review Stendhal's *"so very commonplace" Promenades dans Rome* for the *Foreign Quarterly Review*, only to get one hundred fifty pounds from Colburn when she expected at least the three hundred he had given for *The Last Man*. (Colburn gave Godwin four hundred fifty pounds for *Cloudesley*, perhaps subsidizing the old man at his daughter's expense.) In fact, until 1833 the times would be bad for publishing: "despair and convulsion reign over the country," she wrote Trelawny:[20] financial depression, strikes, and rural riots.

She still intended to repay Murray with her next book. He was doing her various gentlemanly favors and encouraging her sufficiently that through Isabel "Douglas" she asked Benjamin Constant for material for a life of Madame de Staël; alternatively, she proposed a life of Joséphine. For fun as well as research she hoped to visit Paris. But Mérimée had warned that her subjects' love lives would shock the English public; Murray declined both.

Meanwhile, Mary Shelley was "trying her fate in the world," above all hoping for erotic cum supportive love, for a home, and perhaps for another child. Romantic attachment to a woman was no longer an option, and while she was drawn to Shelleyan qualities in a man, he no longer had to be a Shelley.

She needed as well to get and give affection with friends, and, though

more realistic, she neither could nor would forgo committing herself quix-
otically in certain cases, the conjunction of "ready sympathy and too eager
a heart," as she said, with her ideal of generosity. Still, she required freedom
of action, and she often found the Robinson girls too constant companions. "It is strange that independant as I am I cannot arrange an agreable
mode of life . . . ," she noted. "Meanwhile I will be patient, occupied,
quiet — I will dismiss this feverish restlessness nourished by my exclusive
life with women — for we are all alike — we live by detail — & feel too
sensibly every passing incident."[21] "D'etre agitée," she added (having dropped
Italian for intimate entries), was her natural state in unnatural sexual deprivation.

She wanted as well what most people want, what she had enjoyed in
Paris, what Shelley had wanted when he decided they should settle in
Pisa: "a society of our own class, as much as possible, in intellect and
feelings." That society had in fact been refined, highly educated, and upper
class. But the now accepted view, originated by Trelawny and Claire
Clairmont, that she wanted to join "society" is erroneous. As has been
said, only chronology prevents one from calling the smart society of the
1830s *fin de siècle:* luxurious, licentious, mannered — all antipathetic to
her. As she might have said from a longer vantage point, it was as if the
future whispered to the present to eat, drink, and make merry before the
Victorian age arrived. By "society" Mary meant association with people,
just as she opposed "social man" to self-absorbed or atomized individuals.

Nor, Trelawny to the contrary notwithstanding, was she trying to become "respectable." Later, in an angry moment, she would declare that
disengagement from the liberals who had mistreated her was her "first act
of freedom." Her new society, in fact, would be composed of writers,
artists, intellectuals, and so on, and of cultivated, mostly liberal, sometimes
outré, men and women of the world — the very same society that Trelawny
frequented. What is more, at every risk to her own vulnerability, she made
friends with and stood by women who had transgressed sexual mores.
And having a new circle did not mean abandoning the old: she now helped
Jeff Hogg place his magazine articles, gradually restored much of her
intimacy with Jane, and would always admire and aid Leigh Hunt.

"Social enjoyment in one form or another is the alpha and omega of
existence," Shelley had also said; he liked a tiny homogeneous circlet; she
liked variety and scope. Besides, she spent the greater part of her time
writing and studying, usually harassed by cares, often prey to her "domestic
enemy." She needed diversion, attention, and glamour; high time she
enjoyed herself, one might add. As Proust has said, "we are all of us obliged,
if we are to make reality endurable, to nurse a few little foibles in ourselves."

Mary Shelley had not lived in London for six years, so at first she saw people she already knew — except Lord Dillon, who was retired with a heart ailment that killed him in 1832. Julia Robinson was in love with a socially prominent Chester man, and Mary, "as usual — absorbed by & given away to sympathy," assisted Julia and, though dubious, did not advise. When Moore was in town they had movable visits doing errands in a shared cab. Once he took her to Sir Thomas Lawrence's, to whom he was sitting for a portrait, so that she had a chance to talk art with a master. Teasing Moore about his "aristocratic acquaintance," she brought him together with Bowring, until Peacock condemned Moore's life of Byron in Bowring's *Westminster*. "This is not the way to make me regret the sphere of society I have chosen for myself," Moore told her huffily.[22] She herself was enthusiastic about his Byron work and "not unsatisfied" with his account of Shelley.

By winter she was invited out a little and was an instant success, being a legendary personage, and, in good company, another woman to the one Eliza Rennie described; frank, free, amusing, original, even bewitching, reported Maria Jewsbury, who came to tea with her fellow-author Anna Jameson: "she struck me in the light of a matured child, a union of buoyancy and depth; a something that brought to my remembrance Shelley's description of Beatrice in his preface to the Cenci":

> To those she loves her manners would be caressing; to a stranger they are kind and playful, less from a desire to please, than from a habit of amicable feeling. Her hilarity, contrasted with the almost sadly profound nature of her remarks . . . is not the hilarity assumed by worn minds in society, — it is simple — natural — and like Spring full of sweetness, but I doubt her being a happy woman, and I also doubt her being one that could be distinctly termed melancholy. . . . She reminded me of no person I ever saw . . .[23]

Doors had opened; however, Mary could not always enter. "People like me & flatter & follow me, & then I am left alone again, Poverty being a barrier I cannot pass — still I am often amused & sometimes interested," she noted.[24] Her well-to-do new acquaintances lived at considerable distances from her; she could not walk to engagements in evening dress and often could not afford cabs, or the theater if asked to join people; and she was too proud to take favors unless she could recompense in some form, emotional or material. Of all her long-gone luxuries she most missed a carriage.

Compared with Italy's or France's, the social system also limited her.

She had nothing but herself to offer in England, where, she later said, "your income, your connections, your position, make all the weight." And hypocrisy cemented that society. Lady Holland, for one, was still ostracized by many women after thirty unimpeachable married years, because she had been divorced for adultery the year after Mary was born, while dissolute wives were received everywhere as long as their husbands did not disown them.

True, by 1828 there were many who believed she had been a virtuous wife and more sinned against by Shelley than sinning. Godwin's young friend Edward Bulwer (later Bulwer-Lytton) published a best-selling novel, *Pelham,* which included a Shelleyan aristocrat who fell in love with a plebeian girl, "took advantage of her love — her youth — her innocence — she fled with me — *but not to the altar.*" The same year saw Heinrich Marschner's opera *Der Vampyr,* whose pure heroine is seduced from her loving father by a patrician vampire.

For others, however, Mary Shelley was the daughter successor of "licentious, profligate, and shameless" Wollstonecraft.[25] For the generality of women she was taboo because of her youthful liaison. Sometimes she was insultingly snubbed; as she wrote in *Perkin,* "the fallen woman fears women, their self-sufficient virtues and cold reprobation."[26] Mainline feminists shunned her as an exemplar of sexual freedom that the movement generally repudiated for decades. Maria Jewsbury, who considered updating Wollstonecraft's *Rights of Woman,* met Mary only because a friend made it impossible to decline politely. It was, she said, the most interesting evening of her life, adding that Mary was not one "to sit with and think ill of, even on authority," but, understandably if sadly, she had nothing further to do with her. As the climate shifted to Victorianism, the cloud over Mary Shelley was to thicken.

Moreover, her superiority was a handicap in a society in which literatae were savagely caricatured; gushing over but hating one another; "redoubtable" spinsters; or an "awful female Historian." As Horace Walpole had called Mary Wollstonecraft a "hyena in petticoats" so Trelawny dubbed Mary Shelley "a hurricane in petticoats." Moore disliked literary people, loathed "blue Diablessess." "I have long since discovered that I must be prepared for enmity I have never provoked," said Laetitia Landon. "God knows that if, when I do go into society, I meet with more homage and attention than most, it is dearly bought. What is my life? One day of drudgery after another . . . envy, malice . . . these are the fruits of a successful literary career for a woman."[27]

Mary Shelley made friends and acquaintances, nevertheless, and if few were as brilliant as Paris had provided, she could not pick and choose freely. Most would have been welcomed among the Pisan Circle (the Williamses had hardly been great intellects), and her new friends were kinder to her. Almost by definition, the women who befriended her were courageous, nonconformist, or too attracted to care about "authority."

Through Georgiana ("Gee") Paul, daughter of the patrician Beauclerks and wife of the banker John Paul the younger, she knew the Paul clan. Gee's sister-in-law, Anne Frances Paul Hare, who had royal blood through her mother, promptly became Mary's dearest friend. Gentle, accomplished, an elegant woman of the world, but no pattern of womanhood, when Mrs. Hare had her third son in Italy, she gave him to a childless relative in England. "If any one else would like one," she airily said, "would you kindly recollect that we have others."[28] Her husband, Francis, was a radical baronet who refused to use his title. Educated in Italy by his mother's friend, the Greek scholar Clotilda Tambroni, and by the great linguist Mezzofanti, Hare was steeped in the classics, an authority on Italy, and withal a spirited, irreverent man. It was Hare, Walter Savage Landor's friend, who had encouraged Landor to include Shelley in *Imaginary Conversations*.

When Trelawny met the Hares, he told Mary that Anne was "a dish of skimmed milk" and Francis "a pedantic blockhead" (which may indicate that they did not care for him), mocking as well the Robinsons and their "chaffy set." He took sadistic pleasure in denigrating her friends.

As the Hare set gathered for the 1830 season, Mary Shelley noted with justifiable pleasure that they included "some of the best people around town," meaning cosmopolitan or talented rather than pedigreed. She became friendly with the Roderick Murchisons, both notable in the comparatively new science of geology, which had interested her for a decade; and Ellen Manners-Sutton, Lady Blessington's sister, a "lively, hearty Irishwoman," herself under a cloud. She had left her first husband for Charles Manners-Sutton, popular Tory Speaker of the House, whom she married upon her husband's death. If Moore observed that befriending Mary "does not look well for her advance [in society],"[29] Mary was equally careless of self-interest. Hare's brother Julius, who had written an article on Shelley, was a liberal, some said heretical, clergyman, and mentor to the Apostles — Shelley enthusiasts at Trinity College, Cambridge, for whom Shelley was a spiritual as well as poetic inspiration in a period in which many young intellectuals were turning to religion.

Never one to husband money, Mary Shelley had a soirée and an evening tea that spring for some fifteen eclectic guests. She bought a piano; Moore, the Robinsons, and the visiting Italian baritone, Antonio Tamburini, sang. The soirée was "a far better show" than Moore expected, the tea "an odd party as usual" except for Washington Irving; Moore left early, "*very* glad to be off."[30] She had Godwin and her old friends James Kenney and Frederic Reynolds along with new, and recent acquaintances such as Lady Mary Shepherd, author of philosophic essays (a "crazy metaphysician," some said), Edward and Rosina Bulwer, and the painter Richard Rothwell.

On the advice of her physician, William Lawrence, Mary took Percy to Southend for his summer holidays. Despite two years in the city, she was still so sensitive to Nature that she invariably knew when the tide ebbed and flowed by the fluctuations of her own vitality. Though she disliked "crouded rooms where I shall not know a soul scarcely," she came up by packet boat to swell the feminine contingent at Mrs. Manners-Sutton's official ball, as many politicians' wives refused to attend. From August to November she stayed with the Robinsons at Paddington to enjoy autumn.

That year two stage versions of "The Sisters of Albano" played in London; *The Keepsake* contained a spoof on *The Last Man:* "A Dialogue For The Year 2130 . . . From the Album of a Modern Sibyl"; and John Martin painted the second of three *Last Man* pictures. Nevertheless, Mary Shelley now learned that although *The Athenaeum* had ranked her as the most distinguished contemporary English woman of letters, hers was a succès d'estime, not d'argent. What all authors fear happened with *Perkin Warbeck;* just before it came out on May 13, 1830, another novel on Perkin was published. Reviewers praised her versatility and power, though some regretted her gloomy story and pessimistic tone.* But her novel did not sell. The age of literary Romanticism was in decline, and with it the demand for her speciality.

Despite dwindling funds, she made a final effort to repay Murray with a work for his Family Library, proposing various works in her field of competence: lives of Mohammed, the English philosophers, or celebrated women; histories of the conquests of Mexico and Peru, or of eighteenth-century English and Continental manners and literature; women or of chivalry; a book on geology and prehistoric archaeology. Knowing the last would entrench "upon *orthodoxy,*" she assured Murray she had "a great distaste for obtruding any opinions, even if I have any, differing from general belief, of which I am not aware."[31] She offered also to review for the *Quarterly*, "liberal as that publication has become." As Murray declined all these ideas, she had to let the debt stand, assuring him "that *I shall never forget it.*"[32]

Of course, Murray feared her opinions, for whereas she had never

---

* One critic caught her in a minor error that she corrected for a possible second edition, which did not appear until 1857.

written to promulgate, she always had and always would assert them. In *Perkin Warbeck* she had upheld the adulteress Jane Shore, condemned capital punishment, and obliquely declared her sympathy with current working-class protests: " 'Why, while there is plenty in the land, should we and our children starve?' " ask the despairing artisans during Perkin's wars, and take arms against their oppressors.[33] And by "general belief" she meant the shared views of her enlightened contemporaries, and on that spectrum she was liberal to radical. When she was anxious or defensive, she tended to make over- or understatements. For example, she gave as qualification for reviewing only her first *Westminster* review (in which she had described her illicit elopement tour), though she had contributed regularly since.

Mary Shelley was by now so discouraged that she suppressed her ambition for added literary fame. As for finances, she might have done better if she had tried other publishers, or if Sir Timothy and her own reticence had not made her shrink from the magazine features, mentions in the press, and so on that made celebrities and best-sellers of less gifted authors. Laetitia Landon got three hundred pounds for her novels; some authors eight hundred.

Periodical work, therefore, continued to be essential to her income, probably bringing in fifty pounds a year at most. She now sold two articles to the *New Monthly* (possibly having written "Byron and Shelley on the Character of Hamlet" in the November issue.)[34] She also sent a piece to *Blackwood's,* which had asked for contributions, but it rejected the article, and in her current poverty she even offered to write for the *Court Journal.* She disliked having to keep her stories as short as the Annuals required, but every year through 1838 (except 1835) she would publish as many as three tales, and occasionally original poems, in each *Keepsake,* less frequently in other Annuals.

That winter of 1830–1831 her seasonal low spirits were prolonged by disappointment of other "fair expectations." Her closest friend, Mrs. Hare, had left for twelve years in Italy. "Happy one, how I envy you," Mary would write to her at Bagni di Lucca, recalling its dramatic thunderstorms, and recommending Naples for the winter. "Love me, and return to us . . . for it is all very stupid and unamiable without you."[35] Isabel Robinson returned to England, passing as Mrs. Douglas, no longer fascinating, and indifferent to Mary. "Good heavens — is this the being I adored," noted Mary, who, as a greeting, had just published a passionate poem to Isabel, "A Night Scene," in *The Keepsake.* "Old — shy," "desperately poor," she refused the invitation of Mrs. Somerville Wood, an idiosyncratic, free-thinking hostess who shocked her snobbish acquaintances by mixing "respectable" and notorious celebrities, plebeian liberals, and strange foreigners.[36]

Mary Shelley needed a financial success. She planned her first modern novel, *Lodore*, which Ollier advised her to complete before getting a contract with Colburn and his new partner, Richard Bentley. But being generous about assisting people professionally, she took the time to help Trelawny, who sent her his autobiography to make publishable and to publish in gentlemanly anonymity, knowing his authorship would be obvious. Enthusiastic about what was in fact a romantic thriller, she supplied chapter mottoes from Shelley and Byron, edited, and advised that half his audience, women, would not read it unless certain coarse words and scenes to which she herself objected were altered; wisely, she delegated Horace Smith to do so. She acutely titled the work *Adventures of a Younger Son*, and in protracted negotiations with Colburn got Trelawny three hundred pounds.

The one bright spot was political. In June 1830 George IV had died and was succeeded by William IV, who leaned to the Whigs. The largely bloodless July Revolution in France had overthrown the Bourbons, put Louis-Philippe on the throne, and fired uprisings in Italy, Belgium, and Poland. She wrote to congratulate Fanny Wright and Lafayette on the triumph of the cause in Europe. Meanwhile, demands for reform of Parliament surged in England. After fifty years' dominance, the Tories fell in November. The Whigs introduced a drastic reform bill, supported by mass demonstrations.

"The Whigs triumphed gloriously in the boldness of their measure," Mary wrote Trelawny. "England will be free if it is carried."[37] It was to fail, though another would carry in 1832. "Will not our Children live to see a new birth for the world!" she wrote Fanny Wright. "The people *will* be redressed — will the Aristocrats sacrifice enough to tranquillize them — if they will not — we must be revolutionized —" Her personal life, she added, was futile. "Yours is a brighter lot, a nobler career. Heaven bless you in it, dear Girl . . . You have chosen the wiser path . . ."[38] Ironically, Frances Wright had returned to France, pregnant by a colleague, Philippe Darusmont, whom she later married.

"My sanguine disposition and capacity to endure have borne me up hitherto," Mary wrote Trelawny, "but I am sinking at last — but to quit so stupid a topic," she went on to give him news of his many London "loves."[39] With spring, however, she went into debt to get about, enjoying two evenings at Mrs. Wood's with, among others, Payne, Godwin, George Birkbeck, founder of an institution for the education of working-class men, and the Leicester Stanhopes: scintillating Elizabeth Stanhope, one of the "blue Diablesses" Moore could not stand, and with whom Mary struck up a friendship, was Mrs. Wood's daughter. Her husband had fought in the Greek war for the republic, for which he invented a portable press, and had accompanied Byron's body to England. Thanks to Payne, Mary heard Paganini — who threw her and many of the audience into hysterics well worth her expensive ticket — and hired an opera box, taking Julia, whose beau was in town; once they went to Ascot to meet him, and "were a good deal amused."

Since Mrs. Hare's departure, Mary's most intimate friend had become Gee Paul, eight years her junior. When Gee visited her father, who lived near the Shelleys, she talked to Sir Timothy about Mary and Percy, so discomfiting the old man that he gave her a sovereign for the boy. Mary composed Percy's thank-you letter, "dictated artfully," growled Sir Timothy. The Pauls took Mary to Temple Church to hear Dr. Benson, who turned out to be "the only preacher I ever liked."[40] A low churchman, Benson believed the clergy had power "only to *beseech* men in Christ's stead to be reconciled with God," not to judge or absolve them,[41] and preached commonality in a time of increasing sectarianism. Thereafter she occasionally took Percy to Temple Church services, to liberalize the religious instruction he got at Slater's.

Gee's mother introduced Mary to the Beauclerk family at Sunday dinner, and it may have been the Whig Beauclerks who took her to watch William IV's coronation in the Duke of Norfolk's box, a splendid spectacle, though inferior to those of Rome, with ludicrous touches, as when the "poor king" had to poke his pen to get ink to sign his name. Gee's parents-in-law, Sir John and Lady Paul, invited her to hear Gabriele Rossetti (father of the future Pre-Raphaelites Dante and Christina) improvise in the Italian mode. Through Sir John, who owned John Martin's celebrated *Belshazzar's Feast,* or through Godwin, who now became a regular at the intellectuals' suppers given by the painter, a great admirer of Godwin,[42] she met Martin.

By 1831 Mary Shelley's new attachments took tonic effect. The year before she had been so phobic that she hesitated to sign a few lines for Bowring's autograph album, but now, when Bentley published her revised edition of *Frankenstein* for his Standard Novels series (for which she got some fifty pounds), she wrote a preface sketching her early writing career and the genesis at Geneva of her "hideous progeny."[43] (Such was the continuing controversy about *Frankenstein* that Henry Crabb Robinson now read it for the first time and found it "disgusting." Amazingly, he also said it should have been set in medieval rather than in modern times.) Of course, she minimized herself, omitted the fact that she had published as a child, skimmed over serious matters with the humor Jewsbury had remarked, and said she was now "infinitely indifferent" to fame, but at least she wrote the preface. She sat to Rothwell, but apparently stopped because she could not afford a portrait.*

"Gaunt privations" dogged her intermittent pleasures. Moreover, of a balmy day she wandered in the Robinson garden, feeling "the languor & voluptuousness" of desire, and longed for love. In 1830 gossip had had her wed to Joshua Robinson, whom she probably could have married had she been willing to compromise: "To be loved by those one cares not for is not love," she had noted.[44] By mail, Trelawny proposed. "My name will *never* be Trelawny," she returned. "I am not so young as I was . . . but I am as proud — I must have the entire affection, devotion & above all the solicitous protection of any one who would win me — You belong to womenkind in general — & Mary Shelley will *never* be yours —"[45]

---

* The 1831 portrait of a lady by Samuel J. Stump, once thought to be Mary Shelley and still reproduced as such, was removed from display by the National Portrait Gallery in 1937 as questionable at best, in my opinion definitely inauthentic.

18   "The great disappointment of my life"

IN LATE 1829 and again the following May, Mary Shelley asked Sir Timothy, in vain, to see Percy, which he had ceased to do, and to talk to her about the boy's future education, which, she observed to Whitton, the Shelleys in reality directed through their pursestrings. She had opened a campaign to give Percy a better and more costly education than at Slater's, preferably at Eton.

In the exemplary but fallacious Mary Shelley legend, originating in 1887 with Trelawny's by then ancient friend Fanny Kemble Butler, she asks Mrs. Butler how she should educate Percy. When advised that he be taught to think for himself, Mary Shelley exclaims: "Oh, my God, teach him rather to think like other people!"[1] Patently fabulous (the two women did not meet until 1837, when Percy entered Cambridge), the idea that she wanted Percy to develop into an average baronet by sending him to Shelley's former school makes no sense. "Independence of thought is the greatest of human blessings," she declared in 1835.[2] Her happiest moments were when she thought Percy was growing "more and more like Shelley," one of Eton's many nonaverage, nonconformist products, and Percy was a quirky character, boy and man.

In *Matilda* of 1819, and later in *The Last Man,* she had expressed her admiration of the independence, sense of community, and leadership that Eton instilled, qualities she felt Percy needed. He was a bright youngster but antisocial, indolent, and "tractable — which is not quite the virtue of his fathers family," she quipped to Whitton.[3] As Godwin had said of her, she wanted him "to be excited to industry," and to be a classics scholar as well.

Shelley, moreover, had wished his elder son, Charles, and Percy, to attend public school (Eton specifically for Percy).[4] If he had lived to send Percy, one doubts that posterity would have criticized the father as it has the mother, both of whom believed that the benefits outweighed the ills. Mary was well aware of the drawbacks: no modern languages, history, or science, considerable license for the boys, and the fagging system, to her the great evil.[5] There were, however, no schools that incorporated all she wished for Percy.*

Realpolitik also influenced her choice. She was determined for Percy to have the privileges to which his future position should automatically have entitled him. Slater's boys did not have gentlemen's accent and manners, then as now aspects of a crucial, cruel English class division. She wanted Percy to have ties to his peers, which she could not get through the Shelleys or provide herself; to know the real world and to experience life's limits at an early age, as she had not.

Sir Timothy refused Eton, saying, perhaps rightly, that Percy would be hurt by his father's mutinous record there, but he also objected to Mary's second choice, Byron's former school, Harrow. Since Sir Timothy seemed to prefer tutors who boarded a few boys in their homes, Mary consulted Julius Hare about the best tutors, a choice that was not her preference: "Too great security destroys the spirit of manhood . . . ," she had written in *Perkin Warbeck*.[6] Both tutors and Harrow cost one hundred fifty pounds a year, and she was already spending fifty for Percy's clothes and other expenses.

Mary was positive she could move the old man if he saw her and (possibly on Gee Paul's authority) that Lady Shelley was "terrified" she might. It was Lady Shelley, Mary declared, who was her bitter enemy for mercenary reasons, so that she poisoned her husband's mind with tales of Mary's supposed love affairs — as she herself had had affairs and was the kind of woman who accused others.[7] Sir Timothy hardly needed poisoning. He was determined to hold Mary to three hundred pounds a year, partly through avarice, partly through spite. He wanted Percy to be obscure and second-rate and was galled that Mary had friends among eminent Londoners.

Sir Timothy countered with a restrictive bond, about which Mary consulted Samuel Amory, and signed in June 1831.[8] When she inherited her legacy, she would have to repay the Shelley estate all she had been given, with 5 percent interest, and that sum could not exceed six thousand pounds. She already owed the estate forty-three hundred; her allowances since 1823 totaled some twenty-three hundred pounds, so possibly Sir Timothy agreed to repay loans she had contracted elsewhere. In any case she had seventeen hundred pounds in all until he, then seventy-nine, died or re-

---

* In 1830, the Owenite Julian Hibbert offered Godwin to educate Percy privately in order to form the principles of a boy who would someday have wealth and power. Both Godwin and Mary Shelley, however, wanted Percy to go to public school, which she felt was "best suited to form the character of social man."

negotiated. She asked for an annual four hundred, obviously anticipating his death within four years. He would give only three hundred. The following year she used what he called her "Scurrilous Pen" to write him that she supposed he was afraid he would not get his money back: "surely there may be some chance by her dying or her son before me,"[9] he told his solicitor, doubtless hanging tighter to life.

In the spring of 1832 Sir Timothy replaced the ailing Whitton, who died that summer, with another solicitor, John Gregson. Mary again asked for four hundred a year and somewhat mollified Sir Timothy by announcing that when Percy went to Harrow she would economize by moving out of London. Gregson took her part. Sir Timothy granted the four hundred, sneering to Gregson that "Her Diamond Eyes had cut your Glass Heart."[10] Mary entered Percy at Harrow for the fall term, and decided to take him to the seashore at Sandgate in August to harden him up.

Being in debt, she considered moving from London right away. She had lost that part of her income derived from the *Westminster Review*, which had been purchased by J. Perronet Thompson, formerly a military man. According to Thompson, an active editor who could overrule Bowring, the *Westminster* had been criticized for not dealing well with belles lettres, which to him apparently meant rigorously. He objected to the praise with which Mary Shelley ended her review of Fenimore Cooper's *Bravo*. She changed the end and even inserted one of his suggested criticisms — "I care so little for my authorship," she told Hunt. Thompson published the review in February, then objected to her review of Bulwer's *Eugene Aran*, which, he claimed, an acquaintance said could have been written by a girl of thirteen.[11] She wrote no more for him.

But everything else was going so well that Mary Shelley lingered in London. For the last year her spirits had been fortified by having a congenial circle: notably the Pauls, the Manners-Suttons, Mrs. Wood, Mrs. Stanhope, Lady Anne Murray (Lord Normanby's cousin and widow of a general and art patron), Miss Gore, and two of Gee Paul's brothers: Aubrey Beauclerk, the eldest son and heir, who was active in radical politics, and George, an army captain, who had written and illustrated a well-received book, *Journey to Morocco*, and who told Mary that the "Aristocratick chain" kept him from realizing his potential.[12]

Mary had lost Gee Paul's company, however, after seeing her through an ordeal the previous winter. The young Pauls, who had one child, a son named for Gee's eldest brother, Aubrey, were an incompatible couple; he stiff, righteous, and chary; she lively, affectionate, and possessed of what Mary called the Beauclerk "mania" for helping the poor. Paul discovered that Gee had a lover, a dandy whose attentions to Gee had worried Mary, cast her out of his house, keeping their little boy, and began separation procedures. He had the legal right to forbid Gee to see the child, but Mary helped negotiate visiting privileges. She was with Gee when she signed the separation papers, after which Gee, whose mother had just died, retired in disgrace to a Beauclerk relative in Ireland for two years. Though her own son was the injured party, Lady Paul was so impressed by Mary that she became devoted to her.

Perhaps also as a result of Mary's courage and loyalty toward his sister, Aubrey Beauclerk began to fall in love with her, and Mary was seriously attracted to him, though she could not let herself believe that Fate would favor her in love. Thirty-one, four years her junior, Aubrey was what a more ordinary Shelley might have been: gentle in private life yet passionately susceptible to women, a radical idealist but not a rebel. Though his parents had thirteen children, some were probably fathered by lovers of Mrs. Beauclerk (Lord Dudley's longtime mistress), who had waxed "droll" about her incompatible marriage to Beauclerk, son of Dr. Johnson's friend Topham Beauclerk and Lady Diana Spenser. A shy intellectual who lived quietly on his Horsham estate, Beauclerk saw to his sons' education, and while the daughters were dancing in Pisa with their mother, he had taken the boys to lectures in Geneva. At seventeen Aubrey entered the army, lived at periods in Corfu, Malta, and Italy, and had retired a major. Meanwhile, at twenty-two he fathered an illegitimate son, Charles; four years later he was in love with a cousin, Lady Holland's daughter; when he was twenty-nine his illegitimate daughter, Charlotte, was born. He gave both children his name and secured their futures.[13]

"Liberty must and will raise her head o'er the grave of bigotry and ignorance," Aubrey wrote the newly elected Irish M.P. Daniel O'Connell in 1828.[14] Since 1830, during the turbulent months of agitation for a reform bill, he had worked his way into the respect of Francis Place, the veteran reformer who had formerly aided Godwin (and who initially chided Aubrey for his "Utopian theories"), and cut his political teeth forming committees and advertising for the cause. After the bill passed in June 1832, Aubrey, who had recently inherited the estate of his maternal grandmother, the Duchess of Leinster, prepared to run for Parliament as an independent radical.

That spring Mary was also heartened by hope that the Whigs would give her father a sinecure job, which she and Edward Bulwer were helping him to solicit, on grounds of a lifetime of service to the cause and a right to security during his last years. Godwin, melancholy and clinging, was deteriorating, having trouble getting publishers, and asking Mary for ideas for his new novel, *Deloraine* — in which he paid her tribute in the character of Catherine.

With Mary's encouragement, new Shelley publications were appearing, as the reform victory had vindicated his political opinions and created a favorable climate. Bulwer, now editor of the *New Monthly,* had asked her for Shelley material; at her express desire, Jeff Hogg wrote a series of articles on Shelley at Oxford, which Bulwer published during 1832. Jane Hogg sent *Fraser's Magazine* two of Shelley's poems to her; Hunt published Shelley's polemic "Masque of Anarchy," and *The Athenaeum* his "Lines on Castlereagh," which Thomas Kelsall provided from Mary's transcript.[15]

John Murray was publishing a complete edition of Byron's poems with notes, for which Mary described what she knew of the periods of their composition, and Byron's frame of mind: anticipating her own future edition of Shelley's works. Every action of Byron's life, she observed, and every line he wrote was influenced by chagrin at his clubfoot. She also agreed to let William Finden make an engraving of Shelley's portrait for inclusion among the illustrations.

In April Teresa Guiccioli arrived in England for an eight-month visit. Mary returned Teresa's letters to Byron, which Pietro Gamba had put in her safekeeping, and Teresa showed her Byron's love letters, which she had brought.[16] Mary saw little of her, being too poor to entertain her or to attend the parties given for her; Byron's Italian mistress and her artless flouting of British proprieties had society agog. But when Mary learned that the unscrupulous Lady Blessington was publishing *Conversations with Lord Byron* in the *New Monthly,* she asked Teresa to ask her not to expose Claire Clairmont and to print little about herself. Mary also warned Bulwer that Claire had friends who could attack Lady Blessington, and asked what was said about herself; Bulwer reassured her on both counts. In revenge, Lady Blessington told people that Byron had said Mary was vulgar, a liar, artificial, unworthy of Shelley, and that Teresa had been able to recover her letters from Mary only in exchange for Lady Blessington's agreeing to Mary's appeal to "forbear." "I am thankful to her as I would thank someone who had been threatening me with a stiletto, and then spared me," Mary told Teresa.[17]

Teresa interceded for Claire, whom she detested, knowing that she herself was rich, free, and uninjured by her affair with Byron. (Her future French husband would introduce her as Byron's mistress.) But *autre temps autre moeurs,* even in Italy. Teresa resented that in his book on Byron Moore had not referred to her and Byron as friends — *amica* and *amico,* as Italians themselves said — but as lovers. Mary sympathized and herself used "friend" about such relationships in the future. Teresa would not now have written so candidly for Moore, nor would Mary have encouraged her.

As was her practice with publications she disapproved, Mary read neither Lady Blessington's work nor Medwin's memoir of Shelley serialized in the *Athenaeum* that year, which included some unpublished poems. Medwin had only praise for Mary, save for one dig for not having published Shelley's prose. Possibly he did not yet know of Sir Timothy's prohibition, for Mary had given Medwin up. Having impoverished his wife, he had left her and their children in Florence — where Trelawny gave them charity. Thereafter Medwin wrote professionally and lived between England and the Continent.

In May Trelawny returned, to find that Mary's edition of his *Adventures of a Younger Son* had established his reputation as a Corsair, grand eccentric, and friend of Shelley and Byron. He and Mary were again quite close. In June, earlier than planned, Mary took Percy to Sandgate. Shades of *The Last Man,* a cholera epidemic had spread from the east to Europe, driving English tourists before it, and was presently in England. "Fear is its great auxiliary," Mary declared, but kept Percy at Sandgate until September.

"I can never write verses except under the influence of strong sentiment . . . ," Mary would tell Maria Gisborne.[18] Perhaps thinking of Aubrey Beauclerk, that summer she wrote "Stanzas" for *The Keepsake:* "I must forget thy dark eyes' love-fraught gaze"[19] (see Appendix A), in addition to two stories for the Annual. She also made progress on her novel *Lodore.*

Although she knew it would confirm rumors that she and Trelawny were lovers, she took in his daughter Julia, his total opposite, nice, foolish, and "unidea'd." Trelawny, however, stayed at a nearby inn. Mary thought he might run for Parliament, though he was too violent a radical for her taste, but while he was gloomy at being at loose ends he made no such effort. And he resented her present social success as well as her past refusal to marry him. Now understanding him, she made the definitive statement in her journal: "He is a strange yet wonderful being — Endued with genius — great force of character & power of feeling — but destroyed by *being nothing* — destroyed by envy & internal disatisfaction —"[20]

On September 8 William Godwin, Jr., died of cholera, leaving a wife, Emily. The family was shaken, though Claire told Jane Hogg they had never appreciated him: "in our family, if you cannot write an epic poem or a novel that by its originality knocks all other novels in the head, you are a despicable creature . . ."[21] Claire was now a day governess at Pisa and lived with Mrs. Mason. Speaking of envy and internal dissatisfaction,

Claire rhapsodized in her journal about Mary's genius and "the surpassing beauty" of her mind; but, "She has given up every hope of imaginary excellence," "sneaked" into society despite its "depravity." "Others still cling round the image and memory of Shelley. . . . Would to God she could perish . . . so the brightness of his name might not be darkened by the corruptions she sheds upon it."[22] Depraved society notwithstanding, at Claire's request Mary tried to get her a position as companion to Lord Normanby's wife. Claire also sent Mary a story to edit and finish, "The Pole," drawn from the Shelleys' romance. Mary was able to publish it in *La Belle Assemblée* by signing it "Author of Frankenstein," and found a publisher for an article of Claire's.

In certain things, Claire wrote Mary, she was the most daring woman she had ever known: after her misfortunes to expose Percy to the "fatal" dangers of public school. Mary saw to it that Percy learned to swim, Shelley having been unable even to keep himself afloat, but she was determined not to hover. In mid-September she took him to Harrow. When it turned out that she could not put him with the headmaster, an acquaintance of Gee's, she placed him in the house of Benjamin Kennedy, a former Cambridge Apostle, noted scholar, passionate lover of poetry, a liberal, and an energetic, witty, inspiring teacher. She stayed with Lady Paul at the Pauls' Harrow cottage, and spent a good deal fitting Percy out. She meant to live near the Robinsons, who had moved to Thames Ditton, but on Kennedy's assurance that Percy's annual expenses would be one hundred fifty pounds, she returned to Somerset Street. She was relieved that only two of Percy's housemates had the power to fag.

"I write my novel — of Lodore — read 12 books of the Iliad — & am peculiarly cheerful — tranquil & content —" she noted at the turn of 1833. She was meeting interesting people; such as Mrs. Stanhope's friend Mrs. Caroline Norton, the gifted, stunningly beautiful young granddaughter of Sheridan and herself an author; Sir John Paul's ward, the popular novelist Mrs. Catherine Gore; Laetitia Landon and Jane Porter; Aubrey Beauclerk's political colleagues, including Erskine Perry, son of the late owner of the *Morning Chronicle;* George's mistress, Mrs. Wyndham Lewis, future wife of Disraeli. She followed Aubrey's successful November campaign for a seat for East Surrey on a platform advocating wider suffrage, army retrenchment, a graduated property tax, Irish relief from Anglican tithes, abolition of slavery, aid to the poor, and an end to primogeniture.[23]

After Mary visited Thames Ditton, Julia and Rosa Robinson stayed with her in March. She saw Teresa, possibly Mérimée, who came to observe the elections, and Trelawny before he, being "America-mad," left for the United States. Payne had resettled in the States and may have gotten

Frankenstein, The Last Man, and *Perkin Warbeck* published in Philadelphia, though Mary was not paid, since there was no international copyright. Poor Marianne Hunt had taken to soliciting money behind Hunt's back, and at one point broke with Mary when she declined to raise a post-obit for Hunt. But Shelley himself could not have been more steadfast and generous with Hunt than Mary, who now wrote a story for a volume published for his benefit, and possibly put him in touch with the Hares' cousin Mrs. Amelia Dashwood, who became his patron.[24]

Although she did not complete it for another year, Mary had written a good deal of *Lodore* in this period, at a time when the Byronic tone was passé, and political and high society novels were the rage. *Lodore* was none of these but distinctly Mary Shelley in an unforced, contemplative mood. One of her messages is to act justly by ourselves and to others, for the sight of their pain and the sense of self-condemnation entail pangs. More darkly: "the consequences of our actions *never die.*"

In the disguises of the novel she reappraises aspects of the past with significant insight. At thirty-four, world-weary Lord Lodore marries sixteen-year-old Cornelia Santerre, a partial stand-in for Harriet Shelley, and evidence that Mary now saw Harriet as an estimable, spirited, mis-guided young woman. Like Harriet's elder sister, Eliza Westbrook, Cor-nelia's mother divides the couple, pushing Cornelia to live in society and neglect her infant, Ethel.

In despair, Lodore kidnaps Ethel, takes her to the wilds of America, and brings her up in solitude: another version of Mary Shelley's old fantasy of living alone with Godwin, with echoes of *Matilda,** except that she deplores the dependence Lodore fosters in his daughter. En route to England when Ethel is sixteen, Lodore is killed. She marries young Edward Villiers. Their tribulations resemble Mary and Shelley's in their early days, and Mary Shelley contrasts the couple's assurance of a lifetime of happiness and mutual support to the fear and humiliation felt by a secret adulteress (like Gee Paul) " 'living in sin and fear.' " Eventually, Ethel's young mother, Cornelia, gives up society and finds happiness in devotion to her daughter.

In three heroines, Mary Shelley distributes reflections of herself. Cor-nelia has Wollstonecraft potential enervated by a bad education; in Sparta she would have been a heroine, in a period of war or revolution would unflinchingly have met calamity, sustaining and leading her own sex. Love-dependent Ethel is "weak and impatient," yet loyal. The most original is

---

* Mary could not publish her incest story, but may have had it in mind as she wrote *Lodore.* Later, Maria Gisborne asked her about her "beautiful Mathilda." Claire Clairmont, who had Byron on the brain, complained that Lodore was Byron, but he is Byron neither in tem-perament nor actions, and is more likely drawn from the Beauclerk brothers.

Fanny Derham, trained by a gentle Godwinian father, intellectual, asexual, confident, calm, and unswerving in dedication to justice: "Words," she says, "have more power than any one can guess; it is by words that the world's great fight . . . is carried on. I never hesitated to use them, when I fought any battle for the miserable and oppressed."[25] Though the girl lacks the independent income necessary for a single female, "She fancied that she could enter on the career — the only career permitted her sex — of servitude, and yet possess her soul in freedom and power."[26] Despite calumny, errors, and trials, she will be uncontaminated by the world and by life. Mary Shelley suggests that she may someday go on with Fanny's career as an encouragement to young women who would imitate her.

By early 1833 Mary had resolved to move to Harrow, because the only way she could afford to keep Percy there was to have him board with her; his first of three term bills amounted to seventy-five pounds. It was time she left expensive London, Sir Timothy had been saying, and friends who "were somewhat of Her class,"[27] specifically the adulterous Gee Paul, but he refused to give the "Haughty Dame!" fifty pounds for moving expenses. Lady Paul, who would be Mary's neighbor, meant to help furnish her prospective house. "It is hard on my poor dear Father —" Mary wrote Mrs. Gisborne, who now lived in Plymouth. "And I sometimes think it hard on myself — to leave a knot of acquaintances I like —" but added that she could not afford to accept half her invitations and was in debt for the times she did.[28]

She remained in London through Easter, however, and one reason was Aubrey Beauclerk: "mes esperance, ma joie naissait avec cette anneè . . ." she was to write in her journal on the last day of 1833. Together with an unprecedentedly large, aggressive group of new radical members (known as O'Connell's "Tail" because they voted with that militant), Aubrey was participating in exciting sessions in the House of Commons, which she probably attended. At this intoxicating time, he seems to have told Mary that he was in love with her, and she had come to love him deeply. Possibly they became lovers, for she was to recall moments of "ineffable bliss" with him.

She would never have agreed, however, to a secret liaison, and Sir Timothy would cut her off if she lived with Aubrey, so their long-term relations were contingent on marriage. Both she and he knew that she was a dubious *parti* for the heir of a great family and an ambitious politician. Indeed, perhaps Aubrey himself had been "hooked by a dolphin" (as Virginia Woolf has brilliantly written of Imlay and Wollstonecraft) when he had been reared for a less exotic catch. "Does it not provoke you . . . ," Caroline Norton would ask Mary Shelley, "how 'in vain' the gift of genius is for a woman? how so far from binding her more closely to the admiration and love of her fellow-creatures, it does in effect create that 'gulf across which no one passes?' "[29]

Mary herself tried not to hope; too much evil had dogged her, but hope surged nonetheless at the prospect of enduring love, a home, an end of poverty and care, a father for Percy, another child: "the aspect of my life is changed — I enjoy myself much yet nothing is certain," she noted at the end of April. Meanwhile, she had Aubrey to dinner with Godwin, to whom Lord Grey had just given the job of Yeoman Usher of the Exchequer, "a tiny shabby place" but with two hundred pounds a year and lodgings in Westminster Palace. She also gave a small dinner for Godwin, Jane Hogg, the John Martins, and several other artists. She caught influenza, and Lady Paul died of it, a sad omen for Harrow, Mary noted, "were it not for the change that I anticipate." Albeit she did not "quite like appearing in public thus," she agreed to be included in the illustrations in Murray's edition of Byron's work; since there was no portrait of her, she was to sit to Finden. On April 25 she contracted with Bentley to finish *Lodore* in a year, and was undisturbed that she would get only one hundred pounds, fifty more if it sold six hundred copies.[30]

Shortly after, she moved to Harrow. She had restored her intimacy with Jane Hogg, whom she probably told about Aubrey (previously she had promised to tell Jane if she were ever in love): "I hope things will turn out well — *I trust they will* —"[31] If she was "stupidly lodged," not having found a house, it was an Italian spring, the countryside was enchanting, and her dreams of the future radiant; though Percy was happy living with her and her present income could not afford it, she meant to move that fall near Putney. On June 7 she had a relapse of flu, and recovered slowly. Julia Robinson spent July with her. "The tide of Time was at my feet," but then receded, she wrote in a poem on the twenty-sixth, in what she must later have thought premonition. She took Percy to London for his summer vacation, staying at the Robinsons' townhouse.

"August . . . Dark night shadows the world," she notes. Apparently without telling Mary, Aubrey became engaged to the young daughter of a baronet, Ida Goring, who could help his career. In her initial gush of prostrating anguish, no doubt pleading recurrence of flu to the Robinsons, Mary sent for Jane, warning her to show no alarm to anyone: "My only Friend Come — to the deserted one."[32] At her thirty-sixth birthday she wrote Claire that she had reached her first "climacteric"; this she believed was the age at which her mother had died, and before the year was out she expected to be "translated to Paradise."

Despite "frightful calamity," however, she saw her circle, sat to George Clint or his son Alfred for a miniature for Jane,* and grew calm and cheerful. On September 7 she went to Putney with Julia for three weeks, and hiked for as much as fourteen miles, then took Percy to Harrow and rented a house, for which Sir John Paul lent her furniture, with a pleasant garden. Examining herself, she had the courage to admit that besides being wretched she was mortified. "It is not only misery — but annoyance — God help me . . . & from unmerited misfortune my soul rises calm & firm & *free* — May the mood endure —"[33]

The friendship and gratitude of Aubrey's sister Gee (now returned from Ireland) soothed her. She visited London to see her circle, who "afford balm to wounded vanity": Mrs. Stanhope, Mrs. Wood, Miss Gore, George Beauclerk. If they may have suspected, she betrayed nothing. And she contracted for a five-year project for Dr. Dionysius Lardner's *Cabinet Cyclopaedia,* to which Moore and Sir Walter Scott contributed. Lardner assigned her to write three volumes of *Lives of the Most Eminent Literary and Scientific Men of Italy, Spain and Portugal,* the first two volumes the Italian, to be followed by two volumes of French lives. Julia and Ellen Robinson visited for a month, before leaving for two years in Brussels.

In late November Mary Shelley was alone at Harrow. Lady Paul was dead; Mary does not seem to have contacted Mrs. Trollope, Fanny Wright's former friend, who had written critically about Fanny and who in any case left Harrow in 1834. "This is a dull inhospitable place . . . ," she wrote Mrs. Gisborne, "and I live in a silence & loneliness — not possible any where except in England where people are so *islanded* individually in habits —"[34] It was an insidiously erosive situation in which, for Percy's sake, she was to remain for two and a quarter years.

She had Percy, her work, her daydreams, but despite striving to forget, at times she brooded over the past. Like "a shirt of Nessus" Harrow (well named in her case) recalled her previous hopeful spring there; possibly Aubrey had even visited her. She believed that he, like Jane Hogg, had only pretended to love her. (It would be six years before she learned that he had struggled with love for her, and probably that he had not been able to face her.) The wound of Jane's deception reopened, doubly angry.

---

* George Clint had painted Jane and Edward Williams. Jane now commissioned his son Alfred (not George, as has previously been assumed) to paint an improved copy of Amelia Curran's portrait of Shelley, which was bequeathed to the National Portrait Gallery by the Hoggs' daughter Prudentia Lonsdale in 1897. (Richard Walker, *Regency Portraits,* 2 vols. [London: National Portrait Gallery, 1985], I:448–449.) The Clint miniature of Mary Shelley also passed to Prudentia Lonsdale, and was bought at auction after her death by Colonel Shelley Leigh Hunt, Leigh Hunt's grandson. I have been unable to trace its whereabouts.

"Had I not been *deceived* . . . ," she notes.[35] Fate seemed to have demanded another, uncannily similar atonement for Harriet Shelley's death; Mary's fear of woes to come revived.

In November Sir Timothy was so ill as to be given up. She began copying Shelley's letters from abroad, excised of private material, in preparation for publishing his works, and engaged with Edward Moxon, a young friend of Hunt's, to publish her edition. When Sir Timothy "came out as fresh as ever" she delayed the edition but continued preparing Shelley's letters and poems so that she was pervaded by memories of their union, some fanged by Jane, others full of joy or tragedy. The body of Claire's Allegra, incidentally, was buried in Harrow chapel.

Nevertheless, Mary was usually in good spirits for the first year. In November she began the Italian *Lives*, for which she made a list of authors from Thomas Roscoe's *The Italian Novelists* and already had their works in her library. By April she completed *Lodore*, having done some revision.* When she later reviewed the "querulous" journal entries of her Harrow residence (some dozen in all, mostly written in winter), she would observe that they gave an imperfect picture, being the record of her feelings, not of her imagination. For as always when lonely — "Loneliness has been the curse of my life" — she shielded and pleasured herself with fantasies, "my Kubla Khan . . . my butterfly winged dreams . . ."[36]

She went to London for brief monthly visits and for Percy's holidays to enjoy her circle, "where wit, & good humour, & talent, & the art of pleasing reign . . . and forget sorrow in amusement . . ."[37] — though for economy that first Christmas vacation she had to stay with Julia Trelawny, now Mrs. Burley, and could not get around as much as she wished. Her aunt, Everina Wollstonecraft, a disagreeable old woman who supported herself by hack writing, had settled in London; Mary took her back to Harrow for a few unpleasant days, reproaching herself for being "blameably intollerant of annoyance." She had a note from Aubrey, "pour me tourmenter," and was in London on February 12, but returned so as not to attend his wedding on the thirteenth. "Farewel," she noted simply that day.

In the spring *Lodore*'s printer mislaid part of volume III, forcing Mary to put aside *Lives* to rewrite it. "Had I nothing else to do it were still rather hard to come upon me to rewrite . . . ," she told Ollier, when the manuscript might be found "in some odd corner . . ."[38] Then Bentley delayed publication for a year. "I live on my hill, descending to town now and then," she wrote Trelawny in May. "I should go oftenor if I were

* Whether premonition or revision, the young widow, Cornelia, is grieved and mortified to learn that her sweetheart has married another woman.

richer —" adding, as usual with him, that she intended to marry when she found a person she wanted, though still certain she would never change her name, "a pretty & a dear one —"³⁹

Sir Timothy, who regularly pored over her accounts, had long been waiting for June, when she exhausted her six thousand pounds, meaning to give her no more unless the future were settled. In 1824 he had wished to buy her expectant possession of Field Place so Lady Shelley could remain there after his death, but offered only five thousand pounds; now he broached it again. On advice of Amory and Jeff she asked for an outside valuation, which Sir Timothy refused. He demanded to know what she meant Percy to be. A philosopher, she replied. "I can do nothing in any Profession but the Army or Navy," he said.⁴⁰ He may now have allotted her less than the previous six thousand pounds, and took steps to depreciate the value of the estate Percy would inherit. Unless he paid for Percy's university education, she would have seriously to invade her own legacy. Though she wished only to "guardare e passare" ("look and pass on," a quote from Dante's *Inferno*) the Shelleys, at times she hated them: "my father-in-law's prolonged life will ruin me . . . ," she wrote Mrs. Gisborne, "meanwhile he does all he can to injure the future prospects of Percy & myself."⁴¹

That summer holiday she spent much of her time with her father while the ailing Mrs. Godwin took a vacation; her stepmother's care of the declining Godwin so warmed Mary that she called her "Mamma." Otherwise Mary splurged: stayed off Grosvenor Square near her circle, gave a small dinner, went to the theater. Moore called on her. She met Aubrey, whom she had not seen for a year, and doubtless at his suggestion, in order to seem natural, later sent him a letter to frank, as he had done previously. She heard the Lords debate Irish tithes, and probably saw Frances Wright, who was lecturing in London and who called on Godwin.

She was too poor to revisit the city for five months, except on Christmas Day when Mrs. Wood had her to a family dinner with Godwin. In extended solitude she became anxious, "timid." She had long since canceled her portrait for Murray's Byron edition, and felt "doubts, fears & danger" when she did get to London. And she began to feel genuine empathy for Harriet, remorse for not having understood her plight, and revived fear of a biography of Shelley. Moxon had asked to publish Shelley's works with notes and a biography; previously she meant to ask someone else to write the life, probably Jeff, but now she said a life was out of the question.

Claire, moreover, reinforced Mary's awareness of another of Shelley's faults, duplicity, for Mrs. Mason (who died in 1835) had showed her his letters. Claire was shocked to see that while telling her how much he loved her he had criticized her to Mrs. Mason and Byron. Claire now turned lovingly to Mary, but seemed to have learned little, declaiming on the ecstasy of unwed motherhood and happy communities of outcast women as if their own experience to the contrary had never happened.

From this point on Mary Shelley struggled against unprecedented bitterness. She saw herself as a Prometheus "chained to my rock," and even though she told Mrs. Gisborne that she was too much given "to devour my own heart," she felt that she was a victim of English society, a victim of deceit not only by Aubrey and Jane but also by Shelley, and a victim of a Fate not simply retributive but unrelentingly malevolent: ". . . instead of being lucky as I was once called, I am peculiarly the mark of disaster & pain," she noted on December 2. She hoped for nothing but eventually to leave her wasting solitude: "I to whom sympathy — companionship — the interchange of thought is more necessary than the air I breathe . . ."[42] Her sense of injury and desolation was so strong that she could not force herself to walk beyond her garden. Mostly her imagination was dormant, though she had conquered her "sluggish" mind for the Italian *Lives,* "my life & reason have been saved by these 'Lives.' "[43]

"Of [Percy] I think, — life & hope are over for me," she wrote Mrs. Gisborne (who had suspicions of Aubrey, "the amico").[44] "Fate shews her determination to drive me to him alone . . . [I need] something not so *unnatural* as my present life. Not that I often feel ennui — I am too much employed — too much a being of dreams — but . . . it destroys the spring of my mind . . . makes me at once over sensitive with my fellow creatures, & yet their victim & dupe — it takes all strength from my character —"[45] As if from a walled-off world, she heard from a few friends. She had another letter from Aubrey. On February 13, 1835, a year after his wedding day: "An anniversary Strange & sad! —— & bitter," she noted.

Meanwhile, she was desperate about her father, whose job was to be eliminated as part of the Whig reforms. Torn by internal dissension between aristocrats and Benthamites, unpopular for their arrogance and a cruel poor law, forced left by the radicals (who made a practice of disrupting Commons, shouting, hooting, stomping their feet), the Whigs had fallen in November. After new elections, in which Aubrey was returned with fewer radicals, the Tories took office. Mary appealed to Manners-Sutton, and ironically it was the Tories who graciously restored Godwin's job; "They have not the *Morgue* of our Whigs," she told Hunt.[46] Whigs and radicals combined to depose Manners-Sutton from the Speakership. But when the government changed hands, "I was going to congratulate you on the rise of the Tories," she wrote an acquaintance, "& am now obliged instead to congratulate myself on the restoration of the Whigs."[47]

This time the Whigs kept Godwin on. Mary, however, had arrived at the situation of a liberal who had repeatedly been hurt by "the Liberals," meaning left Whigs and radicals, so that she indicted their failings at the same time that she rejected the right's policies.

These years of sacrifice to keep Percy at Harrow were unwholesome for both mother and son. "I should be free & die if —— but no — He is a blessing," she wrote Mrs. Gisborne. She hoped to be rewarded by him in future and told him she lived only for him. " 'Suppose when you grew to be a Man — you would leave me all alone,' " she asked. " 'O Mamma,' " he said, " 'how do you think I could be so shabby . . .' "[48] Indeed, he was never to leave her. As she said, though inexpressive he loved her more than he knew.

Love for him did not blind her to the realization that he had none of the family genius, even though Hunt had said that few boys had such illustrious descent "heaped" on them, and Claire, that he would become England's greatest poet and philosopher. Mary confided to Mrs. Gisborne that he was a good-humored, clever, true-hearted, considerate boy, like Mary reserved with strangers and tenacious when he wanted something, but he had no ambition, no great talents, and little apparent sensibility. Moreover, to her extreme mortification, he had become fat. Because she had always aspired to emulate great people, it would take time before she understood that poor Percy retreated, feeling incompetent to live up to her, Shelley, Godwin, and Wollstonecraft, and that his indolence and social "haughtiness" were the defenses of a boy as shy, proud, and sensitive as his mother. That he liked only a few people (and was to be mad about sailing) may have been his way of being, there at least, like his father.

"I . . . have bartered my very existence for his good," she noted when he wished he could have stayed in Kennedy's house, and yet pitied him.[49] His schoolmates teased him for being a home boarder. She encouraged him to have them to breakfast, borrowed to pay for his mandatory tail coat, wished she could afford a horse for him. In the spring of 1835 Teresa Guiccioli was back in London, where Mary saw her, but at the prospect that Teresa might visit her, "imagine the talk," she exclaimed, knowing the boys would rag Percy about Byron's notorious mistress.

During this period Mary Shelley finished and edited William Godwin, Jr.'s novel, *Transfusion*, for publication with a memoir by Godwin, and wrote a fragment of a story for youngsters, "Cecil." In late 1834 she finished the first volume of the Italian *Lives;* the following fall the second volume, for which she consulted Gabriele Rossetti about the modern poets; in both, all but two of the short biographies were hers. They received no special notice, being published in an encyclopedia, but they are very

fine. She was master of her material and the mis-en-scène, and took particular pleasure in doing justice to Italy. (It galled her that Bulwer, after
five months in Italy, not speaking the language and deaf besides, judged
Italians harshly — "si da retta a un tale forse!" [as if one listens to such a
man], she wrote Mrs. Gisborne.) Her original contribution derived from
being herself a writer who had lived with poets: her discussion of the
creative process, the artistic nature, and the influences of education, experience — and climate.

And these and the succeeding *Lives* gave her wider scope. While noting
that some of her subjects were not the sort of persons who are inspired
by political passions, she ardently admires those so energized, at the same
time praising "the blessed spirit of toleration." Repeatedly, she supports
"noble struggle" for civil and political liberty, from the French Revolution
to recent failed Italian uprisings: "however perilous the passage from slavery to liberty, it must be attempted and persevered in, with all its attendent
evils, if men are to be brought back from that cowardice, indolence, and
selfishness which mark the slave, to the heroism, patience, and intellectual
activity which characterize the freeman."[50] And she applies her determinism
to nations, citing the enduring baneful effect of the Inquisition on Spanish
society and culture.

On March 11, 1835, Mary copied two passages from Coleridge's *Poetical
Works* and *Aids to Reflection* into her journal: the first, a hymn to enduring
marital love; the second: "All things strive to ascend & ascend in their
striving. Shall man alone stoop?" Although she had expected to destroy
her journals postdating Shelley's death, she now decided to preserve them
for Percy; for eighteen months she did not "stoop" to write another entry.
But she was wearing thin. That May she went to a party at Dr. Lardner's,
and, through Godwin, had dinner with the veteran novelist Lady Morgan,
only to be again "buried alive." Furthermore, the Annuals were "cashing
in" on middle-class snobbery by appointing socialites as editors and reducing first-rate fiction,[51] and though Lady Blessington had published a
story of Mary Shelley's in her *Book of Beauty, The Keepsake*'s new editor,
Caroline Norton, neglected to ask her to contribute.

Mrs. Gisborne urged her to summon her genius (as did Claire) to write
a tragedy, or more poems, which Godwin and Jane had presumably praised.
She wished she had not let Godwin talk her out of drama years before,
Mary replied, for then she had powers, but not now, adding that due to
their "material mechanism" women lacked the higher grades of intellect,
and that she herself was weak and vacillating. "My Mother had more
energy of character — still she had not sufficient fire of imagination."
Moreover, Godwin and Jane had disparaged her "best" poem, "A Dirge,"

to Shelley, if for reasons Mary perceived with bitter acuity. "Papa loves not the memory of S— because — he feels he injured him [Shelley]," and Jane's claim to have been Shelley's love "make[s] it distasteful to her that I should feel — & above all be thought by others to feel & to have a right to feel —"[52]

In early July, Mary succumbed to such a serious illness that Jane came to nurse her. She spent the month of August at Dover recovering, followed by two inspiriting weeks in London and a visit to the Stanhopes' Putney house, though she was still weak. She tried to rectify an error she had made in the contract of Trelawny's book, got Peacock to be his arbitrator with Bentley, and saw Trelawny's sister, Charlotte Trevanion, who was ostracized after having been divorced for adultery. When she got back to Harrow, she had a relapse.

Trelawny had returned from America and enchantment with Fanny Kemble Butler to go into society, be captivated by Caroline Norton, and get excited about politics. Though he offered Mary money he avoided her, and wrote Claire that while Mary's head "might be put upon the shoulders of a Philosopher," her "disease" was increasing: "her pining after distinction and the distinguished of fortune."[53] At the same time, he assured Mary of their sacred ties. "I live in total retirement, buried, where my mind is sufficiently at ease in my books," she replied. "The world is now nothing more to me, I am so far from it — at least in imagination, that not even a sound of its distant turmoil and turbulence reaches my ear. I do not like professions. How many covenants equally solemn have I not seen you break . . . How strangely unwise in you to talk to me of 'sacred' ties, when I hear that word I know that every outrage of neglect, contempt and selfishness is to follow."[54]

Fortunately for her morale, *Lodore* had more success than any of her novels since *Frankenstein*.[55] Reviewers praised her quieter style, thoughtfulness, originality, and imagination, her combination of energy and delicacy. *Fraser's* was almost convinced that she, not Shelley, had written *Frankenstein*. She wrote Bowring, searching for books for her third volume of *Lives*, which covered the more obscure Spanish and Portuguese literati. "The best is that the very thing which occasions the difficulty makes it interesting — namely — the treading in unknown paths & dragging out unknown things — I wish I could go to Spain."[56] She also asked Mrs. Gisborne, a fine Iberian scholar, to send her lists of authors she should cover.

In the Italian *Lives* she had analyzed herself in analyzing the necessary qualities of an author; he has "something to say . . . puts down the overflowing of his mind — ideas and notions which, springing up spontaneously, force a birth . . . and acquire an existence through their own native energy and vitality. . . . An Author, therefore, is a human being whose thoughts do not satisfy his mind . . . he requires sympathy, a world to listen, and the echo of assent. . . . [In addition] pride . . . leads him to desire to build up an enduring monument . . . vanity . . . to introduce himself to the reader, and to court the notoriety which usually attends those who let the public into the secret of their individual passions or peculiarities."[57]

She had not thought to write more novels, but when Ollier asked for another, *Falkner*'s story presented itself vividly: not a continuation of autonomous Fanny Derham's, but rather one "to display" the opinion she had come to, that fidelity was the first of human virtues. She half-finished it that winter, since it "wrote itself."

She was also writing for money to go back to London. Since living with her kept Percy from other boys anyway, she decided to put him with a tutor in the spring when he finished the fifth form. She had a third, especially lonely Harrow winter, rarely going to London because she had to save money for her move. In January Jane Hogg had a little girl, Prudentia, to whom Mary stood godmother, envious to the point of bitterness, thinking of her two dead children and others she might have had with Aubrey. Mrs. Hare asked her to come to Italy for a visit, but she could not afford it. About March 25, 1836, she returned to London.

19 "Do not awaken the deep waters"

"OPPRESSION" EXERCISES "the first of its effects," Mary Shelley had written in the Italian *Lives*, "the demoralisation of its victim, before the second stage . . . that of producing a noble and impatient disdain of servitude."[1] At Harrow, she had passed into a third stage: acknowledgment that liberation was probably hopeless. She arrived in London in March 1836, a misgiving, frail, embittered woman of thirty-eight.

Being low on money, she took dreary lodgings at 14 North Bank at Regent's Park. Shortly after, her father fell terminally ill. She and Mrs. Godwin took turns at his bedside, and both were in the room on April 7 when they heard a slight rattle and felt for his stopped heartbeat. In accordance with his will he was buried in Mary Wollstonecraft's grave at St. Pancras, despite thirty-five years of marriage to poor Mrs. Godwin. It was one of fate's fillips that Trelawny, who had orchestrated Shelley's Homeric cremation, helped make Godwin's modest funeral arrangements.

After the funeral Percy went to the tutor Mary had chosen to prepare him for Cambridge, the vicar of Stoneleigh in Warwickshire, a classics scholar recommended by the Master of Wadham College, Oxford, and by Chandos Leigh (for whom Hunt had been named; his father had been tutor to Chandos's father), who lived nearby and would be attentive to the boy.

Some one hundred pounds was all Godwin had to leave his ailing seventy-year-old widow, who now depended upon Mary. He had made Mary his literary executor, instructing her to publish whatever would enhance his name from a huge cache — the miscellaneous papers of a man who had kept everything written by, to, and about himself for forty years. Knowing his passion for fame, she undertook the formidable task of writing a major memoir that would include his fragmentary autobiography and his significant correspondence; Colburn was to publish it, the fee to go to Mrs. Godwin. Mary, with help from her stepmother, wrote many of Godwin's former colleagues for additional letters, and began organizing, editing, and writing the work. No doubt her happiest task was describing her mother as a radiant, once-in-a-generation genius, bold to fight injustice, generous, and sympathetic — if also a peacemaker, more Mary's ideal than Wollstonecraft's.[2]

Godwin had decided that one of his last works, an anti-Christian tract, would bring Mrs. Godwin a thousand pounds, and, though he knew Mary would disapprove, he directed Mary to publish it. Not only was his estimate wild, his gift for mistiming continued to the end, for in the dawn of Victoria's reign atheism was more than ever equated with maleficence and subversion. Mary did not even consider publishing it. On the proceeds of his manuscripts and library auctioned at Sotheby's, Mrs. Godwin moved to Kentish Town with Emily, widow of William, Junior.

Mary Shelley was exhausted, mourning, sick of unending struggle and burdens. Mrs. Gisborne had also died, shortly after the death of her husband. Claire decided to return to England. As Mary did not ask her to live with her, she complained that Mary had deserted her: "as if I could desert one I never clung to —" Mary told Trelawny, "we were never friends . . . she poisoned my life when young . . . I respect her now much — & pity her deeply . . . but she has still the faculty of making me more uncomfortable than any human being — a faculty she, unconsciously perhaps, never fails to exert whenever I see her —"[3] Claire arrived in October to be governess to the daughters of Henry Grey Bennett, a prominent humanitarian and reformer.

Trelawny had joined a new group of aggressive left-wing intellectuals known as the Philosophic Radicals, notably John "Tear'em" Roebuck and wealthy young John Temple Leader, on whose Putney estate they met.* Trelawny's daughter Zella had come to England; he asked Mary to outfit her before he placed her with his mother, and Zella in old age still remembered with delight the gowns and straw bonnet Mary selected.[4]

As Trelawny's friend Caroline Norton was close to Whig Prime Minister Lord Melbourne — so close that her husband was bringing sensational suit for divorce with Melbourne as corespondent — Mary requested her to ask Melbourne for a subsistence for Mrs. Godwin, resulting in a grant of three hundred fifty pounds from the King's Bounty Fund. Amid vicious publicity, though Melbourne was acquitted, Mrs. Norton was divorced in June and lost custody of her young children to her husband, who kept her from even seeing them. She was replaced as *Keepsake* editor by Lady

---

* Isabel Douglas's future husband, William Falconer, was sometimes present, though not affiliated with this group. In the 1840s he visited Via Reggio to see where Shelley had been cremated; Trelawny gave him manuscripts so that he could question an old sailor about how Shelley's boat had gone down.

Emmeline Stuart Wortley, and ostracized by many women, Anna Jameson declaring that she was hard, profligate, and little to be pitied. But Mary wrote her supportive notes throughout the ordeal and invited her to tea in September, and it was to see Mary Shelley that she came out of seclusion.

" 'I was nervous,' " Mrs. Norton wrote Trelawny; " 'it was my first visit to any one — and there is a gentle frankness in her manner, and a vague remembrance [of] the thought and feeling in her books, which prevents my being . . . as with a 'visiting acquaintance.' "[5] And though Mary considered her a supremely fascinating young woman, she did not intend to "press" herself, knowing that Caroline's family, the brilliant Sheridans, worried that Caroline would be further tarnished by associating with her. Nevertheless, the two quickly found commonality and became friends; indeed, Caroline understood Mary as well as anyone ever would. Sharing as she did the penalties of being a superior woman, she realized that Mary was, partly in consequence, shy, proud, and sensitive "in spite of the freest, frankest, and prettiest manner that ever took my fancy."[6]

Since April, except for seeing Mrs. Stanhope and going to one or two parties, Mary Shelley had been hard at work on Godwin's memoir, and, with the same rapidity as since its inception, on *Falkner*. "My best it will be — I believe," she noted in her journal on June 7; a "strong conjuring up of fictitious woes" from a sense of real woe and injury so unmediated that *Falkner*, and "The Parvenue," which she wrote that summer for *The Keepsake*, are uniquely revealing in painful biographical specificity.

"Lovely from her birth," as Shelley had said of Mary, Elizabeth Raby is an orphan. Her father had been cast out by his father (one of two Sir Timothy figures in *Falkner*), and her young widowed mother's death had been hastened by the old man's refusal of financial aid. Little Elizabeth is adopted by Falkner, who resembles a farouche Shelley, violent in his youth, and passionate to serve the oppressed. Falkner's soul is eaten by a secret inadvertent crime: a transmogrification of Shelley's "act"; Falkner had abducted his beloved, an unhappy but faithful wife, Alithea Neville, who had drowned (as had Harriet Shelley) trying to escape him.

Falkner and Elizabeth adore each other. The girl's reading of history and biography inspires her to enthusiasm for noble conduct, but unlike *Lodore*'s Fanny Derham she enacts it in her private circle. She and Alithea's son Gerard, a milder Shelley type, fall in love. Having broken with his father, who believes that Alithea freely eloped, Gerard has as his mission to clear his mother's name. To that end, Falkner confesses, is accused of murder, and imprisoned. Elizabeth defies "fictitious notions" of female propriety, and goes to him. Gerard gets proof of Falkner's innocence, despite his mother's ruin by Falkner. Gerard and Elizabeth marry and live in seclusion near Falkner.

Thus fidelity redeems all.* Moreover, Mary Shelley fantasizes that Godwin and Shelley give up their tearing at her dual loyalty: Elizabeth is her sole heroine to end with a lover and a father, rather than losing one or both. Indeed Mary condemned both father and husband in "The Parvenue," the story of the lowborn wife of an aristocrat whose duty to her importuning father impels her to extort money from her selfish husband and thereby destroys her marriage.

Mary Shelley told Hunt that *Falkner* needed a "sort of softening in the tone, & something to diversify the continual pressure on one topic."[7] On a deeper plane she was speaking of herself. In October, before finishing the book, she gave out emotionally and physically in a minor breakdown. As Bentley did not give advances and she resented the low prices he paid her, she sold the novel to Sanders and Otley, and went to Brighton with Julia Robinson. During her three and a half months there she completed but could not revise *Falkner*.

Irony of fidelity ironies: on Christmas Eve Julia left Mary for a year's stay with Aubrey and Ida Beauclerk at his Ardglass Castle in Ireland. "Love . . . in these days," Mary had written in *Falkner*, "carries on its tragedies more covertly — and kills by the slow, untold pang . . . exerts its influence rather by teaching deceit, than instigating to acts of violence . . ."[8] More passionately, thinking of Jane and Shelley's duplicity, "Let all be true and open," she would write the next year. "Let all be faithful and single-hearted, or the poison-harvest reaped after death may infect with pain and agony one's life of memory."[9]

By early January Mary was almost well except for feeling "a little odd" at times. She had a letter from Caroline Norton describing a pamphlet she was publishing, *Observations on the Natural Claim of a Mother to the Custody of Her Young Children* (which initiated a successful campaign in Parliament to reform the custody law), and Mary wrote back with specifics. "It was a great triumph to me to see how *alike* what I had written and part of your letter were," replied Caroline, and improved one passage by adding Mary's observation.[10]

Both for her philosophic ideals and emotional stability, Mary Shelley felt that bitterness endangered her, and she now resolved on the equivalent of a rest cure. Rather than be further battered, she would protect herself. Fate, not people, had been her enemy, she told Trelawny: "I have no wish to encrease her animosity or her power, by exposing more than I possibly

* The theme of fidelity also attracted George Sand in this period, namely in *Mauprat*, written in 1835–1837.

can to her rancourous attacks."[11] To the degree that she tried not to blame people, however, she resented real enemies, and her first step was to foil them, as well as to avoid perilous "mental annoyances." Worrying her had been fear that presenting Godwin's views on religion in her memoir would raise a cry against her for irreligion, damage Percy, and doom her coming attempt to get Sir Timothy (who had not seen his grandson in more than five years) to pay for Percy's fees and personal expenses at Cambridge. Now she decided to shelve the memoir until Percy was solidly launched.

Trelawny accused her of being afraid to publish Godwin's political views. At that Mary exploded. It was not a question of "*politics*, but *religion*," she wrote him. Moreover, he was dividing his time between the Philosophic Radicals and society while mocking her present isolation. "The society of agreable — gifted — congenial-minded beings is the only pleasure worth having . . . ," she retorted; "you seem in the midst of it . . .

> What can I care for the parties that divide the world — or the opinions that possess it? — What has my life been   what is it Since I lost Shelley — I have been alone — & worse — I had my father's fate for many a year a burthen pressing me to the earth — & I had Percy's education & welfare to guard over — & in all this I had no one friendly hand stretched out to support me. Shut out from even the possibility of making such an impression as my personal merits might occasion . . . I toiled on my weary solitary way . . . [with only the affection of the Robinson sisters], those dear girls whom you chose so long to abuse — Do you think that I have not felt, that I do not feel all this? — If I have been able to stand up . . . it has been by a sort of passive dogged resistance . . . My happiness, my health, my fortunes all are wrecked — Percy alone remains . . . to do him good — is the sole aim of my life. One thing I will add — if I have ever found kindness it has not been from liberals — to disengage myself from them was the first act of my freedom — the consequence was that I gained peace & civil usage . . . You are a Man at a feast . . . you naturally scoff at me & my dry crust in a corner . . . but it is useless to tell a pampered Man this.[12]

Toward the end of her letter she calmed down. "I am obliged to guard against low spirits as my worst disease . . . & usually I am not in low spirits — Why then do you awaken me to thought & suffering by forcing me to explain the motives of my conduct .Could you not trust that I thought anxiously — decided carefully . . . and I would also guard myself from the sense of woe which I tie lead about & sink low low — out of sight or fathom line."[13] "Of Fate I ask only a grave," she said, but in fact she meant "to render the surface safe sailing."

That decision entailed suppressing her creativity. Shortly after she returned to London in February, *Falkner* appeared. A few reviewers attacked her for defending a criminal, or, conversely, for moralizing, but the majority were favorable. *Falkner* was among the best of her romances of "thought and feeling" in the Godwinian mode, according to *The Athenaeum*. But to avoid rousing bitter depths, she decided to concentrate in future on writing nonfiction.

Her current project was the one-volume Spanish and Portuguese *Lives* for Lardner's Cyclopedia. She had difficulty obtaining this rare material, as she would not read at the British Museum, then frequented mainly by men, and a fusty, dirty place besides, and Lord Holland declined Moore's request that he lend her books from his private library. After meticulous research, however, she finished the volume that summer and began the two-volume French *Lives*, which interested her less; "yet it is pleasant writing enough — sparing one's imagination yet occupying one & supplying in some small degree the *needful* which is so very needful," she told Hunt.[14]

At Easter she visited Gee Paul at Horsham, and though she went with misgivings, "the gentry there are very willing to be civil to me," she wrote Hunt, especially as they all thought Sir Timothy "something of a fox . . . more of a fool" and hated the disagreeable Lady Shelley and Shelley daughters; ". . . it is gratifying to find one's enemies unworthy & generally disliked."[15] Gee's father, Mr. Beauclerk, had given her a cottage on his estate, and welcomed Mary to his manor house.

Fox or fool, Sir Timothy kept count of how much Mary consumed of the total he had allotted her in 1834. "Surely she will soon pass the Equator; and alter her Course,"[16] he had told Gregson; that is, leave London and forgo Cambridge for Percy, whose university expenses he now refused to pay. At seventeen Percy had developed an enthusiasm for music, taking violin and flute lessons; if he had no great talent Mary was pleased to see him apply himself to something. She borrowed from Sir Timothy for Percy to matriculate at Trinity College in July.

King William died that summer, and young Victoria succeeded, so Mary had again the hateful task of soliciting Melbourne for Mrs. Godwin, with Bulwer's chary help, and with Caroline Norton's advising her to emphasize her "*toils*" and delicate health ("if your proud little spirit will bear it").[17] When she was to join Caroline at the theater, Mary, prouder than ever, sent her a sovereign for a box seat, and when Caroline sent it back, Mary sat in the balcony. Moreover, in December Mary refused to join her peers in a request to the United States Congress for copyright for English authors: "because she had never asked a favor of anyone & never would."[18]

When happy, as Mary Shelley told Jane Hogg, "I seek my friends — when harassed & uncomfortable I shut myself up in my shell,"[19] and she believed in a "philosophy of happiness." Presently ill-lodged in South Audley Street, she wanted a home suitable for entertaining, though she would have to raise money from a source other than Sir Timothy. She considered buying a small house in Berkeley Square and furnishing it, as she possessed nothing but a few portraits, a hip bath, and books stored with Mrs. Godwin. A courtesan had owned the house, however, which made her too nervous, though Caroline Norton said she was being childish. Then in October she had a bad cough, and was fetched by Caroline in her carriage for outings. Finally, in December 1837 she leased a furnished apartment at 41D Park Street, hired her first personal maid, and shortly afterward obtained a loan of two hundred and thirty-eight pounds.[20]

On New Year's Eve, Mary took stock in her journal: "I am happier than I have been in years — not that any thing good has happened — but I have less to annoy me . . . Tho' still too much alone, I am loved by some & that thought is peace to my heart — My mind is more made up to the evils of my lot & therefore more capable of associating good with it —"

Partly fearing loneliness, partly to help the Robinson sisters, who had very little money, she had Rosa live with her until Julia returned, and then Julia joined them. When Percy came to London he was fine, if too short to suit Mary, in a stylish frock coat. She dreaded his catching a venereal disease and had asked Trelawny to tell him how to protect himself "which, as he has a horror of risking health or comfort, will I hope keep him right —"[21] She and his aunt Claire worried because he liked only the few boys he had known since childhood, and either "flew society" or behaved loutishly out of shyness and pride, which intensified when everyone signaled incredulity that two generations of geniuses had produced this stout, inarticulate youth. Here, too, Mary tried to content herself that Percy would be worthy of his antecedents in integrity and goodness.

Mary Shelley's new friends included Caroline Norton's legal aide Abraham Hayward, clever, given to risqué stories, and a man of letters who had translated *Faust;* elderly Lady Morgan, one of the time's most endearing and enduring personalities, who adored lionizing the famous and being lionized; a Colonel Ratcliffe;[22] and Augusta Goring, who was unhappily married to, and periodically separated from, Ida Beauclerk's brother Henry. Aubrey had returned for the elections of 1837, in which he lost his seat along with several other radicals, and now lived with his family on his father's estate.

Beyond this, Mary Shelley was a marginal member of London's society of achievement, a society fragmented compared with that of Italy or France, in which she was limited by poverty and English moralism. "Very small, fair, fragile, and delicate looking," Fanny Kemble Butler remembered her, "having golden hair and *pale* eyes, gray, I think."[23] Others observed that the color of her eyes changed, apparently, from gray to hazel when she was animated. In 1836 a pseudonymous *Reminiscence* in the *Metropolitan Literary Journal* gave a probably made-up account of her at Pisa that nevertheless reflected the views of admirers: amazingly feminine, beautifully spoken, and natural, for the author of *Frankenstein*. "And Shelley, four-famed — for her parents, her lord, / And for the poor lone impossible monster abhorred," Hunt included her in his 1837 "Blue-Stocking Revels." "(So sleek and so smiling she came, people stared, / To think such fair clay should so darkly have dared.)"

Even so, Mary Shelley needed social reassurance and froze when she felt unliked, with good reason. She never knew when someone would cut her because of her early career. Henry Crabb Robinson noted that the rich, philanthropic, liberal Mrs. Daniel Gaskell (whom Mary thought tiresome though worthy) received Mary Shelley at her house "which very few of her station & fortune would think of doing"[24] — an exaggeration born of his own reproval of her liaison with Shelley. But once, Mrs. Gaskell brought Mary up to the aged feminist and admirer of Godwin and Wollstonecraft, Lucy Aikin, to introduce her, whereupon Miss Aikin "resolutely turned her back on the fair widow," to the dismay of Miss Aikin's young nephew, who "was himself enchanted with Mrs. Shelley's beauty and manners."[25]

Trelawny observed that Mary looked older in daylight but "lights up very well at night — and shows to advantage in society," adding disdainfully, "for there she is happy."[26] "I have heard her accused of an overanxiety to be admired . . . ," Thornton Hunt would respond in 1863; "it was a weakness as venial as it was purely superficial. Away from society, she was as truthful and simple a woman as I have ever met, — was as faithful a friend as the world has produced, — using that unreserved directness . . . which is the very crowning glory of friendly intercourse."[27]

In her preferred company of "the wise, the witty and the enlightened," she is described as very clever, lively, pleasing, unaffected, more impressive on second meeting. When the American statesman Charles Sumner met her "dressed in pure white" at Lady Morgan's, she made a faux pas about Americans, which amused him and embarrassed her, after which she had him at one of her evening teas with a number of Italians and French to whom she spoke "quite gracefully" in their respective tongues.[28] Sympathy for Italy had fallen off since the failed 1831 insurrection, so she was eager to promote liberal Italian exiles.

Benjamin Disraeli, whose first novel had impressed her and whose current *Venetia* featured heroes modeled on Byron and Shelley (Disraeli may have consulted her for it), sometimes franked her letters after his election to Parliament. "I wonder if you *will be* what you *can be*," she remarked to the then distrusted dandy. "Were your heart in your career it would be a brilliant one."[29] She knew other London lights, such as the actor William Macready; the former Cambridge Apostle and confrere of Tennyson, Richard Monckton Milnes; Walter Savage Landor; Thomas Campbell; and the Carlyles.

In June 1838 she was particularly delighted when the ancient poet Samuel Rogers began inviting her to his famous select breakfasts: "of such intellectual fascinating society I have had too little in my day," she noted on the thirtieth. Notoriously deprecatory, Rogers loved to get his guests' blood up. The editor John Mitford recalled that once Rogers made Mary read aloud a segment of William Cowley's "continuation" of Byron's *Don Juan*, "Don Juan Reclaimed," and "*jib'd her*" as she hurried through it.[30] Another time, they debated Shakespeare's sonnets, which Rogers dismissed as having no merit. Thereafter he issued invitations "to meet Mrs. Shelley"; Thomas Moore was asked to one such dinner in February 1840 to which she brought Julia and Rosa Robinson; afterward the party attended a violin concert.

Of her old intimates, Mary was close to Jane* and as usual sparred with Jeff, who had "played the conservative" to forward his career, was mean to his family, and sarcastic about Mary's setting up in the West End. She had tried to get him on the board of a bank some of whose members she knew, and urged Peacock to recommend him for some position. Now on cordial terms with Peacock, she was fond of his daughter Mary Ellen, a thoughtful, well-educated, liberated girl. She paid duty calls on her aunt, Everina, who was devoted to her and whom she helped support with the aid of her cousin, Eliza Wollstonecraft Berry, now living with her husband in Australia. When Claire came to town from the Bennetts' country home, Mary introduced her to her friends, though Claire shrank from people who were cognizant of her past; oppression resulting from her early years had taken its toll on her, too; young people's happiness in life, she told Mary, depended on their having a wise guide.

---

* Jane of course had to live retired, and even so was harrowed in 1838 when the editor of *The Satirist* confused her with another Mrs. Hogg, whom he accused of deserting her real husband and living in Italy as mistress to another man before marrying Mr. Hogg. Jane's husband died in 1840, but she and Hogg never married.

As she approached her forty-first birthday in the summer of 1838, Mary Shelley had managed for a year and a half to keep stimulated while avoiding depression and bitterness. She sometimes felt "tied by the leg" to Julia and Rosa, who had nothing to do except be with her. "It is hazardous for a woman to marry a woman . . . ," she would tell Claire; "I struggled hard to retain personal independance."[31] But it was better than loneliness. Sometimes she went to church, trying to incorporate "Christian teachings" of patience, resignation, and attainment of greater wisdom and goodness through trials and self-denial.

What with London's expense and bad effects on her health, she meant to live a few miles out in Putney when she could afford to move. Her long-run plans depended on what sort of life Percy would choose, either to make a quiet home for him or, best of all, to help him in a public career. The greatest happiness of a woman, she told Sumner, is to be the wife or mother of a distinguished man.

She began writing for Lardner's *Monthly Chronicle*, which had started publication in March 1838,[32] helped Jeff place articles there, and now wrote what were probably her last contributions to *The Keepsake*, a story and two poems. The French feminist Flora Tristan, who visited London in 1839, would remark on her "vers pleins de mélodie et de sentiment."[33] Recently, she had finished a fine chapter on Rousseau for the French *Lives*, in which she upheld the virtue of women who live out of wedlock and are faithful to their lovers; "whoso fails in [fidelity], either man or woman, degrades human nature . . ."[34] Her "Tale of the Passions" was republished in the first number of *The Romanticist and Novelist's Library*. Whether she missed writing novels, she may have considered drama, for this year she complimented Bulwer on his first play with professional acuity, and helped Hunt with his *Legend of Florence*.

Generally, she felt more her own woman. "This may often be observed with women," she wrote the next year in French *Lives*. "When young, they are open to such cruel attacks, every step they take in public may bring . . . irreparable injury to their private affections, to their delicacy, to their dearest prospects. As years are added they gather courage; they feel the earth grow steadier under their steps; they depend less on others . . ."[35]

And so she emerged from her rest cure. That July of 1838, she decided the time had come to perform what she considered her sacred duty to publish Shelley's complete works. Sir Timothy, now eighty-five, had given over his affairs to Gregson and succumbed periodically to illness, but he always recovered so there was no use waiting. Moreover, she felt stable enough to reawaken memories of the past. With Gregson's endorsement she asked Sir Timothy for permission to publish Shelley's poems, on grounds that several pirated editions had already appeared.

She underestimated or refused to accommodate her vulnerability, however. She and Trelawny had reached the stage where he talked liberty and scorned marriage, and she talked duty and wished she had had less freedom. That same month he asked her to write a pamphlet on women's rights for the Philosophic Radicals. She refused, whereupon he took to abusing her at large for lukewarmness in the liberal cause of her "real" friends in that she had never written to support it, and for loving society. She believed other "pretended friends" were chiming in, most likely his clique, as far as her writing was concerned; no other contemporaries seem to have done so. Probably he asked her out of sadism, knowing she would not agree, and in point of political fact the pamphlet needed respectable female sponsors, perhaps one reason it was dropped. Even Caroline Norton believed that women should be given rights only in their special sphere, and Flora Tristan ruefully observed that none of England's female authors embraced the cause of woman's liberation.

Mary Shelley kept disdainful but dispirited silence at Trelawny's abuse, until October 21, when she wrote a long apologia in her journal, angry, "querulous," defensive, and not as positive as it should have been — "that those who love me may hereafter know that I am not all to blame — . . . Being stung I write with irritation . . . Irritability of disposition is indeed my great great fault. In the hour of struggle & action it disappears — but in inaction & solitude it frets me unworthily —"

Rightly fair to herself, she stated that she, unlike her parents and Shelley, did not have "a passion for reforming the world" to their particular opinions, though she "respected" (more accurately, admired) such disinterested, tolerant, and lucid reformers. "My accusers — after such as these — appear to me mere drivellers"; what attracted Trelawny to his short-lived clique, their absolutism and belligerence, repelled her (as she had not been repelled by Frances Wright or Aubrey Beauclerk). And with her historical perspective she feared the radicals would provoke a reaction to the progressive flow under way since 1830.

"I have never written a word that is not in favour of liberalism" — which she changed to "a word in disfavour of liberalism." (In 1847 a critic was to place her oeuvre in the Godwinian school of "warfare with society.") As for not supporting it specifically in her writing, "I feel the counter arguments too strongly . . . on some topics (especially with regard to my own sex) I am far from making up my mind." Also fairly, she did not believe in "taking away all restraining law" from women — or men; prudently, "I will not put myself so far forward — for then I . . . shall be dragged further."

At the same time, she was ashamed of refusing Trelawny. What inhibited her nonetheless was fear and pent-up anger; "Then, I recoil from the vulgar abuse of the inimical press; I do more than recoil . . . Proud & sensitive, I act on the defensive — an inglorious position . . . To hang back, as I do, brings a penalty," for she thought of her old ambitions and love of glory, and despised herself. But she defended that hanging back in a recapitulation of her loneliness, neglect, and ill usage in England since Shelley's death, her poverty and anxiety, her old friends' enmity, above all Jane's treachery.

Fairly, too, she rejected Trelawny's charge of worldliness. "I like society . . . books do much — but the living intercourse is the vital heat . . . But I never crouched to society — never sought it unworthily — If I have never written to vindicate the Rights of women I have ever befriended women when oppressed — at every risk I have defended and supported victims to the social system [for example, Claire Clairmont, Jane Williams Hogg, Mary Diana Dods, Isabel Robinson, Ellen Manners-Sutton, Gee Paul, Charlotte Trevanion, Caroline Norton, Augusta Goring] . . . I do not say aloud — behold my generosity & greatness of mind — for in truth it is simple justice . . .*

"And as I grow older I grow more fearless for myself . . . firmer in my opinions," she wrote toward the end, adding that she might yet ally her name "to the 'good Cause.' " Possibly she was referring to her edition of Shelley's works, which she was preparing. Sir Timothy had agreed to publication, but forbidden a biography. She planned four volumes of the poetical works of Percy Bysshe Shelley, grouped by dates of composition, to be followed by two volumes of essays, letters from abroad, translations, and fragments. Apparently she had intended to ask Jeff to write Shelley's life; to get around Sir Timothy's prohibition, she decided to include biographical material in her critical notes. Moxon bought the copyright for five hundred pounds.

She had in hand printed copies of many poems; many others had to be copied for the printer, for which she hired a secretary to help her; some poems needed correcting or collating. When she was unsure of dates of composition, she deduced them from content, placement in Shelley's note-

* In *Threading My Way* (1874), after this (expurgated) journal entry had been published, Robert Dale Owen quoted it at length, entirely approving it. Most of Trelawny's colleagues were not radical enough for John Stuart Mill, who was currently unable to rouse them to support voting by ballot, except for William Molesworth and Temple Leader, "two raw boys." See *The Life and Labours of Albany Fonblanque*, edited by his nephew Edward Barrington de Fonblanque (London: R. Bentley, 1874), 31. John Roebuck later became a conservative.

books, and letters. As she stated in her Preface, her purpose was "to lay the first stone of a monument due to Shelley's genius, his sufferings, and his virtues," and as he was generally still considered misguided, immoral, and pernicious,[36] her notes were meant to vindicate him "in worthy language." Hunt offered to help, but she wanted the notes to be hers alone.

She began with energy and burning purpose, meanwhile had people for tea, went to the theater, enjoyed the company of Mrs. Hare, who was visiting England. In November she ran into trouble. She intended to publish the whole of Shelley's adolescent *Queen Mab*, though he had deplored its republication by populist radicals, called it "villanous trash" injurious to the cause, and expressed relief that the "foolish" Dedication to Harriet was left out. Moxon wanted to omit two atheistic portions for which he could be prosecuted for blasphemy. Jeff, Peacock, and Hunt advised doing whatever Shelley would do if he were alive; she duly omitted the portions and the Dedication. While rejecting Jeff's opinion that the less said about Shelley's life the better, she agreed with him and Peacock that she should say nothing about Harriet Shelley, and so announced in her Preface: "This is not the time to relate the truth; and I should reject any colouring of the truth"; and in one note: "in all [Shelley] did, he, at the time of doing it, believed himself justified to his own conscience . . ."[37]

But as she advanced in her work, she was lacerated by memories. And when the first volume appeared in late January 1839, two reviewers criticized her omissions in *Queen Mab*. Trelawny was enraged by the cuts — infuriated, she said it was almost worth doing for that — while Jeff insinuated that she was jealous of Harriet (and of Jane); "I began to be fed on poison at Kentish Town . . . ," she returned, "you have mixed the biggest [dose] you possibly could & I am proportionately obliged to you."[38] She informed Moxon that both omissions must be restored in a planned one-volume second edition.

She fell into an acute agitated depression: "I am torn to pieces by Memory . . . ," she noted on February 12. "Poor Harriet to whose sad fate I attribute so many of my own heavy sorrows as the atonement claimed by fate for her death . . . There are other verses I should well like to obliterate for ever," namely, Shelley's sad poems of 1818–1822. "One looks back with unspeakable regret and gnawing remorse to such periods," she wrote in her note, "fancying that had one been more alive to the nature of his feelings and more attentive to soothe them, such would not have existed."[39] Equally distressing was *Epipsychidion*, which she printed with no note.

Volume II came out in early March. By then she was so possessed by a "sort of unspeakable sensation of wildness & irritation,"[40] she afterward told Hunt, that she thought she might go insane. Taking "about a hundredth part" of the opium dose her physician ordered, she "ordered" herself the country, hurriedly moving in mid-month to Layton Cottage in Putney with Julia and Rosa. Between relapses, when she could not work at all, she completed volume III for April publication. When Moxon asked if she wished to delay volume IV, she replied that the "passed" would disturb her whenever she returned to it, and had it ready in early May. Though she had done her best, that best was not her best, she told Hunt. Illness spread "sinister influence over these Notes," she wrote in her last note. "I dislike speaking of myself, but cannot help apologizing to the dead, and to the public . . ."[41]

Although editing Shelley's prose would not be so painful, she could not shake off the remains of her illness. By July 20, however, she finished the last chapter of the French *Lives*, on Madame de Staël. This chapter is of particular interest to Mary Shelley biography. "Too eager a desire for happiness . . . impatience of life under sorrow," she characterizes the younger de Staël of *Delphine* and *Corinne*, declaring that in this she had been "the founder of the Byronic school." She suggests that de Staël might also have impressed men with the misery their falsehood produces, "a story as ancient as Dido . . . For the dignity of womanhood it were better to teach . . . resignation or fortitude enough to endure . . . and rise wiser and better from the trial."[42]

As it happened, that passage was an admonishment to herself. For a strange tragedy had occurred in late April. Aubrey Beauclerk's wife, Ida, died, and of all deaths by drowning — in a pond on the Beauclerks' Horsham estate — leaving four children.[43]

To make her one-volume second edition of Shelley's poems quite complete, Mary did the "confusing & tantalizing" work of going through his numerous workbooks "full of scraps of finished or unfinished poems — half illegible."[44] In August she began editing Shelley's translations, then retrieved the prose manuscripts Peacock had kept since 1824, and finished editing his letters. Such was Shelley's odium still that Peacock and Horace Smith asked her to omit their names as addressees.*

Percy, who had gotten into a "fracas" over one girl, then briefly engaged to another, was spending his summer holidays rowing on the Thames, playing the flute and piano, helping to copy Shelley's letters, and being a darling. "He is the dearest treasure ever Mother was blest with," she wrote Hunt, whom she consulted regularly about Shelley's prose. "I wish he

---

* Both Jeff Hogg and Claire Clairmont withheld Shelley's letters to them as well as other papers, though Claire assured Mary that she had shown her everything in her possession. Ollier wanted money.

would study more — that is all of defect I see — he is passionately fond of Metaphysics."[45] Indeed, a chip off the parental block, he wrote an antireligion fantasia in the Lucianic mode into the notebook he was using to copy his father's letters.[46]

Because of boarding Julia and Rosa, Mary did not have the money to see her London acquaintance: "I prefer the friends —" she confided to Hunt, "but should be glad of both . . . acquaintance . . . serve as flying gibs & top royals to make one speed gaily over life — they are not necessary it is true like the mainsail." Actually, the Robinsons "as a necessity" were becoming intolerable. "I am very easily put under *soggezione*," she later told Claire, "but while under it I hate it."[47] Trelawny was living nearby on Temple Leader's estate, but though Mary had gotten over her anger she never saw him, for he was secluded with Augusta Goring, who had fallen in love with him and borne his child.

In late September, Mary was correcting the essay proofs, and shortly decided to reserve the more controversial for a second prose edition (for which she collected additional letters). She announced in her Preface that she was not now publishing all his prose but only "the most interesting portion," while his *Philosophical View of Reform* and other pieces would appear in a later complete edition. Religion, not politics, was her probable reason; the reform essay was moderate except for several anti-Christian passages. By mid-December the prose volumes and the one-volume edition of the poems were out. The reviews of the prose were generally favorable, though *The Athenaeum* criticized her omissions, and according to *The Spectator* the prose hardly warranted publishing; that reviewer must be a half-witted, ignorant coxcomb, Mary told Moxon. The prose sold slowly, so she held up a second edition, and in any case she remained too unstable to do serious work.

Mary Shelley's edition of Shelley's works established him as one of England's greatest poets, and her notes remain a mine for Shelley scholars. It has been said that attempts to relate a poet's works to the circumstances under which they were written originate with her. If Victorians would love Shelley's lyrical and pathetic poems, which were already, she noted in her Preface, more popular, she declared that his major works breathed his dedication to "the struggle for human weal": "To defecate life of its misery and its evil, was the ruling passion of his soul . . ."[48] Her presentation of his political views was at once forthright and accurately modulated, and she identified herself with them, as distinct from his utopianism. Cogent also was her view that he had anticipated and influenced development of social policy and ideals. What most repelled the public, his sexual opinions and atheism, she softened: the defensiveness of a widow, and one who believed her husband had not always been right. She emphasized the centrality of love in his thought and asserted her own faith that spiritual improvement in this life prepares the way to a higher existence, where she expected to join his spirit. Unfortunately for her own stature, she passed over her part in his intellectual life, except in discussing "The Witch of Atlas" and *The Cenci*, which she judged his finest work.

When she wrote her Preface to Shelley's prose, she had come to enough peace with his duplicity to cite it as his one fault in their "union," excusing it as the by-product of his tender heart and desire to make people better (illustrated by a Goethe quote that Thomas Carlyle identified for her): "he praised too much . . . it may be argued that truth and frankness produce better fruits than the most generous deceit."[49] But in fact she had an additional, deep reservation, for which she had overcompensated in her Preface to the poems by her sole effusion: that whatever faults Shelley had (in regard to Harriet Shelley) proved him human, otherwise his soul was so exalted as to raise him into something divine.

That December of 1839 Hunt asked her to help George Lewes, a Shelley enthusiast, with a projected critical biography. "That I — who if I wished to write a biographical notice of the lost one would do it — any one may guess," she told Hunt;

> the reasons that prevent me & will prevent me are so tragical —
> that I could never bring myself to converse on them to my nearest
> friend . . .
>
> Time . . . adds only to the keeness & vividness with which I
> view the past . . . for when tragedies & most bitter dramas were
> in the course of acting I did not feel their meaning & their con-
> sequences as poignantly as I now do — I cannot write or speak
> of Shelley to any purpose according to my views without taking
> a seal from a fountain, that I cannot bring myself yet to let flow.[50]

About this time she sat to her friend Rothwell. He was not skilled enough to capture her charm, but this is the only certain portrait done from life that has yet been found. For its exhibition in the Royal Academy in 1840, the catalogue printed Shelley's description of her in the Dedication of *The Revolt of Islam*. Dressed in unadorned deep-decolletée black, her plain coiffure smoothed from her high forehead by a thin gold fillet, she looks still and straight into the observer's eye, at once tragic, appealing, firm, and proud.

Once her editions of Shelley's works were published, she felt increasingly satisfied with her accomplishment, and from now on was largely at peace about their union. More fundamental, although she had new and extreme warning to guard against emotional strain, and dreaded unending evil, she countered with conviction that submission would be worse. And she had already found reason to hope.

From September 6 to 18 she had visited Gee Paul on the Beauclerk estate and seen the widowed Aubrey. Himself prone to melancholy, he turned to her in his suffering. She solaced him, and they began seeing each other. By October he told her that he had struggled between love for her and his career before marrying Ida, and they reached an apparent understanding that they might marry once his grief spent itself. He was to be her prop; her sincere attachment to him would impart "permanent" pleasure to his blighted life and revivify it. She had forebodings. "I feel that the great disappointment of my life is renewing itself & spreading desolation over those feelings which I too well know to be pregnant with moments of ineffable bliss," she wrote in her journal on October 5. And yet she had twice faced her own death with faith that her spirit would be received by a gentle, beneficent Power; "Why not . . . cherish the same belief that all would be good, could I but beleive it to be such." On November 27, "Can I have another hope [other than Percy]? A friendship secure helpful — endu[r]ing — a uni[o]n with a generous heart — & yet a suffering one whom I may comfort & bless . . . I can indeed confide in A's unalterable gentleness & true affecti[o]n but will not events place us asunder . . . We shall see!"

That winter Prince Mavrocordato, currently Greek envoy to London, came to pay his respects and present his wife. She had Abraham Hayward, an epicure, to a modest dinner. "Alas — I am an Igorama," she told him, and if willing to try "any little *esoteric* but simple dish" next time, she drew the line at his recipe for partridge pie "with beefsteak *over* as well as under."[51] After years of obscure struggle, Hunt was having a play produced: they talked over the problematic finale. She, Percy, who liked Hunt exceedingly, and Rothwell, who gave them a pre-theater dinner, attended the successful premiere.

She was still unable to write, Bentley had declined her proposal to republish *Valperga*, and Rosa Robinson had had an expensive illness, so that by March she was strapped for money and worried about Percy's future. She asked Bulwer about getting him an attachéship, to which he replied that she lacked political clout. Julia and Rosa temporarily went back to their father in Richmond, while Mary rented a small house near them, and got her cook another job. She became depressed, weak, and anxious. "I feel wrecked again & tossed on the waves of life — my own fault this time," she told Jane. "I might have 'kept it when I got it' . . . But I have not spent it on myself."[52]

That spring she did a bit of work on Godwin's memoir and consulted a new publisher for it.[53] A Mr. Mynott dedicated a song to her. By May, her anxiety about her future with Aubrey diminished: "May — 11 — 12 — 13 amore redivivus," she noted. She gave him time, however, especially because she was to revisit Italy again, after seventeen years, with Percy, Julian Robinson, and another young Cantabridgian, George Deffell, who had invited her to summer with them on Lake Como while they studied to take their degrees the following winter.

In late May she preceded Percy to Brighton. On June 1, a balmy night with a crescent moon over the soft seas, she was irradiated by pantheistic peace. "Years have — how much! cooled the ardent & swift spirit . . . My health impaired by a thousand mental sufferings has cast chains on my soul — Yet . . . though I no longer deem all things attainable — I enjoy what is . . . the enduring affection of a noble heart . . . & Percy . . . Surely this world, stored outwardly with shapes & influences of beauty & good, is peopled in its intellectual life by myriads of loving spirits that mould our thoughts to good . . . minister to the destiny of Man . . . & make part of that atmosphere of love, so hushed, so soft, on which the soul reposes & is blessed."

When it stormed on embarkation day she became so terrified of Percy's drowning at sea that she could not board. They drove by carriage along the coast to Dover, where on a fine mid-June morning she sailed for Calais.

20 "Amore redivivus"

TRAVEL HAD ALWAYS done wonders for Mary Shelley, and now it only took escape to the Continent to reconnect her to her romantic self. She was seasick on the crossing, but when she stepped ashore, exhausted, at Calais with Percy and her maid, Mary Ann Henry, she felt lightsome. They had to be careful with money, so it was a rigorous trip for a forty-two-year-old woman even if she had not been debilitated. They ate *table d'hôte* and traveled mostly by diligence. The first leg was overnight to Paris; here they met Julian Robinson and George Deffell, who showed her on a map their month-long route to Como via Germany. "I feel a good deal of the gipsy coming upon me," said Mary,[1] eager to forget past and present evils on this vacation with fresh, zestful young men. As her first published book had been *History of a Six Weeks' Tour* of 1817, so her last would be *Rambles in Germany and Italy in 1840, 1842, and 1843.*

After a week in Paris they left early on June 25, traveling hard to Trèves. They hired a boat to go along the Moselle and Rhine, Mary longing to explore, then took the train to Frankfurt. At Zurich she had an anxiety attack when Percy went sailing, but on reaching Italian territory she preened at the boys' amazement over her fluency. With "its aspect, its language, its ways of going on, its dear, courteous, lying, kind inhabitants, & its divine climate . . . it was returning to my own land — a land and a period of enjoyment . . . ," she wrote Hayward.[2] To be sure, the return was mixed with tragic memories, and, on arrival at Como on July 14, secret terror for Percy; she let him think that she herself was frightened of sailing, and he promptly had a small boat built.

For eight weeks they stayed in an albergo at Cadenabbia, with its ravishing views. Being near mountains, "the aspiration of earth to reach the heavens," gave her a sense of ineffable content. During midday heat the boys studied; she read Tasso, Dante's *Paradiso*, embroidered, and wrote letters on her box-desk. At sunset she went down to sit in her private *bellevue*, on rocks at the shoreline under an olive grove, to savor a favorite sight she had described in *Perkin Warbeck*, as shadow crept up the Alps to the glowing summits. She returned at night and sometimes went into ecstatic trances. Gradually she forced herself to subdue her fear about Percy's boating and particularly loved sailing with him in moonlight. "For the hundredth time" she did what she had determined a hundred times not to do — neglected to settle on a fixed fee, this time for an Italian master she hired for the boys, and was finely overcharged.

Only chagrin at Austrian occupation of the area disturbed her until three weeks before she was to leave, when the shadow of England's climate, penury, and struggle fell across her. "Why am I condemned to it?" she noted late on August 18, having just come up from the lake. "And then when I thought of A[ubrey] — his sorrows — his passionate love — his struggles — & how hemmed in & impotent are our powers of sympathy & communication — tears rushed into my eyes — And I prayed for peace to all — And still the Supreme Beauty brooded over me & promised peace — at least there [in afterlife] where change is not, & love & power will not oppose each other."

Particularly happy on her forty-third birthday, she prayed in her journal in faulty Italian, for the preservation of Percy's life and health and of the fidelity and affection of " ———— " (Aubrey). On September 9 they left for Milan, stopping at Bergamo, where they heard Rossini's *Moïse*. Her remittance for the trip home had apparently not arrived at Milan, so while waiting, they visited a factory that made fabric out of a compound with glass. "I love the mysterious, the unknown, the wild, the renowned," she wrote in *Rambles*,[3] and felt similarly about new technology, especially railroads and steamboats, a blessing to the traveler "who loves to roam far and free." As the boys had to get back to Cambridge, she gave them minimal funds to leave on the twenty-third, and stayed on.

After going to the post office every day, she found her misdirected remittance and decided to see Geneva again. At five in the morning of the twenty-ninth she and Mary Ann, along with three intrepid Scottish ladies, set out by *vetturino*. At Maggiore she alone had the energy to visit Isola Bella, where she had one of her daydreams: to live there with a few English friends and Italian intellectuals, to be a focus emanating light for the area, "a school for civilization." Crossing the Alps at Simplon, she got out to walk and enjoy the views. After seeing Diodati and Maison Chapuis, where she had spent the summer of 1816 with Byron and begun *Frankenstein*, all the aftermath years seemed to be a "phantasmagoria."

On her way to Paris she observed that the French had become rude, dating, said some, from the Revolution of 1830: "as the fruits of liberty, we wish to perceive the tendency of the low to rise to the level of the high," she would affirm in *Rambles*, "not the high to be dragged down to the low. This, we are told by many, is the inevitable tendency of equality of means and privileges. I will hope not: for on that hope is built every endeavour to banish ignorance, and hard labour and penury, from political society."[4]

She was in Paris by October 12. Aubrey's brother Charles had lent her his rooms in the Rue de la Paix, a blessing since she had so little money that she had to take public transportation. She spent time with Madame de Boinville and her family and Claire's friend Marianna Hammond, went to art galleries, and through Hayward made acquaintance with Sainte-Beuve. She reintroduced herself to Claude Fauriel, whom she had known in 1828, and probably visited Mary Clarke's salon, currently frequented by Lamartine and George Sand. It was a tense period, with France and England at flashpoint as the result of war between Egypt and the Ottoman Empire. Sainte-Beuve, like all the French, "sighs to wash out Waterloo," she wrote Hayward; "they will not remember that they brought Waterloo on themselves."[5] She heard Louis-Philippe address the Chamber of Deputies; he actually wept on his throne, which made her tear up, but, as she noted in *Rambles*, since his occupation of Ancona in 1832 she had suspected his imperialist designs on Italy as well as the Middle East.

After the threat of war subsided, English friends arrived, Mrs. Manners-Sutton (now Lady Canterbury) and Richard Monckton Milnes, whom she invited to stop in "sans ceremonie" during her at-home hours, four to six. Milnes lent her his new book of poems, and on a frigid December 18 they went to see Napoleon's body, which had been brought from St. Helena, entombed at Les Invalides. She thought the body should have been left on its rock, but there was one fine moment, she wrote Eliza Berry; "a breathless silence" while sailors passed quickly down the aisle carrying the ponderous bier "(they could not have supported it long)" and then "a burst of inspiriting music" after they deposited the coffin on a catafalque.[6]

And yet it was a trying time; only London seemed so much worse that she stayed until January. While she had felt imminent evil at times in Italy, when she got to Paris she saw it. One almost hesitates to go on, but she learned that Aubrey Beauclerk and Rosa Robinson had matched up since her departure and were to marry on December 7. Call it quixotic commitment to the unfortunate, resurgent Eros, self-punitive neurotic compulsion, or terrible luck; however interpreted, these repetitions in Mary Shelley's career indicate a fatal inflexibility.

As for the newlyweds, Aubrey was no cad but a grieving, emotional man of thirty-nine susceptible to pretty girls, with four motherless children, and whether Rosa knew that her elder friend and benefactor of many years was on intimate terms with him, she made the most of her own opportunity. It was too bad that Rosa was marrying a middle-aged widower, Claire wrote Mary, yet good for Rosa because she and Julia were so poor that they had been Mary's dependents; "All your acquaintance are glad you will no longer have to maintain any body but yourself and Percy, though they honour you for the generosity with which you have always treated them."[7]

At Como Mary had noted that memories of religious ecstasies were more precious than those of sensual love, but never again would she seek transcendence. Though she meant to complete Godwin's memoir, she became as ill as when she left home. "Do not think of writing the memoirs," wrote Claire, urging her to take care of herself as Percy needed her. To make matters worse, a radical editor was testing the right of free publication by prosecuting Moxon on blasphemous libel charges for publishing *Queen Mab*, though Caroline Norton wrote to assure Mary that the edition would sell the quicker and that Moxon's defense counsel was the astute Thomas Noon Talfourd.

When Mary got to London in early January 1841, she took lodgings at 84 Park Street: "unhappy — betrayed, alone!" she noted in Italian on the eleventh. "My God . . . Preserve my son — make him worthy of his father — and more happy. Grant that I may return to Italy and never more see this country of ingrates, traitors . . . I am . . . bewildered, desperate . . . the blow received is so fatal [?fated] . . ." Soon after, however, she wrote Hayward to come congratulate her on her return. Percy had turned twenty-one in November, and his grandfather at last granted him an allowance, of four hundred pounds, in addition to her four hundred. Percy, who took his B.A. degree in January, chose to live with his mother, now and thereafter.

That Mary Shelley was not a burnt-out case seems incredible. On the contrary, on the rebound from Aubrey's marriage and with this minor bonanza she began a final risorgimento that reminds one of her own fictions about Romans revivified in modern times; inalienable hope in alien latter days. This was the last and hence nonnegotiable reach for her youthful star by a woman without the means to grasp it, and one who had been through too much for her emotional makeup. The lingering nervous illness brought on by editing Shelley's poems was now chronic in greater or lesser degree commensurate with the thwarting of her aspirations. In time, she would have trouble with her head. Usually she was tranquil, but her renewed energy, desires, enthusiasm, and trust quickly swung to distrust, agitation, and a "temper quick and brooding." These feelings she vented mostly to Claire, to whom she was very close in this decade.

Como had rekindled her love of Italy, but she intended to publish new editions of Shelley's works, and Percy was happy studying music, seeing his few friends, and familiarizing himself with estate law at Gregson's suggestion. "A dark spell has been over me since my return," she wrote Harriet de Boinville, adding that she must forgo her dream of touring that autumn to Constantinople, where she knew the English chargé d'affaires and his wife (Sir John Paul's daughter), and Athens, where Mavrocordato was prime minister.[8] Mary resumed her normal social and working life, except that when she tried to write, she could not; in fact, it would be three years before she undertook original works. "Have the storms & wrecks of the last years destroyed my intellect, my imagination, my capacity of invention . . ." she wrote in her journal on February 26:

> This is a moment of crisis . . . London with society would doubt-less amuse me . . . did we definitively settle here — but to take a house . . . Percy perhaps wandering away — & I chained by poverty alone in dark London — this fate I should find unendurable . . . I beleive travelling would be best for him . . . [in Italy] I might live — as once I lived — hoping — loving — aspiring enjoying . . . I am placid now, & the days go by — I am happy in Percy's society & health — but no adjuncts . . . gild the quiet hours & dulness creeps over my intellect — Well that is not the worst — as long as I am not dispirited — yet . . . that will come . . .

Again in April she recorded a spasm of misery. That, however, would be her last entry for three and a half years, and her last journal protest.

In May she and Percy toured Cowes for a week, which, she wrote Fanny Kemble Butler, "has cured all the nervous wretchedness that London makes me endure."[9] On their return they moved into a furnished apartment at 34 Half Moon Street. She bought, on sale, a cottage piano, two arm-chairs, and a writing table, and hung her portraits of Godwin, Wollstone-craft, Shelley, Byron, Trelawny, and William Shelley. Her and Percy's possessions fit into five packing cases, one small trunk, and a bandbox.

Though she could not go on with Godwin's memoir, she published her second edition of Shelley's prose, with the additional letters she had already gathered but not the controversial essays she had once thought to include. Then she began preparing another edition of his poems without *Queen Mab*, owing to the suit against Moxon, but with an essay on Shelley's life and work, which she assigned Jeff Hogg to write.

She avoided Aubrey and Rosa Beauclerk, and if she needed an excuse to break with Julia Robinson, Julia provided it, having told Claire that she and her sisters had given up brilliant society for Mary. Their brother Charles, however, Mary helped launch in Australia, through her cousin Eliza Berry.* She herself was avoided by Trelawny and Augusta Goring. Augusta's husband divorced her, after which she and Trelawny married and later retired to Usk. Mary's old intimates were in their usual bad straits. Claire was rushing to and fro by horse-tram, giving music lessons and attending her invalided mother. Mary and Percy chipped in to pay half Hunt's rent, while Jane Hogg's mutinous daughter Dina was in love with the Hunts' son Henry, to whom Jane and Jeff violently objected.

On June 17 Mrs. Godwin died. Shortly after her burial at St. Pancras, Mary Shelley and Percy went to Dolgelly in Wales, staying through August. Moxon was found guilty but not sentenced, the prosecution caring only for the principle. The liberals had used him, she wrote Moxon, then left him to pay the trial's expenses, for which she intended to ask Lord Normanby to raise a subscription; though Moxon declined that idea, she added a postscript censuring the trial to her volume of Shelley's poems.

For unclear reasons, that edition was never published. But she stayed alert to possess every scrap of Shelley's writings. The following year, when Southey died, she asked his widow for Shelley's letters: many were about Harriet Shelley, so she did not want them to be published, but Mrs. Southey said that she could find none.† For more positive reasons she would try to get his letters to Mrs. Mason, who, it turned out, had destroyed his, Mary's, and Claire's.

Like Mary, though damaged by years of hardship, Claire seized her chance for revitalization after her mother's death. She made a foray to Paris, where she decided to live, as England was expensive and she wanted society, and bought a small annuity on her future legacy from Shelley. Having given her one hundred pounds to get settled, "I congratulate you that you are now free,"[10] Mary wrote, and sent her introductions to friends who would accept Claire in spite of her past, including Frances Wright Darusmont, who, Claire reported, longed to see Mary again. Claire hoped to marry Jane's Dina to someone in Paris, just as she later had girls in mind for Percy. When Dina had a baby by Henry Hunt in 1842, Claire agreed to take in mother and child, but the infant died. Dina and Henry married; since Jeff would not reconcile, they lived with the Hunts: "so

---

* Aubrey Beauclerk's illegitimate son Charles considered emigrating with Charles Robinson, but instead went into the merchant marine. In August 1844, Claire Clairmont heard that Julia had married; possibly this was the Julia-Frances Robinson, daughter of "Henry" Robinson, whose marriage to Pierce-Alfred Netterville the *Gentleman's Magazine* had noted that June.

† In 1881 Shelley's letters to Southey were published by Edward Dowden.

dear is liberty that Dina in Hunts squalid home will rejoice at having escaped [Jeff's] iron rule," Mary said.[11]

Mary Shelley returned from Wales charged with ambition to form a social circle that would stimulate and establish Percy and put him in touch with eligible girls, as he was already stimulated in that regard but knew few. She had a great deal to offer her son in her own contacts and through Rogers, Lady Morgan, Hayward, Fanny Butler, and Milnes, who among them entertained everybody of intellectual note. Mounting interest in the Romantics, moreover, added to her luster. Milnes, who published the first life of Keats in 1848, noted in his Commonplace Book her revelations about Byron's private charities and about Coleridge's poetry. Her new acquaintances included the painter Joseph Severn, who had nursed Keats on his deathbed in Rome; General Guglielmo Pépé, whose book on Italian relations with Britain and France she had tried through George Lewes to get published in England; and Felix Bachiocchi, Eliza Bonaparte's husband. At Rogers's she met Alexis François Rio, whose seminal book on painting, *De la Poesie chrétienne* . . . (untranslated until 1854), had impressed English intellectuals,[12] and who stimulated her to study the history of painting.

Even so, she was infuriated and frustrated, respectively, by two particular situations she had previously accepted. Beyond her choice, free-thinking circle, now that she looked to offer Percy the cultivated or influential society from which she had been debarred, she discovered that, owing to Victorian moralism, that society was more likely to turn its back on her than heretofore. Whether justifiably or reactively, she felt that even Gee Paul, who had returned to her husband, seemed cooler. From this point on, she abominated London, the heart of everything English she detested; mortification, Mammon, hypocrisy.

Moreover, she could lead Percy to water but could not make him drink. He was a short, stout, fair young man, with a round, smooth face and her quiet high-toned voice. Gentle and lovable with her, though undemonstrative, with everyone else he had a thinly humorous, lounging, self-possessed manner, and when he was expected to shine he turned stubborn and acted oafish. "I spent more than I ought trying to form a society in which he might improve himself," she later told Claire, "but the ban under which I am prevented my doing more than introducing him to a few distinguished people whom he refuses to cultivate & when he did go into society he put on an air of stupidity anything but attractive . . . This is all horribly selfish & distorted — forgive me . . ."[13]

Sans Mary, the Shelleys invited Percy to Field Place, where, after a young lifetime of rejection, he was pulled between ancient Sir Timothy and his grandmother, Lady Shelley, and his maiden aunts, Margaret and Hellen. "Mrs. Paul says that Sir Tim has taken a fancy to Percy & the women are outrageously jealous," Mary gleefully wrote Claire.[14] Percy also began to visit Ianthe Esdaile, his father's daughter by Harriet Shelley, a melancholic young woman who had married a well-to-do gentleman in Somerset.

Mary Shelley took great pleasure in Percy's more gifted Cambridge friends. In part, she cultivated them, hoping their initiative would rub off on him; in part, to help their careers. They admired her immensely, and moreover, they attracted her. In the French *Lives*, she had approved Madame de Staël's last love affair with John de Rocca, twenty-two years her junior, and called her "singularly timid" for keeping their marriage secret for fear of ridicule — but added that de Staël was also averse to changing her name.

Her favorite was a charming twenty-three-year-old extrovert, Alexander Andrew Knox, to whom Trelawny and Milnes also were devoted. Predictably reminiscent of Shelley, he had been rejected by his father and was a poet and classicist, poor, nervous, and ailing, with an enlarged heart: "the sun does not shine on him poor fellow — it never does on my [*sic*] friends," she told Claire.[15] Another of Percy's acquaintances was Henry Hugh Pearson, a musician who set several Shelley poems to music, and one of hers — "O listen while I sing to thee" — which Percy probably performed at home, as he was taking harmony and singing from a Signor Negri; Mary hated English singers' "abominable style."

In January 1842 Mary Shelley had resolved to go abroad with Percy that June, to tour through the autumn of 1843, a trip that she hoped might end with his deciding they would live in Italy. By late April she could hardly wait to leave, and yet she feared the journey, because she did not feel well and her head ached when she tried any "mental applications," even writing letters. She and Percy spent a month at Cowes, where she improved somewhat. Knox joined them, and they invited him to come along to Italy — though Mary would have to pay part of his expenses, and, unbeknownst to her, a few of her friends were whispering about their relationship. After Cowes they spent the first week of June at Exbury with a Mr. Brett.

Before sailing, Mary was again embittered. She saw Gregson to get an account of what she would inherit from Shelley (eventually, Sir Timothy being "excessively well") minus all she owed the Shelley estate, and found that she was poorer than she supposed. Because she was not a woman his fiancée could know, a newly engaged friend of Percy's stopped seeing her. Rogers invited Wordsworth to meet her, but following this memorable occasion she wrote Claire merely that Rogers was "the only person in London" who went out of his way for her, and likewise Mrs. Hare, who sent introductions to people in Florence, "the only person who ever treated me kindly," though she had letters from Severn and one from General Pépé for his brother in Naples.

Having given up her apartment in Half Moon Street, she, Percy, Knox, and her maid, Mary Ann, sailed to Antwerp about June 10, and went on to Kissengen to take the cure. Here they met Marianna Hammond, who was governess to the children of a summer visitor, and stayed a "stupid" month. Her general health was much better, though her head was not well and felt "strangely" when she used it, so that she had to curtail her study of German, a great disappointment.

But when they began touring she adored "the perpetual novelty — the exhaustless current of new ideas," the participation: "We must become a part of the scenes around us, and they must mingle and become a portion of us, or we see without seeing and study without learning," she says in *Rambles*.[16] Knox never forgot the experience of traveling with her, "That gifted and enthusiastic woman who had borne her part in the fervour of those days, which gave to the world a poetic epoch!" a friend of his would write.[17]

Mary Shelley was seeing as never before through a romantic prism of imagination, her own and the creations of others. "German" meant "a race in which women are respected — a race that loves justice and truth," profound intellect, a land of forests and heroes, of intellectual liberty, and currently of great music and of progress. En route to meet Hugh Pearson in Dresden, her party passed through Hesse Cassel, from which England had impressed Hessian troops to fight in the American Revolution. "And yet what act of cruelty and tyranny may not be reacted on the stage of the world, which we boast of as civilized," she wrote; "if one man has uncontrolled power . . . the unwritten story of Russia may hereafter tell."[18] At Wartburg Castle she saluted Luther's struggle, "the most fearful human life presents, with antique mis-beliefs and errors upheld by authority."[19] At Weimar she saw the homes and graves of Goethe, Wieland, and her favorite Schiller, and in Berlin explored the art museum and searched out a steel factory to see molten metal: "a new sensation to the soul."

Even a republican, she said, must be impressed that in autocratic Germany, public education of the poor promised to create more social justice than in England with its "gigantic fortunes . . . and squalid penury." Otherwise the reality of modern Germans disillusioned her: "I cannot exercise my imagination about Germans," she wrote Claire, for she found them ugly, graceless, and arrogant.

Her party remained at Dresden for a month so hot that when she tried to see the sights she got ill. Knox was writing a tragedy, Pearson composing an opera; Percy took up the trumpet. Pearson accompanied them to Italy. On August 26 they began a three-week journey to Venice via Prague and Salzburg; Mary loved the scenery and the Tyrol, whose people had fought Napoleon and Bavaria for independence. Barging the Brenta Canal, where in 1818 she had held the dying Clara en route to Venice, she recognized every landmark, and arrived melancholy.

Thanks to Mrs. Mason's daughter Laura, now the wife of Prince Galloni and a resident of Florence, some pleasant Venetians helped her find inexpensive lodgings off the Grand Canal, where they remained a month. Hiring two gondolas, they leisurely explored, she revisited famous sites, galleries, Byron's former palazzo, Lido beach, and Clara's grave. Temple Leader was there, and though Mary disliked his cold, repulsive manner and his clique in England, she cultivated him because Percy wanted to ally himself with the "extra-liberals."

On October 19 they left for Florence, where Mary, the only Italian speaker, finally found just the *lung'Arno* apartment she wanted for their four-month stay: cheap, clean, and facing the sun. It was a muggy winter, and her head felt "as it were pressure on the brain . . . accompanied by mingled agitation & depression of spirits."[20] That was understandable. Laura Galloni, a gifted young woman, was unhappily married and confined by family duties; her sister, Nerina Cini, was ill. Some friends, Reverend and Mrs. John Sandford, were in town — both came from distinguished families, but she was under a cloud because her first husband, Lord Cloncurry (who had once loved Amelia Curran), had divorced her for adultery. Mary, however, hated their dull English set. When she took the boys into more desirable society, Lord Holland, secretary of the English embassy, was rude to her, and other people were uncivil to the boys as well; that showed her that "the *great* will not receive me," she wrote Claire, "& I don't like underate gaities."[21] Then and there she swore never again to enter "*society,* as it is called," and be humiliated. As always, she was to be a woman of her word.

At least she had the pleasure of cutting Mrs. Hoppner dead, knowing she was still telling people that Claire had had a child by Shelley. Another pleasure, "Did I tell you," she wrote Claire, "that I got a ridiculous letter from Gee some time ago, asking me to confide to her my marriage with Knox": "*surmises*" that Mary assumed came from Julian Robinson and his sisters.[22]

Pearson, furthermore, made trouble among her, Percy, and Knox. Though she eased him out by helping pay his way to Vienna, Percy and Knox were alienated. Percy resented Knox's cavalier preference for his mother, while she admired Knox's knack with people and language, and his drama, which she had him send to Macready and herself recommended to the actor. While Knox took full advantage of seeing Italy with her, she was annoyed with Percy, who shrank from girls or any other society, fooled around playing his trumpet, and cared nothing for paintings, antiquities, and historical sites. "Clash and struggle" was her prescription. "He ought to be thrown entirely on his own resources in some strange wild place where he would be excited to activity of mind & body," she wrote Claire.[23]

Her major occupation, however, was systematic study of Florentine painting by period and school, using Rio's book on Christian art as her guide. In *Rambles*, she summarized his thesis that the most glorious centuries of Italian painting were those when artists were inspired by Christian piety, prior to Renaissance sensuousness and paganism, and went on to say that while she herself believed that in all the arts the greatest embodied the purest and most elevated conceptions, artists must be free to work as they chose: "Bigotry is ever to be eschewed in all that pertains to man."[24]

As soon as a north wind cleared the air, she got well, but Percy was tired of Florence. They went by steamer to Rome, arriving in mid-March 1843 for the Easter ceremonies, and stayed two months at Amelia Curran's former house in Via Sistina above the Spanish Steps.

In "delicious" Rome she spent much of her time with Rio and his wife, whom she had run into in Dresden and arranged to meet. Rio's authoritative, delightful company (Milnes said his conversation rang like churchbells) intensified her pleasure in Rome's treasures and visits to modern painters' studios. She and Percy read books in the Colosseum and the Baths of Caracalla, and visited Shelley's grave in the Protestant cemetery, set under a crumbling wall tower, with ivy and shrubs and wild flowers; Keats was buried nearby, but she never found her son William's grave.

On May 10 they went to Sorrento for two perfect months. Her bedroom looked north to mountains; orange trees along the terrace overlooking the Mediterranean perfumed the air. Knox's brilliant Cambridge friend Robert Leslie Ellis joined them for lunch picnics and moonlight sails. Once they sailed to Capri, later to Amalfi, where thirty bearers "vociferated" to carry them up the precipitous path to Ravello, and she hired all thirty. She longed to winter, to settle in Italy, but Percy said he would die out of England. Knox's sole relative had died, so they left Sorrento early, on July 10, and sailed from Naples to Marseilles, squeezing every penny, as they now paid entirely for Knox. While the young men went on to London so Percy could attend a series of lectures on aerial navigation (besides, he hated Paris), Mary stayed a month in Paris with Claire.

The difference between the stepsisters had never seemed clearer to Mary than now, in Claire's obsessive anger at the Boinville family, who disliked her and whom she insisted Mary not see, and at a friend who had proved as treacherous as Jane Williams had been to Mary. "Ma guarda e passa," warned Mary, be glad that one's injurers are at fault and not oneself, and dismiss self-destructive resentment from one's mind, or it will become monomania. But Claire had interesting friends — some made through Mary, notably Mrs. Sandford's glamorous, erratic daughter, Lady Sussex Lennox; some Russian aristocrats from her own years as companion; and, most exciting, a group of exiled Italian patriots.

Among the last, Mary Shelley found what she saw as the embodiment of the best of Young Italy in the person of Ferdinando Luigi Gatteschi, who was then nearing thirty. In fact, Gatteschi was a genuine hero, with a fascinating personality, as well as cultivated, clever, and extremely handsome. Furthermore, he had had a career that paralleled Shelley's, in that he was the son of a wealthy Arezzo nobleman, brought up in luxury and great expectations and cast out by his family at eighteen for sexual and political reasons. His father's mistress, whose advances he spurned, and his own discarded mistress turned his family against him, and the boy alienated them permanently when he joined the Carbonari and fought in the 1830–1831 insurrection against Austria.

When the uprising was crushed, Gatteschi fled to Corsica with other young patriots, including Carlo Guitera, son of a Corsican soldier-diplomat who had served with Pasquale Paoli. French authorities consigned them to Mâcon. After organizing a Societa dei Veri Italiani, the band returned to Italy, melded their society into Mazzini's Giovine Italia, and worked underground. They were found out more than once, and eventually were exiled.[25] Gatteschi, Guitera and his wife, and a few comrades settled in Paris. Guitera got a pittance from youthful Count Martini (possibly Martini Giovio della Torre di Crema, a coming leader of Italian liberation). Gatteschi was destitute.

"There is something in his position that makes one *frisonner*," Mary told Claire: an educated gentleman, noble in obscurity, proud in poverty, his talents dulled by misfortunes, ardent for his country, and so beautiful that Claire said no English father would let him into his family as tutor. Gatteschi (as well as Guitera), however, was also on the lookout for rich women, though he was attracted to Mary Shelley herself as well as to her celebrity. She persuaded him to write about the 1831 insurrection and French occupation of Ancona, and despite his apparent mortification she borrowed from Claire so he could pay half of his debts. "It is, & has been, the curse of ones life to have this desire to serve others without the means," she told Claire.[26] (In *Rambles* she would quote Ben Jonson's message to Charles I upon receipt of a niggardly gift: "Tell him his soul lives in an alley.")

"Dragged back" to London in late August, Mary landed in the rain, "of course," and to rooms Percy had taken, so wretched that they moved to Putney on September 11. The house she rented on the bank of the Thames, White Cottage, was shabby and had no spare bedroom. Percy promptly bought a boat, which kept her frightened, and she could not get him to read or stop meandering about; all her plans for him were frustrated by "Old Sir Tim or rather Eternity"; at ninety he had recovered from an illness. Aunt Everina had died ("of natural decay aided by her determination to do nothing she was told") in debt to her caretakers, which Mary gradually paid since her cousin Eliza Berry did not contribute. Knox wanted to write, but poverty forced him back to Cambridge for a law degree.

Gatteschi wrote her about his tormenting destitution, while she and Claire (who, of course, by now was just as taken with him as Mary was) tried to help without humiliating him. He was mad to participate in a new Italian insurrection, but claimed that honor forbade his reneging on his debts in Paris. If his writing was good, Mary meant to make a book of it for Moxon, or an article for an important magazine, and give him the fee.

Until then, Mary was determined to write for money for Gatteschi and for her own uses, "though I die for it." On September 20 her "luckless head" made her skeptically consider trying homeopathy,* "one of the fashionable quackeries of the day which consisting chiefly of diet & exercise are just suited to me." Five days later the weather turned cool, her head was good, and she thought of writing articles on French, Italian, or Spanish literature for the *Foreign Quarterly Review* or *Monthly Chronicle*. Moxon was eager to publish a book by her. She considered a novel, but told him that she was much better at nonfiction. In two days she had looked through her notes of her recent tour and decided to write about it.

She began *Rambles* with extreme ambivalence; in fact, she felt so bitter about her social ban that she wished never to publish again, "that never my name might be mentioned in a world that oppresses me."[27] Only because Mrs. Hare set a loving example, she felt, did Gee Paul show affection. Nevertheless, she suppressed her bitterness — and totally forgave

* In homeopathic theory and practice, disease is to be cured by administering minute doses of remedies that in healthy people produce effects similar to the complaint of the patient.

"poor" Aubrey Beauclerk, whose oldest daughter by Ida had died; besides, she admired him and Rosa, pregnant with a second child, for having his illegitimate daughter, Charlotte, live with them.

Once started on *Rambles*, she worked fast and with pleasure, but her head and nerves were bad at times, and her eyes got so weak and inflamed that she wrote only until noon. She decided on two volumes, the first about her 1840 tour for which she used her letters to Claire, and obtained a sixty-pound advance from Moxon. In late October, Gatteschi's manuscript arrived and confirmed her best hopes. He had the substance of greatness in him, she wrote Claire; "What a wonderful people the Italians are." She could use his material in her second volume, and asked him to write more for chapters on the Papal States and the Carbonari.

Meanwhile, except for making Percy's friends at home, she economized in her "comfortable cot" and went to London only for Rogers's breakfasts. She had Paris in prospect, however, as Claire was pressing her to return to Paris for reasons to be kept secret from Percy; Claire was afraid that if she served Gatteschi he and others would think she was in love with him. "You certainly have a most active imagination . . . ," Mary replied. "I am never afraid of loving a man who does not love me — and if I am suspected . . . manco male steady conduct soon puts that out of people's heads — & if it does not . . . life is too short . . . I am so entirely exiled from the good society of my own country on account of the outset of my life that I *can* care for nothing but the good opinion of a few near & dear friends — & of my own conscience."[28]

When Percy went to see Ianthe Esdaile in mid-December, Mary visited Claire, having announced that she would often be with Mrs. Hare, currently in Paris, and that Claire must leave her free; "I am sadly & savagely independant — & this arises from defects in my character I cannot surmount."[29] In Paris she almost finished the first volume of *Rambles*, Gatteschi was at her feet, and when she left in late January 1844 she was infatuated, imaginatively rather than erotically, with him. Afterward, her letters to him were not only encouraging but fond, and confidential about her past and current life. "Flashes of light about his character penetrated," she admitted later, but she would not look.

Young Count Martini was also Mary Shelley's beneficiary and admirer. He owned a Titian painting that he wished to sell, *The Adulteress Brought before Christ*. She thought it belonged in the National Gallery, asked Severn to interest the English government in purchasing it, had it shipped, and took Samuel Rogers, a connoisseur, to see it. At her advice, Martini came over with Guitera to promote the sale, otherwise spending most of his time with Mary, who had the Italian educator and patriot Enrico Mayer to dinner for him. The market was glutted by fake Titians,[30] and since there was some question of this painting's authenticity, it was bought by a private collector.*

Meantime, her last romance began to thicken into an imbroglio of intrigue, rancor, and venality. Gatteschi was in despair at her departure, reported Claire. But as he and Guitera put Claire off and fixed on Mary, who could do more for them, Claire reverted to her old ambivalence (for years to come her health would be as bad as Mary's). Gatteschi plied Mary with letters about his troubles that made it hard for him to write, while she, who at times got so nervous when she took "pen in finger" that she could hardly think straight, completed her research for *Rambles;* since she was in no condition with her limited German to get certain information to be found only in histories written in German, she consulted two friends who were experts, Hayward and Miss Rose Stewart, a scholar who lived in Paris "among the learned."

In mid-April, Sir Timothy began at last to sink into death. Mary's head was *"far* from well," probably owing to anxiety; she felt guilty about her joy at her old enemy's imminent death, and, especially because Mary Ellen Peacock's husband had just drowned at sea, she feared a "Parthian kick from fate at the last instant" for Percy. Godwinian to the bone, nevertheless, after twenty-one years of scrimping she could not wait for Sir Timothy's death to begin sharing her fortune. With Percy's assistance, she sent Gatteschi money, and promised Hunt one hundred and twenty pounds a year, to go to Marianne if she survived him; because of the Hunts' fecklessness, and her own indebtedness to the estate, Mary chose not to give Hunt outright the two thousand she had pledged in 1826, but engaged to pay any pressing debt if she could. Aubrey sent her a lawyer, but she decided to use Gregson and Shelley's former adviser Walter Coulson. Peacock was executor of Shelley's will.

On April 24 Sir Timothy expired, and Mary Shelley and the new Sir Percy plunged into complicated business. Shelley's eighty-thousand-pound estate — consisting of Field Place, and of rented farms and houses producing an annual income of five thousand — was entailed on Percy, and yet Shelley had been able to bequeath it because he had had the expectant power to end the entail. Mother and son cut that Gordian knot by simply undertaking to share everything equally: properties, income from rents, and encumbrances that, they now discovered, amounted to fifty thousand pounds.

Shelley had willed Mary the residue of the estate after his bequests,

---

* The painting, which had also been cut down from its original size, is now in the Glasgow art museum, and is thought to be by Giorgione.

totaling twenty-two and a half thousand pounds, to Claire Clairmont, Ianthe Esdaile, Jeff Hogg, and Peacock were paid. But Mary owed Lady Shelley thirteen thousand for everything Sir Timothy had lent her, with interest, since 1823. The estate had also to pay the five thousand Sir Timothy had left his two daughters, and Shelley's post-obit loan of forty-five hundred to his brother, John.

In order to pay out the nearly fifty thousand pounds, Gregson got a mortgage costing almost two thousand a year. But the total fixed annual outgo came to twenty-four hundred, because of Lady Shelley's jointure of five hundred a year. Sir Timothy left Percy nothing; his personal assets went to his eighty-year-old wife, including everything under Field Place's roof. Thus Mary and her son would divide an income that turned out also to be twenty-four hundred pounds. Each was to put six hundred into joint expenses and obligations (such as Hunt's annuity); each had six hundred to use as he or she wished. If and when Percy married, each would take half the income of half their assets, while he got the income of the other half.[31]

As Mary had predicted years before, she did not have a large fortune to manage, and she did so with great anxiety and generosity. In buying power, she and Percy together had two hundred pounds more than Shelley had had in Italy, and they themselves reduced it to less. Presumed richer than was the case, they were besieged by "heart-breaking" petitioners: Hunt, to whom they gave two hundred pounds for debts after Mary failed through Milnes, a Tory M.P., to get him a government grant; the widow of William Godwin, Junior, to whom Mary allotted fifty pounds a year; plus bare acquaintances and strangers.

Claire, furthermore, was at her most difficult. Shelley had left her six thousand pounds outright, and six thousand for Allegra, whose death postdated the will, to be invested by Peacock. She wanted the second six in her own hands, accused Mary of withholding it, and, advised by her brother Charles, threatened to go to court. Counsel ruled for Claire, to Mary's relief. She begged Claire to come over to get sound advice about investing the legacy, but as White Cottage had no spare bedroom (and Percy did not want Claire around for weeks), Mary meant Claire to stay elsewhere. Claire thereupon refused to come.

Still, Mary Shelley felt that fate had done her justice at long last, and foresaw power, enjoyment, greater generosity, Percy's taking his fit station, and his chance to become someone. Her bitterness subsided, her mistrust of Gee Paul vanished. When Marianna Hammond offered to visit for a few hours en route to her job, "I never heard of any thing so abominable,"

Mary exclaimed, had her stay several days, and took her to the opera and French theater for some fun before she was "buried."

And Lady Shelley, who was moving out of Field Place with her daughters, broke the ice of twenty-one years by inviting Mary to inspect what Mary found to be a "desperately" dull place. Milnes, among other friends, told Mary to urge Percy to live there, but "he would either spend all his money in going away from it," she wrote Claire, "or be forced from sheer ennui to make love to the dairy maid," nor did she mean "to vegetate in absolute solitude."[32] Percy bought a larger boat, and she invited a party, including Adelaide Sartoris, Fanny Butler's sister and a famous singer, to see the Thames regatta from her Putney garden.

From now on she cherished Percy not only for his virtues but also (though still with chagrin) for inadequacies she attributed with considerable justification to the Shelleys' miserliness and rejection during his formative years. She also recognized that Knox had not treated him well. To her joy, and perhaps in part to give her joy, Percy had an ambition to stand for Parliament for Horsham. To establish himself locally he tried to get appointed deputy lieutenant for Sussex and was refused on good grounds — though Mary suspected that the Whigs, who "have always been disagreeable to us," had not endorsed him. Inexperienced, he looked to her for guidance, "and I of course so earnestly wish to guide right, that I feel uncomfortable," she wrote Milnes.[33] In November Milnes notified her that there might be an open election for the Horsham seat.

But by then their income was two thousand pounds, owing to estate upkeep, which Sir Timothy had badly neglected, so Percy decided against spending money for the race. He took this disappointment with characteristic cheerful contentment that his mother found hard to muster; "he . . . is the sheet anchor of my life," she wrote Claire.[34] They leased White Cottage for another year, and rented out run-down Field Place, which Lady Shelley stripped of everything except the fireplace grates, for sixty pounds a year.

In July, Mary Shelley finished her last published works. Her unsigned two-part review of Caroline A. Halsted's *Richard the Third*, a sympathetic revisionist history that she felt went a bit too far, was *The Athenaeum*'s lead article in two issues, August 3 and 10.[35] *Rambles*, which she dedicated to Samuel Rogers, came out August 1. Except for Gatteschi's contributions, which she had translated and edited, "It seems to me such a wretched piece of work," she told Hunt, "written much of it in a state of pain that makes me look at its pages now as if written in a dream."[36]

She had not published an original work under her own name for seven years, so a new book of hers was an occasion. Two years before, George Dibdin Pitt's revived play on the Last Man was advertised as "partly [very partly] founded on Mrs. Shelley's thrilling novel." In *La Muse du Département* (1843), Balzac, who had been influenced by *Frankenstein* in his *Peau de chagrin*, cited her and Ann Radcliffe as proof that women outdo men in imaginative invention. Currently, R. H. Horne devoted a chapter to her in *The New Spirit of the Age* (with which Robert Browning assisted), in which he observed that the imaginative romance was almost extinct but gave *Frankenstein* first place in the genre, and praised *Valperga* as worthy of her gifts and "her high rank in the aristocracy of genius as the daughter of Godwin and Mary Wollstonecraft, and the widow of Shelley." The illustrator Joseph Noel Patton dedicated his *Compositions from Shelley's Prometheus* to her in admiration of "Her Genius and Worth."

If *Rambles* could not climax her career, it is an important recapitulation of her experience and thought, a final tribute to Italy, and overall her most uninhibited self-presentation: a semi-epistolary account of her travels and her states of mind, interwoven with recollections of her past, commentary on history, social issues, politics and art, and useful information. It was one of her most favorably reviewed works, though it was disliked by Browning, who expected concrete, original description but nevertheless sent the book to Elizabeth Barrett. In fact, parts of *Rambles* convey an anachronistic Romanticism.

"If I saw any opening for G[atteschi]," Mary had told Claire, "I would have him over here & serve him all I could." Now she could help him try for a literary career (he spoke no English), and meanwhile get him pupils for Italian lessons by which Knox, also an admirer of Gatteschi, said he could make two hundred pounds a year. She asked him to come — without telling Claire, who heard it from Lady Sussex Lennox, who heard it from Guitera, who had become her lover. Then Gatteschi accused Mary and Claire of telling people she had given him money and said he would not come. Though Mary knew Guitera had told about the gifts, she tried to get him a job on a French railroad.

By mid-August, shortly before her forty-seventh birthday, Gatteschi was in England,[37] and Mary was ignoring Claire's warning that he would get on not by giving lessons but by his looks. While he had convinced Mary of his "peculiar & glorious characteristic — independance of mind," between being a teacher and a gigolo he had no conflict if appearances were preserved, but what he wanted was to marry her. If she had loved him, she might have accepted, but she declined. He seemed inconsolable; she assured him of her continuing devotion and help, and gave him her portrait. He was to write a drama that she would translate into English verse and get Macready to star in.

In early September Gatteschi left for Paris. Mary's letters to him were probably more forthcoming than before. At the end of the month she ran down to Sandgate to spend a few days with the Aubrey Beauclerks and bathe in the "sunny & fresh" sea. On October 2 she was reading Burke's letters to his son, and copied one passage in her journal:

> Preserve always a habit of a giving (but still with discretion), however little, as a habit not to be lost. The first thing is justice. Whatever one gives ought to be from what one would otherwise spend, not from what one w^d otherwise pay. To spend little & give much, is the highest glory man can aspire to.

That would be her last journal entry, and one she may subsequently have thought should stand as such, no matter how the ideal had seduced her into indiscretion.

Meantime, Claire fell out with the Italians and felt surrounded by enemies, to which Mary returned that Claire had a suspicious nature. In early December Claire wrote that Lady Sussex Lennox was in love with Gatteschi; that in itself did not surprise Mary. By the turn of 1845, with grim pleasure and lurid detail, Claire reported that Lady Sussex Lennox openly called Gatteschi her beloved and demanded that he renounce Mary, while he rode the boulevards in a carriage and allowed his mistress to make their affair public. Even so, Mary offered friendship and aid, which he refused, having a gaudier, more prodigal bird in hand.

Mary Shelley disengaged from Gatteschi without animus, hoping that he would resume some worthy career, as eventually he was to do. That winter she lived quietly at Putney. One of her rare excursions to London was to inspect Severn's painting of Shelley in the ruins of Rome, for which she had taken him Shelley's portrait. She disliked his depiction of the face, made suggestions, and had the Hunts do likewise. Knox wrote a comedy for which she got him an introduction to the actor Charles Mathews, but it was not accepted and Knox went to Paris in search of other opportunities.

Sometimes she felt ennui, Mary wrote Claire in June 1845, "but vehement regrets & desires have faded away — & the calm of years is a comfortable port to reach at last."[38] In fact, however, she would retire from life vehemently, as she had begun it.

21 "I will sit amidst the ruins and smile"

"NEAR YOU AND PERCY it is impossible to be unhappy," Claire Clairmont told Mary Shelley in May 1845, "for your unity is so charming, and there is so much calm and happiness in you, it imparts a most beneficial influence . . . and then your conversation so nice and so universal draws one out of the narrow cares of self."[1]

Claire had just returned to Paris from a four-month stay in England. Mary had her sleep nearby, otherwise, except for business in London in regard to Shelley's legacy, she was at White Cottage, momentarily enchanted and toned by its atmosphere. Before she left, Mary had a little dinner for her and lent her fifty pounds.

"God put us here — one is sorry one has not done better," Mary wrote Claire, "but it is all over . . . To do a little good — to watch over those dear — to enjoy quiet — & if one can be a little amused *voila tout* . . ."[2] When Charles, now a respected teacher in Vienna, visited Claire in Paris, he expected Mary to hold a grudge over the money he had made her raise for him in 1829; instead, she sent him ten pounds for his children, proof, he said, of her infinite kindness and generosity.

Percy ordered a yacht that moderated her secret terror — not "dazzling" like his father's fatal *Don Juan* but a sturdy cutter — and joined the Royal Thames Yacht Club. For his current German music mistress Mary had consulted her old friend Vincent Novello, whose family she invited to her regatta party that summer, an al fresco gathering in her garden overlooking the Thames, festive with swooping, flag-dressed yachts. Her two intimate friends, as they had been for many years, were Gee Paul, who accommodated to her sorry marriage and worked in various charities, and whose lively affection, Mary said, "shed a charm over my life"; and the more sophisticated Mrs. Hare, with whom she had an added bond of mutual longing for Italy. The Aubrey Beauclerks and his brothers George and Charles were family friends, and Hunt later said that Putney was almost the only place to which he was invited during this period.

Mary kept in touch with widowed Lady Morgan and was sought after by the Italophile Mrs. Susanna Milner-Gibson, a prominent literary and political hostess. At Rogers's that June she impressed Crabb Robinson as "better than clever — quiet and agreeable. Yet she talked . . . ,"[3] adding enthusiastically after a July breakfast that she was the worthy descendent of her parents and "consort" of Shelley.

As so many people had felt since she was a girl, Mary Shelley emanated serenity and thoughtfulness, and her present desire for contented aging was genuine. All the same, that desire was more for refuge from longing, regret, and protest than for quietude in and of itself.

Her ambition for Percy was irrepressible. She pitied and yet sighed at his stultification when, as a new baronet, he was presented to Queen Victoria and Prince Albert; knowing no one, he went alone and stood around by himself, feeling that he was in a false position. As for quiet, inactivity had always been bad for her, and while she continued to read widely and to help other authors, she herself could not write. To "quicken her blood" and avoid being cross, she sometimes tippled.

Her hatred of London intensified with the kind of humiliation she met when Lord Dillon's widow cut her during a call on Trelawny's friend Lady Dorothea Campbell (who had formerly lost her young children in a custody case): "you may guess how gladly I shelter myself in solitude & Putney from these pieces of impertinence," she wrote Claire.[4] "Lady Dillon is an old fool," Claire replied; "Envious creature," she added (betraying her own animus), "she wants to annoy you because she thinks you fortunate."[5] Before Mary would meet some acquaintances of Claire's, Claire had to assure her they would "venerate your superiority."

Percy's current penchant to live at Castle Goring, the huge, romantic white elephant built by his great-grandfather Sir Bysshe, appealed to Mary, but they needed a great deal of money to furnish it — not to mention live in it. "Ah! with your head — why don't you speculate! and with your luck," wrote Claire, "If I had your head I'd speculate all day long."[6] Mary invested in railroads, but railroads had been overexpanding, and shares fell in value.

By July she and Percy were overdrawn at the bank; they sold their shares and some land. Between depressed farm rentals and a rainy summer that ruined crops, their income was fifteen hundred pounds, while people "in crowds" asked for money: starving villagers whom they helped; Hunt, to whom they gave two hundred pounds, which they had to borrow; and the creditor of one of Shelley's post-obits whom they owed forty-five hundred. Isabel Booth was near destitution, nursing her aged, epileptic husband. After Mary failed, again through Milnes, to get Booth a government grant, Percy obtained forty pounds from the Royal Literary Fund for Booth.

As the lease on White Cottage ran out in the fall, they planned to winter cheaply in Naples; Mary hoped for Athens as well. In August she could not afford to join Percy at Cowes, where he and Gee's son, Aubrey Paul, tried out his yacht — which proved a failure and was sold at a loss.

"Your expressions towards me are very flattering — dear Claire," Mary answered Claire's latest encomium in a depressed mood. "I have been pursued all my life by lowness of spirits which superinduces a certain irritability which often spoils me as a companion . . . To be as I ought to be towards others (for very often this lowness does not disturb my inward tranquillity) I need to be a little tipsey . . . any thing of emotion . . . makes me not so much a happier as a better person . . . I hate & despise myself for it . . ."[7]

Shortly, she was seized by paroxysmal emotion. After months of silence, she began receiving, and replying to, increasingly abusive letters from Gatteschi accusing her of leading him on to expect great things, perhaps marriage, which he could "prove" by her letters to him, and leaving him destitute. He never hinted at money but had his friend Guitera demand a large sum, and harassed Claire. Mary became frantic with shame and fear of what exposure would mean for herself and for Percy, from whom she hid everything. She had an attack of what her physician called "functional [as opposed to organic] derangement in the nerves or brain." About September 10 she confided in Knox, who had returned from Paris.

If she could retrieve her letters, she would be saved from the worst, and she had a drastic plan for Knox, her emotions notwithstanding. Keeping her name secret, he was to appeal to the Paris prefect of police, Gabriel Delessert, to foil Gatteschi's blackmail by seizing her letters and portrait and giving them to Knox. Knox was also to notify an important Italian liberal, Ettore Peronne (future foreign minister of Piedmont). Knox needed credentials, so, without specifying the reason, she asked Trelawny to write Delessert. Knox wanted to use Gatteschi's letters to her about coming uprisings in Italy; that, she said, would be an unconscionable betrayal. Before Knox rushed to Paris, he advised her not to open Gatteschi's letters and get away from Putney. On October 1 she left with Percy for Brighton.

In a flood of agitated letters, "I am indeed humbled — & feel all my vanity & folly & pride,"[8] she wrote Claire, and asked for forgiveness for not being kinder. And again: ". . . with my letters in his possession, he can destroy me . . . O happy are you, dear Claire not to be devoured by humiliating and remorseful thoughts . . . that there are bad people in the world I always knew — and to treat one of the worst as if he were an angel, was a piece of folly that nothing can excuse —"[9] And yet, "I do not wish him to be injured & insulted,"[10] and she feared for his lover, Lady Sussex Lennox.

Though she asked Claire to burn these letters, Claire kept and copied them (starting from the fall of 1843, as well as other letters, until 1849) to have a record of Mary's relations with Knox as well, and her apologies. Some letters she endorsed: "says Knox acted ill towards Percy"; "She calls Mr. Knox my Knox"; "She confesses . . . how ill she requited my kindness."

Percy noticed how subdued his mother was, which she attributed to bad health. On October 13 she heard that Knox had her letters. (What happened to her portrait, presumably a miniature, is unknown.) As *Le National* and *Le Constitutionnel* indignantly reported, on the eleventh five gendarmes appeared at Gatteschi's apartment and despite his protest that his papers were personal took them on grounds of his being implicated in an uprising in Rimini; proceeding to Guitera's, they did likewise. Next day, *Le Messager* denied for the government that the requisitions had anything to do with Italian affairs but said nothing about the motives.[11]

"It is an awful power this seizure," Mary wrote Claire, though she could not regret using it. Hugely relieved, overflowing with gratitude and praise for Knox, she took Percy back to Putney, for they had been seeing the Horace Smiths and she worried that because he normally shut himself off from girls he would fall in love with the Smiths' "pretty nice little" daughter, who was not what she wanted for him; "he sadly wants to marry," she told Claire, wishing she could find a good wife for him, or he for himself.

Once the crisis was over, however, she felt defeated on all sides, and, worst of all, doomed to live in London. Now almost twenty-six, Percy was tired of having no home or occupation and wanted them to buy a townhouse. To pay for it and the forty-five-hundred-pound post-obit he sold Castle Goring, and, of all unaspiring occupations, began reading conveyance law. "My brilliant star — What a mockery," Mary broke out to Claire.[12]

Nor had she heard the last of purloined letters. In October one "G. Byron," who claimed to be Byron's son, offered her, through Shelley's old friend Thomas Hookham, eight Shelley letters (six to her), and several of her own. She thought they were among many more they had left in Paris in 1814 and at Marlow, but offered as little as possible to another rogue for what she considered her stolen property and got her own letters for thirty pounds. In February "Byron" threatened to publish Shelley's letters and two from Harriet Shelley unless she paid him five pounds each; she refused to give more than one, counterthreatened an injunction against publication, and he withdrew for the time.

In November, meanwhile, Claire reported that Lady Sussex Lennox was furious over the seizure of Gatteschi's papers, and that the lovers were calumniating Mary and plotting revenge. But Mary had burned her letters to Gatteschi and refused to fear. That business ended with her repaying Knox for all he had done for her. Knox was temporarily living at White Cottage while struggling to pay obligations contracted when he resided in Paris. She had spent so much on the retrieval of her letters to Gatteschi that she had to get her banker to advance her the money for Knox's debts.

"My poor poor Percy . . . ," she wrote Claire, "when money that would have been the making of him is thrown into the gulph."[13] ("She says would she were dead for robbing Percy . . . of money to give Knox," Claire noted on her copy of that letter.) By fits and starts Percy hoped to get into Parliament if he had the money, and at just this time Mary had her heart set on it, for, she wrote Eliza Berry's recent widower, Alexander (a conservative), "my friends the Whigs" might return to power and call an election.

Prime Minister Robert Peel, seizing on the bad harvest compounded by the potato famine in Ireland, proposed repealing the Corn Laws, which kept grain prices high. Members of his Tory party and the Whigs were on both sides of the issue, but, though it went against Mary and Percy's interests as landowners, she supported Peel. "I am very political," she said, and got inside information from Knox, who now started a brilliant career as a journalist. Peel fell. Percy tried for the Duke of Norfolk's endorsement for Parliament, though Mary fumed at the duke's idiotic pro–Corn Law speech — worse, she said, than anything ever recorded in "the history of the government of the aristocracy" — telling the poor to assuage their hunger with hot water flavored with curry powder. The Whigs could not form a government, to her disgust, and Peel returned.

But had there been an election, she despaired of Percy's success given his lack of quickness and address. Recently, for example, she had gotten him to go to a Milner-Gibson dinner, where he mumbled among such influentials as the liberal editor Albany Fonblanque, Harrison Ainsworth, the actor William Macready, and Mrs. Catherine Gore, and doubtless went off in a corner with the host, who owned a famous yacht.

In December they bought and she began furnishing a four-story house at 24 Chester Square in Pimlico, the first house she had ever owned. To her it meant domestic annoyances, humiliations when she tried to form a social circle for Percy, and the need to spend their money mostly on themselves — "a thing I have not yet been able to do, poor or rich." She got "rhumatic pains" and felt weak. At the turn of 1846, "Thank God I am at last *acclimatié*," she wrote Claire (herself beset by nervous irritability), who was returning to England to stay, but she was "frightfully" nervous, and when they moved in early March, the house hung "like a mill stone round my spirits."

On March 12 she had some kind of an attack. One of her new neighbors was Dr. Gideon Mantell, with whom she had corresponded about a Shelley letter in 1839; he was a physician, since retired with a painful spinal tumor, and a geologist whose publications fascinated her. That day he and Dr. John Ayrton Paris, president of the Royal College of Physicians, were called in to Mary Shelley: "Found her very ill from neuralgia of the heart."[14]

Whether she had chest pains, they disappeared; probably Mantell was consulted on suspicion of spinal disease, for her attacks began with acute pain in her back; as it subsided, the spinal nerves felt "all alive," and when she walked or made any exertion, "as if the spine would altogether give up the ghost." Extreme nervousness accompanied this illness, which she would suffer, with remissions, along with the "nervous rhumatism," for most of her remaining years. She had not complained of trouble with her head since September 1845, and would not again until October 1848. Shortly thereafter, she manifested indubitable signs of the brain tumor that killed her in early 1851, but her new symptoms fluctuated too, while some of the old continued; the brain tumor would not be diagnosed until near the end.

Besides nervous rheumatism, the doctors diagnosed "neuralgia," then a generic name for a number of "obstinate," fluctuating disorders thought to be caused by irritation of the nerves in a particular part of the body, in her case false (or blind) neuralgia resulting from compression of the spinal nerves by some "body." The usual treatment was narcotics and doses of iron, and as her physicians made little of her illness, they may have believed there was not much to be done for women who had bad nerves to start with.

She evidently did have sciatica or perhaps a disk problem. But from her past history and the evidence up until autumn of 1848, it appears that her major illness was the one suffered by many upper-class Victorian women (and by men as well), later termed conversion hysteria by Charcot and his pupil Freud, today known as somaticization disorder.[15] Thus, a few months before Elizabeth Barrett arose from the sofa on which she had spent twenty-five years with a weak back and under her father's domination, married Robert Browning and went to Italy, Mary Shelley became more or less an invalid. It was as if she broke the back of her protest; or, like a Prometheus, drove the vulture away by agreeing to make her bed on the rock. She would be a courageous, resilient patient, who herself believed, too long, unfortunately, that much of her trouble was emotionally induced.

She and Percy spent five weeks at Cowes, then a week in Berkshire with Lady Shelley, who was fatally ill, and Percy's aunts. In May she was "well in all respects" save for an uncomfortable and weak spine. Then out of the blue she heard from Tom Medwin that he had written a *Life of Shelley* for which he would get two hundred and fifty pounds, and which would include the first full account of the Chancery suit, Harriet Shelley's pregnancy by a lover, and her suicide.

A book on Shelley's work she would have welcomed; she had detested Bulwer's recent charge that his poetry was obscurantist, "glittering and fantastic"; Bulwer "thinks to gain popularity by truckling to the times," she told Moxon, adding astutely, "& mistakes the spirit of the times . . ."[16] But because of the "English world" she asked Medwin not to publish Shelley's life, above all no information that would harm the living, namely, Harriet's daughter, Ianthe, but also Claire, who had attained a degree of peace. "I have done all that can be done with propriety at present. I vindicated the memory of my Shelley and spoke of him as he was . . . a celestial spirit given and taken away, for we were none of us worthy of him — and his works are an immortal testament . . ."[17]

Medwin claimed that he would publish in six weeks (the latest of several publishers rejected the book that very day because it lacked her approval), but offered to suppress the *Life* for two hundred and fifty pounds, seemingly the third of her recent extortion experiences. She did not answer and heard no more from him for over a year. By June 25 she was so well that she called at seven in the evening on Mantell, who got out of his sickbed, and kept him up talking until one.

In mid-July Mary Shelley left Claire in charge of Chester Square and went to Baden-Baden with Mrs. Hare, who intended to take the cure. It was probably there that Mary met a Shelley enthusiast, Wilhelm Hamm, who took "hints" from her discussions of Shelley for an 1858 fictional biography of the poet, concentrating on his love for Emilia Viviani (when Mary learns of it she tries suicide, but eventually accepts losing him).

Otherwise, Mary Shelley kept to herself, except for Mrs. Hare, because the spa's English residents subjected her to the same humiliations as in London. After a week she walked upstairs fast and got spinal pain. A few days later she consulted a Dr. Guggert, who confirmed that she had neuralgia and nervous rheumatism, but added that she would suffer until the "things" pressing on her spinal nerves were dissolved. She improved with his prescribed baths and mineral water. Then she took a long walk and went to bed with acute pain and extreme nervousness — an attack that she concluded had also been caused by thinking about Chester Square, "a Million lb. weight round my neck."

"My birthday — helas! not a very gay one," she wrote Claire on August 30, asking her not to alarm Percy. He had a bad back himself, so she was anxious for him to consult Guggert, and, after attending the funeral of Lady Shelley, who died on August 21, he came to Baden. He reported that "G. Byron's" solicitor had given Hookham copies of the Shelley letters that "Byron" intended to publish, and after writing Knox she authorized Hookham to keep the copies, but told him not to go to the police or courts for the originals. Later, "Byron" would sell forgeries of these and other materials by celebrities.

After her return to Chester Square that October, Mary Shelley kept as active as her condition permitted. Sometimes she lay on her sofa upstairs and scrawled a few letters. In that position she wrote Marianna Hammond, who informed her that Laura Galloni had written a novel, *Inez*, being printed at Naples, was working on a second, and wanted Mary's help to get them published in England. Too often, Mary replied, women's minds "are tempered to *enfanter* (alluding to the Socratic mixture theory —) great actions or works . . . Had Laura been the wife of a great man — she had found in action a scope & aim — As it is she writes — I hope & trust . . . that her work will be such as to bear the impress of her intellect —

"Most people are ill or bad," she added, "from sheer ennui."[18] She had Laura send *Inez* via General Pépé's brother and subsequently began translating it. Laura Galloni would become a popular writer under the name Sara.

At other times, Mary enjoyed a few luxuries; she and Percy were richer by the five hundred pounds a year they had paid for Lady Shelley's jointure, although their properties needed twice that sum for repairs. She took rides in a newly bought carriage, accepted invitations from Lady Morgan and Mrs. Milner-Gibson, gave a breakfast for the famous visiting German novelist Countess Ida Hahn-Hahn, and had friends for quiet dinners, wearing beautifully made long, soft, gray gowns. A new acquaintance noted the curious color change in her eyes when she was keenly interested. She inspected Mantell's fossil collection, and read his latest work on microbes, as well as her usual range of literature. When she was in pain, Moxon provided her with light reading, sea tales such as Dana's *Two Years Before the Mast*, and current novels.

She felt isolated, often dull, but not forgotten. The January *Westminster Review* published an article by George Lewes in which he stated that "if original conception could make a poet, [E.T.A.] Hoffmann and Mrs.

Shelley would have precedence over Homer, Milton, or Shakespeare."[19] Walter Savage Landor, Abraham Hayward, and other authors sent her their new publications. At Milnes's request she sent him a Shelley holograph for his friend the German diplomat-historian K. A. Varnhagen von Ense, with a covering note, both of which Milnes forwarded to his friend. That winter she wrote to the Royal Literary Fund for Isabel Booth, whose husband had died, and she later gave and solicited money for a hospital for the poor. When the Whigs, "a shabby cold-blooded set," finally awarded Hunt a pension, she told him it should have been larger — but stopped paying his debts.

She followed politics and foreign affairs, and again hoped that Percy would be elected from Horsham after the coming dissolution of Parliament. He spent a good deal of time and money in that notoriously corrupt district, before taking his fellow radical Aubrey Beauclerk's advice against risking over two thousand pounds on a campaign he would probably lose. Instead, he bought his first cruising yacht.

In early 1847 Mary apparently changed to a physician who agreed with Guggert that relieving pressures on her spinal nerves would cure her: this Dr. Smith probably was Thomas Southwood Smith, a physiologist and renowned initiator of public health programs for the poor.[20] In mid-March Smith performed operations that left her "locally weak," but calm, cheerful, confident, and improving, but by late May she could just "crawl" about, sitting up was intolerably painful and she had a small growth besides. Smith prescribed Brighton for the summer, so Percy left for a seven-week cruise in the Baltic on his yacht. She hid her fear, gave him her mother's *Letters from Sweden*, and took heart from Peacock, who wrote her reassuringly and quoted Southey's lines eulogizing Wollstonecraft, a poem Mary had not known.

From mid-June through August Mary stayed at Brighton with Gee Paul, herself ill from an undiagnosed obstruction (which killed her that winter, a sad loss). She bathed in the sea, had Isabel Booth visit, and used a wheelchair to get about. She had never liked Brighton, and was bored. She had another attack in July when she learned that Medwin's *Life of Shelley* would soon be published. She asked Hunt to request friendly newspapers not to publicize the book; Hunt's journalist son Thornton offered to ask Medwin's publisher to suppress it, but she agreed with Hunt that that would only arouse attention. Besides, she herself doubted that the book was as bad as Medwin had threatened.

The return drive to Chester Square on August 31 left her back in "vile" pain, but Dr. Smith attributed it to reactivated neuralgia. Her growth had disappeared. He prescribed quinine and quiet. She and Percy drove to Monmouthshire in an open carriage Mary had been wanting — Lady Shelley's, ironically enough, which Mary bought when they visited the Shelley ladies en route. She especially loved the idyllic Vale of Usk. Freedom from Chester Square soothed her, but she did not feel up to contacting the Trelawnys, who lived at Usk.

By the time she got back to Chester Square, Medwin's *Life of Shelley* had been published. It contained both considerable new fact and error about Shelley, revelations about Claire, mean remarks about Mary's youthful looks and radicalism, and corrections of her "misinformation." He made notes treating her more roughly for a second edition he never published.[21]

In December, Mary Shelley was the subject of an essay in *Tait's Edinburgh Magazine* by George Gilfillan, a friend of Carlyle and De Quincey, which was reprinted in two other journals. In the last fifty years, Gilfillan wrote, there had been only one British literary school, that of a common master, Godwin, "a common philosophical as well as poetical belief, common training, that of warfare with society," comprised of Godwin, Wollstonecraft, Charles Brockden Brown, Shelley, and Mary Shelley. After *Frankenstein*, Gilfillan suggested, association with and idolatry of Shelley had narrowed Mary Shelley's genius. "She has much, however, of his imaginative and of his speculative qualities — her tendency, like his, is to the romantic, the ethereal, and the terrible . . . her protest against society is his, copied out in a fine female hand. . . ."[22]

Gilfillan concluded by reminding Mary Shelley that only she could write the fully knowledgeable biography of Shelley that the public still anticipated from her. That long-felt obligation, intensified by Medwin's publication, finally made Mary Shelley resolve to write her biography of Shelley; she began to gather her papers.[23] (It may have been now that she burned some of her own correspondence, Aubrey Beauclerk's letters, Godwin's crueler communications, and all of her own to her father; only one note has survived.) When Trelawny visited London that winter, she probably sought material from him.

The French revolution of 1848 broke out in February. By mid-March, Mary Shelley vehemently opposed it, as the issue of that violent class struggle had gone beyond the establishment of a political republic to a socialist state, based on "wicked and desolating principles" of equality that were being enacted by dictatorial measures. Christian Socialism, which organized in response to 1848, would have been closer to her ideas; equality achieved by liberty and fraternal spirit, and in raising "the low to the high" to the furtherance of peace and high civilization. George Sand, she told Claire that July, must lose by supporting the revolution — "all *Artistes* must."[24] By then, however, Sand herself had drawn back.

Similarly, Mary supported the concurrent German and Austrian liberal revolutions but not the socialist uprising (Claire asked her to cool the fervor of Charles Clairmont's son), and she was appalled by the German peasant revolts. "Barbarism — Countless uncivilized men, long concealed under the varnish of our social system, are breaking out with the force of a volcano & threatening order — law & peace," she wrote Alexander Berry.[25] Apparently preparing to dominate Europe again, the French were propagandizing, "even exciting" the hitherto peacefully petitioning English Chartists, and rousing the Irish: "One half of Ireland detests the other half," she added. Meanwhile, England's leaders "perpetually make the grossest mistakes." After a moderate French Assembly was elected, the radicals were brutally crushed, but she was struck by a prediction Bulwer had made in 1841 that the effects of Napoleonism — to which she now presciently added "revolutionism" — had only begun.

Italy was entirely another matter. When liberals won constitutions in three major states and war against Austria began, she sent Nerina Cini bandages for the wounded and asked for details of the struggle. Her faith in Gatteschi was redeemed; he rushed back to Italy, was appointed to the Tuscan National Council and thereafter elected Deputy for Arezzo. Austria eventually prevailed, but Mary must have known that its years in Italy were numbered.

March 1848 found Mary Shelley well and happy. The Horsham radical party had slated Percy to run for Parliament, and if the Whig candidate won he could be unseated for corruption.[26] But, ironically, Mary herself flouted this ambition for him because of another. She had a houseguest, Mrs. Jane Gibson St. John, a young widow whom she and Percy had met the previous year at the behest of mutual friends (probably including Knox's friend Robert Leslie Ellis, then coediting Bacon's works with James Spedding, a relative of Jane St. John's), one of whom had told Mrs. St. John she would be a perfect wife for Percy, and probably said the same to Percy.

Jane St. John, Mary Shelley now told a friend, "is a prize indeed . . . the best & sweetest thing in the world."[27] Socially speaking, she was a misprize, being illegitimate, one of her attractions to Mary Shelley. Her banker father, Thomas Gibson of Newcastle on Tyne, had never married the mother of their nine children.[28] Jane was twelve when he died in 1832, and was sent with a favorite brother to live with the John Spedding family near Bassinghurst in the Lake District; Mrs. Spedding was their paternal aunt.

In 1841 Jane married an ailing aristocrat (a distant cousin of Aubrey Beauclerk), Charles St. John, the youngest of three legitimate sons of Lord Bolingbroke, among a bevy of illegitimates, and though Jane told Mary that St. John had none of the family defects, he himself had an illegitimate son. The couple lived in the country. She nursed him until his death in 1844 left her a widow at twenty-four, just as Mary Shelley had been. Since then she had lived quietly in Dorsetshire. When she visited a relative in London following a tour abroad in 1847, she was too in awe of Mary Shelley to approach her, but Mary called to introduce herself. Jane, who had hagiographical inclinations, was instantaneously bewitched.

> I said to myself, "Who are you — you lovely being?" . . . rising gently, she came towards me and said very softly, "I am Mary Shelley" . . . She was tall and slim [sic], and had the most beautiful deep-set eyes I have ever seen.[29]

Neither a beauty nor an intellectual, Jane was short and plump with a Greek nose and strong jaw, but "She looks all she is, all goodness and truth," Mary wrote Augusta Trelawny, with some failure in acumen. Nicknamed "Wren," Jane was softly affectionate with people she loved and possessed extraordinary vitality, initiative, and pluck, but more determination than scruples. Mother and son would gain a wren of iron, prone to nervous attacks, but indomitable. Mary had worried that Percy might marry a young girl whom he was not cut out to guide or educate, whereas Jane was just a year younger than he, and already shared his tastes. Many people had advised Percy to marry an heiress, and Rosa Beauclerk had exaggerated the size of Jane's fortune, but Percy and Jane were made for each other. On March 24 they became engaged.

That Jane loved simple domesticity and had no worldly ambition may have been a relief to Percy, who withdrew his candidacy (another radical would be seated). He decided to settle at Field Place, the lease of which had to be bought back, oversee the farm, improve the estate, and help his tenants.

The couple were married on June 22 at St. George's, Hanover Square. During their honeymoon month in the Lake District, Mary Shelley stayed in Sandgate: again ill and weak, frightened about money for Field Place, as well as ambivalent about living there. On July 29 she joined the newlyweds at Field Place.

The rather ordinary, comfortable house, sited in a hollow, was full of workmen, but from Shelley's boyhood bedroom, which she chose for her own, she could see groves of great trees and the setting sun. Jane and Percy made flying trips to London to buy furnishings with Mrs. Hare's guidance. Ennui loomed, however. Besides, it was a "vile" rainy autumn, and the low-lying house was "the dampest isle in Xendom," Mary wrote Claire; "the scissors & knives get rusty — the whole place is a swamp."[30]

Apparently Mary planned to write her biography of Shelley in the house in which he was born, but she never began it, because her health took a new turn for the worse,[31] with increasingly bad "nervous attacks" — actually, these were early signs of the brain tumor. But, as poor Percy said after her death, "Her illness puzzled the doctors so long, and presented so many different appearances that they could not make out what was the matter with her."[32]

Because of Field Place's dampness, Mary went to Brighton, where she told Claire she had a new malady, dizziness and "swimming" in the head. Claire recommended calomel for her bowels. "I am Semele to Jove," she replied, "it would soon send me to the other world," but tried it anyway. She was much better in late November but when Percy and Jane visited, she had a violent nervous attack, which she attributed to excitement, and renewed spinal symptoms.

She went to London to be under Dr. Smith's care, staying at Knox's house since Chester Square was empty and for let. Smith prescribed cod-liver oil: "fine weather w^d be the best cure," she wrote Claire, who was at Brighton, "& we have had two days very fine (how the sea must sparkle) . . ."[33] The dizziness diminished, but she had several fits of weakness, often in the head, and pain in her legs, right hand, and one eye. Her condition may have been exacerbated by fear for Jane, who was in London dangerously ill from what was finally diagnosed as a kidney infection.

They all went back to Field Place in late January 1849, but, shortly after, Jane got worse and Percy took her to London for treatments. Mary, who may now have changed physicians, stopped taking all medicines, being convinced that her sick nerves were simulating other diseases. She became better, walked well, took rides on a pony, went up to see Jane. But she could not complete her translation of Laura Galloni's novel, because her head got the old "strange feelings" when she used it, shortly followed by bad headaches and alarming episodes "resembling" paralysis in the right arm and leg that "brought on" tremors. When these attacks stopped, she had pain at the top of her head. Yet she improved in mid-April, when Jane was well enough for Percy to bring her home.

"I never deserved such peace & happiness as I enjoy with them," Mary would write Augusta Trelawny. Jane's doctor said it was essential for her to spend the next winter in a warm climate, and Mary was determined to go with her children, whose perfectly felicitous union embraced her. "No mother and son were ever bound together by such ties of love . . . ," declared Jane; "she had been to me more than a mother, sister, friend . . ."[34]

Jane idolized Mary, whom she described as tender, gentle, lovely, noble, suffering in silence and totally selfless, and admired her "wondrous intellect" and eloquence. Mary talked to her about her childhood; already a Wollstonecraft admirer, Jane duly respected Godwin and loathed Mrs. Godwin. Although Mary never discussed Harriet Shelley with Percy or Jane, Jane witnessed Mary's refusal to purchase forged Shelley letters, her care of his papers, her assessment of people who asked to see his holographs. If Jane hyperbolized in old age that Mary referred "to what he might think, or do, or approve of, almost as if he had been in the next room,"[35] Mary certainly instilled adoration of Shelley in Percy's more energetic co-heir to the poet's reputation and, as it turned out, to Mary's, Godwin's, and Wollstonecraft's.

None of them cared to partake of local society, but Mary kept up with the neighboring Beauclerks; Aubrey had become melancholic and reclusive. Guests at Field Place consisted of Knox and Jane Hogg (Mary gave her goddaughter, Prudentia Hogg, Xenophon's *Cyropaedia*); Peacock and his daughter Mary Ellen (who married George Meredith in 1849); members of Horace Smith's family; Percy's friends, including John Touchet, a lawyer with literary interests; and Jane's relatives and her first husband's illegitimate son, whose guardian she was. Mary transacted some business and paid taxes on the estate. They gave a great deal to the poor, and Mary obtained a grant from the Royal Literary Fund for Edward Holmes, her old friend of the Novello circle.

In May, Claire came for her first long stay. Driven a little crazy by Mary's good fortune, her loving children, her imagined elegant county society, Claire had been intolerably disagreeable, saying that no one must think she was paying court to her rich relatives. Jane so disliked her that she meant to absent herself, until Mary, hitherto discreet about Claire, asked not to be left alone with her, "the bane of my existence" since early childhood. Claire brought along her niece Clairy, Charles's daughter, and made constant trouble. One day when Mary was ill in her room, Clairy, sobbing and terrified, begged Jane to save her from Claire, who was cursing her because she would not misinform her parents that she was married so that Claire could be rid of her. Setting her considerable jaw, Jane locked Mary in her room lest she get worse by intervening, and ordered Claire to bed.

Soon after, Claire was infuriated when Clairy and Mary's favorite Knox got engaged. She accused Mary ("Mephistopheles") of making the match (actually, Mary wondered if the girl loved Knox), and broke permanently with her. Percy was through with Claire, while fiercer Jane took pains to make it clear that Claire was not Mary Shelley's blood relation.

Jane was well that summer and Mary in better health than in years. But when rain began in September, Jane's infection flared up, driving the Shelleys to Paris. Mary closed up the house, saw Peacock in London, and followed with her maid, Mary Ann. They proceeded to Nice, where Jane's condition continued alarming. Mary had sporadic convulsions and re-newed rheumatism, so that she was unable to walk, though she took donkey rides along the shore and into the hills. Jane had enlightened Percy about Mary's fear of his sailing, so he never sailed again until after his mother's death.

That winter of 1849–1850 a homeopathic doctor treated Jane, who improved "as by magic," said skeptical Mary. But having nothing to lose, she started a regime he prescribed for her, which included sipping wine. Nice, she remarked, was as far south as her beloved Tuscany, and suddenly remembered that years before, Trelawny had picked up for her in Florence her 1819 portrait by Amelia Curran. She wrote him for it, more than once, but he would not give it back.

At Percy and Jane's desire, they went to Lake Como in May on the way home, but it poured, so they left as soon as the Alps were passable. On June 17 they reached England.

Once Mary Shelley got over the journey, she had no more convulsions and few rheumatic attacks. "We live very quietly and happily," she wrote Augusta Trelawny in August, wishing only that Jane would get pregnant and that destiny had located Field Place in the Vale of Usk. Jane's London homeopathic doctor had dismissed her as cured, and she frisked about "as plump as a partridge and as gay as a lark." Mary felt so well that she wondered if she had benefited not just from absence of fear about Jane but from homeopathy. "Such is the force of prejudice (or reason)," she told Augusta, "that I cannot bring myself to beleive in homæopathy . . . but I half think that I ought to ascribe the *very* much better that I am than last year, to homæopathic medicine . . ."[36]

Field Place had its pleasures, a flower garden, a dovecote, Percy's dogs sporting about, a "stumping clattering" ghost that one guest saw on the stairs. Religious posters were put up in the vicinity by a "brother," she reported to Touchet, expressing the hope "there might be some limitation to the torments of the wicked, & to express this hope, the placards bear on them H— fire for ever!" And of a female sectarian, "She is of the sect which delights rather in little fish & triangles — of one sect you must be; & both equally enjoy the advantage of the prospects held out in the . . . placard for those who differ from you."[37]

But Jane's illness returned with September's rains. Percy arranged to buy a new home near Bournemouth, Boscombe Manor; meanwhile, they all moved back to Chester Square.

By November the headaches that had plagued Mary in 1849 must have returned and become persistent, severe when she lay down, and she may have had some weakness on the right side of her body. On the fifteenth she wrote the Royal Literary Fund for another grant for Isabel Booth, starting off with careful script and ending four pages later in a scrawl. Jane and Percy, true believers, called in homeopathic physicians, who were more mystified than alarmed, not that anything could have been done by then.

Starting with a numb right leg and minor speech impairment, paralysis began to set in. On December 17 Dr. Richard Bright, discoverer of Bright's disease, and an eminent brain specialist, was consulted. He diagnosed brain tumor.

Jane did not want Percy to know, so Bright told him his mother might get no worse, that he had ordered her not to read or write. Isabel Booth wanted to come to her, but Percy told her not to make an unnecessary journey. Mary Shelley, however, knew she was dying. She was profoundly serene about Percy's future and she had never feared death. Hers was in the stoic tradition. She conspired with Jane to keep Percy hopeful, and told her she wished to be buried at St. Pancras next to her father and mother. Though Trelawny had offered her his plot adjacent to Shelley's, transporting her body to Rome, she said, would be too costly and troublesome. She spoke of William, whose portrait hung on her bedroom wall, the child whose death thirty-three years ago had seemed her ultimate tragedy. When Percy knew the truth, she asked him to give Isabel Booth fifty pounds a year and a mourning suit.

Now almost completely paralyzed, her speech going, in agony, she lay propped up until January 23, 1851, when she had a succession of terrible convulsions, then fell unconscious, giving no sign of life except for breathing. On February 1, Percy, Jane, and Mary Ann stood by as her breathing stopped. Isabel Booth, with whom she had first experimented with premonitions when they were girls in Scotland, had a presentiment that day that she was dead.

"And now she has left us most mournful and wretched," Percy wrote Isabel in simple truth. He was so unstrung that his mother's oldest friend and Hunt were among the few he could notify, and the death was registered by Mary Ann Henry. "Mary Wollstonecraft Shelley, Female, 53 Years,

Widow of Percy Bysshe Shelley Esq.," reads the certificate, "Cause of death Disease of the brain Supposed Tumour in left hemisphere of long standing certified." Some said she died of "a *Cancer* of the Brain," as Hookham told John Mitford, who recalled the time Samuel Rogers teased her about Byron at one of his breakfasts.[38] "Lately died Mrs. Shelley, a woman of genius, leaving a son born after her marriage with the unfortunate poet . . . ," noted Crabb Robinson, mindful to the end of her early liaison.[39]

People rarely do justice to those who do not do justice to themselves. So exalted above herself had Mary Shelley helped to make Shelley that her most extensive obituary, in *The Athenaeum*, after delicately noting their liaison by quoting his Dedication of *The Revolt of Islam*, went on to say that he had "winged and nerved" her youthful genius to produce *Frankenstein*, though adding that her subsequent works were unfairly neglected. "It is not . . . as the authoress even of *Frankenstein* . . . that she derives her most enduring and endearing title to our affection," stated the *Literary Gazette*, "but as the faithful and devoted wife of Percy Bysshe Shelley." "See'st thou a skylark," George Meredith began a poem recalling Shelley's ode. For George Lewes and Thornton Hunt's relatively radical *Leader*, her death first recalled Wollstonecraft and Godwin, then her illustrious "most christian hearted" husband, and last, the author of *Frankenstein*, "one of those books that become the parent of whole generations of romances," *The Last Man, Lodore,* "etc."

One who mourned the dead with action, Jane determined to bury Mary Shelley with her parents in the graveyard of St. Peter's in Bournemouth, rather than St. Pancras: "it would have broken my heart to let her loveliness wither in such a dreadful place," she declared, as the once pastoral grave-yard was choked in one of the ugliest parts of London. Percy and Jane took Mary Shelley's coffin and the exhumed bodies of Godwin and Woll-stonecraft to Bournemouth for burial, leaving the second Mrs. Godwin ignobly behind. In the 1870s W. P. Frith made a sketch of Wollstonecraft's original tombstone at which young Mary and Shelley had declared their love, for a painting of that event.[40] Subsequently the graveyard was dug up for St. Pancras station, but the tombstone remains.

Percy could not bear to be in the house where his mother died or to let anyone touch her things.* He and Jane moved to Boscombe Manor and sold Chester Square. Not until the first anniversary of Mary Shelley's death did they open the box-desk she had always kept near her bed and

---

* Mary Shelley left Percy and Jane a lock of Mary Wollstonecraft's hair in a packet on which she wrote: *"My mother's Hair / for Percy & Jane to respect"*; they cut tresses of Mary's hair, labeling the packet "Our beloved Madre's hair Feby 1st 1851," and sent locks of it to Isabel Booth and John Touchet. (Bodleian Shelley Relics 32, items i, iv.)

found relics she had not shown even them: her copy of Shelley's *Adonais* with one torn-out leaf folded around a piece of silk that held a bit of his ashes and the remnant of his heart, and a box containing a workbook they had shared and locks of hair of her dead William and Clara.

That Mary Wollstonecraft Godwin Shelley asked to be buried with her parents, however, was her final affirmation of identity with what they stood for, and one that had accrued odium in orthodox circles. When the American Moncure Daniel Conway (a Unitarian minister who had been dismissed for abolitionist advocacy, edited *The Dial*, lectured in England for the North, and stayed as pastor of an ultra-liberal congregation) made pilgrimage to the grave in 1868, he was informed by the statesman-author Sir Henry Taylor, Percy and Jane's neighbor, that the rector of St. Peter's had refused to bury the heretical trio. "But Lady Shelley was determined," reported Conway, "and one day actually came . . . in her carriage, following a hearse which bore the bodies":

> She sat in her carriage before the locked iron gates, and expressed her resolution to sit there until the bodies were admitted for burial. The rector, dreading perhaps the scandal, . . . yielded; the gravedigger did his work with haste; and by night, without any ceremonial, the bodies were let down into their grave.[41]

That night, without religious service, Mary Shelley was laid between her parents in a common grave on the high, sloping burial ground. The rector protested again when Percy and Jane planned to place a flat marble tomb slab with inscriptions to Godwin, "Author of 'Political Justice'," and to Mary Wollstonecraft, "Author of 'Vindication of the Rights of Women.' " Lady Shelley asked if he had read Wollstonecraft's book, Conway continues, "and he having confessed he had not, she said he had better read it and state his objections afterward. So she sent him the volume. . . . He then said he could not find fault with it, and so the inscription went on," as did Godwin's.

"Mary Wollstonecraft Shelley, Daughter of Willm & Mary Wollstonecraft Godwin, and Widow of the late Percy Bysshe Shelley" reads the third inscription — without "Author of Frankenstein." Her masterpiece was then, and has remained, more of a challenge to orthodoxy than those of her parents. Little more than a decade ago, when the Greater London County Council agreed to put up an official plaque to Mary Shelley at Chester Square, now the parsonage of St. Michael's Church, church authorities would not allow "Author of Frankenstein" to appear on it. The council refused to place it without the citation. The impasse was broken by a member of the Keats-Shelley Memorial Association, Mrs. Beatrice

Hanss, who had a white marble plaque made to Mary Shelley, "Author" and "Wife of the Poet." Mrs. Hanss's teenage grandson nailed up the plaque, which was unveiled on June 21, 1977, in the presence of a committee of the Memorial Association, friends, and the Dean of Westminster.

In the intervening century and a quarter, however, Mary Shelley's reputation had undergone a distorting sea change, for the contest over her burial was clean-cut compared with that which began a few years after over her memory and has not been resolved to this day.

22 Romance and Reality

ONE OF MARY SHELLEY'S valid prophecies turned out to be the predilection of her alter ego in *The Last Man*, Lionel Verney, for historical figures who had "been traduced, or about whom clung obscurity and doubt." For she is a striking example of a posthumous reputation bent out of shape by admirers and, more lastingly, by traducers.

This situation derives from Mary Shelley's association with Shelley, and is loaded with instructive ironies. Whether, as Keats said, writers lead allegorical lives, the issue in the Shelleys' case has been the nature of the allegory. Mary Shelley's daughter-in-law, Lady Shelley, has borne the brunt for liberal Victorian sentimentalization of Shelley, and she could likewise be charged about Mary Shelley. But this obscures the fact that both ideal-izers and defamers of controversial figures select qualities relevant to larger arguments of their own times. For nineteenth-century conservatives the Shelleys exemplified immoral, subversive views enacted in a liaison that drove his first wife to suicide. Shelley engendered his own legend in reaction to such opprobrium; Mary Shelley, Hunt, the Cambridge Apos-tles, and innumerable others developed aspects of it to counter his critics, and after her death in 1851 liberal Victorians incorporated her in the leg-end — before her adoring children, themselves liberals, spearheaded the cause. Sentimentality, moreover, can be an expression of genuine feelings and longing for the ideal that made strong men weep over Rousseau's and Richardson's novels in the eighteenth century, Dickens's in the nineteenth, and that manifests itself today in tragic situations, fictional and real.

As Victorian liberals apologized for or overlooked Shelley's radicalism, so they excused Mary Shelley's liaison with him and her early radicalism, romanticized their union, took for granted her punishment by society, and ignored the social and political content of her works. Indeed, pro-gressives also romanticized the pair. A few weeks after Mary Shelley's death, George Lewes's and Thornton Hunt's *Leader* published "Lines on the Death of Mrs. Shelley" by "E.W.L.," eulogizing her as a genius among blessed immortals; Shelley's beloved, inspiration, and inconsolable mourner:

> Another, yet another, snatch'd away,
> By death's grasp, from among us! Yet one more
> Of Heaven's anointed band, — a child of genius, —
> A peeress, girt about with magic powers, —
> That could at will evoke from her wild thought
> Spirits unearthly, monster-shaped . . .
>
> Mourn her not, Earth! her spirit, disenthrall'd,
> No more shall droop in lonely widowhood . . .
>
> Mourn her not, Earth! she is at rest with him,
> The mighty minstrel of the impassion'd lay, —
> The Poet-martyr of a creed too bright,
> Whose lofty hymnings were so oft attuned
> Unto the music of her own pure name,
> The theme and inspiration of his lyre . . .

This was Sir Percy and Lady Shelley's favorite eulogy. The couple could have lived a peaceful uncomplicated existence in "Moon-country," as neighbors called the coastscape near Bournemouth. Their spacious Boscombe Manor was sited in woods that thinned near the heathered cliff tops into dwarfed wind-slanted thickets, with hillocks of sand dunes descending to the sea. Jane became a yachtswoman, sailing with Percy off Bournemouth, and in 1853 took her first cruise with him to the Mediterranean, which he described in a newspaper article. They made a number of such voyages until she hurt her neck in a boating accident. Between 1854, when Percy was elected to England's premier sailing club, the Royal Yacht Squadron, and 1887, he owned a total of ten cruising yachts and boats for cup-racing, two of which, *Ginevra* and *Queen Mab*, he named for his father's poems.[1] Jane encouraged his dilettante talents in a perfect vocation; he built a beautiful little theater at Boscombe, painted the curtain with a scene of Casa Magni, and put on plays, sometimes writing book and music, in which he and Jane acted. In time, their stage productions grew so professional that they gave benefits for charities at their Chelsea house on the Embankment — and were legally enjoined to cease. Being unable to have children, they adopted Jane's niece Bessie Florence Gibson.

An endearing eccentric in conventional surroundings, Percy had the shrewdness of an innocent child, a quaint wit, and "a curious strain of a somewhat furtive, illusive, inarticulate fantasy, almost as far removed from the everyday world as was his father's soaring poetic imagination."[2] At one point he retired to Chelsea in some disgrace, having painted the ribs of several greyhounds white and let them run around the area looking like skeletons. He was also prone to melancholia (his half sister, Ianthe Esdaile, ended a melancholic recluse), "vigorously met" by Jane.[3]

Their mission, however, for which Jane rightly said they suffered much, was the Shelleys. Jane had a romantic temperament of the Trelawny type; she was a fierce lover and hater who heightened and masked reality, though she did not make things up as Trelawny did. But Percy felt just as strongly about his parents, and if he let his wife take the lead and had a drier tone, they were partners. Add to this the couple's unworldliness, and the fact that the more, sometimes unscrupulous, opposition their tactics evoked, the more fanatic Jane grew.

The ugly incident at St. Peter's over burying Mary Shelley started them off in a beatifying reaction. They commissioned Henry Weekes for a large memorial sculpture à la Michelangelo's *Pieta:* Mary on one knee clasping Shelley's drowned body. St. Peter's refused to install the work; they placed it at nearby Christchurch Priory. Jane made her boudoir into a museum displaying relics, manuscripts, and portraits, an entirely appropriate undertaking if she had not called it "the sanctum" and expected admittees to be church-reverent. Jane Hogg thought this ludicrous, yet she herself stood up and bowed whenever Shelley's name was spoken.

Percy and Jane made a survey of Mary Shelley's great cache of manuscripts, her own, her parents', and Shelley's, a trove in private hands perhaps unequaled in the world. Their priorities approximated hers: first, a life of Shelley, which would serve as well as a partial biography of her until they authorized a complete life; then a biography of Godwin incorporating and modeled upon her unfinished memoir of her father, in which she had also begun to rehabilitate her mother; and additional restitution of Wollstonecraft in some form.

Near the sixth anniversary of Mary Shelley's death, in early 1857, they invited Hogg, Peacock, and Trelawny to a reunion, in order to choose the Shelley biographer who would present the poet according to their own lights. Trelawny declined to attend (and began his own book); Peacock was too cool, and besides mentioned that Mary had sometimes annoyed him in the early days of their association. Hogg was entrusted with the task, assuring Percy that he would give Mary, whose life and Shelley's had been "blended," due importance. His first two volumes, ending before Shelley's separation from Harriet, came out in 1858, a vivid but facetious, self-servingly manipulated work that so offended Percy and Jane they refused Hogg access to their papers for the sequel. Peacock agreed with that prohibition for reasons of his own: Hogg intended to hint that Peacock had been Harriet's lover — and had already so misinformed Boscombe Manor.

That same year, Trelawny published his *Recollections of the Last Days of Byron and Shelley*, in which Mary Shelley is a highly gifted personage, attractive woman, and a deeply loving if individual mate to an eccentric genius.* Percy and Jane were quite pleased. It would be a quarter of a century before they were to authorize another biographer, however. Instead, they decided to publish *Shelley Memorials*, a biography of both Shelleys, with selected papers. Jane was editor-in-chief; as her aide they engaged twenty-four-year-old Richard Garnett, who had been working with Anthony Panizzi, Librarian of the British Museum, for eight years. A precocious scholar, Garnett had much to learn about public relations. Leigh Hunt and John Touchet also helped with *Shelley Memorials*, which was published in 1859.

There is a natural antagonism between family and other parties whose job or pleasure it is to ferret out problematic information, or who must defend themselves. *Shelley Memorials* combined illumination, defense, manipulation of truth, and hagiography, and set off a long train of consequences. It was not too far off the mark to state, for example, that while Shelley never deviated from championing "the poorer classes," Mary's sympathy, encouragement, and entire "self-devotion" divested him of hostile bitterness in his attacks on social and political abuses. ("The editor, Lady Shelley, is quite a liberal," observed Crabb Robinson.)[4] But the work minimized the Shelleys' marital problems, and Christianized his religious views. As for Mary Shelley's career after his death, *Shelley Memorials* skimmed over it, leaving out its heterodox aspects, while noting her "noble energy of character" in struggles with poverty and loneliness, and her major works, with expurgated correspondence and extracts from her journals.

In the vital matter of Shelley's treatment of Harriet Shelley, *Shelley Memorials*, like Hogg's life of Shelley, defended the poet by implying that she had been unfaithful to him. Boscombe Manor had Shelley's letters so stating, plus Hogg's "information" about Peacock and Harriet, but published no specifics — as Mary and Shelley had not — to protect Harriet's daughter, Ianthe Esdaile. *Shelley Memorials* also duplicitously reinforced Hunt's "fiction," which Mary had deplored, that she and Shelley began their liaison only after the separation.

---

* Though Trelawny had been responsible for the unseaworthy design of Shelley's *Don Juan*, in this work he blamed it entirely on Edward Williams, even declaring that he himself had objected to it.

Infuriated, and threatened, the aged Peacock published his corrective "Memoirs of Shelley" in *Fraser's Magazine* between 1858 and 1860, in which he introduced a fiction of his own: that Shelley had been happy with Harriet until he met Mary, and that Harriet had been a faithful wife. He went so far as to include Eliza Westbrook's deposition for the Chancery court suit of 1817, stating that Mary had "cohabited" with Shelley before the separation, and Shelley's letter telling Eliza that she could excusably consider Mary the cause of Harriet's ruin.

Now Jane felt engaged in holy war, and was probably worried as well about her susceptible husband's distress. A believer in spiritualism, she "received" messages from Mary Shelley in automatic writing: "Don't mind Mr Peacock — he wont live another year you will get more letters more papers by waiting dear Janey. . . . Dear Love Never pray me to come to you but I charitably wait for our meeting . . ."[5]

Meantime, in *Fifty Years' Recollections* Cyrus Redding had praised Mary Shelley's truthfulness and assistance for the biographical sketch of Shelley he wrote for his 1829 edition of Shelley's poems. Another of her old friends, Eliza Rennie, published *Traits of Character* with a chapter on Mary Shelley in widowhood, in the liberal Victorian mold; emphasizing her character and integrity, her sadness and shrinking from notice, her "correct" behavior, her supposed belief that publishing was "unfeminine," and giving no glimpse of her complexity, depth, or ambition.

In 1863 the radical Thornton Hunt gave a truer and yet partly unfortunate picture of Mary Shelley in an important article on Shelley in the *Atlantic Monthly*. "She was, indeed, herself a woman of extraordinary power, of heart as well as head," he wrote, with her mother's magnanimity, "a masculine capacity for study" all her life, command of history, imaginative power and daring originality in her fiction. Moreover, "While the biographers of Shelley are chargeable with suppression, the most straightforward and frank of all of them is Mary . . . while she has nobly abstained from telling those things that other persons should have supplied . . ."[6] Informed by his parents, aided by Lady Shelley, who was avid to get back at Peacock despite Ianthe Esdaile's feelings, and making deductions from Mary Shelley's fiction, Thornton gave the most accurate story of Shelley and Harriet yet published.

He affirmed both Mary Shelley's community of spirit with Shelley and her "stubborn" independent outlook. But he reported what he had absorbed from his father, Leigh Hunt (Thornton had been about seven when he knew the Shelleys as a couple); that in youth she was physically unattractive, a bit of a sloven, given to "peevishness" (Leigh Hunt had referred to her "irritability" in his condolence letter to Sir Percy), and not fully appreciative of Shelley until after his death, though he added that Shelley had not fully appreciated her either.

Furthermore, he suggested that her education had been spotty, making her subsequent achievement overly dependent on Shelley and adding a new dimension of credence to her own self-denigration in that regard. Here Thornton was misled by Lady Shelley, who out of hatred for the Clairmonts claimed to one and all that young Mary had been a Cinderella, relegated to household drudgery while Claire enjoyed all the advantages. Thus, Thornton wrote, Shelley was Mary's "great school." And thus, noting that *Frankenstein*'s "leading idea has been ascribed to her husband," Thornton said only, "but, I am sure, unduly." In 1876, the "fact" that Godwin had neglected her education was established in *William Godwin* by C. Kegan Paul, the Godwin biographer chosen by Boscombe Manor — and authorized to republish Mary Wollstonecraft's letters to her lover Gilbert Imlay.*

Two years later Trelawny transmogrified these misinterpretations and introduced worse in a brutal character assassination. William Michael Rossetti had begun interviewing him for a memoir of Shelley in 1869. The current generation considered Trelawny *the* authority, since by now Hunt, Peacock, and Hogg were dead, and no one had any idea that Trelawny had not been as close to Shelley as he claimed, nor a consistent friend of Mary Shelley's. Then a reclusive, ignored old bear, Trelawny was simmering with animus against her that had been reignited by the "cant" about both Shelleys (to which he himself admittedly had bowed in his *Recollections*) and by his loathing of Jane Shelley, a "nasty devil," he told Rossetti, and Percy, a "beer-swilling lout." Pumped for information, he gave it slashingly, and decided to write another book himself.

He knew little about the Shelleys prior to Pisa, so he got that information from Claire Clairmont, who had converted to Catholicism and was living with her niece Pauline in Florence.† Shortly after Mary Shelley's death Claire had considered writing her own memoirs, and more recently thought of writing about Shelley in order to deplore his sexual theories, which had wreaked such havoc in her life. That Mary Shelley was in malign hands is clear from Claire and Trelawny's correspondence and appallingly so in his *Records of Shelley, Byron, and the Author*, published in 1878. He

* Paul was an Anglican cleric who left holy orders to become a publisher, and who had ties to the Christian Socialist movement.
† Ferdinando Luigi Gatteschi called on Claire, Pauline reports, "a most fascinating man — old now & fat . . . & rather deaf — but clever! — amiable and cultivated"; whereupon Claire furiously demanded that Pauline choose between them. (*CC Journals*, p. 220, fn. 56.)

got added ammunition from H. Buxton Forman's recent publication of Mary Shelley's poem "The Choice," in which she accused herself of "cold neglect" of Shelley.

Reared "perfectly orthodox" by Godwin, Trelawny's Mary Shelley never believed in her mother's views and never had sympathy with any of Shelley's, while she conformed to the rules of the world as wife and widow, longing only to be respectable and accepted into society. (After his cremation she indifferently gave Shelley's heart to Leigh Hunt.) Whenever she could she went to church, partly to show that she did not agree with his atheism. Her torso was too long for her legs. She was shrewish, jealous, a bad housewife. Shelley stayed with her, enduring "the utmost malice of fortune," for fear she would commit suicide.

> Mrs. Shelley was of a soft, lymphatic temperament, the exact opposite of Shelley in everything; she was moping and miserable when alone, and yearning for society. Her capacity can be judged by the novels she wrote after Shelley's death, more than ordinarily commonplace and conventional. . . . The memory of how often she had irritated and vexed him tormented her after-existence, and she endeavoured by rhapsodies of panegyric to compensate. . . .[7]

Records has reverberated from that day to this. Though many readers were disgusted by Trelawny's coarseness, his book entered a vastly disproportionate wedge between the Shelleys, shifted the ground so that the woman renowned for heterodoxy, character, and talent came to be thought conventional and more or less deficient, and bombed Boscombe Manor into defensive measures that made correction impossible.

Garnett answered Trelawny's charges (and at more length exposed his inaccuracies about Shelley and Byron) in an article in the *Fortnightly Review*. He asserted that Mary Shelley had eminently understood and sympathized with Shelley, conceded that the poet at times was dissatisfied, and concluded that her initial overwrought self-reproach had been moderated by a "chastened" heart.[8] "The charge of excessive orthodoxy is very new, and calculated to excite inextinguishable hilarity," he stated simply. What was self-evident to him, however, required proof twenty-seven years after Mary Shelley's death. Only a full biography by an independent, forthright author who had access to all of Boscombe Manor's primary source material could definitively have refuted Trelawny and set the record straight.

And now was the time, while the Romantic Mary Shelley still had life. George Eliot's hero in "The Lifted Veil" (1859) possesses her gift of prevision; the heroine of *Daniel Deronda* (1876), Gwendolyn Harleth, is reminiscent of Mary Shelley. Bulwer-Lytton's futurist *The Coming Race* (1871) owes something to *The Last Man*. In 1880 Eliza Lynn Linton published *The Rebel of the Family*, whose auburn-haired, hazel-eyed heroine, Perdita, is a modernized Mary Godwin; "that complex and bewildering Perdita, whom no one understood, and whom so many afflicted": tactless, alternately silent and impassioned, a republican and democrat, who is saved from a man-hating feminist "Illuminati" by love for a plebeian whom she marries against her family's wishes.

Tributes to Mary Shelley's intellect and liberalism were published by Robert Dale Owen in the early 1870s. *Perkin Warbeck* had been republished in 1857, and *Frankenstein* remained in print; in an 1887 dramatization the monster was manufactured by a girl named Mary Ann. Mary Shelley was included in French encyclopedias, in the American Sarah Josepha Hale's *Woman's Record; Or, Sketches of all Distinguished Women, From 'The Beginning' Till A.D. 1850*. A passage from *Valperga* was printed in S. Austin Allibone's *Prose Quotations: From Socrates to Macaulay*, published in Philadelphia in 1876.

Lady Shelley, to whom Sir Percy had given carte blanche with the family papers, took the precise wrong course. "I believe that your hands alone are pure enough to touch her,"⁹ she had told Garnett. When he got out of writing Mary Shelley's life on grounds that he would be discounted as a special pleader, Jane spent five years editing the Shelleys' major correspondence and the journals and privately printing some dozen copies of this censored material, titled *Shelley and Mary*, on which biographers would have to depend. She omitted about a fifth of the journals dating in Mary Shelley's widowhood, all references to "A" (Aubrey Beauclerk), and two passages that she had already printed in *Shelley Memorials*, which she now considered too revealing and cut out of the original notebooks with a penknife. It was probably she who also cut out other such segments, though Mary Shelley herself might have destroyed some.

To give credit where credit is due, nevertheless, Jane preserved the vast majority of the original manuscripts — unlike Cosima Wagner or Albertine de Staël or Hallam Tennyson and others who destroyed quantities of their relatives' private papers — except for giving some holographs to admirers of the Shelleys. Percy purchased additional material as it became available, excepting Claire Clairmont's; they remained on such bad terms that he refused her offer to sell him her papers.

Claire died in 1879 and was buried in a shawl Shelley had given her. (The contest for her papers, which Buxton Forman eventually won, would inspire Henry James's *The Aspern Papers*.) Trelawny died in 1881, having rewarded his wife Augusta for all she had undergone for him by bringing a young mistress into their home, been honored as Shelley's magnificent old rebel friend by Swinburne, and been painted by Millais. He capped his mendacity in the epitaph on his tombstone next to Shelley's: "let not their bones be parted. / For their two hearts in life were single-hearted." Shelley would have been startled, to say the least.

In 1882, on Garnett's recommendation, Lady Shelley chose Edward Dowden to write Shelley's life and Florence T. (Mrs. Julian) Marshall to write Mary Shelley's. By then, although they did not swallow Trelawny whole, these biographers and most of Mary Shelley's admirers were influenced by him. This applied to the American Helen Moore, who published *Mary Shelley*, the first biography, in 1886. Lady Shelley, meanwhile, insisted that Mary Shelley had been a saint, claiming, for instance, that a pencil portrait of Mary that Sir Percy and she had found at Casa Magni had been worshiped as the Virgin by a local peasant. Moore quoted extensively from *Shelley Memorials* and included passages from Thornton Hunt and Trelawny, along with Lady Shelley's statement that Mary Shelley was the most tender, gentle, pure, and noble woman who ever trod this earth, and that no thought of self had ever occurred to her. In Moore's interpretation, Mary Shelley had no life separate from Shelley, and, like de Staël and Wollstonecraft, was the kind of female author who influences her male colleagues but whose works have no lasting importance.

Similarly, in Dowden's *Life of Shelley*, which was also published in 1886, Mary Shelley plays, often behind the scenes, the role of Shelley's steadfast, loving pupil and best friend, herself devoid of genius. From girlhood "naturally more conservative" than Godwin and Wollstonecraft, she exercised wholesome restraint on Shelley. Claire Clairmont was far more vivid. (Ironically, a hostile conservative, John Cordy Jeaffreson, gave a truer picture of Mary's youthful dissidence in *The Real Shelley*.) That same year William Michael Rossetti stated in a memoir of Shelley that Mary Shelley contributed to the development of Shelley's poetic power, but judged her "essentially simple." Hereafter, many people would say that a separate biography was unwarranted.

Mary Shelley's son may not have read her biography by Mrs. Marshall, as Sir Percy died after an extended illness on December 5, 1889, not long after the work appeared. Lady Shelley buried him with his mother and grandparents, with Shelley's heart in a silver urn. A charming eulogy came from Samoa from Robert Louis Stevenson, with whom the couple had been intimate during his residence in Bournemouth, and who loved Percy for his sweet nature and "strange, interesting, simple thoughts; . . . he had the morning dew upon his spirit . . . ," Stevenson wrote, "so a poet's son — to the last."[10] In fact, Percy was much like his mother. Stevenson had already done Mary Shelley poetic justice, however, for at Bournemouth he too had a fertile nightmare that inspired his *Dr. Jekyll and Mr. Hyde*, in the *Frankenstein* genre.

Florence Marshall opened her *Life and Letters of Mary Wollstonecraft Shelley* with a cogent review of her subject's status: "She has been variously misunderstood . . . idealized as one who gave up all for love, and to be condemned . . . for the very same reason . . . extolled for perfections she did not possess, and decried for the absence of those she possessed in the highest degree . . . lauded as a genius, and depreciated as one over-rated. . . . To her husband she has been esteemed alternately a blessing and the reverse."[11] But being restricted to *Shelley and Mary*, dogged by Lady Shelley, and herself a product of her times, Marshall furthered her subject's eclipse. She stated that Mary Shelley abdicated her individuality for Shelley, offered up her whole life at the shrine of one "transcendently greater." She gave Godwin little credit as Mary's educator, and claimed that Shelley had adversely affected her because their early union checked talents and activity that might have surpassed Wollstonecraft's. The widowhood is worthy and dull; there is no passion for Jane Hogg, no Beauclerk or Gatteschi, and the works are scanted. The success of her life was "the moral success of beauty of character."

Marshall denied Trelawny's charges of Mary Shelley's orthodoxy by defensive generalities. Concurrently, Matthew Arnold published Fanny Kemble Butler's story about Mary Shelley's wishing Percy "to think like everyone else," and that became the exemplary Mary Shelley quotation down to today.

In 1890 a critical biography, *Mrs. Shelley*, was published by Lucy Madox Rossetti, W. M. Rossetti's wife, for the Eminent Women series. She added some illuminating facts about the life, such as Godwin's supervision of Mary's education and the Gatteschi episode, but she deprecated the works, claiming, for instance, that Mary Shelley had "affectedly" and continually portraitized Shelley and Byron, who were "too subtle and complex to be unravelled by her."* The following year Garnett published Mary Shelley's *Keepsake* stories, to mixed reviews, *The Athenaeum* noting "some imaginative power and generous sympathy with all that is noble." Garnett, however, fixed the impression of her subsidiary importance in his essay for the definitive *Dictionary of National Biography:* "Nothing but an absolute magnetising of her brain by Shelley's can account for her having risen so far above her usual self as in *Frankenstein*."

* Lucy Rossetti had seen Trelawny's portrait of Mary Shelley by Amelia Curran, since lost, a stiff amateurish work depicting Mary Shelley with an oval face, high forehead, gray eyes tending to brown near the iris, and thin mouth.

Opinion about Mary Shelley continued to be polarized. For one turn-of-the-century follower of Marshall, Mary "broke over [Shelley's] head the precious vase of her heart's love, and wiped his feet with the hairs of her head."[12] Another defamed Shelley: "She was a lily, whom evil fate, in the garb of false philosophy, led to strike the roots of a pure and innocent nature into the shifting morass of a fickle heart . . ."[13] On the other side, William Graham, who claimed to have interviewed Claire Clairmont, wrote that Mary became "prim and proper," enjoying, as she supposedly did, respectable Sussex society, and had always had great respect for "Mrs. Grundy," while Mark Twain observed that she had set her "masculine grip" on Shelley.

Lady Shelley had her final say in 1897, in *Talks with Lady Shelley* by Maud Brooke Rollaston, daughter of a Fabian clergyman whose advocacy of socialism influenced Oscar Wilde.* Long ailing with kidney disease, Lady Shelley died on June 24, 1899, at Boscombe Manor and was buried in the common family grave at St. Peter's. But she extended her grasp on the Shelleys' papers. She had already given a third of her collection, mostly Shelley material, to the Bodleian Library with the proviso that it be filed away until 1922. Another third, Mary Shelley's journals, workbooks, unpublished papers, and much of her correspondence, she gave to her heir, Baron Abinger, and the remaining, miscellaneous third to the Shelley-Rolls family, who succeeded to the Shelley baronetcy. The Abinger and Shelley-Rolls heirs restricted their materials until the 1940s.

In 1907 W. M. Rossetti published what by then seemed to be an obsolete tribute to Mary Shelley — actually written on the thirtieth anniversary of her death — as the daughter of radical parents and Shelley's chosen, immortal "heart-mate" in *Democratic Sonnets*, a volume whose sentiments had seemed so revolutionary that publication was delayed. Three years later her personal repute suffered fresh Trelawnyan damage from which it has yet to recover when H. Buxton Forman published Trelawny's letters; a long succession to Claire Clairmont arraigned Mary Shelley, "a conventional slave," for loving society and for hypocritical piety. Forman took a more moderate position in his preface, stating that after talking with Florence Marshall he thought better of Mary Shelley, but that she was too vain and worldly to be a good wife. Subsequently, Roger Ingpen, a rising Shelley scholar who sympathetically presented the facts

* Lady Shelley gave University College, Oxford, a life-sized sculpture of the recumbent, drowned Shelley, which she commissioned from Onslow Ford, later a surrealist. The work has been unfairly said to have contributed to the Victorian legend of Shelley as a sexless angel, for the poet is pagan-stark naked.

of her financial situation in widowhood in *Shelley in England*, commented that what she really loved was society.

What Stendhal would have termed a negative crystallization had formed. Mary Shelley's detractors sneered and accreted cause for so doing, an appetite that has fed upon itself. In 1918 Franklin B. Sanborn published *The Romance of Mary W. Shelley, John Howard Payne and Washington Irving*, her and Payne's correspondence which was interpreted as her using Payne to try to marry Irving. (A 1930 embellishment declared that she "never embarked upon any emotional adventure without a return ticket in her pocket.")[14]

In the great disillusionment following World War I, modernist critics and political radicals alike deprecated Shelley; debunkers saw Mary Shelley as hypocritical. In 1920, a well-meaning bumbler wrote in a letter to the *Times Literary Supplement* that the relics in Boscombe Manor's sanctum had included pen and paper Shelley used just before his death, and that (possibly a Lady Shelleyism) Mary Shelley had put a glass cover over them and carried them from Italy to England on her knees (it was Percy she had on her knees, had she gone in for that sort of display).[15] "That's her final give-away for me," Katherine Mansfield wrote John Middleton Murry. "Did everybody know? Oh, *didn't* they just? I've done with her."[16] A. H. Kozul introduced Mary Shelley's poetic dramas "Proserpine" and "Midas" in 1922 by remarking at once on her "feminine" nimble invention and on *Frankenstein* as "that most unwomanly of all feminine romances."

Even so, Mary Shelley retained respect. Murry himself, and the *Times Literary Supplement*, reviewed her poems favorably, the latter observing that besides her acknowledged intellectual power, she had a tender, emotional side. Murry also lauded her "measured" commentary on Shelley's poems. In an introduction to a small edition of her letters and in an essay, Henry H. Harper praised her gifts. Walter Edwin Peck used and in some instances misused passages from her fiction to vivify *Shelley: His Life and Works*, as finding the-persons-in-the-fiction had become a major rationale for reading her work. Richard Church published *Mary Shelley* for the Representative Women series in 1928 — a slender but exceptionally perceptive biography, though Church devoted only nine pages to her life after Shelley's death.

Frankenstein, moreover, had launched on the cinematic career that has imprinted Mary Shelley's story on mass imagination throughout the world. The first American film adaptation of 1910 was followed by Italian, Mexican, Spanish, and additional English-speaking versions. In 1931 Boris Karloff became the monster for millions, and the rest is history. As for the original author, relatively few people have ever known more than Mary

Shelley's name, if that, while her authorship, instead of clarifying her image for the cognoscenti, has mystified many and changed few minds. Thus the Shelley scholar Ellsworth Barnard, in 1936: "It ought to be obvious to the student of Shelley's life that Mary Shelley, for all her merits, was quite incapable, both morally and intellectually, of understanding her husband's opinions, much less of sharing them."[17]

Such gross misbelief is excusable insofar as all scholars must rely upon secondary sources and in restating them may overstate. All the same, the very romanticization for which they berate Lady Shelley has led some to make Shelley into a sort of Christ militant, with Mary Shelley as mythic foil, a lachrymose, dense, bourgeois Judas, and Claire Clairmont his Magdalen.* Besides, one's own superiority is enhanced by having an object to look down on. And finally, if new research is not exhaustive, it can ratify an established image.

Until the mid-twentieth century Mary Shelley was of interest mainly to Shelleyans. What has remained a standard life, *Mary Shelley*, was published in 1938 by Rosalie Glynn Grylls (later Lady Mander). Alone of any biographer until the late 1940s, Grylls was given access to the Abinger and Shelley-Rolls collections for lives of Godwin, Mary Shelley, Claire Clairmont, and Trelawny. While she included new correspondence and a dozen new selections from the journals, she did not thoroughly investigate Mary Shelley's years after Shelley's death. Grylls saw her as the only one of his loves worthy to have been his wife, yet as a morbid moper, basically anti-Bohemian, conflicted between the feminine and the artist, between trying to be "like everybody else" and being unable to be so. If she did not become quite Trelawny's conventional slave, Grylls concluded in *Claire Clairmont*, she could not be recognized as Wollstonecraft's daughter.

Newman Ivey White's monumental critical biography, *Shelley*, published in 1940 when the intelligentsia embraced progressive heroes, reestablished the centrality of Shelley's sociopolitical ideas. He did Mary Shelley considerable justice during her union with Shelley, but believed that later she minimized his radicalism, yearned for respectability, and, furthermore, manipulated her editions of his poems in order to conceal her supposed revulsion from him after her children's deaths. (White similarly assumed that Sir Percy intended to run for Parliament as a conservative rather than as a radical.)

In 1944 Frederick L. Jones published seven hundred and five of Mary

---

* See Max Beerbohm's irreverent "but for Missolonghi" observation that our images of Shelley and Byron would be different if they had lived into middle and old age: Byron probably fat, balding, bewhiskered, grumpy; Shelley producing masses of dull poetry. It is equally possible that Shelley might have led about the same quotidian life as Sir Percy's at Boscombe Manor.

Shelley's letters as a resource for Shelley scholars. He stated that while some gaps remained (notably her letters to Hogg, which were published shortly thereafter), his edition gave an adequate picture of her. But many came from imperfect copies that left out amusing or colorful passages; other letters he did not know about, and he was not permitted to see the letters in two important collections: that of Lord Abinger and that of the American private collector Carl H. Pforzheimer. Jones declared that she was a remarkable woman in her own right, praised *Valperga*, and accused a succession of malicious and unsound scholars of injuring "the name of a good and noble woman." Yet he himself claimed that she was possessive, doleful, dependent, "insatiably" eager to associate with talented people. In 1947 Jones published her journals, perforce comprised of what had already been published, which he believed to be nearly perfect.

The reaction of one Shelley scholar, Carl Grabo, bespoke the now traditional outlook. He declared that Mary Shelley's letters after Shelley's death showed that she had little sympathy with liberal ideas, was preoccupied with society and trivial material things, and wrote mostly hack work, rarely showing "a gleam of intellectual curiosity." Then, Robert Metcalf Smith in *The Shelley Legend* claimed to expose a long sequence of "fraudulent and mistaken" efforts from their originator, Mary Shelley, down to White, by which Shelley had been made into a "Victorian angel" and Claire Clairmont deprived of her place as his lover. He also accused Mary Shelley of forging the letter in which Shelley charged Harriet Shelley with several love affairs. White and Jones exploded the forgery charge, and Jones denied the beatification, but the stain adhered.

With the centenary of Mary Shelley's death, interest in her revived, and has steadily grown. Muriel Spark led off in 1951 with *Child of Light: A Reassessment of Mary Wollstonecraft Shelley*, a short, sympathetic, and yet misleading, biography based on then available printed sources, with a critical study and an abridgement of the almost forgotten *The Last Man*. Spark published a retouched version, *Mary Shelley: A Biography*, in 1987. In 1953 Elizabeth Nitchie published *Mary Shelley*, the first critical biography to utilize the Shelley-Rolls and Abinger collections, which had been opened to scholars. Her assessment of the works was mixed and superficial. Not having investigated Mary Shelley's private life afresh, Nitchie felt that she would have been better and nobler had she not "compromised with conventional society." She cited works, however, demonstrating that Mary had remained a liberal — supposedly up until the last several years of her life. In 1959, Nitchie also published *Mathilda* (*Matilda*), Mary Shelley's previously unknown novella of father-daughter incest.

Among ground-breaking books since have been Jean de Palacio's *Mary*

Shelley dans son oeuvre (1968), the most exhaustive critical study yet of her works, her place in literature, her thought and psychology; another critical study by William Walling (1972); W. H. Lyles's annotated bibliography (1975); Charles E. Robinson's edition of *Mary Shelley: Collected Tales and Stories* (1976); and *The Endurance of Frankenstein* (1979), a collection of essays edited by George Levine and U. C. Knoepflmacher. Many editions of *Frankenstein*, one of *The Last Man*, numerous scholarly articles, graduate studies, and several popularized books and biographies have also been published. At last count, *Frankenstein* has been translated into eighteen languages, its film and stage adaptations seem inexhaustible, and television is its latest media outlet.

The woman's movement has had revolutionary impact on social history and literary studies. Beginning with the late Ellen Moers's *Literary Women* (1976), followed by Sandra M. Gilbert and Susan Gubar in *The Madwoman in the Attic: The Woman Writer and the Nineteenth-Century Literary Imagination* (1979), many feminist scholars see Mary Shelley as an impressive contributor to a female literary tradition.

Despite all of this, however, Mary Shelley's reputation remains unsettled, even poor, largely owing to traditional misconceptions that cling in the absence of complete information about her. Whatever some contemporary academics may say about works being all and lives nothing, the urge to integrate lives and works goes irresistibly on, while interpretation of works can be affected by perception of lives. So, as *Frankenstein* seems to be an aberration, some scholars used it in the 1970s to illuminate Shelley's or Godwin's or even Byron's thought; James Rieger declared that Shelley was her "co-author with final authority for the text." Shelley's poems have been studied on a new level of scholarship, educing books and articles on Mary's editorship. But instead of creating the consensus of appreciation of her extraordinary achievement that might be expected from Shelley's admirers, these publications range from highly laudatory, to mixed, to picayune, to condemnatory, the last often attributing her editorial "flaws" to her presumed sentimentality, gentility, or even "vulgarity."

By the 1980s some influential Romantic scholars were reevaluating Mary Shelley's oeuvre with new respect, which, however, did not necessarily include her life, and character, while elsewhere the worst case against her is still being made.

That case was presented by Sylva Norman, witty author of *Flight of the Skylark: The Development of Shelley's Reputation*, and a 1970 essay in *Shelley and his Circle*, in other respects a model of modern scholarship. In sum, her girlhood education was irregular; Shelley awoke her vigor and inde-

pendence. She had insufficient sympathy for him, developed convention-
ality during their union, and withdrew from him after her childrens' deaths.
As a widow she was dazzled by lords, frequented fashionable parties,
otherwise had "homely" friends like the Hares. Glad that Percy thought
like everyone else, she "insisted" on exiling herself to Harrow. She deluded
herself about her past happiness, prettified Shelley, and "simulated" ardor
for democracy. In 1979, Trelawny's mendacity in regard to his own career
was exposed by his biographer William St. Clair, and yet not applied to
Trelawny's criticisms of Mary Shelley, who is said to have "gone over to
the enemy." A *New York Times* review of Ken Russell's 1987 film *Gothic*
refers to her "renowned prudery." The feminist Mary Poovey reads her
as passively submitting to the feminine ideal of her times except for the
"defiance" of authorship.

This biographer is in no position to be indignant about Mary Shelley's
negative repute, however she may regret it. Rather, I am testimony to its
potency. It took two years of research, from 1975 to 1977, before I realized
how dubious that repute was, and then it was necessary to start afresh in
order to study her with an open mind. In 1980, 1983, and 1988, meanwhile, Betty T. Bennett has published three volumes of the first complete
edition of Mary Shelley's letters, with important notes and introductions.
In a review of Bennett's first volume, Richard Holmes, who had belittled
Mary in his *Shelley: The Pursuit,* declared that he had never realized the
breadth of independence of Mary Shelley's thought, her unconventional
years following Shelley's death, or her restless spirit. Mary Shelley's complete *Journals* (1987), edited by Paula R. Feldman and Diana Scott-Kilvert,
provides an additional invaluable resource.

Current studies of Mary Shelley, including this biography, will not be
the final word, but they can be based on data that approach the complete,
and without which human beings cannot be comprehended as they deserve, in all their complexity, in the context of their times as well as their
significance to our own. As Mary Shelley quoted Edmund Burke in her
last journal entry: "The first thing is justice."

Mary Shelley was an important Romantic who survived into the Victorian age. Her private life, career, and works are a rich resource for that
historical evolution, a broader mine than those of her great associates,
Shelley and Byron, whom kind death saved from erosion. Far from being
subjected to romantic turbulence, she chose it. Aspiration, enthusiasm,
challenge, active mind and spirit, and optimism were among her cardinal
qualities, contrary to the impression that she was temperamentally cool,
quiet and pessimistic, and it was her incapacity for resignation to cold
reality that eventually wore her down.

She should be recognized as indeed her mother's daughter, heir to Wollstonecraft's Romantic feminism and to a fuller measure of punishment for it. From *Frankenstein* to *Rambles*, her heroes and heroines are those who confront custom, power, and unjust authority. Moreover, her creative and scholarly works establish her as a major literary figure of the first half of the nineteenth century. She belongs among the great editors for her editions of Shelley's works, even among the great disciples, given the veneration she also won for his character and ideas.

Perhaps she will be best remembered for her perception in *Frankenstein* and *The Last Man*, that the Promethean drive is at the heart of human progress and yet a bringer of new ills if not focused on ethical means and ends; and even so, if Nature shrugs we perish. In that ambiguity she may be said to have heralded the consciousness that distinguishes the Post-Modern from the Modern Age.

APPENDIXES

SHORT-TITLE LIST

CHAPTER NOTES

INDEX

Appendix A

"STANZAS"

I must forget thy dark eyes' love-fraught gaze,
   Thy voice, that fill'd me with emotion bland,
Thy vows, which lost me in this 'wild'ring maze,
   The thrilling pressure of thy gentle hand;
And, dearer yet, that interchange of thought,
   That drew us nearer still to one another,
Till in two hearts one sole idea wrought,
   And neither hoped nor fear'd but for the other.

I must forget to deck myself with flowers:
   Are not those wither'd which I gave to thee?
I must forget to count the day-bright hours,
   Their sun is set — thou com'st no more to me!
I must forget thy love! — Then let me close
   My tearful eyes upon unwelcome day,
And let my tortured thoughts seek that repose
   Which corpses find within the tomb alway.

Oh! for the fate of her who, changed to leaves,
   No more can weep, nor any longer moan;
Or the lorn Queen, who, chilling as she grieves,
   Finds her warm beating heart grow calm in stone.
Oh! for a draught of that Lethean wave,
   Mortal alike to joy and to regret! —
It may not be! not even that would save!
   Love, hope, and thee, I never can forget!

Printed in *The Keepsake for MDCCCXXXIII*, Frederic Mansel Reynolds, ed. (London: Longman, Rees, Orme, Brown, Green, and Longman; Paris: Rittner and Goupil; Frankfurt: Charles Jügill, 1832): 52. Mary Shelley's fair copy for the printer is in The Berg Collection, The New York Public Library.

Appendix B

MARY SHELLEY'S WORKS

* Newly attributed.
? Possibly by Mary Shelley.

NOVELS

Frankenstein: Or, The Modern Prometheus. 3 vols. London: Lackington, Hughes, Harding, Mavor, & Jones, 1818.

Frankenstein; or, The Modern Prometheus. [With an Introduction by "M.W.S."] London: Henry Colburn and Richard Bentley; Edinburgh: Bell and Bradfute; Dublin: Cumming, 1831. A revised one-volume edition.

Matilda. Written 1819–1820; published as *Mathilda*, Elizabeth Nitchie, ed. Chapel Hill, N.C.: University of North Carolina Press, 1959.

Valperga: Or, the Life and Adventures of Castruccio, Prince of Lucca. 3 vols. London: G. and W. B. Whittaker, 1823.

The Last Man. 3 vols. London: Henry Colburn, 1826.

The Fortunes of Perkin Warbeck, A Romance. 3 vols. London: Henry Colburn and Richard Bentley, 1830.

Lodore. 3 vols. London: Richard Bentley, 1835.

Falkner. A Novel. 3 vols. London: Saunders and Otley, 1837.

DRAMAS

"Proserpine, a Mythological Drama in Two Acts." *The Winter's Wreath* for 1832 (1831), 1–20. (Completed April 1820.)

"Midas." *Proserpine & Midas. Two unpublished Mythological Dramas by Mary Shelley*, A[ndré] H[enri] Koszul, ed., 45–89. London: Humphrey Milford, 1922. (Written 1820.)

A tragedy (unfinished and lost), 1824.

STORIES AND SEMIFICTIONAL ESSAYS

"Hate" (unfinished and lost), 1814.

"Valerius; the Reanimated Roman" (unfinished), 1819. *Mary Shelley: Collected Tales and Stories*, Charles E. Robinson, ed., 345–346. Baltimore and London:

The Johns Hopkins University Press, 1976. Hereafter cited as *Collected Tales*.

"An Eighteenth-Century Tale" (fragment) [?1819]. *Collected Tales*, 332–344.

A story for Leigh Hunt's *The Indicator* (unpublished and lost), 1821.

"A Tale of the Passions." *The Liberal: Verse and Prose from the South* 2 (1823): 289–325. Anon.

"Recollections of Italy." *London Magazine* 9 (January 1824): 21–26.

"The Bride of Modern Italy." *London Magazine* 9 (April 1824): 351–363. Anon.

"Roger Dodsworth: The Reanimated Englishman," 1826. Cyrus Redding, *Yesterday and To-day*, II:150–165. 2 vols. London: T. Cautley Newby, 1863. "Mrs. Shelley."

"Lacy de Vere." *Forget-Me-Not* for 1827 (London: Rudolf Ackermann, 1826): 275–294. Anon.

* "The Ritter von Reichenstein." *The Bijou* for 1828 (London: W. Pickering, 1827): 114–138.

"The Sisters of Albano." *The Keepsake for MDCCCXXIX* (London: Hurst, Chance, and Co., 1828): 80–100. By the Author of Frankenstein. (Unless otherwise noted, Mary Shelley's *Keepsake* contributions are signed "the Author of Frankenstein.") Two stage versions of this story were produced in 1830: *The Sisters of Charity*, by Richard Brinsley Peake, at the English Opera House; and *The Italian Sisters; or The Brigands of Albano*, at the Adelphi.

"Ferdinando Eboli: A Tale." *The Keepsake for MDCCCXXIX* (1828): 195–218.

* ?"The Magician of Vicenza." *Forget-Me-Not* for 1829 (1828): 273–283.

"The Mourner." *The Keepsake for MDCCCXXX* (1829): 71–97.

"The Evil Eye." *The Keepsake for MDCCCXXX* (1829): 150–175.

"The False Rhyme." *The Keepsake for MDCCCXXX* (1829): 265–268.

"Transformation." *The Keepsake for MDCCCXXXI* (1830): 18–39.

"The Swiss Peasant." *The Keepsake for MDCCCXXXI* (1830): 121–146.

"The Dream." *The Keepsake for MDCCCXXXII* (London: Longman, Rees, Orme, Brown, and Green, 1831): 22–38.

"The Brother and Sister, An Italian Story." *The Keepsake for MDCCCXXXIII* (London: Longman, Rees, Orme, Brown, Green, and Longman, 1832): 105–141.

"The Invisible Girl." *The Keepsake for MDCCCXXXIII* (1832): 210–227.

"The Smuggler and His Family." *Original Compositions in Prose and Verse . . .* , 27–53. London: Edmund Lloyd, 1833. "Mrs. Shelley."

"The Mortal Immortal: A Tale." *The Keepsake for MDCCCXXXIV* (1833): 71–87.

"The Trial of Love." *The Keepsake for MDCCCXXXV* (1834): 70–86.

"The Elder Son." *Heath's Book of Beauty. 1835* (London: Longman, Rees, Orme, Green, and Longman, 1834): 83–123. "Mrs. Shelley."

"The Parvenue." *The Keepsake for MDCCCXXXVII* (1836): 209–211. "Mrs. Shelley."

?"The Pilgrims." *The Keepsake for MDCCCXXXVIII* (1837): 128–155.

"Euphrasia: A Tale of Greece." *The Keepsake for MDCCCXXXIX* (1838): 135–152. "Mrs. Shelley."

"The Heir of Mondolfo." Probably written during 1825–1827. *Appleton's Journal: A Monthly Miscellany of Popular Literature* (New York), n.s. 2 (January 1877): 12–23.

For possible additional works, see *Collected Tales*, xviii–xix.

POEMS

"Orpheus," with Percy Bysshe Shelley, 1820–1821. *Relics of Shelley*, Richard Garnett, ed., 20–25. London: E. Moxon & Co., 1862.

"The Choice." Written July 1823. *The Choice. A Poem on Shelley's Death by Mary Wollstonecraft Shelley*, H[arry] Buxton Forman, ed. London: Printed for the Editor for Private Distribution, 1876.

"On Reading Wordsworth's Lines on Peel [*sic*] Castle; 'It is with me, as erst with you.'" Written Dec. 8, 1825. R[osalie] Glynn Grylls, *Mary Shelley: A Biography*, 302–303. London, New York: Oxford University Press, 1938.

"Fragment; (To Jane with the Last [Man]) 'Tribute for thee, dear solace of my life.'" Written January 1826. Grylls, *Mary Shelley*, 303.

"Absence; 'Ah! he is gone — and I alone! —.'" *The Keepsake for MDCCCXXXI* (1830): 39.

"A Dirge; 'This morn, thy gallant bark, love.'" *The Keepsake for MDCCCXXXI* (1830): 85.

"A Night Scene; 'I see thee not, my gentlest Isabel.'" *The Keepsake for MDCCCXXXI* (1830): 147–148. "By Mary S."

"Alas I weep my life away." Journal entry, Sept. 4, 1831. Elizabeth Nitchie, *Mary Shelley: Author of "Frankenstein,"* 235. New Brunswick, N.J.: Rutgers University Press, 1953.

"Struggle no more, my Soul with the sad chains." Journal entry, Sept. 16, 1831. Nitchie, *Mary Shelley*, 235.

* "Stanzas: 'I must forget thy dark eyes' love-fraught gaze.'" *The Keepsake for MDCCCXXXIII* (1832): 52. Unsigned. In the same volume: ?"Stanzas: 'To love in solitude and mystery,'" 28; ?"Stanzas: 'It is because amid the crowd,'" 307–308.

?"Fame." *Forget-Me-Not* for 1833 (1832): 92.

"La Vida es sueno; 'The tide of Time was at my feet.'" Written July 26, 1833. Nitchie, *Mary Shelley*, 233–234.

"Tempo e' piu di Morire / Io ho tardato piu ch' i' non vorrei; 'Sadly borne across the waves.'" Written 1833. Nitchie, *Mary Shelley*, 231–233.

"O listen while I sing to thee." Written March 12, 1838. Nitchie, *Mary Shelley*, 234–235. Published under this title as a canzonet with accompaniment for harp or piano by Hugh H. Pearson. London: D'Almaine & Co. [c. 1842].

"Stanzas: 'How like a star you rose upon my life.' " *The Keepsake for MDCCCXXXIX* (1838): 179.

"Stanzas: 'O come to me in dreams, my love!' " *The Keepsake for MDCCCXXXIX* (1838): 201.

Although it has been suggested that poems by Mrs. Godwin in *The Keepsake* were by Mary Shelley, they were written by Mrs. C. G. Godwin, "author of Wanderer's Legacy, Sappho, etc." See Andrew Boyle, *An Index to the Annuals (1820–1850)* (Worcester: Andrew Boyle, 1967). "Ode to Ignorance," *The Metropolitan Magazine* 9 (January 1834): 29–31, signed "M.W.S.," has been attributed to Mary Shelley but is not likely to be hers.

TRANSLATIONS OR ADAPTATIONS

Apuleius's Cupid and Psyche (unpublished), 1817.

* " The Stars," from Schiller's *Turandot, Prinzessin von China,* 1823. See *The Journals of Mary Shelley 1814–1844,* Paula R. Feldman and Diana Scott-Kilvert, eds., II:271. 2 vols. Oxford: The Clarendon Press, 1987.

* ?Translation of Guidiccioni's "Sonnet to Italy." *New Monthly Magazine and Literary Journal* 10 (March 1824): 222. "S."

* " 'The Divysion of The Earthe' in Imitation of Spenser, from the German of Schiller." *The Bijou* for 1829 (1828): 164–165. "M.S."

* " 'The Song of the Sword' from the German of C. T. Korner." *The Bijou* for 1829 (1828): 174–177. "M.S."

"Ritratto di Ugo Foscolo" ("Portrait of Ugo Foscolo"). *The Bijou* for 1830 (1829): 40–41. "M.S."

* "To Glory. From the Italian of Ciapetti." *The Bijou* for 1830 (1829): 98. "M.S."

* " 'Ode, from the German of Klopstock, To Meta.' " *The Bijou* for 1830 (1829): 225–226. "M.S."

* Laura Tighe Galloni d'Istria, *Inez de Medine* (uncompleted and unpublished), 1846–1848. (Chapters VIII and IX are in the Abinger MSS.)

TRAVEL WORKS

[with Percy Bysshe Shelley.] *History of a Six Weeks' Tour through a Part of France, Switzerland, Germany, and Holland: with Letters Descriptive of a Sail round the Lake of Geneva, and of the Glaciers of Chamouni.* London: T. Hookham, Jun.; and C. and J. Ollier, 1817.

Rambles in Germany and Italy, in 1840, 1842, and 1843. 2 vols. London: Edward Moxon, 1844.

BIOGRAPHIES

The life of Jean Baptiste Louvet de Couvray (unfinished and lost), 1814.

[with James Montgomery and Sir David Brewster.] *Lives of the Most Eminent Literary and Scientific Men of Italy, Spain, and Portugal.* Volumes I and II: volumes 86 and 87 of The Cabinet of Biography, Conducted by the Rev. Dionysius Lardner (Lardner's Cabinet Cyclopedia). London: Longman, Orme, Brown, Green, & Longman; and John Taylor, 1835. In volume I, except for those of Dante and Ariosto, Mary Shelley wrote all the lives: Petrarch, Boccaccio, Lorenzo di Medici,

Marsilio Ficino, Giovanni Pico della Mirandello, Angelo Poliziano, Bernardo Pulci, Luca Pulci, Luigi Pulci, Cieco da Ferrara, Burchiello, Matteo Maria Bujardo, Francesco Berni, and Machiavelli. In volume II, she did not write the lives of Galileo and Tasso. She did write those of Pietro Metastasio, Carlo Goldoni, Vittorio Alfieri, Giambattista Marino, Vincenzo Monti, and Ugo Foscolo; she probably wrote the remaining lives: Francesco Guicciardini, Vittoria Colonna, Giovanni Battista Guarini, Gabriello Chiabrera, Alessandro Tassoni, and Vincenzo da Filicaja.

Lives of the Most Eminent Literary and Scientific Men of Italy, Spain and Portugal. Volume III: volume 88 of The Cabinet of Biography, Conducted by the Rev. Dionysius Lardner (Lardner's Cabinet Cyclopedia). London: Longman, Orme, Brown, Green & Longman; and John Taylor, 1837. Mary Shelley wrote all the lives, except possibly that of Alonzo de Ercilla; these include lives of Juan Boscán, Garcilaso de la Vega, Diego Hurtado de Mendoza, Luis Ponce de León, Fernando de Herrera, Jorge de Montemayor, Cristóbal de Castillejo; under Early Dramatists, Cervantes, Lope de Vega, Vicente Espinel, Esteban de Villegas, Luis de Góngora, Francisco Gómez de Quevado, and Pedro Calderón de la Barca; under Early Poets of Portugal, [Bernardim] Ribeyra [Ribiero], Gil Vicente, Francisco de Sá de Miranda, Antonio Ferreira, and Luíz Vaz de Camoëns.

Lives of the Most Eminent Literary and Scientific Men of France. Volumes I and II: volumes 102 and 103 of The Cabinet of Biography, Conducted by the Rev. Dionysius Lardner (Lardner's Cabinet Cyclopedia). London: Longman, Orme, Brown, Green, & Longman; and John Taylor, 1838–1839. Volume I: lives of Montaigne, Rabelais, Corneille, La Rochefoucauld, Molière, La Fontaine, Pascal, Madame de Sévigné, Boileau, Racine, and Fénélon; volume II: Voltaire, Rousseau, Condorcet, Mirabeau, Madame Roland, and Madame de Staël.

Unfinished life of Percy Bysshe Shelley. Portions printed in Thomas Jefferson Hogg, *Life of Percy Bysshe Shelley,* I:v–vii, viii–ix, 27, 31–34, 40–41. 2 vols. London: Edward Moxon, 1858. Original MS. at the Bodleian Library, Oxford.

Unfinished memoir of William Godwin. Portions printed in C[harles] Kegan Paul, *William Godwin: His Friends and Contemporaries,* I:25–26, 36–37, 47, 64, 73–74, 76, 78–83, 120–121, 123–125, 129–135, 161–162, 231–232, 238–239, 332–333. 2 vols. London: Henry S. King, 1876. Original MS. in the Abinger MSS., Bodleian Library, Oxford.

ARTICLES AND REVIEWS (unsigned, except as noted)

"Madame D'Houtetôt." *The Liberal: Verse and Prose from the South* 3 (1823): 67–83.

"Giovanni Villani." *The Liberal* 4 (1824): 281–297 [printed "197"].

"On Ghosts." *London Magazine* 9 (March 1824): 253–256. Signed Σξ.

"Rome in the First and Nineteenth Centuries." *New Monthly Magazine and Literary Journal* 10 (March 1824): 217–222.

An anonymous tribute to Lord Byron upon his death, written for the *London Magazine* (unpublished and lost).

"Defense of Velluti." *The Examiner* 958 (June 11, 1826): 372–373. Letter signed "Anglo-Italicus." "Mary Shelley's Second Defense of Velluti." *The Letters of Mary W. Shelley.* Frederick L[afayette] Jones, ed., II:354–356 (Appendix III). 2 vols. Norman, Okla.: University of Oklahoma Press, 1944.

"The English in Italy." *Westminster Review* 6 (October 1826): 325–341. Review of *The English in Italy; Continental Adventures. A Novel;* and *Diary of an Ennuyée.*

"A Visit to Brighton." *London Magazine* 16 (December 1826): 460–466.

* ?"The Italian Novelists. Translated from the Italian, by Thomas Roscoe. 4 vols. London. 1825." *Westminster Review* 7 (January 1827): 115–116. Review.

"Illyrian Poems — Feudal Scenes." *Westminster Review* 10 (January 1829): 71–81. Review of Prosper Mérimée's *La Guzla, La Jacquerie; Feudal Scenes, followed by the Family of Carvajal, a Drama.*

"Modern Italy." *Westminster Review* 11 (July 1829): 127–140. Review of Best, *Italy as it is;* and J. Sismond[i], *A Tour in Italy and Sicily.*

Review of *The Loves of the Poets. Westminster Review* 11 (October 1829): 472–477.

Review of *Cloudesley; a Tale. Blackwood's Edinburgh Magazine* 27 (May 1830): 711–716.

Review of *1572 Chronique du Temps de Charles IX — Par l'Auteur du Théâtre de Clara Gazul. Westminster Review* 13 (October 1830): 495–502.

?"Byron and Shelley on the Character of Hamlet," *New Monthly Magazine and Literary Journal* 29 (November 1830): 327–336.

"Memoirs of William Godwin." In *Caleb Williams,* by William Godwin, iii–xiii. London: Colburn and Bentley, 1831.

?"Living Literary Characters, No. II. The Honourable Mrs. Norton." *New Monthly Magazine and Literary Journal* 33 (February 1831): 180–183.

?"Living Literary Characters, No. IV. James Fenimore Cooper." *New Monthly Magazine and Literary Journal* 33 (April 1831): 356–362.

Review of "The Bravo; a Venetian Story. By the Author of 'The Pilot,' 'The Borderers,' etc." [James Fenimore Cooper]. *Westminster Review* 16 (January 1832): 180–192.

Review of *Eugene Aram* by Edward Bulwer, written for *Westminster Review,* early 1832, and rejected.

* ?"Modern Italian Romances." *The Monthly Chronicle* 2 (November 1838): 415–428.

* ?"Portuguese Literature." *The Monthly Chronicle* 3 (January 1839): 20–34.

* ?"Spanish Romantic Drama. Life, A Dream." *The Monthly Chronicle* 3 (June 1839): 488.

* "Richard the Third, as Duke of Gloucester and King of England. By Caroline A. Halsted. 2 vols. Longman & Co." *The Athenaeum* 875, 876 (Aug. 3 and 10, 1844): 707–708, 728–731. Review.

Mary Shelley may also have published in *The Foreign Quarterly Review* in 1829–1839 and 1844, and in *The Monthly Chronicle* in 1844.

Attributed to Mary Shelley but not by her:

"Narrative of a Tour round the Lake of Geneva, and of an Excursion through the

Valley of Chamouni." *La Belle Assemblée, or Court and Fashionable Magazine* n.s. 28 (July 1823): 14–19. Unsigned.

"Recollections of the Lake of Geneva." *The Spirit and Manners of the Age* 2 (December 1829): 913–920. "M.W.S."

EDITED WORKS

Percy Bysshe Shelley. *Posthumous Poems of Percy Bysshe Shelley*. London: John and Henry L. Hunt, 1824.

[Edward John Trelawny]. *Adventures of a Younger Son*. London: Colburn and Bentley, 1831.

[Claire Clairmont]. "The Pole." *The Court Magazine and Belle Assemblée* 1 (August and September 1832): 64–71, 129–136. Signed "By the Author of 'Frankenstein.'"

William Godwin, Jun. *Transfusion; or, The Orphan of Unwalden*. London: Macrone, 1835.

Percy Bysshe Shelley. *The Poetical Works of Percy Bysshe Shelley*. Mrs. Shelley, ed. 4 vols. London: Edward Moxon, 1839.

Percy Bysshe Shelley. *The Poetical Works of Percy Bysshe Shelley*. Mrs. Shelley, ed. London: Edward Moxon, 1840 [1839]. One-volume edition with Postscript added.

Percy Bysshe Shelley. *Essays, Letters from Abroad, Translations and Fragments, By Percy Bysshe Shelley*. Mrs. Shelley, ed. 2 vols. London: Edward Moxon, 1840 [1839]. Second edition, 1841.

WORKS FOR CHILDREN

"Mounseer Nongtongpaw; or the Discoveries of John Bull in a Trip to Paris." London: Proprietors of the Juvenile Library [M.J. Godwin & Co.]. 1808. Four editions published by Godwin. Two editions published in the United States.

A story for Mrs. Mason's daughter (unpublished and lost), 1820.

"Maurice." Sent to Godwin in 1821 (unpublished and lost).

"Cecil." Uncompleted novella, c. 1834. Abinger MSS.

The following three works cannot be positively attributed to Mary Shelley, but internal and circumstantial evidence supports the conjecture that she used the pseudonym Mrs. Caroline Barnard — for whose independent existence I have been unable to find proof:

* ?*The Parent's Offering; or, Tales for Children*. By Mrs. Caroline Barnard. 2 vols. London: M.J. Godwin & Co., Juvenile Library, 1813. An "improved edition" published 1823. *The Parent's Offering; Or, Interesting Tales For Youth of Both Sexes*. By Mrs. Caroline Barnard. A New Edition, with the Addition of "The Noise," "The Refusal," and "The Heap of Stones." London: Baldwin and Cradock, 1829.

* ?*The Prize: Or, The Lace-Makers of Missenden*. By Mrs. Caroline Barnard. London: M.J. Godwin & Co., Juvenile Library, 1817.

* ?*The Fisher-Boy of Weymouth: to which are added, The Pet-Donkey, and The Sisters*. London: M.J. Godwin & Co., Juvenile Library, 1819. Advertised as *The Fisherboy; or, Worth in humble life, and other tales*. By Mrs. C. Barnard.

Short-Title List

The following short titles are used in the chapter notes. For the convenience of the reader, all of Mary Shelley's works are grouped at the end of this list.

Abinger MSS.

Papers of Mary Shelley and her family, owned by Lord Abinger; on deposit at the Bodleian Library, Oxford. Most of these papers have been microfilmed.

Byron Letters

Byron's Letters and Journals. Leslie A. Marchand, ed. 12 vols., Cambridge: The Belknap Press of Harvard University Press, 1973–1982.

CC Journals

The Journals of Claire Clairmont. Marion Kingston Stocking, ed., with the assistance of David Mackenzie Stocking. Cambridge: Harvard University Press, 1968.

Dowden, *Shelley*

Edward Dowden. *The Life of Percy Bysshe Shelley*. 2 vols., London: Kegan Paul, Trench & Co., 1886.

Gisborne, Williams

Maria Gisborne and Edward E. Williams: Shelley's Friends, Their Journals and Letters. Frederick L. Jones, ed. Norman: University of Oklahoma Press, 1951.

Grylls, *Claire Clairmont*

R[osalie] Glynn Grylls (Lady Mander). *Claire Clairmont, Mother of Byron's Allegra*. London: John Murray, 1939.

Hogg, *Shelley*

Thomas Jefferson Hogg. *The Life of Percy Bysshe Shelley*. 2 vols., London: Edward Moxon, 1858.

Houghton MSS.

The papers of Richard Monckton-Milnes, First Baron Houghton. Trinity College Library, Cambridge University.

Hunt, "Shelley"

[Thornton] Hunt. "Shelley. By One Who Knew Him." *Atlantic Monthly* 11 (February 1863): 184–204.

Marshall, *Mary Shelley*

Mrs. Julian Marshall [Florence T.]. *The Life and Letters of Mary Wollstonecraft Shelley*. 2 vols., London: Richard Bentley & Son, 1889.

Murray MSS.

The manuscripts of John Murray, publisher of Lord Byron, held by John Murray VI.

Palacio, *Mary Shelley*   Jean de Palacio, *Mary Shelley dans son oeuvre: Contri-*
                                 butions aux études shelleyennes. Paris: Editions Klinck-
                                 sieck, 1969.

Paul, *Godwin*   C. Kegan Paul. *William Godwin: His Friends and Con-*
                                 temporaries. 2 vols., rpt. New York: AMS Press, 1970.

PBS Letters   *The Letters of Percy Bysshe Shelley.* Frederick L. Jones,
                                 ed. 2 vols., Oxford: The Clarendon Press, 1964.

Peacock, *Memoirs*   Thomas Love Peacock, "Memoirs of Percy Bysshe Shel-·
                                 ley." *The Works of Thomas Love Peacock,* vol. VIII,
                                 H.F.B. Brett-Smith and C. E. Jones, eds. (Halliford
                                 Edition). 10 vols., London: Constable & Co. Ltd,
                                 1934.

Rennie, *Traits*   [Eliza Rennie]. *Traits of Character: Being Twenty-Five*
                                 Years' Literary and Personal Recollections By A Con-
                                 temporary. 2 vols., London: Hurst and Blackett, 1860.

Rossetti, *Mrs. Shelley*   Lucy Madox Rossetti. *Mrs. Shelley.* Eminent Women
                                 Series. London: W. H. Allen, 1890.

Shelley and his Circle   *Shelley and his Circle.* Vols. I–IV, Kenneth Neill Cam-
                                 eron, ed.; vols. V–VIII, Donald H. Reiman, ed.
                                 Cambridge: Harvard University Press, 1961, 1970,
                                 1973, 1986.

The following short titles are used for works written or edited by Mary Shelley
(for full bibliographical citations, if not included here, see Appendix B):

Collected Tales

Falkner

Frankenstein, 1818

Frankenstein, 1831

The Last Man

Lives, 1835–1837

Lives, 1838–1839

Lodore

Matilda

MWS, *Godwin*

MWS Journal   Journals of Mary Wollstonecraft Shelley, Abinger MSS.
                                 See also *The Journals of Mary Shelley 1814–1844.*
                                 Paula R. Feldman and Diana Scott-Kilvert, eds. 2
                                 vols., Oxford: The Clarendon Press, 1987.

MWS Letters   *The Letters of Mary Wollstonecraft Shelley.* Betty T. Ben-
                                 nett, ed. 3 vols. Baltimore and London: Johns Hop-
                                 kins University Press, 1980, 1983, 1988.

PBS Poems

Perkin Warbeck

Rambles

Valperga

The following abbreviations are used in the reference material in the chapter notes and in the index: CC, Claire Clairmont; WG, William Godwin; MWS, Mary Wollstonecraft Shelley; PBS, Percy Bysshe Shelley; EJT, Edward John Trelawny.

Chapter Notes

1 "My brilliant star"

1. MWS Journal, Oct. 21, 1838.
2. *The Remains of the Late Mrs. Richard Trench*, Richard C. Trench, ed. (London: Parker, Son, and Bourn, 1862), 359.
3. WG, *St. Leon*, 4 vols. (London: G.G. and J. Robinson, 1799), II:41.
4. MWS, *Godwin*.
5. WG to Joseph Gerrald, Jan. 25, 1794, Paul, *Godwin*, I:128.
6. For a study of utopianism, see Frank E. and Fritzie P. Manuel, *Utopian Thought in the Western World* (Cambridge: The Belknap Press of Harvard University Press, 1979).
7. Anna Seward, *Letters of Anna Seward: Written between the Years 1784 and 1807* (1811; rpt. New York: AMS Press, 1975), 344.
8. MWS, *Godwin*, in Paul, *Godwin*, I:135.
9. WG, autobiographical notes, Abinger MSS.
10. Anna Laetitia [Aikin] Le Breton, *Memories of Seventy Years, by One of a Literary Family*, Mrs. Herbert Martin, ed. (London, Edinburgh: Griffith & Farran, 1883), 81.
11. WG to ?, Sept. 19, 1797, Abinger MSS.; *Anima Poetae: From the Unpublished Note-Books of Samuel Taylor Coleridge*, Ernest Hartley Coleridge, ed. (London: W. Heinemann, 1895), 56.
12. WG, *The Enquirer* (London: G.G. and J. Robinson, 1797), 11.
13. Paul, *Godwin*, I:289–290.
14. *Autobiography of Henry Taylor, 1800–1875*, 2 vols. (London: Longman's, Green & Co., 1885), I:19.
15. Una Taylor, *Guests and Memories: Annals of a Seaside Villa* (London, New York: Humphrey Milford, Oxford University Press, 1924), 28.
16. WG, *St. Leon*, I:119–120.
17. Ibid., 118–119.
18. Louisa Jones to WG, undated, Abinger MSS.
19. Ibid.
20. WG, *St. Leon*, II:27–28.
21. Lady Margaret Mount Cashell to WG, Apr. 6, 1801, Abinger MSS.
22. S. T. Coleridge to WG, May 21, 1800, Paul, *Godwin*, II:3.
23. Ibid.; and Coleridge to WG, Sept. 11, 1800, ibid., 3, 8.
24. See WG to William Cole, Mar. 2, 1802, ibid., 118–120.
25. Lady Mount Cashell to WG, Aug. 6, 1801, Abinger MSS.: "[you mention] in your last letter that you send your little girl of four years old to school." Godwin was sometimes confusing about ages. Mary was in her fourth year after her third

birthday, in her eleventh after her tenth birthday, and so on. She herself always believed that her mother died at thirty-six rather than thirty-eight. Frank Cole, director of Libraries and Arts, London Borough of Camden, has found no record of such day schools in Somers Town, but often these were informally organized.

26. WG to James Marshall, [July 11, 1800], Paul, *Godwin*, I:365.

27. Ibid., 358.

28. Godwin's *Scripture Histories* was published in 1802. I am indebted to William St. Clair for this information.

29. *Valperga*, I:199.

30. *Lodore*, I:30–31.

31. WG to ?, Aug. 29, 1801, Paul, *Godwin*, II:74.

2 "TO BE SOMETHING GREAT AND GOOD"

1. *Dictionnaire historique et bibliographique de la Suisse* (Neuchâtel, 1933), VII:116. The Vials were originally from Trièves in Dauphiny, and became citizens of Geneva in the early eighteenth century. The second Mrs. Godwin's history has been explored but never thoroughly illuminated. Godwin's *Fleetwood* probably contains hints. William St. Clair's forthcoming biography of Godwin and his family promises to clarify her pre-Godwin career.

2. WG to Mary Jane Godwin, Apr. 5, 1805, Abinger MSS. Godwin may have played down Wollstonecraft before his remarriage, perhaps under the impact of his persecution. In 1799, her girlhood friend Jane Arden Gardiner offered him Wollstonecraft's early letters to her, which he did not take. Possibly, however, it was a question of money.

3. WG, *Letter of Advice to a Young American* (London: M.J. Godwin & Co., 1818), 7–8.

4. I conjecture that "Caroline Barnard" was a pseudonym for Mary Godwin. See Chapter 3, n. 29.

5. "The Elder Son," *Collected Tales*, 244.

6. *MWS Letters*, I:296.

7. *Valperga*, III:100, 243.

8. MWS Journal, Oct. 21, 1822.

9. Hunt, "Shelley," 198.

10. WG, Journal, Feb. 8, 1806, "Explanation w. Fanny," Abinger MSS.

11. *Frankenstein*, 1831, v–vi.

12. MWS, *Godwin*.

13. WG, "My dear child," Sept. 20, 1806, Abinger MSS.

14. MWS, *Godwin*, in Paul, *Godwin*, I:232.

15. William Austin, *Letters from London Written during the Years 1802 & 1803* (Boston: W. Pelham, 1804), 204.

16. Paul, *Godwin*, II:213–214. This letter has been taken as evidence of Godwin's lack of time or interest in Mary's education, whereas it shows that he did not agree with all of Wollstonecraft's theories and employed his own.

17. *Valperga*, I:198–199.

18. CC to EJT, c. 1870, Grylls, *Claire Clairmont*, 274.

19. MWS to Abraham Hayward, Dec. 22, 1839, *MWS Letters*, II:334.

20. MWS to Jane Williams, July 23 [1823], *MWS Letters*, I:350.

21. WG to PBS, Dec. 10, 1812, *PBS Letters*, I:340–341, fn. 3; WG to Marmaduke Martin, Feb. 10, 1798, *Shelley and his Circle*, I:206.

22. WG, *History of England* (London: M.J. Godwin & Co., 1806), vi.

23. MWS, *Godwin*, in Paul, *Godwin*, I:36–37.

24. WG, *History of Greece* (London: M.J. Godwin & Co., 1822), vii.

25. Rossetti, *Mrs. Shelley*, 28.

26. WG to ?, Jan. 2, 1808, *A Nursery Companion*, Iona and Peter Opie, eds. (Oxford: Oxford University Press, 1980), 128. See pp. 118–122 for the poem and illustrations. A portion of Godwin's letter was quoted in Lowe Brothers Ltd. catalogue #1200 of Dec. 2, 1960, but Mihai Handrea, curator of the Carl H. Pforzheimer Shelley and his Circle collection, has advised me that it was sold to an unknown party.

27. WG to W. T. Baxter, June 8, 1812, *Shelley and his Circle*, III:102.

28. WG, *Fleetwood*, 3 vols. (London: Richard Phillips, 1805), II:186–187.

29. WG, *Essay on Sepulchres* (London: W. Miller, 1809), 76.

30. MWS, draft of *Frankenstein*, Abinger MSS. She altered the words but not the sentiment in her fair copy.

31. WG, *Fleetwood*, II:170.

32. "Boccaccio," *Lives*, 1835–1837, I:127.

33. See *Valperga*, I:194–195; *Lodore*, III:8.

34. These heroines include Elizabeth Lavenza in *Frankenstein*, who (like Wollstonecraft's Maria) speaks up in court for justice; *Valperga*'s Euthanasia, who chooses political justice over love, and Beatrice, who gives herself to Castruccio; dissident Fanny Derham in *Lodore*; Elizabeth Raby in *Falkner*, who defies female proprieties for nobler duties.

35. Mary Wollstonecraft, *Letters Written During a Short Residence in Sweden, Norway, and Denmark* (London: J. Johnson, 1796), 66.

36. Iris Origo, "Allegra," *A Measure of Love* (New York: Pantheon Books, 1957), 27.

3 "THE TIME OF MY GIRLISH TROUBLES"

1. WG to P. Patrickson, Jan. 4, 1813, Paul, *Godwin*, II:198.

2. WG to Francis Place, Sept. 11, 1814, *Shelley and his Circle*, III:379.

3. Henry Crabb Robinson, *On Books and Their Writers*, Edith J. Morley, ed., 3 vols. (London: J. M. Dent & Sons, 1938), I:14.

4. Mary Jane Godwin to Lady Mount Cashell, Nov. 15, 1814, Feb. 7, 1815, Dowden, *Shelley*, Appendix B, II:546, 547.

5. CC to MWS, Nov. 6, 1835, Abinger MSS.

6. Her own translation is among the Abinger MSS.

7. MWS to Maria Gisborne, Dec. 28, 1819, *MWS Letters*, I:122.

8. *Falkner*, I:75.

9. Alfred Thomas Story, *The Life of John Linnell*, 2 vols. (London: Bentley and Son, 1892), I:54. Story notes as an afterthought (p. 65) that Charles Clairmont also took lessons from Linnell. So little has been known of Mary's early years that Godwin has been reproached for giving Charles but not Mary instruction by Linnell.

10. MWS Journal, Dec. 2, 1834.

11. WG, *Thoughts Occasioned by the Perusal of Dr. Parr's Spital Sermon* (London: Taylor and Wilks, 1801), 81–82.

12. Lucy Aikin, *Epistles on Women* (London: J. Johnson, 1810), 80–81.

13. Jane West, *Letters to a Young Lady, in Which the Duties and Character of Women Are Considered* (Troy, N.Y.: O. Penniman and Co.; New York: I. Riley and Co. 1806), 28.

14. Mary Wollstonecraft, *The Wrongs of Woman: or, Maria. Posthumous Works of the Author of "A Vindication of the Rights of Woman,"* William Godwin, ed. (1798; rpt., 4 vols. in 2, Clifton, N.J.: Augustus M. Kelley, Publishers, 1972), II:147.

15. WG, *The Pantheon* (London: M.J. Godwin & Co., 1806), 63.

16. WG to Mary Jane Godwin, May 24, 1811, Paul, *Godwin*, II:185.

17. WG to Mary Jane Godwin, May 18, 1811, ibid., 184.

18. Letter to the author from C. E. Busson, Ramsgate Branch Libraries, Kent County Council. The former school building is now 66 High Street.

19. Mary Jane Godwin to WG, June 10, 1811, Abinger MSS.

20. *Shelley and his Circle*, III:75.

21. Two sheets in Mary's youthful hand on the subject as illustrated in ancient history, perhaps her draft for an essay, are among the Abinger MSS. The Egyptians' "hatred of innovation, the never-failing attendant on a mind which has learnt every thing from imitation, and nothing from itself, was the natural consequence of the arbitrary government they obeyed," whereas in the history of the ancient Greeks, "bred in liberty and independence," we find "the triumph of human nature." "The names of Ninus and Semiramis . . . are preserved by the bloody hallo [halo] with which glory and victory always decorate its worshippers. . . ."

22. WG to W. T. Baxter, June 8, 1812, *Shelley and his Circle*, III:100–101.

23. Marshall, *Mary Shelley*, I:33. Marshall interviewed the then aged Christina Baxter.

24. William John Fitzpatrick, *The Life, Times, and Contemporaries of Lord Cloncurry* (Dublin: J. Duffy, 1855), 516–517.

25. WG to ?, undated, Paul, *Godwin*, II:214.

26. *CC Journals*, 431. The Carl H. Pforzheimer Shelley and his Circle Collection has a lock of Mary's hair, probably somewhat faded in color, which she pinned to a letter to T. J. Hogg.

27. Dowden, *Shelley*, Appendix B, II:546.

28. The Rev. John Stirton, *Pastime Papers* (Farfor, Scotland: W. Shepherd, 1917), 98–99.

29. It is possible that all or some of the eight stories Godwin published in the two-volume *Parent's Offering* in late 1812 by "Mrs. Caroline Barnard" were written by Mary Godwin. As noted in Chapter 2, the family situation of young Matilda in "The Widower Remarried" pertains to Mary's. The heroine of Mary's *Matilda* (1819) has the same name. That might mean only that the earlier Matilda's story attracted her. But considering a normal development between "Mounseer Nong-tongpaw" at ten and *Frankenstein* at nineteen, she would have been capable of writing *The Parent's Offering*; indeed, one would expect her to write publishable stories. When she eloped with Shelley, she brought along her writings for him to see, and they could have been in book form. Moreover, as will appear, later stories by "Mrs. Barnard" published by Godwin dovetail with Mary's circumstances and his need for money.

30. See James Stuart, *Reminiscences* (London: privately printed, 1911), 51 and passim for information about the Baxters and Mary's stay by Isabel Baxter's grandson. See also *The Dundee Advertiser*, Sept. 7, 1897; later (less reliable) articles by A. H. Millar in *The Dundee Advertiser*, Dec. 2, 1911, *The Dundee Courier*, July 8, 1922, and *The Bookman* 62 (July 1922).

31. See John Graham Dalyell, *The Darker Superstitions of Scotland* (Glasgow: Griffin, 1835), passim, and 542. Mary may well have been told about, even have read about (in Thomas Pennant's *Tour in Scotland in 1772*), the alleged former existence of these gigantic humanoids who are so provocative of *Frankenstein*. One, a female, Cailleachvear, sent destructive tempests; another, a male or female called Glaslich, haunted the coast of Inverness-shire. Dalyell adds that a medieval scholar, Cassiano, reported similar beings on the Continent, known as Bacuceous and described as proud.

32. MWS to Jane Williams, May 31, 1823, *MWS Letters*, I:340.

33. George Gilfillan, "Mrs. Shelley," *Tait's Edinburgh Magazine* 14 (December 1847): 852.

34. *Matilda*, 11.

35. Rossetti, *Mrs. Shelley*, 62. Rossetti's informant, who apparently toured with Mary and the Baxters, was named Miller; he became an Edinburgh publisher and may have been connected with Constable.

36. *Falkner*, I:112.

37. *Shelley and his Circle*, III:105.

4 "MY CHOICE!"

1. *Lodore*, I:208–209.

2. Fanny Godwin to MWS, July 29, 1816, Dowden, *Shelley*, II:39.

3. Fanny Burney, *The Wanderer; or, Female Difficulties*, 5 vols. (London: Longman, Hurst, Rees, Orme, and Brown, 1814), I:403, 435.

4. *Rambles*, I:175.

5. Mary Wollstonecraft, *The Wrongs of Woman: or, Maria*, I:140.

6. Bodleian MS. Shelley adds. c. 5, folder 1, 1.

7. Hogg, *Shelley*, I:55–56.

8. Ibid., 96.

9. Note on *Queen Mab*, *PBS Poems*, I:98, 101.

10. Ibid., 99.

11. Peacock, *Memoirs*, VIII:95.

12. Harriet Shelley to Catherine Nugent, Jan. 24, [1815], *PBS Letters*, I:424, fn. 3.

13. PBS to T. J. Hogg, Oct. 3 [for 4], 1814, ibid., 402.

14. Percy Bysshe and Mary W. Shelley Notebook, Manuscript Division, Library of Congress.

15. Grylls, *Claire Clairmont*, Appendix D, 277.

16. *Lodore*, II:4.

17. Hogg, *Shelley*, II:147–148.

18. CC to EJT, Aug. 30–Sept. 21, 1878, *Shelley and his Circle*, IV:787.

19. PBS to T. J. Hogg, Oct. 3 [for 4], 1814, *PBS Letters*, I:402.

20. MWS Journal, June 8, 1824.

21. MWS note written into her copy of PBS's *Queen Mab*. This book is catalogued RP 114869 in the collections of the Huntington Library of San Marino, California; this and succeeding passages are reproduced by permission.

22. Huntington Library *Queen Mab*.

23. Peacock, *Memoirs*, VIII:92.

24. PBS to Harriet Shelley, July ?14, 1814, *PBS Letters*, I:390.

25. Mary Jane Godwin to Lady Mount Cashell, August or September 1814, Dowden, *Shelley*, Appendix B, II:543. Whereas there is no reason to doubt Mrs. Godwin's report in this and other instances, Dowden wisely warned that she deliberately perverted the truth in several important matters and, moreover, that her letters to Lady Mount Cashell exist only in copies heavily edited by the not always trustworthy Claire Clairmont.

26. Ibid., 544.

27. Mary Jane Godwin to Lady Mount Cashell (dated by Claire Clairmont Sept. 2, 1814, Aug. 16, or Aug. 20), Grylls, *Claire Clairmont*, Appendix D, 276–277.

28. CC to EJT, ca. 1870, Grylls, *Claire Clairmont*, Appendix C, 270.

29. MWS Journal, July 29, 1814.

5 "FRANCE . . ."

1. MWS, "The English in Italy," *CC Journals*, Appendix A, 442. A book review, this was originally published in the *Westminster Review* 12 (October 1826).

2. CC's Journal, Aug. 21, 1814, *Shelley and his Circle*, III:351.

3. MWS Journal, Aug. 7, 1814.

4. CC's Journal, Aug. 19, 1814, *Shelley and his Circle*, III:349. For the lovers' itinerary, see pp. 357–370.

5. Ibid., Aug. 18, 1814, 348.

6. Ida Saint Elme, in *Les Mémoires d'une Contemporaine* (Paris: Ladvocat, 1827–1828), 391–392, made up an episode in which Shelley gallantly gave up this "chambre d'honneur" to her when they supposedly met at Dessein's in 1820.

7. CC's Journal, Aug. 20, 1814, *Shelley and his Circle*, III:350.

8. Ibid., Aug. 18, 1814, 347.

9. Ibid., Sept. [Aug.] 19, 1814, 349.

10. MWS, *History of a Six Weeks' Tour* (London: T. Hookham, Jr., 1817), 49–50.

11. MWS Journal, Aug. 28, 1814.

12. PBS to Harriet Shelley, Sept. 14, 1814, *PBS Letters*, I:395.

13. "Motto" written inside the back cover of Journal Book I. Some seven years later, when Mary wanted Jane (then Clare) Clairmont to live independently, and Shelley wished Jane to stay, Jane jotted "3 still / Clare" inside the back cover of Shelley's notebook. Bodleian MS. Shelley e. 2.

14. MWS Journal, Sept. 25, 1814.

15. MWS to PBS, Oct. 25, [1814], *MWS Letters*, I:1.

16. PBS to MWS, Oct. 27, 1814, Nov. 1, 1814, *PBS Letters*, I:412, 415.

17. PBS to MWS, Oct. 27, 1814, *PBS Letters*, I:413.

18. MWS to PBS, Oct. 28, 1814, *MWS Letters*, I:3.

19. MWS to PBS, Nov. 3, 1814, ibid., 4–5.

20. MWS Journal, Dec. 8, 1814.

21. Ibid., Nov. 16, 1814.

22. Dowden, *Shelley*, I:508–509; Newman Ivey White, *Shelley*, 2 vols. (New York: Knopf, 1940), I:394–397.

23. MWS Journal, Oct. 14, 1814.

24. Ibid., Nov. 20, Nov. 29, 1814.

25. MWS to T. J. Hogg, Apr. 25, 1815, *MWS Letters*, I:12.

26. MWS to T. J. Hogg, Jan. 24, 1815, ibid., 9.

27. MWS to T. J. Hogg, Mar. 6, 1815, ibid., 11.

28. MWS to T. J. Hogg, Apr. 25, 1815, ibid., 12.

29. MWS to T. J. Hogg, Apr. 26, 1815, ibid., 14.

30. PBS to MWS, [?Summer 1815], *PBS Letters*, I:426.

31. MWS to PBS, July 27, 1815, *MWS Letters*, I:15.

6 "A TRANQUIL RESIDENCE . . ."

1. *The Last Man*, I:186.

2. Ibid., I:338.

3. PBS to MWS, Oct. 27, 1814, *PBS Letters*, I:413.

4. Note on *The Cenci*, *PBS Poems*, II:272.

5. CC to MWS, "Friday September" [1816, Bath], Abinger MSS.

6. PBS to W. T. Baxter, Dec. 30, 1817, *PBS Letters*, I:587.

7. CC to MWS, July 4, 1845, Abinger MSS.

8. CC to Byron [Spring 1816], Murray MSS.

9. PBS to T. J. Hogg, Nov. 28, 1817, *PBS Letters*, I:568. Shelley usually left his letters to Hogg open for Mary to add a note if she chose, which she rarely did.

10. Burke began with an account of history in terms of butcheries in each of a sequence of wars, totaling the dead at about 36 million. In one of her notebooks,

now in the Library of Congress, Mary added his figures and got 35,400,000.

11. See Jean de Palacio, "Mary Shelley's Latin Studies: Her Unpublished Translation of Apuleius," *Revue de littérature comparée* 38 (October–December 1964): 564–571.

12. The Faustian aspect of Victor Frankenstein has been thought to have filtered to Mary through Shelley's report to her via "Monk" Lewis, who had translated *Faust* and whom Shelley met in August 1816. However, she knew of *Faust* well before she conceived *Frankenstein*. De Staël includes Faust's evocation of the Earth Spirit and his despairing soliloquy as he contemplates suicide. Probably Mary chose Ingolstadt as young Frankenstein's university because de Staël identified it as the place where experimental scientific work was under way, and also as the headquarters of the political visionary Adam Weishaupt, founder of the Illuminati. Furthermore, de Staël remarks that hideous objects suggest evil by association, and that it is above all in the human form that we are taught what is extraordinary and unknown in the harmonies of mind and body.

13. *Frankenstein*, 1831, vi–vii.

14. See Godwin's descriptions of his and Wollstonecraft's association in the *Memoirs* and *St. Leon*.

15. PBS to MWS, Aug. 15, 1821, *PBS Letters*, II:335.

16. MWS to T. J. Hogg, Feb. 28, 1823, *MWS Letters*, I:316.

17. Prior to that time Shelley's poems featured the passionate girl of *Alastor* and Ianthe's "burning, moving" frame in "The Daemon of the World," both written at Bishopsgate; glowing Cythna in *The Revolt of Islam*, Helen's flaming union with Lionel in *Rosalind and Helen*, and the lovers' "mingled unreserve" in "The Sunset." His cooler image of Mary as the moon appears after 1819.

18. MWS Journal, Oct. 2, 1822.

19. Hunt, "Shelley," 199.

20. Thornton Hunt, from his unpublished "Proserpina," in Edmund Blunden, *Leigh Hunt* (London: Cobden-Sanderson, 1930), Appendix 2, 359.

21. PBS to MWS, Nov. 4, 1814, and PBS to T. J. Hogg, Oct. 4, 1814, *PBS Letters*, I:419, 403.

22. Note on *The Revolt of Islam*, *PBS Poems*, I:374. Mary does not specify when Shelley chose poetry over philosophy, but her journal shows that he studied the Greek, Italian, and English poets and portions of Scripture after their elopement, in London and Bishopsgate.

23. *Shelley and his Circle*, VII:1–12. Contrary to the accompanying Commentary, however, Peacock never seems to have regarded Mary's education before she met Shelley as imperfect.

24. See Richard Monckton-Milnes, Lord Houghton, Commonplace Book for 1842–1843, Houghton MSS #202: "Mrs. Shelley says she knew the horror that Coleridge meant to attach to the Ladie in Christabel was two eyes in her bosom."

25. "Monti," *Lives*, 1835–1837, II:310.

26. "Camoëns," ibid., III:313.

27. MWS Journal, Feb. 16, 1815.

28. CC to MWS, Sept. 16, 1834, Abinger MSS. Printed in Palacio, *Mary Shelley*, 264–265. Claire's own lying-in a year later would be miserable.

29. PBS to WG, Mar. 6, 1816, *PBS Letters*, I:459. Many of Shelley's letters to Godwin of this period were in Claire's possession at her death. Apparently she either took them from or was given them by the Godwins. On his letter to Godwin of Feb. 26–27 Shelley used his famous Judgment of Paris seal for the first time. Thereafter Mary and Claire would also use it on occasion.

30. PBS to WG, Mar. 29, 1816, *PBS Letters*, I:466.

31. Fanny Godwin to MWS, May 29, 1816, Dowden, *Shelley*, II:24.

32. CC to Byron, [March–April 1816], Murray MSS.

33. CC, Manuscript, *Shelley and his Circle*, VI:577.

34. CC to Byron, Sept. 29, 1816, Murray MSS.

35. Claire seems to have been frightened as the moment of truth, her first intercourse with Byron, approached; "On Saturday a few moments may tell you more than you yet know," she wrote him. "Till then I am content that you should believe me vicious and depraved." [Spring 1816], Murray MSS. Byron later wrote Douglas Kinnaird that "she *had not* lived with S[helley] during the time of our acquaintance" and therefore he had reason to think that her "brat" was his own. Byron to Douglas Kinnaird Jan. 20, 1817, *Byron Letters*, V:162.

36. CC to Byron, May 6, 1816, Murray MSS.

7 "SWITZERLAND — BATH"

1. MWS to Fanny Imlay, May 17, 1816, *MWS Letters*, I:18. Mary published this and a second letter, probably edited from the originals, in *History of a Six Weeks' Tour*.

2. "We debate with ourselves in wonder . . . ," Shelley wrote in an unpublished review; "what could have been the series of thoughts — what could have been the peculiar experiences that awakened them — which conduced, in the author's mind, to the astonishing combinations of motives and incidents, and the startling catastrophe, which compose this tale." *The Complete Works of Percy Bysshe Shelley*, newly edited by Roger Ingpen and Walter E. Peck, 10 vols. (New York: Gordian Press, 1965), VI:263. His wonderment was in part disingenuous, meant to disguise his relationship to Mary. Certainly he was astounded by her mastery of the "elementary feelings of the human mind," her "tremendous" and pathetic scenes, the novel's accumulating suspense and momentum. But he knew there were indeed "peculiar experiences" that galvanized her and that neither he nor she ever discussed publicly.

3. *Rambles*, I:139.

4. John Polidori, *The Diary of Dr. John William Polidori, Relating to Byron, Shelley, etc.*, William Michael Rossetti, ed. (London: Elkin Mathews, 1911), 99, 101, 106.

5. PBS to T. L. Peacock, May 15, 1816, *PBS Letters*, I:476. "Mary is engaged in writing . . ." She may have begun *The Prize; or The Lace-Makers of Missenden*, which Godwin published late that year as by Mrs. Caroline Barnard; it is noteworthy that Mary read several of Madame de Genlis's books for children at Geneva. When she had visited Peacock at Great Marlow from Bishopsgate, she had been struck by the plight of the female cottage workers who made lace. (See her Note on *The Revolt of Islam* in *PBS Poems*.) Set in Little Missenden, *The Prize* is a formula novelette with little social criticism, but striking connections with Mary. It features a model industrious girl and her flighty younger sister who gets into trouble because she fails to confide in the older girl, and a benevolent young squire and his wife who settle, as the Shelleys were to do, in a renovated local house. There is also a Quaker character named Pemberton; at Bishopsgate Shelley knew a Quaker, and his former doctor in London was named Pemberton.

In late September 1816, Shelley gave Godwin only two hundred of the three hundred pounds he had promised. Possibly Mary then proceeded to complete and send to Godwin her story so that he could publish it and make a hundred pounds from it. Her journal entry for Nov. 5 notes "£100" and "M.G. 100"; on December 6 "Letter from Mrs. G. & £100 — write to Mrs. G." Godwin might have offered to reimburse Mary, with whom he still refused any contact.

6. MWS Journal, July 22, 1816; MWS to Fanny Imlay, May 17, 1816, *MWS Letters*, I:18.

7. Emily W. Sunstein, "Louise Duvillard of Geneva, the Shelleys' Nursemaid,"

Keats-Shelley Journal 29 (1980): 27–30. Elise's mother had an infant William's age, who I conjecture was nicknamed "Aimée." Elise herself may possibly have had an illegitimate child named Aimée, but the very complete records of Geneva do not so indicate, and it is hard to imagine that Mary and Shelley would not have wished Elise to bring her child with her to England.

8. Mary would refer to this point in *Lives*, 1838–1839; see "Rousseau," II:129.

9. MWS to Fanny Imlay, June 1, 1816, *MWS Letters*, I:20.

10. MWS Journal, Sept. 3, 1824. The other men were probably Edward Williams and Prince Alexander Mavrocordato. In Thomas Medwin's notes for a possible second edition to his *Life of Percy Bysshe Shelley* (1847), he stated that everyone believed Byron's sonnets to Ginevra were written to Mary. Medwin, then antagonistic to Mary, added that she did not care for Byron's reference therein to the Magdalen. See Thomas Medwin's "Corrections and Emendations in the Life of Shelley," The Pierpont Morgan Library. Actually, Byron wrote these sonnets two years before meeting Mary.

11. MWS Journal, May 15, 1824.

12. Medwin claimed that Byron told him that Shelley married Mary because of Byron's persuasion.

13. Canto III records the summer's storms, sailing, conversations, the Wordsworthian sense of oneness with Nature that Shelley and Mary temporarily inspired in Byron, and her loving play with William, which made Byron regret his own Ada and possibly contributed to his current attempt to reconcile with Lady Byron. Mary later wrote an account of Geneva for Thomas Moore's *Life of Byron*.

14. Mary's copy of the third canto's first 111 lines — apparently made before Byron added the final verses addressed to his daughter — is in the University of London Library, S.L.C.V. 6. On it Byron noted: "This was copied out by M.W.G. from the original M.S. sent by me to England." He gave it to someone in Milan.

15. Polidori, *Diary*, June 18, 1816, 127.

16. Mary's 1831 Preface to *Frankenstein*, written sixteen years after the event, gives the gist of what she called "History of the Inconstant Lover," and of "Portraits de famille" in which a sinner is doomed to kill the children of his line. She remembered them because by then she had lost two children, and believed that fate had demanded their deaths as an atonement for Harriet Shelley's death. In two other stories, men are awakened by vengeful revenants opening their bedcurtains. James Rieger, in "Dr. Polidori and the Genesis of *Frankenstein*," *Studies in English Literature* 3 (1963): 461–472, has accused Mary of deception in the Preface. He takes Polidori's note of June 15 about a conversation with Shelley on "principles — whether man was merely an instrument" to be the conversation on the principle of life, in which case MWS had her nightmare the night after she claimed to have had it. But Polidori's diary is not perfectly accurate, and moreover the subject of the conversation sounds more like free will and determinism. Rieger also accuses her of concealing Polidori's influence on *Frankenstein*.

17. Thomas Moore, *Letters and Journals of Lord Byron: With Notices of his Life*, 2 vols. (London: John Murray, 1830), II:31.

18. Polidori, *Diary*, June 17, 1816, 125.

19. *Frankenstein*, 1831, ix.

20. Possibly at Geneva Mary saw Saint-Simon's early *Lettres d'un habitant de Genève* (1803), which assigns a leading role to scientists in the conflict between propertied and unpropertied classes and proposes that scientists should rule society.

21. *Frankenstein*, 1831, x–xi.

22. Muriel Spark has observed that Mary did not have the type of creative mind that generates its own flow of inspiration but rather depended on the fluctuating influence of external things. This includes places, names, literary influences.

23. Apparently having completed her previous journal notebook, which has been lost, Mary took a sketchbook (Bodleian MS. Shelley adds. e. 16) to Chamonix in which she made notes, later transcribing them into a new journal notebook, which she used until 1819.

24. MWS Journal, Aug. 21, 1816: "Shelley reads Milton."

25. The *New Monthly Magazine* 63 (Apr. 1, 1819), printed "The Vampyre" as by Byron. The editor states that he has in his possession the outline of "Miss M. W. Godwin's" tale, which Polidori had given one of his Genevan hostesses.

26. Fanny Godwin to MWS, Sept. 26, 1816, Dowden, *Shelley*, II:52.

27. CC to Byron, Sept. 29, 1816, Murray MSS.

28. PBS to Leigh Hunt, Dec. 8, 1816, *PBS Letters*, I:517.

29. CC to Byron, Sept. 12, 1816, Murray MSS.

30. CC to Byron, Sept. 29, 1816, ibid.

31. MWS to PBS, Dec. 5, 1816, *MWS Letters*, I:22.

32. Although it does not seem to be extant, Lady Shelley had Fanny Godwin's Oct. 8 letter to Mary as of Mar. 11, 1872, when she wrote Alexander Berry about it (letter in the Mitchell Library, Sydney, Australia). See also Burton R. Pollin, "Fanny Godwin's Suicide Re-examined," *Etudes Anglaises* 18, no. 3 (July–September 1965): 258–268.

33. *Frankenstein*, 1818, II:8. Justine Moritz does not appear in Victor's account of his boyhood, although later Elizabeth says that she was his favorite; possibly Mary created the character as a tribute to Fanny Godwin. The names Moritz and Krempe, Victor's professors, and Victor's subsequent trip to England are drawn from the travel book by Carl Moritz that she had previously read.

34. Probably because of Byron, whose grandfather had been a midshipman with Anson, Mary reread Anson's *Voyage* for its famous mutiny, an inspiration for the mutiny of Walton's crew, followed by Evert Ide's *Travels*, about his trip across Russia into Tartary, for its account of the icebound north. Doubtless she also recalled voyages she had heard about in Dundee.

35. Page 137 of the *Frankenstein* MS, Abinger MSS. In the first draft, initially meant to be two volumes, volume and chapter divisions differ from their final arrangement. Volume II began at the present third chapter of Volume II.

36. *Frankenstein*, 1831, xi. James Rieger declares that this is another of Mary's deceptions, because the extent of Shelley's assistance makes him not merely her editor but a "minor collaborator." *"Frankenstein" (The 1818 Text)*, James Rieger, ed. (Indianapolis: Bobbs Merrill, 1974), xliv.

E. B. Murray analyzes Shelley's revisions to Mary's draft of about half the novel (about one thousand words to her forty-four thousand — not counting the final twenty-five hundred, which are in his hand except for a few, and which he may have copied from her lost draft). "Shelley's Contribution to Mary's *Frankenstein*," *Keats-Shelley Memorial Bulletin* 29 (1978): 50–68. As Murray notes (correcting Rieger), Mary did not accept all of Shelley's suggestions, and herself revised a few of them. He finds that many of Shelley's changes are "creative," in that they "help to shape atmosphere, incident, character, reader-response."

But that is any editor's job; in this instance he was also a great poet. Even so, not all of Shelley's wording is necessarily for the better. Moreover, Mary made her own, often substantive changes in some six hundred places on the extant drafts. And Shelley shaped only one incident. Mary intended twenty-three-year-old Victor's father to tell him to take a vacation, during which he would decide to make the female in Scotland. Shelley recommended that Victor go to England for the purpose of creating the female, since Mary's gender led her to make Victor overly dependent upon his father's authority. Even in her revision, Victor needs his father's consent to the trip, just as he had waited impatiently at the university for his father to set the date for his return home.

Leonard Wolf states that while some of Shelley's emendations are substantive, they are "no more or less valuable than those that working writers accept from their editors." *The Annotated Frankenstein* (New York: Clarkson N. Potter, 1977), 3. Wolf is correct. That Shelley's editing was in no way vital to *Frankenstein* is why Mary did not mention it in her Preface.

37. This very long chapter was revised. The present Chapter VI of Volume II was originally V. For the story of the De Lacy son's fiancée, Safie, Mary consulted her mother's *Vindication of the Rights of Woman*. By December 15 Mary probably had finished at least the present Chapter VI.

38. MWS to PBS, Dec. 5, 1816, *MWS Letters*, I:22.

39. Ibid., 23.

40. PBS to MWS, Dec. 16, 1816, *PBS Letters*, I:520.

41. MWS to PBS, Dec. 17, 1816, *MWS Letters*, I:24–25.

42. PBS to Eliza Westbrook, Dec. 18, 1816, *PBS Letters*, I:523. For Harriet Shelley's suicide note, see *Shelley and his Circle*, IV:802.

43. Mrs. Godwin revealed the fullness of her hatred by writing Lady Mount Cashell that Mary had blackmailed Shelley into marriage by threatening to kill herself and little William, a lie Claire Clairmont repeated to Trelawny years after Mary's death.

44. MWS to PBS, Jan. 17, 1817, *MWS Letters*, I:28.

45. MWS to Byron, Jan. 13, 1817, ibid., 26.

46. Byron to Douglas Kinnaird, Jan. 20, 1817, *Byron Letters*, V:162.

47. In her journal, Mary copied Charles Lamb's poem to Hunt's son Thornton, written when Hunt was in prison for libeling the Prince Regent.

48. David Booth to Isabel Booth, Jan. 9, 1818, *Shelley and his Circle*, V:390–391.

49. *Frankenstein*, 1818, II:155. "Day after day, week after week, passed away . . . and I could not collect the courage to recommence my work," Victor begins the present Volume III, the first two chapters of which, particularly in manuscript, evidence a letdown in drive and control.

50. Ibid., III:177.

8 "Marlow"

1. Robert Southey to William Wordsworth, [May 5 and 8, 1817], *New Letters of Robert Southey*, Kenneth Currey, ed., 2 vols. (New York and London: Columbia University Press, 1965), II:156.

2. PBS to WG, Mar. 9, 1817, *PBS Letters*, I:535.

3. Henry Crabb Robinson, *On Books and Their Writers*, Edith J. Morley, ed., 3 vols. (London: J. M. Dent & Sons, 1938), I:204. Thornton Hunt, who turned seven this year, would recall almost fifty years later that Mary was not attractive in looks or dress at this time; Hunt, "Shelley," 189. But the opinion of Kenney, a man of the theater accustomed to handsome actresses, is surely more reliable. Thornton's memory may have been affected by the fact that Mary was pregnant and wore loose clothing.

4. MWS to PBS, May 29, 1817, *MWS Letters*, I:36.

5. Leigh Hunt to Vincent Novello, June 24, 1817, Charles and Mary Cowden Clarke, *Recollections of Writers* (1878; rpt. Fontwell, Sussex: Centaur Press, 1969), 197.

6. Noted (by Edward Silsbee?) in a Shelley notebook, MS Eng. 258.3, Hough-

ton Library, Harvard University. Through the notebook that Shelley gave Mary in May 1814 (now in the Library of Congress), one can visualize them at work. On various pages, sometimes turned wrong side up, it includes her translation of the *Aeneid* and Apuleius, his essay on game laws and Preface to *Frankenstein*, and Clare's Italian and Latin exercises.

7. *Falkner*, I:20.

8. Dowden, *Shelley*, II:123.

9. PBS to Lackington, Allen and Company, Aug. 22, 1817, *PBS Letters*, I:553.

10. PBS to Byron. Sept. 24, 1817, ibid., 557.

11. MWS to Leigh Hunt, Mar. 5, 1817, *MWS Letters*, I:32.

12. See Donald H. Reiman, "Shelley as Agrarian Reactionary," *Keats-Shelley Memorial Bulletin* 30 (1979): 5–15.

13. Byron to J. C. Hobhouse, May 11, 1820, *Byron Letters*, VII:99.

14. MWS to PBS, Sept. 30, 1817, *MWS Letters*, I:49.

15. MWS to PBS, Jan. 17, 1817, ibid., 27.

16. MWS to Marianne Hunt, Feb. 24, 1820, ibid., 136.

17. MWS to Leigh and Marianne Hunt, June 30, 1817, ibid., 38.

18. John Keats to Leigh Hunt, May 10, 1817, *The Correspondence of Leigh Hunt*, Thornton Hunt, ed., 2 vols. (London: Smith, Elder and Co., 1862), I:106.

19. Leigh Hunt to PBS and MWS, Nov. 16, 1821, ibid., 174.

20. Robert Southey to Bernard Barton, Nov. 26, 1822, *New Letters of Robert Southey*, II:240.

21. Leigh Hunt in *The Examiner*, Aug. 31, 1817, *Shelley and his Circle*, V:274.

22. CC to Byron, Jan. 12, 1818, Murray MSS.

23. David Booth to Isabel Booth, Jan. 9, 1818, *Shelley and his Circle*, V:392.

24. PBS to Byron, Apr. 23, 1817, *PBS Letters*, I:540.

25. MWS to PBS, Sept. 24, 1817, *MWS Letters*, I:41.

26. MWS to PBS, Sept. 28, 1817, ibid., 46.

27. PBS to MWS, Oct. 6, 1817, *PBS Letters*, I:561.

28. See Robert Buchanan, "Thomas Love Peacock: A Personal Reminiscence," *New Quarterly Magazine* 4 (April 1875): 248–249. Buchanan "fancied" that Peacock never liked Mary. Her daughter-in-law, Lady Shelley, would claim that Peacock told her (Lady Shelley) so himself, because Mary was uncivil to him and contradicted him. Peacock, to be sure, married a young woman who did not contradict him, but he seems to have become quite fond of Mary in their later association.

29. MWS to PBS, Sept. 24, 1817, *MWS Letters*, I:42–43. After this batch the extent of Shelley's corrections of *Frankenstein* proofs is not clear. He probably brought other batches when he came to Marlow on weekends, and may have done others himself before she joined him in London. Byron, too, had given Shelley authority to correct *Childe Harold*.

30. MWS to PBS, Sept. 30, 1817, *MWS Letters*, I:48.

31. MWS to PBS, Sept. 28, 1817, ibid., 45.

32. MWS to PBS, Oct. 18, 1817, ibid., 57.

33. CC to Byron, Jan. 12, 1818, Murray MSS.

34. The Shelleys' wish for anonymity in this work was shaky, and they bowed somewhat to convention. In his preface Shelley described the tour as one taken by the author and "her husband" and "sister"; Mary used their initials and signed her letters from Geneva "M.S." Everyone knew they had been in Geneva, scandalously unmarried, with Clare.

35. CC to MWS, July 4, 1845, Abinger MSS.

36. Shelley went so far as to sign this poem "Pleyel," a character in his favorite Charles Brockden Brown's *Wieland*, who loves a girl named Clara, marries another,

and after she dies in childbirth marries Clara. Similarly, when Clare changed her name to Claire, she may have been thinking of Claire, Julie's relative who loves the hero, in Rousseau's *Nouvelle Héloïse*.

37. PBS to Thomas Moore, Dec. 16, 1817, *PBS Letters*, I:583.

38. In one of his working notebooks (Bodleian MS. Shelley adds. e. 19) Shelley jotted, "See Clarke's Travel Peleponesus." Mary, who was reading Dr. Edward Clarke's *Travels in Various Countries of Europe, Asia, and Africa* in its entirety, started the fourth volume on Greece on Jan. 27, 1818. In his description of Epidaurus, Clarke mentions "a headless marble statue" and a local inhabitant who told him that only "a few broken pieces of marble" remained of a great king's palace and other important buildings (IV:120, 126). Mary may have recommended this to Shelley, who began "Ozymandias" on Feb. 14, 1818, and may have acknowledged her part by signing it "Glirastes." The title of another Shelley poem of this period, *Prince Athanase*, was probably inspired by Helen Maria Williams's nephew, Athanase C. L. Coquerel; Godwin had a copy of Williams's *The Charter* addressed to Athanase, which Mary may recently have seen at Skinner Street.

39. T. J. Hogg to John Frank Newton, Feb. 25, 1818, *Shelley and his Circle*, V:502. E. B. Murray claims that both Mary and Shelley were intent on keeping Shelley's "share" in the novel even more secret than her authorship, adducing her discard of a satiric passage about Oxford, which he had attended. But Murray himself notes that Shelley told Lackington that he had corrected the manuscript. Moreover, the Godwins read it, with Shelley's words written thereon; Claire Clairmont and others of the Shelleys' intimates must also have known about his editing. Mary properly discarded the passage because it was atonal, discursive, and puerile.

40. MWS to PBS, Oct. 18, 1817, *MWS Letters*, I:57.

41. Leigh Hunt to MWS, July 25–27, 1819, *Shelley and his Circle*, VI:846.

42. MWS to PBS, Sept. 24, 1817, *MWS Letters*, I:41.

9 "MILAN . . ."

1. MWS to Leigh and Marianne Hunt, Mar. 22, 1818, *MWS Letters*, I:63.

2. Bodleian MS. Shelley adds. c. 5, f. 92.

3. Here Mary had her first contact with Valperga, the Duchess of Valperga's palazzo being prominent in Turin.

4. CC to Byron, Apr. 27, 1818, Murray MSS.

5. *Valperga*, I:203.

6. MWS to EJT, Jan. 11, 1833, *MWS Letters*, II:181.

7. MWS to Marianne Hunt, Aug. 28, 1819, ibid., I:104.

8. "An Eighteenth Century Tale: A Fragment," *Collected Tales*, 346.

9. MWS to Maria Gisborne, June 15, 1818, *MWS Letters*, I:72–73.

10. MWS to Maria Gisborne, July 2, 1818, ibid., 74.

11. MWS to Maria Gisborne, July 26, 1818, ibid., 75.

12. To provide part of the five hundred pounds, possibly Mary wrote *The Fisher-Boy of Weymouth; to which are added, The Pet-Donkey, and The Sisters* at Bagni di Lucca, and sent it to Godwin, who published the work in 1819 as by Mrs. Caroline Barnard. The title story is reminiscent of Godwin's *Caleb Williams*.

13. Walter Scott, "Remarks on *Frankenstein, or The Modern Prometheus; A Novel*," *Blackwood's Edinburgh Magazine* 2 (March 1818): 611–620.

14. Anonymous review of *History of a Six Weeks' Tour, Blackwood's Edinburgh Magazine* 3 (July 1818): 412, 416.

15. PBS to MWS, Sept. 22, 1818, *PBS Letters*, II:40.

16. MWS to Sir Walter Scott, June 14, 1818, *MWS Letters*, I:71.

17. "Luigi Pulci," *Lives*, 1835–1837, I:178.

18. Mary's comment on *Rosalind and Helen (PBS Poems)* speaks of his view of love.

19. PBS to MWS, Aug. 23, 1818, *PBS Letters*, II:37–38.

20. Byron to John Cam Hobhouse, Nov. 11, 1818, *Byron Letters*, VI:76.

21. "Valerius," *Collected Tales*, 333.

22. *The Last Man*, I:355–356.

23. MWS Journal, Nov. 30, 1818.

24. MWS to Maria Gisborne, Jan. 22, 1819, *MWS Letters*, I:85.

25. *The Manuscripts of the Younger Romantics. A Facsimile Edition, with Scholarly Introductions, Bibliographical Descriptions, and Annotations*, Donald H. Reiman, ed., 3 vols. (New York and London: Garland Publishing, Inc., 1985), III:117. In this poem Shelley says that he will find no refuge until death in friendship or "love's caress," presumably Mary's, for the woman (Harriet) he would fold in "relenting love" is dead. He mentions another "wretch" battered by misfortunes like a northern shore by winter gales, apparently quoting Sophocles on Oedipus. Yet he takes heart in hope of an eventual end to the tyranny that has degraded Italy, and ends with the thought of finding some calm cove with those he loves.

26. MWS to Maria Gisborne, Jan. 22, 1819, *MWS Letters*, I:85–86.

27. Newman Ivey White, *Shelley*, 2 vols. (New York: Knopf, 1940), Appendix VII, II:547. Shelleyans have long hypothesized on the question of Elena's parentage: Elise's child by Shelley or Byron, which seems highly unlikely; or Claire's by Shelley, which is impossible. It seems more sensible to believe Shelley, who told Thomas Medwin and Byron that he took charge of the child to help a young married English lady who had fallen in love with him for his poetry, and whom he met again in Naples. Medwin seems to have known who she was.

28. MWS to Marianne Hunt, Mar. 12, 1819, *MWS Letters*, I:88–89.

29. *Valperga*, I:204, 206.

30. "Valerius," *Collected Tales*, 342. Mary begins at the legendary sites of the Bay of Baie, which she had seen in Naples, including the Sybil's cave with which she would introduce *The Last Man*. The tale foreshadows *Matilda*; frank, tender, Scottish-born young Lady Harley becomes like a daughter to Valerius; the story breaks off as she senses his love for her and becomes uneasy.

31. MWS to Maria Gisborne, Apr. 9, 1819, *MWS Letters*, I:93.

32. See *Shelley and his Circle*, VI:777–781. Polidori committed suicide the following year, possibly because his "Vampyre" had been attributed to Byron.

33. MWS to Jane Williams, May 31, 1823, *MWS Letters*, I:340.

34. MWS to Maria Gisborne, Apr. 9, 1819, ibid., 93–94.

35. MWS to Maria Gisborne, June 5, 1819, ibid., 99.

10 "LEGHORN . . ."

1. MWS to Marianne Hunt, Nov. 24, 1819, *MWS Letters*, I:114.

2. MWS Journal, May 31, 1823.

3. CC to Byron, Mar. 16, 1820, Murray MSS.

4. MWS to Marianne Hunt, June 29, 1819, *MWS Letters*, I:101–102.

5. MWS to Leigh Hunt, Sept. 24, 1819, ibid., 108.

6. MWS Journal, Oct. 10, 1822.

7. *Valperga*, III:45–46, 50–51.

8. CC to MWS, Sept. 11, 1835, Abinger MSS.

9. *Valperga*, I:172.

10. Bodleian MS. Shelley adds. e. 12. Mary saw these outpourings only after his death, though he showed some to friends. Included are "Invocation to Misery," "The Sunset," "That time is dead forever," his "Second Conscience" lines quoted later in this chapter, and later poems. In her 1824 and 1839 editions of his poems she misdated several poems from this notebook, since she had no firsthand knowledge of the precise time of their composition.

11. Shelley wrote "November 5th, 1817" on this poem, probably his faulty recollection of the date of Harriet Shelley's death rather than the date of composition. After Mary found these lines, she wrote an inexact version of them, possibly from memory, on the first page of Journal Book III as a motto.

12. See *Rosalind and Helen* and "The Sunset." In the latter poem, a lady finds her lover dead one morning in their bed, after which she returns to her old father, living on in gentle sadness, a "lost child." Since Shelley set the poem at Bishopsgate, Mary ascribed it to 1816, but from its affinity to *Rosalind and Helen*, its placement in his notebook, and the fact that Leigh Hunt published several lines in *The Literary Pocket-Book for 1823* (published in 1822), the poem may be dated 1819–1820.

13. *Matilda*, 98. This edition includes portions of "Fields of Fancy," the drafts of which are at the Bodleian and repay independent study since Mary wrote them during her initial, most immediate reaction to her children's deaths.

14. A slip of Mary's pen in "Fields of Fancy" suggests Matilda's seductive intent with her father: "Accept," Matilda says, "the pure heart of your unhappy father." Mary then crossed out "father" and substituted "daughter." Bodleian MS. Shelley adds. c. 5, folder 1, f. 1. In *Matilda*, Matilda's father gets rid of several of her suitors — none of them Woodville, whom she does not meet until two years after her father's death. The version in "Fields of Fancy" was too close to what had actually happened. Mary also seemed to associate Godwin with Shelley: Matilda later denies what there is no reason to assume, that Woodville "in no degree reminded me of my father." *Matilda*, 60.

15. *Matilda*, 64–65.

16. Note on Poems Written in 1818, *PBS Poems*, III:159.

17. Note on *Prometheus Unbound*, ibid., II:139.

18. *Matilda*, 16.

19. Ibid., 65.

20. MWS to Amelia Curran, Sept. 18, 1819, *MWS Letters*, I:106.

21. PBS to Leigh Hunt, Aug. 15, 1819, *PBS Letters*, II:109.

22. WG to MWS, Sept. 9, 1819, Abinger MSS.

23. Maria Gisborne to MWS, Oct. 11, 1819, *Gisborne, Williams*, 53. The Shelleys left a crate of books with Mrs. Gisborne when they left Leghorn. For Mary's list of some of the contents, see Jean de Palacio, "Shelley's Library Catalogue," *Revue de littérature comparée* 36 (April–June 1962): 272–276.

24. Mrs. Mason [Lady Mount Cashell] to MWS, [late 1819], Abinger MSS.

25. MWS to Maria Gisborne, c. Nov. 13, 1819, *MWS Letters*, I:112.

26. Helen R[ossetti] Angeli, *Shelley and His Friends in Italy* (1911; rpt. New York: Haskell House, 1973), 98.

27. PBS to WG, Aug. 7, 1820, *PBS Letters*, II:227.

28. MWS to Maria Gisborne, Dec. 2, 1819, and MWS to Marianne Hunt, Nov. 24, 1819, *MWS Letters*, I:118, 114.

29. Mrs. Mason to PBS, "Friday 21," Abinger MSS.

30. MWS to Maria Gisborne, Jan. 12, 1820, *MWS Letters*, I:123–124.

31. MWS to Maria Gisborne, Jan. 18, 1820, ibid., 126.

32. MWS Journal, Oct. 27, 1822.

33. Abinger MSS. Mary also did a synopsis of the First Book of Samuel, probably

on reading Spinoza, who used it to illustrate the difference between primitive history and spurious revelation from divine and spiritual inspiration. The Shelleys supported the contemporary Zionist movement to reestablish "the ancient republic of Jews according to the Mosaic law," which they may have heard of in Leghorn where there was a large Sephardic community. See *The Shelley Memorial Volume*, by Members of the English Club, Imperial University of Tokyo (Tokyo, 1923), 188.

34. Review of *The Revolt of Islam*, *Quarterly Review* 21 (April 1819): 467–468.

35. Anonymous, *Don Juan: With a biographical Account of Lord Byron and His Family; Anecdotes of His Lordship's Travels and Residence in Greece, at Geneva, Etc. Including, Also, a Sketch of the Vampyre Family* (London: William Wright, 1819). This work includes a reference to Mary's *Frankenstein* nightmare in Geneva. "There Frankenstein was hatched — the wretch abhorred, / Whom shuddering Sh—— saw in horrid dress." Last names of women were commonly used in such poems.

36. MWS to Maria Gisborne, Jan. 12, 1820, *MWS Letters*, I:124.

37. MWS to Marianne Hunt, Mar. 24, 1820, ibid., 137–138.

38. *Matilda*, 55.

39. MWS to Maria Gisborne, Apr. ?24 or 25, 1820, *MWS Letters*, I:144.

40. *Gisborne, Williams*, 27.

41. Ibid., 44.

42. PBS to John and Maria Gisborne, Mar. 11, 1820, David M. Stocking and Marion Kingston Stocking, "New Shelley Letters in a John Gisborne Notebook," *Keats-Shelley Memorial Bulletin* 31 (1980): 2–3.

43. Bodleian MS. Shelley adds. e. 12, f. 103a.

44. *CC Journals*, Jan. 11 and Feb. 8, 1820, 116–117, 123.

45. Mary probably knew about Elena by the winter of 1820–21. Shelley may have hoped to put Elena with Leghorn guardians until he could introduce her into his family, but the Naples foster parents seem to have retained her to extract money. Shelley mentions Elena's death in a letter to the Gisbornes supposedly written July ?7, 1820 (*PBS Letters*, II:210–212), which some scholars believe he gave Mary to enclose in hers of July 7 to the Gisbornes. But Shelley mentions an episode of July 2 that occurred between Mrs. Gisborne and Muzio Clementi, which he could not have known about on July 7. The enclosure more probably was his poem "Letter to Maria Gisborne."

46. PBS to WG, Aug. 7, 1820, *PBS Letters*, II:224.

47. Marcel Kessel, in his "The Mark of X in Claire Clairmont's Journal," *PMLA* 66 (December 1951): 1180–1183, detected Claire's record of her menstrual periods in her journal during the time in question.

48. *CC Journals*, July 3 and 4, 1820, 153.

49. PBS to WG, Aug. 7, 1820, *PBS Letters*, II:228.

50. MWS to Maria Gisborne, July 7, 1820, *MWS Letters*, I:153.

51. MWS to Maria Gisborne, July 19, 1820, ibid., 156.

52. Pietro Baratti, "Shelley, Longfellow, Petrarca, Il Vecchio Cimitero Inglese," *Liburni Civitas* (Leghorn: Rassegna di attivita municipale, 1928), 132.

11 "Solitude . . ."

1. MWS Journal, Oct. 9, 1827. Author's translation.

2. Ibid., Dec. 31, 1822.

3. MWS to Maria Gisborne, Oct. 16 or 17, 1820, *MWS Letters*, I:161.

4. *Valperga*, I:34.

5. Thomas Medwin, "Memoir of Shelley," *The Athenaeum* No. 249 (Aug. 4, 1832): 503–504.

6. MWS Journal, May 31, 1823. Thus also Matilda: "Never for one moment when most placid did I cease to pray for death"; *Matilda*, 52.

7. MWS Journal, Oct. 10, 1822.

8. *The Last Man*, II:17–18.

9. MWS Journal, undated; Book 3, third from last page.

10. *Valperga*, I:197.

11. Shelley and others compared Castruccio with Napoleon, but Mary thought of Napoleon as ambition incarnate from the beginning; it was Castruccio's gradual corruption that interested her. Claire stated that Castruccio was Byron and Euthanasia Shelley, but she had Byron and Shelley on the brain. Castruccio is a calculating, ruthless politician, unlike capricious Byron. Though Shelley shared Euthanasia's political principles, he was her opposite in temperament, closer to Beatrice in febrility and self-deluding imagination. Beatrice is often identified with Claire, but much about her corresponds to Mary.

12. MWS Journal, Feb. 8, 1822.

13. Note on Poems of 1820, *PBS Poems*, IV:53.

14. Houghton Library MSS. Eng. 258.2.

15. PBS to CC, Oct. 29, 1820, *PBS Letters*, 2:242.

16. MWS to Leigh Hunt, Dec. 29, 1820, *MWS Letters*, I:171.

17. Ibid.

18. MWS to Leigh Hunt, Dec. 3, 1820, ibid., 166.

19. Emilia Viviani to MWS, Dec. 24, 1820, Newman Ivey White, *Shelley*, 2 vols. (New York: Knopf, 1940), II:476.

20. After Shelley's death Mary came across one of his jottings, which she copied in a notebook with other fragments and which may date from this period: "I more esteem / Her whom I love than that which I desire." Bodleian MS. Shelley adds. d. 7, Item 39.

21. MWS to CC, Apr. 2, 1821, *MWS Letters*, I:187.

22. MWS to Maria Gisborne, c. Feb. 14, 1821, ibid., 183.

23. Prince Alexander Mavrocordato to MWS, Apr. 3, 1821, Abinger MSS.

24. Charles E. Robinson, "The Shelleys to Leigh Hunt: A New Letter of 5 April 1821," *Keats-Shelley Memorial Bulletin* 31 (1980): 54; see also Robinson, "Shelley to the Editor of the *Morning Chronicle*: A Second New Letter of 5 April 1821," *Keats-Shelley Memorial Bulletin* 32 (1981): 55–58.

25. MWS to Leigh Hunt, Apr. 17, 1821, *MWS Letters*, I:189.

26. Note on Poems of 1820, *PBS Poems*, IV:54.

27. Note on Poems of 1821, ibid., 152.

28. MWS to Maria Gisborne, May 28, 1821, *MWS Letters*, I:200.

29. PBS to CC, June 16, 1821, *PBS Letters*, II:303.

30. Bodleian MS. Shelley adds. c. 12, 23 r–v.

31. MWS to Jane Williams, Dec. 5, 1822, *MWS Letters*, I:297.

32. MWS Journal, May 31, 1823.

33. Bodleian MS. Shelley adds. e. 17, f. 3.

34. PBS to MWS, Aug. 8, 1821, *PBS Letters*, II:324.

35. For one, see the Paris-published quarterly *Revue Encyclopédique; où, analyse raisonnée des productions les plus remarquables dans la littérature, les sciences, et les arts* 11 (July 1821).

36. In her 1824 edition of Shelley's poems, Mary attributed this poem to June 1814; in her 1839 edition to 1821. She probably corrected the date after having considered the fact that Shelley wrote the poem in a notebook he used from the earliest, 1816–1821.

37. PBS to MWS, Aug. 7, 1821, *PBS Letters*, II:319.

38. MWS to Isabella Hoppner, Aug. 10, 1821, *MWS Letters*, I:206–207.

39. MWS to PBS, Aug. 10, 1821, ibid., 204.

40. PBS to MWS, Aug. 16, 1821, *PBS Letters*, II:339.

12 "PISA . . ."

1. Inventory of the Shelleys' household goods, which Byron purchased in August 1822, in order to help Mary Shelley financially. Abinger MSS.

2. CC to MWS, March 1834, Abinger MSS. This letter was written after Claire discovered from Mrs. Mason that Shelley had spoken slightingly about her to people other than Byron. She advises Mary to "Accept of friendship all that it has of sweet and bury the rest in oblivion. I had once a friend [Shelley] whom I loved entirely and who certainly loved me much; yet immense were the lies he told of me: I regard this not — he was great and above all pure-minded and I love him still as if he had never spoken ill of me . . . one feels enobled by being the victim of necessity. I wish I could be as blessed with the lies told to me as with those told of me."

3. Teresa Guiccioli to Byron, Sept. 27, 1821, Abinger MSS.

4. MWS to Marianne Hunt, Mar. 5, 1822, *MWS Letters*, I:221.

5. Mary's memory seems to have failed her in the early 1840s, when she stated in *Rambles* that she had recently seen "Cinque Maggio" for the first time. Medwin remembered her reading it in Pisa, and a copy, not in her hand, is included among other poems in the Abinger MSS grouped as "Verses Addressed to Mrs. Shelley."

6. MWS to Maria Gisborne, Feb. 9, 1822, *MWS Letters*, I:218.

7. William St. Clair, *Trelawny: The Incurable Romancer* (New York: Vanguard Press, 1977), 34.

8. EJT to MWS, November 1822, Marshall, *Mary Shelley*, II:49.

9. MWS to EJT, Jan. 7 and 31, 1823, *MWS Letters*, I:303, 310.

10. EJT, *Recollections of the Last Days of Shelley and Byron* (Boston: Ticknor and Fields, 1858), 28–29. Trelawny also writes that Mary was "mournful in solitude" and happy in society, but this is a retrospection rather than fact as of 1822.

11. Jane Williams, "A fragment —," *CC Journals*, Appendix D, 479.

12. "Portrait de Mme. Shelley par le Comte de Metaxa," Abinger MSS.

13. MWS Journal, Feb. 8, 1822.

14. MWS to Maria Gisborne, Jan. 18, 1822, *MWS Letters*, I:214.

15. Emily W. Sunstein, "Shelley's Answer to Leslie's *Short and Easy Method with the Deists*, and Mary Shelley's Answer, 'The Necessity of a Belief in the Heathen Mythology to a Christian,'" *Keats-Shelley Memorial Bulletin* 32 (1981): 53.

16. MWS to Leigh and Marianne Hunt, Jan. 25, 1822, *MWS Letters*, I:217.

17. MWS to Maria Gisborne, Jan. 18, 1822, ibid., 215.

18. MWS to Leigh Hunt, Apr. 13, 1822, ibid., 234.

19. MWS to Maria Gisborne, Feb. 9, 1822, ibid., 218.

20. Bodleian MS. Shelley adds. c. 12, f. 25.

21. Dowden, *Shelley*, II:465.

22. MWS and PBS to CC, [Mar. 20, 1822], *MWS Letters*, I:226, and *PBS Letters*, II:400.

23. PBS to John Gisborne, Apr. 10, 1822, ibid., 406.

24. *Shelley's The Triumph of Life: A Critical Study. Based on a Text Newly Edited from the Bodleian Manuscript*, Donald H. Reiman, ed. (Urbana: University of Illinois Press, 1965), 242. See also pp. 119–121.

25. PBS to John Gisborne, June 18, 1822, *PBS Letters*, II:435.

26. Leigh Hunt to Elizabeth Kent, *Shelley and Keats as They Struck Their Contemporaries*, Edmund Blunden, ed. (London: C. W. Beaumont, 1925), 56.

27. MWS to Jane Williams, May 31, 1823, *MWS Letters*, I:341.

28. *Gisborne, Williams*, 137.

29. PBS to CC, May 28, 1822, *PBS Letters*, II:427.

30. Mrs. Mason to PBS, undated, Abinger MSS.

31. *Perkin Warbeck*, III:169–170.

32. *Gisborne, Williams*, 162.

33. PBS to Mary Jane Godwin, May 29, 1822, *PBS Letters*, II:428.

34. MWS to Maria Gisborne, June 2, 1822, *MWS Letters*, I:236.

35. Leigh Hunt to Elizabeth Kent, c. August 1823, #3:35, Keats-Shelley Memorial House, Rome.

36. EJT, *Recollections*, 125.

37. MWS to Maria Gisborne, Aug. 15, 1822, *MWS Letters*, I:244.

38. MWS to Leigh Hunt, [c. June 30, 1822], ibid., 238.

39. MWS to Maria Gisborne, Aug. 15, 1822, ibid., 246.

40. Ibid., 246–247.

41. *Lady Blessington's Conversations with Lord Byron*, Ernest J. Lovell, Jr., ed. (Princeton: Princeton University Press, 1969), 53.

42. EJT to Byron, [July 13, 1822], Rosenbach Library and Museum.

43. "The Evil Eye," *Collected Tales*, 110.

44. MWS to Maria Gisborne, c. Aug. 27, 1822, *MWS Letters*, I:254.

13 "MAGNIFICENT . . ."

1. Byron to John Murray, Aug. 3, 1822, *Byron Letters*, IX:189.

2. MWS Journal, Oct. 5, 1822.

3. MWS to Thomas Medwin, July 29, 1822, *MWS Letters*, I:243.

4. MWS to Maria Gisborne, c. Aug. 27, 1822, ibid., I:252.

5. Ibid., 252, 254.

6. Ibid., 253.

7. Byron to MWS, Sept. 10, 1822, *Byron Letters*, IX:205.

8. Mary Shelley, "On Ghosts," *London Magazine* 9 (March 1824): 254.

9. MWS to Jane Williams, Sept. 18, 1822, *MWS Letters*, I:264.

10. MWS to Jane Williams, Dec. 5, 1822, ibid., 297.

11. MWS to Maria Gisborne, Sept. 17, 1822, ibid., 261.

12. Mrs. Thomas's note in a copy of *Frankenstein*, now in the Pierpont Morgan Library, which Mary annotated in Albaro and gave her on leaving Italy; Mrs. Thomas, among other kindnesses, agreed to forward back to England Shelley's manuscripts, which Peacock had already shipped.

13. Leigh Hunt to Elizabeth Kent, Nov. 7, 1822, *The Correspondence of Leigh Hunt*, Thornton Hunt, ed., 2 vols. (London: Smith, Elder and Co., 1862), I:200.

14. MWS to Jane Williams, Sept. 18, 1822, *MWS Letters*, I:264. Mary was privately critical of Mrs. Wright for endangering Trelawny in this affair. Mrs. Wright wrote Mary several notes, now among the Abinger MSS.; Mrs. Thomas was so annoyed by Mrs. Wright's importunities that she broke off their acquaintance.

15. Mary adapted bits of this journal for a fragment of her biography of Shelley the following March. In her first entry and another in 1834, she noted that no one would ever see her journals postdating his death. Skeptics may say this was for effect for future readers, but such posturing would be out of character. By spring 1835 she decided to preserve these journals under circumstances that will appear. She always intended to preserve the journals written before Shelley's death.

16. MWS Journal, Oct. 5, 1822.

17. Ibid., Oct. 2, 1822.

18. MWS to Maria Gisborne, Nov. 22, 1822, *MWS Letters*, I:290.

19. MWS Journal, Oct. 10, 1822.

20. Ibid., Oct. 21, Nov. 17, 1822.

21. MWS to Maria Gisborne, Nov. 22, 1822, *MWS Letters*, I:291.

22. MWS Journal, Oct. 21, 1822.

23. Mary had read Pietro Giannone, *Storia civile del regno di Napoli* (1723) for *Valperga*.

24. Quoted in William H. Marshall, *Byron, Shelley, Hunt, and The Liberal* (Philadelphia: University of Pennsylvania Press, 1960), 159–160.

25. Hunt wrote the table of contents of the second issue of *The Liberal* into Mary's workbook (Bodleian MS. Shelley d. 1), apparently while they were working together. She wanted Hunt to publish Trelawny's account of Shelley's funeral rites (which Hunt considered too gruesome), and hoped that Medwin might also publish in the magazine.

26. MWS to EJT, Jan. 31, 1823, *MWS Letters*, I:309.

27. W. M. Rossetti later believed that Mary had hopes of Trelawny, in the mistaken belief that she used Shelley's Judgment of Paris seal only when writing Trelawny. But Mary also used this seal in letters to others.

28. Hogg, *Shelley*, I:vi–vii. Hogg edited these fragments. "Sits umpire my Conscience," she wrote originally, and substituted "Love" for "my Conscience." Bodleian MS. Shelley adds c. 5, f. 114v. It has been conjectured that her fragments, dated Feb. 10, about Shelley's Eton days might have been written in England in 1825, but Dr. Bruce Barker-Benfield, Assistant Librarian of the Bodleian, has found that they were written on Italian paper. Letter to the author, Jan. 30, 1986.

29. MWS to Jane Williams, Dec. 5, 1822, *MWS Letters*, I:295.

30. MWS to Jane Williams, Jan. 12, 1823, ibid., 306.

31. MWS Journal, Dec. 31, 1822.

32. MWS to Jane Williams, Jan. 12, 1823, *MWS Letters*, I:304, 305.

33. Bodleian MS. Shelley adds. d. 5, f. 4. This item consists of *The Literary Pocket-Book for 1822*, published by Hunt, which Mary was using as a memorandum book, pp. 47–126 passim.

34. MWS to Jane Williams, Apr. 10, 1823, *MWS Letters*, I:330.

35. Mary Shelley, "Giovanni Villani," *The Liberal* 4 (1823): 283, 284. At this time the Classic-Romantic controversy was highly politicized in Italy. The young, among them Giuseppi Mazzini, who was then in Genoa, accused the classicists of supporting "Literary Despotism."

Although it has been attributed to her, Mary did not write "A Narrative of a Tour round the Lake of Geneva," published in *La Belle Assemblée*, n.s. 28 (July 1823). The itinerary differs from hers of 1816; she did not climb the Col de Balme. Nor could she have seen Frederick Clissol's Mont Blanc expedition on August 18, 1822. Letter to the author from Bernard Cottard of Les Amis de Vieux Chamonix.

36. MWS to Byron, Feb. 25, 1823, *MWS Letters*, I:315–316.

37. MWS to Jane Williams, May 31, 1823, ibid., 341.

38. MWS to T. J. Hogg, Feb. 28, 1823, ibid., 318.

39. MWS Journal, Mar. 17, 1823.

40. MWS to Jane Williams, Mar. 7, 1823, *MWS Letters*, I:320.

41. MWS to T. J. Hogg, Feb. 28, 1823, ibid., 319.

42. MWS to Jane Williams, Apr. 10, 1823, ibid., 331. "Hunt a deist," she notes, "L. B. if anything an an[glican]." Bodleian MS. Shelley adds. d. 5, f. 4, p. 15.

43. MWS to Jane Williams, May 31, 1823, *MWS Letters*, I:342.

44. Leigh Hunt to Elizabeth Kent, c. August 1823, #3:35, Keats-Shelley Memorial House, Rome.

45. Leigh Hunt to Elizabeth Kent, *Shelley and Keats as They Struck Their Contemporaries*, Edmund Blunden, ed. (London: C. W. Beaumont, 1925), 57.

46. MWS to Jane Williams, July 2, 1823, *MWS Letters*, I:344.

47. MWS to Teresa Guiccioli, July ?2–10, 1823, ibid., 346.

48. MWS Journal, June 3, 1823.

14 "THE REGIONS . . ."

1. MWS to Leigh and Marianne Hunt, July 30, 1823, *MWS Letters*, I:355.

2. Ibid., 356.

3. MWS to Leigh Hunt, Sept. 9, 1823, ibid., 378.

4. Ibid., 379. Interestingly, that winter M.J. Godwin & Co. reissued Mrs. Caroline Barnard's *The Prize* in an "improved" edition.

5. Leigh Hunt to Vincent Novello, July 24, 1823, Charles and Mary Cowden Clarke, *Recollections of Writers* (New York: Charles Scribner's Sons, 1878), 218–219.

6. MWS to Leigh Hunt, Oct. 2–5, 1823, *MWS Letters*, I:393.

7. T. J. Hogg to Jane Williams, Apr. 17, 1823, Abinger MSS.

8. "Petrarch," *Lives*, 1835–1837, I:70.

9. MWS to Leigh Hunt, Oct. 2–5, 1823, *MWS Letters*, I:393.

10. MWS to EJT, Mar. 22, 1824, ibid., 415.

11. MWS to Leigh Hunt, Oct. 20, 1823, ibid., 398.

12. MWS Journal, Dec. 15, 1823.

13. In *Revue Encyclopédique* 22 (October 1823): 132–133, Anne Louise Swanton-Belloc judged *Valperga* inferior to *Frankenstein*, and MWS's Romanticism and her picture of medieval customs, etc., unconvincing. "On aime son talent, son style énergétique, ses images variés, tour-a-tour sombres ou brilliantes, sa peinture si forte de passions les plus exaltées, mais on sent qu'elle manque à tout cela le charme de la verité."

14. See MWS to James Hessey and John Taylor, editors of the *London*, forwarding a tale she expected them to insert in their coming issue (*MWS Letters*, III:401).

15. MWS to Leigh Hunt, Sept. 18, 1823, *MWS Letters*, I:384.

16. MWS to Marianne Hunt, Nov. 27, 1823, ibid., 403.

17. Rennie, *Traits*, II:111.

18. MWS to Marianne Hunt, Nov. 27, 1823, *MWS Letters*, I:403.

19. Edward Holmes to Leigh Hunt, British Library, MSS. 38523, f. 89.

20. See "Beauty's Tear," "Pity's Tear," "The Mother's Tear," Abinger MSS.

21. Clarke, *Recollections of Writers*, 37–38.

22. MWS to Marianne Hunt, Nov. 27, 1823, *MWS Letters*, I:404.

23. MWS to Leigh Hunt, Sept. 18, 1823, ibid., 384.

24. Harriet de Boinville to MWS, Oct. 16, 1829, Abinger MSS.

25. MWS to EJT, July 28, 1824, *MWS Letters*, I:438.

26. *Conversations of James Northcote*, William Hazlitt, ed., *The Collected Works of William Hazlitt*. A. R. Waller and Arnold Glover, eds., 12 vols. (London: J. M. Dent and Co., 1903), VI:334.

27. Thomas Allsop, *Letters, Conversations and Recollections of S. T. Coleridge* (New York: Harper, 1836), 132. None of the other relevant Titians in the Louvre (two Madonnas, *Fête Champêtre*, *Allegoria*, and the Pardo Venus) have the serene, contemplative, somewhat remote smile that, according to many of Mary Shelley's contemporaries, was her usual expression, and that Shelley referred to in "The Witch of Atlas" and *Epipsychidion*.

28. Alan Lang Strout, "Knights of the Burning Epistle," *Studia Neophilogica* 26 (1953–1954): 90.

29. In 1834 Henry Crabb Robinson asked Mrs. Hoppner about Mary's and Byron's love affair.

30. Mary Shelley, "The English in Italy," *CC Journals*, Appendix A, 444. Originally published in *Westminster Review* 6 (October 1826).

31. T. J. Hogg to Jane Williams [July 1823], *After Shelley: The Letters of Thomas Jefferson Hogg to Jane Williams*, Sylva Norman, ed. (London: Oxford University Press, Humphrey Milford, 1934), 16.

32. Paul, *Godwin*, I:82.

33. Elizabeth Rumble to Richard Garnett, July 25, 1877, *Letters about Shelley from the Richard Garnett Papers*, William Richard Thurman, Jr., ed. (University of Texas, Ph.D. dissertation, August 1972), 367. Miss Rumble, the Gisbornes' housekeeper, who disliked Mary, added that she could not keep any of her Italian servants, whereas Mary's Maria was still sending messages in 1834 that she was eager to return to Mary's service whenever she came back to Italy.

34. Cyrus Redding, *Fifty Years' Recollections, Literary and Personal, with Observations on Men and Things*, 3 vols. (Charles J. Skeet: London, 1858), II:338, notes that a circle of women writers and "Blues" met once a week at one another's homes to exchange ideas, and that Lady Caroline Lamb and Lady Charlotte Bury and others provided a link between noble and middle-class literatae. See also Anna Laetitia [Aikin] Le Breton, *Memories of Seventy Years . . .*, Mrs. Herbert Martin, ed. (London, Edinburgh: Griffith & Farran, 1883).

35. MWS Journal, Jan. 18, 1824.

36. I am indebted to William St. Clair for this information.

37. MWS Journal, Sept. 5, 1826.

38. WG to MWS, Feb. 27, 1824, Marshall, *Mary Shelley*, II:108.

39. MWS to John Howard Payne, Jan. 28, 1826, *MWS Letters*, I:510.

40. MWS to EJT, Mar. 22, 1824, ibid., 415, 417.

41. Cyrus Redding, *Yesterday and To-day*, 2 vols. (London: T. C. Newby, 1863), II:149. Redding's favorable review of Godwin's work in the *New Monthly Magazine*, published by Colburn, had been altered by the senior editor, Thomas Campbell.

42. MWS to Teresa Guiccioli, May 16, 1824, *MWS Letters*, I:421.

43. For Mary as Shelley's literary executor and editor, see the commentaries of Donald H. Reiman, ed., in *The Manuscripts of the Younger Romantics. A Facsimile Edition, with Scholarly Introductions, Bibliographical Descriptions, and Annotations*, 3 vols. (New York and London: Garland Publishing, Inc., 1985).

44. Philip Rieff, *Freud: The Mind of the Moralist*, 3d ed. (Chicago: University of Chicago Press, 1959), Preface to First Edition, xiv.

15 "The Union of Kentish Town"

1. MWS to EJT, July 28, 1824, *MWS Letters*, I:436–437.

2. Washington Irving, July 17, 1824, "French Journal, 1823–1826," *The Complete Works of Washington Irving*, Henry A. Pochmann, gen. ed., *Journals and Notebooks*, vol. III, Walter A. Reichart, ed., (Madison: University of Wisconsin Press, 1969), III:366.

3. Mary Cowden Clarke, *Letters to an Enthusiast* (Chicago: A. C. McClurg & Co., 1902), 144.

4. MWS to Marianne Hunt, Oct. 10, 1824, *MWS Letters*, I:453.

5. MWS to Leigh Hunt, Aug. 22, 1824, ibid., 444.

6. Thomas Lovell Beddoes to Thomas Forbes Kelsall, Aug. 25, 1824, *The Letters of Thomas Lovell Beddoes*, Edmund Gosse, ed. (1894; rpt. New York: Benjamin Blom, Inc., 1971), 35.

7. MWS to Leigh Hunt, Aug. 22, 1824, *MWS Letters*, I:445. Gamba showed

Mary the poem Byron had composed on his last birthday, which she copied into her third journal notebook.

8. Ibid.

9. Doris Langley Moore, *The Late Lord Byron* (London: John Murray, 1961), 101.

10. MWS to Teresa Guiccioli, Dec. 30, 1824, *MWS Letters*, I:460.

11. MWS to Arthur Brooke, June 20, 1824, ibid., 429.

12. MWS to T. J. Hogg, Oct. 3, 1824, ibid., 450.

13. Ibid.

14. Sir Timothy Shelley to William Whitton, Apr. 1, 1827. Bodleian MS. Shelley adds. d. 14, f. 12v.

15. MWS to T. J. Hogg, Oct. 3, 1824, *MWS Letters*, I:449.

16. MWS to T. J. Hogg, Aug. 30, 1824, ibid., 446.

17. MWS to Teresa Guiccioli, Dec. 30, 1824, ibid., 460.

18. Frances Wright to MWS, Sept. 29, 1827, Abinger MSS.

19. Jane Williams wrote Claire Clairmont that she had discarded an unnamed lover; Claire replied that it was a pity he did not please Jane.

20. J. H. Payne to Washington Irving, undated, *The Romance of Mary W. Shelley, John Howard Payne and Washington Irving*, with remarks by F. B. Sanborn (Boston: Boston Bibliophile Society, 1907), 28.

21. MWS to EJT, Oct. 12, 1835, *MWS Letters*, II:256.

22. MWS to Leigh Hunt, Apr. 8, 1825, ibid., I:477.

23. MWS to Teresa Guiccioli, Mar. 6, 1825, ibid., 474.

24. Abinger MSS. The paper on which Mary copied these letters is watermarked 1824.

25. MWS to Prince Alexander Mavrocordato, Feb. 22, 1825, *MWS Letters*, I:467.

26. MWS to Leigh Hunt, Dec. 28, 1825, ibid., 508.

27. Stewart March Ellis, *William Harrison Ainsworth and His Friends*, 2 vols. (New York: John Lane Company, 1911), I:122.

28. J. H. Payne to MWS, undated, Sanborn, *Romance*, 30. In a Prefatory Note, Henry Howard Harper stated that Mary "used" Payne to establish a relationship with Irving, a charge that seems patently false. However, in his later Introduction to *Letters of Mary W. Shelley (Mostly Unpublished)* (Boston: Printed only for Members of the Bibliophile Society [Norwood, Mass: The Plimpton Press], 1918), 7–28, Harper warmly praised Mary's critical faculties.

29. MWS to J. H. Payne, May 31, 1825, *MWS Letters*, I:481.

30. J. H. Payne to MWS, undated, Sanborn, *Romance*, 36.

31. MWS to J. H. Payne, May 31, 1825, *MWS Letters*, I:487.

32. MWS to J. H. Payne, June 29, [1825], ibid., 494–495.

33. MWS to J. H. Payne, [July 29, 1825], ibid., 500.

34. MWS to J. H. Payne, June 29, [1825], ibid., 495.

35. MWS to Leigh Hunt, June 27, [1825], ibid., 491.

36. *Perkin Warbeck*, II:236; III:265.

37. Jane Williams, "A Fragment —," *CC Journals*, Appendix D, 479.

38. MWS to Jane Williams, Aug. 7, 1827, *MWS Letters*, I:558.

39. *Lady Morgan's Memoirs: Autobiography, Diaries and Correspondence*, 2 vols. (London: W. H. Allen & Co., 1862), II:525.

40. *The Last Man*, I:1–2.

41. Ibid., II:148.

42. Ibid., III:192.

43. The verses are among the Abinger MSS.; the prediction is contained in an

unsigned letter or review to Leigh Hunt, Bodleian MS. Shelley adds. d. 5, ff. 40–41.

44. Thomas Lovell Beddoes to Thomas Forbes Kelsall, Apr. 1, 1826, Beddoes, *Letters*, 104.

45. MWS to John Poole, May 6, 1826, *MWS Letters*, I:516.

46. MWS to J. H. Payne, Apr. 21, 1826, ibid., 514.

47. MWS to Leigh Hunt, Aug. 12, ibid., 528.

48. MWS to Jane Williams, Aug. 28, 1827, ibid., 573.

49. MWS to Charles Cowden Clarke, June 23, 1826, ibid., 522.

50. By the brilliant sleuthing of Betty T. Bennett, on whose revelations I base my account of Mary Diana Dods and of Isabel Robinson in this and the next chapter. See *MWS Letters*, I:533–534, n. 2, and II:7–8, n. 8.

51. See R. Stanley Dicks, "Mary Shelley: An Unprinted Elegy on Her Husband?," *Keats-Shelley Memorial Bulletin* 28 (1977): 36–41. Betty T. Bennett, however, informs me that Dods wrote this elegy for a beloved woman.

52. Strout, "Knights of the Burning Epistle," 96.

53. "Ma non di me come d'amante . . . ," Abinger MSS.

54. Thomas Moore, a Robinson family friend, may have been referring to Isabel Robinson's affair in his journal entry of May 13, 1824: "Drove to Hampstead to see Miss Robinson; strange scene." *The Journals of Thomas Moore*, Wilfred S. Dowden, ed., 4 vols. (London and Toronto: Associated University Presses; Newark: University of Delaware Press, 1979), II:731.

55. See *MWS Letters*, I:526, 527 fn. 2.

16 "Ingratitude . . ."

1. Mary Shelley, "Illyrian Poems — Feudal Scenes," *Westminster Review* 10 (January 1829): 72.

2. MWS to Teresa Guiccioli, Aug. 20, 1827, *MWS Letters*, I:565.

3. MWS to EJT, Mar. 4, 1827, ibid., 541–542.

4. Rennie, *Traits*, I:106, 107, 109.

5. Lord Dillon to MWS, Mar. 18, 1829, Marshall, *Mary Shelley*, II:197.

6. Cyrus Redding, *Literary Reminiscences and Memoirs of Thomas Campbell*, 2 vols. (London: C. J. Skeet, 1860), II:175–176. Redding refers to Joshua Robinson as "Mr. R————" of Paddington here and in his *Fifty Years' Recollections* (p. 227) and his *Yesterday and To-day* (I:179); so does *The Life and Letters of Thomas Campbell*, William Beattie, ed., 3 vols. (London: E. Moxon, 1849), II:175, 332. See also Rennie, *Traits*, I:171; Rate Books for Paddington; *Alumni Oxoniensis*, Joseph Forster, ed., 3 vols. (Nendeln, Lichtenstein: Kraus Reprint Ltd., 1968), III:1214; Records of St. Mary's, Paddington. Robinson's wife had been Rosetta Tompkins.

7. When Teresa Guiccioli visited England in 1832, the not always veracious Lady Blessington claimed that Teresa complained to her that Mary had shown Moore her letters to Byron. In his biography of Byron, Moore used one letter that he claimed Byron showed him in Venice, gave extracts of two he could have seen there, and quoted from one of July 1821 that Mary might have shown him. But if Teresa had been angry with Mary about this, it is unlikely that she would have shown Mary Byron's letters to her, as she did on this visit. In fact, these letters are of little import compared with the account of her romance with Byron that Teresa herself wrote for Moore. It has been said also that Mary gave Moore a copy of lines Byron had written in Teresa's copy of *Corinne*, but Teresa herself sent them to Moore.

8. MWS Journal, Oct. 21, 1838.

9. *Perkin Warbeck*, II:68.

10. Just before she left she was reminded of the dangers of self-revelation. On July 21, the London *Morning Herald* reported the murder of the Reverend Joshua Waterhouse and discovery of Mary Wollstonecraft's love letters to him. Godwin went to see Mary next day possibly about these letters, now lost, which Godwin may have procured and destroyed.

11. MWS to J. H. Payne, Aug. 22, 1827, *MWS Letters*, I:569.

12. WG to MWS, Oct. 9, 1827, Marshall, *Mary Shelley*, II:182.

13. MWS to J. H. Payne, Aug. 22, 1827, *MWS Letters*, I:568.

14. MWS to Jane Williams Hogg, Sept. 23, 1827, ibid., II:9.

15. "The Ritter von Reichenstein," like Mary's subsequent contributions to *The Bijou*, is signed "M.S." Set in Austria, it combines Othello and Fidelio themes. One inspiration may have been Schiller's account of the legend of the Knight of Taggenburg in *The Sharing of The Earth*. Unjustly suspected of adultery by the knight, his lady becomes a hermitress, and after her death a saint. Mary's heroine is named Appolonia von Santis; names similar to those of Mrs. Gisborne's Italian servant and to Madame du Plantis of Florence. William Fraser and William Pickering edited *The Bijou*.

16. Frances Wright to Robert Dale Owen, Oct. 2, 1827, Historical Society of Pennsylvania.

17. MWS to Frances Wright, Sept. 12, 1827, *MWS Letters*, II:3–4.

18. Ibid., 4–5.

19. MWS to Robert Dale Owen, Nov. 9, 1827, ibid., 17.

20. Frances Wright to MWS, Nov. 9, 1827, Abinger MSS.

21. Robert Dale Owen, *Threading My Way: An Autobiography* (1874; rpt. New York: Augustus M. Kelley, 1967), 322.

22. MWS to Frances Wright, Dec. 30, 1830, *MWS Letters*, II:123.

23. Frances Wright to MWS, Dec. 25, 1827, Abinger MSS.

24. MWS to ?James Robins, Jan. 5, 1828, *MWS Letters*, II:22.

25. MWS to Jane Williams, Feb. 14, 1828, ibid., 25.

26. "It seems as if some one had awakened the *Quarterly* from a long nap," Melusina Trench wrote in 1826, "and enabled it to look around and see that Goethe was not quite an imbecile, elderly gentleman, only known as the author of an improper novel called *Werther*, now out of date; that Shelley was not quite a mad rhymester, equally presumptuous and inane; and that there existed other poets in Europe besides the acknowledged *quintetto*, Scott, Byron, Southey, Rogers, and Campbell." *The Remains of the Late Mrs. Richard Trench*, Richard C. Trench, ed. (London: Parker, Son, and Bourn, 1862), 616.

27. Thomas Moore to John Murray, c. Feb. 18, 1828, Samuel Smiles, *A Publisher and His Friends. Memoirs and Correspondence of the Late John Murray*, 4 vols. (London: John Murray; New York: Charles Scribner's Sons, 1891), II:309–310. Moore wanted access to other Shelley letters to Byron in Mary's possession. She may have shown him that of Feb. 15, 1822, which he printed and which Hobhouse denied furnishing, about Hunt's having gotten money from the two poets. While it told the public nothing not already notorious about Hunt, if Mary showed it to Moore it may have been to counter Hunt's defamatory *Lord Byron and Some of his Contemporaries* (1828).

28. Slater published an edition of "Select Plays" for schools, and a book advocating a revised translation of the Scriptures. He and his wife, Ann, had three sons, the eldest born in 1824, who attended King's College and Cambridge.

29. Apparently Isabel Robinson's audacious stratagem was never discovered

even by her family. The present Mrs. Margaret Drummond-Wolff, whose husband is the grandson of Isabel Robinson's daughter, Adeline, has informed me that Isabel married twice, first Sholto Douglas, then, having been widowed, the Reverend William Falconer, with whom she lived in Italy. Similarly, the *Dictionary of National Biography* entry for Falconer, a translator of Strabo, stated that he married the widow of W. S. Douglas in 1840. Isabella Robinson Falconer died near Pistoia in 1869. Her daughter, Adeline, married Henry Drummond-Wolff, and they, to complete a bizarre circle, became close friends of Sir Percy Shelley and his wife.

30. *The Garnett Letters*, Cecilia Payne-Gaposchkin, ed. (privately printed, 1979), 117. The originals are deposited at the Houghton Library, Harvard University. Quoted by permission of Katherine Haramundanis and the Houghton Library.

31. For this circle, see Mary Elmina Smith, *Une Anglaise intellectuelle en France sous la Restauration, Miss Mary Clarke* (Paris: Champion, 1927); James Fred Marshall, "Les Dames Garnetts, Amies de Stendhal," *Le Divan* 32, nos. 269–276 (Nendeln, Lichtenstein: Kraus Reprint Ltd., 1968); Henri Martineau, *Petit Dictionnaire Stendhalien* (Paris: Le Divan, 1848).

32. MWS to Prosper Mérimée, May 24, 1828, *MWS Letters*, II:40.

33. MWS to Jane Williams, June 5, 1828, ibid., 41.

34. *Garnett Letters*, 225.

35. MWS to Jane Williams, July 17, 1828, *MWS Letters*, II:54.

36. MWS to Jane Williams, June 28–29, 1828, ibid., 51–52.

37. *The Athenaeum* No. 55 (Nov. 12, 1828): 863. Mary would publish a review in *The Athenaeum* in 1844, and may have written for it occasionally in the intervening years. The magazine was originally published by Colburn, then by members of the Apostle group that championed Shelley. A marked file of contributing authors exists — except for the years 1828–1832, 1835, and 1844, in which her name does not appear. See Leslie A. Marchand, *The Athenaeum: A Mirror of Victorian Culture* (Chapel Hill: University of North Carolina Press, 1941), ix. Thus she might have contributed during 1828–1832 and 1835. "On Female Authorship," in no. 42 (Aug. 13, 1828), is suggestive of her.

38. MWS to Jane Williams, June 28–29, 1828, *MWS Letters*, II:50–51.

39. Prosper Mérimée to MWS, July 5, 1828 (trans. Lenora D. Wolfgang), Betty T. Bennett and William T. Little, "Seven Letters from Prosper Mérimée to Mary Shelley," *Comparative Literature* 31:2 (Spring 1979): 142.

40. Prosper Mérimée to MWS, Feb. 4, 1829, ibid., 152.

41. Prosper Mérimée to MWS, July 28, 1828, ibid., 144.

42. MWS to EJT, July 27, 1829, *MWS Letters*, II:82.

43. Prosper Mérimée to MWS, Jan. 12, 1829, Bennett and Little, "Seven Letters," 150.

17 "A NEW KIND OF LIFE"

1. While "Recollections of the Lake of Geneva" in *The Spirit and Manners of the Age* 2 (December 1829) is signed "M.W.S." (no other certain work of Mary Shelley's is so signed), the author had been on Lake Geneva recently; nor would Mary Shelley note that Voltaire, Rousseau, Gibbon, and Byron had "perverted" their genius "to the purpose of infidelity." It is interesting, however, that in 1829 "Mrs. Caroline Barnard" made her last appearance in a new edition of *The Parent's Offering* (London: Baldwin and Craddock) "with the Addition of 'The Noise,' 'The Refusal,' and 'The Heap of Stones' " — stories for boys of Percy Shelley's age.

2. *The Athenaeum* 97 (Sept. 2, 1829): 544–545.

3. *CC Journals*, 432–433.

4. Rennie, *Traits*, 1:105, 110, 104–105, 113–114.

5. MWS to EJT, April [1829], *MWS Letters*, II:72.

6. MWS to EJT, Dec. 15, 1829, ibid., 93–94. The financial situation of Mary's relations may be connected to an auction of "Shelley's library" by William Wise in St. Clement's, Oxford, on Oct. 17, 1829. See John Turner, "Bibliographical Notes," *Antiquarian Book Monthly Review* 6:1 (January 1979): 30–31. I am indebted to Dr. Mihai Handrea for calling my attention to this article and to notes by G. M. Matthews about the contents of Shelley's library. Some of the contents postdated Shelley's Oxford days and may have been included in the Shelleys' library at Marlow and in Italy. Mary could have been forced to sell these books to help Claire, Charles Clairmont, and Godwin.

7. Rennie, *Traits*, I:108–109.

8. See *Perkin Warbeck*, II:299.

9. See Betty T. Bennett, "The Political Philosophy of Mary Shelley's Historical Novels: *Valperga* and *Perkin Warbeck*," in *The Evidence of the Imagination: Studies of Interactions between Life and Art in English Romantic Literature*, Donald H. Reiman, Michael C. Jaye, and Betty T. Bennett, eds., with the assistance of Doucet Devin Fischer and Ricki B. Herzfeld (New York: New York University Press, 1978).

10. *Perkin Warbeck*, III:17–18.

11. Ibid., 351, 352, 353.

12. Ibid., 351.

13. MWS to EJT, July 27, [1829], *MWS Letters*, II:82.

14. MWS Journal, Oct. 21, 1838.

15. Prosper Mérimée to MWS, Feb. 4, 1829 (trans. Lenora D. Wolfgang), Betty T. Bennett and William T. Little, "Seven Letters from Prosper Mérimée to Mary Shelley," *Comparative Literature* 31:2 (Spring 1979): 152. When Mérimée's mother asked him for an autograph of Mary Shelley in 1835, he had by then kept only her first letter, which he subsequently gave a friend.

16. MWS to EJT, July 27, [1829], *MWS Letters*, II:82.

17. MWS to Maria Gisborne, Jan. 16, 1833, ibid., 183.

18. Review of *1572 Chronique du Temps de Charles IX* [sic] — *Par l'Auteur de Théâtre de Clara Gazul, Westminster Review* 13 (October 1830): 502.

19. Review of *The Loves of the Poets, Westminster Review* 11 (October 1829): 475.

20. MWS to EJT, Dec. 15, [1829], *MWS Letters*, II:95.

21. MWS Journal, Apr. 23, 1830.

22. Thomas Moore to MWS, Apr. 3, 1830, *The Letters of Thomas Moore*, Wilfred S. Dowden, ed., 2 vols. (Oxford: The Clarendon Press, 1964), II:698.

23. *Anna Jameson: Letters and Friendships*, Mrs. Steuart Erskine, ed. (London: T. Fletcher Unwin, 1915), 89–90.

24. MWS Journal, Jan. 22, 1830.

25. *The Philadelphia Album and Ladies Literary Gazette* 4:10 (Mar. 6, 1830): 86–87.

26. *Perkin Warbeck*, II:134–135.

27. S. C. Hall, *A Book of Memories of Great Men and Women of the Age, From Personal Acquaintance* (London: Virtue and Co., Ltd., 1877), 266.

28. Augustus J. C. Hare, *The Story of My Life*, 4 vols. (London: George Allen, 1896), I:40. For the Hares, see also his *Memorials of a Quiet Life* (London: Strahan & Co., 1872); Malcolm Elwin, *Landor: A Replevin* (London: MacDonald, 1958); R. H. Super, *Walter Savage Landor: A Biography* (New York: New York University Press, 1954).

29. Mar. 25, 1830, *The Journals of Thomas Moore*, Wilfred S. Dowden, ed., 4

vols. (London and Toronto: Associated University Presses; Newark: University of Delaware Press, 1979), III:1295.

30. Ibid., Mar. 25, June 7, 1830, 1295, 1306. Mary had told Moore to tell Washington Irving, who had come to London the previous fall as secretary of the American legation, that she hoped the two men would spend an evening with her, but Irving put Moore off with one excuse or another. Then Mary met Irving at a dinner party given by the Manners-Suttons on April 10, and in late May asked him to her June 7 party. Ralph M. Aderman, "Mary Shelley and Washington Irving Once More," *Keats-Shelley Journal* 31 (1982): 24–28. Aderman suggests that Mary "used" Moore as she had "used" Payne to bring her and Irving together, that her invitation was for an "intimate meeting," and that Irving feared her romantic interest in him. Clearly, Irving was not interested in her — and may not have wanted further contact with Godwin, who had asked him to get *Cloudesley* published in America — but it seems perfectly natural for her to ask Moore to help her renew the acquaintance of a man she had liked. It was just as natural to Moore and Irving to prefer exclusive spheres, and in fact as Mary realized this she let her friendship with Moore lapse into mutually rewarding acquaintanceship.

31. MWS to John Murray III, Sept. 8, 1830, *MWS Letters*, II:115.

32. MWS to John Murray, Dec. 29, 1830, ibid., 121.

33. *Perkin Warbeck*, III:99.

34. Possibly "The Honourable Mrs. Norton" and "James Fenimore Cooper." Unless it is particularly significant, Mary Shelley's periodical work will not be cited in the text after this chapter. For her complete oeuvre, see Appendix B.

35. MWS to Anne Hare, [September–October 1832], *MWS Letters*, II:172.

36. See *The Journals of Mary Shelley 1814–1844*, Paula R. Feldman and Diana Scott-Kilvert, eds., 2 vols. (Oxford: The Clarendon Press, 1987), Appendix III, II:621.

37. MWS to EJT, Mar. 22–25, 1831, *MWS Letters*, II:133.

38. MWS to Frances Wright, Dec. 30, 1830, ibid., 124.

39. MWS to EJT, Mar. 22–25, 1831, ibid., 132.

40. MWS Journal, Feb. 14, 1831.

41. Christopher Benson, A.M., Master of The Temple, *Discourses upon the Powers of the clergy, prayers for the dead, and the Lord's Supper*, Preached at the Temple Church (London: John W. Parker, 1841), 57.

42. Thomas Balston, *John Martin 1789–1854: His Life and Works* (London: Gerald Duckworth & Co. Ltd., 1947), 157, 163–166.

43. E. B. Murray has advised me that Mary worked from the 1823 edition, which has many minor changes to that of 1818. Whether Godwin or Mary had made those changes, she retained all but one, and made substantial further alterations, many of them reflective of her sad experience since 1816–1817. In her recall in the Preface of the ghost stories read at Geneva, quite accurate after fifteen years, it is significant that Mary remembered elements relevant to Shelley's separation from Harriet Shelley, and to the deaths of his and Mary's children.

44. MWS Journal, Dec. 18, 1830.

45. MWS to EJT, July 26, 1831, *MWS Letters*, II:143.

18 "THE GREAT DISAPPOINTMENT . . ."

1. See Matthew Arnold, "Shelley," *Essays in Criticism*, 2d ed. (London, New York: Macmillan and Co., 1889), 205–206. Arnold heard this story while taking tea at Lady Barbarina Gray's with Mrs. Butler, during which they argued about the color of Mary Shelley's eyes; he said they had been brown, Mrs. Butler insisted

on gray. See also *A Family Chronicle, Derived from Notes and Letters Selected by Barbarina, The Hon. Lady Gray*, Mrs. Gertrude Agnes Lyster [Sullivan], ed. (London: John Murray, 1908), 333.

2. "Monti," *Lives*, 1835–1837, II:315.

3. MWS to W. Whitton, Dec. 2, 1829, *MWS Letters*, II:91.

4. Shelley's designated guardian for Charles had specified that the then three-year-old boy should "be prepared for one of the large or public schools" and eventually sent "to the University," probably Oxford. Roger Ingpen, *Shelley in England* (London: Kegan Paul, Trench, Trubner and Co., 1917), 506–507.

5. For a rather reproving discussion of Mary Shelley's choice, see Palacio, *Mary Shelley*, 236–241. Palacio cites one historian of British education who seems to overstate the case that in the early 1830s controversy "raged" about public schools, with the Tories championing them. Several exposés or critiques were published, and there was some agreement that reforms were needed. Liberals as well as conservatives continued to send their sons to public schools; many of these parents felt as Mary did that boys would learn and develop manliness in a democratic scene, rather than be isolated in private education. In Mary's "Cecil," an unfinished story for youngsters written in this period, Cecil's foster mother sends him to public school, but sees to it that he learns living languages. Abinger MSS.

6. *Perkin Warbeck*, I:141.

7. See MWS to Leigh Hunt, Feb. 3, 1835, *MWS Letters*, II:219.

8. The bond is in the Pforzheimer Collection.

9. Sir Timothy Shelley to John Gregson, Jan. 7, 1833, Bodleian MS. Shelley adds. d. 14, f. 57r.

10. Sir Timothy Shelley to John Gregson, Nov. 20, 1832, Bodleian MS. Shelley adds. d. 14, f. 53r.

11. L. G. Johnson, *General T. Perronet Thompson 1783–1869: His Military, Literary, and Political Campaign* (George Allen and Unwin: London, 1957), 182–183.

12. George Beauclerk to MWS, undated, Abinger MSS. Mary's friend Miss Gore, thought to have been Cecilia, daughter of the novelist Mrs. Catherine Gore, is probably the "A. Gore" on whom Godwin called in November 1834. The Robert Gores of West Ham, Essex, had daughters named Amelia, Annabella, and Arabella, and a son, Henry, who may have been the "dear Henry" whom Percy loved. See MWS to ? Gore, undated, *MWS Letters*, II:193. Miss Gore was a woman of literary interests, with her own home near Grosvenor Square. (Richard Monckton Milnes said that her forehead was bald as a knee.) Cecilia Gore, a young girl at this time, was famous for her wasp waist. In 1843 Mary seems to have misheard that she died (and attributed it to her tight lacing), for she married Lord Edward Thynne in 1853 and died in 1879.

13. For this and subsequent information about Beauclerk, I am indebted to Peter Beauclerk Dewar, coauthor with Donald Adamson of *The House of Nell Gwynn: The Fortunes of the Beauclerk Family* (William Kimber: London, 1974), who generously shared his research with me. See also the Holland House Papers, Francis Place Papers, all in the British Library; The Will of Charles Beauclerk, PRO 11203.

14. Peter Beauclerk Dewar Papers.

15. Irving Massey, *Posthumous Poems of Shelley, Mary Shelley's Fair Copy Book . . .* (Montreal: McGill–Queen's University Press, 1969), 177.

16. "I *know* Ld B. [Byron] left no MS. with Teresa except letters to herself — which I have seen & in which you are not alluded to." MWS to Claire Clairmont, [Sept. 11, 1844], *MWS Letters*, III:150. Mary also told Trelawny that she had

seen Byron's "very fine" love letters to Teresa. "Talks with Trelawny: Part II," *The Athenaeum* No. 2857 (July 29, 1882): 145. Mary could have read this material, which Teresa never let out of her hands, only if Teresa showed it to her. And apparently this was not the first time Teresa had done so. Richard Monckton Milnes recorded in his Commonplace Book for 1840–1841, quoting Mary, who was his friend: "Mrs. Shelley with the Guiccioli routing over Byron's letters at Pisa — finding so many letters of gratitude to him while at Ravenna for charities conferred; 'his avarice was merely a fancy of a certain part of his life and indeed hardly came on until Lade Noel died and he grew rich.' " Houghton MSS. 201.

17. MWS to Teresa Guiccioli, Aug. 15, [1832], *MWS Letters*, II:168.

18. MWS to Maria Gisborne, June 11, [1835], ibid., 246.

19. MWS's press copy of this poem is in The Berg Collection, New York Public Library. It was published in *The Keepsake for 1833*, which contains three other anonymous "Stanzas" in the same mood.

20. MWS Journal, June July August September 1832.

21. Marshall, *Mary Shelley*, II:248.

22. *CC Journals*, 432.

23. "Beauclerk. East Surrey. Croydon Meeting (Extracted from the *Morning Chronicle* of Monday, November 5, 1832)," British Library.

24. It may have been now that Mary gave Hunt her story "The Heir of Mondolfo," on which she had worked for some time, to publish for his benefit. It was found years later among his papers.

25. *Lodore*, III:8.

26. Ibid., 223.

27. Sir Timothy Shelley to John Gregson, Feb. 26, 1832, Bodleian MS. Shelley adds. d. 14, f. 43r.

28. MWS to Maria Gisborne, Jan. 16, 1833, *MWS Letters*, II:183.

29. Caroline Norton to MWS, Jan. 5, [1837], Abinger MSS.

30. British Library MS. 46612.

31. MWS to Jane Hogg, [May 5, 1833], *MWS Letters*, II:189. Jane Hogg seems to have showed Mary the letters Jeff had written Jane during their secret affair. Either Jane or Mary sent them to Maria Gisborne; John Gisborne copied many of these letters into his journals. Abinger MSS.

32. MWS to Jane Hogg, undated, *MWS Letters*, II:248.

33. MWS Journal, September 1833.

34. MWS to Maria Gisborne, July 17, [1834], *MWS Letters*, II:208.

35. MWS Journal, Nov. 14, 1833.

36. Ibid., Dec. 2, 1834.

37. Ibid., Dec. 2, 1834.

38. MWS to [Charles Ollier], Apr. 30, 1834. *MWS Letters*, II:201.

39. MWS to EJT, May 7, 1834, ibid., 203–204.

40. Sir Timothy Shelley to John Gregson, May 8, 1834, Bodleian MS. Shelley adds. d. 14, f. 73r.

41. MWS to Maria Gisborne, Oct. 30–Nov. 7, [1834], *MWS Letters*, II:214.

42. MWS to Maria Gisborne, June 11, [1835], ibid., 245.

43. MWS Journal, Dec. 2, 1834.

44. Maria Gisborne to MWS, Oct. 22, 1835, Abinger MSS.

45. MWS to Maria Gisborne, Oct. 30–Nov. 7, [1834], *MWS Letters*, II:214.

46. MWS to Leigh Hunt, Feb. 3, 1835, ibid., 219.

47. MWS to ?, [?May 29–June 2, 1835], ibid., 244.

48. MWS to Maria Gisborne, July 17, 1835, ibid., 209.

49. MWS Journal, Dec. 2, 1834.

50. "Monti," *Lives*, 1835–1837, II:333.

51. Anne Renier, *Friendship's Offering: An Essay on the Annuals and Gift Books of the 19th Century* (London: Private Libraries Association, 1964), 20 et passim.

52. MWS to Maria Gisborne, June 11, [1835], *MWS Letters*, II:246–247.

53. EJT to CC, Nov. 30, 1835, *The Letters of Edward J. Trelawny*, H. Buxton Forman, ed. (London: Henry Frowde, Oxford University Press, 1910), 194.

54. MWS to EJT, [undated], *MWS Letters*, II:140. I believe that this letter, copied by Trelawny, belongs in this period, and have corrected what I take to be his minor punctuation and spelling errors.

55. "Mrs. Shelley has written a clever novel . . . ," remarked Joseph Jekyll, "in which there is such a pretty, loving couple that the reader feels as if he had dined on sweetness." *Correspondence of Mr. Joseph Jekyll . . . 1818–1838*, Algernon Burke, ed. (London: J. Murray, 1894), 334.

56. MWS to John Bowring, Oct. 3, [1835], *MWS Letters*, II:255.

57. "Alfieri," *Lives*, 1835–1837, II:351.

19 "DO NOT AWAKEN . . ."

1. "Goldoni," *Lives*, 1835–1837, II:213.

2. Paul, *Godwin*, I:231–232.

3. MWS to EJT, [May 14, 1836], *MWS Letters*, II:271.

4. I am indebted to William St. Clair for extracts of notes by Zella's grandson, the late C. M. Trelawny-Irving, of talks with Zella when he was a child, which were prepared for H. J. Massingham c. 1934.

5. EJT to MWS, Sept. 25, 1836, *The Letters of Edward J. Trelawny*, H. Buxton Forman, ed. (London: Henry Frowde, Oxford University Press, 1910), 204. Trelawny quotes an unnamed woman whom some have thought to be Fanny Kemble or Augusta Goring, but who is almost certainly Caroline Norton.

6. Caroline Norton to MWS, Jan. 5, [1837], Abinger MSS.

7. MWS to Leigh Hunt, Apr. 26, [1837], *MWS Letters*, II:285–286.

8. *Falkner*, I:267.

9. "Rochefoucauld," *Lives*, 1838–1839, I:108.

10. Jane Gray Perkins, *The Life of the Honorable Mrs. Norton* (New York: Henry Holt & Co., 1909), 133. Mary Shelley's thoughts are reflected on pages 83–84 of the pamphlet, in which Norton states that a law is dangerous if its severity is so much more apparent than its equity that men side with the sufferer: "for this reason there *is* a permitted discretion . . . in favour of those who have received unendurable provocation." And she cites the case of a woman proved to have stabbed a man but exonerated on grounds that he had insulted her. "Is maternal instinct *weaker*, then, than female modesty? . . ." The copy of this pamphlet that Norton sent Mary is in the Pforzheimer Collection.

11. MWS to EJT, [Jan. 26, 1837], *MWS Letters*, II:281.

12. Ibid., 280–281.

13. Ibid., 282.

14. MWS to Leigh Hunt, [December 1837–March 1838], ibid., 293.

15. MWS to Leigh Hunt, Apr. 26, [1837], ibid., 286.

16. Sir Timothy Shelley to John Gregson, May 17, 1836, Bodleian MS. Shelley adds. d. 14, f. 81r.

17. Caroline Norton to MWS, Bolton Street, undated, Abinger MSS.

18. Henry Crabb Robinson to William Wordsworth, Dec. 11, 1837, Dr. Williams' Library, London.

19. MWS to Jane Hogg, Mar. 10, 1840, *MWS Letters*, II:341.

20. The bond for this debt to one Jane Clarke, for which Peacock went surety, is in the Pforzheimer Collection.

21. MWS to EJT, Jan. 3, [1837], *MWS Letters*, II:278.

22. *The Journals of Mary Shelley 1814–1844*, Paula R. Feldman and Diana Scott Kilvert, eds., 2 vols. (Oxford: At the Clarendon Press, 187), II:617–618 (Appendix III).

23. Lyster, *Family Chronicle*, 333.

24. Henry Crabb Robinson to Thomas Robinson, Apr. 21, 1843, Dr. Williams' Library, London.

25. Anna Laetitia [Aikin] Le Breton, *Memories of Seventy Years . . .* , Mrs. Herbert Martin, ed. (London, Edinburgh: Griffith & Farren, 1833), 81.

26. EJT to CC, Mar. 23, 1836, *Trelawny Letters*, 196.

27. Hunt, "Shelley," 199.

28. Edward L. Pierce, *Memoir and Letters of Charles Sumner*, 2 vols. (Boston: Roberts Brothers, 1893), II:21.

29. MWS to Benjamin Disraeli [?Nov. 15–Dec. 7, 1837], *MWS Letters*, II:290.

30. Notes by John Mitford, British Library MS. adds. 32574, f. 21. Printed, with some apparent error due to illegible writing, in Walter Edwin Peck, *Shelley: His Life and Work*, 2 vols. (Boston, New York: Houghton Mifflin, 1927), II:411.

31. MWS to CC, [Aug. 16, 1842]. *MWS Letters*, III:36.

32. *The Wellesley Index to Victorian Periodicals*, 4 vols. (Toronto: University of Toronto Press, 1966), III:115. A *Monthly Chronicle* advertisement in *The Athenaeum* (Mar. 7, 1840) offered back copies of volumes 1–4 and cited Mary Shelley among the contributors. Possibly she wrote "Modern Italian Romances," vol. 2 (November 1838), "Portuguese Literature," vol. 3 (January 1839), and "Spanish Romantic Drama," vol. 3 (June 1839).

33. Flora Tristan, *Promenades dans Londres* (Paris, London: H.-L. Delloye, 1840), 316.

34. "Rousseau," *Lives*, 1838–1839, II:140.

35. "Madame de Staël," ibid., 340.

36. See William Gladstone's Memo about Shelley of Sept. 26, 1836, British Library MS. adds. 44762, f. 175.

37. *PBS Poems*, I:vi; I:139.

38. MWS to T. J. Hogg, Feb. 11, [1839], *MWS Letters*, II:309.

39. *PBS Poems*, III:162.

40. MWS to Leigh Hunt, July 20, [1839], *MWS Letters*, II:318.

41. *PBS Poems*, IV:226.

42. "Madame de Staël," *Lives*, 1838–1839, II:327, 332.

43. Witnesses at Ida Beauclerk's inquest testified that she sometimes had fits of giddiness and head pains, and moreover had a weak ankle. *The Times* (London), Apr. 27, 1839.

44. MWS to Edward Moxon, Nov. 11, [1839], *MWS Letters*, II:330.

45. MWS to Leigh Hunt, July 20, [1839], ibid., 318.

46. "The Picture of God — A vision," written in Percy Florence Shelley's notebook containing university work and copies of Shelley's letters. Abinger MSS.

47. MWS to CC, Sept. 20, [1843], III:91.

48. *PBS Poems*, I:viii.

49. PBS, Essays, *Letters from Abroad, Translations and Fragments*, Mrs. Shelley, ed., 2 vols. (London: Edward Moxon, 1840), I:xxiv.

50. MWS to Leigh Hunt, [Dec. c. 23, 1839], *MWS Letters*, II:335. " 'The mystery of existence,' " she had quoted de Staël in *Lives*, 1838–1839, 341, " 'is the connection between our faults and our misfortunes. I never committed an error that was not the cause of a disaster.' "

51. MWS to Abraham Hayward, Dec. 22, [1839], *MWS Letters*, II:334.

52. MWS to Jane Hogg, Mar. 10, [1840], ibid., 341.

53. Mary's list of Godwin's letters for her memoir of him is written on paper watermarked 1839. Abinger MSS.

20 "AMORE REDIVIVUS"

1. *Rambles*, I:9.

2. MWS to Abraham Hayward, Oct. 26, [1840], *MWS Letters*, III:5.

3. *Rambles*, I:175.

4. Ibid., 143–144.

5. MWS to Abraham Hayward, Nov. 18, [1840], *MWS Letters*, III:7.

6. MWS to Eliza Berry, Jan. 14, 1842, ibid., 19.

7. CC to MWS, Oct. 30, [1840], Abinger MSS.

8. MWS to Harriet de Boinville [Spring 1841], *MWS Letters*, III:12.

9. MWS to Fanny Butler, May 14, [1841], ibid., 15.

10. MWS to CC, Mar. 4, [1842], ibid., 22.

11. MWS to CC, Nov. 25, [1842], ibid., 47.

12. See David J. DeLaura, "The Context of Browning's Painter Poems: Aesthetics, Polemics, Histories," *PMLA* 95, no. 3 (May 1980): 367–388.

13. MWS to CC, Aug. 30, [1843], *MWS Letters*, III:83, 84.

14. MWS to CC, Mar. 4, [1842], ibid., 22.

15. MWS to CC, ibid., 23.

16. *Rambles*, I:265.

17. Mrs. Andrew Crosse, *Red-Letter Days of My Life* (London: R. Bentley & Son, 1892), 153.

18. *Rambles*, I:205.

19. Ibid., 209.

20. MWS to CC, Mar. 23, [1843], *MWS Letters*, III:62.

21. MWS to CC, Apr. 15, [1843], ibid., 68.

22. MWS to CC, Nov. 25, [1842], ibid., 47. Several lines following, possibly on the subject of marrying Knox, were later cut out of this letter.

23. Ibid.

24. *Rambles*, II:149.

25. Carlo Guitera, *Appunti autobiografica* in *Lo Hymen Hymenae* (Rome, 1897), 7–27.

26. MWS to CC, [Oct. 13, 1843], *MWS Letters:* III:99.

27. Ibid., 101.

28. MWS to CC, Sept. 20, [1843], ibid., 91, 92.

29. Ibid., 90.

30. *The Art-Union* (September 1844), 286. Its editor, S. C. Hall, observed that 102,269 "old masters" were imported between 1833 and 1843, and in 1847 a larger number of "Titians" than Titian had painted in all his long life.

31. See "The Shelley Estate," a document in the Abinger MSS., drawn up upon Percy Florence Shelley's marriage.

32. MWS to CC, June 4 [1844], *MWS Letters*, III:135.

33. MWS to Richard Monckton-Milnes, (c. June 5, 1844), ibid., 138.

34. MWS to CC, Oct. 27, [1844], ibid., 158.

35. See the (unsigned) review of *Richard the Third, as Duke of Gloucester and King of England*, by Caroline A. Halsted, 2 vols., Longman & Co. in *The Athenaeum*, Nos. 875, 876 (Aug. 3 and 10, 1844), 707–708, 728–731. On Aug. 17, 1844, Claire wrote Mary that she had *The Athenaeum* and would let Mary know "what I think of your criticism in it." Abinger MSS.

36. MWS to Leigh Hunt, [?July 30–August 1844], *MWS Letters*, III:146.

37. Gatteschi's name appears in the Home Office Entry Books for 1844 as having arrived between June 29 and August 27. There is no record of his departure.

38. MWS to CC, [?June 6, 1845], *MWS Letters*, III:185.

21 "I WILL SIT . . ."

1. CC to MWS, May 7, 1845. Abinger MSS.

2. MWS to CC, ?June 6, 1845, *MWS Letters*, III:185–186.

3. Henry Crabb Robinson, *On Books and Their Writers*, Edith J. Morley, ed., 3 vols. (London: J. M. Dent & Sons, 1938), II:654.

4. MWS to CC, May 23, 1845, *MWS Letters*, III:182.

5. CC to MWS, [late May 1845], Abinger MSS.

6. CC to MWS, May 7, 1845, Abinger MSS.

7. MWS to CC, Aug. 12, 1845, *MWS Letters*, III:200.

8. MWS to CC, Sept. 15, 1845, ibid., 204.

9. MWS to CC, Oct. 7, 1845, ibid., 211.

10. MWS to CC, Oct. 8, 1845, ibid., 213.

11. No record of Gatteschi or Guitera has survived in the archives of the Préfecture de Police.

12. MWS to CC, Oct. 18, 1845, *MWS Letters*, III:240.

13. MWS to CC, Dec. 11, 1845, ibid., 267.

14. Dennis R. Dean, "Mary Shelley and Gideon Mantell," *Keats-Shelley Journal* 30 (1981): 25. The quotation, from Mantell's journal entry of March 12 (his journal is in the Alexander Turnbull Library of the National Library of New Zealand), clearly reads "neuralgia of the heart," not the "head."

15. For a diagnosis of Mary Shelley's case, I am deeply indebted to Dr. Frank Elliot, consultant to the Elliot Neurological Center of the Pennsylvania Hospital, Philadelphia, who studied a detailed account of her symptoms from 1837 to 1851, as well as her past history. Dr. Elliot, who is familiar with nineteenth-century medical history, points out that headaches, "pressure on the brain," spinal weakness, and fluctuating or changing complaints were and are typical neurotic psychosomatic manifestations. For a different opinion, with which Dr. Elliot disagrees, see *MWS Letters*, III:389 (Appendix I).

16. MWS to Edward Moxon, [?Jan. 30, 1846], *MWS Letters*, III:275.

17. MWS to Thomas Medwin, mid-May 1846, ibid., 284.

18. MWS to Marianna Hammond, undated, ibid., 281–282.

19. George Lewes, "Grote's History of Greece: The Homeric Poems," *Westminster Review* 46 (January 1847): 211.

20. In 1847, Emily Dunstan, a woman whom both Mary Shelley and Claire Clairmont knew, was in prison for debt. She returned money Mary had sent her and asked for the name of an enlightened physician. "I must tell you . . . ," Mary wrote Claire on July 28, "I said, tho' I was not acquainted with him I had heard that Dr. Southwood Smith was both clever & liberal." *MWS Letters*, III:324. Although another Smith could have been her physician, "I must tell you" suggests that Mary was warning Claire to uphold her in a white lie, perhaps fearing that Dunstan might ask her to interest Southwood Smith in her case. Mary was not treated by homeopathic physicians until the winter of 1849–1850.

21. In 1913 H. Buxton Forman published a new edition of Medwin's *Life of Shelley* that included emendations Medwin had made on a copy of the book. Medwin's unpublished notes are at the Pierpont Morgan Library.

22. George Gilfillan, "Female Authors — No. III — Mrs. Shelley," *Tait's Edinburgh Magazine* 14 (December 1847): 850–851, 852.

23. Marshall, *Mary Shelley*, II:380.

24. MWS to CC, July 28, 1848, *MWS Letters*, III:344.

25. MWS to Alexander Berry, June 30, 1848, ibid., 341.

26. William Albery, *A Parliamentary History of Horsham 1290–1885* (London, New York: Longmans, Green and Co., 1927), 403–414.

27. MWS to Charles Robinson, c. Mar. 18, 1848, *MWS Letters*, III:334.

28. Ibid., 334, fn. 1.

29. Maud Rolleston, *Talks with Lady Shelley*, The King's Treasury of Literary Masterpieces (London: George G. Harrap, 1925), 27–28.

30. MWS to CC, Aug. 27–28, 1848, *MWS Letters*, III:346.

31. "But at the same moment that happier and brighter prospects seemed to open to her view, and when she had made arrangements for writing the life of her husband, symptoms of illness, of a threatening character, showed themselves. From time to time they appeared and subsided; but gradually her old energy went . . ." *Shelley Memorials: From Authentic Sources . . .*, Lady Shelley, ed. (London: Henry S. King & Co., 1875), 228.

32. Sir Percy Shelley to Isabel Booth, c. Feb. 6, 1851, *MWS Letters*, III:393–394.

33. MWS to CC, Dec. 10, 1848, ibid., 352.

34. Lady Shelley to Alexander Berry, Mar. 7, 1851, ibid., 394.

35. Marshall, *Mary Shelley*, II:312.

36. MWS to Augusta Goring, Aug. 12, 1850, *MWS Letters*, III:383–384.

37. MWS to John Touchet, Aug. 2, 1850, ibid., 381–382.

38. Notes by John Mitford, British Library Add. MSS. 32574, f. 19.

39. Robinson, *On Books*, I:235.

40. W. P. Frith, *My Autobiography and Reminiscences*, 3 vols. (London, Guilford: R. Bentley & Son, 1888), II:124.

41. M[oncure] D[aniel] Conway, "South Coast Saunterings in England," *Harper's New Monthly Magazine* 38, no. 226 (March 1869): 463. See Paul's more decorous reference, *Godwin*, II:332–333.

22 ROMANCE AND REALITY

1. Montague Guest and William B. Boulton, *The Royal Yacht Squadron* (London: John Murray, 1930), passim.

2. Una Taylor, *Guests and Memories: Annals of a Seaside Villa* (London, New York: Humphrey Milford, Oxford University Press, 1924), 336.

3. Irving Massey, "Some Letters of Shelley Interest," *Keats-Shelley Memorial Bulletin* 19 (1968): 16.

4. Henry Crabb Robinson, *On Books and Their Writers*, Edith J. Morley, ed., 3 vols. (London: J. M. Dent & Sons, 1938), II:791.

5. Abinger MSS.

6. Hunt, "Shelley," 198–199.

7. EJT, *Records of Shelley, Byron and the Author*, 2 vols. (London: Basil Montague Pickering, 1878), Appendix, II:255.

8. Richard Garnett, "Shelley's Last Days," *Fortnightly Review*, n.s. 23 [29] (June 1878): 854–856.

9. *Letters about Shelley from the Richard Garnett Papers*, William Richard Thurman, Jr., ed. (University of Texas, Ph.D. dissertation, August 1972), 130.

10. Robert Louis Stevenson to Lady Shelley, Jan. 15, 1890, Rosalie Glynn Grylls, *Mary Shelley: A Biography* (London: Oxford University Press, 1938), 293.

11. Marshall, *Mary Shelley*, I:3.

12. Elbert Hubbard, *Little Journeys to the Homes of Famous Women* (New York: G. P. Putnam's Sons, 1897), 399.

13. I[sobel] S[tuart], *The London Star*, Mar. 5, 1894.

14. Muriel Norris, "Mary Shelley and John Howard Payne," *London Mercury* 22 (October 1930): 450.

15. J. E. Panton, *Times Literary Supplement* 983 (Nov. 18, 1920): 759.

16. Katherine Mansfield to John Middleton Murry, December 1920, *The Letters of Katherine Mansfield to John Middleton Murry*, 2 vols. (London: Constable & Co., 1928), II:83.

17. Epigraph to Part I, Robert Metcalf Smith, *The Shelley Legend* (New York: Charles Scribner's Sons, 1945), 1; from Ellsworth Barnard, *Shelley's Religion* (Minneapolis, University of Minnesota Press, 1936).

Index

NOTE: subentries are arranged chronologically except in the entries for Lord Byron, Claire Clairmont, William Godwin, Mary Wollstonecraft Godwin Shelley, and Percy Bysshe Shelley, where they are alphabetized for the convenience of the reader.